Public Relations

Strategies and Tactics

Public Relations

Strategies and Tactics

Eleventh Edition
Global Edition

Dennis L. Wilcox
School of Journalism & Mass Communications
San Jose State University

Glen T. Cameron
School of Journalism
University of Missouri

Bryan H. Reber
Grady College of Journalism & Mass Communications
University of Georgia

PEARSON

Boston Columbus Indianapolis New York San Francisco Upper Saddle River
Amsterdam Cape Town Dubai London Madrid Milan Munich Paris Montréal Toronto
Delhi Mexico City São Paulo Sydney Hong Kong Seoul Singapore Taipei Tokyo

Head of Learning Asset Acquisition, Global Edition: Laura Dent
Editor-in-Chief: Ashley Dodge
Senior Acquisitions Editor: Melissa Mashburn
Editorial Assistant: Courtney Turcotte
Director of Marketing: Brandy Dawson
Managing Editor: Denise Forlow
Acquisitions Editor, Global Edition: Vrinda Malik
Project Editor, Global Edition: Daniel Luiz
Media Producer, Global Edition: M. Vikram Kumar
Senior Manufacturing Controller, Production, Global Edition: Trudy Kimber
Program Manager: Maggie Brobeck
Project Manager: PreMediaGlobal
Senior Operations Supervisor: Mary Fischer
Operations Specialist: Mary Ann Gloriande
Art Director: Jayne Conte
Cover Image: © Radu Razvan/Shutterstock
Director of Digital Media: Brian Hyland
Digital Media Project Management: Learning Mate Solutions, Ltd.
Digital Media Project Manager: Tina Gagliostro
Full-Service Project Management and Composition: PreMediaGlobal
Cover Printer: Courier Kendallville

Credits and acknowledgments borrowed from other sources and reproduced, with permission, in this textbook appear on appropriate page within text or on pages 620–624

Pearson Education Limited
Edinburgh Gate
Harlow
Essex CM20 2JE
England

and Associated Companies throughout the world

Visit us on the World Wide Web at:
www.pearsonglobaleditions.com

Authorized adaptation from the United States edition, entitled Public Relations: Strategies and Tactics, 11th edition, ISBN 978-0-205-96064-4, by Dennis L. Wilcox, Glen T. Cameron, and Bryan H. Reber, published by Pearson Education © 2015.

British Library Cataloguing-in-Publication Data
A catalogue record for this book is available from the British Library

10 9 8 7 6 5
19 18 17

Typeset in Janson Text LT Std by PreMediaGlobal USA, Inc.

Printed in Malaysia (CTP-VVP)

ISBN-10: 1-292-05658-4
ISBN-13: 978-1-292-05658-6

Brief Contents

PART 1 Role 27

CHAPTER 1 Defining Public Relations 27
CHAPTER 2 The Evolution and History of Public Relations 65
CHAPTER 3 Ethical Considerations and the Role of Professional Bodies 96
CHAPTER 4 The Practice of Public Relations 121

PART 2 Process 149

CHAPTER 5 The Role and Scope of Research in Public Relations 149
CHAPTER 6 The Public Relations Process 177
CHAPTER 7 Communication Concepts and Practice in Public Relations 197
CHAPTER 8 Evaluation and Measurement of Public Relations Programs 223

PART 3 Strategy 245

CHAPTER 9 Public Opinion: Role, Scope, and Implications 245
CHAPTER 10 Conflict Management and Crisis Communication 274
CHAPTER 11 Audiences 303
CHAPTER 12 Laws and Applications 326

PART 4 Tactics 357

CHAPTER 13 Internet and Social Media: Role & Scope in Public Relations 357
CHAPTER 14 Media Relations Management: Print Media 389
CHAPTER 15 Media Relations Management: Electronic Media 420
CHAPTER 16 Event Management 444

PART 5 Application 471

CHAPTER 17 Communicating Corporate Affairs 471
CHAPTER 18 Public Relations in Entertainment, Sports, and Tourism 499
CHAPTER 19 Public Relations in Government 519
CHAPTER 20 Global Public Relations in an Interdependent World 544
CHAPTER 21 Public Relations in Non-Profit, Health, and Education Sectors 571

Contents

PART 1 Role 27

CHAPTER 1
Defining Public Relations 27

The Challenge of Public Relations 28
A Global Industry 31
A Definition of Public Relations 33
Other Popular Names 35
Stereotypes and Less Flattering Terms 36
Public Relations as a Process 40
The Diversity of Public Relations Work 41
Public Relations vs. Journalism 42
Public Relations vs. Advertising 45
Public Relations vs. Marketing 46
How Public Relations Supports Marketing 47
Toward an Integrated Perspective 47
A Career in Public Relations 49
Essential Career Skills 52
The Value of Internships 55
Salaries in the Field 57
The Value of Public Relations 60
ON THE JOB INSIGHTS: The Nature of Public Relations Work 29
ON THE JOB INSIGHTS: Is Apple's Decision to Build Macs in the United States a "Publicity Stunt"? 38
ON THE JOB ETHICS: Facebook's Attempt at "Spin" Makes No Friends 39
ON THE JOB A MULTICULTURAL WORLD: A Cuban Restaurant in Miami Celebrates Its 40th Anniversary 44
ON THE JOB INSIGHTS: Networking: The Key to Career Success 50
ON THE JOB INSIGHTS: Do You Have the Right Personality for a Career in Public Relations? 53
ON THE JOB INSIGHTS: How to Succeed in Public Relations 54
ON THE JOB SOCIAL MEDIA IN ACTION: Advertising Firm Hires Interns through a Twitter Campaign 55
ON THE JOB INSIGHTS: Can You Complete This Internship Application? 56
ON THE JOB INSIGHTS: Entry-Level Salaries in the Communications Field 58
ON THE JOB INSIGHTS: An Overview of Salaries in the Public Relations Field 59
ON THE JOB INSIGHTS: Looking for an Entry-Level Job in Public Relations? 61
Summary 62
Case Activity: Promoting Beef Jerky as a Healthy Snack 63
Questions for Review and Discussion 63
Media Resources 63

CHAPTER 2
The Evolution and History of Public Relations 65

Early Beginnings 66
The Middle Ages 66
Colonial America 67
The 1800s: The Golden Age of Press Agentry 68
The Legacy of P. T. Barnum 69
Promoting the Westward Movement 69
Politics and Social Movements Take the Stage 72
Early Corporate Initiatives 74
1900 to 1950: The Age of Pioneers 74
Ivy Lee: The First Public Relations Counsel 75
Edward L. Bernays: Father of Modern Public Relations 76
Other Pioneers in the Field 78
Major Contributions by Industrialists, Presidents 81
1950 to 2000: Public Relations Comes of Age 82
The Influx of Women into the Field 84
2000 to the Present: Public Relations Enters the Digital Age 88
Public Relations in the Next Five Years 89
ON THE JOB INSIGHTS: The Social Media of the Reformation 67
ON THE JOB A MULTICULTURAL WORLD: The Beginnings of Public Relations in Other Nations 70
ON THE JOB INSIGHTS: Major Historical Themes over the Centuries 73
ON THE JOB ETHICS: Was Ivy Lee Less than Honest? 77
ON THE JOB INSIGHTS: Four Classic Models of Public Relations 83

PR CASEBOOK: Classic Campaigns Show the Power of Public Relations 85
ON THE JOB INSIGHTS: A Multicultural World: Global Study Identifies Top Issues in Public Relations 90

Summary 93
Case Activity: It's Not Raining Men 94
Questions for Review and Discussion 94
Media Resources 95

CHAPTER 3
Ethical Considerations and the Role of Professional Bodies 96

Understanding Ethics and Values 97
The Ethical Advocate 99
The Role of Professional Organizations 99
The Public Relations Society of America (PRSA) 99
The International Association of Business Communicators (IABC) 101
The International Public Relations Association (IPRA) 101
Other Groups 102
Professional Codes of Conduct 103
Codes for Specific Situations 105
Other Steps toward Professionalism 108
Changing Practitioner Mindsets 108
A Standardized Curriculum 112
Expanding Body of Knowledge 112
Professional Accreditation 113
Ethical Dealings with the News Media 115
Gifts to Journalists 116
Linking Ads with News Coverage 118
Transparency and Disclosure Issues 118

ON THE JOB INSIGHTS: Use of "Front Groups" Poses Ethical Concerns 98
ON THE JOB INSIGHTS: Global Standards for Professional Practice 104
ON THE JOB INSIGHTS: PRSA's Code of Ethics: Guidelines for Professional Practice 105
ON THE JOB SOCIAL MEDIA IN ACTION: Dealing Ethically with Consumer Review Sites 107
ON THE JOB INSIGHTS: Your Job: Ethics Counselor to Senior Management 109
ON THE JOB ETHICS: The Ethical Dilemma of Being a Spokesperson 111
ON THE JOB A MULTICULTURAL WORLD: "Pay for Play" in China 117

Summary 119
Case Activity: Ethical Dilemmas in the Workplace 119
Questions for Review and Discussion 120
Media Resources 120

CHAPTER 4
The Practice of Public Relations 121

Public Relations Departments 122
Corporate Structure Shapes the Public Relations Role 122
Organization of Departments 124
Public Relations as a Staff Function 128
Levels of Influence 130
Cooperation with Other Staff Functions 131
The Trend toward Outsourcing 132
Public Relations Firms 134
Services Provided by Firms 135
Global Reach 138
The Rise of Communication Conglomerates 138
Structure of a Counseling Firm 140
How Public Relations Firms Get Business 141
Pros and Cons of Using a Public Relations Firm 141
Fees and Charges 145

ON THE JOB INSIGHTS: So You Want to Make a Six-Figure Salary? 123
ON THE JOB A MULTICULTURAL WORLD: IBM Has a Global Birthday Celebration 125
ON THE JOB INSIGHTS: Job Levels in Public Relations 128
ON THE JOB INSIGHTS: Wanted: A Public Relations Specialist 129
PR CASEBOOK: 7-Eleven Celebrates Its Birthday with 5 Million Free Slurpees 133
ON THE JOB SOCIAL MEDIA IN ACTION: Sterling Vineyards Finds the Perfect Host 136
ON THE JOB INSIGHTS: The Secret Life of Working in a Public Relations Firm 137
ON THE JOB INSIGHTS: American PR Firms Have Global Clients 139
ON THE JOB INSIGHTS: Top 10 Public Relations Firms 140
ON THE JOB INSIGHTS: Wanted: An Account Executive for a Public Relations Firm 142

ON THE JOB INSIGHTS: Kenya Looks for a Public Relations Firm 144
ON THE JOB ETHICS: PR Firm Dropped by Wal-Mart for Ethical Lapse 145
ON THE JOB INSIGHTS: Your Choice: A Corporation or a PR Firm? 146
Summary 147
Case Activity: Planning a Career in Public Relations 148
Questions for Review and Discussion 148
Media Resources 148

PART 2 Process 149

CHAPTER 5
The Role and Scope of Research in Public Relations 149

The Importance of Research 150
Defining the Research Role 150
Determining the Research Role and Scope 150
Using Research 151
A Variety of Research Techniques 153
Secondary Research 155
Online Databases 155
The World Wide Web 157
Qualitative Research 158
Content Analysis 158
Interviews 159
Focus Groups 159
Copy Testing 161
Ethnographic Techniques 162
Quantitative Research 162
Random Sampling 162
Sample Size 163
Questionnaire Construction 164
Carefully Consider Wording 164
Avoid Loaded Questions 165
Consider Timing and Context 165
Avoid the Politically Correct Answer 165
Give a Range of Possible Answers 165
Use Scaled Answer Sets 165
How to Reach Respondents 166
Mailed Questionnaires 167
Telephone Surveys 167
Personal Interviews 167
Omnibus or Piggyback Surveys 168
Web and E-Mail Surveys 168
Digital Analytics for Public Relations 169
Web Analytics 169
Social Media Monitoring Tools 169
Social Media Participatory Research 170
Web Analytics 170
Social Media Monitoring Tools 171
Social Media Participatory Research 173
ON THE JOB SOCIAL MEDIA IN ACTION: New Brunswick Targets Audiences Using Google Analytics 156
ON THE JOB A MULTICULTURAL WORLD: Reaching a Diverse Audience about Electric Rates 160
ON THE JOB ETHICS: Sex and Alcohol: The AMA's News Release 164
ON THE JOB INSIGHTS: Questionnaire Guidelines 166
PR CASEBOOK: Research Provides Foundation for Cookie Campaign 174
Summary 175
Case Activity: Conducting Research about Rumors in Real Time 175
Questions for Review and Discussion 176
Media Resources 176

CHAPTER 6
The Public Relations Process 177

The Value of Planning 178
Approaches to Planning 178
Management by Objective 178
An Agency Planning Model 180
Elements of a Program Plan 181
Situation 182
Objectives 184
Audience 185
Strategy 186
Tactics 187
Calendar/Timetable 189
Budget 192
Evaluation 192

ON THE JOB INSIGHTS: Social Media in Action 179
PR CASEBOOK: Chase Sapphire Serves Up Foodie Experiences 183
ON THE JOB INSIGHTS: A New Frontier for Strategy 187
ON THE JOB A MULTICULTURAL WORLD: Latinas Don't Walk, They Strut: A Celebration of Latin Style 188
ON THE JOB ETHICS: Grassroots Environmentalism: Conflict of Interest or a Win-Win? 190
ON THE JOB INSIGHTS: The "Big Picture" of Program Planning 194
Summary 195
Case Activity: A Plan for Fair Trade Mojo 195
Questions for Review and Discussion 195
Media Resources 196

CHAPTER 7
Communication Concepts and Practice in Public Relations 197

The Goals of Communication 198
Implementing the Plan 198
A Public Relations Perspective 198
Receiving the Message 201
Five Communication Elements 201
The Importance of Two-Way Communication 202
Paying Attention to the Message 204
Some Theoretical Perspectives 205
Other Attention-Getting Concepts 206
Understanding the Message 208
Effective Use of Language 208
Writing for Clarity 208
Believing the Message 212
Remembering the Message 214
Acting on the Message 215
The Five-Stage Adoption Process 215
The Time Factor 217
How Decisions Are Influenced 217
Word-of-Mouth Campaigns 218
ON THE JOB SOCIAL MEDIA IN ACTION: Nestlé Gets Bruised in Social Media Fight with Greenpeace 203
PR CASEBOOK: Mobile on the John: A Public Relations Firm Scores a Royal Flush 207
ON THE JOB INSIGHTS: Hit Parade of Overused Words in News Releases 211
ON THE JOB INSIGHTS: Are Women Better Communicators Than Men? 213
ON THE JOB INSIGHTS: New and Improved Press Releases Still Achieve Communication Objectives 219
ON THE JOB ETHICS: eWOM Poses Ethical Challenges 220
Summary 220
Case Activity: A New Campaign to Combat Heart Disease 221
Questions for Review and Discussion 222
Media Resources 222

CHAPTER 8
Evaluation and Measurement of Public Relations Programs 223

The Purpose of Evaluation 224
Objectives: A Prerequisite for Evaluation 224
Current Status of Measurement and Evaluation 225
Measurement of Production 226
Measurement of Message Exposure 227
Media Impressions 229
Basic Web Analytics 230
Advertising Value Equivalency (AVE) 230
Systematic Tracking 232
Requests and 800 Numbers 234
Return on Investment (ROI) 234
Measurement of Audience Awareness 235
Measurement of Audience Attitudes 236
Measurement of Audience Action 236
Measurement of Supplemental Activities 239
Communication Audits 239
Pilot Tests and Split Messages 239
Meeting and Event Attendance 240
Newsletter Readership 240
ON THE JOB INSIGHTS: Effectiveness of Measurement Tools 227
ON THE JOB INSIGHTS: Measuring Effectiveness on the Web 228
ON THE JOB A MULTICULTURAL WORLD: YouTube Videos Promote World Water Day 231
ON THE JOB ETHICS: The New Math: Ad Rates versus News Coverage 233

PR CASEBOOK: Ketchum's Evaluation of the DoubleTree CAREavan 237
ON THE JOB SOCIAL MEDIA IN ACTION: Chevy at SXSW: Event Success by the Numbers 241
Summary 242
Case Activity: Evaluating the Success of Tourism Promotion 243
Questions for Review and Discussion 243
Media Resources 244

PART 3 Strategy 245

CHAPTER 9 Public Opinion: Role, Scope, and Implications 245

What Is Public Opinion? 246
Opinion Leaders as Catalysts 247
- *Types of Leaders* 247
- *The Flow of Opinion* 250

The Role of Mass Media 251
- *Agenda-Setting Theory* 251
- *Media-Dependency Theory* 252
- *Framing Theory* 252
- *Conflict Theory* 254

The Dominant View of Public Relations 258
- *Uses of Persuasion* 258
- *Persuasion in Negotiation* 259
- *Formulating Persuasive Messages* 260
- *Findings from Persuasion Research* 262

Factors in Persuasive Communication 262
- *Audience Analysis* 262
- *Source Credibility* 263
- *Appeal to Self-Interest* 265
- *Clarity of Message* 266
- *Timing and Context* 266
- *Audience Participation* 266
- *Suggestions for Action* 267
- *Content and Structure of Messages* 267

The Limits of Persuasion 268
- *Lack of Message Penetration* 270
- *Competing Messages* 270
- *Self-Selection* 270
- *Self-Perception* 270

The Ethics of Persuasion 270

ON THE JOB: Pitt's Project 248
ON THE JOB INSIGHTS: The Life Cycle of Public Opinion 249
ON THE JOB ETHICS: Framing Fracking: What Is the Truth? 253
ON THE JOB A MULTICULTURAL WORLD: What Does It Mean to "Be Authentic" around the World? 255
PR CASEBOOK: Gun Control Advocates and Opponents Work to Shape Public Opinion 256
ON THE JOB INSIGHTS: Six Principles of Persuasion 259
USING SOCIAL MEDIA AND BLOGS: SOCIAL MEDIA IN ACTION: Changing Nutrition Perceptions about McDonald's 261

Summary 271
Case Activity: Persuading People to Help Fund-Raise 272
Questions for Review and Discussion 272
Media Resources 273

CHAPTER 10 Conflict Management and Crisis Communication 274

Strategic Conflict Management 275
The Role of Public Relations in Managing Conflict 277
It Depends—A System for Managing Conflict 281
It Depends: Two Basic Principles 282
- *A Matrix of Contingency Factors* 283
- *The Contingency Continuum* 284

The Conflict Management Life Cycle 285
- *Proactive Phase* 285
- *Strategic Phase* 286
- *Reactive Phase* 286
- *Recovery Phase* 286

Processes for Managing the Life Cycle 287
Issues Management 287
- *Strategy Options* 288
- *Action Plan* 289
- *Evaluation* 289

Conflict Positioning and Risk Communication 289
Variables Affecting Risk Perceptions 290
Crisis Management 291
What Is a Crisis? 291
A Lack of Crisis Planning 292
How to Communicate during a Crisis 293
Strategies for Responding to Crises 293
Reputation Management 295
The Three Foundations of Reputation 295
Image Restoration 296
Déjà Vu—All Over Again 300

ON THE JOB A MULTICULTURAL WORLD: Managing Conflict: Benetton Balances Humanitarian and Business Ideals 279
ON THE JOB INSIGHTS: The Issues Management Process 288
ON THE JOB SOCIAL MEDIA IN ACTION: Social Media Plays Crucial Role after Tornado 292
PR CASEBOOK: Changing Corporate Culture Helps Toyota Turn the Corner 298

Summary 300
Case Activity: Unlikely Coalitions Fight New York over Soda Ban 301
Questions for Review and Discussion 302
Media Resources 302

CHAPTER 11
Audiences 303

A Multicultural Nation 304
Reaching Ethnic Audiences 305
Hispanics 307
African Americans 308
Asian Americans 311
Reaching Diverse Age Groups 314
The Millennial Generation 314
Teenagers 315
Baby Boomers 315
Seniors 316
Gender/Lifestyle Audiences 317
Women 317
The LGBT Community 318
Religious Groups 319
The Disability Community 322

ON THE JOB INSIGHTS: Minorities Assure Obama's Election 306
ON THE JOB SOCIAL MEDIA IN ACTION: Pampers Makes Every Hispanic Baby Special 308
ON THE JOB A MULTICULTURAL WORLD: Pepsi Sponsors Global Latin Music Concert 309
ON THE JOB INSIGHTS: Art Connects Cruise Ship Line with African Americans 310
ON THE JOB INSIGHTS: The Diversity of Education and Income 311
ON THE JOB INSIGHTS: Communicating with Multicultural Groups 313
ON THE JOB SOCIAL MEDIA IN ACTION: Potty Humor for Moms 318
PR CASEBOOK: Ben & Jerry's Celebrates Same-Sex Marriage 320
ON THE JOB ETHICS: Lowe's Stumbles on Sponsorship of All-American Muslim 322

Summary 323
Case Activity: A Campaign to Increase Student Diversity 324
Questions for Review and Discussion 324
Media Resources 325

CHAPTER 12
Laws and Applications 326

A Sampling of Legal Problems 327
Libel and Defamation 328
Avoiding Libel Suits 329
The Fair Comment Defense 330
Invasion of Privacy 330
Employee Communication 330
Photo Releases 331
Product Publicity and Advertising 331
Media Inquiries about Employees 332
Copyright Law 333
Fair Use versus Infringement 334
Photography and Artwork 335
The Rights of Freelance Writers 335
Copyright Issues on the Internet 336
Copyright Guidelines 336
Trademark Law 337
The Protection of Trademarks 339
The Problem of Trademark Infringement 340

Misappropriation of Personality 341
Regulations by Government Agencies 342
Federal Trade Commission 342
Securities and Exchange Commission 344
Federal Communications Commission 346
Other Federal Regulatory Agencies 347
The Food and Drug Administration 347
Equal Employment Opportunity Commission 348
Corporate Speech 349
Nike's Free Speech Battle 349
Employee Speech 350
Employee E-Mail 350
Surfing the Internet 350
Employee Blogs 351
Liability for Sponsored Events 351
The Attorney/Public Relations Relationship 352
ON THE JOB A MULTICULTURAL WORLD: MillerCoors Faces Controversy in a Long-Held Sponsorship 328
ON THE JOB SOCIAL MEDIA IN ACTION: The FTC Tackles Undisclosed Celebrity Social Media Endorsements 343
ON THE JOB INSIGHTS: Are Conversations Between Public Relations Pros and Their Clients Legally Protected? 352
PR CASEBOOK: Coca-Cola Fights Legal Battles on Regulatory and Consumer Fronts 354
Summary 355
Case Activity: Should Employees' Social Media Activities Be Controlled? 356
Questions for Review and Discussion 356
Media Resources 356

PART 4 Tactics 357

CHAPTER 13
Internet and Social Media: Role & Scope in Public Relations 357

The Internet: Pervasive in Our Lives 358
The World Wide Web 359
Making a Website Interactive 362
Managing the Website 363
Webcasts 363
Podcasts 364
Blogs: Everyone Is a Journalist 365
Wikis: Saving Trees 367
The Tsunami of Social Media 368
Facebook: King of the Social Networks 370
Twitter: Saying It in 144 Characters 373
LinkedIn: The Professional Network 376
YouTube: King of Video Clips 376
Flickr and Instagram: Sharing Photos 379
Pinterest 380
The Rising Tide of Mobile-Enabled Content 382
An Ocean of Apps 383
Texting: Not Sexy but Pervasive 386
ON THE JOB INSIGHTS: Ways That Organizations Use Their Websites 361
ON THE JOB ETHICS: The Rules of Social Engagement 367
ON THE JOB SOCIAL MEDIA IN ACTION: Marriage Equality Symbol Goes Viral 369
ON THE JOB INSIGHTS: Some Misconceptions About Being a Social Media Manager 370
ON THE JOB INSIGHTS: Does Justin Bieber Really Have 37 Million Followers? 375
PR CASEBOOK: Social Media Fuel a Solar Decathlon 378
ON THE JOB A MULTICULTURAL WORLD: Adidas, Singapore Campaigns Tap Social Media 384
Summary 386
Case Activity: A Social Media Campaign for Yogurt Program 387
Questions for Review and Discussion 387
Media Resources 387

CHAPTER 14
Media Relations Management: Print Media 389

The Importance of Mass Media 390
The News Release 390
Planning a News Release 391
The Basic Online News Release 391
The Multimedia News Release 394
Publicity Photos and Infographics 396
Infographics 399
Media Kits 400
Mat Releases 401
Media Alerts and Fact Sheets 402
Two Kinds of Fact Sheets 402

The Art of Pitching a Story 404
Tapping into Media Queries 408
Distributing Media Materials 408
Electronic News Services 409
Online Newsrooms 409
Media Interviews 411
Preparing for an Interview 412
The Print Interview 412
News Conferences 413
Planning and Conducting a News Conference 414
Online News Conferences 415
Media Tours and Press Parties 415
Media Tours 415
Press Parties 416

ON THE JOB A MULTICULTURAL WORLD: Sensitivity Required for Global News Releases 393
ON THE JOB ETHICS: The Blurring Line Between *"Earned"* and *"Paid"* Media 404
ON THE JOB INSIGHTS: Media Relations: How to Get a Date with a Reporter 406
PR CASEBOOK: A Successful Pitch Pays Dividends 407
ON THE JOB INSIGHTS: Working with "Citizen" Journalists 408
ON THE JOB SOCIAL MEDIA IN ACTION: Samsung Smartphone Has Media's Number 413

Summary 417
Case Activity: Promoting the Opening of a New Library 418
Questions for Review and Discussion 418
Media Resources 419

CHAPTER 15
Media Relations Management: Electronic Media 420

The Reach of Radio and Television 421
Radio 421
Audio News Releases 422
Radio PSAs 424
Radio Media Tours 426
Television 427
Video News Releases 428
The New "Normal": B-Roll Packaging 430
Television PSAs 430
Satellite Media Tours 431
News Feeds 432
Guest Appearances 433
Talk Shows 434
Magazine Shows 435
Pitching a Guest Appearance 436
Product Placements 437
Issues Placement 439
DJs and Media-Sponsored Events 440

ON THE JOB A MULTICULTURAL WORLD: Broadcast Media Has Large Hispanic Audience 422
ON THE JOB INSIGHTS: Radio PSAs Should Have Varying Lengths 425
PR CASEBOOK: Video PSA Warns About Use of Decorative Contact Lenses 431
ON THE JOB INSIGHTS: Guidelines for a Satellite Media Tour 433
ON THE JOB ETHICS: Should Television Guests Reveal Their Sponsors? 438
ON THE JOB SOCIAL MEDIA IN ACTION: Brand Journalism Extends the Reach of Television 440

Summary 441
Case Activity: Getting Broadcast Time for Peanut Butter 442
Questions for Review and Discussion 442
Media Resources 443

CHAPTER 16
Event Management 444

A World Filled with Events 445
Group Meetings 445
Planning 445
Registration 450
Program 450
Banquets 451
Working with Catering Managers 453
Logistics and Timing 454
Receptions and Cocktail Parties 454
Open Houses and Plant Tours 457
Conventions 458
Planning 458
Program 460
Trade Shows 462
Exhibit Booths 462

Hospitality Suites 463
Pressrooms and Media Relations 463
Promotional Events 464
Using Celebrities to Attract Attendance 465
Planning and Logistics 466
ON THE JOB INSIGHTS: A Job Listing for an Events Manager 446
PR CASEBOOK: Solid Promotional Strategy Makes Picasso a Hit in Seattle 447
ON THE JOB INSIGHTS: How to Plan a Meeting 448
ON THE JOB INSIGHTS: Making a Budget for a Banquet 453
ON THE JOB INSIGHTS: Asking the Right Questions After an Event 456
ON THE JOB SOCIAL MEDIA IN ACTION: Making Reservations on the Web 461
ON THE JOB A MULTICULTURAL WORLD: Beer, Rum, Vibrators, and Garlic: The World of Promotional Events 467
ON THE JOB INSIGHTS: Corporate Sponsorships: Another Kind of Event 468
Summary 469
Case Activity: Plan an Event 470
Questions for Review and Discussion 470
Media Resources 470

PART 5 Application 471

CHAPTER 17
Communicating Corporate Affairs 471

Today's Modern Corporation 472
The Role of Public Relations 475
Media Relations 477
Customer Relations 479
Reaching Diverse Markets 480
Consumer Activism 481
Consumer Boycotts 483
Employee Relations 485
Layoffs 486
Investor Relations 487
Marketing Communication 487
Product Publicity 488
Product Placement 488
Cause-Related Marketing 489
Corporate Sponsorships 490
Viral Marketing 491
Environmental Relations 493
Corporate Philanthropy 493
PR CASEBOOK: Wal-mart Scandal Highlights Role of Investor Activists 473
ON THE JOB INSIGHTS: Study Finds Trust in Leaders Is Low 477
ON THE JOB SOCIAL MEDIA IN PRACTICE: Duke Energy Uses Social Media to Tell Its Story 481
ON THE JOB INSIGHTS: Boycotts Come From All Directions 484
ON THE JOB INSIGHTS: Nudist Group Makes Pitch for Corporate Sponsors 495
Summary 496
Case Activity: A Corporate Wellness Campaign 497
Questions for Review and Discussion 497
Media Resources 497

CHAPTER 18
Public Relations in Entertainment, Sports, and Tourism 499

A Major Part of the American Economy 500
The Cult of Celebrity 500
The Public's Fascination with Celebrities 502
The Work of a Publicist 503
The Business of Sports 506
Community Relations 507
The Tourism Industry 509
Phases of Travel Promotion 511
Appeals to Target Audiences 511
Coping with Threats and Crises 513
ON THE JOB SOCIAL MEDIA IN ACTION: A Royal Birth Generates Record Coverage 501
ON THE JOB INSIGHTS: Wanted: A Press Coordinator for a Network 504
ON THE JOB INSIGHTS: How to Promote a Play 506

ON THE JOB INSIGHTS: The Super Bowl: An Economic Engine on Steroids 508
ON THE JOB A MULTICULTURAL WORLD: Chinese Tourists Flood the World 510
ON THE JOB INSIGHTS: Fifty Shades of Travel Promotion 512
ON THE JOB INSIGHTS: How Many "Freebies" to Accept? 513
PR CASEBOOK: Poop on the Deck: Carnival Cruise Line Has a Crisis 515

Summary 516
Case Activity: Promoting a Resort 517
Questions for Review and Discussion 517
Media Resources 517

CHAPTER 19
Public Relations in Government 519

Government Organizations 520
Basic Purposes of Government Public Relations 520
The Federal Government 521
The White House 522
Congress 523
Federal Agencies 524
State Governments 529
Local Governments 531
The Case for Government Public Information and Public Affairs 532
Government Relations by Corporations 533
Lobbying 535
Pitfalls of Lobbying 537
Grassroots Lobbying 538
Election Campaigns 539

PR CASEBOOK: Election Campaign Team Turns Policy Campaign Team After Obama's Re-Election 521
ON THE JOB INSIGHTS: "Partnership" Stretches Federal Funds 525
ON THE JOB SOCIAL MEDIA IN ACTION: Centers for Disease Control and Prevention Get Help From Zombies 528
ON THE JOB INSIGHTS: Google Flexes Its Muscle in Washington 534
ON THE JOB ETHICS: Student Loan Industry Engages In "Aggressive" Lobbying 536

Summary 541
Case Activity: How Do You Communicate Proactively? 542
Questions for Review and Discussion 542
Media Resources 543

CHAPTER 20
Global Public Relations in an Interdependent World 544

What Is Global Public Relations? 545
Development in Other Nations 545
International Corporate Public Relations 549
The New Age of Global Marketing 549
Language and Cultural Differences 551
Foreign Corporations in the United States 554
U.S. Corporations in Other Nations 555
Public Relations by Governments 560
American Public Diplomacy 566
Opportunities in International Work 567

ON THE JOB A MULTICULTURAL WORLD: Reaching Out to the Muslim World 552
ON THE JOB INSIGHTS: English Is the World's Dominant Language 553
ON THE JOB INSIGHTS: Traveling Abroad? How to Make a Good Impression 554
ON THE JOB ETHICS: Would You Buy a T-Shirt Made in Bangladesh? 557
PR CASEBOOK: NGO Campaign Goes After Fishing Subsidies 559
ON THE JOB SOCIAL MEDIA IN ACTION: Wars and Conflict: Governments Enlist Social Media as a Weapon 561
ON THE JOB INSIGHTS: U.S. Firms Represent a Variety of Nations 562
ON THE JOB INSIGHTS: A CNN Report on Kazakhstan: News or Propaganda? 563
ON THE JOB INSIGHTS: China's Educational Outreach to the World 565

Summary 568
Case Activity: Promoting Tourism for Turkey 569
Questions for Review and Discussion 569
Media Resources 570

CHAPTER 21
Public Relations in Non-Profit, Health, and Education Sectors 571

The Nonprofit Sector 572
Competition, Conflict, and Cooperation 572
Membership Organizations 574
Professional Associations 574
Trade Groups 575
Labor Unions 575
Chambers of Commerce 576
Advocacy Groups 578
Public Relations Tactics 578
Social Service Organizations 579
Foundations 579
Cultural Groups 580
Religious Groups 581
Public Relations Tactics 581
Health Organizations 582
Hospitals 582
Health Agencies 583
Educational Organizations 584
Colleges and Universities 585
Key Publics 586
Fund-Raising and Development 588
Motivations for Giving 588
Fund-Raising Methods 590
ON THE JOB A MULTICULTURAL WORLD: Global Strategic Communication Helps African Females Avoid Brutality 573
ON THE JOB ETHICS: Chamber of Commerce Tempers Its Position on Global Climate Change 577
ON THE JOB SOCIAL MEDIA IN ACTION: Need Info about Sex?: Text a Question 584
ON THE JOB INSIGHTS: Universities Tap Alumni Through Social Media 587
ON THE JOB INSIGHTS: Charitable Donations Top $316 Billion 589
ON THE JOB INSIGHTS: A New Fund-Raising Technique: Crowdfunding 593
Summary 593
Case Activity: A Social Media Presence for Goodwill Industries 594
Questions for Review and Discussion 594
Media Resources 595

Directory of Useful Web Sites 596
Bibliography of Selected Books, Directories, Databases, and Periodicals 597
Index 604
Credits 620

Preface

A textbook should be more than packaged information arrayed in page after page of daunting gray type that makes a reader's eyes glaze over. It should be written and designed to engage readers with attractive photos and charts, concise summaries of key concepts, and plenty of practical examples from today's practice that actively engages the reader. It must have clear learning objectives for every chapter and actively engage students in critical thinking and problem solving.

That's why this new edition of *Public Relations: Strategies & Tactics* continues its widely acclaimed reputation as the most readable, comprehensive, up-to-date, introductory public relations text on the market. This 11th edition, like others before it, continues to successfully blend theory, concepts, and actual programs and campaigns into a highly attractive format that is clear and easy for students to understand.

Students will find interesting examples, case studies, and illustrations throughout that will encourage them to actively engage in learning the basic concepts of professional practice. This text will also challenge them to develop their creative problem-solving skills, which is essential for a successful career in public relations.

The book also appeals to instructors who want their students to thoroughly understand the basic principles of effective public relations and be able to apply them to specific, real-life situations. Indeed, many instructors report that this text does an outstanding job of instilling students with a deep understanding of what it means to be a public relations professional with high standards of ethical responsibility.

This new edition, like others before it, is consistent in offering a comprehensive overview of today's public relations practice, the issues facing the industry, and highlighting programs and campaigns that set the standard for excellence. Students learn from award-winning campaigns, but they also learn from situations where an organization's efforts were less than successful and have even bordered on a lack of ethical responsibility. That's why the "good, the bad, and the ugly" is included in this book.

New in the 11th Edition

The authors have considerably revised and updated every chapter of the book to reflect today's diverse public relations practice on the local, national, and international level. The suggestions of adopters and reviewers regarding the 10th edition have been given serious consideration and have helped make this edition even better than the last one.

Consequently, this edition contains the best of previous editions but, at the same time, has replaced all dated material with new information and case studies that reflect the pervasive use of the Internet and social media that has revolutionized the public relations industry. This makes this edition particularly relevant to students and instructors. The following highlights the new approach and content:

New Coauthor

We are pleased to add Dr. Bryan H. Reber, professor of public relations at the University of Georgia, as our new co-author. He is an experienced academic with more than 15 years of professional experience that and teaches a range of undergraduate and graduate courses in public relations. This not only gives him expertise but valuable insights on how to write and present material that help students learn and clearly understand basic concepts. He is well-known among fellow academics for his research and is highly regarded as a leader in public relations education.

New Social Media in Action Features

The use of the Internet and social media in public relations is pervasive throughout this new edition, but a new feature, Social Media in Action, spotlights particular programs that extensively used social media to accomplish their objectives or issues that involved the use of social media by various organizations. Some examples include the following:

- An ad agency hires interns through a Twitter campaign (Chapter 1)
- Dealing ethically with consumer websites (Chapter 3)
- Sterling Vineyards finds the perfect online host (Chapter 4)
- Google analytics guides a tourism campaign by New Brunswick (Chapter 5)
- Using social media in a national campaign for Hilton Double Tree hotels (Chapter 6)
- Nestle gets in social media fight with Greenpeace (Chapter 7)
- Chevy at SXSW (Chapter 8)
- Changing nutrition perceptions about McDonald's (Chapter 9)
- Getting the word out via social media after a tornado (Chapter 10)
- Clorox develops "potty humor" for moms (Chapter 11)
- FCC goes after celebrity social media endorsements (Chapter 12)
- Marriage equality symbol goes viral (Chapter 13)
- Samsung introduces its new Galaxy Note (Chapter 14)
- Red Bull uses website for "storytelling" (Chapter 15)
- Registering for conventions and events on the Web (Chapter 16)
- Social media helps Duke Energy communicate in wake of Hurricane Sandy (Chapter 17)
- A royal birth generates record Web traffic (Chapter 18)
- Centers for Disease Control (CDC) gets help from Zombies (Chapter 19)

New Features on Ethical Practice

Ethical practice in the real world is rarely a black-white situation. These new features focus on questionable practice and ask students to evaluate the situation from their own perspective and what they have learned about professional standards. Some samples:

- Facebook and its public relations firm conducts a stealth campaign against Google (Chapter 1)
- Was Ivy Lee less than honest during labor problems at a Colorado mine? (Chapter 2)
- Cash "bribes" for coverage in China (Chapter 3)

- Wal-Mart drops public relations firm for ethical lapse (Chapter 4)
- A grassroots campaign pits business against environmentalists (Chapter 6)
- Word-of-Mouth (WOM) campaigns raise concerns (Chapter 7)
- Lowe's stumbles on sponsorship of All-American Muslim (Chapter 11)
- Employers standards for employee blogs, social media outreach (Chapter 13)
- The blurring line between "earned" and "paid" media (Chapter 14)
- Student loan industry does "aggressive" lobbying (Chapter 19)
- Would you buy a T-shirt made in Bangladesh? (Chapter 20)

New Features Highlighting Award-Winning Campaigns

A key selling point of this new edition is new casebooks that make today's practice of public relations more "real" to students. A special effort has been made to focus on campaigns that would interest students and include brands that are familiar to them. Some samples include the following:

- A Miami Cuban restaurant celebrates its 40th anniversary (Chapter 1)
- IBM has a global birthday celebration (Chapter 4)
- 7-Eleven celebrates its birthday with free Slurpees (Chapter 4)
- Chase bank creates awareness of its new, premier credit card (Chapter 6)
- Infographic about using cell phones on the toilet is a hit (Chapter 7)
- Pampers campaign makes every Hispanic child special (Chapter 11)
- Ben & Jerry's celebrates same-sex marriage (Chapter 11)
- Social media fuel a solar decathlon by the U.S. Department of Energy (Chapter 13)
- Campaigns by Adidas, Singapore tap social media (Chapter 13)
- Video warns young people about decorative contact lenses (Chapter 15)
- A winning promotional strategy for a Picasso exhibit (Chapter 16)
- Mini-cases on promoting beer, garlic and even vibrators (Chapter 16)
- Fifty shades of tourism promotion: four mini-cases (Chapter 18)
- "Above the Influence" campaign by Drugfree.org (Chapter 19)

New Insights about Working in Public Relations

The theory and principles of public relations are important, but students considering a career in public relations also need to know about current trends and issues in the field, including guidelines on how to do a specific tactic. The following are a sampling of highlighted features that give students such insights:

- Traits needed to succeed in a public relations career (Chapter 1)
- The social media of the reformation in the 15th century (Chapter 2)
- The characteristics of a typical woman who is a VP of public relations (Chapter 2)
- A global study identifies the top issues facing public relations executives (Chapter 2)
- Three examples of foreign clients served by U.S. public relations firms (Chapter 4)

- Kenya issues a Request for Proposal (RFP) to promote tourism (Chapter 4)
- The "big picture" of how to do a program plan (Chapter 6)
- Are women better communicators than men? (Chapter 7)
- News releases are still valuable in the digital age (Chapter 7)
- How Ketchum evaluated its Double Tree hotels campaign (Chapter 8)
- How companies can become more "authentic" (Chapter 9)
- How to communicate with various ethnic groups (Chapter 11)
- Are conversations between clients and public relations counsel legally protected? (Chapter 12)
- The top ten organizations with Facebook and Twitter followers (Chapter 13)
- How to write a multimedia news release (Chapter 14)
- Edelman annual survey finds low trust about business (Chapter 17)
- The Super Bowl: An economic engine on steroids (Chapter 18)
- Obama's campaign team becomes a policy promotion team (Chapter 18)
- Google increases its Washington lobbying (Chapter 19)
- Crowdsourcing as a new way of fundraising (Chapter 21)

Updated Stats about the Public Relations Industry

This new edition provides the latest published statistics about the public relations industry and advances in the Internet and social media. Some samples include the following:

- The most recent salaries based on experience, gender, and job level (Chapter 1)
- The Global Alliance for Public Relations sets new standard of professional responsibility in the Melbourne Mandate (Chapter 3)
- The top ten public relations firms in the United States by income and employees (Chapter 4)
- Internet penetration and use throughout the world (Chapter 13)
- Share of audience by the leading social media sites (Chapter 13)
- The top four languages in the world in terms of speakers (Chapter 20)
- A breakdown of charitable giving in the United States by sources and recipients (Chapter 21)

Expanded Information on Diverse and Multicultural Audiences

Communicating with diverse, multicultural audiences is a necessity in today's society. A sampling of the following features will help students better understand the opportunities and the pitfalls:

- A campaign to highlight Hispanic lifestyles (Chapter 6)
- Minorities assure Obama's re-election (Chapter 11)

- Pepsi sponsors a global Latin music festival (Chapter 11)
- Educational levels and income of various ethnic groups (Chapter 11)
- Broadcast media has large Hispanic audience (Chapter 15)
- Chinese tourists flood the world (Chapter 18)
- Reaching out to the Muslim world (Chapter 20)

New Features on Conflict and Crisis Communications

Conflict and crisis often make the headlines, and students need to know that both advocates and opponents extensively use public relations to influence public opinion and legislation. The following new features, often from yesterday's headlines, will provide students with a good context for understanding the concepts of conflict and crisis management:

- Framing fracking: What is the truth? (Chapter 9)
- Gun control advocates and opponents square off (Chapter 9)
- Benetton faces criticism for using Bangladesh sweatshops (Chapter 10)
- Changing corporate culture helps Toyota recover its business (Chapter 10)
- MillerCoors faces controversy in sponsorship of Puerto Rican Day parade (Chapter 12)
- Coca Cola battles threats from regulatory and consumer groups (Chapter 12)
- Wal-Mart deals with angry investors after a bribery scandal (Chapter 17)
- A Chinese boycott affects Japan's automakers (Chapter 17)
- Carnival lines faces a crisis when a ship gets disabled (Chapter 18)
- Syria, other nations use social media as a weapon of war (Chapter 20)
- Campaign to combat the practice of female mutilation in Africa (Chapter 21)
- Apple resigns from U.S. Chamber of Commerce over global warming issues (Chapter 21)

Expanded Information on Internet and Social Media Analytics

The buzzword, Big Data, has now entered the mainstream and public relations professional are now using new software metrics and analytics for both research and measurement. Some examples for this new edition:

- Web analytics, use of dashboards, monitoring mentions on social media, conducting research surveys using social media (Chapter 5)
- How Hilton's DoubleTree hotels and Ketchum used research to plan a national campaign (Chapter 8)
- Measuring effectiveness on the Web (Chapter 8)
- The power and reach of Facebook by the numbers (Chapter 13)
- Does Justin Bieber really have 37 million followers? (Chapter 13)

Short Essays by Young Professionals

This new edition adds a new dimension by having young professionals tell students in their own voice about working in the trenches. Their writing style is breezy and personal, which students will enjoy.

- Robin Carr, director of public relations for Xoom, tells students to do more networking (Chapter 1)
- Kellie Bramlet, account executive at Black Sheep Agency, tells about the hectic life of working in a public relations firm (Chapter 4)
- Michelle Kraker, an experienced public relations professional, writes that being a social media manager is not all fun and games (Chapter 13)

Actual Job/Intern Postings in Public Relations

Students are curious about the type of jobs that are available in public relations. This edition provides some sample job descriptions and what qualifications are needed.

- What Ogilvy Public Relations expects in an application for an internship (Chapter 1)
- An entry-level position for a New York City public relations firm (Chapter 1)
- A Phoenix company seeks a public relations specialist (Chapter 4)
- A New York City firm seeks an experienced account executive (Chapter 4)
- A Los Angeles company seeks an event manager (Chapter 16)
- NBC Universal seeks a press coordinator (Chapter 18)
- Empire State College looking for a director of communications (Chapter 21)

Organization of the Book

This edition also continues its tradition of organizing the contents into five parts in order to give a complete overview of the field: These parts are (1) role, (2) process, (3) strategy, (4) tactics, and (5) application. Such an organization allows instructors the flexibility of selecting what parts of the book best fits the objectives and length of the course.

Part 1 is the role of public relations in society, which describes what public relations is and what kinds of specialization are available in the industry. It also gives a brief history of public relations, the development of professional practice, and how public relations department and firms do business.

Part 2 is the process of public relations that includes a chapter each on research, planning, communication, and evaluation.

Part 3 deals with strategy, which includes the concepts of public opinion and persuasion, conflict management and crisis communications, reaching diverse audiences, and the legal aspects that affect public relations practice.

Part 4 is an overview of the actual tactics used by public relations professionals such as the use of the Internet and social media, preparing materials for mass media, placements on radio and television, and how meetings and events advance public relations goals.

Part 5 shows how public relations is used by various segments of society. Corporate public relations leads off and is followed by entertainment, sports, and tourism. The last three chapters deals with politics and government, global public relations, and non-profits in health and education.

Student Learning Tools

Each chapter of *Public Relations: Strategies and Tactics* includes several learning tools to help students better understand and remember the principles of public relations, and to give them the practice they need to apply those principles to real-life situations. This edition continues the tradition of providing key student learning aids at the beginning and end of every chapter. In each chapter, you will find:

- **Chapter-Opening Preview.** Learning objectives for students are succinctly stated at the beginning of every chapter.
- **End-of-Chapter Summary.** The major themes are summarized at the end of each chapter.
- **End-of-chapter Case Activity.** A public relations situation or dilemma based on actual cases is posed, and students are asked to apply what they have just read in assigned chapter. These case problems can be used either for class discussion, group projects, or as written assignments. The following are some new case activities in this edition:
  - Promoting beef jerky as a healthy snack (Chapter 1)
  - Do men and women have different perceptions of public relations as a career? (Chapter 2)
  - Three ethical dilemmas in the workplace (Chapter 3)
  - Conducting research to determine a course of action in fighting a rumor (Chapter 5)
  - Promoting increased public awareness of "fair trade" coffee (Chapter 6)
  - A new campaign to combat heart disease (Chapter 7)
  - How to evaluate the success of Mexico's tourism campaign (Chapter 8)
  - Convincing fellow students to do fundraising for a cause (Chapter 9)
  - Business and minority groups fight a soda ban in New York City (Chapter 10)
  - A campaign to increase student diversity at a university (Chapter 11)
  - Should employers restrict social media use by employees? (Chapter 12)
  - Planning special events to promote a luxury handbag (Chapter 16)
  - Planning a corporate wellness campaign (Chapter 17)
  - Planning a promotion for a Colorado resort (Chapter 18)
  - A health campaign about a possible flu epidemic (Chapter 19)
  - A social media campaign for Goodwill Industries (Chapter 21)
- **Questions for Review and Discussion.** A list of questions at the end of each chapter helps students prepare for tests and also stimulates class discussion.

- **Media Resources.** These updated end-of-chapter lists of readings and websites give students additional references for exploring topics brought up in the chapter.
- **Useful Websites and Bibliography.** This updated collection of selected books, periodicals, and directories at the end of the book provides a more complete list of references for students wishing to conduct further research.

Instructor Resources

Name of Supplement	Description
Instructor's Manual and Test Bank	This comprehensive instructor resource provides learning objectives, chapter outlines, sample syllabi, class activities, and discussion questions. The fully reviewed Test Bank offers more than 700 test questions in multiple-choice, true/false, and essay format. Each question is referenced by page. Available for download at www.pearsonglobaleditions.com/Wilcox (access code required).
PowerPoint™ Presentation Package	This text-specific package provides lecture slides based on key concepts in the text. Available for download at www.pearsonglobaleditions.com/Wilcox (access code required).

To learn more about our programs, pricing options, and customization, visit www.pearsonglobaleditions.com/Wilcox.

Acknowledgments

We would like to thank the following reviewers for their expertise and their helpful and insightful suggestions for the development of this text:

Josh Boyd, Purdue University
Karyn Brown, Mississippi State University
Christopher Caldiero, Farleigh Dickinson University
Robert A. Carroll, York College of Pennsylvania
Jennifer Chin, University of North Carolina, Wilmington
Janine W. Dunlap, Freed-Hardeman University
Gregg Feistman, Temple University
W. Gerry Gilmer, Florida State University
Randy Hines, Susquehanna University
Steve G. Mandel, Pennsylvania State University
Teresa Mastin, Michigan State University
Ronda L. Menke, Drake University
Maureen Taylor, Rutgers University
Kelly Kinner Tryba, University of Colorado at Boulder

Beth Wood, Indiana University
Brenda J. Wrigley, Syracuse University
Alan Adelman, Santa Monica College
Lily Ungar, University of California, Los Angeles
Maxey Parish, Baylor University
Susan Hunt-Bradford, Saint Louis Community College
Christopher Bond, Missouri Western State University

Pearson wishes to thank the following people for their work on the content of the Global Edition:

Contributor:

Jaishri Jethwaney, Indian Institute of Mass Communication, New Delhi

Reviewers:

Matt Grant, School of Arts and Communication, University of Southern Queensland, and School of Public Health, Tropical Medicine and Rehabilitation Sciences, James Cook University, Queensland, Australia
Iqbal Sachdeva
Archana Singh, School of Communication Studies, Panjab University, Chandigarh, India

About the Authors

Dennis L. Wilcox, Ph.D., is professor emeritus of public relations and past director of the School of Journalism & Mass Communications at San Jose State University, California. He is a Fellow and accredited (APR) member of the Public Relations Society of America, former chair of the PRSA Educator's Academy, and past chair of the public relations division of AEJMC. Among his six books, Dr. Wilcox is the lead author of *Public Relations: Strategies and Tactics* and *Think: Public Relation, and Public Relations Writing and Media Techniques.* His honors include PRSA's "Outstanding Educator," the Xifra Award from the University of Girona (Spain), and an honorary doctorate from the University of Bucharest. He is currently a member of the International Public Relations Association (IPRA) and the Arthur W. Page Society, a group of senior communication executives. Dr. Wilcox regularly gives presentations at international conferences and to students and professionals in such diverse nations as Thailand, India, Latvia, Serbia, and Argentina. Dennis.Wilcox@sjsu.edu

Glen T. Cameron, Ph.D., is Gregory Chair in Journalism Research and founder of the Health Communication Research Center at the University of Missouri. Dr. Cameron has authored more than 300 articles, chapters, and award-winning conference papers on public relations topics. In addition to being coauthor of *Public Relations: Strategies and Tactics*, he is also coauthor of *Think: Public Relations and Public Relations Today: Managing Competition and Conflict*. A popular lecturer internationally, Dr. Cameron has received the **Baskett-Moss** and **Pathfinder** awards for career achievement. Dr. Cameron gains ongoing public relations experience by managing over $42 million in external funding of health public relations projects for sources such as NIH, NCI, Missouri Foundation for Health, USDA, CDC, the U.S. Department of Defense, and Monsanto. Camerong@missouri.edu

Bryan H. Reber, Ph.D., is professor of public relations at the University of Georgia's Grady College of Journalism and Mass Communication. He teaches introduction to public relations, management, writing, and campaigns. On the graduate level he teaches management, persuasion, campaign research, and public opinion. His research focuses on public relations theory, practice, pedagogy, and health communication. Dr. Reber regularly presents his research at national and international conference and has published his research in such publications as the *Journal of Public Relations Research* and *Public Relations Review*. He is the coauthor of several books, including *Think: Public Relations, Public Relations Writing & Media Tactics*, and *Public Relations Today: Managing Competition and Conflict*. Dr. Reber worked for 15 years in public relations at Bethel College, Kansas. He has conducted research for the Sierra Club, Ketchum, and the Georgia Hospital Association, among others. Reber@uga.edu

chapter 1

Defining Public Relations

After reading this chapter, you will be able to:

Be familiar with the global scope of the public relations industry

Have a good definition of public relations

Understand that public relations is a process, not an event

Know the difference between public relations, journalism, advertising, and marketing

Assess the skills needed for a public relations career and what salary to expect

The Challenge of Public Relations

It is 9 A.M. and Anne-Marie, a senior account executive in a San Francisco public relations firm, is at her desk getting ready for a full day of busy activity. She takes a few minutes to answer some text messages, scan her e-mails, and tweet a printing firm about the status of a brochure. She also quickly flips through the local daily, reviews the online editions of the *Wall Street Journal* and the *New York Times*, and checks her Google Alerts list to catch up on any late-breaking news or postings about the firm's clients.

She downloads a *Wall Street Journal* article about the increasing risk of tainted food from foreign suppliers and makes a note to have her student intern do some more research about this issue. One of Anne-Marie's clients is a restaurant chain, and she senses an opportunity for the client to capitalize on the media interest by informing the press and the public about what the restaurant chain is doing to ensure the quality and safety of their meals.

She then finishes a draft of a news release about a client's new tablet computer and forwards it to her supervisor, a vice president of client services, for review before it is e-mailed to the client. She will also attach a note that an electronic news service can deliver it to newspapers across the country later in the day. Anne-Marie's next activity is a brainstorming session with other staff members in the conference room to generate creative ideas about revamping a Facebook page for a microbrewery that will generate more interest and "likes."

When she gets back to her office, she finds more text messages, tweets, and voicemails. A reporter for a trade publication needs background information on a story he is writing; a graphic designer has finished a rough draft of a client's new logo; a catering manager has called about final arrangements for a VIP reception at an art gallery; and a video producer asks Anne-Marie to preview a video clip of a celebrity giving a testimonial about a client's new designer jeans. Once the video is finalized, it will be uploaded to YouTube, the company's web page, and distributed by satellite to television stations throughout the nation.

Lunch is with a client who wants her counsel on how to position the company as environmentally conscious and dedicated to sustainable development. After lunch, Anne-Marie walks back to the office while talking on her phone to a colleague in the New York office about an upcoming satellite media tour (SMT) to announce a national food company's campaign to reduce childhood obesity. She also calls an editor to "pitch" a story about a client's new product. He's interested, so she follows up by sending some background material via a tweet providing links to several websites. Back in the office, Anne-Marie touches base with other members of her team, who are working on a 12-city media tour by an Olympic champion representing Nike.

Then it's back to the computer. She checks several online databases to gather information about the industry of a new client. She also reviews online news updates and postings on popular blogs to find out if anything is being said about her clients. At 5 P.M., as she winds down from the day's hectic activities, she reviews news stories from an electronic monitoring service about another client, an association of strawberry producers. She is pleased to find that her feature story, which included recipes and color photos, appeared in 150 dailies and were also used by several influential food bloggers.

But the day isn't quite done. Anne-Marie is on her way to attend a chapter meeting of the Public Relations Society of America (PRSA), where the speaker will discuss trends in reputation management. It's her way of continuing her education since her graduation from college four years ago with public relations major and a minor in marketing. After the meeting, she networks with several other members over a glass of wine and a quick dinner. It's a nice respite from the constant deluge of text messages, e-mails, and tweets on her mobile phone that must be dealt with before she calls it a day.

As this scenario illustrates, the profession of public relations is multifaceted and public relations professionals have many roles as shown in the infographic on page 43. A public relations professional must have skills in written and interpersonal communication, media relations and social media, research, negotiation, creativity, logistics, facilitation, problem solving, and strategic thinking.

Indeed, those who want a challenging career with plenty of variety often choose the field of public relations. The U.S. Bureau of Labor Statistics (www.bls.gov/ooh) estimates that the field already employs more than 300,000 people nationwide, and its 2012–2013 *Occupational Outlook Handbook* projects a 23 percent growth rate in public relations specialists through 2020, faster than the average for all occupations. The handbook notes that the growth of the public relations occupation ". . . will be driven by the need for organizations to maintain their public image in a high-information age and with the growth of social media." The handbook also gives a good description of what public relations managers and specialist do; as can be seen in the Insights box which follows.

More good news: A public relations although battered by the recent economic recession, seems to be somewhat resilient. Jim Rutherford, executive vice president (EVP) of private equity firm Veronis Suhler Stevenson (VSS), quipped to *PRWeek*, "The economy may have been in a downturn, but even companies in bankruptcy protection had to communicate to their stakeholders."

on the job INSIGHTS

The Nature of Public Relations Work

The *Occupational Outlook Handbook 2012–13*, published by the U.S Bureau of Labor Statistics (www.bls.gov/ooh), describes the various activities of public relations specialists and managers:

Duties

Public relations managers and specialists typically do the following:

- Write news releases and prepare information for the media.
- Identify main client groups and audiences and determine the best way to reach them.
- Respond to requests for information from the media or designate an appropriate spokesperson for information source.
- Helps clients communicate effectively with the public.
- Develop and maintain their organization's corporate image and identity, using logos and signs.
- Draft speeches and arrange interviews for an organization's top executives.
- Evaluate advertising and promotion programs to determine whether they are compatible with the organization's public relations efforts.
- Develop and carry out fundraising strategies for an organization by identifying and contacting potential donors and applying for grants.

(continued)

Public relations specialists, also called communication specialists and media specialists, handle an organization's communication with the public, including consumers, investors, reporters, and other media specialists. In government, public relations specialists may be called press secretaries. They keep the public informed about the activities of government officials and agencies.

Public relations specialists must understand the attitudes and concerns of the groups they interact with to maintain cooperative relationships with them.

Public relations specialists draft news releases and contact people in the media who might print or broadcast the material. Many radio or television special reports, newspaper stories, and magazine articles start at the desks of public relations specialists. For example, a news release might describe a public issue, such as health, energy, or the environment, and what an organization does to advance that issue. In addition to publication through traditional media outlets, releases are increasingly being sent through the Web and social media.

Public relations managers review and sometimes write news releases. They also sponsor corporate events to help maintain and improve the image and identity of their organization or client.

In addition, they help to clarify their organization's point of view to its main audience through media releases and interviews. Public relations managers observe social, economic, and political trends that might ultimately affect the organization, and they recommend ways to enhance the firm's image based on these trends. For example, in response to a growing concern about the environment, an oil company may create a public relations campaign to publicize its efforts to develop cleaner fuels.

> Public relations managers and specialists create and maintain a favorable public image for their employer or client. They write material for media releases, plan and direct public relations programs, and raise funds for their organizations.
>
> —*U.S. Bureau of Labor Statistics*

In large organizations, public relations managers may supervise a staff of public relations specialists. They also work with advertising and marketing staffs to make sure that advertising campaigns are compatible with the image the company or client is trying to portray. For example, if the firm has decided to emphasize its appeal to a certain group, such as younger people, the public relations manager ensures that current advertisements will be well received by that group.

In addition, public relations managers may handle internal communications, such as company newsletters, and may help financial managers produce an organization's reports. They may help the organization's top executives by drafting speeches, arranging interviews, and maintaining other forms of public contact. Public relations managers must be able to work well with many types of specialists to accurately report the facts. In some cases, the information they write has legal consequences. They must work with the company's or client's lawyers to be sure that the information they release is both legally accurate and clear to the public.

In addition to the ability to communicate thoughts clearly and simply, public relations specialists and managers must show creativity, initiative, and good judgment. Decision-making, problem-solving, and research skills also are important. People who choose public relations as a career should have an outgoing personality, self-confidence, an understanding of human psychology, and an enthusiasm for motivating people. They should be assertive but able to participate as part of a team and be open to new ideas.

A Global Industry

Public relations, however, is not just an American activity. It is also a worldwide industry. The global dimensions of public relations can be illustrated in several ways. The following gives some background on (1) the global market, (2) the number of practitioners, (3) regions of major growth, and (4) the growth of public relations as an academic discipline.

Global Expenditures on Public Relations In terms of economics, the public relations field is most extensively developed in the United States. Private equity firm Veronis Suhler Stevenson (VSS), which has been tracking the communications industry for the past 15 years, reported that spending on public relations in the United States was $3.7 billion in 2009. CNN, however, estimated that about $5 billion was spent by U.S. companies on public relations in 2012, a somewhat small amount compared to the $150 billion spent annually on advertising.

A major factor in the recent growth of the public relations industry is the overwhelming presence of the Internet. According to the *Economist*, "The rise of the Internet and social media has given PR a big boost. Many big firms have a presence on social networking sites, such as Facebook and Twitter, overseen by PR staff. PR firms are increasingly called on to track what consumers are saying about their clients online and to respond directly to any negative commentary."

Increased use of social media also is expected to increase employment growth for public relations specialists. These new media outlets will create more work for public relations workers, increasing the number and kinds of avenues of communication between organizations and the public.

U.S. Department of Labor

The amount spent on public relations for the rest of the world is somewhat sketchy and not well documented. One major reason is that public relations can include a number of activities that overlap into such areas as marketing, promotion, direct mail, event sponsorships, and even word-of-mouth advertising. The *Holmes Report*, which also ranks the 250 biggest PR firms in the world, estimates that public relations was a $10 billion global business in 2012. Other research estimates that about $3 billion of this amount comes from European spending on public relations due to the expansion of the European Union (EU) and the emerging economies of Russia, Ukraine, the Czech Republic and the Baltic nations. There is also considerable growth in other regions of the world, particularly China, which will be discussed shortly.

An Estimated 3 Million Practitioners The Global Alliance (www.globalalliancepr.org), with about 40 national and regional public relations associations representing 160,000 members, estimates that some 3 million people worldwide practice public relations as their main occupation. This includes the estimated 320,000 practitioners in the United States, and also the estimated 50,000 located in the United Kingdom (UK). It's also estimated that there are between 7,000 and 10,000 public relations firms in the United States, and the directory *Hollis Europe* lists almost 3,000 public relations firms (consultancies) in 40 European nations. In addition, there are now an estimated 10,000 firms in China, according to the *Holmes Report*.

Many of these firms are one-person operations, but also included are firms with hundreds of employees. There are, of course, literally thousands of companies, governmental organizations, and nonprofits around the world that also have in-house public relations departments and staffs.

There is also about 200 national and regional public relations organizations around the world. A partial list that shows the geographic diversity includes the following: Public Relations Institute of Southern Africa (PRISA), the Spanish Association of Communicators (DIRCOM), the Public Relations Institute of Australia (PRIA), the Public Relations Society of Serbia, the Canadian Public Relations Society (CPRS), the Public Relations Society of Kenya (PRSK), the Institute of Public Relations (United Kingdom), the Romania Public Relations Association (RPRA), the Public Relations Agencies Association of Mexico (PRAA), Relaciones Publigas America Latina (ALARP), the Consejo Professional de Relaciones Publicas of Argentina, the Public Relations Society of India (PRSI), and the Middle East Public Relations Association (MEPRA).

An Explosion of Growth in China, Other Nations Major growth is also occurring in Asia for several reasons. China is literally the "new frontier." Since opening its economy to market capitalism 30 years ago, China today is the world's second largest economy after the United States. And the public relations industry is increasing at the rate of 20 percent annually, according to *PRWeek*. The China International Public Relations Association (CIPRA) reports that the industry employs about 500,000 people and every major global public relations firm now has offices in the country. According to the *Economist*, the Chinese public relations market is about $2 billion annually.

China's membership in the World Trade Organization (WTO) opened the floodgate for more public relations activity by international companies engaged in a fierce competition for the bonanza of reaching more than a billion potential customers. The biggest trend, according to the *Economist*, is now a soaring demand for public relations among Chinese companies as they actively seek local consumers, foreign investments, and international outlets for their goods. The 2008 Beijing Olympics and the 2010 Shanghai World Expo further fueled the dynamic growth of public relations in China.

Other nations, such as Malaysia, Korea, Thailand, Singapore, Indonesia, and India, are also rapidly expanding their domestic and international markets, which creates a fertile environment for increased public relations activity. India has great economic and public relations potential because, like China, it has over 1 billion people and is also moving toward a more robust market economy. Africa and Latin America also present growth opportunities, stimulated in part by hosting international events. South Africa hosted the World Cup soccer championship in 2010 and Brazil will host the Summer Olympics in 2016. A more detailed discussion of international public relations is found in Chapter 20.

A Proliferation of University Courses Large numbers of students around the world are studying public relations as a career field. One study by Professor Elizabeth Toth and her colleagues at the University of Maryland surveyed English-only websites and found 218 degree, certificate, and diploma programs offered in 39 countries. In another study by Chunhui He and Jing Xie at Zheijiang University's Communications Studies Institute, they report that more than 300 universities in China have now added public relations to their course offerings.

A similar number of U.S. colleges and universities have bachelor and graduate degrees in public relations, according to *PRWeek*. In addition, many other universities offer one or more public relations courses in such areas as communication studies and business administration. Most majors, however, are in departments or schools of journalism. In these units, the 2012 annual survey of journalism and mass communication enrollment by Lee Becker and his associates at the University of Georgia (www.grady.uga.edu/annualsurveys) reported that almost a third of the students (66,000) were studying public relations, strategic communications, or advertising.

In Europe, an estimated 100 universities also offer studies in the subject. Unlike the United States, however, many courses are taught in a faculty of economics or business. Public relations study is popular in such nations as the Netherlands, Germany, Serbia, Romania, Latvia, Estonia, and Finland. Many Asian universities, particularly those in Thailand, Korea, Indonesia, India, and the Philippines, also offer major programs. Australia and New Zealand have a long history of public relations education.

In South America, particularly in Argentina, Chile, and Brazil, public relations is taught at many universities. South African universities have the most developed public relations curriculum on the African continent, but programs of study can also be found in Nigeria, Ghana, and Kenya. The Middle East, particularly the United Arab Emirates, introduced public relations into university curriculums during the mid-1990s. In sum, public relations is a well-established academic subject that is taught and practiced on a global scale.

A Definition of Public Relations

Public relations has been defined in many ways. Rex Harlow, a Stanford professor and founder of the organization that became the Public Relations Society of America, once compiled more than 500 definitions from almost as many sources. The definitions ranged from the simple, "Doing good and getting credit for it," to more verbose definitions. Harlow's collective definition, for example, is almost 100 words.

One early definition that gained wide acceptance was formulated by the newsletter *PR News*: "Public relations is the management function which evaluates public attitudes, identifies the policies and procedures of an individual or an organization with the public interest, and plans and executes a program of action to earn public understanding and patience."

> Public relations is a strategic communication process that builds mutually beneficial relationships between organizations and their publics.
>
> *Public Relations Society of America*

Other definitions are provided by theorists and textbook authors. One of the first major textbooks the field, *Effective Public Relations* by Scott Cutlip and Allen Center, stated, "Public relations is the management function that identifies, establishes, and maintains mutually beneficial relationships between an organization and the various publics on whom its success or failure depends." The management function was also emphasized more than 25 years ago in *Managing Public Relations* by James E. Grunig and Todd Hunt. They said, "Public relations is the management of communication between an organization and its publics."

National and international public relations organizations, including the PRSA, also have formulated definitions. Here are two examples:

- "Public relations is influencing behaviour to achieve objectives through the effective management of relationships and communications." (British Institute of Public Relations, whose definition has also been adopted in a number of Commonwealth nations)
- "Public relations practice is the art and social science of analyzing trends, predicting their consequences, counseling organization leaders, and implementing planned programs of action which serve both the organization's and the public's interest." (1978 World Assembly of Public Relations in Mexico City and endorsed by 34 national public relations organizations)

A good definition for today's modern practice is offered by Professors Lawrence W. Long and Vincent Hazleton, who describe public relations as "a communication function of management through which organizations adapt to, alter, or maintain their environment for the purpose of achieving organizational goals." Their approach promotes the idea that public relations should also foster open, two-way communication and mutual understanding, with the idea that an organization—not just the target audience—changes its attitudes and behaviors in the process.

The most recent rendition of a definition was formulated by the PRSA in 2012. After considerable research and feedback from its members, the organization announced the following: "Public relations is a strategic communication process that builds mutually beneficial relationships between an organization and their publics." The infographic below shows the numerous words that are associated with the concept of public relations.

Figure 1.1 Words That Describe Public Relations

A number of concepts and words are associated with a definition of today's public relations. This infographic from the Public Relations Society of America (PRSA) shows the words in larger type that are most frequently associated with public relations.

The PRSA definition and other modern definitions of public relations emphasize the building of mutually beneficial relationships between the organization and its various publics. A more assertive approach, however, is offered by Professor Glen Cameron, at the University of Missouri School of Journalism. He defines public relations as the "strategic management of competition and conflict for the benefit of one's own organization—and when possible—also for the mutual benefit of the organization and its various stakeholders or publics."

It isn't necessary, however, to memorize any particular definition of public relations. It's more important to remember the key words that are used in most definitions that frame today's modern public relations. The key words are:

- **Deliberate.** Public relations activity is intentional. It is designed to influence, gain understanding, provide information, and obtain feedback from those affected by the activity.
- **Planned.** Public relations activity is organized. Solutions to problems are discovered and logistics are thought out, with the activity taking place over a period of time. It is systematic, requiring research and strategic thinking.
- **Performance.** Effective public relations is based on actual policies and performance. No amount of public relations will generate goodwill and support if the organization has poor policies and is unresponsive to public concerns.
- **Public interest.** Public relations activity should be mutually beneficial to the organization and the public; it is the alignment of the organization's self-interests with the public's concerns and interests.
- **Two-way communication.** Public relations is not just disseminating information but also the art of listening and engaging in a conversation with various publics.
- **Management function.** Public relations is most effective when it is a strategic and integral part of decision making by top management. Public relations involves counseling, problem solving, and the management of competition and conflict.

To summarize, you can grasp the essential elements of effective public relations by remembering the following words and phrases: deliberate . . . planned . . . performance . . . public interest . . . two-way communication . . . strategic management function. The elements of public relations just described are part of the process that defines today's public relations.

Other Popular Names

Public relations is used as an umbrella term on a worldwide basis. Most national membership associations, from the Azerbaijan Public Relations Association to the Zimbabwe Institute of Public Relations, identify themselves with that term.

Individual companies and other groups, however, often use other terms to describe the public relations function. The most popular term among Fortune 500 companies is *corporate communications*. This description is used by such companies as McDonald's, BMW of North America, Toyota, Walt Disney, and Walgreens. Other companies, such as GM and Xerox, just use the term *communications*.

A number of corporations also use combination titles to describe the public relations function within the organization. IBM, for example, has a senior vice president (SVP) of marketing and communications. At Facebook, the public relations executive is in charge of *communications and public policy*. Johnson & Johnson goes with *public affairs and corporate communications*, while L'Oreal USA uses *corporate communications and external affairs*. Other companies think in more global terms. The public relations executive at Coca-Cola, for example, is in charge of *worldwide public affairs and communications*, and FedEx uses *worldwide communications and investor relations*.

The use of *corporate communications* is based, in part, on the belief that the term is broader than *public relations*, which is often incorrectly perceived as only *media relations*. Corporate communications, many argue, encompasses all communications of the company, including advertising, marketing communications, public affairs, community relations, and employee communications.

Public information and *public affairs* are the most widely used terms by nonprofits, universities, and government agencies. The implication is that only information is being disseminated, in contrast to persuasive communication, generally perceived as the purpose of public relations. Social services agencies often use the term *community relations*, and the military is fond of *public affairs*. Increasingly, many nonprofits are using the term *marketing communications*, as they reorient to the idea that they must sell their services and generate donations in a highly competitive environment.

Other organizations use a term that better describes the primary activity of the department. It is clear, for example, that a department of investor relations deals primarily with stockholders, institutional investors, and the financial press. Likewise, a department of environmental affairs, community relations, or employee communications is self-explanatory. A department of marketing communications primarily emphasizes product publicity and promotion. The organization and functions of communications departments are discussed in Chapter 4.

Like departments, individuals specialize in subcategories of public relations. A person who deals exclusively with placement of stories in the media is, to be precise, a *publicist*. Publicists are specialists that concentrate on finding unusual news angles and planning events or "happenings" that attract media attention—a stunt by an aspiring Hollywood actress, for example, or an attempt to be listed in the *Guinness Book of Records* by baking the world's largest apple pie. *Publicist* and *Press Agent* are honorable terms in the entertainment and celebrity business, but such titles are rarely used by the mainstream public relations industry. Chapter 18 discusses the work of New York and Hollywood publicists.

Public Relations Hollywood Style

Samantha Jones (Kim Cattrall) leads aglamorous life as the owner of a public relations firm in the television series *Sex and the City*. In the second movie sequel, she even goes to Abu Dhabi to plan a public relations campaign for a luxury hotel. Public relations work, however, requires more than wearing designer clothes and going to dinner parties.

Stereotypes and Less Flattering Terms

Unfortunately, the public often has a much different image of public relations. A common stereotype is that public relations is a glamorous field because public relations practitioners meet exciting and interesting people, go to parties, and generally spend the day doing a lot of schmoozing.

The reality, of course, is less glamorous. CareerCast, for example, lists "Event Coordinator" as the sixth most stressful job in America, followed by "PR Executive" in seventh place. The major stress, reports CareerCast, is that "these professionals are in a very competitive field, which often includes highly visible, tight deadlines." In addition, ". . . some PR executives are required to interact with potentially hostile members of the media, especially after a disaster." Practitioners also have to deal with the stress of working with clients and employers who often have unrealistic expectations.

Women, in particular, are stereotyped. "Pop culture," says Adrianna Giulani of Devries Public Relations, "is chock full of stereotypes of women in PR. All you have to do is tune into E!, HBO, and TBS to see 'power girls' wield control at the doors of parties. . . ." She adds, "The danger of these portrayals is that, as we all know in our business, media not only reflects popular opinion but it shapes it. While sensationalized images of women living in 'spin city' might be more entertaining to watch . . . I would say the 'PR girls' that rule today are more likely to worship hashtags than shoes."

Other television programs and movies also give somewhat negative stereotypes about public relations. An early example of glamorizing the field was Samantha Jones (Kim Cattrall) as the owner of a public relations firm in the television series *Sex and the City*, plus two movie sequels, who seemed to spend most of her time meeting men and wearing designer clothes. ABC's *Spin City*, on the other hand, featured Michael J. Fox as the deputy mayor of New York, who protected his bumbling boss from the media and public. More recently, Bravo launched a reality show, *Kell on Earth*, that the *New York Times* described as "a reality show that follows a publicist, Kelly Cutrone, as she bullies and cajoles her way through the underbelly of the New York fashion world." *Mad Men*, a series about an advertising firm in the 1960s, has also portrayed public relations as a somewhat dubious activity with no moral compass.

Some films are satires, but still project a negative image of public relations. *Thank You for Smoking*, a movie adapted from the book by Christopher Buckley, is a particularly good satire about a public relations person defending the tobacco industry. *Wag the Dog*, starring Dustin Hoffman and Robert DeNiro, is also a satire focusing on how an embattled president creates a fake war with the help of public relations pros to improve his image. A more recent film, *Bruno*, with leading actor Sacha Baron Cohen, played up the "dumb blonde" syndrome. At one point in the film, Sacha's fictional character asks two sisters who run a public relations firm in Los Angeles, "What charities are hot now?" They replied, "Darfur." He then asked them where Darfur is, and they didn't have a clue.

Other negative stereotypes are perpetuated by journalists who use terms such as "PR stunt" or "PR fluff." One journalist once described public relations as "the art of saying nothing." Joe Norcera, a business columnist for the *New York Times*, once expressed his frustration with Apple public relations reps by writing "This is another Apple innovation: the robotic spokesman who says only what he's programmed to say." See the Insights box about Apple being accused of a doing a "PR stunt."

Norcera and other journalists often express frustration when they feel that public relations personnel are stonewalling, providing misleading information, or not being readily accessible to fully answer questions. This is traditionally a problem of effective media relations and, quite frankly, incompetence occurs in all fields, including public relations. Chapters 14 and 15 discuss the responsibilities of public relations personnel to provide assistance to media personnel.

Public relations is also referred to as *spin*. This term first appeared in a 1984 *New York Times* editorial about the activities of President Ronald Reagan's reelection campaign. In the beginning, the meaning of *spin* was restricted to what often were considered the unethical and misleading activities and tactics of political campaign consultants. Today, however, the media widely use the term to describe any effort by an individual or organization to interpret an event or issue according to a particular viewpoint. On occasion, however, spin can lead to a question of ethics, which is highlighted in the Ethics box on page 39. A more academic term for spin is the concept of *framing*. Multiple research studies show how journalists, as well as public relations personnel, "frame" issues. See Chapter 9 for more on the theory of framing.

on the job INSIGHTS

Is Apple's Decision to Build Macs in the United States a "Publicity Stunt"?

Apple's CEO Tim Cook made headlines in December 2012 when he announced that the company would make a $l00 million investment to make Macs in the United States. Although many lauded the decision as a major contribution to the "made in America" movement, others were less than impressed, calling the decision a "PR stunt" or simply just a "PR initiative," inferring that the Apple decision didn't have much substance.

The cynics pointed out that Apple could have done more because it was sitting on more than $120 billion in cash reserves and that the $l00 million investment was only 1 percent of Apple's annual $l0 billion that it spends on capital expenditures. Others say the rationale for the decision was primarily a public relations decision to get some favorable press to counteract criticism by human rights groups about the safety incidents and high working hours in Chinese factories where the vast majority of its products are assembled. *San Jose Mercury News* columnist Mike Cassidy, who covers Silicon Valley, was more forgiving. He wrote, "OK, maybe it takes a little zip out the Apple-comes-to-America story. But why dwell on the negative? A journey of 1,000 miles—or from Shenzhen to the United States, for that matter, starts with a first step."

What do you think? Was Apple's decision only a "PR stunt" without much substance or a decision by a socially responsible corporation to bring manufacturing jobs back to the United States?

Figure 1.2 Public Relations as "Image Building"

The image of an organization is made up of many factors, and public relations is only one of them. (Copyright © The New Yorker Collection 2004. Mick Stevens from www.cartoonbank.com. All rights reserved.)

on the job ETHICS

Facebook's Attempt at "Spin" Makes No Friends

There's nothing wrong with the use of "spin," presenting information in the most favorable light for an organization, but it does raise ethical issues when there is a lack of disclosure regarding the source of the information. This was the case when Burson-Marsteller, a major public relations firm, attempted to hide Facebook as its client when it launched a "whisper campaign" to discredit Google's privacy policies.

Two B-M staffers, both former journalists, contacted major tech bloggers and reporters at major publications to offer information and help them write opinion articles criticizing Google. When several suspicious bloggers asked them the name of their client, they refused to answer. It didn't take long for *USA Today* and the *Daily Beast* to figure out that B-M was engaging a "spin" campaign on behalf of its client, Facebook.

The fallout was immediate. Many publications picked up the story and the issue went viral on the Internet. The headlines said it all: "Facebook waged stealth PR war on Google" and "Facebook unmasked as Burson-Marsteller's mystery client." Leading bloggers also criticized both Facebook and B-M for a lack of disclosure and transparency. Fraser Seitel, a public relations counselor in New York, told *Ragan's PR Daily*, "If Facebook has problems with Google, then it should have the confidence and decency to express the reasons why, from the mouth of a Facebook executive."

Others in the public relations community also slammed Burson-Marsteller for a lack of professional ethics for agreeing to hide Facebook as a client. Rosanna Fiske, chair of the Public Relations Society of America wrote that the core tenet of the PRSA code is honesty. "Under the PRSA code," she said, "B-M would be obligated to reveal its client and disclose the client's intentions, which appear to mount an attack on Google's practices." Steve Barrett, editor of *PRWeek*, also wrote, "In not disclosing Facebook as its client, Burson engaged in activity that contravenes industry guidelines and is considered unethical."

Both Facebook and Burson-Marsteller suffered major damage to their reputations and sought to minimize the negative coverage by doing some more "spin." Facebook, for example, denied that the company had engaged in a "smear campaign" and was only trying to bring a privacy problem to the attention of the public. Burson-Marsteller, no longer representing Facebook, said that the failure to disclose its client was against its policies and that it was redistributing its code of ethics to all employees to ensure that it would not happen again.

Another term with a long history is *flack*. These words are derisive slang terms that journalists often use for a press agent or anyone else working in public relations. It's like calling a journalist a "hack." Although in recent years most publications, including the *Wall Street Journal*, have refrained from using the "F" word in news stories, columnists still occasionally use the word.

The term has a mixed history. According to Wes Pedersen, a former director of communications for the Public Affairs Council, the term *flack* originated in 1939 in *Variety*, the show business publication. It began using *flack* as a synonym for *press agent*, he says, "in tribute to the skills of Gene Flack in publicizing motion pictures." Others say the word flack was used during World War I to describe heavy ground fire aimed at enemy aircraft, and journalists often feel they also are bombarded with a barrage of news releases.

Within the public relations community, feeling also exists that *PR* is a slang term that carries a somewhat denigrating connotation. The late Sam Black, a public relations consultant in the United Kingdom and author of several books on public relations, said, "The use of 'PR' probably originated as a nickname for 'press relations,'" the primary activity of public relations in its early years (see Chapter 2).

Although PR is now more than press relations, the nickname is commonly used in daily conversation and is widely recognized around the world. A good compromise, which this book uses, is to adopt the style of spelling out "public relations" in the body of a text or article but to use the shorter term, "PR," if it is used in a direct quote.

Public Relations as a Process

Public relations is a process—that is, a series of actions, changes, or functions that bring about a result. One popular way to describe the process, and to remember its components, is to use the RACE acronym, first articulated by John Marston in his book *The Nature of Public Relations*. Essentially, RACE means that public relations activity consists of four key elements, which are explained in Chapters 5–8:

- **R**esearch. What is the problem or situation?
- **A**ction (program planning). What is going to be done about it?
- **C**ommunication (execution). How will the public be told?
- **E**valuation. Was the audience reached and what was the effect?

Another acronym, ROPE, is also used to explain the public relations process. Jerry Hendrix, in his book *Public Relations Cases*, says **R** is research, **O** is objectives in terms of setting content output and impact, P is programming and execution, and **E** is evaluation. Yet another acronym for the public relations process is R-O-S-I-E for research, objectives, strategies, implementation, and evaluation.

In all cases, the process is a never-ending cycle in which six components are links in a chain. Figure 1.3 shows the process.

1. **Step 1: *Research and Analysis.*** This consists of inputs that determine the nature and extent of the public relations problem or opportunity. These may include feedback from the public, media reporting and editorial comment, analysis of trend data, other forms of research, personal experience, and government pressures and regulations.
2. **Step 2: *Policy Formulation.*** Public relations personnel, as advisors to top management, make recommendations on policy and what actions should be taken by the organization.
3. **Step 3: *Programming.*** Once a policy or action is agreed on, public relations staff begin to plan a communications program that will further the organization's objectives. They will set objectives, define audiences, and decide on what strategies will be used on a specific timeline. Budget and staffing are also major considerations.
4. **Step 4: *Communication.*** Public relations personnel execute the program through such vehicles as news releases, media advisories, newsletters, Internet and Web postings, special events, speeches, and community relations programs.
5. **Step 5: *Feedback.*** The effect of these efforts is measured by feedback from the same components that made up the first step. Did the media mention the key messages? Did people change their attitudes or opinions? Did sales go up? Did the organization preserve or enhance its reputation?

We provide a voice in the marketplace of ideas, facts, and viewpoints to aid informed public debate.

—Public Relations Society of America, defining the role of public relations in today's society

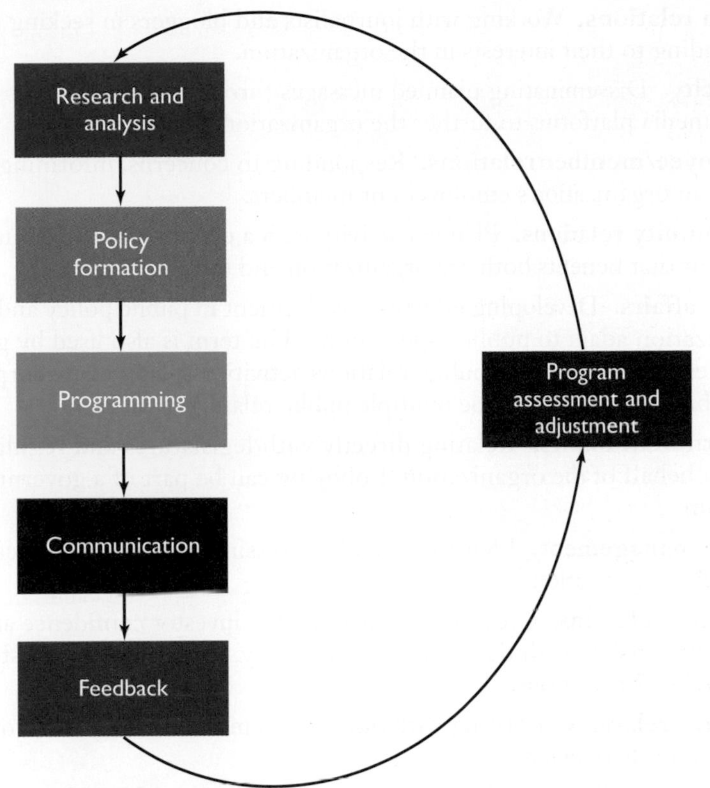

Figure 1.3 **The Public Relations Process**

The conceptualization of public relations as a cyclical process, feedback, or audience response leads to assessment of the program, which becomes an essential element in the development of another public relations project.

6. **Step 6: *Assessment.*** The cycle is then repeated. The success or failure of the policy or program is assessed as a way of determining whether additional efforts are needed, or whether new issues or opportunities must be addressed. Thus, it is a continuing loop process.

Note that public relations plays two distinct roles in this process, thus serving as a "middle ground" or "linking agent." On one level, public relations interacts directly with external sources of information, including the public, media, and government, and relays these inputs to management along with recommendations. On a second level, public relations becomes the vehicle through which management reaches the public with assorted messages to accomplish organizational goals.

The Diversity of Public Relations Work

The basic process of public relations, just described, is manifested in a variety of ways. The PRSA Foundation lists the various aspects of public relations activity that are done by individuals working in the field. In addition, see the many roles of a public relations professional on page 43.

- **Counseling.** Providing advice to management concerning policies, relationships, and communications.
- **Research.** Determining attitudes and behaviors of publics in order to plan public relations strategies. Such research can be used to (1) generate mutual understanding or (2) influence and persuade publics.

- **Media relations.** Working with journalists and bloggers in seeking publicity or responding to their interests in the organization.
- **Publicity.** Disseminating planned messages through traditional mass media and social media platforms to further the organization's interests.
- **Employee/member relations.** Responding to concerns, informing, and motivating an organization's employees or members.
- **Community relations.** Planned activity with a community to maintain an environment that benefits both the organization and the community.
- **Public affairs.** Developing effective involvement in public policy and helping an organization adapt to public expectations. The term is also used by government agencies to describe their public relations activities and by many corporations as an umbrella term to describe multiple public relations activities.
- **Government affairs.** Relating directly with legislatures and regulatory agencies on behalf of the organization. Lobbying can be part of a government affairs program.
- **Issues management.** Identifying and addressing issues of public concern that affect the organization.
- **Financial relations.** Creating and maintaining investor confidence and building good relationships with the financial community. Also known as investor relations or shareholder relations.
- **Industry relations.** Relating with other firms in the industry of an organization and with trade associations.
- **Development/fund-raising.** Demonstrating the need for and encouraging the public to support an organization, primarily through financial contributions.
- **Multicultural relations/workplace diversity.** Relating with individuals and groups in various cultural groups. A good example is the 40th anniversary celebration of a Cuban restaurant in Miami on page 44.
- **Special events.** Stimulating an interest in a person, product, or organization by means of a well-planned event; also, activities designed to interact with publics and listen to them.
- **Marketing communications.** Combination of activities designed to sell a product, service, or idea, including advertising, collateral materials, publicity, promotion, direct mail, trade shows, social media, and special events.

These components, and how they function, constitute the substance of this textbook. The next sections, however, will help you more fully understand the differences between public relations and the related fields of journalism, advertising, and marketing.

Public Relations vs. Journalism

Writing is a common activity of both public relations professionals and journalists. Both also do their jobs in the same way. They interview people, gather and synthesize large amounts of information, write in a journalistic style, and are trained to produce good copy on deadline. In fact, many reporters eventually change careers and become public relations practitioners.

Figure 1.4 **The Many Roles of a Public Relations Professional**

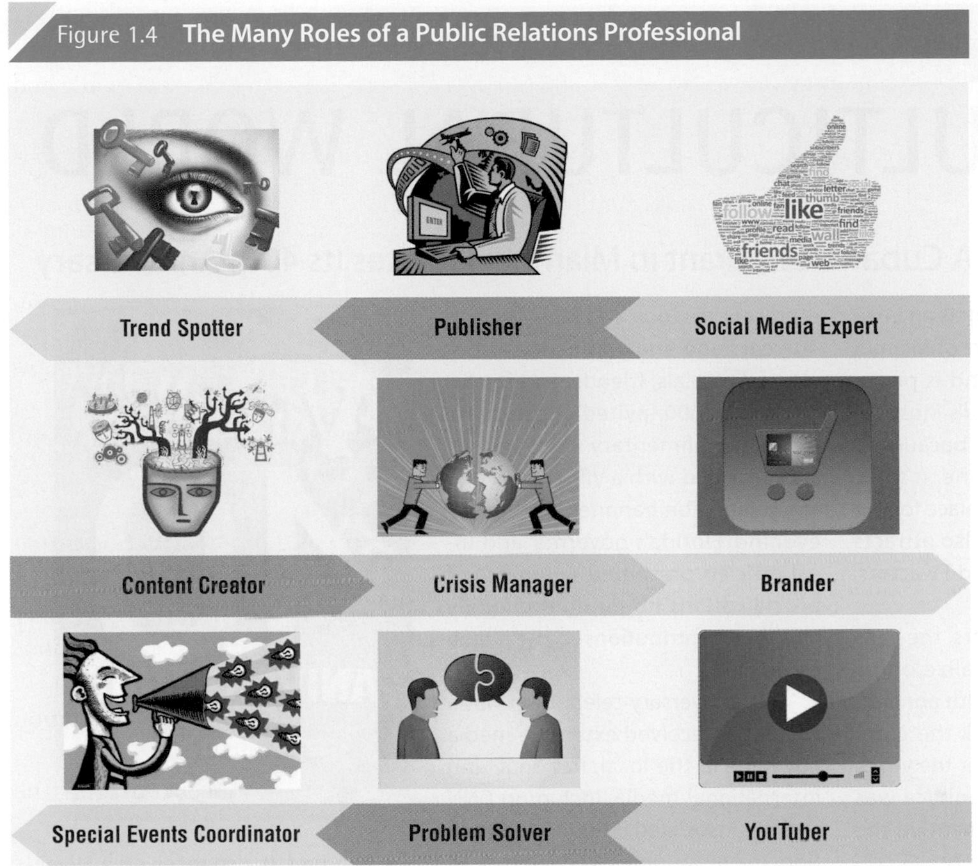

Source: Alfredo Vela, TICs y Formacion, Spain (http://ticsyformacion.com).

This has led many people, including journalists, to the incorrect conclusion that little difference exists between public relations and journalism. For these people, public relations is simply being a "journalist-in-residence" for a nonmedia organization. However, despite the sharing of many techniques, the two fields are fundamentally different in scope, objectives, audiences, and channels.

Scope Public relations, as stated earlier, has many components, ranging from counseling to issues management and special events. Journalistic writing and media relations, although important, are only two of these elements. In addition, effective practice of public relations requires strategic thinking, problem-solving capability, and other management skills.

Objectives Journalists gather and select information for the primary purpose of providing the public with news and information. Public relations personnel also gather facts and information for the purpose of informing the public, but the objective is not only to inform but also to change people's attitudes and behaviors in order to further an organization's goals and objectives. Harold Burson, chairman of Burson-Marsteller, makes the point: "To be effective and credible, public relations messages must be based on facts. Nevertheless, we are advocates, and we need to remember

on the job

A MULTICULTURAL WORLD

A Cuban Restaurant in Miami Celebrates Its 40th Anniversary

Versailles Restaurant is an institution in the heart of Miami's "Little Havana" and is popularly known as "The World's Most Famous Cuban Restaurant" because of its excellent Cuban cuisine. It's not only a popular gathering place for the Cuban community, but also attracts famous musicians, film and TV actors, and even U.S. presidents.

The restaurant's owners, the Valls family, decided to capitalize on its reputation by having a 40th anniversary celebration to thank the community for its support over the years. Public relations firm Republica was engaged to plan and executive the celebration. Its goals were (1) celebrate Versailles' iconic role within the community, (2) make Versailles top-of-mind among all generations, (3) reaffirm its renowned position, (4) thank the community for its devoted support throughout the last 40 years, and (5) own the claim, "World's Most Famous Cuban Restaurant."

Republica started by creating a 40th anniversary logo that included the tagline, "World's Most Famous Cuban Restaurant" that was used on all collateral materials. A block party was also organized that gave customers items from its original l971 menu at 1971 prices. It was also an opportunity to announce renderings of Versailles' upcoming renovations and distribute commemorative 40th anniversary posters and branded coffee cups.

An invitation to a second event, held in a large tent adjacent to the restaurant, used "Spanglish" text to represent the look and feel of Miami 40 years ago and was sent to VIPs, elected officials, friends, and family. More than 600 Invited guests were given complimentary valet service and provided with a VIP entrance to the celebration banquet. During the evening, Florida's governor and local officials presented a number of proclamations honoring the family and their contributions to the Miami community.

The anniversary celebration was a success. It received extensive media coverage in the local, national, and international media, including CNN and the Associated Press (AP). In addition, the restaurant's website rose to 3,000 unique visitors a month, and its Twitter account generated about 1,000 postings during the evening of the banquet. It also received a Silver Anvil Award from the Public Relations Society of America (PRSA) in the category of events and observances.

Felipe Valls, Sr. is interviewed by the media at the 40th anniversary celebration of the family-owned restaurant, Versailles.

that. We are advocates of a particular point of view—our client's or our employer's point of view. And while we recognize that serving the public interest best serves our client's interest, we are not journalists. That's not our job."

Audiences Journalists write primarily for a mass audience—readers, listeners, or viewers of the medium for which they work. By definition, mass audiences are not well defined, and a journalist on a daily newspaper or a TV station, for example, prepares material geared to a general audience. A public relations professional, in contrast, carefully segments audiences into various demographic and psychological characteristics. Such research allows messages to be tailored to audience needs, concerns, and interests for maximum effect.

Channels Most journalists, by nature of their employment, reach audiences primarily through one channel—the medium that publishes or broadcasts their work, or even a Web news site such as *Huffington Post*. Many, of course, also have their own blog or Twitter account, but the fact remains that public relations professionals use a variety of channels to reach a variety of audiences. The channels and platforms used may be a combination of traditional media outlets newspapers, magazines, radio, and television. Or they may also include direct mail, brochures, posters, newsletters, trade journals, special events, podcasts, blogs, websites, Facebook, Pinterest, Twitter, YouTube, and even mobile-enabled apps.

Public Relations vs. Advertising

Just as many people mistakenly equate publicity with public relations, there is also some confusion about the distinction between publicity (one area of public relations) and advertising.

Although publicity and advertising both utilize mass media for dissemination of messages, the format and context each uses are different. Publicity—information about an event, an individual or group, or a product—appears as a news item or feature story in the mass media or online. This is called *earned media* because editors, also known as gatekeepers, make the decision to use the material as a new item and the organization doesn't pay for the placement.

> We're beginning to see research that supports the superiority of PR over advertising to launch a brand.
>
> —*Al and Laura Ries, authors of* The Fall of Advertising and the Rise of Public Relations

Advertising, in contrast, is *paid media*. Organizations and individuals contract with the advertising department of a media outlet to buy space or time. An organization writes the content, decides the type and graphics, and controls where and when the advertisement will be used. In other words, advertising is simply renting space in a mass medium or on a website. The lion's share of revenue for traditional media and even Facebook or Google comes from the selling of advertising space.

Other differences between public relations activities and advertising include:

- Most advertising is placed in mass media outlets such as television, radio, magazines, and newspapers. Public relations, however, often relies on what is called *owned media*. In other words, organizations produce and distribute content for media platforms "owned" or controlled by the organization. This can include newsletters, brochures, podcasts, websites, intranet, blogs, Facebook brand pages, Twitter handles, and videos.

- Advertising is primarily directed to potential buyers of goods and services; public relations presents its message to specialized external audiences (stockholders, vendors, community leaders, environmental groups, and so on) and internal publics (employees) that are not necessarily purchasers of the product or service.
- Advertising is readily identified as a specialized communication function; public relations is broader in scope, dealing with the policies and performance of the entire organization, from the morale of employees to the amount of money given to local community organizations.
- Advertising is often used as a communication tool in public relations, and public relations activity often supports advertising campaigns. Advertising's primary function is to sell goods and services; public relations' function is to create an environment in which the organization can thrive. The latter calls for dealing with economic, social, and political factors that can affect the organization's brand or reputation.

The major disadvantage of advertising is the cost. A full-page color ad in *USA Today* on a week day is $200,000. Advertising campaigns on network television, of course, can run into millions of dollars. Advertisers, for example, paid $3.8 million for a 30-second Super Bowl ad in 2013. Consequently, companies often use a tool of public relations—product publicity—that is more cost effective and often more credible because the message appears in a news context. One poll by Opinion Research Corporation, for example, found that online articles about a product or service were more persuasive than banner ads, pop-up ads, e-mail offers, and sponsored links.

Public Relations vs. Marketing

Public relations is distinct from marketing in several ways, although their boundaries often overlap. Both disciplines deal with an organization's external relationships and employ similar communication tools to reach the public. Both also have the ultimate purpose of ensuring an organization's success and economic survival. Public relations and marketing, however, approach this task from somewhat different perspectives or worldviews.

Objectives The purpose of marketing is to sell goods and services through attractive packaging, competitive pricing, retail and online promotions, and efficient distribution systems. The purpose of public relations is to build relationships with a variety of publics that can enhance the organization's reputation and establish trust in its policies, products, and services.

> Marketing is transaction oriented. While public relations can be part of a marketing strategy, it has a much larger responsibility within the organization.
>
> *—Dave Imre, an executive at Imre Communications, Baltimore*

Audiences The primary audiences for marketing are consumers and customers. Public relations (often called "corporate communications") deals with a much broader array of audiences, or publics. They may include investors, community leaders, environmental groups, vendors, government officials, and even employees, who can affect the organization's success and profitability through boycotts, legislation, and the generation of unfavorable publicity.

Competition vs. Opposition Marketing professionals tend to rely exclusively on competitive solutions, whereas public relations professionals often perceive the problem as effectively dealing with opposition. When meeting opposition to a product, marketing often thinks the solution is lower pricing or better packaging. However, public relations professionals realize that pricing doesn't make any difference if consumers perceive that the product has defects or the company is associated with poor environmental practices or the use of sweatshop labor in developing nations.

Role in Management An organization, to be successful in the marketplace, must pay constant attention to its reputation and have policies that enhance trust and credibility among its multiple publics. Public relations, in its ideal form, directly deals with upper management to shape and promote the organization's core values. In sum, a brand is created through the expression of an organization's values, actions, and effective public relations strategies—not through a glitzy ad or marketing campaign.

How Public Relations Supports Marketing

Philip Kotler, professor of marketing at Northwestern University and author of a leading marketing textbook, says public relations is the fifth "P" of marketing strategy, which includes four other Ps—Product, Price, Place, and Promotion. As he wrote in the *Harvard Business Review*, "Public relations takes longer to cultivate, but when energized, it can help pull the company into the market."

When public relations is used to support an organization's marketing objectives directly, it is called *marketing communications*. Thomas Harris, author of *The Marketer's Guide to Public Relations*, prefers the term *marketing public relations*. This, he says, distinguishes the function from *corporate public relations* that defines the corporation's relationships with its noncustomer publics.

Dennis L. Wilcox, in his text *Public Relations Writing and Media Techniques*, lists eight ways in which public relations activities contribute to fulfilling marketing objectives:

1. Developing new prospects for new markets, such as people who inquire after seeing or hearing a product release in the news media
2. Providing third-party endorsements—via newspapers, magazines, radio, and television—through news releases about a company's products or services, community involvement, inventions, and new plans
3. Generating sales leads, usually through articles in the trade press about new products and services
4. Creating an environment for a new product by raising an issue or situation that can be solved through using the new product or service
5. Stretching the organization's advertising and promotional dollars through timely and supportive releases about it and its products
6. Providing inexpensive sales literature, because articles about the company and its products can be reprinted as informative pieces for prospective customers
7. Establishing the corporation as an authoritative source of information on a given product
8. Helping to sell minor products that don't have large advertising budgets

Toward an Integrated Perspective

Although well-defined differences exist among the fields of advertising, marketing, and public relations, there is an increasing realization that an organization's objectives can be best accomplished through an integrated approach.

This understanding has given rise to such terms as *integrated marketing communications (IMC)*, *convergent communications*, and *integrated communications*. Don Schulz, Stanley Tannenbaum, and Robert Lauterborn, authors of *Integrated Marketing Communications*, explain the title of their book as follows:

> A concept of marketing communication planning that recognizes the added value of a comprehensive plan that evaluates the strategic roles of a variety of communication disciplines—e.g., General Advertising, Direct Response, Sales Promotion, and Public Relations—and combines these disciplines to provide clarity, consistency, and maximum communication impact.

Several factors have fueled the trend toward IMC. (See the IMC model in Figure 1.5.) First is the downsizing of organizations. Many of them have consolidated departments and have also reduced staff dedicated to various communication disciplines. As a result, one department, with fewer employees, is expected to do a greater variety of communication tasks.

> It comes down to economics. If you're coming up with one idea that can be used across five different marketing disciplines, it just makes the idea much stronger, that much more cohesive when you are communicating it to your audience, and it makes your dollar work that much harder.
>
> —*Andrea Morgan, EVP of consumer brands for Euro RSCG*

Second, organizational marketing and communication departments are making do with tighter budgets. Many organizations, to avoid the high cost of advertising, look for alternative ways to deliver messages. These may include (1) building buzz via word of mouth, (2) targeting influentials, (3) Web marketing, (4) grassroots marketing, (5) media relations and product publicity, and (6) event sponsorship.

Third is the increasing realization that advertising, with its high costs, isn't the silver bullet that it used to be. The problem is the increasing clutter of advertising, the fragmentation of audiences among multiple media, and a general lack of credibility among consumers.

Al and Laura Ries, authors of the popular book (at least among public relations people) *The Fall of Advertising and the Rise of PR*, write, "We're beginning to see research that supports the superiority of PR over advertising to launch a brand. A recent study of 91 new product launches shows highly successful products are more likely to use PR-related activities than less successful ones."

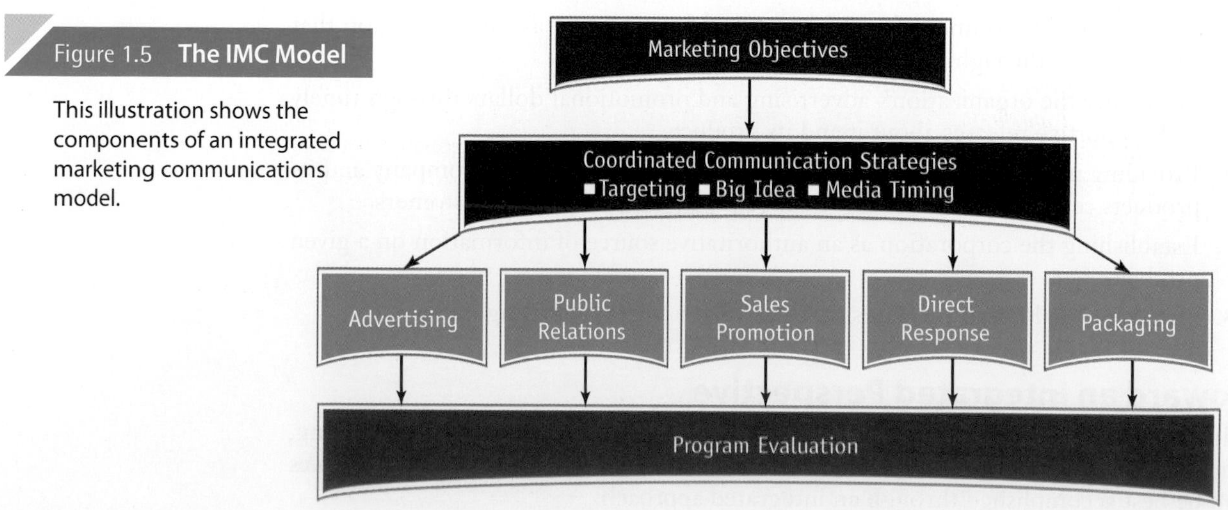

Figure 1.5 The IMC Model

This illustration shows the components of an integrated marketing communications model.

Fourth, it is now widely recognized that the marketing of products and services can be affected by public and social policy issues. Environmental legislation influences packaging and the content of products, a proposed luxury tax on expensive autos affects sales of those cars, and a company's support of Planned Parenthood or health benefits for same-sex partners may spur a product boycott.

The impact of such factors, not traditionally considered by marketing managers, has led many professionals to believe that organizations should do a better job of integrating public relations and public affairs into their overall marketing considerations. In fact, David Corona, writing in the *Public Relations Journal* some years ago, was the first one to advance the idea that marketing's sixth "P" should be public policy.

The concept of integration, therefore, is the ability of organizations to use a variety of strategies and tactics to convey a consistent message in a variety of forms. The metaphor might be the golfer with a variety of clubs in her bag. She may use one club (public relations) to launch a product, another club (advertising) to reinforce the message, and yet another club (Web and social media marketing) to actually sell the product or service to a well-defined audience.

The golf metaphor also reflects a realization on the part of management and marketing executives that public relations is an effective strategy in several important areas. A *PRWeek* survey of marketing executives, for example, found that public relations ranked higher in effectiveness than advertising or marketing in nine areas: (1) brand reputation, (2) corporate reputation, (3) cultivating thought leaders, (4) strategy development, (5) launching a new product, (6) building awareness, (7) generating word of mouth, (8) message development, and (9) overcoming a crisis.

A good example of an integrated marketing campaign is Sony's PlayStation campaign to get a wider audience for its game, *Unchartered 3: Drake's Deception* series. The creative idea was to feature the hero, Nathan Drake, as an example of the "half-tucked shirt" look that was becoming a fashion trend in Hollywood. The campaign was launched during New York Fashion Week and Sony took a tongue-in-cheek approach, using Drake to parody the new half-tucked shirt fashion trend.

The integrated communications team hosted a pop-up half-tuck dressing room in New York's Herald Square and invited people on the street to receive a Nathan Drake half-tuck makeover. The team also released celebrity photos illustrating the half-tuck look in popular culture and also engaged a fashion expert, Jay Manuel, to talk up the trend in various media interviews. The company also purchased a half-tuck Facebook tab and placed a humorous half-tuck ad on a Times Square billboard during Fashion Week.

The campaign is a good example of what is now called *brand journalism* or what others call *content marketing*, in which advertising (paid media) played a minor role. It generated almost 300 news stories in game publications and mainstream consumer publications and was covered by E!, NBC, and the *Today Show*. As a result, Sony exceeded sales expectations and shipped 3.8 million copies on the launch day of the new game.

A Career in Public Relations

The growth of public relations as a career field has spawned any number of public relations courses, sequences, and majors.

The Commission on Public Relations Education, which includes public relations educators and representatives from all of the major professional organizations, has set the standard by specifying a minimum of five courses that should be required in a public relations major. They are:

- Introduction to public relations (including theory, origin, and principles)
- Public relations research, measurement, and evaluation
- Public relations writing and production
- Supervised work experience in public relations (internship)
- An additional public relations course in law and ethics, planning and management, and case studies or campaigns

> PR people are the story tellers. It's our job to help find the authenticity at the core of our companies and clients, and tell those stories to the world in real words that will really be heard.
>
> *—Fred Cook, president of Golin Harris public relations*

In addition, the Commission highly recommends that students take courses in such areas as marketing, management, economics, social psychology, and multicultural communication. Other experienced professionals agree that coursework is important, but also feel networking skills should not be overlooked. See the Insights box about a first-person account.

Public relations in the United States has traditionally been taught in departments and schools of journalism. Consequently, a number of journalism graduates also consider employment in public relations, as job opportunities on newspapers and other traditional media continue to decline. Lindsey Miller, in a www.ragan.com article, writes, "As curricula diversify and career options widen, many J-school grads are seeing the more stable and better-paying corporate communications field as fertile ground for their skills. They're armed not only with the ability to write a good article, but they can also tell a good story on a range of platforms, using a variety of media."

on the job

INSIGHTS

Networking: The Key to Career Success

By Robin Carr

We all take different paths to reach our professional and personal goals. Whatever you do, be sure to network, network and network some more. Every job I have ever had has been the direct result of networking and I cannot stress this enough.

And while social media sites such as LinkedIn and Twitter are great tools to network and learn, there's nothing like getting out and meeting people face to face. Go to monthly luncheons, mixers and attend business conferences with interesting speakers and panels. Collect business cards, follow up with an email or LinkedIn invitation, and your network will grow.

Even while you are still in school, take the time to go to various mixers and events and meet people. IABC (International Association of Business Communicators) and PRSA (Public Relations Society of America) have open events and you don't have to be a member.

Social channels have realized the importance of face-to-face

Robin Carr

interaction. LinkedIn, for example, has hundreds of online groups that you can join and they often have meetings and conferences. They can be for PR or whatever other interests and hobbies you may have. Same with Twitter and their "tweet-ups" and Google+ gatherings—these all great examples of the best of both on and off-line interactions.

While in school, get actively involved with your PRSSA (Public Relations Student Society of America) chapter. Often times, your area PRSA chapter will host PRSSA students and create professional partner programs. This is an excellent way to not only network, but find a mentor or two.

The terrific thing about public relations as a discipline is that you can apply it to practically anything.

After graduation, I worked at a PR agency for nearly two years to get general experience in the work world. Agencies are very good places for PR graduates to start. There are a variety of clients and you can learn and discover what your interests are and, of course, network. There are many agencies that have different specialties: start-up companies, technology, environmental, consumer products, and hospitality, to name a few.

While I learned a lot at my time at the agency, my first love was sports, so I was able to land an informational interview with the Publicity Director for the San Francisco Giants. There are very limited PR openings in sports, however, and while I felt discouraged at the time, I was told to be patient and wait for an available opportunity. Sure enough, about six months later, I attended a Giants game and I ran into the gentleman I had interviewed with. He said "call me tomorrow—my assistant quit today!" So I got the job as an administrative assistant in the publicity department. It was very entry level, but it was a foot in the door. And the Giants had always promised me that I would move up and I was promoted several times. I worked there 10 years, before moving on to Nike and EA Sports.

The terrific thing about public relations as a discipline is that you can apply it to practically anything. I worked in sports public relations for 18 years; however, my career path has included video gaming, retail, technology and fashion. There are also networking events besides PR groups that you can join that are catered to your field of PR. For instance, I'm a member of the Association for Women in Sports Media, WISE (Women in Sports/Entertainment) and the National Sports Marketing Association.

Finally, if possible, do more than one internship—two preferably. Take advantage of opportunities when they come up and get in on the ground floor if you have to. Be patient—if you really want to move up to the next level, work hard and prove yourself. It will pay off.

Robin Carr has worked almost 30 years in public relations, including stints at the San Francisco Giants, Nike, EA Sports. Ubisoft, Gap, Inc., and Kodak. She is currently director of public relations for Xoom, a global digital money transfer company in San Francisco. Robin is a graduate of the public relations degree program at San Jose State University.

Such skills, of course, are important in public relations work, but there's some debate whether journalism majors have the training and temperament that lead to higher management positions in public relations. Richard Mintz, managing director of the Harbour Group in Washington, D.C., told an *Atlantic* magazine blogger, "Journalists, by their nature, don't make great advocates or public relations people, because they're trained to be objective rather than take sides. They also tend to work alone, and they have no business experience." And journalist Mary Ellen Arch who decided to get a master's degree in public relations after being laid-off from a newspaper told a *New York Times* reporter, "Working in the newsroom does not prepare you for a job in public relations." Many journalists, however, have found that their talents are somewhat in demand by organizations who are using "brand journalism" and "content marketing" to reach consumers with informative articles about their organizations, products, and services.

In sum, there are many paths to a career in public relations. Majoring in public relations, or at least taking some basic courses in the subject, is considered the best preparation, but majors from other fields such as journalism, communication studies, and marketing also have skills that are valued by many employers. Former TV news producer Bev Carlson, a board member of Nebraska's chapter of the PRSA, told www.ragan.com, "It all depends on the person and their willingness to be flexible and learn."

There's also some thought that public relations courses should be in a school of business instead of a journalism department or school. The argument is that today's public relations is no longer exclusively a journalistic-type activity that involves working with the media. James Lukaszewski, a well-known consultant and speaker in the public relations field, is quite blunt. He wrote in *The Strategist*, "At minimum, PR programs belong in marketing sequences rather than journalism sequences. The sooner we can reflect a more management-like perspective, the more quickly we'll find ourselves called in for our advice and counsel." Some success along this line has occurred as the result of efforts by the Public Relations Society of America and the Arthur W. Page Society, a group of senior-level public relations executives, to have public relations included in MBA programs.

Many European universities, for example, offer a public relations curriculum as part of a business curriculum. At the University of Belgrade in Serbia, for example, public relations is located in the Faculty of Economics. And in Latvia, the strongest public relations program in the country is taught at Turiba Business University. Management schools in India also offer the most courses in public relations and corporate communications. In the United States, however, the vast majority of public relations programs continue to be part of schools or departments of journalism or communication.

Essential Career Skills

A student's choice of a major in college is important, but equally important is participating in campus clubs, taking internships, and even working part-time at jobs that develop essential skills for a successful career in public relations. The essential skills are (1) writing skill, (2) research ability, (3) planning expertise, (4) problem-solving ability, (5) business/economics competence, and (6) expertise in social media.

1. **Writing skill.** The ability to put information and ideas onto paper clearly and concisely is essential. Good grammar and good spelling are vital. Misspelled words and sloppy sentence structure are unacceptable. The importance of writing skill is emphasized in a career advice column in *Working Woman*: "I changed careers, choosing public relations as having the best potential, but found it difficult to persuade employers that my writing and interpersonal skills were sufficient for an entry-level job in the profession."

2. **Research ability.** Arguments for causes must have factual support instead of generalities. A person must have the persistence and ability to gather information from a variety of sources, as well as to conduct original research by designing and implementing opinion polls or audits. Too many public relations programs fail because the organization does not assess audience needs and perceptions. Skillful use of the

on the job INSIGHTS

Do You Have the Right Personality for a Career in Public Relations?

Take a look at this checklist. How many of the personality traits do you have? Check each item that you think accurately describes you. If you check fewer than 15 of the 25 items, a career in public relations may not be the best fit for you. If you check 20 or more, then such a career may fit you like a hand in a glove.

_____ Do you have a good sense of humor?

_____ Are you generally positive and optimistic?

_____ Is it easy for you to meet people? Do you consider yourself "friendly"?

_____ Do you converse easily with most anyone?

_____ Do you handle rejection and frustration well?

_____ Are you able to easily persuade people?

_____ Do you present yourself professionally? Do you maintain a well-groomed, business-like appearance?

_____ Are you a showman?

_____ Do you like creative endeavors?

_____ Would friends describe you as considerate and tactful?

_____ Are you a skilled wordsmith?

_____ Are you able to gain and maintain the trust of your boss?

_____ Do you like being with people?

_____ Are you a good listener?

_____ Do you like solving problems for people?

_____ Do you consider yourself curious or interested in a variety of subjects?

_____ Do you enjoy reading on diverse subjects?

_____ Do you have a determination to bring projects to completion?

_____ Are you a high-energy person?

_____ Do you deal well with emergencies or crises?

_____ Do you view mistakes as a way to learn?

_____ Are you good at being factual and objective?

_____ Are you respectful of others' points of view?

_____ Do friends think you're perceptive and sensitive?

_____ Are you a quick learner?

Internet and computer databases is an important element of research work. Reading current newspapers and magazines also is important.

3. **Planning expertise.** A public relations program involves a number of communication tools and activities that must be carefully planned and coordinated. A person needs to be a good planner to make certain that materials are distributed in a timely manner, events occur without problems, and budgets are not exceeded. Public relations people must be highly organized, detail-oriented, and able to see the big picture. Caryn Alagno, vice president of Edelman Worldwide, adds, "Pay attention to details . . . and when it comes to the 'small stuff,' make sure you treat all tasks like a big deal."

4. **Problem-solving ability.** Innovative ideas and fresh approaches are needed to solve complex problems or to make a public relations program unique and memorable. Increased salaries and promotions go to people who show top management how to solve problems creatively.

5. **Business/economics competence.** The increasing emphasis on public relations as a management function calls for public relations students to learn the "nuts and bolts" of business and economics. According to Joel Curren, senior vice president of CKPR in Chicago, "The greatest need PR people have is understanding how a business

Students should not only know how to use social media tools such as Facebook and Twitter, but also how to apply critical thinking to the selection, implementation, and evaluation of such tools in achieving client or employer goals

Commission on Public Relations Education

and, more importantly, how a public company operates." Rachel Beanland, a professional interviewed by *Public Relations Tactics*, noted that almost all of the recent public relations grads she talked to wished they had taken a marketing course. In sum, students preparing for careers in public relations should obtain a solid grounding by taking courses in economics, management, and marketing.

6. **Expertise in social media.** Employers still value expertise in mainstream media relations, but it's now just as important to have social media savvy. A survey of employers by online MarketingVOX found 80 percent of the respondents agreed that knowledge of social networks is either important or very important. The three most important skills for job applicants are social networking, blogging, and tweeting. Employers also prefer job applicants who know about podcasting, search engine optimization (SEO), e-mail outreach, Web content management, and social bookmarking.

It should be noted, of course, that all jobs in public relations don't require all these essential skills in equal proportion. It often depends on your specific job responsibilities and assignments. Other skills required for today's practitioner are in the Insights box below. You may also want to take the personality quiz on page 53.

on the job INSIGHTS

How to Succeed in Public Relations

Various research studies have identified the personal characteristics that lead to a successful career in public relations. The following list was compiled by the Commission on Public Relations Education (www.commpred.org):

- A high-quality liberal arts education
- A cosmopolitan worldview
- Intellectual curiosity
- Excellent mass and interpersonal communication skills
- Depth and breadth knowledge of public relations theory
- An interest in life-long learning
- A fascination with the public relations environment, both within the organization and external to it
- Empathy, wisdom and understanding of diverse populations
- Focus on a professional role, both within the organization as well as its external environment
- Analytical problem-solving skills
- Respect for the frequent need for urgency in practitioners' responsibilities
- An orientation to goal achievement while thriving on hard work
- An ability to complete multiple tasks that are often a combination of strategic, tactical and technical responsibilities, all of which have tight deadlines
- A strong work ethic
- The understanding that public relations practitioners commonly work hours far in excess of a traditional 40-hour week

on the job

SOCIAL MEDIA IN ACTION

Advertising Firm Hires Interns through a Twitter Campaign

Campbell Mithun, a Minneapolis advertising agency specializing in brand-image communications, had its own brand-image problem. The firm was perceived as a traditional firm (founded in 1933) and not being very digital savvy despite its strength in this area.

It needed a big idea to showcase its digital capabilities and engaged Hill & Knowlton public relations to come up with a creative solution. The decision was to turn the routine operation of hiring 13 interns into a social media event by having applicants submit an employment application composed entirely of 13 tweets. Applicants had 13 days to submit 13 tweets as part what was dubbed as the Lucky 13 Internship.

Campbell's employees were trained in Twitter tips and how to track responses to tweets from applicants. Hill & Knowlton also conducted an extensive campaign to publicize the "contest" by placing stories in local, state, and national media. Business writers were encouraged to monitor the tweets and also tweet about the campaign. The agency also set up a dedicated #L13 website, blogged about the hiring process, and even uploaded a YouTube video about the campaign. There was also a ripple effect as L13 applicants tweeted their followers and posted comments on their Facebook pages.

The campaign generated coverage in such publications as *Advertising Age*, the *New York Times*, the *Minneapolis Star Tribune*, and the *St. Paul Business Journal*. In addition, it was covered by *Mashable*, *Gawker*, and *FastCompany*. About 100 blogs mentioned the campaign, and the agency's website traffic went up 400 percent. The campaign generated 425 applicants (as compared to the typical 150). Post-campaign surveys indicated that Campbell Mithun was able to improve perceptions in the business community that it was an agency with digital capabilities.

The Value of Internships

Interships are extremely popular in the communications industry, and a student whose résumé includes practical work experience along with a good academic record has an important advantage. The Commission on Public Relations Education believes the internship is so important that it is one of the five basic courses it recommends for any quality college or university public relations curriculum.

An internship is a win-win situation for both the student and the organization. The student, in most cases, not only receives academic credit, but also gets firsthand knowledge of work in the professional world. This gives the student an advantage in getting that all-important first job after graduation. In many cases, recent graduates are hired by their former internship employers because they have already proved themselves.

> Internship programs can be much more than a means to get young, inexpensive talent. Designed properly, they can offer a significant return on investment for agencies.
>
> *Mark Hand, reporter for* PRWeek

Indeed, *PRWeek* reporter Sara Calabro says:

> Agencies and corporate communications departments are beginning to see interns as the future of their companies, not merely as gophers that they can pass the grunt work off to. While a few years ago, it was typical for an intern to work for nothing, it is almost unheard of for an internship to be unpaid these days.

Many major public relations firms have formal internship programs. At Edelman Worldwide, for example, students enroll in "Edel-U," an internal training program that exposes them to all aspects of agency work. The summer internship program at Weber Shandick in Boston is called "Weber University." Calabro cites Jane Dolan, a senior account executive, who says that upper management is always incredibly impressed with the work that interns do for their final projects. "It is amazing to see them go from zero to 100 in a matter of months," says Dolan.

Hill & Knowlton also has an extensive internship training program in its New York office, taking about 40 interns a year. In its view, the internship program is "the cheapest and most effective recruiting tool available." Ketchum also gets about 800 résumés each year for 12 to 14 summer positions, which pay a weekly stipend. According to Scott Proper, SVP at Ketchum, "You can walk the halls any day and find former interns in pretty senior positions."

It's not always possible, of course, for a student to do an internship in Chicago or New York. However, many opportunities are available at local public relations firms, businesses, and nonprofit agencies. It is important, however, that the organization have at least one experienced public relations professional who can mentor a student and ensure that he or she gets an opportunity to do a variety of tasks to maximize the learning experience. See the Insights box below for what Ogilvy Public Relations expects in an internship application.

Most reputable national and international firms pay interns, and the going rate is about $12 to $15 per hour. This often is not the case at the local level. Many smaller companies and nonprofits claim that they cannot afford to pay, or that the opportunity to receive college credit is sufficient compensation. Part of the problem, writes Ross Perlin in the *New York Times*, is that "Colleges and universities have become cheerleaders and enablers of the unpaid internship boom, failing to inform young people of their rights or protect them from the miserly calculus of employers."

Perlin points out that many internships violate U.S. Department of Labor guidelines that specify that unpaid internships are only acceptable if the experience is similar to that offered in a vocational school, does not displace a regular employee, and

on the job INSIGHTS

Can You Complete This Internship Application?

Employers use a variety of techniques to select students for internships. In addition to personal interviews, they also test students on their knowledge of basic public relations concepts and ask for samples of their writing ability. A good example is Ogilvy Public Relations, with offices in 60 cities around the world that offers a 10-week summer paid internship program.

How to Apply

- You must be a college junior to apply.
- You must be available for the 10-week internship from June to August.
- Hint: Think of a creative way to 'package' yourself when submitting the below items. This is your chance to impress us about why you should work at Ogilvy this coming summer. A cover letter is not required but if you feel you need one, go for it.

Please submit the following required items:

(Sorry, if it's not all there when you apply, it won't be accepted. Has something to do with attention to detail.)

- First things first: create a profile in order to upload the below items
- Resume
- In a Word document, list your top two areas of interest (healthcare, corporate/public affairs, media relations, digital influence, insights and research, or consumer marketing). For more information on our practices, please visit www.ogilvypr.com
- Two professional or educational letters of reference
- Writing samples: Please answer only two of the following four questions, each in fewer than 300 words.
  1. You can invite three people to dinner on Friday, one from the past, the present, and the future. Who are you inviting and why?
  2. Your client comes to you with little or no budget and needs a marketing plan. How would you leverage your social media expertise to help them achieve their goals?
  3. Your client has just briefed you on a revolutionary new product that the company intends to call "the bicycle." The bicycle is described as a light, two-wheeled steerable machine propelled by human power. It can be used for transportation, as well as sports and leisure. Write a press release on this new product. You can add any information you feel necessary, within reason, but please follow the appropriate format of a press release to announce this product.
  4. Social media has changed the way brands interact with consumers. How do we ensure that our clients are building brand equity in this new territory?

What you'll learn in the internship

You will learn the craft of client services and its function in the PR industry in our 10-week paid summer internship program. You'll participate in weekly seminars to learn about our 360-degree offerings, all while planning a client presentation/pitch. You'll be mentored by some of the best and brightest in the building and you'll learn what it means to balance the art & science of public relations.

What's in it for us:

You have the instincts of a business person plus a creative edge
You are digitally savvy
You have excellent written and verbal communication skills
You are passionate about marketing and public relations
You take a rigorous and creative approach to problem solving
You have a fine appreciation and respect for creative work
You are intellectually curious
You are persistent and take initiative

that the employer derives "no immediate advantage" from the student's work. In other words, if an intern's work is generating income for an organization such as a public relations firm who is billing clients for work done by an intern, the student deserves some form of compensation. PRSA's *Professional Standards Advisory PS-17: Ethical Use of Interns* can be found at www.prsa.org.

Salaries in the Field

Public relations work pays relatively well compared to other communications professions. Many practitioners say they like the income and opportunities for steady advancement. They also enjoy the variety and fast pace that the field provides. Blogger Todd Defren of www.pr-squared.com writes, "PR is hard work, strategic work, under promoted and infinitely interesting work—hard to describe or appreciate until you're in the trenches."

Several surveys have attempted to pinpoint the national median annual salary for recent graduates in their first full-time jobs in the public relations field. Probably the most definitive survey is the one conducted by Lee Becker and his associates at the University of Georgia. They work with journalism and mass communications programs throughout the nation to compile a list of recent graduates, who are then surveyed (www.grady.uga.edu/annualsurveys/).

In their survey of 2012 graduates from 82 departments and schools of journalism and mass communications, they found that recent public relations graduates as of May 2013 were earning a median annual salary of $33,000. Please note that median is the mid-point of salaries reported. The below chart gives the median entry-level salaries by communications field.

Other surveys focus on salaries for practitioners in the field. The *Occupational Handbook for 2012–13* by the U.S. Department of Labor reports that public relations and fundraising directors earn a median salary of $91,810. Public relations managers earn $57,550 and public relations specialists earn $52,090. This is compared to $33,840 for all occupations indexed by the Department of Labor. The annual salary survey, conducted by *PRWeek*, places a more optimistic figure on salaries in public relations. Its 2013 survey of median salaries, for example, found that experienced practitioners in the corporate world earned $119,000 annually compared to $90,000 for those working in public relations firms. Nonprofit public relations paid the least amount, $74,550. See the Insights box below for a breakdown of salaries by title and gender.

The Arthur W. Page Society, a group of senior communication executives representing many of America's Fortune 500 corporations, also conducts an annual survey of its members regarding budgets and executive compensation. In general, compensation for the top communications officer in a large corporation ranges from $269,000 to $500,000+. There are, of course, other forms of compensation. Former Edelman

on the job INSIGHTS

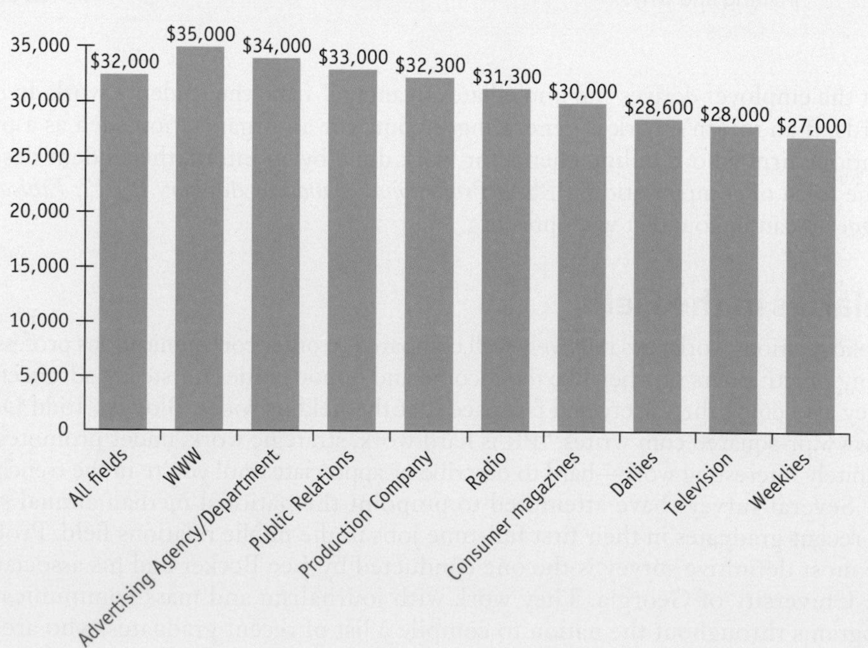

Source: Becker, L., Vlad, T., and Simpson, H. (2013, November). 2012 Job Market for JMC Grads Hold Steady. AEJMC Newsletter, 15.

on the job

INSIGHTS

An Overview of Salaries in the Public Relations Field

PRWeek conducts an annual survey of salaries. The following charts are excerpted from the 2013 survey, which is compiled from 1,071 respondents to the survey. Respondents were 63 percent female and 37 percent male, and averaged 13 years of professional experience. Salaries are reported as medians, which means that 50 percent of the responses were above the amount reported and 50 percent earned less.

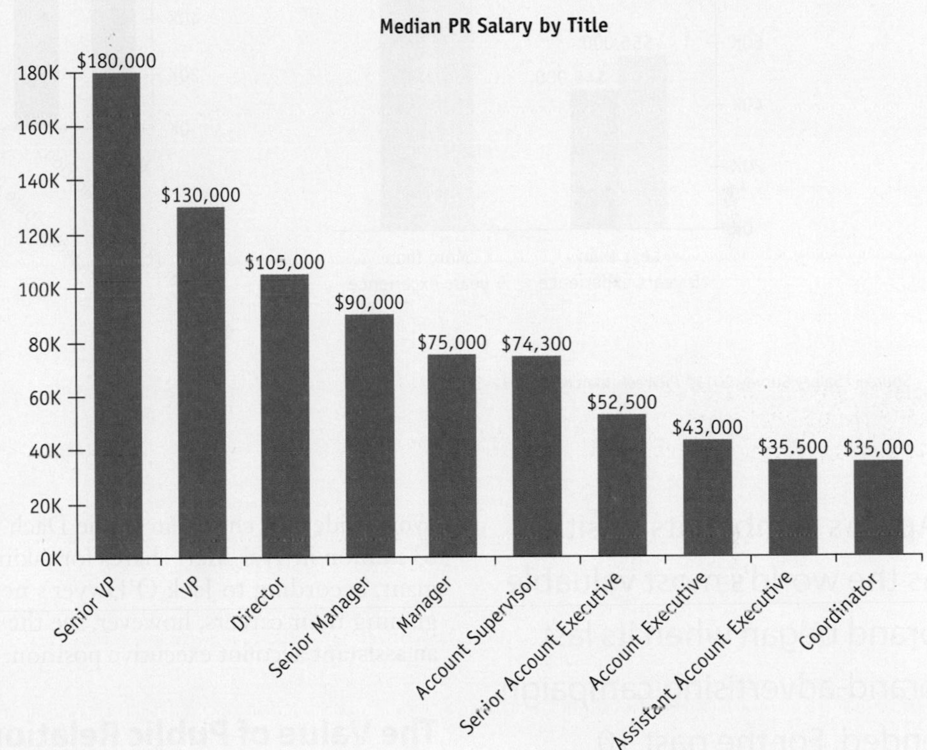

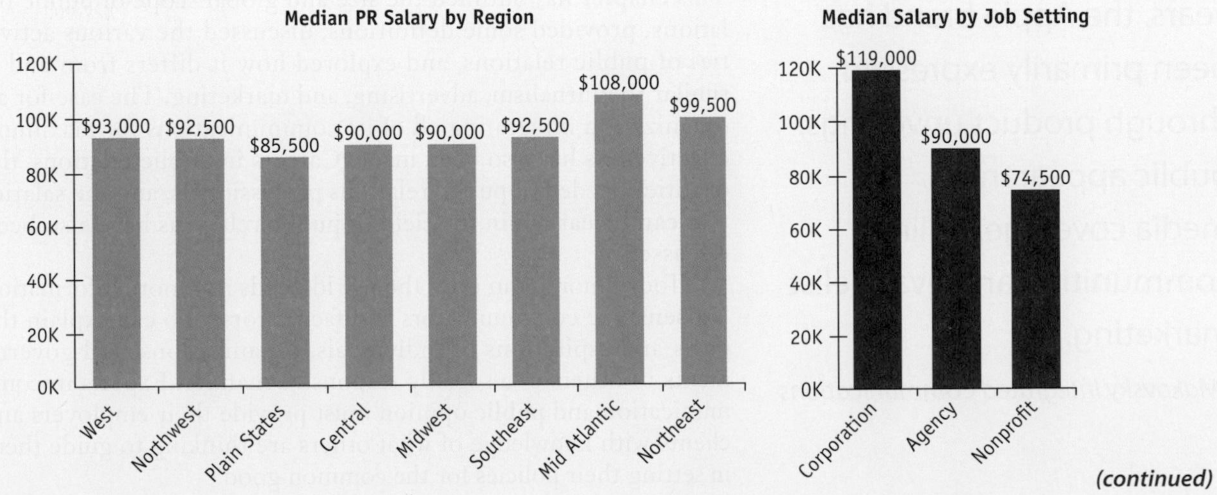

(continued)

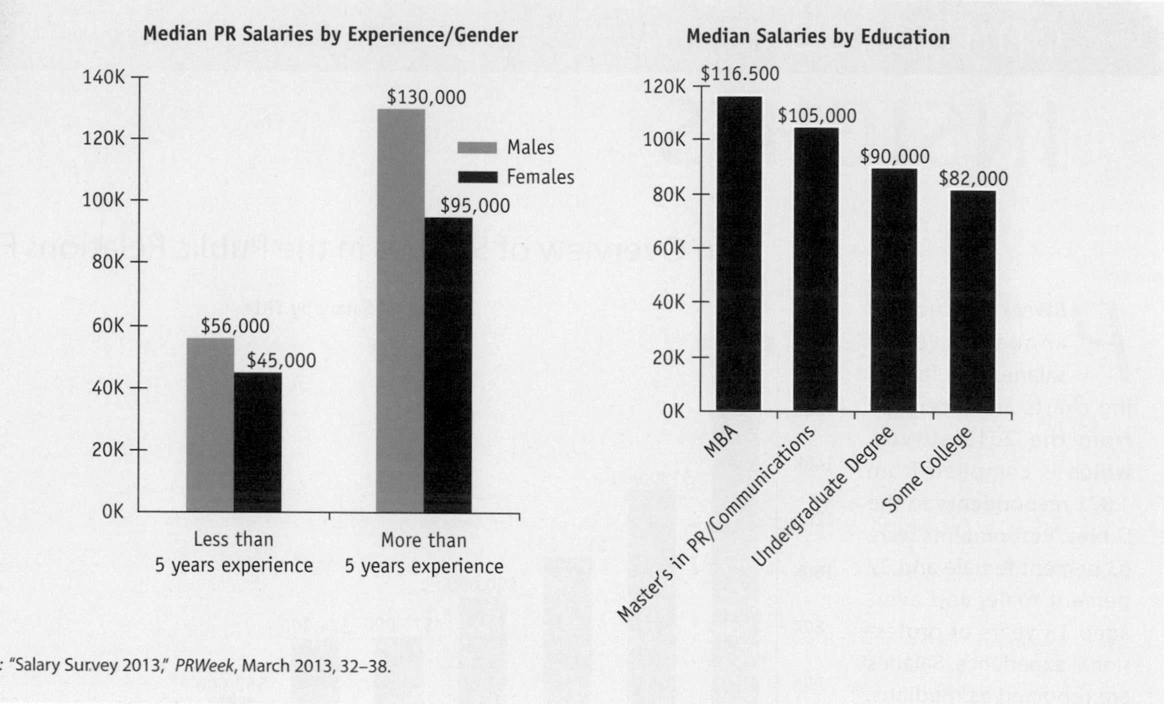

Source: "Salary Survey 2013," *PRWeek*, March 2013, 32–38.

Apple's climb to its position as the world's most valuable brand began when its last brand-advertising campaign ended. For the past 10 years, the Apple brand has been primarily expressed through product unveilings, public appearances, media coverage, online communities, and evangelist marketing.

Makovsky Integrated Communications

Worldwide vice chairman Leslie Dach is reported to have received $3 million in Wal-Mart shares for taking the EVP post at the retail giant, according to Jack O'Dwyer's newsletter. For those just beginning their careers, however, see the Insights box on page 61 for an assistant account executive position.

The Value of Public Relations

This chapter has outlined the size and global scope of public relations, provided some definitions, discussed the various activities of public relations, and explored how it differs from and is similar to journalism, advertising, and marketing. The case for an organization integrating all of its communications for maximum effectiveness has also been made. Careers in public relations, the qualities needed in public relations professionals, and the salaries that can be earned in the field of public relations have also been discussed.

Today more than ever, the world needs not more information but sensitive communicators and facilitators who can explain the goals and aspirations of individuals, organizations, and governments to others in a socially responsive manner. Experts in communication and public opinion must provide their employers and clients with knowledge of what others are thinking to guide them in setting their policies for the common good.

on the job INSIGHTS

Looking for an Entry-Level Job in Public Relations?

Many recent graduates find their first job in a public relations firm as an "account coordinator" or "assistant account executive." The following is a job description posted on LinkedIn by a public relations firm in New York City:

Job Description:

Are you looking for work at an award winning PR and social media agency in New York City? Are you looking for a fun and engaging work atmosphere and supportive team? Then we have the job for you! We are currently looking for an account coordinator (AC) or Assistant Account Executive (AAE) to be core team members on client accounts and perform various public relations and social media tasks.

Specific Job Responsibilities

- Contribute as core team member on client accounts
- Create and maintain media lists, editorial calendars, speaking, and award matrices
- Monitor daily news of clients
- Submit speaking abstracts and award nominations
- Distribute news releases
- Write, proof, and edit a variety of PR, marketing, and social media materials
- Help develop compelling pitches to journalists and key bloggers
- Respond to journalist queries
- Develop agency agendas, recap reports, clip, and monthly reports
- Assist with development of strategic PR, marketing, and social media plans
- Participate in social media engagement for clients and agency

Desired Skills and Experience

- Bachelor's degree in public relations, communications, or related field
- 1–3 years in PR (experience in high-tech preferred)
- Strong written and verbal communication skills
- Solid media skills
- Team oriented and ability to take lead on relevant projects
- Proficiency in Microsoft Office and using social media platforms
- Experience with Vocus, Cision, and other PR software programs a plus

Indeed, in this era of heightened environmental concern, accountability, and transparency, no organization exists solely for its own purposes; it must also serve society as a whole. Another way of expressing this point is the idea that no organization can exist without the express permission of the government and society at large.

Tom Glover, writing in *Profile*, the magazine of the Institute of Public Relations in the United Kingdom, believes "clear and consistent communication helps organizations achieve their goals, employees to work to their potential, customers to make informed choices, investors to make an accurate assessment of an organization, and society to form fair judgments of industries, organizations, and issues."

Public relations provides businesses and society with a vital service. On a practical level, Laurence Moskowitz, chairman and CEO of Medialink, says that public relations is ". . . informative. It's part of the news, the program, the article, the stuff readers and viewers want . . ." Indeed, the Harris Interactive/PRSA survey previously mentioned also found that 71 percent of its respondents agreed with the statement that public relations professionals can "help raise awareness about important issues that the public might not know about."

Richard Edelman, CEO of Edelman Worldwide, adds that the value and evolution of public relations is toward public engagement. He told the World Public Relations Forum in Melbourne, Australia: "Public engagement is a reflection of public relations' multi-stakeholder perspective. We understand deeply that it is not enough to sell to consumers alone. We engage with NGOs, regulators, policy makers, academics, and those new influencers—the impassioned consumers, empowered employees, and social activists. We also find common ground between humanity and science."

Summary

The Challenge of Public Relations

- Public relations is well established in the United States and throughout the world. Growth is strong in Europe and Asia, particularly China.
- Common terms in most definitions of public relations are *deliberate*, *planned*, *performance*, *public interest*, *two-way communication*, and *strategic management function*.
- Organizations use a variety of terms to describe the public relations function, calling it *corporate communications*, *public affairs*, *communication*, and even *external affairs*. Less flattering terms used in the media include *flack* and *spin doctor*.

Public Relations as a Process

- The public relations process can be described with the RACE acronym: **R**esearch, **A**ction, **C**ommunication, and **E**valuation. The process is a constant cycle; feedback and program adjustment are integral components of the overall process.
- Public relations work includes the following specializations: counseling, media relations, publicity, community relations, governmental affairs, employee relations, investor relations, development/fund-raising, special events, and marketing communications.
- Public relations is a distinct discipline separate from journalism, advertising, and marketing. Although the disciplines share basic concepts of effective communication, public relations is much broader in scope and works to build relationships with multiple publics.
- An organization's goals and objectives are best achieved by integrating the activities of advertising, marketing, and public relations to create a consistent message. Integration requires teamwork and the recognition that each field has strengths that complement and reinforce one another.

A Career in Public Relations

- The recommended path to a career in public relations is to major or take courses in the subject. Journalism majors and communication majors, however, are also attracted to the field. Students, in addition to having excellent writing skills, should also take courses in management, marketing, and economics.
- Those who plan careers in public relations should be competent in the following areas: writing, research, planning, problem solving, business/economics, and social media.
- Students should participate in internships throughout college as part of their preprofessional training in public relations. Paid internships are the most desirable.
- Entry-level salaries are higher in public relations than in many other communications fields. An entry-level person can earn a salary in the $30,000 to $40,000 range. A more experienced professional can earn a salary in six figures.

Case Activity **Promoting Beef Jerky as a Healthy Snack**

Tom Jones Beef Jerky is naturally high in protein and low in fat, calories, and carbs that make it an ideal snack for active, health-conscious individuals. The only problem is that consumer research shows that many have the perception that jerky is unhealthy. The company wants to change this perception and to increase sales to men and women, aged 18 to 34, who actively exercise and lead healthy lifestyles.

Your public relations firm is hired to (1) increase awareness of Tom Jones' products through sponsoring an event that would appeal to a "work hard and play hard" audience, (2) provide samples at such an event to showcase the brand's health snack message, and (3) generate local print, online, and broadcast coverage. There is no budget for advertising. What would you recommend?

Questions **For Review and Discussion**

1. Why does an organization require public relations?
2. Is public relations a management function? Does public relations support other executive functions within an organization through engagement of relevant stakeholders and the insights these engagements bring?
3. What key words and phrases are found in most definitions of public relations?
4. What does the acronym RACE stand for?
5. "Public relations is a process and not an event." Support or refute the statement with arguments.
6. Public relations is known by various other popular terms worldwide. What are they?
7. What are the components of basic public relations practice? Which one sounds the most interesting to you as a possible career specialty?
8. Public relations is often stereotyped in pop culture and media as bold, glamorous, and without substance. Do you agree or disagree? Why?
9. What are the three insights you have gathered from various public relations definitions about the profession per se?
10. How does public relations differ from the fields of journalism, advertising, and marketing?
11. Internships are popular in many fields. Under what circumstances should interns be given some compensation for their work?
12. Who coined the term "spin" to mean public relations? How has the usage of the term changed over time?
13. Name any six activities listed by the Public Relations Society of America that are pursued by public relations practitioners.
14. Discuss entry-level salaries in public relations. Are they about what you expected? What about the salaries for experienced professionals?
15. After reading this chapter, do you think you would enjoy a career in public relations? Why or why not?

Media Resources

Ashooh, N. and others (2012, April). Master Class: How must education evolve to address the PR professional's expanding role? *PRWeek*, 51–52.

Becker, L., Vlad, T., and Simpson, A. (2013, 2012 Annual Survey of Journalism and Mass Communications Enrollments. Journalism & Mass Communications Educator, 68(4), 305-334.

Becker, L.B., Vlad, T., & Simpson, H. (2013, November). 2012 Job Market for JMC Grads Holds Steady. *AEJMC Newsletter*, 1-12-16.

Bureau of Labor Statistics. (2012). *Occupational outlook handbook 2012–13: Public relations managers and specialists*. Retrieved from www.bls.gov/ooh/management/public-relations-managers-and-specialists.htm

Celsi, C. (2011, February 23). Twenty tips for mastering an internship interview. Retrieved from www.prdaily.com

Chung, W., & Choi, J. (2012). Professionalism in public relations pedagogy: A comparative analysis of public relations curricula among the United States, United

Kingdom, and South Korea. *Journalism and Mass Communication Educator, 67*(4), 375–392.

Crenshaw, D. (2011, May 10). How to break into PR: 9 tips for new graduates. *Ragan's PR Daily*. Retrieved from www.prdaily.com

Elliott, S. (2011, November 21). Redefining Public Relations in the Age of Social Media. *NewYork Times*. Retrieved from www.nytimes.com

Garcia, A. (2012, January 9). The top five reasons PR is so darn stressful. *PRNewser*. Retrieved from www.mediabistro.com/prnewser

Greenhouse, S. (2010, April 2). Growth of unpaid internships may be illegal, officials say. *New York Times*. Retrieved from www.nytimes.com

Holmes, P. (2012, July 23). Global PR industry up eight percent to $10bn. *Holmes Report*. Retrieved from www.holmesreport.com

McDonald, F. (2011, February 10). Paid or unpaid, time to evaluate PR's use of interns. Retrieved from http://prsay.prsa.org

Perlin, R. (2011, April 12). Unpaid interns, complicit colleges. *New York Times*. Retrieved from www.nytimes.com

Public relations defined: Reshaping the future of the profession, (2012, Spring). *The Strategist*, 6.

Public relations defined: A modern definition for the new era of public relations, (2012, April 11). Retrieved from www.prsa.org

Sebastian, M. (2012, January 5). PR is now the seventh-most stressful job in America. *Ragan's PR Daily*. Retrieved from www.prdaily.com

Siegriest, L. (2011, February 10). PRSA updates guidelines on ethical use of interns. Retrieved from www.prweekus.com

Soriano, M. (2012, August 1). How did you know? Reflections on joining the public relations adventure. *Council of Public Relations Firms*. Retrieved from www.prfirms.org

The Evolution and History of Public Relations

chapter 2

After reading this chapter, you will be able to:

Understand the evolution of public relations from ancient empires to today's practice

Know how public relations tactics have contributed to American independence, the settlement of the West, and social causes such as voting rights for women

Appreciate the contributions of visionaries such as Ivy Lee and Edward Bernays, who laid the foundation of today's practice

Have insight into the reasons for the influx of women into the field

Be knowledgeable about current developments and trends in the field

Early Beginnings

The concept of public relations is probably as old as human communication itself. In many ancient civilizations, people were persuaded to accept the authority of government and religion through common public relations techniques such as interpersonal communication, speeches, art, literature, staged events, and publicity. None of these endeavors were called public relations, of course, but their purpose and effect were often the same as those of today's modern practice. Indeed, some common themes regarding public relations activity are consistent over the centuries, as shown in the Insights box on page 73.

Herodotus, writing about the Persian Wars, noted that the Greeks carved messages on stones near watering holes to demoralize the Ionian fleet. And Alexander the Great publicized his battlefield victories by sending glowing reports back to the Macedonian Court. In India, Emperor Asoka (273–326 B.C.) was communicating with his subjects through messages on large stone pillars erected at major crossroads. The Rosetta Stone, dating back to 196 B.C., was basically a publicity release touting an Egyptian pharaoh's accomplishments. Similarly, the ancient Olympic Games were promoted to enhance the aura of athletes as heroes in much the same way as the 2012 games in London.

Julius Caesar was probably the first politician to publish a book, *Commentaries*, which he used to further his ambitions to become emperor of the Roman Empire. He also organized elaborate parades whenever he returned from a successful battle to burnish his image as an outstanding commander and leader. After Caesar became a consul of Rome in 59 B.C., he had public proceedings posted on walls throughout the city. These *Acta Diurna*, or "Daily Doings," was probably one of the world's first newspapers.

Saint Paul, the New Testament's most prolific author, also qualifies for the public relations hall of fame. According to James Grunig and Todd Hunt, authors of *Managing Public Relations*:

> The apostles Paul and Peter used speeches, letters, staged events, and similar public relations activities to attract attention, gain followers, and establish new churches. Similarly, the four gospels in the New Testament, which were written at least 40 years after the death of Jesus, were public relations documents, written more to propagate the faith than to provide a historical account of Jesus' life.

Emperor Asoka

Emperor Asoka of India used stone pillars as early as 300 B.C. to publicize his accomplishments and policies.

The Middle Ages

The Roman Catholic Church was a major practitioner of public relations throughout the Middle Ages. Pope Urban II used symbolism, staged events, and propaganda to persuade thousands of followers to join the Crusades. Six centuries later, the Church was among the first to use the word *propaganda*, with the establishment by Pope Gregory XV of the College of Propaganda to supervise foreign missions and train priests to propagate the faith.

Meanwhile, in Venice, bankers in the 15th and 16th centuries practiced the fine art of investor relations and were probably the first, along with local Catholic bishops, to adopt the concept of corporate philanthropy by sponsoring such artists as Michelangelo.

It was also during the Middle Ages that Gutenberg developed the printing press (1450), which profoundly influenced the gathering and distribution of information for the next 500 years. The printing press essentially made it possible for individuals and organizations to communicate directly with the public and to publicize any number of endeavors. See the Insights box below about how Martin Luther's reformation went viral.

Colonial America

The United States was first settled by immigrants, primarily those from England. Various land companies with a license from the Crown actively promoted colonization to generate revenues from what the colonists were able to manufacture or grow. In other words, colonization was strictly a commercial proposition. As early as 1584, for example, Sir Walter Raleigh was sending back glowing accounts to England of what was actually a swamp-filled Roanoke Island. The Virginia Company, in 1620, distributed flyers and brochures throughout Europe, offering 50 acres of free land to anyone willing to migrate.

on the job INSIGHTS

The Social Media of the Reformation

Today's social media has made the dissemination of information more rapid, but the concept is not a new idea. Martin Luther's "95 Theses" that launched the protestant reformation more than 500 years ago also went viral in a matter of weeks because of advances in printing and the interaction of various social networks.

It all started with Luther nailing his complaint about the selling of indulgences by the Catholic Church on the church door in Wittenberg in 1517 that, like today's bloggers, set off a public debate. Within a few weeks, his "theses" were reprinted in pamphlets and broadsheets throughout Germany in much the same way as today's network of friends "like," retweet, and post links to the original source. According to the *Economist*, "The unintentional but rapid spread of the '95 Theses' alerted Luther to the way in which media passed from one person to another could quickly reach a wide audience." In other words, the message was amplified in much the same way as what occurs in today's social media networks.

Luther's ideas were also amplified through music and visual images that reached people beyond the educated and literate elite. Ballads were a popular medium used by both reformers and Catholics to spread information and attack their enemies. In addition, woodcuts with bold graphics and some text were published in broadsheets that conveyed messages to the illiterate and served as visual aids for preachers. Luther's observation that "without images we can neither think nor understand anything" is still reflected today by the extensive use of visuals and infographics on websites and various networks such as YouTube and Instagram.

The cascade of pamphlets, mass-produced broadsheets, ballads, and graphic woodcuts that were produced by Luther and his network of supporters in the years after 1517 is a prime example of the multimedia campaign. It ultimately made the Reformation an overwhelming and unstoppable movement, and the rest is history.

Source: How Luther Went Viral: Five Centuries before Facebook and the Arab Spring, social media helped bring about the Reformation, (2011, December 17). *Economist*, 93–95.

After the American colonies were well established, publicity and public relations techniques were used to promote various institutions. In 1641, Harvard College published a fund-raising brochure and sent representatives to England to raise funds. In addition, 10 other colleges founded between 1745 and 1775 also raised funds through promotional brochures, special events, lotteries, and cultivating wealthy donors. King's College (now Columbia University) issued its first news release in 1758, which announced its commencement exercises.

Public relations also played an active role in American independence. A major promoter of independence was Sam Adams, whom one historian once called "The father of press agentry." Adams was the founder of the Sons of Liberty and organized rallies and demonstrations in the 1760s to protest the Stamp Act. By the early 1770s, Adams had polished his organizing and publicity skills. For example, he is credited with organizing the Boston Tea Party—which *PRWeek* has called "... the greatest and best-known publicity stunt of all time ..."—in which a group of colonists dressed as Indians threw crates of tea from a British trade ship into Boston Harbor as a symbolic protest of British taxation, which received widespread publicity throughout the colonies. Another major success of Adams was to label the killing of five colonists by British troops at a demonstration as the "Boston Massacre," which further inflamed public opinion against Great Britain. Adams had a refined sense of how symbolism could sway public opinion.

Also instrumental in bringing lukewarm citizens around to the cause of American independence was Tom Paine's *Common Sense*. More than 120,000 copies of the pamphlet were sold in three months, an early example of political communication to a national audience. After independence, Alexander Hamilton, John Jay, and James Madison wrote the *Federalist Papers* to rally public support for the ratification of the U.S. Constitution. The effort laid the foundation for distributing syndicated opinion pieces via the mass media, a concept that is still being used today in public relations.

The 1800s: The Golden Age of Press Agentry

The 1800s was a period of growth and expansion in the United States. It also was the golden age of the press agent, which Webster's *New World Dictionary* defines as "a person whose work is to get publicity for an individual, organization, etc." The period was also the age of hype, which is the shrewd use of the media and other devices to promote an individual, a cause, or even a product or service, such as a circus.

Press agents were able to glorify Davy Crockett as a frontier hero to draw political support away from Andrew Jackson, attract thousands to the touring shows of Buffalo Bill and sharpshooter Annie Oakley, make a legend of frontiersman Daniel Boone, and promote hundreds of other personalities.

These old-time press agents played on the credulity of the public in its longing to be entertained. Advertisements and press releases were exaggerated to the point of being outright lies. Doing advance work for an attraction, the press agent dropped complimentary tickets on the desk of a newspaper editor, along with the announcements. Voluminous publicity generally followed, and the journalists and their families flocked to their free entertainment, with scant regard for the ethical constraints that largely prohibit such practices today.

The Legacy of P. T. Barnum

The individual who best represents the hype and press agentry of the 19th century is Phineas T. Barnum, the great American showman. He was the master of what historian Daniel Boorstin calls the pseudoevent, which is a planned happening that occurs primarily for the purpose of being reported. Barnum used flowery language, exaggeration, controversy, massive advertising, and publicity to promote his various attractions in an age when the public was hungry for any form of entertainment.

Barnum first gained fame in 1835 as the exhibitor of Joice Heth. She was an African American who was billed as George Washington's nursemaid, which would have made her 161 years old. Barnum and his advance man, Levi Lyman, encouraged public debate about her background and age because it generated not only media coverage but the sale of tickets as the public came to see for themselves. In the 1840s, another Barnum exhibit that generated controversy (and much media coverage) was the Fejee Mermaid, a stuffed creature that was half-monkey and half-fish. Barnum quoted some clerics who said it might be possible to merge species, but that the public should come to his American Museum in New York and judge for themselves—which they did in great numbers.

> He [Barnum] is a direct ancestor of everything from Bat Boy in the *Weekly World News* to all those pseudoscience shows on the History Channel like 'MonsterQuest' to . . . the creators of reality television.
>
> *James Hynes, reviewing a book by Candace Fleming,* The Tremendous, Stupendous Life of Showman P. T. Barnum

Thanks to Barnum, Tom Thumb became one of America's first media celebrities. He was a midget, standing just over 2 feet and weighing 15 pounds, but he was exceptional at singing, dancing, and performing comedy monologues. Barnum made a public relations event of the marriage of "General" Tom Thumb to another midget. He even got extensive European bookings for Thumb by introducing him to society leaders in London, who were enchanted by him. An invitation to the palace followed, and from then on Thumb played to packed houses every night. Barnum, even in his day, knew the value of third-party endorsement.

Another Barnum success was the promotion of Jenny Lind, the "Swedish Nightingale." Lind was famous in Europe, but no one in America knew about her beautiful voice until Barnum took her on a national tour and made her one of America's first pop icons. He obtained full houses on opening nights in each community by donating part of the proceeds to charity. As a civic activity, the event attracted many of the town's opinion leaders, whereupon the general public flocked to attend succeeding performances—a device still employed today by entertainment publicists.

Promoting the Westward Movement

Throughout the 19th century, publicity and promotion helped to populate the western United States. Land speculators distributed pamphlets and other publicity that described almost every community as "the garden spot of the West," which one critic of the time called "downright puffery, full of exaggerated statements, and highwrought and false-colored descriptions." One brochure about Nebraska, for example, described the territory as the "Gulf Stream of migration . . . bounded on the north by the 'Aurora Borealis' and on the south by the Day of Judgment." Other brochures were more down-to-earth, describing the fertile land, the abundant water, and the opportunity to build a fortune.

on the job

A MULTICULTURAL WORLD

The Beginnings of Public Relations in Other Nations

The British scholar J. A. R. Pimlott once wrote, "Public relations is not a peculiarly American phenomenon, but it has nowhere flourished as in the United States. Nowhere else is it so widely practiced, so lucrative, so pretentious, so respectable and disreputable, so widely suspected, and so extravagantly extolled."

It's important to realize, however, that other nations have their own histories. The following is a representative sample.

Germany

Railroads and other large business enterprises began publicity efforts as far back as the mid-19th century. Alfred Krupp, who founded the Krupp Company, the premier industrial firm in Germany and eventually the base of the Nazi war power, wrote in 1866, "We think . . . it is time that authoritative reports concerning factory matters, in accordance with the facts should be propagated on a regular basis through newspaper reports which serve an enlightened public." In the 1870s, German Chancellor Otto von Bismarck set up a press office in the Foreign Ministry to do media relations, arrange interviews, and organize news conferences.

Great Britain

The Marconi Company, a world leader in wireless telegraphy, established a department in 1910 to distribute news releases about its achievements and operations. In 1911, the first government public relations campaign was launched by the Insurance Commission to explain the benefits of the National Insurance Act.

The Air Ministry appointed the first government press officer in 1919, and a year later the Ministry of Health appointed a director of information. The government then launched the British Broadcasting Corporation (BBC) in 1922 as a way to communicate British values and viewpoints to its colonies and other nations. Professional public relations counseling for business was introduced in the country in 1924, when Basil Clarke started a firm in London. His first client was a dairy group that wanted to promote milk pasteurization, an innovation that had met with some resistance from the public.

Australia

Public relations in Australia largely consisted of publicity efforts until after World War II. When U.S. General Douglas MacArthur arrived after his escape from Corregidor in 1942, he introduced the term *public relations* and, with a highly skilled staff, demonstrated numerous ways of promoting his image and the war effort.

The industry grew steadily and, in 1960, the Public Relations Institute of Australia (PRIA) was formed. Notable practitioners included Eric White, who, according to one source, "virtually created the public relations industry" in Australia. As early as the 1960s, White oversaw extensions of his firm to six Pacific Rim countries.

India

Although India has a long history of kings and emperors who used various methods of communication and propaganda, modern public relations probably began during World War I, when the government set up publicity boards throughout the country to mobilize support for the war. According to C. V. Narasimha Reddi, editor of the *Public Relations Voice*, "Public relations or public communication played an active role in Indian independence." Gandhi, for example, used musicians, roadside meetings, rallies, speeches, and media interviews to reach both the urban and the rural populations to create awareness of the freedom struggle. Indeed, several Indian scholars have called Gandhi the "father of Indian public relations." TATA, now one of India's largest corporations, began programs in community relations and employee communications as early as 1912.

The Philippines

The public relations industry in the Philippines was transplanted from the West in the 1940s. In fact, the country is considered the "Pacific birthplace of public relations." U.S. Army public information officers regularly issued news releases to the Philippine press during World War II. An early Filipino pioneer was Pete Teodoro, public relations director for a paint manufacturer. He is credited with undertaking the first organized public relations campaign to generate goodwill and business from local contractors and architects. In 1966, the San Miguel Corporation, known worldwide for its beer, established the first public relations department.

Spain

The growth of public relations in Spain started in the 1950s and paralleled political, economic, and media developments in Spain. An advertising agency, Danis Advertising of Barcelona, launched a public relations campaign in 1955 to build community goodwill for a corporate client and its product. One of the directors of that campaign, Joaquin Maestre, started his own public relations firm in 1960. According to one historian, the advent of public relations consultancies "marked the beginning of a 'dynamic consumer market' for public relations services, which led to setting up the first public relations agencies as a direct response to the 'market demand for services.' "

The Russian Federation

The collapse of the Soviet Union in 1991 ushered in a free-market economy and democratic reforms that caused the rapid growth of the public relations field in government and private business. With the new openness, global companies began selling products and services in the new Russia, with the assistance of Western-style advertising, public relations, and promotion.

In addition, Russian companies began to understand the importance of publicizing their products and services. Before that time, most "public relations" was conducted by the government. In the mid-1990s, a Russian association of public relations professionals was organized to promote standards and provide continuing education.

South Africa

Although the government established an information bureau in 1937 to distribute official information, the concept of public relations as an occupation wasn't established until 1943 when the first public relations practitioner was appointed by South African Railways. Five years later, the first public relations firm was founded in Johannesburg. Today, the public relations industry is considered the most developed on the African continent and the Public Relations Institute of Southern Africa, founded in 1957, has about 1,200 members.

Thailand

Public relations in Thailand, as in many nations, dates back to the 1950s. Esko Pajasalmi from Finland is credited with starting the first public relations firm in Thailand. He started his firm, Presko, after serving more than a decade as a Christian missionary in northern Thailand. Presko eventually became the nation's largest public relations firm and set the standard for other firms that followed.

One early Presko campaign was for Colgate-Palmolive, after its toothpaste was falsely accused of containing pork fat. The Muslim community was horrified, and Colgate immediately lost 100 percent of the market in southern Thailand. Pajasalmi contacted Muslim leaders, took them to inspect the factories, and convinced them that the rumors were unfounded. Business boomed again.

United Arab Emirates

Rapid business and economic development in the past two decades, particularly in Dubai, has encouraged the growth of public relations. By the mid-1980s, the majority of government departments and other major institutions had created a public relations department. In addition, a number of international public relations firms arrived in the mid-1980s to service the operations of multinational companies with operations in the Middle East.

American railroads, in particular, used extensive public relations and press agentry to attract settlers and expand operations. As Andy Piasecki, lecturer at Queen Margaret University College in Edinburgh, Scotland, describes it:

> The expansion of the railroads was dependent on publicity and promotion. This is hardly surprising that any investment in western expansion was dependent on finding a population. Many railroad companies were colonization agencies as much as they were transport companies. Without people, no railroads could be sustained and because there were, at this time, few people out West, they had to be brought in . . . .

Consequently, such companies as the Burlington and Missouri Railroad promoted Western settlement from England and other European nations. The company set up an information office in Liverpool that distributed fact sheets and maps and placed stories in the local press. In addition, the railroad promoted lectures about migrating to the American West. According to Piasecki, "The pièce de resistance for the Burlington was a kind of early road show . . . an elaborately illustrated lecture with 85 painted views, each covering 250 square feet."

The publicity and promotion paid off. Piasecki notes, "During the 1870s and the 1880s, the railroads attracted an estimated 5 million people to the Midwestern states, and they were responsible for the establishment there of almost 2 million farms. None of this could have been achieved without complex communication strategies closely linked to business objectives . . . ."

Near the end of the 19th century, the Santa Fe Railway launched a campaign to lure tourists to the Southwest. It commissioned dozens of painters and photographers to depict the dramatic landscape and show romanticized American Indians weaving, grinding corn, and dancing.

Politics and Social Movements Take the Stage

The early 1800s also saw the development of public relations tactics on the political and activist front. Amos Kendall, a former Kentucky newspaper editor, became an intimate member of President Andrew Jackson's "kitchen cabinet" and probably was the first presidential press secretary.

Kendall sampled public opinion on issues, advised Jackson, and skillfully interpreted Jackson's rough ideas, putting them into presentable form as speeches and news releases. He also served as Jackson's advance agent on trips, wrote glowing articles that he sent to supportive newspapers, and probably was the first to use newspaper reprints in public relations; almost every complimentary story or editorial about Jackson was reprinted and widely circulated. Article reprints are still a standard tactic in today's modern practice.

Supporters and leaders of such causes as abolition, suffrage, and prohibition employed publicity to maximum effect throughout the century. In 1848, for example, the organizers of the first women's rights convention in Seneca Falls, New York, used a variety of public relations tactics to promote the meeting and their cause. This included news releases, brochures, legislative petitions, special events, speaking tours, and even early concepts of issues management.

The Women's Christian Temperance Union (WCTU), during the 1870s and beyond, also used a variety of public relations strategies to ban alcohol and promote the suffrage movement. Some of its techniques were (1) distributing information kits and fact sheets to the press, (2) establishing coffee houses, (3) holding demonstrations in front of liquor stores, and (4) going door to door to persuade voters. Both Annie Wittenmyer and Francis Willard, early presidents of the WCTU, had a sophisticated understanding of effective media relations and made sure journalists were always accommodated at the group's conventions. Willard once wrote that media coverage could mean reaching up to "tens and hundreds of thousands, millions, while the proceedings in the auditorium will be known to only a few thousand."

Another activist group, the Anti-Saloon League of America, used pamphlets, posters, lectures, and lobbying, which ultimately led to the enactment in 1920 of the Eighteenth Amendment, banning the selling and consumption of alcoholic products in the United States.

on the job INSIGHTS

Major Historical Themes over the Centuries

The evolution of public relations can be placed on a timeline from ancient beginnings to today's practice, but there are also basic themes that transcend time and place. Margot Opdycke Lamme, at the University of Alabama, and Karen Miller Russell, at the University of Georgia, contend ". . . that the public relations function has remained remarkably consistent over time . . . " and there are five major historical themes.

Profit

In the historical literature, profit is consistently a motivation for the public relations function. In the 1500s, Pope Clement VIII used public relations tactics to raise money. Fifty years later, Harvard College was the first college in America to begin a development campaign. American railroads, in the 1800s, used media relations, exhibits, and press junkets to increase ticket sales.

Recruitment

Lamme and Russell write, "By the Middle Ages, Irish Monks, the Crusades, and the Catholic Church in Spain all employed public relations methods to recruit armies of the faithful." The Sons of Liberty, in the mid-1700s, used pamphlets, demonstrations, and staged events to recruit members opposed to British colonial rule.

Legitimacy

Third-party endorsements have been used throughout history to give legitimacy to causes and institutions. Glastonbury Abbey appropriated the King Arthur legends to legitimize England's rule over the Celts. P. T. Barnum and the railroads often engaged opinion leaders such as scholars and clerics to give their activities credibility.

Agitation

The temperance and woman's suffrage movements used agitation to rally the public against drunkenness and gender discrimination. Lamme and Russell also note, "The 1890s battle between Westinghouse and Edison for current included exploitative pathos and logos, while Standard Oil engaged in public relations to battle antitrust proponents."

Advocacy

Public relations tactics were used in the abolition movement to ban slavery, and were also used by Standard Oil to advocate its position against antitrust legislation. At the end of the 19th century, the Sierra Club's John Muir was advocating for conservation and the establishment of national parks.

Lamme and Russell note, "Collectively, these five motivations drove an enormous variety of tactics, such as brochures, pamphlets, and books, and other print materials, plays, music, art, third-party endorsements, slogans and symbols, media coverage, and showmanship and publicity stunts." Thus, they conclude, "The concept of public relations development over time is therefore relevant primarily to the scale at which tactics were employed and to the gradual development of the rules of engagement."

Source: Lamme, M. O., & Russell, K. M. (2010, Winter). Removing the spin: Toward a new theory of public relations history. *Journalism Communication Monographs, 11* pp. 281–362 (4).

Other activists in the latter half of the 19th century focused on racial discrimination. Ida B. Wells was born a slave in 1862, and was just 22 when she refused to move when a railroad conductor ordered her to give up her seat. (This was more than 70 years before Rosa Parks, who became the symbol of the 1960s civil rights movement.) Ida went on to own and edit an antisegregationist newspaper (which was later burned down by a white mob) and also be an advocate for antilynching laws, after three of her friends were lynched by a mob in Memphis. She wrote articles and books, gave hundreds of speeches, and skillfully crafted arguments to change

Ida B. Wells

Her writings and use of public relations tactics were instrumental in bringing antisegregation ideas to the forefront of American thinking.

public opinion in America and Europe. She was also a founder of the National Association for the Advancement of Colored People (NAACP) and became one of the most influential black leaders of her time.

There was also an environmental movement during the last half of the 19th century. In the 1860s, naturalist John Muir began a lifelong quest to protect wilderness areas and to establish national parks. He wrote several books and dozens of magazine articles, sent thousands of telegrams, and lectured throughout the country. In 1889 he worked with the influential *Century Magazine* to promote a campaign requesting congressional support to create Yosemite National Park. The activist public relations campaign succeeded, and today's citizens continue to enjoy the benefits of a protected Yosemite.

Early Corporate Initiatives

The wave of industrialization and urbanization that swept the nation after the Civil War created many new businesses that competed in the marketplace.

One department store owner, John Wannamaker of Philadelphia, was one of the first major retailers to use the tactics of public relations to attract customers. In the 1870s, he published a magazine that was given free to customers. Wannamaker also placed image ads about the quality of merchandise and service in his stores and even organized a lecture bureau to bring in noted speakers.

Another department store, Macy's, introduced its first Christmas window in 1870 that attracted the public to the store. Its greatest public relations coup, however, was the creation of the Macy's Thanksgiving Day Parade, which was started in 1924. By 1933, more than a million people lined the parade route in New York City. Today, the annual parade still draws large crowds and a national television audience.

Westinghouse Corporation established what is believed to be the first in-house publicity department, to promote the concept of alternating current (AC) versus Thomas Edison's direct current (DC) system. George Westinghouse eventually won a bruising public relations battle with Edison, and AC became the standard in the United States. In 1897, the term *public relations* was first used, in a company listing, by the Association of American Railroads.

1900 to 1950: The Age of Pioneers

By the start of the 20th century, public relations had begun to reinvent itself along journalistic lines, as the emphasis shifted from the hype and press agentry of the Barnum era to the idea that facts and information were more effective strategies. Two factors were involved in this shift. First, the press agent model didn't really fit the operations and objectives of large corporations. Second, the new field of public relations attracted journalists, who were more comfortable with objectivity and the dissemination of information.

Ivy Lee: The First Public Relations Counsel

The leading pioneer in this new approach to public relations was Ivy Ledbetter Lee, a former business journalist for the *New York Times*, the *New York World*, and the *New York American*. He began as a publicist, but shortly expanded that role to be regarded as the first public relations counsel.

When Lee opened his public relations firm, Parker and Lee, in 1905, he issued a declaration of principles that signaled a new model of public relations practice: public information. Lee's emphasis was on the dissemination of truthful, accurate information rather than distortions, hype, and exaggerations.

One of Lee's first clients was the Pennsylvania Railroad, where he was retained as a "publicity counselor" to handle media relations. His first task was to convince management that the policy of operating in secret and refusing to talk with the press, typical of many large corporations at the time, was a poor strategy for fostering goodwill and public understanding. When the next rail accident occurred, Lee provided press facilities, issued what is claimed to be the first news release of the modern age, and took reporters to the accident site. Although such action appeared, to the conservative railroad directors, to be reckless indiscretion, they were pleasantly surprised that the company received fairer press comment than on any previous occasion.

It wasn't long before other railroads also adopted a more open information policy. By 1912, Lee had become the executive assistant to the president of the Pennsylvania Railroad, which Scott Cutlip, in his comprehensive history of public relations, calls "the first known instance of a public relations person being placed at the management level."

One of Lee's major accomplishments was the 1913–1914 railroad freight hike campaign. The Pennsylvania Railroad, after years of rising expenses, needed a 5 percent railroad freight rate hike to remain in business, but there was considerable public opposition and also a skeptical Interstate Commerce Commission (ICC). Lee believed the public and the ICC could be persuaded to accept higher rates if they were given the facts and made aware of the situation.

Burton St. John III, in a *Public Relations Review* article, recounts how Lee conducted his campaign. He not only widely distributed the railroad industry's case to the press, but he also broke with past publicity practices by clearly identifying the source of the information. After each ICC hearing, he distributed the railroad's testimony to the press, railroad employees, railway riders, congressmen, state legislators, college presidents, and other opinion leaders such as the clergy. Other techniques were leaflets and bulletins for railway riders and community opinion leaders, a speaker's bureau, and reprints of speeches.

All these efforts paid off. Public opposition declined, and chambers of commerce around the country bombarded the ICC with resolutions supporting the railroad. The ICC approved the 5 percent rate hike. St. John concludes, "Lee's propaganda campaign for the Pennsylvania Railroad is a landmark in the history of public relations."

Lee counseled a number of companies and charitable organizations during his lifetime, but he is best known for his work with the Rockefeller family. In 1914, John D. Rockefeller Jr. hired Lee in the wake of the vicious strike-breaking activities, known as the Ludlow Massacre, at the Rockefeller family's Colorado Fuel and Iron Company (CF&I) plant. Lee went to Colorado to do some fact-finding (research) and talked to both sides. He found that

> Through his 20th century principles and practices, Ivy Lee, more than any other communicator in history, heralded the commencement of the 21st century practice of PR.
>
> *Fraser P. Seitel, author of* The Practice of Public Relations

labor leaders were effectively getting their views out by talking freely to the media, but that the company's executives were tight-lipped and inaccessible. The result, of course, was a barrage of negative publicity and public criticism directed at CF&I and the Rockefeller family.

Lee, drawing on his rate hike experience, proposed a series of informational bulletins by management that would be distributed to opinion leaders in Colorado and around the nation. The leaflets were designed to be thought pieces about various issues concerning mining, manufacturing, and labor. In all, 19 bulletins were produced over a period of several months and sent to a mailing list of 19,000. Even at this early time, Lee recognized the value of directly reaching opinion leaders, who, in turn, were highly influential in shaping public discussion and opinion.

Lee organized a number of other public relations activities on behalf of CF&I during 1914 and 1915, including convincing the governor of Colorado to write an article supporting the position taken by the company. Lee also convinced Rockefeller to visit the plant and talk with miners and their families. Lee made sure the press was there to record Rockefeller eating in the workers' hall, swinging a pickax in the mine, and having a beer with the workers after hours. The press loved it. Rockefeller was portrayed as being seriously concerned about the plight of the workers, and the visit led to policy changes and more worker benefits. As a result, the United Mine Workers failed to gain a foothold. Some critics, however, say that Lee was not always honest or accurate in his defense of the mine owners. See the Ethics box on page 77.

Edward L. Bernays

This legendary figure in public relations had a career spanning about three-quarters of a century; he died at the age of 103 in 1995. He became known as the "father of modern public relations."

Lee continued as a counselor to the Rockefeller family and its various companies, but he also counseled a number of other clients. For example, he advised the American Tobacco Company to initiate a profit-sharing plan, the Pennsylvania Railroad to beautify its stations, the movie industry to stop inflated advertising, and the New York Subway to promote various stops along its route, such as the Museum of Natural History, as a way to increase ridership.

He is remembered today for his four important contributions to public relations: (1) advancing the concept that business and industry should align themselves with the public interest, (2) dealing with top executives and carrying out no program without the active support of management, (3) maintaining open communication with the news media, and (4) emphasizing the necessity of humanizing business and bringing its public relations down to the community level of employees, customers, and neighbors.

Edward L. Bernays: Father of Modern Public Relations

Lee's public information model is still used today, but a new approach to the practice of public relations, introduced in the 1920s, emphasized the concept of "scientific persuasion." A leading proponent of this new approach was Edward L. Bernays, who, through brilliant campaigns and extensive self-promotion, became known as the "Father of Modern Public Relations" by the time of his death in 1995 at the age of 103.

on the job

ETHICS

Was Ivy Lee Less than Honest?

The pioneering efforts of Ivy Lee to establish public relations as a legitimate profession and management counsel are widely recognized, but he has also been criticized for not always living up to his declaration of principles for truth and honesty as mentioned on page 75. The series of informational pamphlets and news releases that he distributed in 1914 while working for the Rockefeller family during labor strife at a Colorado mine, say some critics, were not always truthful or accurate. In one news release, according to the *Economist*, he accused Mother Jones, an elderly labor activist, of being a prostitute and a brothel keeper.

After the strike was settled, Lee testified before the U.S. Commission on Industrial Relations and said "none whatever" when asked if he checked the facts given to him by the mine owners. He went on to say, according to *O'Dwyer's Communications & New Media*, that he had ". . . no responsibility for the facts and no duty beyond compiling them and getting them into the best form for publicity work." In another statement, he said, "What is a fact? The effort to state an absolute fact is simply an attempt to give you my interpretation of the facts."

Lee's statements continue to raise questions for today's public relations practitioners. Do public relations practitioners have an ethical responsibility to actually check the "facts" provided by an employer or client before distributing the information to the media and the public? Or is it only their job to compile such "facts" into what Lee describes as "the best form for publicity"?

Bernays, who was the nephew of Sigmund Freud, believed public relations should emphasize the application of social science research and behavioral psychology to formulate campaigns and messages that could change people's perceptions and encourage certain behaviors. Unlike Lee's public information model, which emphasized the accurate distribution of news, Bernays's model was essentially one of advocacy and scientific persuasion. It included listening to the audience, but the purpose of feedback was to formulate a more persuasive message. Professor Emeritus James Grunig of the University of Maryland, a major theorist in public relations, has labeled this the two-way asymmetric model, one of four classic models that are outlined on page 83.

Bernays became a major spokesperson for the "new" public relations through his 1923 book *Crystallizing Public Opinion*, which outlined the scope, function, methods, techniques, and social responsibilities of a public relations counsel—a term that was to become the core of public relations practice.

The book, published a year after Walter Lippmann's insightful treatise on public opinion, attracted much attention, and Bernays was even invited by New York University to offer the first public relations course in the nation. Bernays, over the course of his long career, had many successful campaigns that have become classics. Here is a sampling:

- **Ivory Soap.** Procter & Gamble sold its Ivory Soap by the millions after Bernays came up with the idea of sponsoring soap sculpture contests for school-aged children. In the first year alone, 22 million schoolchildren participated in the contest, which eventually ran for 35 years. Bernays's brochure with soap sculpture tips, which millions of children received in their schools, advised them to "use discarded models for face, hands, and bath."

■ **"Torches of Liberty."** During the Roaring 20s, Bernays was hired by the American Tobacco Company to tap the women's market by countering the social taboo of women smoking in public. His solution was to have beautiful fashion models march in New York's popular Easter Parade, each waving a lit cigarette and wearing a banner proclaiming it a "torch of liberty." By making smoking a symbol of liberation, the sale of cigarettes to women skyrocketed. Later in his life, Bernays said he would have refused the account if he had known the dangers of tobacco.

He [Bernays] was the first to demonstrate for future generations of PR people how powerful their profession could be in shaping America's economic, political, and cultural life.

Larry Tye, author of Father of Spin: Edward L. Bernays & the Birth of Public Relations

■ **Light's Golden Jubilee.** To celebrate the 50th anniversary of Thomas Edison's invention of the electric light bulb, Bernays arranged the worldwide attention-getting Light's Golden Jubilee in 1929. It was his idea, for example, that the world's utilities would shut off their power all at one time, for one minute, to honor Edison. President Herbert Hoover and many dignitaries were on hand, and the U.S. Post Office issued a commemorative two-cent postage stamp. Bill Moyers, in an interview with Bernays in 1984, asked, "You got the whole world to turn off its lights at the same time. That's not influence, that's power." Bernays responded, "But you see, I never thought of it as power. I never treated it as power. People want to go where they want to be led."

Journalist Larry Tye has outlined a number of campaigns conducted by Bernays in his book *The Father of Spin: Edward L. Bernays & the Birth of Public Relations*. Tye credits Bernays with having a unique approach to solving problems. Instead of thinking first about tactics, Bernays would always think about the "big idea" of how to motivate people. The bacon industry, for example, wanted to promote its product, so Bernays came up with the idea of doctors across the land endorsing a hearty breakfast. No mention was made of bacon, but sales soared anyway, as people took the advice and started eating the traditional breakfast of bacon and eggs.

Bernays, during his long, 20th-century-spanning life, constantly wrote about the profession of public relations and its ethical responsibilities—even to the point of advocating the licensing of public relations counselors. One historian described him as "the first and doubtless the leading ideologist of public relations."

Although he was named by *Life* magazine in 1990 as one of the 100 most important Americans of the 20th century, it should be noted that Bernays had a powerful partner in his life, Doris E. Fleischman, who was a talented writer, ardent feminist, and former Sunday editor of the *New York Tribune*. Fleischman was an equal partner in the work of Bernays's firm, interviewing clients, writing news releases, editing the company's newsletter, and writing and editing books and magazine articles.

Other Pioneers in the Field

Ivy Lee and Edward Bernays were the most prominent pioneers in the public relations profession from 1900 to 1950, but the field is populated with a number of other brilliant practitioners and colorful personalities. The following gives a brief sketch of other leading historical figures:

■ **George Creel.** The public information model that Lee enunciated in his counseling was also used by George Creel, who was also a former newspaper reporter. He was asked by President Woodrow Wilson to organize a massive public relations effort to unite the nation and to influence world opinion during World War I.

In their book *Words That Won the War*, James O. Mock and Cedric Larson write: "Mr. Creel assembled a brilliant and talented group of journalists, scholars, press agents, editors, artists, and other manipulators of the symbols of public opinion as America had ever seen united for a single purpose." Among its numerous activities, the Creel Committee persuaded newspapers and magazines to contribute volumes of news and advertising space to encourage Americans to save food and to invest heavily in Liberty Bonds, which were purchased by more than 10 million people.

Such a massive publicity effort had a profound effect on the development of public relations by demonstrating the success of these techniques. It also awakened a public awareness of the power of mediated information in shaping public opinion and behavior.

■ **Arthur W. Page.** Page became vice president of the American Telephone & Telegraph (AT&T) Company in 1927 and is credited with establishing the concept that public relations should have an active voice in higher management. Page also expressed the belief that a company's performance, not press agentry, comprises its basis for public approval. More than any other individual, Page is credited with laying the foundation for the field of corporate public relations. He served on the boards of numerous corporations, charitable groups, and universities.

> . . . all business in a democratic country begins with public permission and exists by public approval.
>
> *Arthur W. Page*

After his death in 1960, a group of AT&T associates established a society of senior communication executives in his name. The Arthur W. Page Society, comprising more than 500 senior-level public relations executives, has several meetings a year and publishes various monographs on communications management. The society posts on its website (www.awpagesociety.com) the six principles of public relations management developed by the society's namesake. In summary, Page's principles are: (1) tell the truth, (2) action speaks louder than words, (3) always listen to the consumer, (4) anticipate public reaction and eliminate practices that cause conflict, (5) public relations is a management and policy-making function that impacts the entire company, and (6) keep a sense of humor, exercise judgment, and keep a cool head in times of crisis.

■ **Benjamin Sonnenberg.** It was Sonnenberg who suggested that Texaco sponsor performances of the Metropolitan Opera on national radio. Sponsorship of the Saturday-afternoon series, which began in 1940, continued for a half-century and enhanced Texaco's reputation as a patron of the arts. Biographer Isadore Barmash described Sonnenberg as "the most influential publicist of the mid-twentieth century." He had an opulent townhouse in New York and entertained many of America's most powerful men and women. Asked what the secret of his success was, he quipped, "I build large pedestals for small people."

■ **Rex Harlow.** Considered by many to be the "father of public relations research," Harlow was probably the first full-time public relations educator. As a professor at Stanford University's School of Education, he taught public relations courses and also conducted multiple continuing education workshops around the nation for working practitioners. Harlow founded the American Council on Public Relations, which later became the Public Relations Society of America (PRSA). In 1952, he founded *Social Science Reporter*, one of the first newsletters in the field.

■ **Leone Baxter.** Baxter and her partner, Clem Whitaker, are credited with founding the first political campaign management firm in the United States. The firm handled several California governor and U.S. Senate campaigns, advised General Dwight Eisenhower when he ran for president in 1952, and counseled Richard Nixon on the famous "Checkers" speech that saved his career as vice president.

■ **Warren Cowan.** *Portfolio* magazine called Cowan the "consummate Hollywood PR man" because his firm, Rogers and Cowan, was one of the first firms to serve the movie industry in the 1930s. Cowan represented such celebrities as Judy Garland, Cary Grant, Frank Sinatra, Gary Cooper, and Paul Newman during his lifetime and is credited with mentoring today's leading Hollywood publicists. He once said, "If we don't have anything to publicize, let's create it." When Cowan died at age 87 in 2008, he was buried with his cell phone in his hand.

■ **Eleanor Lambert.** The "grande dame" of fashion public relations, Lambert is credited with putting American designers such as Bill Blass and Calvin Klein on the map when Europeans dominated the industry. She also compiled the "Best-Dressed" list for 62 years, which always received extensive media publicity.

■ **Elmer Davis.** President Franklin D. Roosevelt appointed Davis head of the Office of War Information (OWI) during World War II. Using the Creel Committee as a model, Davis mounted an even larger public relations effort to promote the sale of war bonds, obtain press support for wartime rationing, and encourage the planting of "victory gardens." The Voice of America (VOA) was established to carry news of the war to all parts of the world, and the movie industry made a number of feature films in support of the war. The OWI was the forerunner of the U.S. Information Agency (USIA), which was established in 1953. Its operations are now part of the U.S. State Department's public diplomacy efforts.

■ **Moss Kendrix.** "What the public thinks counts!" was the mantra of Kendrix, who founded his own public relations firm in 1944. He is credited with being the first African American to acquire a major corporate account, the Coca-Cola Company. During his lifetime, he designed countless public relations and advertising campaigns for major corporations. The Museum of Public Relations (www.prmuseum.com) notes: "He educated his corporate clients about the buying power of the African American consumer, and helped to make America realize that African Americans were more complex than the derogatory images depicted in the advertising of the past."

■ **Dan Edelman.** The operations and scope of today's public relations firms owe much to the pioneering efforts of Dan Edelman, who launched his Chicago firm in 1952. Over the years, until his death at age 92 in 2013, he built the world's largest independent public relations firm (Edelman Worldwide) that is now headed by his son, Richard Edelman. The firm now employs more than 4,500 worldwide and generates revenues of more than $600 million annually. Edelman pioneered the idea that public relations was a more effective way to market a company's reputation and brands than advertising and proved it through successful campaigns for such clients as Sara Lee, Starbucks, Butterball Turkeys, and even the Mormon Church. His firm also pioneered in expanding the activities of public relations firms to do everything from crisis management to political lobbying.

Major Contributions by Industrialists, Presidents

Major contributions to the development of public relations have also been made by nonpractitioners who had the vision to successfully harness many of its basic concepts. Some leading examples are Henry Ford, Samuel Insull, and Teddy Roosevelt.

Henry Ford Henry Ford was America's first major industrialist, and he was among the first to use two basic public relations concepts. The first was the notion of positioning, the idea that credit and publicity always go to those who do something first. Second was the idea of being accessible to the press. Joseph Epstein, author of *Ambition*, says, "He may have been an even greater publicist than mechanic."

In 1900, Ford obtained coverage of the prototype Model T by demonstrating it to a reporter from the *Detroit Tribune*. By 1903, Ford achieved widespread publicity by racing his cars—a practice still used by today's automakers. He garnered further publicity and became the hero of working men and women by being the first automaker to double his worker's wages to $5 per day. A populist by nature, he once said, "Business is a service, not a bonanza," an idea reiterated by many of today's top corporate executives, who believe in what is now called corporate social responsibility (CSR).

Teddy Roosevelt
Theodore Roosevelt and conservationist John Muir combined forces to create Yosemite National Park.

Samuel Insull At the corporate level, the Chicago Edison Company broke new ground in public relations techniques under the skillful leadership of its president, Samuel Insull. Well aware of the special need for a public utility to maintain a sound relationship with its customers, Insull created a monthly customer magazine, issued a constant stream of news releases, and even used films for public relations purposes. In 1912, he started the "bill stuffer" by inserting company information into customers' bills—a technique used by many utilities today. He did much to expand the market for electricity by promoting electrical appliances, with the theme that they liberate women from household drudgery.

Teddy Roosevelt President Theodore Roosevelt (1901–1909) was a master at promoting and publicizing his pet projects. He was the first president to make extensive use of news conferences and press interviews to drum up public support when Congress was resistant. He was an ardent conservationist and knew the publicity value of the presidential tour. For example, he took a large group of reporters and photographers to see the wonders of Yosemite National Park, as a way of generating favorable press coverage and public support for the creation of additional national forests and national parks.

While president, Roosevelt set aside 150 million acres for public recreational use and essentially became the "father" of the American conservation movement. Even his nickname, "Teddy," comes from the publicity that was generated after he spared a small bear on a hunting trip and a toy maker began to market "Teddy" bears in recognition of the president's humane gesture. He's probably the only U.S. president to have a stuffed animal named after him, a name that survives to this day.

President Franklin D. Roosevelt apparently took notes from his cousin Teddy. His supporters organized nationwide birthday balls in 1934 to celebrate his birthday and raise funds for infantile paralysis research. This led to the creation of the March of Dimes. The campaign by Carl Byoir & Associates, a leading public relations firm at the time, orchestrated 6,000 events in 3,600 communities and raised more than $1 million.

1950 to 2000: Public Relations Comes of Age

During the second half of the 20th century, the practice of public relations became firmly established as an indispensable part of America's economic, political, and social development.

The booming economy after World War II produced rapid growth in all areas of public relations. Companies opened public relations departments or expanded existing ones. Government staffs increased in size, as did those of nonprofits, such as educational institutions and health and welfare agencies. Television emerged in the early 1950s as a national medium and as a new challenge for public relations expertise. New counseling firms sprang up nationwide.

The growth of the economy was one reason for the expansion of public relations, but there were other factors, too:

- Major increases in urban and suburban populations
- The growth of a more impersonalized society, represented by big business, big labor, and big government
- Scientific and technological advances, including automation and computerization
- The communications revolution in terms of mass media
- Bottom-line financial considerations often replacing the more personalized decision making of a previous, more genteel society

Many citizens felt alienated and bewildered by such rapid changes, cut off from the sense of community that had characterized the lives of previous generations. They sought power through innumerable pressure groups, focusing on causes such as environmentalism, working conditions, and civil rights. Public opinion, registered through new, more sophisticated methods of polling, became increasingly powerful in opposing or effecting change.

Both physically and psychologically separated from their publics, American business and industry turned increasingly to public relations specialists for audience analysis, strategic planning, issues management, and even the creation of supportive environments for the selling of products and services. Mass media also became more complex and sophisticated, so specialists in media relations who understood how the media worked were also in demand.

Typical of the public relations programs of large corporations at midcentury was that of the Aluminum Company of America (ALCOA). Heading the operation was a vice president for public relations and advertising, who was aided by an assistant public relations director and advertising manager. Departments included community relations, product publicity, motion pictures and exhibits, employee publications, the news bureau, and speech writing.

The 1960s saw Vietnam War protests, the civil rights movement, the environmental movement, interest in women's rights, and a host of other issues. Antibusiness sentiment was high, and corporations adjusted their policies to generate public goodwill and understanding. Thus, the idea of issues management was added to the

on the job INSIGHTS

Four Classic Models of Public Relations

A four-model typology of public relations practice was formulated by Professors James Grunig of the University of Maryland and Todd Hunt of Rutgers University in their 1984 book *Managing Public Relations*. The models, which have been used widely in public relations theory, help to explain how public relations has evolved over the years.

Press Agentry/Publicity

This is one-way communication, primarily through the mass media, to distribute information that may be exaggerated, distorted, or even incomplete in order to "hype" a cause, product, or service. Its purpose is advocacy, and little or no research is required. P. T. Barnum was the leading historical figure of this model during the 19th century. Sports, theater, music, film, and the classic Hollywood publicist are the main fields of practice today.

Public Information

One-way distribution of information, not necessarily with a persuasive intent, is the purpose of public information. It is based on the journalistic ideal of accuracy and completeness, and the mass media are the primary channel. There is fact-finding for content, but little audience research regarding attitudes and dispositions. Ivy Lee, a former journalist, was the leading historical figure during this model's development from about 1910 into the 1920s. Government, nonprofit groups, and other public institutions are primary fields of practice today.

Two-Way Asymmetric

In this model, scientific persuasion is the purpose and communication is two-way, with imbalanced effects. The model has a feedback loop, but the primary purpose of the model is to help the communicator better understand the audience and how to persuade it. Research is used to plan the activity and establish objectives as well as to learn whether an objective has been met. Edward Bernays was the leading historical figure during the model's beginning in the 1920s. Marketing and advertising departments in competitive businesses and public relations firms are the primary places of practice today.

Two-Way Symmetric

Gaining mutual understanding is the purpose of this model, and communication is two-way with balanced effects. Formative research is used mainly to learn how the public perceives the organization and to determine what consequences organizational actions/policy might have on the public. The result may counsel management to take certain actions or change policies. The idea, also expressed as "relationship building" and "engagement," is to have policies and actions that are mutually beneficial to both parties. Arthur W. Page is considered a leading advocate of this approach. Educators and professional leaders are the main proponents of this model, which has been around since the 1980s. The fields of practice today include organizations that engage in issue identification, crisis and risk management, corporate social responsibility, and long-range strategic planning.

job description of the public relations manager. This was the first expression of the idea that public relations should be more than simply persuading people that corporate policy was correct. During this period, the idea emerged that perhaps it would be beneficial to have a dialogue with various publics and adapt corporate policy to their particular concerns. Grunig labeled this approach *two-way symmetrical communication* because there's balance between the organization and its various publics. In other words, the organization and the public can influence each other.

The 1970s was an era of reform in the stock market and investor relations. The Texas Gulf Sulfur case changed investor relations forever by establishing the idea that a company must immediately disclose any information that may affect the value of its stock. The field of investor relations boomed.

By the 1980s, the concept of public relations as a management function was in full bloom. The term *strategic* became a buzzword, and the concept of management by objective (MBO) was heavily endorsed by public relations practitioners as they sought to prove to higher management that public relations does indeed contribute to the bottom line. Many definitions from this time emphasized public relations as a management function. As Derina Holtzhausen of Oklahoma State University notes, "Public relations management highlights organizational effectiveness, the strategic management of the function through strategic identification of publics, and issues management to prevent crisis." The PRCasebook on page 85 highlights some classic campaigns.

Reputation, or *perception*, management was the buzzword of the 1990s. Burson-Marsteller, one of the largest public relations firms, decided that its business was not public relations but, rather, "perception management." Other firms also declared that their business was "reputation management." Inherent in this was the idea that public relations personnel should be experts in issues management, crisis communications, and environmental monitoring to build credibility and trust among internal and external audiences and enhance the organization's reputation for corporate responsibility.

The Influx of Women into the Field

The period between 1950 and 2000 also marked the transformation of public relations from a male-dominated field to one in which women now constitute about 70 percent of practitioners.

The shift occurred over several decades. In 1979, women made up 41 percent of the public relations field. By 1983, they had become the majority (50.1 percent) of the public relations workforce. A decade later, the figure stood at 66.3 percent. By 2000, the percentage had leveled off at about 70 percent, where it remains today. National organizations also reflect the trend. About 75 percent of the membership in the International Association of Business Communicators (IABC) are now women, and the Public Relations Society of America (PRSA) estimates that about 70 percent of its members are now women.

Such numbers also reflect the influx of women into the American workforce at all levels. Today, women make up 61 percent of the labor force in the United States and also in many European nations. This can be somewhat explained by the massive influx of women into the nation's colleges and universities that has also taken place in the past several decades. The National Center for Educational Statistics, for example, estimated that the class of 2013 had 1.74 million bachelor degree candidates and women accounted for 57 percent of them.

PRCasebook

Classic Campaigns Show the Power of Public Relations

During the last half of the 20th century, a number of organizations and causes have used effective public relations to accomplish highly visible results. *PRWeek* convened a panel of public relations experts and came up with some of the "greatest campaigns ever" during this time period.

- **The Civil Rights Campaign.** Martin Luther King Jr. was an outstanding civil rights advocate and a great communicator. He organized the 1963 civil rights campaign and used such techniques as well-written, well-delivered speeches; letter writing; lobbying; and staged events (nonviolent protests) to turn a powerful idea into reality.
- **NASA.** From the very beginning NASA fostered media accessibility at Houston's Johnson Space Center. For example, NASA director Chris Kraft insisted that television cameras be placed on the lunar lander in 1969, and in later years reporters were invited inside mission control during the Apollo 13 mission. According to *PRWeek*, "Those historic moments have helped the public overlook the huge taxpayer expense and numerous technical debacles that could otherwise have jeopardized the future of the organization."
- **Cabbage Patch Kids.** Public relations launched the craze for the adoptable dolls and created a "must-have" toy. The campaign set the standard for the introduction of a new product and showed what a strong media relations program can do for a product.
- **Seat Belt Campaign.** In the 1980s, the U.S. automotive industry got the nation to "buckle up" through a public relations campaign. Tactics included winning the support of news media across the country, interactive displays, celebrity endorsements, letter-writing campaigns, and several publicity events, such as buckling a 600-foot-wide safety belt around the Hollywood sign. Notes *PRWeek*, "The results of one of the biggest public relations campaigns of all time were phenomenal, with the number of people 'buckling up' rising from 12 to 50 percent—it is now even higher."
- **Hands Across America.** The largest human gathering in history was a public relations stunt in 1986 that saw 7 million people across 16 states join hands to form a human chain to raise money for the hungry and the homeless. Even President Ronald Reagan participated.
- **Tylenol Crisis.** This has become the classic model for a product recall. When Johnson & Johnson found out that several people had died from cyanide-laced Tylenol capsules, a national panic erupted. Many thought the company would never recover from the damage caused by the tampering. However, the company issued a complete recall, redesigned the packaging so that it is tamper-proof, and launched a media campaign to keep the public fully informed. The result was that Tylenol survived the crisis and again became a best-seller.
- **Windows 95 Launch.** This campaign is easily in the product launch hall of fame. Microsoft, through media relations and publicity, achieved an unprecedented 99 percent awareness level among consumers before the product even hit the shelves.
- **Understanding AIDS.** This successful health education campaign changed the way that AIDS was perceived by Americans. In addition to a national mailing of a brochure titled "Understanding AIDS," there were grassroots activities that specifically targeted African Americans and Hispanics.

Source: The greatest campaigns ever. (2002, July 15). *PRWeek*, 14–15.

Sheryl Battles, VP of corporate communications, Pitney Bowes

Kathryn Beiser, EVP of corporate communications, Hilton Worldwide

Beth Comstock, SVP and chief marketing officer, General Electric

Diane Gage Lofgren, SVP and COO of brand communication, Kaiser Permanente

Ellen East, EVP and CCO of Time Warner Cable

Zenia Mucha, EVP and CCO of The Walt Disney Company

Christine Owens, SVP of communications, UPS

Cynthia Round, SVP of marketing and external relations, Metropolitan Museum of Art

Carol Schumacher, VP of investor relations, Wal-Mart

Women in Public Relations

This group of senior executives exemplifies the rise of women to major positions in large corporations and public relations firms.

Women traditionally earned degrees in such subjects as education, social work, and library science, but that has also changed. Today, women earn more college degrees than men in all fields except the physical sciences, math, engineering, and business. This is particularly true in the communications field, according to the annual survey of journalism and mass communications departments at 490 colleges and universities conducted by Lee Becker and his associates at the University of Georgia. In 2012, for example, women made up 64 percent of the undergraduate enrollments, 67 percent of the master's degree candidates, and 59 percent of the doctoral (Ph.D.) students.

A number of reasons are given for the major influx of women into the field of public relations. Some of these reasons include the following:

- Women find public relations work a more flexible environment for juggling family responsibilities.
- Women earn higher salaries in public relations than in comparable fields such as newspapers, radio, and television.
- A woman can start a public relations firm without a lot of capital, or even work out of her home as an independent consultant.
- Women are perceived to have better listening and two-way communication skills than men.
- Women, because of college courses in the humanities and the liberal arts, are often considered better at such skills as writing, giving presentations, and organizing events.

At the same time, a number of studies show that the majority of women in public relations earn less money than their male counterparts (see the salary survey information in Chapter 1). This, however, also reflects American society, where statistics show that full-time female workers in all fields earn only about 80 percent as much as the typical male.

A number of research studies have investigated the role and status of women in public relations. Some studies have explored the female/male salary gap and have come to various conclusions. Some scholars say that the gap is the result of women having less work experience in the field than typical males, so they are more likely to perform lower-paying tactical functions instead of management duties. Other researchers have found that women have fewer mentors and role models than men, which limits their career aspirations. Still others have concluded that male-dominated corporate structures still impose a "glass ceiling" that limits a woman's ability to rise in the organization.

Although the executive ranks in the public relations field are still predominantly male, female representation in higher management has increased in recent years. According to one study by Catalyst, the female share of executive roles in business increased from 14 percent in 1960 to 43 percent in 2008. Another positive note is the membership of the Arthur W. Page Society, which is composed of senior-level communication executives. It's now about 50 percent female. A representative grouping of female executives who are members of the Page Society is on page 86. Also, refer to the infographic on page 88 about the "Most Typical VP Working in American PR." It's also notable that *PRWeek*'s 2013 list of the 50 most powerful people in public relations now includes 20 women executives.

This industry doesn't look at gender, but rather attracts, nurtures, and promotes those who can provide business insights to their clients, understand influence and the power of storytelling, and drive business results.

Melissa Waggener Zorkin, CEO and founder of Waggener Edstrom public relations

Figure 2.1 **The Characteristics of a Female Public Relations Professional**

PRWeek, in its annual salary survey, found that the average vice president in corporate public relations is female, married, and makes $137,000 annually.

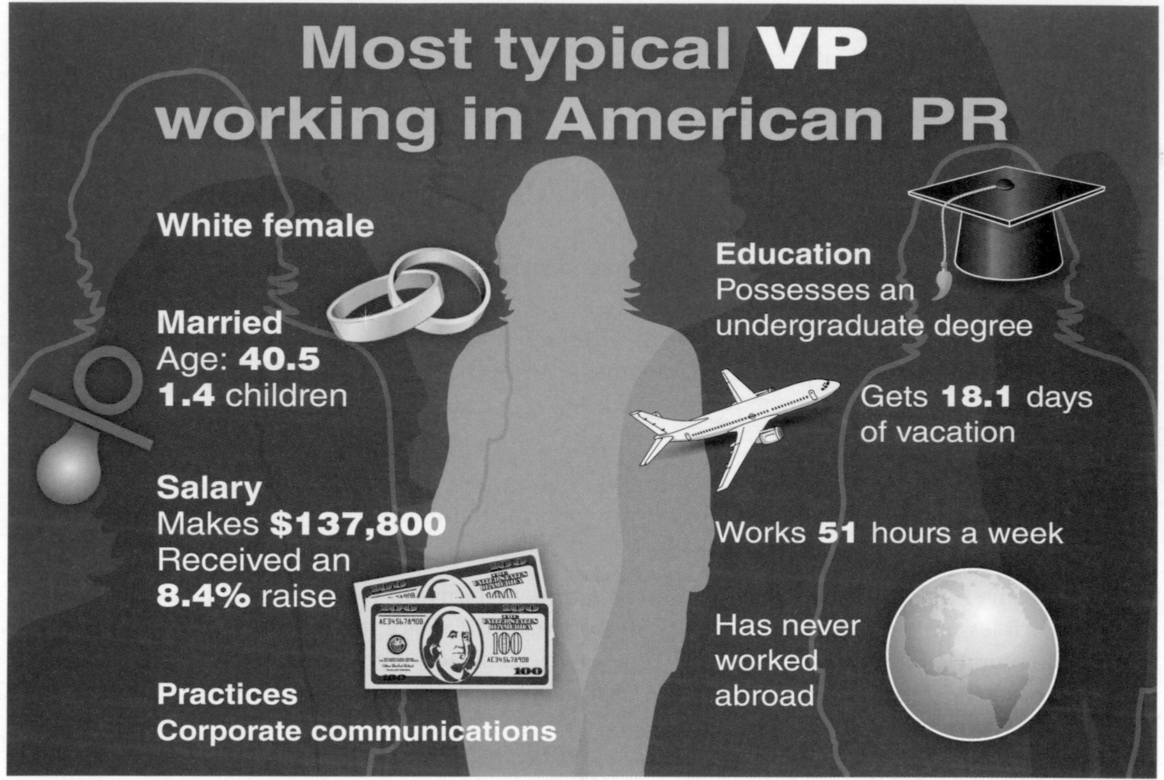

Source: PRWeek, March 2012, page 33.

2000 to the Present: Public Relations Enters the Digital Age

The rapid expansion of the Internet and the rise of social networks such as Facebook, Twitter, YouTube, and LinkedIn have caused a major revolution in how public relations is practiced today. The traditional model of one-way communication was replaced with a new emphasis on such buzzwords as "engagement" and "dialogue" to build mutually beneficial relationships with well-defined publics. In addition, this period marked the advent of the "democratization of information" in which almost anyone could become a publisher and reach literally millions of people without the filter of traditional mass media.

By the beginning of the century, a number of scholars and practitioners also began to conceptualize the practice of public relations as "relationship management," the basic idea being that public relations practitioners are in the business of building and fostering relationships with an organization's various publics. The idea has also caught on in marketing; *relationship marketing* is an effort to form a solid, ongoing relationship with the purchaser of a product or service.

Relationship management builds on Grunig's idea of two-way symmetrical communication, but goes beyond this by recognizing that an organization's publics are, as Stephen Bruning of Capital University notes, "active, interactive, and equal participants of an ongoing communication process." Bruning continues, "Typically, organizations are fairly effective at fulfilling content communication needs (communicating to key public members what is happening), but often fall short of fulfilling key public member relational communication needs (making the key public members feel they are valued in the relationship)."

An extension of relationship management is the *dialogic* (dialogue) model of public relations that has emerged since 2000. Michael Kent of Montclair University and Maureen Taylor of Rutgers University wrote in a *Public Relations Review* article that "A theoretical shift, from public relations reflecting an emphasis on managing communication, to an emphasis on communication as a tool of negotiating relationships, has been taking place for some time." Kent and Taylor say that good dialogic communication requires skills such as the following:

> . . . listening, empathy, being able to contextualize issues within local, national and international frameworks, being able to identify common ground between parties, thinking about long-term rather than short-term objectives, seeking out groups and individuals with opposing viewpoints, and soliciting a variety of internal and external opinions on policy issues.

The concept of dialogue places less emphasis on mass media distribution of messages and more on interpersonal channels. Kent and Taylor, for example, say that the Internet and World Wide Web are excellent vehicles for dialogue if the sites are interactive. They write, "The Web can be used to communicate directly with publics by offering real-time discussions, feedback loops, places to post comments, sources for organizational information, and postings of organizational member biographies and contact information."

Another development is the concept that public relations should do more than build relationships. Professor Glen Cameron of the University of Missouri, and co-author of this book, says public relations should be more assertive and is best defined as the strategic management of competition and conflict in the best interests of the organization and, when possible, also in the interest of key publics. This concept is discussed further in Chapter 10.

Public Relations in the Next Five Years

Throughout history, the practice of public relations has been a reflection of social, cultural, and economic forces that have shaped and influenced society through the centuries. The field of public relations is constantly evolving, and a number of ongoing developments will shape the practice of public relations in the coming years. The following are some current trends:

A Multicultural World We now live in a multicultural world that requires sensitivity and knowledge of multiple audiences. Minorities, for example, will comprise more than one-third of the U.S. population by 2016 and constitute a major voting bloc with considerable purchasing power. In terms of global economic growth, China will surpass the United States and become the world's largest economy by as early as 2025. The other BRIC nations—Brazil, India, and Russia, will also become major players in the world economy, which will change how companies launch new products in a diverse, multinational economy. For example, Dow Chemical already has 80 percent

on the job INSIGHTS

A Multicultural World: Global Study Identifies Top Issues in Public Relations

Various challenges have risen as public relations has evolved over the years, and today's practitioners must deal with some new issues during the next several years. The Plank Center for Leadership in Public Relations at the University of Alabama conducted an online survey of nearly 4,500 practitioners in 23 nations and compiled the following top 10 issues in descending order by percentage of mentions by respondents:

ISSUE	PERCENT OF RESPONDENTS
Dealing with the speed and volume of information flow	23.0%
Managing the digital revolution and rise of social media	15.3%
Improving measurement of communication effectiveness	12.2%
Effectively dealing with crises that may arise	11.9%
Dealing with the growing demands of transparency	8.4%
Improving employee engagement and commitment	7.9%
Finding, developing, and retaining top talent	7.5%
Meeting demands for corporate responsibility	6.1%
Meeting communication needs in diverse cultures	5.3%
Improving the image of the profession	2.5%

of its employees located at 156 manufacturing plants outside the United States; and Starbucks plans 30,000 stores worldwide in the coming years.

The world is also getting more connected; Internetworldstats.com reports that 2.5 billion people were already on the Internet in 2012 and the International Telecommunications Union (ITU) reports that the number of mobile phone subscribers totaled 6.9 billion in 2013 with the fastest growth in the developing nations. Fred Cook, president of Golin Harris, says, "The seismic shift to globalization and multiculturalism will transform communication. It will not be enough to address emerging cultures by simply creating separate practices to focus on individual ethnic groups. In the coming decades, the current ethnocentric approach to public relations will be replaced by a more holistic perspective." See Chapter 11, "Audiences."

> The public relations industry, long an enclave of well-paid, college-educated, white professionals, is finally waking up to the reality that it needs to do better PR to attract people of color.
>
> *Tannette Johnson-Elie, columnist,* Milwaukee Journal-Sentinel

Recruitment of Minorities A continuing challenge is recruitment of a diversified workforce in public relations, one that more accurately reflects the demographics of the U.S. population.

According to the U.S. Census Bureau, the fastest-growing, and now largest, group comprises Hispanics. They are now 16 percent of the population, compared with 12.2 percent for African Americans. Asians make up 4.7 percent, and Native Americans comprise 1 percent of the population. Unfortunately, not much has changed in the public relations industry. Whites still comprise nearly 90 percent of public relations specialists in the United States, according to the U.S. Bureau of Labor Statistics, compared to only 63.7 percent of the nation's population.

Many public relations departments and firms have initiated programs in diversity recruitment, but one obstacle is a shortage of qualified candidates. Racial or ethnic minority groups constitute only about a third of the students enrolled in journalism and mass communications programs. The shortage is also reflected in the membership of the Public Relations Student Society of America (PRSSA) with chapters on about 300 campuses. Less than 5 percent of the group's members are African American.

The Public Demand for Transparency Instant global communications, corporate finance scandals, government regulation, and the increased public demand for accountability have made it necessary for all of society's institutions, including business and industry, to be more transparent in their operations and to become more "authentic" as a trusted source of information.

A position paper by Vocus, a communications software firm, says it best: "An organization's every action is subject to public scrutiny. Everything—from the compensation provided to a departing CEO to the country from which a manufacturing plant orders its materials—is considered open to public discourse." Sir Martin Sorrell, CEO of communications conglomerate WPP, adds, "It is, like it or not, a more transparent world. Everything a company does and says will be dissected and discussed."

The Institute of Public Relations (IPR) in the United Kingdom says that the role of public relations has changed considerably over the last decade: "Instead of being used primarily as a way to influence and secure media coverage, organizations are using public relations to communicate with their stakeholders as society demands more transparency."

Expanded Role for Public Relations Professionals have already repositioned public relations as being more than media relations and publicity, but those hard fought gains will need to be reinforced in the coming years by taking more active leadership in organizations as marketing, technology, and communications converge. Tom Gable, a public relations counselor in San Diego, says, "Our challenge and opportunity will be to own the areas of positioning, branding, reputation management, and building relationships for the long term with multiple constituencies." Increasingly, public relations personnel will play an even greater role in planning and executing integrated communications campaigns.

PR pros have always been charged with managing the dialogue between the organization and the public, and will emerge as trendsetters in the social space by providing valuable communication counsel and achieving results that directly influence the clients' bottom lines.

Sandra Fathi, founder and president of Affect, a social media firm in New York

Corporate Social Responsibility (CSR) Global warming, environmental integrity, sustainable development, fair treatment of employees on a global basis, product quality and safety, and ethical supply chains are now on the agenda of all organizations. All elements of the organization are involved in the creation of the socially responsible corporation, but public relations will play a central role. James Murphy, global managing director of communications for Accenture, expresses it well: "PR staffs are in the forefront of building trust and credibility—and coordinating corporate social responsibility efforts. These are the people who deal with trust issues all the time; therefore, we're in a good position to address them." CSR is further discussed in Chapter 17 "Communicating Corporate Affairs."

Increased Emphasis on Measurement The global public relations industry is reaching consensus on standards of measurement that demonstrate how public relations contributes to an organization's bottom line. One example is the Barcelona Principles crafted at the 2nd European Summit on Measurement in 2010. They specifically state that (1) advertising rate equivalency for "earned" media does not equal the value of public relations, (2) measuring outcomes is preferred to measuring outputs, and (3) the effect of public relations on business results should be measured.

In 2012, the Coalition for Public Relations Research Standards consisting of several major international groups created a broad platform of standards for public relations research, measurement, and evaluation. Increasingly sophisticated software programs that can measure all aspects of a public relations program are facilitating the drive for higher standards of measurement.

One dimension of measurement is the return on investment (ROI). According to Kathy Cripps, chair of the Council of Public Relations Firms, two other important dimensions of measurement are: (1) measuring outcomes—the long-term effectiveness of a public relations program; and (2) measuring outputs—how well a program was executed and how effective its tactics were. Measurement and evaluation are further discussed in Chapter 8 "Evaluation and Measurement of Public Relations Programs."

Managing the 24/7 News Cycle The flow of news and information is now a virtual flood that occurs every minute of the day. Public relations personnel will need to constantly monitor, analyze, and curate large amounts of data and respond to what is being reported or discussed in everything from traditional media to blogs, chat groups, and other social media. In addition, the demand for instant response and the distribution of even more information often leave little or no time for reasoned response or even ensure accuracy. A major challenge for today's practitioners is how to create relevant content on multiple platforms to reach a variety of segmented publics.

Continued Growth of Digital Media Public relations personnel will continue to expand their digital toolbox as new social media platforms and thousands of new apps are created. The greatest area of growth today and in the coming years will be the creation of mobile-enabled content. Gartner research, for example, reports that by 2016, two-third of all Internet traffic will be viewed on mobile devices.

The decline of audience for traditional media has also led to the realization that all organizations are now in media business. Public relations and marketing professionals are increasingly using "storytelling" techniques to develop content "hubs" for distribution across multiple platforms. It's called "brand journalism" because a story distributed by Nissan may not necessarily have anything to do with its cars. Studies also show that 70 percent of consumers and 80 percent of business executives prefer to get company information via short articles instead of ads.

Increasingly, visual content will become the standard for most Web-based platforms. An example of "storytelling" are short videos

The public relations implications are obvious. Optimizing your content for social media channels and mobile are critical. Producing content with more video and visuals is key.

Jeff Domansky, social PR strategist and CEO of Peak Communications

produced by Intel that tell personal stories about how its technology is used by individuals in their business or personal lives. An example is the rapid rise of Instagram and Pinterest. See Chapter 13, "Internet and Social Media: Role & Scope in Public Relations."

Outsourcing to Public Relations Firms The outsourcing trend developed some years ago, but now it's almost universal. A survey published in *The Strategist* notes, "The use of agencies is now the norm in American business across all revenue categories and industries in this study: 85 percent of respondents (corporate executives) work with outside PR firms." This is not to say that corporate public relations departments are disappearing, but, increasingly, such tactics as media relations, annual reports, and sponsored events are being outsourced to public relations firms. In addition, it's entirely possible that basic tactics such as preparation of digital news releases and other collateral materials will be outsourced to places such as India. See Chapter 4, "The Practice of Public Relations."

The Need for Lifelong Professional Development Public relations personnel, given the rapid additions to knowledge in today's society, will need to continually update their knowledge base just to stay current with new developments and even hundreds of new Internet-based applications. Deirdre Breakenridge, coauthor of *Putting the Public Back in Public Relations*, wrote on a PRSA blog (comprehension.prsa.org), "Social media is forcing a reform of the public relations industry and now requires public relations and communication professionals to act as research librarians, sociologists, cultural anthropologists, and content managers, among other responsibilities."

Summary

Early Beginnings

- Although public relations is a 20th-century term, the roots of the practice go back to the ancient empires of Egypt, Greece, Rome, and India.
- The Catholic Church in the Middle Ages, as well as Martin Luther in the Reformation, extensively used public relations tactics to promote their respective points of view.
- Private companies attracted immigrants to the New World through promotion and glowing accounts of fertile land. The American Revolution, in part, was the result of such staged events as the Boston Tea Party and the writing of the *Federalist Papers*.

The 1800s: The Golden Age of Press Agentry

- P. T. Barnum, the master showman of the 19th century, pioneered many techniques that are still used today in the entertainment industry.
- The settlement of the West was due in large part to promotions by land developers and American railroads.
- The first presidential press secretary dates back to the administration of Andrew Jackson in the 1820s.
- Social movements for women's rights, racial equality, prohibition, and preservation of wilderness used multiple tools of publicity to influence public opinion.
- The Wannamaker department store in Philadelphia and Macy's in New York were the first to use public relations techniques to attract customers in the 1870s.
- The United States adopted alternating current (AC) in the 1890s, partly as a result of a successful public relations campaign by George Westinghouse, who competed with Thomas Edison's advocacy of direct current (DC).

1900 to 1950: The Age of Pioneers

- Ivy Lee and Edward Bernays are considered the two outstanding pioneers who did much to establish the foundation for today's public relations practice.
- Another visionary who dominated the field is Arthur W. Page, probably the first practitioner to establish public relations as an integral part of high-level corporate management.
- The pioneers also included a number of colorful personalities, including Hollywood publicist Warren Cowan and fashion publicist Eleanor Lambert.

1950 to 2000: Public Relations Comes of Age

- The field of public relations greatly expanded after World War II as a result of changes in American society. These changes included urbanization, the development of mass media including television, and the overall expansion of business.
- The concept of public relations as just media relations and publicity began to shift; the concepts of "reputation management" and "relationship building" became more prominent in the literature and in practice.
- Public relations matured as a management function at the highest levels of the organization.
- Public relations, traditionally a male domain, experienced the massive influx of women into the field, to the point that an estimated 70 percent of today's public relations practitioners are female.

2000 to the Present

- Public relations, in the era of the Internet and social media, places increased emphasis on listening, engagement, and dialogue with respective publics.
- Current, ongoing trends in public relations include the effort to have a more diverse workforce, practice on a global scale, and the revolutionary shift from traditional mass media to digital media, including the Internet and social media.
- The concept of corporate social responsibility (CSR) and the necessity for transparency become mainstream in terms of widespread acceptance by all organizations.

Case Activity **It's Not Raining Men**

Is there a gender gap in public relations? Why does the field attract more women than men? How does each gender perceive careers in public relations? Focus groups with majors at three universities (Arkansas State, Virginia Commonwealth University, and Texas Tech) provided some themes:

- The "people skills" stereotype holds for both genders, but more so for females.
- Females are more likely to define public relations as "party planning" and "having fun" primarily as an influence of how television and film portray females in public relations.
- Males are more attracted to the strategy and management side of public relations.
- Both genders expect to be in management positions, but males are more likely to pursue corporate settings.
- Both genders perceive certain female stereotypes as being strengths in the profession.
- Both genders like the variety of the profession. There's always something new.
- Both genders like the versatility of the educational experience. You can do a lot of different things with the degree.

Working in groups of 5 to 10 students, conduct your own discussion of these themes. Does the group agree or disagree with them and in what way? In the group's view, why are there so few men studying public relations or, to put it another way, why does the field attract so many women?

Questions **For Review and Discussion**

1. The roots of public relations extend deep into history. What were some of the early antecedents to today's public relations practice?
2. Name any five pioneers from the field of PR over the last century, and at least one contribution of each to the profession.
3. The Boston Tea Party has been described as the "greatest and best-known publicity stunt of all time." Would you agree? Do you feel that staged events are a legitimate way to publicize a cause and motivate people?
4. Which concepts of publicity and public relations practiced by P. T. Barnum should modern practitioners use? Which should they reject?
5. What are the four classic models of public relations? Describe each in a few sentences.
6. Has technology made a difference in the way the PR profession is practiced today? How?
7. What's your assessment of Ivy Lee's work for the Rockefeller family in the Colorado Fuel & Iron Company labor strife? Do you think his approach was

sound and ethical? What would you have done differently?

8. Summarize the major developments in the philosophy and practice of public relations from the 1950s to 2000. In what way have the concepts changed since 2000?
9. James Grunig outlined four models of public relations practice. Name and describe each one. Do the models help explain the evolution of public relations theory?
10. Public relations is now described as "relationship management." How would you describe this concept to a friend?
11. The data from various countries suggest that more and more women are joining the world of public relations. What in your opinion are the strengths they bring and what possible constraints could they face?
12. Describe several recent trends in the public relations field that will shape the field in the next five years.

Media Resources

Cutlip, S. M. (1994). *The unseen power: A history of public relations*. Mahwah, NJ: Lawrence Erlbaum.

Frohlich, R., & Peters, S. B. (2007). PR bunnies caught in the agency ghetto? Gender stereotypes, organizational factors, and women's careers in PR agencies. *Journal of Public Relations Research, 19*(3), 229–254.

Koeneman, C., & Giuliani, A. (2012, September). Do you think that the PR industry is a boys' club at executive levels? *PRWeek*, 17.

Lamme, M. O. (2011). Shining a calcium light: The WCTU and public relations history. *Journalism & Mass Communications Quarterly, 88*(2), 245–266.

Lamme, M. O., & Russell, K. M. (2010, Winter). Removing the spin: Toward a new theory of public relations history. *Journalism & Communication Monographs, 11*(4), 281–362.

Martinelli, D. K., & Mucciarone, J. (2007, March). New Deal public relations: A glimpse into FDR Press Secretary Stephen Early's work. *Public Relations Review, 33*(1), 49–57.

Public relations: Rise of the image men. (2010, December 18). *Economist*, 126–128.

Social media in the 16th century: How Luther went viral. (2011, December 17). *Economist*, 93–96.

St. John, B. (2006). The case for ethical propaganda within a democracy? Ivy Lee's successful 1913–1914 railroad rate campaign. *Public Relations Review, 32*(3), 221–228.

Sullivan, J. (2011, May/June). True enough: The second age of PR. *Columbia Journalism Review*, 34–39.

The PR professional of 2015: Analyzing the future of public relations. (2012, March). *Public Relations Tactics*, 11–12.

Working, R. (2011, March). Women dominate the PR industry: Why? *Ragan Report*, 17–18.

chapter 3

Ethical Considerations and the Role of Professional Bodies

Bernie Madoff epitomized the worst in ethical standards.

After reading this chapter, you will be able to:

Understand the role of the ethical advocate

Appreciate the role that professional groups play in setting standards

Be familiar with the progress being made toward professionalism

Define the characteristics of being a public relations professional

Be ethical when working with the media

Understanding Ethics and Values

There is some confusion about the difference between ethics and values, but public relations professionals should know the difference, as a framework for their daily work. The Markula Center for Applied Ethics at the University of Santa Clara in California says, "Ethics refers to the standards of conduct which indicates how one *should behave* based upon moral duties and virtues rising from principles of right and wrong." Values, however, are "central beliefs which determine how we *will behave* in certain situations."

"An ethical public relations professional," says University of South Carolina Professor Shannon Bowen, "should have such values as honesty, openness, loyalty, fair-mindedness, respect, integrity, and forthright communication." These values are usually incorporated into codes of ethics, which will be discussed shortly. The reality, however, is that individuals interpret basic values in different ways as they struggle to assess what is "right" or "wrong" in a particular situation.

Public relations professionals also have the burden of making ethical decisions that take into consideration (1) the public interest, (2) the employer's self-interests, (3) the standards of the public relations profession, and (4) their personal values. In an ideal world, these four spheres would not conflict, and clear-cut guidelines would make ethical decisions easy. In reality, however, making the right ethical decision is often a complex process involving many considerations.

One consideration is your "discomfort" level. Google cofounder Sergey Brin, being interviewed by the *Wall Street Journal* about the company's exit from China because of censorship restrictions, said, "Ultimately, I guess it is where your threshold of discomfort is, so we obviously as a company crossed that threshold of discomfort." In other words, how comfortable would you feel if you were asked to (1) exaggerate the qualities of a product, (2) defend a company's poor environmental record, (3) speak on behalf of the tobacco or liquor industry, or (4) organize a "citizens' group" funded by the gun industry? See the Insights box that follows.

Your answers to these questions reflect your values. If your orientation is Kant's *absolutist* philosophy, that something is either completely "right" or "wrong," you would refuse to do some of these activities. Or you might take Aristotle's *existential* approach, which calls for a balance between two extremes, and undertake the assignment but execute it in such a way that it doesn't cross your threshold of "discomfort." You could, for example, organize the "citizens' group" but also disclose its sponsor.

A third philosophical path is the *utilitarian* approach advocated by John Stewart Mill. He believed that the end could justify the means as long as the result caused the least harm and most good or happiness for the greatest number of people. The National Rifle Association (NRA), for example, takes the utilitarian approach to promoting gun ownership. The most good accrues to its 4 million members and the constitutional right of Americans to

Public Relations Ethics

This *New Yorker* cartoon, although humorous, gives the impression that the purpose of public relations is to twist the facts. In reality, the moral imperative for public relations professionals is to tell the truth.

"Hold everything! The P.R. department just sent over this chart."

on the job

INSIGHTS

Use of "Front Groups" Poses Ethical Concerns

Citizens' Protest

Special interest groups such as political parties, labor unions, and industry trade groups often organize and fund a rally by a "citizens" group.

The proliferation of so-called front groups waging purported grassroots campaigns to achieve public relations goals has created much debate in the field in recent years.

Almost every "save the environment" organization has spawned a countergroup. For example, the timber industry paid Burson-Marsteller $1 million to form the Forest Alliance of British Columbia (FABC) to oppose the International Coalition to Save British Columbia's Rainforests. The purpose of the alliance, claiming to be a grassroots movement, was to convince the public that environmental destruction has been exaggerated and to persuade lawmakers to abolish unprofitable environmental regulations.

Names given to many of the organizations are confusing, if not downright deceptive. Northwesterners for More Fish was the name chosen for a "grassroots" coalition of utilities and other companies in the Northwest who were under attack from environmental groups for depleting the fish population. A pro-hunting group known as the Abundant Wildlife Society of North America also works to convince people that wildlife is so plentiful that no additional legislation was needed to protect it. The controversy over fracking has also generated any number of "citizen" groups. The American Petroleum Association, for example, funds Energy Citizens, which places ads featuring ordinary citizens saying that they "vote" for more domestic energy and energy independence for America.

Questioned about the tactics used in so-called grassroots campaigns, more than half of the professionals surveyed by *PRNews* said that it is unethical for parties to not publicly disclose the special interests that organize and fund such efforts. PRSA also condemns "front groups" that "seek to influence the public policy process by disguising or obscuring the true identity of their members or by implying representation of a much more broadly based group than exists."

bear arms. Other groups, such as the Mayors Against Illegal Guns, believe the least harm and the greatest good would be more controls on gun ownership.

The Ethical Advocate

Another consideration of students, as well as public relations critics, is whether a public relations practitioner can ethically communicate at the same time that he or she is serving as an advocate for a particular client or organization. To some, traditional ethics prohibits a person from taking an advocacy role because that person is then "biased" and trying to "manipulate" people.

David L. Martinson of Florida International University makes the point, however, that the concept of role differentiation is important. This means that society, in general, expects public relations people to be advocates, just as society expects advertising copywriters to make a product sound attractive, journalists to be objective, and attorneys to defend someone in court. Because of this concept, Martinson believes that "Public relations practitioners are justified in disseminating persuasive information so long as objective and reasonable persons would view those persuasive efforts as truthful." He continues, in a monograph published by the public relations division of the Association for Education in Journalism and Mass Communications:

> Reasonable persons recognize that public relations practitioners can serve important societal goals in an advocacy (role defined) capacity. What reasonable persons require, however, is that such advocacy efforts be directed toward genuinely informing impacted publics. Communication efforts . . . will not attempt, for example, to present false/deceptive/misleading information under the guise of literal truth no matter how strongly the practitioner wants to convince others of the merits of a particular client/organization's position/cause. . . . Role differentiation is not a license to "lie, cheat, and/or steal" on behalf of clients whether one is an attorney, physician, or public relations practitioner.

We are advocates of what we believe to be the truth and not merely blind advocates for our organizations. We need to take all of this very seriously and on a very personal level.

W. D. (Bill) Nielsen, former VP of public affairs for Johnson & Johnson, speaking at the 44th annual lecture of the Institute for Public Relations

The Role of Professional Organizations

Professional organizations have done much to develop the standards of ethical, professional public relations practice and to help society understand the role of public relations. A primary objective has been the development of professionals through continuing education in terms of publications, conferences, short courses, seminars, and speakers at local, regional, and national meetings. Although such organizations represent only a small percentage of the total number of individuals working in public relations, they set the professional standards by which the entire industry is judged. The following sections give a thumbnail sketch of the largest professional groups serving the public relations profession.

The Public Relations Society of America (PRSA)

The largest national public relations organization in the world is the Public Relations Society of America (PRSA); the group's website can be found at www.prsa.org. PRSA is headquartered in New York City. It has almost 22,000 members organized into

110 chapters nationwide. It also has 20 professional interest sections that represent such areas as employee communications, counseling firms, entertainment and sports, food and beverages, multicultural communications, public affairs and government, nonprofit organizations, travel and tourism, and even public relations educators.

A fourth of PRSA members work in a corporate environment. Another 20 percent work for a public relations firm, and 17 percent work for nonprofits and associations. See Figure 3.1 on page 102. The top four responsibilities in rank order for PRSA members are: (1) media relations, (2) writer/editor, (3) marketing communications, and (4) corporate communications. In terms of gender, 70 percent of PRSA's membership is now female.

PRSA has an extensive professional development program that offers short courses, seminars, teleconferences, and webcasts throughout the year. Some typical topics from a recent listing of online seminars available to members included social media for crisis communications, using text messaging to engage employees, and the opportunities for games and gamification in public relations.

In addition to workshops and seminars, PRSA holds an annual meeting and publishes two major periodicals. *Public Relations Tactics* is a monthly tabloid of current news and professional tips. *The Strategist* is a quarterly magazine that contains in-depth articles about the profession and issues touching on contemporary public relations practice. The organization also sponsors the Silver Anvil and Bronze Anvil awards, which recognize outstanding public relations campaigns. The Bronze Anvils recognize outstanding examples of tactical communication vehicles such as blogs, newsletters, videos, and websites. A number of these award-winning campaigns and materials are included in this book.

PRSA's Publication

The Strategist and *Tactics* magazines are published by the Public Relations Society of America (PRSA) as one way of providing professional development for its members.

PRSSA PRSA is also the parent organization of the Public Relations Student Society of America (PRSSA), whose website can be found at www.prssa.org. This group celebrated its 45th anniversary in 2012 and is the world's largest preprofessional public relations organization, having 300 campus chapters (including one in Argentina) with almost 10,000 student members.

The student group, which has its own national officers, serves its members at the local chapter level through a variety of campus programs and maintains a close working relationship with the local sponsoring PRSA chapter. It has a national publication, *Forum*, and sponsors a national case study competition so that students have the opportunity to exercise the analytical skills and mature judgment required for public relations problem solving. The organization awards a number of scholarships, holds regional and national conventions, and actively promotes mentoring between students and professionals in the field. PRSSA members, after graduation, are eligible to become associate members of PRSA.

The International Association of Business Communicators (IABC)

The second largest organization is the International Association of Business Communicators (IABC). The group's website can be accessed at www.iabc.com. It has 14,000 members in 70 nations, but about 90 percent of the membership is from the United States and Canada. The Toronto chapter is the largest, with more than 1,600 members; the three largest chapters outside North America are in Australia, the United Kingdom (UK), and South Africa. According to an IABC profile of members, 40 percent of the membership work in a corporate environment, 16 percent work for a public relations firm, and another 11 percent work in the nonprofit sector. The top four responsibilities for IABC members in rank order are (1) corporate communications, (2) employee communications, (3) marketing communications, and (4) media relations. In terms of gender, 75 percent of IABC's membership is now female.

IABC, headquartered in San Francisco, has similar objectives as the PRSA. Its mission is to "provide lifelong learning opportunities that give IABC members the tools and information to be the best in their chosen disciplines." It does this through sponsoring year-round workshops, publishing reports, and holding an annual meeting. The organization also has an awards program, the Gold Quill that honors excellence in business communication. The IABC online publication is *Communication World*; it features professional tips and in-depth articles on current issues. IABC also has student chapters on various campuses, with a combined membership of about 900 students.

The International Public Relations Association (IPRA)

A third organization, one that's thoroughly global in scope, is the International Public Relations Association (IPRA) with headquarters in London. The group's website is at www.ipra.org. IPRA has about 1,000 members in about 80 nations. Its membership is primarily senior-level public relations executives, and its mission is "to provide intellectual leadership in the practice of international public relations by making available to our members the services and information that will help them to meet their professional responsibilities and to succeed in their careers."

The international orientation of IPRA makes it somewhat different from national groups. It bases its code of ethics on the charter of the United Nations. The first point of its 13-point code states that members shall endeavor "to contribute to the achievement of the moral and cultural conditions enabling human beings to reach their full stature and enjoy the rights to each they are entitled under the 'Universal Declaration of Human Rights.' " In terms of dealing with misinformation, IPRA states that members shall refrain from "Circulating information which is not based on established and ascertainable facts."

IPRA organizes regional and international conferences to discuss issues in global public relations, but it also reaches its widespread membership through its website and *Frontline*, its major online publication. In addition, it issues Gold Papers on

Figure 3.1 **Employment Categories of PRSA and IABC Members**

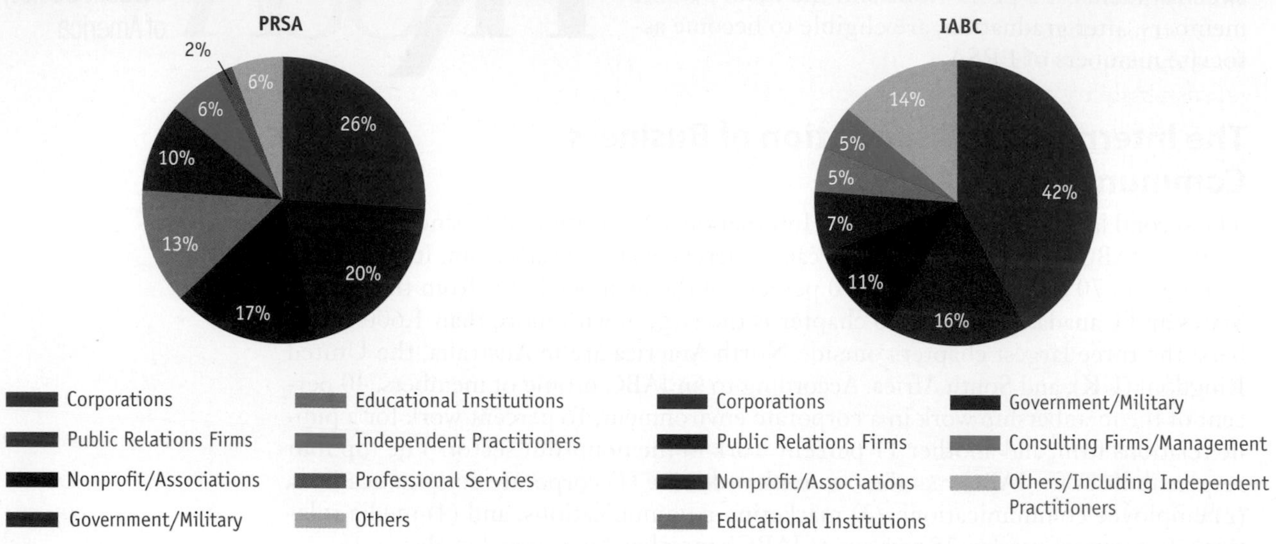

public relations practice and conducts an annual Golden World Awards competition to honor outstanding public relations programs and campaigns around the world. A continuing project of the organization is a transparency campaign to encourage media in various nations not to accept bribes in exchange for news coverage. See the Multicultural box on page 117.

Other Groups

The PRSA, IABC, and IPRA are the largest broad-based membership organizations for communicators and public relations professionals. In addition, there are more specialized organizations in the United States. They include:

- Council for the Advancement and Support of Education (CASE), www.case.org (3,200 colleges and universities)
- National Investor Relations Institute (NIRI), www.niri.org (4,000 members in the financial industry)
- National School Public Relations Association (NSPRA), www.nspra.org (school communicators, K–12)
- National Black Public Relations Society (NBPRS), www.nbprs.org (about 1,000 members)
- Hispanic Public Relations Society (HPRA), www.hpra-usa.org (network of Hispanic communicators)
- The Arthur W. Page Society, www.awpagesociety.com (senior-level communication executives in major corporations and public relations firms)
- Council of Public Relations Firms, www.prfirms.org (association of 100 public relations firms)

On an international level, the Global Alliance for Public Relations and Communication Management (www.globalalliancepr.org) is an umbrella group of more than

70 national organizations representing more than 160,000 professionals. The group's mission is to (1) unify the profession on a global basis, (2) raise professional standards, and (3) "to work in the public interest for the benefit of the profession." In June 2010, for example, alliance representatives approved *The Stockholm Accords* that further outlined the responsibilities of public relations professionals in such areas as environmental sustainability, organizational governance, management, internal communications, and external communications. The full text of the accords are found on the Global Alliance website. See the Insights box on page 104 about the group's Melbourne Mandate.

Professional Codes of Conduct

Virtually all codes of ethics begin with the duty to tell the truth, and the code of ethics for the field of public relations is no exception. The first article in the Code of Brussels, enacted by the IPRA, says, "Act with honesty and integrity at all times so as to secure the confidence of those with whom the practitioner comes in contact." And the first principle of the Arthur W. Page Society is simply, "Tell the Truth."

Similar concepts about honesty are elaborated upon in the codes of national public relations groups. The Public Relations Society of America, for example, has a fairly extensive code of conduct that is summarized on page 105. In addition, the organization issues interpretations of its code when new situations arise. The PRSA code, for example, was written before the age of the Internet, so it issued a statement condemning deceptive online practices, saying, "Any attempts to mislead or deceive an uninformed audience are considered malpractice." Internet transparency is further discussed on page 105.

Most national organizations place heavy emphasis on educating their members about professional standards rather than having a highly structured grievance process in place. They do reserve the right, however, to censure or expel members who violate the organization's code or who are convicted of a crime in a court of law.

The IABC's code is based on the principle that professional communication is not only legal and ethical, but also in good taste and sensitive to cultural values and beliefs. Members are encouraged to be truthful, accurate, and fair in all of their communications.

According to IABC, the organization "fosters compliance with its code by engaging in global communication campaigns rather than through negative sanctions." The code is published in several languages and distributed annually to members. In addition, the organization includes panels on ethics at its annual meeting and encourages chapters to include ethics in their local programs. PRSA and other organizations have similar programs.

A more aggressive form of enforcement, however, is conducted by the German Council for Public Relations, which is the umbrella organization for three German public relations associations. It actively investigates complaints about unethical behavior and publicly issues warnings and rebukes to organizations that violate professional standards. The council, however, evaluates the behavior of organizations only, not the behavior of individuals.

The common complaint about ethic codes, however, is they are "toothless" in terms of enforcement. There's really no punishment for an individual who is unethical and unprofessional. About the only penalty that an organization can impose is to expel a person from the organization, which doesn't stop the offender from continuing to work in public relations.

on the job

INSIGHTS

Global Standards for Professional Practice

The Global Alliance for Public Relations and Communication Management, representing about 160,000 practitioners around the world, established a new mandate for professional practice at the 2012 World Public Relations Forum in Australia.

The Melbourne Mandate calls for public relations professionals to (l) define and maintain an organization's character and values, (2) build a culture of listening and engagement, and (3) instill responsible behaviors by individuals and organizations. The entire document can be downloaded from www.globalalliancepr.org, but given next are some excerpts relating to the personal conduct of individual practitioners.

Public relations and communication professionals have a mandate to:

Demonstrate societal responsibility by:

- Creating and maintaining transparent—open, honest, and accessible—processes and credible communication that balance public interest with organizational needs.
- Supporting the sustainability strategies of the communities from which the organization obtains resources and its license to operate.
- Ensuring that communication on behalf of employers, clients, and brands does not overstate the value of products and services, which would distort the expectations of consumers and other stakeholders.
- Defining accountability metrics against which contributions to society would be measured and improved.

Demonstrate professional responsibility by:

- Understanding, abiding by and operating in accordance with the relevant professional codes of ethics.
- Communicating the professional standards that guide public relations and communication to internal and external stakeholders.
- Maintaining competence by continually pursuing education and learning so as to perform responsibly and effectively.

Demonstrate personal responsibility by:

- Ensuring one's personal communication is always truthful, and that one's actions reflect the imperatives of doing good and creating mutual benefit over the long term.
- Recognizing and appreciating differences between one's personal values and those of organizational stakeholders and communities, in line with societal expectations.
- Taking personal ownership of the professional standards by which day-to-day decisions and actions are governed.
- Being willing to make tough decisions—and understanding the consequences—when circumstances, society, or the organization create conditions that prevent or contradict one's personal standards.
- Being accountable for one's decisions and actions.

There are also regional associations such as the Federation of African Public Relations Association (FAPRA), the Association of Latin American Public Relations Professionals (ALARP), the European Public Relations Confederation (CEPR), and the European Public Relations Education and Research Association (EUPRERA).

Problems with code enforcement, however, are not unique to public relations groups. Professional organizations, including the Society for Professional Journalists, are voluntary organizations, and they don't have the legal authority to ban members from the field, because no licensing is required. Such organizations run a high risk of being sued for defamation or restricting the First Amendment

on the job

INSIGHTS

PRSA's Code of Ethics: Guidelines for Professional Practice

The Public Relations Society of America (PRSA) has a fairly comprehensive code of ethics for its members. The group's values and provisions for conduct are summarized as follows:

PRSA Values

ADVOCACY. We serve the public interest by acting as responsible advocates for those we represent.

HONESTY. We adhere to the highest standards of accuracy and truth in advancing interests and communicating with the public.

EXPERTISE. We acquire and responsibly use specialized knowledge and experience.

INDEPENDENCE. We provide objective counsel to those we represent.

LOYALTY. We are faithful to those we represent, while honoring our obligation to serve the public interest.

FAIRNESS. We deal fairly with clients, employers, competitors, peers, vendors, the media, and the general public.

PRSA Provisions of Conduct

FREE FLOW OF INFORMATION. Advancing the free flow of accurate and truthful information is essential to serving the public interest.

COMPETITION. Healthy competition among professionals preserves an ethical climate while fostering a robust business environment.

DISCLOSURE OF INFORMATION. Open communication fosters informed decision making in a democratic society.

SAFEGUARDING CONFIDENCES. Client trust requires appropriate protection of confidential and private information.

CONFLICTS OF INTEREST. Avoiding real, potential or perceived conflicts of interest builds the trust of clients, employers and the public.

ENHANCING THE PROFESSION. Public relations professionals work constantly to strengthen the public trust in the profession.

Source: Public Relations Society of America (www.prsa.org/ethics)

guarantee of free speech if they try to publicly censure a member or restrict his or her occupation.

Consequently, most professional groups believe that the primary purpose of establishing codes of ethics is not enforcement, but rather education and information. The Global Alliance strongly endorses professional development and states that members should "actively pursue personal professional development." Thus, all groups seek to enunciate standards of conduct that will guide members in their professional lives. It seems to work. Several studies have shown that the members of PRSA and other organizations have a much higher awareness of ethics and professional standards than do nonmembers.

Codes for Specific Situations

Various organizations, as noted, have established codes for the general practice of public relations. There also are established guidelines for ethical practice in such areas as (1) Internet transparency, (2) video news releases, (3) financial information, and (4) corporate practice.

Internet Transparency Public relations personnel are constantly using the Web and social networks to communicate information about their employers and clients, but they should do so within an ethical framework. The PRSA, for example, categorically states " . . . that misrepresenting the nature of editorial content or intentionally failing to clearly reveal the source of message contents is unethical." The Arthur W. Page Society, an organization of senior-level communication executives, and 10 other major public relations organizations have endorsed the following guidelines:

- The source of any material must be clearly identified. Any attempt to mislead or deceive the blogger or the intended audience is considered unethical.
- You must identify yourself and your connection to any employer or client in any postings in which you are promoting and publicizing a product or service.
- You must disclose your affiliation with a client or employer in any chat room postings, particularly if the affiliation is relevant to the topic or the conversation. If you want to make a personal comment about your client or employer's products or policies, you need to say something such as, "This is my personal opinion and doesn't necessarily reflect the policies or positions of my employer."
- It's considered unethical to offer cash or "gifts" to bloggers in return for posting favorable reviews concerning a product or service. Under new Federal Communications Commission (FTC) guidelines, both you and the blogger are liable if any payments, free products, or gifts are not disclosed in the posting.
- The owners of blogs, Facebook pages, and Twitter accounts must be clearly identified and disclosed. In other words, you can't use your name to establish a fake blog to promote a product or cause when the actual source/owner is the client or employer.
- Respect copyrights, trademarks, and fair use guidelines if you post material from other sources.
- Respect your audience. Don't use ethnic slurs, personal insults, or obscenity, or engage in any conduct that is not acceptable in the workplace.

More recently, it has been estimated by research firm Gartner that 10 to 15 percent of the reviews for products, hotels, and restaurants on various consumer sites such as YELP or TripAdvisor are "fake reviews" posted by the organizations or by individuals that are paid to post good reviews. Such activity is considered unethical and a violation of professional public relations practice. See the Social Media in Action box on page 107.

Video News Releases Controversy about the use of video news releases (VNRs) by television stations and whether the viewing public has been informed about the source of information also has prompted greater attention to ethical behavior by the stations and the public relations industry that produces VNRs for any number of clients. On one hand, television stations are faulted for failing to tell viewers the source of video footage to give the impression that the video material was prepared by the station's own news staff.

On the other hand, producers of VNRs have been criticized for not properly identifying the sponsor (or client) of the material. One technique, for example, has been to have an actor pose as a newsperson on the VNR and simply say, "This is Jane Doe, reporting from Washington."

As a result of criticism from media watchdog groups and concerns by the Federal Communications Commission (FTC) about the lack of disclosure of third-party information in newscasts, the National Association of Broadcast Communicators (NABC) established new ethical guidelines that included (1) intentionally false and misleading information must be avoided, (2) the sponsor must be clearly identified at

on the job

SOCIAL MEDIA IN ACTION

Dealing Ethically with Consumer Review Sites

It's estimated that 80 percent of consumers now consult reviews on such sites as Yelp, Amazon, and TripAdvisor before they buy a product or even make a restaurant or hotel reservation. In addition, various surveys have found that almost 90 percent say they are influenced by such reviews in making a purchase decision.

Crowdsourced review sites, however, are a mixed blessing for business. Positive reviews add credibility to a product or service, but unfavorable reviews can quickly damage a company's brand and affect sales. Consequently, companies must include consumer websites as part of their overall public relations strategy.

The first rule is join the conversation says Kat Grusich, a senior account executive with Cookerly Public Relations. Organizations should respond quickly and publicly to any negative comments by showing concern for the customer's bad experience, making an apology if appropriate, and attempting to solve the problem. "If people walk away from a discussion pleased with your response, they are more likely to have a better impression of your brand," says Grusich, writing in *Ragan's PR Daily*.

On occasion, however, it's also necessary to proactively respond if a review is erroneous, completely out of left field, and even fake. In such cases, the company needs to contact the administrators of the review site with information documenting the inaccuracies. "With enough proof, sites such as Yelp, TripAdvisor, and Insider Pages have deleted false reviews," says Grusich.

The second rule is to never post a fake review on behalf of your employer or client. It is considered unethical for public relations staff or other employees to pose as ordinary consumers and post glowing reviews of your organization. It's also considered unethical to pay individuals to post favorable reviews. Grusich says, "Remember, reviews are all about public perception—and the public can pick up pretty quickly on phony feedback. Should you attempt to improve your reputation through positive anonymous reviews, it could come back to haunt you."

Grusich concludes, "How you manage your online reputation can help make the difference between five-star success and one-star failure."

the opening of the video and on all advisory materials and scripts, and (3) any persons interviewed must be accurately identified by name, title, and affiliation.

Financial Information The National Investors Relations Institute (NIRI), for example, has adopted a 12-point code of ethics in the wake of corporate financial scandals such as Enron, WorldCom, and Tyco. NIRI (www.niri.org) requires all its members to affirm the code in writing. The code holds members responsible for such things as (1) exercising independent professional judgment, (2) keeping track of financial laws and regulations, and (3) ensuring full and fair disclosure. Members who violate the law or SEC regulations are expelled from the organization.

Corporate Practice Many public relations firms and companies also have established codes of conduct and regularly schedule training sessions for their employees. Ketchum, a large international firm, has a code that covers (1) truth and accuracy in communications, (2) how to handle confidential information, (3) what gifts and entertainment are acceptable and not acceptable, (4) fair dealings with suppliers and vendors, (5) safeguarding of client proprietary information, and (6) abuse of "inside" information.

On occasion, however, a firm is "outed" for violating its own professed standards. In such cases, the firm usually issues an apology and promises to further "educate" its employees about its code of ethics. This was the case when Burson-Marsteller had to admit that two staffers violated company policy by conducting a stealth campaign against Google without disclosing that the client was Facebook, which was highlighted in Chapter 1, page 39.

Of course, it is one thing to have a code of conduct in the employee handbook and another to actually practice what is being preached. Public relations executives have the responsibility to ensure that ethics becomes an integral part of the "corporate culture" and also that ethical considerations are part of senior management's policy decisions and how the organization responds to various situations. See the Insights box on page 109.

Other Steps toward Professionalism

So what is a profession? C. V. Narasimha Reddi, an elder statesman of public relations in India and editor/publisher of *Public Relations Voice*, says there are five prerequisites for a profession like public relations. They are:

- **Education.** A body of knowledge for learning skills
- **Training.** Instruction, continuing education to improve and update skills
- **Literature.** Textbooks, case studies, reference books, and academic journals
- **Research.** Evaluation and measurement of programs and campaigns
- **Code of Ethics.** Standards that generate trust and credibility

Professor Reddi's prerequisites, for the most part, have been achieved in the public relations field, and some of his concepts have already been discussed, such as organizations having codes of conduct. The making of a profession, however, is an evolutionary process that includes a number of steps. They include (1) changing the mindset of many practitioners in the field who have no formal training in public relations, (2) establishing public relations as an academic discipline, (3) expanding the body of knowledge, (4) promoting certification and accreditation of practitioners, and (5) even moving toward required continuing education for members of professional organizations. The following sections outline what progress has been made.

Changing Practitioner Mindsets

Among public relations practitioners, there remains differences of opinion about whether public relations is a craft, a skill, or a developing profession. Certainly, at its present level, public relations does not qualify as a profession in the same sense that medicine and law do. Public relations does not have prescribed standards of educational preparation, a mandatory period of apprenticeship, or even state laws that govern admission to the profession. This also means that anyone can work in "public relations" even if they don't have the educational preparation or have never been "socialized" into the basic standards of professional practice.

on the job INSIGHTS

Your Job: Ethics Counselor to Senior Management

The traditional role of a public relations manager is to build relationships and trust in an organization, but an equally important role is to counsel management about incorporating ethics and the organization's core values into every decision. Professor Shannon Bowen of the University of South Carolina, in a monograph published by the Institute for Public Relations Research (IPR), gives some guidelines on how to become an ethics counselor to management:

Learn about Ethics

- Take courses in ethics while in college to build a framework for decision making.
- Once on the job, learn about the value systems of the organization.
- Incorporate those values into planning public relations activities for the organization.

Know Your Own Values

- Assess your own values and what is most important to you.
- Determine if your values match the values espoused by your client or employer.
- If they match, you have a solid foundation on which to build a professional career.
- If they don't match, you should find an organization more supportive of your values.

Spot Ethical Issues

- Be an early warning system in terms of identifying issues that pose ethical dilemmas for the organization.
- Early identification allows the organization to avoid loss of reputation and to take a proactive stance in managing an issue.

Identify and Shape the Organization's Core Values

- Identify what values are expressed in the organization's mission statement, code of ethics, and other policies.
- Actively educate all employees about the organization's values.
- Encourage an atmosphere of open discussion about ethical issues.

Educate Management

- A public relations manager should provide ethical advisement to management using the concepts of issues management, research, and conflict resolution.

... the public relations function is ideally informed to counsel top management about ethical issues.

Shannon Bowen, University of South Carolina

- Management often doesn't realize the many ways that public relations can contribute to solving and preventing ethical problems, so public relations managers must continually educate management about such capabilities.
- Being accepted as an ethics counselor will give the public relations function more power and status in the organization.

Source: S. A. Bowen. (2010). Ethics and public relations. *Institute for Public Relations*. Retrieved from www.instituteforpr.org

Adding to the confusion about professionalism is the difficulty of ascertaining what constitutes public relations practice. John F. Budd Jr., a veteran counselor, once wrote in *Public Relations Quarterly*: "We act as publicists, yet we talk of counseling. We perform as technologists in communication, but we aspire to be decision-makers

Staffers who feel their ethics aren't compromised by clients or colleagues will more likely succeed and do their best work.

Ted McKenna, reporter for PRWeek

dealing in policy." The debate whether public relations is a profession no doubt will continue for some time. But, for many who aspire to be true professionals, the most important principle is for the individual to act like a professional. This means that a practitioner should have:

- A sense of independence.
- A sense of responsibility to society and the public interest.
- Manifest concern for the competence and honor of the profession as a whole.
- A higher loyalty to the standards of the profession and fellow professionals than to the employer of the moment.

Unfortunately, a major barrier to professionalism is the mindset that many practitioners themselves have toward their work. As James Grunig and Todd Hunt state in their text *Managing Public Relations*, many practitioners tend to hold more "careerist" values than professional values. In other words, they place higher importance on job security, prestige in the organization, salary level, and recognition from superiors than on the four values just listed.

On another level, many practitioners are limited in their professionalism by what might be termed a "technician mentality." These people narrowly define professionalism as the ability to do a competent job of executing the mechanics of communicating (preparing news releases, brochures, newsletters, etc.), even if the information provided by management or a client is in bad taste, is misleading, lacks documentation, or is just plain wrong.

Another aspect of the technician mentality is the willingness to represent issues or products that go against one's own beliefs and moral code. One survey on ethical awareness, conducted by Professors Lee Wilkins at the University of Missouri and Renita Coleman at the University of Texas, asked advertising personnel whether they would take a multimillion-dollar beer account even though they were against alcohol consumption. Most of respondents answered yes to this and similar questions, causing advertising to be ranked somewhat near the bottom of the list of occupations in terms of ethical awareness. Public relations personnel, given the same questions, did somewhat better; they ranked sixth on the list of occupations for ethical awareness.

Some practitioners defend the technician mentality, however, arguing that public relations people are like lawyers in the court of public opinion. In their view, everyone is entitled to his or her viewpoint, and whether the public relations person agrees or not, the client or employer has a right to be heard. Thus, a public relations representative is a paid advocate, just as a lawyer is. The only flaw in this argument is that public relations people are not lawyers, nor are they in a court of law where judicial concepts determine the roles of defendant and plaintiff. In addition, lawyers have been known to turn down clients or resign from a case because they doubted the client's story.

Public relations practitioners, like lawyers, must also make choices. Will I lie for my employer? Will I deceive to gain information about another agency's clients? Will I cover up a hazardous condition? Will I issue a news release presenting only half the truth? Will I use the Internet to post anonymous messages promoting a client's product? Will I quit my job rather than cooperate in a questionable activity? In other words, to what extent, if any, will I compromise my personal beliefs? Being a spokesperson for a celebrity or an organization also has its ethical dilemmas, which is highlighted in the Ethics box on page 111.

on the job

ETHICS

The Ethical Dilemma of Being a Spokesperson

Credibility Lapse

At a news conference, Governor Mark Sanford of South Carolina admits to having an affair. In 2013, two years after the scandal, he relaunched his political career by being elected to Congress.

One duty of a public relations practitioner is to serve as an organization's official spokesperson. What the practitioner tells the media is not considered his or her personal opinion, but management's response or stance on an issue or situation. Lauren Fernandez, a public relations professional who also blogs about the field, says, "As PR professionals, we represent a client, brand, and organization."

An ethical challenge arises, however, when spokespersons are asked to say things on behalf of management that are misleading and even untrue. In such a situation, many practitioners take the approach that they are only the messengers and are not responsible for the accuracy of the message. An Apple spokesperson, for example, told the media that CEO Steve Jobs was taking a six-month leave of absence to correct a "hormonal imbalance." This was only partially true; Jobs secretly went to Memphis to get a liver transplant in his unsuccessful battle against cancer.

Being loyal to your client and employer is an admirable trait in a spokesperson, but there are limits if a person's own values and credibility is on the line in terms of distributing false or misleading information.

Joel Sawyer, communications director for South Carolina Governor Mark Sanford, lost considerable credibility and finally resigned after reporters "outed" him for lying to them about his boss hiking on the Appalachian Trail when, in fact, a married Sanford was seen boarding a flight to Argentina to see his mistress. The resulting scandal forced Sanford to resign and the State Ethics Commission charged him with ethics violations noting that he had also "directed members of his staff in a manner that caused them to deceive and mislead the public."

The communications director and the press secretary of New York's governor David Paterson also resigned after the governor was involved in a scandal in which he used his influence to suppress charges of domestic violence against one of his closest aides. Peter E. Kauffmann, the communications director, announced that he could no longer "in good conscience" continue to serve because he had come to doubt the truthfulness of what Governor Paterson wanted him to say about the allegations.

The role of spokesperson raises some ethical questions for you to think about. What would you do as a spokesperson if a client or employer gave you information that you knew was false or misleading? Would you justify your actions by saying that you were only the "mouthpiece," or would you quit? Is there anything else between these two extremes you would do?

Lying makes a problem part of the future; truth makes it part of the past.

Rick Pitino, college and professional basketball coach, quoted in Feeding Frenzy: Crisis Management in the Spotlight *by Jon F. Harmon*

You are your reputation. Never go against your beliefs, ethics, or morals. Trust is something that is easy to lose and almost impossible to gain back.

Jon Harris, SVP of global communications, Sara Lee

These and similar questions plague the lives of public relations personnel, although surveys do show that a high number hold such strong personal beliefs and/or work for such highly principled employers that they seldom need to compromise their personal values. If employers make a suggestion that involves questionable ethics, the public relations person often can talk them out of the idea by citing the possible consequences of such an action—adverse media publicity, for example. "Richard Levick, a crisis communications consultant in Washington, D.C., has a simple axiom: "If you can't justify it to your mother, don't do it."

In sum, professionalism in public relations really begins with the self-image of the individual as a professional who adheres to a high standard of honesty and integrity in his or her daily work. Although it is important to show loyalty to an employer, you must never allow a client or an employer to rob you of your self-esteem or undermine your reputation.

A Standardized Curriculum

Public relations as an academic discipline is an important step toward professionalism. PRSA, IABC, and other organizations such as the National Communication Association (NCA) and the Association for Education in Journalism and Mass Communications (AEJMC) have worked toward professionalism by standardizing the curricula of public relations at the undergraduate and master's degree levels.

One result of this cooperation is the Commission on Public Relations Education (www.commpred.org), which consists of leading educators and practitioners representing a number of professional communication groups. The commission, also mentioned in Chapter 1, has called for more involvement by practitioners in the educational process. It noted, "While the record of broad support for public relations education by professional groups is growing, there is a critical need for similar action by individual practitioners and the firms, companies and organizations . . . ."

The commission has also set the standard for coursework in public relations, saying it should comprise 25 to 40 percent of all undergraduate credit hours. Of that coursework, at least half should be clearly identified as public relations courses covering such topics as (1) principles, (2) case studies, (3) research and evaluation, (4) writing and production, (5) planning and management, (6) campaigns, and (7) supervised internships. One measure of success in establishing a standard curriculum is PRSSA's rule that a chapter cannot be established on a university campus unless the institution offers a minimum of five courses in public relations—and there are now more than 300 campuses with chapters.

Expanding Body of Knowledge

Every profession is based on an accumulation of knowledge in the field. Various groups have added to the body of knowledge of public relations through the years by commissioning research studies, monographs, books, and reports. IPRA, for example, has issued a number of "gold papers" over the years on such topics as environmental communications and sustainability, consumerism, and corporate social responsibility. IABC has published a number of books and monographs on such topics as intranets, communication management, and employee communications. These organizations also publish magazines and newsletters, as mentioned earlier.

The two major academic journals in public relations are the *Public Relations Review* and the *Journal of Public Relations Research*. Both publications publish a variety of scholarly articles about public relations and communications theory, in-depth analyses of public relations issues and campaigns, and survey research. In addition, the body of knowledge is constantly expanding through trade publications such as *PRWeek*, *Ragan.com*, and *O'Dwyer's PR Report*, *Adweek*, and various newsletters. There are also about 3,000 blogs and numerous LinkedIn discussion groups devoted to public relations.

Major Centers of Research The best-known think tank for public relations research is the Institute for Public Relations (IPR), which celebrated its 50th anniversary in 2006. Headquartered at the University of Florida, IPR is an independent, nonprofit organization of educators and practitioners "that builds and documents research-based knowledge in public relations, and makes this knowledge available and useful to practitioners, educators, and their clients." Research papers and other information are available for free on its website (www.instituteforpr.org). In recent years, it has commissioned a number of studies regarding the metrics of public relations measurement and even has a free online database of articles and research about social media (instituteforpr.org/scienceofsocialmedia). The IPR motto says a lot: "Dedicated to the science beneath the art."

Another research center is the Strategic Public Relations Center at the University of Southern California (USC) Annenberg School for Communication. It conducts an annual survey, among other research, that primarily documents public relations as a management function. Statistics on public relations evaluation methods, departmental budgets, level of staffing, and management reporting relationships are compiled. The center has an online database, PR Management Database (PRMD), that is available free of charge at www.annenberg.usc.edu/sprc.

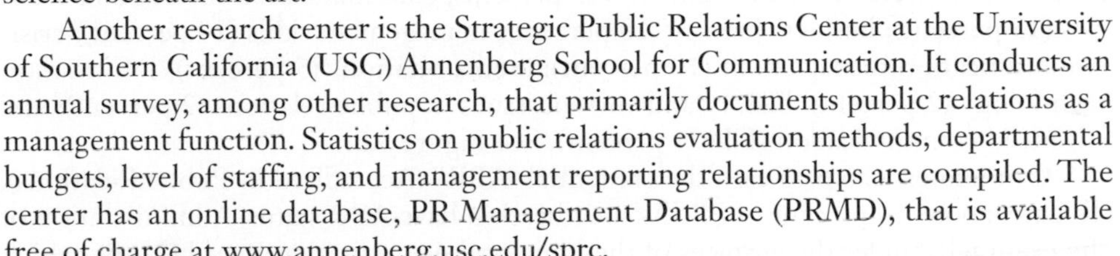

Three other centers of public relations research are worth noting. One is the Arthur W. Page Center (www.thepagecenter.comm.psu.edu) at Pennsylvania State University. Its goal is "the study and advancement of ethics and responsibility in corporate and public communication." The Center has teaching modules on ethics and an extensive oral history video collection. The second center is the Plank Center for Leadership in Public Relations (www.plankcenter.ua.edu) at the University of Alabama. Its primary mission is "to help develop and recognize outstanding leaders and role models in public relations" through research and professional education efforts. For students and practitioners who want to increase their knowledge of international public relations, there is the Center for Global Public Relations (http://www.egpr.nccc.edu) at the University of North Carolina, Charlotte.

Public relations and public affairs are becoming more scientific and professional. It's less a case of who you know. And more a case of what you know.

Sir Martin Sorrell, CEO of WPP communications conglomerate, London

Professional Accreditation

One major step to improve standards and professionalism in public relations around the world has been the establishment of accreditation programs. This means that practitioners voluntarily go through a process in which they are recognized by a national organization, to be competent, qualified professionals.

PRSA, for example, began its accreditation program about 60 years ago. Other national groups, including the IABC, the Canadian Public Relations Society (CPRS), the British Institute of Public Relations (BIPR), to name just a few, also have established accreditation programs.

The IABC Model The approach used by most national groups is to have written and oral exams and to have candidates submit a portfolio of work samples to a committee of professional peers. IABC, for example, places a major emphasis on the individual's portfolio as part of its ABC (Accredited Business Communicator) certification. The candidate must also have a minimum of five years' experience and pass a four-hour written and oral exam. Only about 8 percent of IABC's members, however, have earned ABC designation.

The PRSA Model PRSA was the first public relations group in the world to establish an accreditation program, and so it's worth examining in some detail how it works. First, candidates are required to take a preview course (available online), complete a "readiness" questionnaire, and show a portfolio of work to a panel of professional peers before taking the written exam, which is available at test centers throughout the United States.

The two-and-a-half-hour exam tests knowledge of the field and gives proportional weight to various core topics: research, planning, execution, and evaluation of programs (30 percent); ethics and law (15 percent); communication models and theories (15 percent); business literacy (10 percent); management skills (10 percent); crisis communication management (10 percent); media relations (5 percent); information technology (2 percent); history and current issues in public relations (2 percent); and advanced communication skills (1 percent). See Figure 3.2.

Candidates who pass earn the credential "APR" (Accredited in Public Relations). To date, about 20 percent of PRSA's membership have APR status. Administration of the exam falls under the auspices of the Universal Accreditation Board (UAB), which was created by PRSA in 1998 (www.praccreditation.org). It allows non-PRSA members from other professional groups that have affiliated with UAB to take the accreditation exam. The vast majority of those taking the exam, however, are members of PRSA.

Required Continuing Education Some groups are beginning to require continuing education as a prerequisite for professional certification. Australia's PRIA, for example, requires its members to maintain Certified Practitioner (CP) status by completing 40 hours of continuing education each year. This, however, is the exception. The vast majority of national groups—including IABC and PRSA—have no continuing education requirements for their accredited members, let alone the rank and file. The failure to establish minimum continuing education requirements for members, quite frankly, gives public relations less status as a profession than other groups that require continuing education, such as dietitians and teachers, and even hair stylists.

Indeed, more than one expert has pointed out that there is a great deal of difference between "accreditation," which only requires a one-time exam, and "certification" that requires continued education and professional development to remain certified. They advocate the establishment of an industry-wide certification program that would have more credibility among clients and employers. The idea is that anyone can be public relations practitioner, just like anyone can be an accountant, but being a Certified Public Accountant (or Certified Public Relations Professional) is an earned designation that brings more status and even higher potential income.

Figure 3.2 **The Core Areas of Knowledge in PRSA's Accreditation Exam**

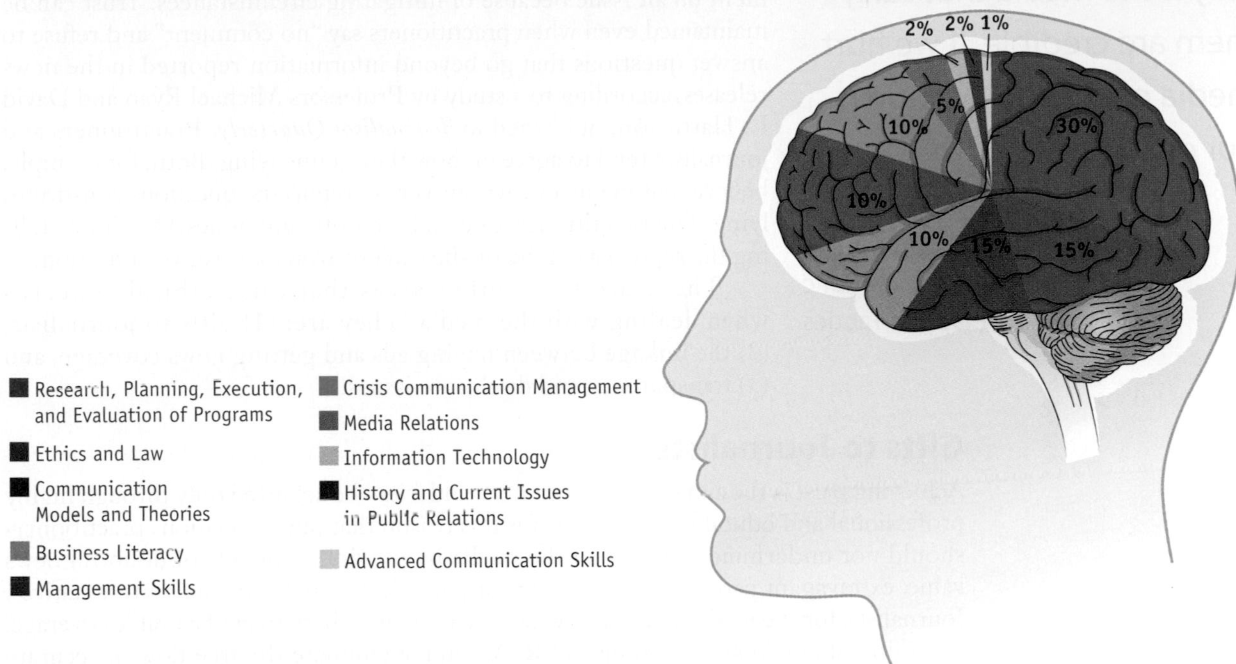

In addition, certification can add "teeth" to enforcement because individuals who violate professional standards could be de-certified in a way that would be legally defensible because it would not restrict them from just calling themselves a generic public relations practitioner.

Shel Holtz, a public relations professional for more than 30 years and also ABC, wrote in his blog (www.holtz.com), "The sooner the profession enacts certification as an industry-wide requirement, the better our chance of saving the entire information ecosystem from deteriorating into a cesspool of content nobody can trust." Holtz, however, is a voice in the wilderness. So far, there has been little movement by public relations organizations and individual practitioners to combine forces and create an industry-wide certification program, despite the idealistic resolutions of various groups for improved professional practice.

Ethical Dealings with the News Media

The most practical consideration facing a public relations specialist is his or her dealings with the news media. The standard rubric is that he or she must be totally honest to maintain credibility and gain the trust of journalists and editors.

But the axiom "The devil is in the details" also applies. Honesty, for example, doesn't automatically mean that public relations professionals must answer every question that a reporter might ask. They often have to use discretion because of their obligation to represent the best interests of their clients or employers. There may be proprietary information or detailed information about organizational plans that cannot be released for public consumption. There also may be personal information about executives or employees that are protected by privacy laws.

Our messages are credible only if the media that carry them are credible. If we hurt media credibility, we hurt our own.

Tim Yost, communications director for ASC, a Detroit automotive manufacturer, in Public Relations Tactics

Consequently, it is also "honest" for a practitioner to tell a reporter that he or she cannot provide information or make a comment on an issue because of mitigating circumstances. Trust can be maintained even when practitioners say "no comment" and refuse to answer questions that go beyond information reported in the news releases, according to a study by Professors Michael Ryan and David L. Hartinson, published in *Journalism Quarterly*. Practitioners and journalists tend to agree on how they define lying. Both, for example, believe that giving evasive answers to reporters' questions constitutes lying. The practitioner is much better off (and honest) by simply telling the reporter that he or she can't or won't answer the question.

There are three other areas that raise ethical concerns when dealing with the media. They are: (1) gifts to journalists, (2) the linkage between buying ads and getting news coverage, and (3) transparency and disclosure issues.

Gifts to Journalists

Achieving trust is the aim of all practitioners, and it can be achieved only through highly professional and ethical behavior. It is for this reason that public relations practitioners should not undermine the trust of the media by providing junkets of doubtful news value, extravagant parties, expensive gifts, or personal favors for media representatives. Journalists, for the most part, will view these actions as bribery to get favorable coverage.

Gifts of any kind, according to PRSA, can contaminate the free flow of accurate and truthful information to the public. See the Multicultural box on page 117. Although the exact words "corrupting the channels of communication" are no longer used in the PRSA code, there are still the same strictures about gifts of products, travel, and services to reporters and even bloggers (see page 105 about guidelines for Internet transparency). There is some blurring of lines, however, when it comes to such items as coffee mugs, T-shirts, or even a bottle of ketchup that is enclosed in media kits as a promotional gimmick. In most cases, such items are of little value and not considered a "gift." Some dailies, however, have a policy of not accepting even such minor items.

In most cases, publicists know it's not "cool" to offer reporters and bloggers gifts in return for coverage, and thus engage in a more indirect approach. De Vries public relations and its client, Pantene, for example, were heavily criticized for sending out a survey to journalists, asking them what types of gifts they would like to receive, among other questions. And a publicist for the television series *The Good Wife* also earned the ridicule of entertainment bloggers when she sent them a news release with the note "As a thank you for considering the story, I would love to send you a $20 Amazon gift certificate." Ann Taylor also generated considerable criticism when it offered bloggers a chance to be in a lottery for up to $500 in cash if they posted a favorable review.

Although gift giving is considered unethical in the United States, other nations have different standards. A survey conducted by Insight and MediaSource, for example, found that two out of five Arabic-language journalists in the Middle East might be more inclined to use a news release if it came with a gift. Another area of ethical concern is paying a reporter's expenses for covering an event or news conference. Although the practice is not done in the United States, it's not uncommon in other nations. In one survey, almost a third of European journalists said they expect public relations people to pay their expenses. The percentage rises to almost 60 percent in Asian nations. The issue of "pay for play" in China is discussed in the Multicultural box that follows.

Some people might assume that public relations representatives would benefit from being able to influence journalists with gifts, but this is not the case. A major selling point of public relations work is the third-party credibility of reporters and editors. The public trusts journalists to be objective and somewhat impartial in their dissemination of information. If the public loses that trust because they feel the media can be "bought," the information provided by public relations sources also becomes less credible.

on the job

A MULTICULTURAL WORLD

"Pay for Play" in China

China is somewhat different than the United States and Western Europe in the respect that public relations firms commonly pay to get their clients in the print and broadcast media. A one-minute interview with an executive on a Chinese TV news program, for example, costs $4,000. Or if a company wants a story about a new product in the Chinese edition of *Esquire*, the going rate is $10,000 per page, according to reporter David Barboza, of the *New York Times*.

The concept of "pay for play" also comes into play with Chinese journalists. A Shanghai business executive told Barboza, "If one of my companies came up with a cure for cancer, I still couldn't get any journalists to come to the press conference without promising them a huge envelope filled with cash."

Junkets, however, can also work. One leading Chinese daily, for example, published an interview with the president of Moet Hennessy after the company paid the airfare, lodging, and food costs of nine journalists to visit the company's chateau in western China.

China, of course, isn't the only nation that has a "pay for play" media culture. Russia and its former republics also have a reputation for publishing articles and doing broadcast interviews for pay. In the Republic of Georgia, for example, the two major TV stations even have a rate card for guests who appear on news programs and in talk shows. Media in various African and Middle Eastern nations also have similar practices.

Several international organizations such as the International Public Relations Association (IPRA), the International Federation of Journalists, and Transparency International have condemned such practices. They contend that "news material should appear as a result of the news judgment of journalists and editors, not as a result of any payment in cash or any other kind of inducements."

The concept of "pay for play" in some cultures, such as China, raises some ethical questions. Although such practices are considered unethical in an American or European context, public relations firms and international companies operating in China often justify "pay for play" because that's the way media relations is done in China. As they say, "When in Rome, do as the Romans do."

What do you think? If you were assigned to Shanghai to do public relations work for an American company, would you adhere to American standards of professional practice, or would you go with the flow and pay media outlets, including the "expenses" of journalists, for coverage?

Source: D. Barboza. (2012, April 4). In China Press, best coverage money can buy. *New York Times*, A1, B2.

Linking Ads with News Coverage

"I don't think it's as blatant as putting cash in an editor's hand," says Mark Hass, chief executive of Manning, Selvage, and Lee, in a *New York Times* interview. He says it is often an implied agreement that the organization will buy advertising in the publication as long as an article or a product review will be part of the package. Indeed, a survey of marketing communication managers by *PRWeek* found that almost 20 percent of the respondents had purchased advertising in return for a news story.

Magazines serving a particular industry, such as home decorating, bridal fashions, or autos, often blur the line between news features and advertisements. Tony Silber, who writes about the magazine industry, told *PRWeek*, "If you look at shelter magazines, they are going to have advertisers' products in their decorated spreads of homes." There's also considerable suspicion that the Car of the Year on the cover of an auto magazine is the result of an automaker's extensive purchase of advertising space in that magazine. Is this just coincidence, or part of an "understanding"?

Editors, however, defend the practice, arguing that organizations who receive coverage should also help the publication survive by buying advertising. That may be true, but the question still remains an ethical one for public relations practitioners. At what point does the transaction become "pay for play"?

Transparency and Disclosure Issues

Is it ethical for a public relations firm, for example, to hire a freelance writer to write favorable stories about its client? The Lewis Group, according to *PRWeek*, paid more than $10,000 to a freelancer to write flattering stories in the local newspaper about its client, Health South's Richard Scrushy, who was on trial for fraud. Again, there is some blurring of lines here. Whose responsibility was it to inform the public that the freelancer was being paid by Health South? Was this the obligation of the public relations firm, or the responsibility of the writer to inform the newspaper's editors or acknowledge payment in her article?

> If something as basic as honesty does not appear to be instilled in the fabric of the PR department, I begin to question the entire PR program on down to its products and services.
>
> *Rose Gordon, news editor of* PRWeek

Transparency and disclosure are issues in the broadcast industry also. Should a spokesperson on a television talk show reveal his or her employer? This question came to the forefront when it was revealed in the press that the Toy Guy (Christopher Byrne), who appears on scores of local and national television shows with his selections of the best and hottest toys for the Christmas season, is actually paid hundreds of thousands of dollars by various toy companies to promote their products.

Celebrities appearing on talk shows such as NBC's *Today* show also raise the issue of transparency. Actress Kathleen Turner, for example, told Diane Sawyer on ABC's *Good Morning America* about her battle with rheumatoid arthritis and mentioned that a drug, Enbrel, helped ease the pain. What Turner didn't reveal, and Sawyer didn't tell the audience, was that Turner was being paid to appear by the company that manufactures the drug. After the *New York Times* broke the story, the networks said they would initiate a policy that viewers would be told about a celebrity's ties to a corporation or particular cause.

The blurring of lines in today's media continues to be a major concern for both public relations professionals and journalists. Indeed, a PRSA/Bacon's Inc. survey found that the greatest single challenge facing practitioners is "upholding credibility within an environment where the lines between PR, advertising, and journalism are growing increasingly vague."

Summary

Understanding Ethics and Values

- Ethics is the study of how we should behave. Values drive our actual behavior in a given situation.
- It is possible to be an advocate and conduct yourself in a manner that is honest, open, and fair.
- Society understands that the advocate is operating within an assigned role, much like a defense lawyer has an assigned role in court.

The Role of Professional Organizations

- Groups such as PRSA, IABC, and IPRA play an important role in setting the standards and ethical behavior of the profession.
- A major mission of professional groups is to provide continuing education to its members and to raise standards in the industry.

Professional Codes of Conduct

- Virtually all professional organizations have published codes of conduct that set standards for professional behavior.
- There also are specialized codes of conduct for such areas as financial relations, production of video news releases, and working with bloggers and social media networks.

Other Steps toward Professionalism

- An occupation becomes a profession through an evolutionary process that involves many steps including the acceptance of professional standards by practitioners with no formal training in the field.
- Public relations can be considered a profession in several ways. It has a body of knowledge, is now widely accepted as a discipline in colleges and universities, and has academic centers for research.
- Major groups such as IABC and PRSA have accreditation programs in which members submit work portfolios and pass oral and written exams.
- True public relations professionals have a loyalty to the standards of the profession and the public interest.

Ethical Dealings with the News Media

- Both public relations and journalism groups condemn gift giving to journalists because the practice undermines the media's credibility and the public's trust.
- Other ethical issues that may come up when dealing with the media include advertising influencing news coverage and the lack of disclosure about the affiliation of celebrities on television talk shows.

Case Activity **Ethical Dilemmas in the Workplace**

A number of situations can raise ethical questions in the public relations business. Resolving these situations often involve sifting through a number of factors including your philosophical orientation, your personal belief system, and your understanding of professional standards. What ethical concerns are raised in the following situations? What would you do in each situation?

- Your company has a great product, and the management wants a higher profile on such consumer review sites as Yelp and Amazon. Several freelance writers contact you with an offer. They will post multiple favorable reviews of your product under various anonymous names and only charge $25 for every posted review.
- The president of the company decides it would be "good PR" and visibility for her to have a personal Twitter account and write a weekly blog. She, of course, doesn't have much time for this so she asks you, the public relations director, to "ghost-write" the tweets and the blog in her name.
- Your public relations firm has a luxury resort hotel in Hawaii as a client. It's important to get articles about the hotel in various leading travel magazines. One idea is to invite influential travel writers and their families for a one-week stay at the hotel, all expenses paid, with the understanding that they would write a favorable article about their experience.

Questions For Review and Discussion

1. What ethical points should be considered when acting as a spokesperson for an organization?
2. What role do professional organizations play in setting the standards of public relations practice?
3. Describe, in general, the activities of PRSA, IABC, and IPRA.
4. A number of professional groups have codes of ethics. What are some common characteristics of these codes?
5. How should companies respond to critical consumer reviews on such sites as YELP or TripAdvisor?
6. What ethical rules apply to Internet public relations and participation in social networking sites?
7. Is it a good idea to speak the truth and come clean on an issue or be selective in sharing the truth in the interest of an organization's image? Discuss with arguments on either side.
8. In what ways do the concepts of "careerism" and "technician mentality" undermine the concept of public relations as a profession?
9. How does accreditation help practitioners and the profession?
10. What is the difference between certification and accreditation? Would an industry-wide certification program be better than accreditation offered by various organizations such as PRSA?
11. What is a "front" group? Why are they considered unethical?
12. Should public relations personnel give gifts to journalists? Why or why not?
13. "Quid pro quo" has been used to describe the relationship between PR and news media, often in the form of advertisements in exchange for coverage. Do you think the practice is unethical? Why?
14. Should celebrities who appear on television talk shows disclose what company or organization is paying them to appear?

Media Resources

Barboza, D. (2012, April 4). In China, best coverage money can buy. *New York Times*, A1, B2.

Bowen, S. A. (2007). Ethics and public relations. *Institute for Public Relations*. Retrieved from www.instituteforpr.org

Bruell, A. (2011, April). Ethics.com. *PRWeek*, 28–29.

Bustillo, M., & Zimmerman, A. (2009, April 23). Paid to pitch: Product reviews by bloggers draw scrutiny. *Wall Street Journal,* pp. B9, B16.

Coleman, R., & Wilkins, L. (2009). The moral development of public relations practitioners: A comparison with other professions and influences on higher quality ethical reasoning. *Journal of Public Relations Research, 21*(3), 318–340.

Fullerton, J.A,, Kendrick, A., and McKinnon, L. (2013). Advertising Ethics: Student Attitudes and Behavioral Intent. *Journalism & Mass Communications Educator, 68*(1), 33–49.

Gingerich, J. (2012, February). Front groups wage PR warfare in 'fracking' debate. *O'Dwyer's PR Report*, l8–19, 21.

Goodness has nothing to do with it: Utilitarians are not nice people. (2011, September 24), *Economist*, 102

Gower, K. K. (2007). *Legal and ethical restraints on public relations.* Prospect, IL: Waveland Press.

Grusich, K. (2012, October 9). Guide to Practicing (Ethical) PR on Yelp and Other Review Sites. *Ragan's PR Daily.* Retrieved from www.Ragan.com

Hazley, G. (2012, July). PR groups: pros shouldn't edit Wikipedia pages. *O'Dwyer's PR Report*, 8.

Holiday, R., & Astor, L. (2012, October). Should PR agencies pay bloggers for coverage promoting their clients? *PRWeek*, 27.

Holtz, S. (2011, July 15). Sweeping out the dark, ugly corner of Public Relations. *Shel Holtz blog*. Retrieved from www.holtz.com

Holtz, S. (2012, July 31). Jaw-dropping abuses labeled as PR signal that the time is now for certification. *Shel Holtz's blog*. Retrieved from www.holtz.com

Pogebin, R. (2013, August 7). Fake Comments Muddy a Debate. New York Times, C1, 6.

Putting words into action: PRSA's new social media policy. (2011, March). *Public Relations Tactics*, 18.

Should PR Leaders serve as the conscience of an organization? (2010, September). *Public Relations Tactics*, 16–18.

chapter 4

The Practice of Public Relations

After reading this chapter, you will be able to:

- Understand the role and functions of a public relations department
- Be more knowledgeable about the staff function of public relations
- Understand the structure of a public relations firm and its various activities
- Know the difference between working in a department and working in a firm

Public Relations Departments

A department of public relations, now usually called corporate communications or a similar term, has been an integral part of American business and industry for almost 150 years.

In the beginning, the primary objectives of a public relations department were promotion and publicity. American railroads in the 1870s, as explained in Chapter 2, had public relations departments that promoted settlement of the West. Also in the 1870s, department stores such as Wannamaker's in Philadelphia and Macy's in New York used public relations to attract customers. Of course, there is also George Westinghouse, who started a public relations department in 1889 to promote alternating current (AC) and his new company. Henry Ford also recognized the value of a public relations staff in promoting his cars in the early 1900s.

Today, public relations has expanded from its traditional functions and now exercises its influence on the highest levels of management. In a changing environment, and faced with the variety of pressures previously described, executives increasingly see public relations not as publicity and one-way communication, but as a complex and dynamic process of negotiation and compromise with a number of key audiences, which are often called "publics." James Grunig, now professor emeritus of public relations at the University of Maryland, calls the new approach "building good relationships with strategic publics," which requires public relations executives to be "strategic communication managers rather than communication technicians."

Grunig, head of a six-year IABC Foundation research study on excellence in public relations and communications management, continues:

> When public relations helps that organization build relationships, it saves the organization money by reducing the costs of litigation, regulation, legislation, pressure campaign boycotts, or lost revenue that result from bad relationships with publics—publics that become activist groups when relationships are bad. It also helps the organization make money by cultivating relationships with donors, customers, shareholders and legislators.

The results of an IABC study seem to indicate that chief executive officers (CEOs) consider public relations to be a good investment. Another survey of 200 organizations shows that CEOs give public relations operations a 184 percent return on investment (ROI), a figure just below that of customer service and sales/marketing.

Ideally, professional public relations people assist top management in developing policy and communicating with various groups. Indeed, the IABC study emphasizes that CEOs want communication that is strategic, is based on research, and involves two-way communication with key publics. See the Insights box on page 123 about the attributes that a CEO wants in a chief communications officer.

Corporate Structure Shapes the Public Relations Role

Research indicates, however, that the role of public relations in an organization often depends on the type of organization, the perceptions of top management, and even the capabilities of the public relations executive.

Large and complex organizations, for example, have a greater tendency to include public relations in the policy-making process. Companies such as IBM and Cola-Cola, which operate in a highly competitive environment, are more sensitive to policy

on the job
INSIGHTS

So You Want to Make a Six-Figure Salary?

CEOs of major corporations have high expectations for their chief communications officers (CCOs) who are commonly called vice president (VP) or even senior vice president (SVP) of corporate communications. The Arthur W. Page Society, an elite group of senior communications executives, surveyed CEOs to find out what key attributes they look for in a senior-level communications executive.

Detailed knowledge of the business. Be an expert in communications, but you should also have knowledge of business in general and the details of the company in particular.

Extensive communications background. Experience and extensive relationships are assumed, but you need expertise in what the company needs. A company in a highly regulated industry, for example, puts a premium on government and political experience.

A crystal ball. You need to anticipate how different audiences will react to different events, messages, and channels.

C-Suite credibility. It's crucial to be accepted in what is called the "C-Suite." Experience in actually running a business or a division is one form of earning one's "credentials."

Extensive internal relationships. You need to have your finger on the pulse of the company and know employees at every level of the operation.

Team player. Decisions are made on a collaborative basis. You thus need to have strong relationships with colleagues and the respect of the CEO's inner circle.

Educator. CEOs want you to educate them and the rest of the company on communications skills in general, and how to develop strategies for communicating the company's values.

issues, public attitudes, and corporate reputation. Consequently, their public relations departments place more emphasis on establishing interactive social media sites, regular contact with traditional media, sponsorship of events, writing executive speeches, and counseling management about issues that could potentially affect the bottom line.

In such organizations, which are classified as *mixed organic/mechanical* by management theorists, the authority and power of the public relations department are quite high; public relations is part of what is called the "dominant coalition" and has a great deal of autonomy.

In contrast, a small-scale organization of low complexity that offers a standardized product or service feels few public pressures and little governmental regulatory interest. It thus has scant public relations activity, and staff members perform basic duties such as producing the company newsletter and issuing routine news releases. Public relations in a traditional organization have virtually no input into management decisions and policy formation.

Research also indicates that the type of organization involved may be less significant in predicting the role of its public relations department than are the perceptions and expectations of its top management. In many organizations, top-level management perceives public relations as primarily a journalistic and technical function—media relations and publicity. In large-scale mechanical organizations of low complexity, there is also a tendency to think of public relations as only a support function of the marketing department.

Such perceptions by top management severely limit the role of the public relations department as well as its power to take part in management decision making. In such instances, public relations is relegated to being a tactical function, one of simply preparing messages without input on what should be communicated in those messages. In many cases, however, public relations personnel self-select technician roles because they lack a knowledge base in research, environmental scanning, problem solving, and managing total communications strategies. Research also suggests that many practitioners prefer and choose the technician roles because they are more personally fulfilled by working with tactics than with strategy.

The most admired *Fortune* 500 corporations, in terms of reputation, tend to think of public relations as more of a strategic management tool. A study by the University of Southern California (USC) Annenberg Strategic Public Relations Center (www.annenberg.usc.edu/sprc) found that these companies, compared to others, dedicate a larger percentage of their gross revenues to public relations activities, extensively use outside public relations firms to supplement their own large staffs, and don't have public relations personnel report to the marketing department.

PRWeek, summarizing the survey, said, "PR Departments that closely align their own goals with their companies' strategic business goals receive greater executive support, have larger budgets, and have a higher perceived contribution to their organizations' success." See the Multicultural World box on page 125 for a case study of a successful anniversary program by IBM that involved more than 400,000 employees.

The primary indicator of a department's influence and power, however, is whether the top communications officer has a seat at the management table. To gain and maintain a seat at the management table should be an ongoing goal of public relations practitioners. Experts indicate that it is increasingly common for the top public relations practitioner in an organization to report to the CEO. One survey of 500 senior-level practitioners, conducted by the Annenberg Strategic Public Relations Center, found that 64 percent of all respondents and 77 percent of *Fortune* 500 respondents report to the "C-Suite" (CEO, COO, or chairman). The report adds, "They were much more likely to indicate that their CEOs believe PR contributes to market share, financial success, and sales, than those reporting to other parts of the organization."

Julie O'Neil of Texas Christian University researched the sources influencing corporate public relations practitioners. She reported in a *Public Relations Review* article that having influence in the company is based on four factors: (1) perception of value by top management, (2) practitioners taking on the managerial role, (3) reporting to the CEO, and (4) years of professional experience. In another study published in the *Journal of Public Relations Research*, Juan Meng from the University of Georgia found that the top three attributes of excellent public relations managers were (1) strategic decision-making capability, (2) ability to solve problems and produce results, and (3) communication knowledge and expertise.

Organization of Departments

The executive in charge of a corporate communications department usually has one of three titles: manager, director, or vice president. A vice president of corporate communications may have direct responsibility for the additional activities of advertising and marketing communications. Another title, which is promoted by the Arthur W. Page Society, is *chief communications officer* (CCO), to match the common management rubric of CMO (chief marketing officer), CFO (chief financial officer), or even CEO (chief executive officer). The various job levels in public relations are outlined in the Insights box on page 128.

on the job

A MULTICULTURAL WORLD

IBM Has a Global Birthday Celebration

IBM marked its 100-year anniversary with a global celebration that involved more than 400,000 employees in 170 nations. A centennial milestone for a technology company is a rarity, so the company decided to celebrate by involving its employees in a year-long program to refresh public perceptions of IBM around the world.

The campaign had four objectives: (1) connect with all employees during the centennial, (2) extend employee engagement beyond a one-day anniversary event, (3) improve employee understanding of IBM's history and impact on the world, and (4) engage the IBM workforce in volunteering time and expertise on a "Day of Service" to help nonprofit and other civic groups in local communities.

The following strategies were used:

- The corporate communications staff sought stories from each country and business unit that aligned with one of three themes—Pioneering the Science of Information, Making the World Work Better, and Reinventing the Modern Corporation. They curated more than 850 submissions and country teams often added local details.
- A guidebook for local communications teams was developed, speeches and presentations offered talking points, and materials about IBM's centennial helped decorate offices and provided signage for local events.
- Two films by award-winning directors were produced and made available in eight languages that focused on IBM's history and culture of innovation. The films were posted on the company's intranet sites and on YouTube.
- A Twitter hashtag was created for employees to share comment and images of their volunteer contributions at the local level.
- Major exhibits about IBM's history and contributions to society were mounted in 14 nations.
- A book titled *Making the World Work* was printed in seven languages and mailed to the home of every employee.

The campaign produced the following results:

- Employees around the world completed 3.1 million hours of volunteer service to charitable organizations in their local community—making the effort the largest corporate volunteerism initiative in history.
- More than 5,000 employee volunteer projects in 120 countries helped 10 million people.

- The two films were shown at hundreds of employee events and received more than 1 million views on YouTube.
- Almost 550,000 copies of the book, *Making the World Better*, were distributed to all full- and part-time employees and another 20,000 were downloaded from the company's intranet.
- Surveys found that the vast majority of employees said they had a greater appreciation of IBM's impact on the world, were more confident of IBM's future, and had a better understanding of what makes IBM different from other companies.
- More than a thousand articles in local media commented on IBM's commitment to service.
- IBM gained 8 points in brand value in the annual Interbrand's most valuable global brand study.
- The campaign received a PRSA Silver Anvil award in 2012 for best overall campaign of the year.

They need to be able to anticipate the reactions of governments, private interest groups, shareholders, factions, and so forth, in real time.

CEO of a large corporation on what he expects in a chief communications officer, in a survey by the Arthur W. Page Society

A public relations department usually is divided into specialized sections, each of which has a coordinator or manager. Common sections found in a large corporation are media relations, investor relations, consumer affairs, governmental relations, community relations, marketing communications, and employee communications.

Large, global corporations such as IBM and General Motors have more than 500 employees in various areas of corporate and marketing communications, and the IBM organizational chart (Figure 4.1) is a good example of how a large operation is structured. Corporate communications, under a senior vice president (SVP) of marketing, communications, and citizenship, has 13 vice presidents overseeing such areas as (1) marketing, (2) corporate affairs, (3) executive communications, (4) employee communications, and (5) communications for various business units. See also the AT&T organization chart on page 127.

Figure 4.1 **IBM's Organization Chart**

IBM's organization chart shows the integration of global marketing and communications under a senior vice president, Jon Iwata, who is a graduate of the public relations degree program at San Jose State University. There are 13 divisions headed by a vice president.

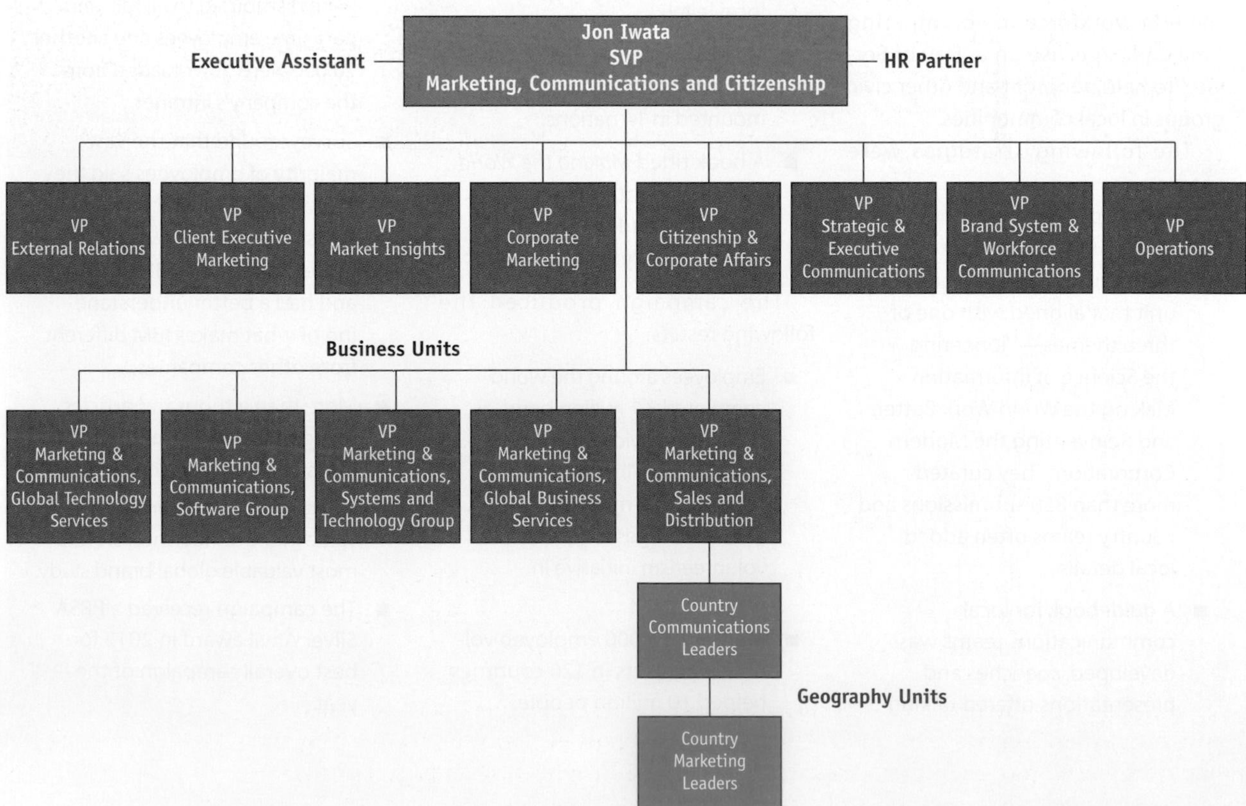

Figure 4.2 AT&T's Organization Chart

The chart shows the divisions within corporate communications at this giant telecom. In addition to the 200 communication staffers at corporate headquarters, each of AT&T's business units also have public relations professionals that coordinate with corporate communications.

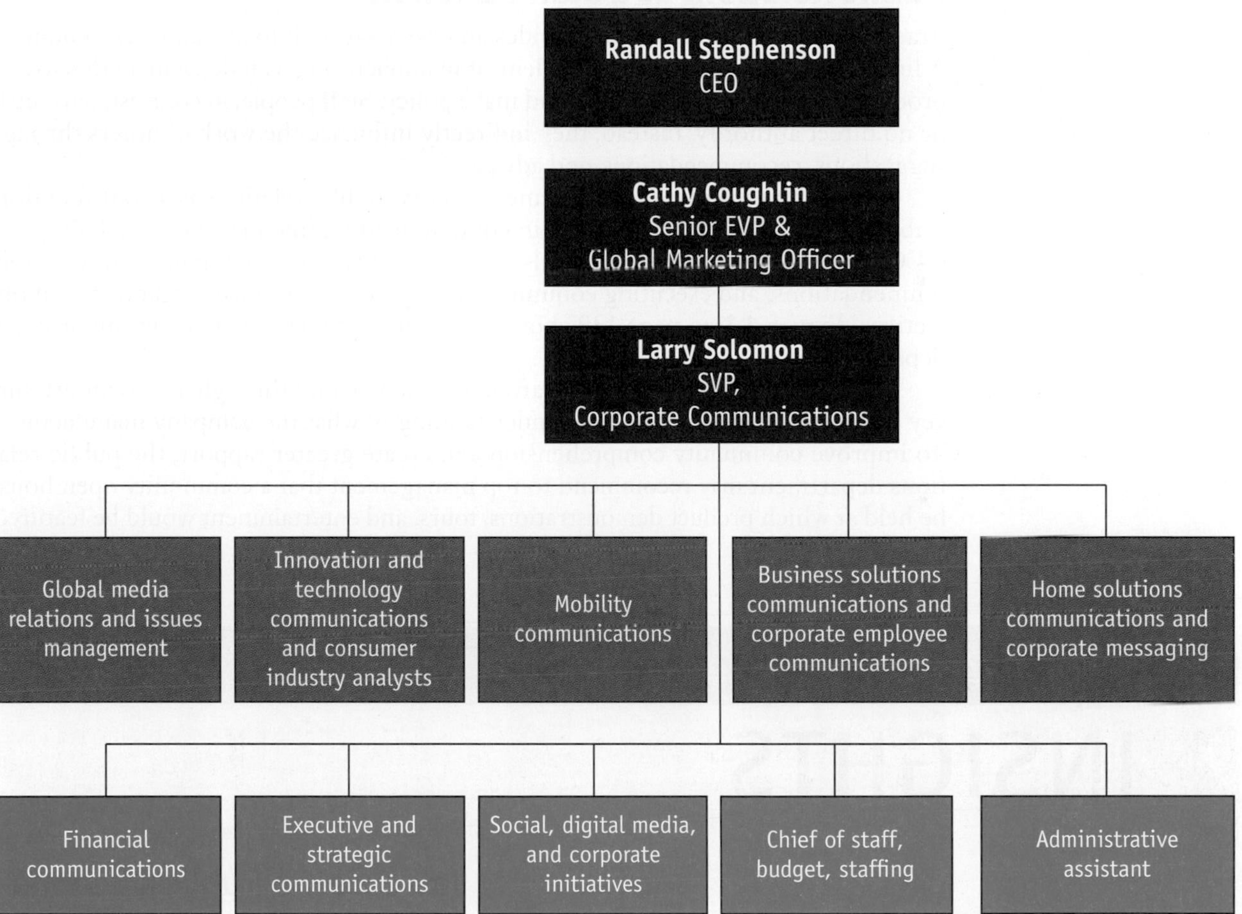

Source: PRWeek, March 2013.

This example, however, should not mislead you about the size and budget of public relations departments. The USC Annenberg study found that *Fortune* 500 companies typically have 24 professionals in the corporate communications/public relations department. The majority of companies are much smaller in size and have fewer staff in the public relations area. One study of medium-sized U.S. corporations by the Conference Board found that the typical public relations department has nine professionals. Another survey, by PRSA and Bacon's Information, Inc., found that only 13 percent of the respondents work for an organization that has more than 10 employees in public relations. Another 45 percent work in a department with two to five employees. Almost a third of the respondents reported that they are the only public relations employee in their organization. See the Insights box on page 129 for an entry-level position for a public relations specialist.

Public relations personnel may also be dispersed throughout an organization in such a manner that an observer has difficulty ascertaining the extent of public relations activity. For example, some personnel may be found in the marketing department working exclusively on product publicity, while others may be assigned to human resources as communication specialists who produce newsletters and announcements posted on the organization's intranet. Decentralization of the public relations function, and the frictions it causes, will be discussed later in this chapter.

Public Relations as a Staff Function

Traditional management theory divides an organization into *line* and *staff* functions. A line manager, such as a vice president of manufacturing, can delegate authority, set production goals, hire employees, and make policy. Staff people, in contrast, have little or no direct authority. Instead, they indirectly influence the work of others through suggestions, recommendations, and advice.

According to accepted management theory, public relations is a staff function. Public relations people are experts in communication; line managers, including the CEO, rely on them to use their skills in preparing and processing data, making recommendations, and executing communication programs to meet organizational objectives. Figure 4.3 on page 130 shows the primary functions of a communications department.

For example, public relations staff members may find through a community survey that people have only a vague understanding of what the company manufactures. To improve community comprehension and create greater rapport, the public relations department may recommend to top management that a community open house be held at which product demonstrations, tours, and entertainment would be featured.

on the job INSIGHTS

Job Levels in Public Relations

- **Entry-Level Technician.** Uses technical "craft" skills to disseminate information, persuade, gather data, or solicit feedback
- **Supervisor.** Supervises projects, including planning, scheduling, budgeting, organizing, leading, controlling, and problem solving
- **Manager.** Constituency and issue-trend analysis; departmental management, including organizing, budgeting, leading, controlling, evaluating, and problem solving
- **Director.** Constituency and issue-trend analysis; communicating and operational planning at departmental level, including planning, organizing, leading, controlling, evaluating, and problem solving
- **Executive.** Organizational leadership and management skills, including developing the organizational vision, the corporate mission, strategic objectives, annual goals, businesses, broad strategies, policies, and systems

Source: Adapted from Public Relations Society of America. *Public Relations Professional Career Guide.*

on the job INSIGHTS

Wanted: A Public Relations Specialist

The following is a job description for an entry-level position that was posted on LinkedIn by a company in the Phoenix, Arizona, area:

Job Description

The public relations specialist will develop, execute and measure strategic communications, marketing and public relations plans under the direction of the firm's Public Relations Director. Typical projects may include developing brochures and marketing materials, newsletter and web content, editing monthly client reports, planning events, creating webinars, and filming and editing videos.

Many projects will be completed in coordination with subject-matter experts and/or vendors, such as graphic or web designers.

Key Responsibilities:

- Research, develop, execute and track communication plans on behalf of clients throughout the country
- Write and edit content for both print and electronic mediums
- Coordinate the design and production of print pieces, websites and videos, in conjunction with appropriate creative vendors and contractors
- Work closely with PR director to ensure client communication and public relations goals are being met; adjust plans when needed
- Manage a variety of projects from start to finish, keeping key stakeholders apprised of their status
- Maintain client websites
- Engage in media relations on behalf of clients and the firm
- Travel (in state and out of state) to client meetings to make presentations and identify potential new projects based on discussions and follow up

Desired Skills & Experience

- One to four years of public relations, marketing or journalism experience
- Ability to write persuasively on behalf of trade unions and other construction trades groups
- Ability to write well, manage multiple projects and meet deadlines in a fast-paced environment
- Understands business uses of social media or has willingness to learn
- Strong knowledge of MS Office, including Word, Excel, PowerPoint, Publisher and Outlook
- Fluent in AP Style
- Detail-oriented, self-directed and proactive work style
- Enjoys working as part of a team
- Bachelor's degree in public relations, communication, journalism or marketing

Other Requirements:

- Available for early morning, evening and weekend meetings and events, as necessary
- Access to reliable transportation for attending meetings, events and other client-related activities
- Available for occasional travel to in-state and out-of-state meetings or conferences

You should note that the department can only recommend this action. It would have no direct authority to decide on its own to hold an open house or to order various departments within the company to cooperate. If top management approves the proposal, the department may take responsibility for organizing the event. The CEO, as a line manager, has the authority to direct all departments to cooperate in the activity. Although public relations departments can function only with the approval of top management, there are varying levels of influence that these departments may exert. These levels will be discussed shortly.

Figure 4.3 **The Functions of a Corporate PR/Communications Department**

A number of functions are performed by corporate communications departments. The number-one function, according to a national survey by Corporate Communications International (CCI) of Baruch College/CUNY in New York is communications strategy, with 100 percent of the departments reporting that they perform that function. This list lists the top ten functions:

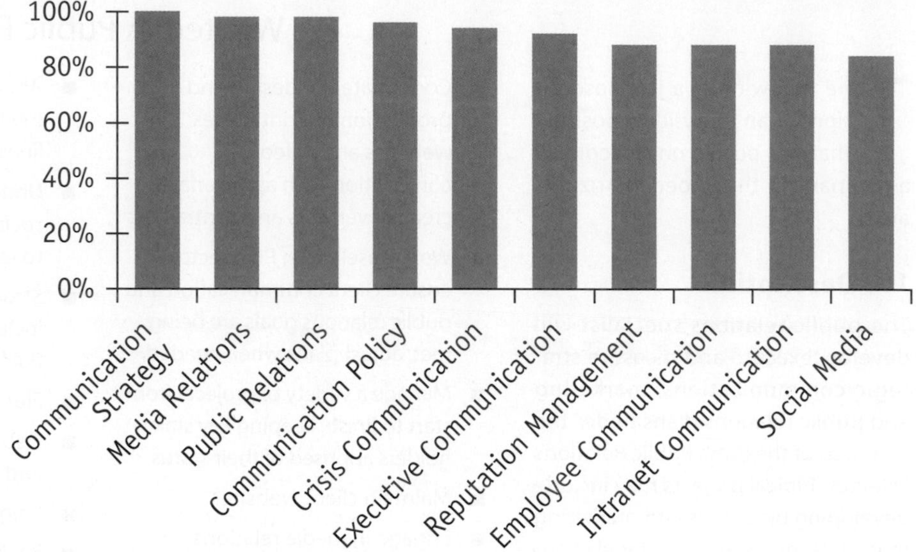

Source: "CCI Corporate Communication Practices and Trends, 2011, United States," page 29, by Corporate Communications International (CCI) of Baruch College/CUNY.

Access to Management The power and influence of a public relations department usually result from access to top management, which uses advice and recommendations to formulate policy. That is why public relations, as well as other staff functions, is located high in the organizational chart and is called on by top management to make reports and recommendations on issues affecting the entire company. In today's environment, public acceptance or nonacceptance of a proposed policy is an important factor in decision making—as important as costing and technological ability. This is why the former president of RJR Nabisco, F. Ross Johnson, told the *Wall Street Journal* in an interview that his senior public relations aide was "Numero Uno" and quipped, "He is the only one who has an unlimited budget and exceeds it every year." Being part of the executive suite also has its rewards. Citigroup's EVP of global public affairs, according to the *Wall Street Journal*, was hired at an annual salary of $1 million.

A significant part of our function has to do with strategic communications—altogether too much crisis communications.

John Buckley, EVP of corporate communications for AOL

Levels of Influence

Management experts state that staff functions in an organization operate at three levels of influence and authority: advisory, compulsory-advisory, and concurring authority.

Advisory On the lowest level, the staff function may be only *advisory*: Line management has no obligation to take recommendations or even request them. When public relations is purely advisory, it is often ineffective. A good example is the Toyota recall.

The auto company generated a great deal of public, legislative, and media criticism because its public relations department was relegated to a low level and was, for all practical purposes, nonexistent in the early stages of the crisis that caused Toyota's reputation for quality to fall off the charts.

Compulsory-Advisory Under the *compulsory-advisory* concept, organization policy requires that line managers (top management) at least listen to the appropriate staff experts before deciding on a strategy. Don Hellriegel and John Slocum, authors of the textbook *Management*, state: "Although such a procedure does not limit the manager's decision-making discretion, it ensures that the manager has made use of the specialized talents of the appropriate staff agency."

Johnson & Johnson is a good example. The Tylenol crisis, in which seven persons died after taking capsules containing cyanide, clearly demonstrated that the company based much of its reaction and quick recall of the product on the advice of its public relations staff. In this case, public relations was in a compulsory-advisory position, which is the most effective level of influence.

Concurring Authority This concept places public relations in the position of reviewing and approving all materials and communications with external audiences. For instance, an operating division wishing to publish a brochure or newsletter cannot do so unless the public relations department approves the key messages and design. If differences arise, the parties must agree before work can proceed.

Many firms use this mode to prevent departments and divisions from disseminating materials that do not conform to company graphic standards. In addition, the company must ascertain that its trademarks are used correctly to ensure continued protection. *Concurring authority*, however, may also limit the freedom of the public relations department. Some companies have a policy that all employee magazine articles and external news releases must be reviewed by the legal staff before publication. The material thus cannot be disseminated until legal and public relations personnel have agreed on what will be said.

Cooperation with Other Staff Functions

Ideally, public relations is part of the managerial subsystem and contributes to organizational strategy. Public relations is, say professors James and Larissa Grunig, "the management of communication between an organization and its publics." However, other staff functions also are involved in the communication process with internal and external publics. The four areas that require cooperation to avoid possible friction and turf battles are: (1) legal, (2) human resources, (3) advertising, and (4) marketing.

Legal The legal staff is concerned about the possible effect of any public statement on current or potential litigation. Consequently, lawyers often frustrate public relations personnel by taking the attitude that any public statement can potentially be used against the organization in a lawsuit. Conflicts over what to release, and when, often have a paralyzing effect on decision making, causing the organization to seem unresponsive to public concerns. This is particularly true in a crisis, when the public demands information immediately.

Human Resources The traditional personnel department has now evolved into the expanded role of "human resources," and there is often confusion over who is responsible for employee communications. Human resources personnel believe they should control the flow of information. Public relations counters that satisfactory external communications cannot be achieved unless effective employee relations are conducted simultaneously. Layoffs, for example, affect not only employees, but also the community and investors.

We're no longer in silos where marketing does its own thing, and PR does its own thing.

Kim Plaskett, director of corporate communications for Greyhound

Advertising Advertising and public relations departments often collide because they compete for funds to communicate with external audiences. Philosophical differences also arise. Advertising's approach to communications is, "Will it increase sales?" Public relations asks, "Will it make friends?" These differing orientations frequently cause breakdowns in coordination of overall strategy.

Marketing Marketing, like advertising, tends to think only of customers or potential buyers as key publics, whereas public relations defines publics in a broader way—any group that can have an impact on the operations of the organization. These publics include governmental agencies, environmental groups, neighborhood groups, and a host of other publics that marketing would not consider to be customers.

Logic dictates, however, that an organization needs a coordinated and integrated approach to its communications strategy. The following suggestions may help achieve this goal:

- Representatives of departments should serve together on key committees to exchange information on how various programs can complement each other to achieve overall organizational objectives. If representatives from human resources, public relations, legal, and investor relations present a united front to senior managers, their influence would likely be increased exponentially.
- Collaboration or coalition building among departments with shared interests in communication issues can also help achieve organization-wide business goals.
- Heads of departments should be equals in job title. In this way, the autonomy of one department is not subverted by that of another.
- All department heads should report to the same superior, so that all viewpoints can be considered before an appropriate strategy is formulated.
- Informal, regular contacts with representatives of other departments help dispel mindsets and create understanding and respect for each other's viewpoint.
- Written policies should be established to spell out the responsibilities of each department. Such policies are helpful in settling disputes over which department has authority to communicate with employees, create and control content on the organization's website, or alter a news release.

The Trend toward Outsourcing

A major trend in business today has been the outsourcing of services, whether they be telecommunications, accounting, customer service, software engineering, or even legal. The trend line is also for more organizations to outsource their communication activities to public relations firms and outside contractors. Indeed, the USC study found that *Fortune* 500 companies now spend 25 percent of their public relations budgets on outside firms. In addition, almost 90 percent of those companies use outside public relations counsel to varying degrees. See the PR Casebook on page 133 about a 7-Eleven campaign that used outside counsel.

We use agencies almost as extensions of our internal staff. We work as partners.

Paul James, communications manager of Harley-Davidson

PRCasebook

7-Eleven Celebrates Its Birthday with 5 Million Free Slurpees

The nation's largest convenient store chain, 7-Eleven, celebrates its birthday on July 11 every year by giving a free Slurpee to its customers. The year 2011, however, called for a special once-in-a-lifetime celebration because the date would be 7/11/11. The idea was to have a campaign that would transform its ordinary 84th birthday celebration into a major event.

Ketchum was retained to spearhead the public relations campaign with the theme "Our Birthday: Your Bash." There were two objectives to capitalize on the unique 7/11/11 date: (1) increase store traffic and sales, and (2) enhance the visibility of 7-Eleven and its Slurpee brand through national media coverage, social media conversation, and grassroots engagement. The campaign had three components:

First Phase

- The "Year of 7-11" is launched on Facebook and Twitter.
- On the seventh day of every month, fans are asked to answer 7-Eleven trivia questions using the hashtag "#YearOf711."

Second Phase

- Downloadable party hats/confetti and a free Slurpee coupon redeemable on 7/11 are posted. Facebook fans are asked to post birthday photos/videos.
- A video is distributed showing a Slurpee drink-themed cake designed by the "Cake Boss" and birthday expert Buddy Valastro.
- News releases and features are distributed to print, online, and broadcast outlets.

Third Phase

- The birthday celebration takes place at 7-Elevens across the country.
- Morning talk show hosts and DJs sip Slurpees on air, local media covers in-store celebrations, and in-store games are held in 18 markets.

Results

- Five million Slurpees are given away on 7/11.
- A new record is set in single-day store traffic and sales.
- There were 3,000 media placements, including *Good Morning America, CNN, MSNBC, USA Today, New York Times,* and *Huffington Post.*
- The Slurpee drink received 15 minutes of airtime during *Today's* 7/11/11 broadcast.
- There was a 38 percent increase in Facebook fans, raising the total to 865,000.
- 7-Eleven and Slurpee ranked #1 and #3 on U.S. *Google Trends Hot Searches* on 7/11.

The campaign received a 2012 PRSA Silver Anvil Award in the marketing consumer products category.

A national survey by *PRWeek* found that companies of all sizes spend more than 40 percent of their public relations budget on the services of outside firms. In high technology, the percentage was even higher—a whopping 66 percent of the corporate budget. In contrast, nonprofits allocate an average of 38 percent of their budget for external public relations services.

The most frequent reason given for outsourcing is to bring expertise and resources to the organization that can't be found internally. A number of outside providers, for example, provide software programs for monitoring and measuring a client's publicity efforts. A second reason is the need to supplement internal staffs during peak periods of activity. The most frequently outsourced activities, according to a study by Bisbee & Co. and Leone Marketing Research, are, in descending order, (1) writing and communications, (2) media relations, (3) publicity, (4) strategy and planning, and (5) event planning.

Public relations firms, and the services they offer, are discussed next.

Public Relations Firms

American public relations firms have proliferated in proportion to the trend toward outsourcing, which has just been mentioned. The growth of the global economy has also helped. As American companies expanded into booming domestic and worldwide markets, many corporations felt a need for public relations firms that could provide

Figure 4.4 This ad from Ruder Finn focuses on its creative capabilities to serve clients

them with professional expertise in communications to reach specific publics at the national and international level.

Executives of public relations firms predict even more growth, as more countries adopt free-market economies and as Internet applications continue to expand. The major growth is in the BRIC nations—Brazil, Russia, India, and China.

Services Provided by Firms

Today, public relations firms provide a variety of services:

- **Marketing communications.** This involves promoting products and services through such tools as news releases, feature stories, special events, brochures, and media tours.
- **Executive speech training.** Top executives are coached on public affairs activities, including personal appearances.
- **Research and evaluation.** Scientific surveys are conducted to measure public attitudes and perceptions.
- **Crisis communication.** Management is counseled on what to say and do in an emergency such as an oil spill or a recall of an unsafe product.
- **Media analysis.** Appropriate media, including social media, are examined for their ability to target specific messages to key audiences.
- **Community relations.** Management is counseled on ways to achieve official and public support for such projects as building or expanding a factory.
- **Events management.** News conferences, anniversary celebrations, rallies, symposiums, and national conferences are planned and conducted.
- **Public affairs.** Materials and testimony are prepared for government hearings and regulatory bodies, and background briefings are prepared.
- **Branding and corporate reputation.** Advice is given on programs to establish a company brand and its reputation for quality.
- **Financial relations.** Management is counseled on ways to avoid takeover by another firm and effectively communicate with stockholders, security analysts, and institutional investors.

"Young people today need heroes—that's why I hired a P.R. firm."

on the job

SOCIAL MEDIA IN ACTION

Sterling Vineyards Finds the Perfect Host

Sterling Vineyards, a well-established winery, had an image problem. It was well respected (the official wine of the Academy Awards for five years in a row), but was perceived as a bit stodgy and less appealing to a new, more contemporary consumer.

The winery engaged public relations firm Taylor Global to come up with an integrated campaign that would use social media to advance the brand. The strategy was to create the Ultimate Host Challenge that would use an online competition to reach the target audience personified as "Eve." This imaginary woman was 37, married with one daughter, stylish, and living in suburban Southern California. She had a flair for hosting informal gatherings, used social media channels, and consumed online information about food and entertainment. To reach "Eve," Sterling created "The Sterling Ultimate Host" campaign to find the woman who could be a brand ambassador to personify Sterling as an authentic, open, and accessible brand for every occasion.

The campaign was launched on Sterling's Facebook page supplemented with point-of-purchase displays and advertising. The competition to find the "Ultimate Host" was conducted on Facebook with four challenges: Entertaining on a Dime, Date Night, Wine & Foodie Movie, and Host's Choice. A winner of each challenge was selected and competed in a grand finale in New York City. The top prize was being named "Sterling Ultimate Host," a cash prize, a trip to Sterling Vineyards, and a position as brand spokesperson for six months. Hosting the campaign was renowned foodie and chef Padma Lakshmi who issued the challenges via video postings on Sterling's Facebook page. Fans were encouraged to enter by submitting videos, text, and photos. Lakshmi was also featured in *Wine Spectator*, *Real Simple*, and *Sunset* magazines. In addition, outreach was made to national media outlets, women's lifestyle writers, and influential wine bloggers.

The campaign had the following results:

- Sales increased by more than 10 percent.
- Almost 60 national placements were achieved, which included *Fox & Friends*, *People*, and *Wine Spectator*.
- Facebook fans increased from 2,400 to 34,700 and Sterling was perceived as more youthful, playful, and fresher for younger consumers.
- Wine distributors reported that stores stocked more Sterling wines.

The Sterling campaign received a Silver Anvil Excellence Award from PRSA in the category of integrated communications—consumer products.

Public relations firms also offer specialty areas of service as trend lines are identified. Burson-Marsteller now has a practice specialty in labor to help corporations deal with unions. Earlier, the firm set up a specialty area in environmental communications. Other firms offer specialty services in such areas as integrated marketing, crisis management, technology, and health care. Fleishman-Hillard has even formed an animal care practice group to serve the growing interest in the health of the country's pets. More recently, many public relations firms have added digital and social media as a specialty area of practice. Weber Shandwick, for example, has created a division focused on content creation and distribution under the rubric of "branded journalism." This is further discussed in Chapter 13.

The variety of services and counseling offered to clients has also led many firms to rebrand themselves in recent years. One result is that only 6 of the 50 largest firms

on the job INSIGHTS

The Secret Life of Working in a Public Relations Firm

By: Kellie Bramlet

Public relations agency life is not for the timid. Nor the dull nor the dependent upon eight hours of nightly sleep. Agency life is for the bold, the creative and the iPhone-addicted. Luckily for us, there's no short supply of those qualities around these parts.

It's not all glamorous parties and getting paid to spend hours on Facebook (although there is some of that too). Agency life is tough work, but rewarding too. Here's a look at what drives our days.

Constant Creative Demand

Whether it's delivering a gorilla suit, learning the secret language in "A Clockwork Orange," or letting an antique deli scale ride shotgun, it's all in a day's work for a PR agency pro. There's just no "typical day." While others are idling away in cubicles, watching the clock tick-tock, we're dreaming up crazy catchy campaign slogans, dashing to drop off media deliveries and crafting infographic press releases.

We're the ones saving ideas on their cell phones during dinner with friends on a Friday night. We're the ones taking notes at a music festival because we've drawn some parallel between the crowd interaction and potential client engagement tactics. We're the ones fighting the urge to text and drive because we drove past something that made us think. We're always on. Because inspiration is everywhere—and our brains never stop.

Continuous Gear Shifting and Learning

Health care legislation on tap one day and restaurant menu writing the next day. Or maybe the next hour. Working at an agency requires a quick-shifting mind and a continuous burn to learn. Because we're always working with new clients in new industries, boredom just doesn't exist behind agency walls.

Fun? Yes. Easy? Hardly. Agency life requires you to know a lot about a lot. Your clients expect you to be on your game every day. So brush up, take notes and study hard. Do that and you'll always get the facts right. And just remember when in doubt, don't just double check. Triple check.

Multiple Personalities. Or At Least Perspectives

PR pros have to be able to communicate to a wide variety of audiences, from your Pinterest-obsessed best friend to your dad, who just called and asked you to teach him to post Facebook photos over the phone. In order to do that effectively, we have to be able to consider how each of these very different groups will interpret each message. Yes, empathy isn't just a quality that will make you a great friend, but it will make you a great agency staff member.

A ~~Little~~ A LOT of Initiative

Public relations professionals get to make stuff happen. We're never

waiting around for the story to break. We're out and about, building the buzz ourselves.

That's what you've got to do to stay ahead. Your clients don't want to tell you what to do. You're the expert, so get out there, and start doing it. Pitch stories about the amazing work your clients are doing or help them do some amazing work. Come on. Who doesn't love knowing what's on the front page before everybody else?

Yep. We're pretty lucky to be in the gig we're in. Never bored and always on the go. That's agency life in a nutshell. Sure it's crazy, but we wouldn't have it any other way.

Kellie Bramlet is an account executive at The Black Sheep Agency, a Houston-based firm specializing in public relations, social media, and marketing. A version of this essay appeared on the firm's blog and was further distributed by www.ragan.com

in the United States now have "public relations" in their name. Instead they just use a name such as Edelman, Ketchum, or even Cohn &Wolfe. Jacqueline Kolek, a senior director at Peppercomm, told *PRWeek*, "We've evolved as the industry has into a truly integrated communications firm."

Increasingly, public relations firms emphasize the counseling aspect of their services, although most of their revenues still come from implementing tactical aspects such as writing news releases and organizing special events or media tours. The transition to counseling is best expressed by Harold Burson, chairman of Burson-Marsteller, who once told an audience, "In the beginning, top management used to say to us, 'Here's the message, deliver it.' Then it became, 'What should we say?' Now, in smart organizations, it's 'What should we do?' "

Because of the counseling function, we use the phrase *public relations firm* instead of *agency* throughout this book. Advertising firms, in contrast, are properly called *agencies* because they serve as agents, buying time or space on behalf of a client.

A good source of information about public relations counseling is the Council of Public Relations Firms, which has about 100 member firms. The group provides information on its website (www.prfirms.org) about trends in the industry, how to select a public relations firm, and career advice.

Global Reach

Public relations firms, large and small, usually are found in metropolitan areas. On an international level, firms and their offices or affiliates are situated in the world's major cities and capitals. Edelman Worldwide, the world's largest independently owned firm, has about 4,600 employees and 63 offices in almost 30 nations. Fleishman-Hillard has 2,600 employees in 85 offices around the world. Ketchum, another major international firm, has about 75 offices and 2,500 employees. Some examples of campaigns conducted in other nations are highlighted in the Insights box that follows on page 139.

International outreach is important because most major public relations firms generate substantial revenues from international clients, including U.S. companies with operations abroad. The MSL Group and Hill+Knowlton, for example, get an estimated 60 percent of their revenue from foreign clients. And Burson-Marsteller gets about 55 percent. See the chart of the top 10 public relations firms on page 140.

International work isn't only for large firms. Small- and medium-sized firms around the world have also formed working partnerships with each other to serve international client needs. The largest in terms of revenues is PR Organization International (PROI) with 56 independent partners in 50 nations. Another major group is Worldcom, with 110 partners in 48 nations. A new network, PRBoutiques International has 32 partner firms in 11 nations. Essentially, firms in such networks as PROI cooperate with each other to service clients with international needs. A firm in India, for example, may call its partner in Los Angeles to handle the details of events and news coverage for a visiting trade delegation from India. More information about global public relations is found in Chapter 20.

The Rise of Communication Conglomerates

Today, both public relations firms and advertising agencies have become part of large, diversified holding companies with global reach. In fact, an estimated 60 percent of the global business in public relations is now conducted by firms owned by holding companies that also own not only public relations firms and advertising agencies, but also marketing firms, billboard companies, direct mail firms, and specialty shops in social media, events, and celebrity placements. The following are the four major holding companies, according to *PRWeek*'s 2012 rankings.

WPP Group This London-based conglomerate is the largest with revenues of $15.4 billion. It has a stable of major public relations firms, including Hill+Knowlton Strategies, Burson-Marsteller, Ogilvy PR Worldwide, and Cohn & Wolfe.

Omnicom This holding company, with headquarters in New York, has worldwide revenues of $13.9 billion. It owns such leading public relations firms as Ketchum, Porter Novelli, Fleishman-Hillard, and Cone Communications.

Publicis Groupe Based in Paris, this holding company has revenues of $7.8 billion. Its major public relations firm in the United States is MSL Group, but the holding company also owns major firms in Europe and Asia.

Interpublic Group IPG, based in New York, has $7 billion in worldwide revenues. In addition to several major advertising agencies, it has several major public relations firms, including Weber Shandwick, GolinHarris, Carmichael Lynch Spong, and DeVries PR. It, like the other major holding companies, is continually expanding operations in such developing markets as Brazil, India, Russia, and China.

on the job INSIGHTS

American PR Firms Have Global Clients

The client list of American public relations firms often includes foreign companies and governments.

Ogilvy Asia-Pacific. The firm helped Nestle (a Swiss-based company) launch an integrated social media campaign in China to promote its new banana-shaped ice cream product, BenNaNa. Part of the strategy was to highlight the product's "peel-able" nature and target "kiddults," ages 18 to 31, who were encouraged to post photos, videos, and designs on Weibo, a Chinese microblogging site. Within three months, BenNaNa generated more than 4.6 million Weibo tweets and was the top trending topic for two weeks. The company encouraged photos of individuals peeling or eating the product by offering a banana-shaped pillow, which resulted in 86 percent of the original tweets being posted with a photo. In addition, Ogilvy created a microsite, which included photos and stories. Three BenNaNa prank videos received more than 150,000 views and inspired consumers to submit their own pranks. As a result, the new product rapidly became Nestle's #1 ice cream brand in sales volume.

Colangelo & Partners Public Relations. This New York firm worked with the Japan Sake and Shochu Makers Association to introduce shochu, a distilled beverage popular in Japan, to the American public. Using the theme, "The National Spirit of Japan," the firm created Facebook and Twitter pages and promoted various events. It arranged for free tastings at three upscale restaurants in New York City and also worked with the Astor Center in New York, a prominent wine institute, to have a tasting seminar led by an expert mixologist. More than 200 industry representatives and 400 consumers attended. Coverage included the *New York Times* and *Time* magazine.

Ketchum. The firm has represented the Russian Federation since 2006, and one of its recent campaigns was to position Russia as "Europe's Bright Light of Growth" in order to generate more foreign investment in the country. Another objective was to improve Western perceptions of two-time Russian President Vladimir Putin's government. One strategy was the placement of op-eds by various business executives in such media as the *Huffington Post* and *CNBC* that carried out the theme of Russia being the "most dynamic place on the continent."

on the job

INSIGHTS

Top 10 Public Relations Firms

PRWeek annually ranks public relations firms by global revenue. Its 2013 ranking of the top 10 are listed below. The figures shown are educated estimates because all the firms, except independently owned Edelman, are part of conglomerates that don't officially release revenues of its various units.

NAME OF FIRM	TOTAL GLOBAL REVENUE IN $ MILLIONS	PERCENT FROM U.S. INCOME	PERCENT FROM FOREIGN INCOME	EMPLOYEES WORLDWIDE
Edelman Worldwide	665	61	39	4,600
Weber Shandwick	535	72.8	27.2	n/a
Fleishman-Hillard	550	66.3	33.7	2,650
Ketchum	450	64.4	35.6	2,500
Burson-Marsteller	450	45.5	54.5	2,300
MSL Group	485	38.1	61.9	3,400
Hill+Knowlton Strategies	380	39.4	60.6	2,500
Ogilvy PR	300	50	50	2,000
GolinHarris	150	66.6	33.4	n/a
Porter Novelli	140	71.4	28.6	n/a

Source: Compiled and adapted from Agency business report (2013, May). *PRWeek*, 25–85.

Large conglomerates acquire public relations firms for several reasons. One is the natural evolutionary step of integrating various communication disciplines into "total communication networks." Supporters of integration say that no single-function agency or firm is equipped with the personnel or resources to handle complex, often global, integrated marketing functions efficiently for a client. In addition, joint efforts by public relations and advertising professionals can offer prospective clients greater communications impact, help them generate more business, and help them expand the number of their geographical locations around the world. London-based WPP, for example, now employs 69,000 people in more than 100 nations because most campaigns, even global ones, must still be tailored to local customs, ethnic groups, and religious preferences.

Structure of a Counseling Firm

You should not conclude, however, that all public relations firms have large staffs and global outreach. Of the 1,600 firms listed in *O'Dwyer's Directory of Public Relations Firms*, most have less than 10 employees. A small public relations firm may consist only of the owner (president), a vice president, and several account executives and administrative assistants. Larger firms have a more extended hierarchy.

The organization of Ketchum in San Francisco is fairly typical. The president is based in Ketchum's New York office, so the executive vice president is the on-site director in San Francisco. A senior vice president is associate director of operations. Next in line are several vice presidents, who primarily do account supervision or special projects.

An account supervisor is in charge of one major account or several smaller ones. An account executive, who reports to the supervisor, is in direct contact with the client and handles most of the day-to-day activity. At the bottom of the list is the assistant account executive, who does routine maintenance work, compiling media lists, gathering information, and writing rough drafts of news releases.

Recent college graduates usually start as assistant account executives. Once they learn the firm's procedures and show ability, promotion to account executive may occur within 6 to 18 months. After two or three years, it is not uncommon for an account executive to become an account supervisor.

Executives at or above the vice presidential level usually are heavily involved in selling their firm's services. In order to prosper, a firm must continually seek new business and sell additional services to current clients. Consequently, the upper management of the firm calls on prospective clients, prepares proposals, and makes new business presentations. In this very competitive field, a firm not adept at selling itself frequently fails. See the Insights box on page 142 for a job description for an account executive at a public relations firm.

How Public Relations Firms Get Business

Organizations, even if they have internal public relations staff, often use the services of public relations firms because they need supplemental staffing, help with a special project, or specific expertise in a particular situation. In fact, the Strategic Public Relations Center at the University of Southern California (USC) reports that public and private companies spend about 25 percent of their total public relations budget on the services of public relations firms.

A common approach to engaging the services of a public relations firm is to issue what is called a "Request for Proposal," known as an RFP. Firms are invited to make a presentation regarding their capabilities and express their ideas about what program they would create to address the potential client's particular needs.

A typical RFP was one issued by Dow Chemical to select a firm to support its sponsorship of the 2014 Sochi Winter Olympics. Several major public relations firms were asked to bid on the $1 million account. Needless to say, this is a highly competitive situation and firms use their most skilled presenters to "sell" their services and ideas. See the Insights box on page 144 about an RFP issued by the Kenya Tourism Board.

Pros and Cons of Using a Public Relations Firm

Because public relations is a service industry, a firm's major asset is the quality of its people. Potential clients thinking about hiring a public relations firm usually base their decisions on that fact, according to a survey of *Fortune* 500 corporate vice presidents.

Basic attributes that an organization wants from a firm, according to another survey of 600 clients, are (1) understanding your business and the industry, (2) responding

on the job INSIGHTS

Wanted: An Account Executive for a Public Relations Firm

Recent graduates often begin their careers at a public relations firm. The following job description for an assistant account executive/account executive was posted on LinkedIn by a New York public relations firm. The firm received almost 350 applications.

Responsibilities

Media Relations

- Understand how to approach different media outlets and know their deadlines
- Develop a strong knowledge of the traditional media and social media that influence your client's customers, prospects, and investors
- Draft media result reports; analyze campaign results through use of PR measurement tools, develop executive summaries and reports based on campaign objectives, package results for your clients
- Maintain and continue to develop strong relationships with journalists who cover your clients' business and industries
- Build and maintain editorial and speaking calendars

Client Services

- Demonstrate expertise in your clients' business and industry, and know your clients' competitors
- Enhance your knowledge about your clients' competitive environment by reading industry trade publications and monitoring competitive activity
- Serve as the "go to" client contact for information
- Participate in client conference calls and attend meetings

Administrative

- Scan media for accurate coverage of clients, draft meeting agendas, and compile media clips

Required Expertise

Writing Skills

- Refined writing skills with understanding of your target audience
- Ability to do compelling narratives and storytelling
- Write and edit first drafts of news releases, fact sheets, Q&As, pitch letters, bios, and activity reports
- Proficiency to proofread and edit materials and client correspondence

Presentation Skills

- Assist in development of materials for presentations
- Be able to clearly express yourself and present in front of a group

Additional Skills

- Know how to use media databases and other software programs
- Be able to do time management and prioritize tasks on multiple accounts
- Exhibit resourcefulness in asking questions and looking for answers
- Proficient use of Microsoft Office, Outlook

Background Requirements

- Bachelor's degree in public relations or related field
- 1–3 years relevant experience
- Strong interest in financial services, technology, and business-to-business (b2b) communications
- "Team player" mindset and willingness to work collaboratively with peers

to all your needs and requests in a timely manner, and (3) working within your budget. Clients also give high priority to (1) accurate work, (2) high-quality staff, (3) consistent delivery of key messages to target audiences, (4) outstanding client service, (5) a measurable return on investment, and (6) creative programs that meet business objectives.

Both firms and potential clients also consider possible conflicts of interest. A firm, for example, cannot ethically represent two clients that are direct competitors such as Coca-Cola and Pepsi. Other concerns can also come up. Chevron, for example, cancelled its contract with Ogilvy PR because the firm was also working with Environmental Defense, a nonprofit that supported a multi-billion dollar lawsuit against a Chevron subsidiary. See the Ethics box on page 145 about a client cancelling a contract with a public relations firm.

Public relations firms must also be careful about "poaching" each other's employees, especially if a person moves to another firm and takes an account with them. Weber Shandwick, for example, sued Hill+Knowlton (H+K) when two employees left the firm and then solicited staffers and clients to join them at H+K.

Advantages Public relations firms offer several advantages:

- **Objectivity.** The firm can analyze a client's needs or problems from a new perspective and offer fresh insights.
- **A variety of skills and expertise.** The firm has specialists, whether in speech writing, trade magazine placement, investor relations, or identifying influential bloggers.
- **Extensive resources.** The firm has abundant media contacts and works regularly with numerous suppliers of products and services. It has research materials, including data information banks, and experience in similar fields.
- **Offices throughout the country.** A national public relations program requires coordination in major cities. Large firms have on-site staffs or affiliate firms in many cities around the world.
- **Special problem-solving skills.** A firm may have extensive experience and a solid reputation in desired areas. For example, Burson-Marsteller is well known for its expertise in crisis communications, health and medical issues, and international coordination of special projects. Hill+Knowlton is known for its expertise in public affairs, and Ketchum is the expert in consumer marketing.
- **Credibility.** A successful public relations firm has a solid reputation for professional, ethical work. If represented by such a firm, a client is likely to get more attention among opinion leaders in mass media, government, and the financial community.

Disadvantages There are also drawbacks to using public relations firms:

- **Superficial grasp of a client's unique problems.** Although objectivity is gained from an outsider's perspective, there is often a disadvantage if the public relations firm does not thoroughly understand the client's business or needs.
- **Lack of full-time commitment.** A public relations firm has many clients. Therefore, no single client can monopolize its personnel and other resources.
- **Need for prolonged briefing period.** Some companies become frustrated because time and money are needed for a public relations firm to research the organization and make recommendations. Consequently, the actual start of a public relations program may take weeks or months.
- **Resentment by internal staff.** The public relations staff members of a client organization may resent the use of outside counsel, seeing it as an implication that they lack the ability to do the job.

on the job INSIGHTS

Kenya Looks for a Public Relations Firm

Its common practice for organizations seeking public relations counsel to issue a Request for Proposal (RFP). The Kenya Tourism Board, for example, issued a 57-page RFP to solicit proposals from public relations firms to promote the country as a major destination for commercial visitors and tourists.

The RFP calls for separate applications from public relations firms based in such areas as the United States, China, Europe, India, and the Middle East. The winning firms would be expected to do such activities as (1) create and distribute publicity about Kenya's game parks and other attractions, (2) organize seminars and tours of the country by travel writers, (3) organize news conferences in select markets to enhance a positive image of the country abroad, and (4) emphasize that Kenya is safe to visit despite some outbreaks of ethnic violence in rural areas and along the Kenya–Somali border.

The RFP outlines a detailed process for evaluating proposals and the qualifications of public relations firms that may wish to apply. The following are some requirements that are evaluated on a point system:

- Any public relations firm is automatically disqualified if they already represent other African destinations, including Indian Ocean nations such as the Seychelles.
- Account personnel must have more than five years experience in marketing a destination.
- The firm must demonstrate experience in managing a high-budget integrated campaign that includes digital, electronic, print, and interactive media.
- Experience in working with tour operators, airlines, travel agents, and other members of the tourism industry.
- A description of the firm's organization and an outline of recent experience on assignments of a similar nature.
- A detailed CV of the firm's employees that would be assigned to the account.

- A detailed list of strategies that would be used and a breakdown of the cost per activity.
- A certified audit regarding the financial health and stability of the public relations firm.

Responding to an RFP requires considerable thought on the part of a public relations firm. It must first decide if it has the staffing and capabilities to successfully compete. Second, they have to decide whether the size of the potential contract is worth the time and effort of their staff to develop a comprehensive proposal. And finally, the firm has to realistically assess the odds of getting the contract.

- **Need for strong direction by top management.** High-level executives must take the time to brief outside counsel on the specific objectives sought.
- **Need for full information and confidence.** A client must be willing to share its information, including the skeletons in the closet, with outside counsel.
- **Costs.** Outside counsel is expensive. In many situations, routine public relations work can be handled at lower cost by internal staff.

on the job

ETHICS

PR Firm Dropped by Wal-Mart for Ethical Lapse

Mercury Public Affairs in Los Angeles was dropped by Wal-Mart after one of its senior associates posed as a University of Southern California (USC) student journalist at a union meeting urging Wal-Mart employees to unionize.

Stephanie Harnett, a 26-year-old employee of Mercury Public Affairs, was "outed" by Warehouse Workers United after she attended a news conference as "Zoe Mitchell" and even interviewed a worker, according to the group. The Mercury firm, at the time, was retained by Wal-Mart to lobby officials at Los Angeles City Hall over a proposed Wal-Mart grocery in the Chinatown area which had met with community and labor opposition.

Mercury executives issued a statement that Harnett's actions "were in no way approved, authorized, or directed by Wal-Mart or Mercury." The statement further stated, "She showed very poor judgment and Mercury takes full responsibility. We are taking the necessary disciplinary actions."

The fallout, however, was immediate. Harnett left the firm and Wal-Mart cancelled its contract with Mercury Public Affairs. Steve Restivo, senior director of community affairs for Wal-Mart issued a statement saying, "Our culture of integrity is a constant at Wal-Mart and by not properly identifying herself, this individual's behavior was contrary to our values and the way we do business."

Coverage of this situation in the public relations trade press caused some raised eyebrows among public relations professionals who wondered whether Harnett would have posed as a journalist on her own without the knowledge of her supervisors. They also wonder if she, at her lower level position, became the scapegoat in an attempt to save the account. What do you think? What lesson can you learn from this situation?

Fees and Charges

A public relations firm charges for its services in several ways. The three most common methods are:

- **Basic hourly fee, plus out-of-pocket expenses.** This method is commonly used by attorneys, accounting firms, and management consultants. The number of hours spent on a client's account is tabulated each month and billed to the client. Work by personnel is billed at various hourly rates. Out-of-pocket expenses, such as cab fares, car rentals, airline tickets, and meals, are also billed to the client. In a typical $100,000 public relations campaign, about 70 percent of the budget is spent on staff salaries.
- **Retainer fee.** A basic monthly charge billed to the client covers ordinary administrative and overhead expenses for maintaining the account and being "on call" for advice and strategic counseling. Many clients have in-house capabilities for executing communication campaigns but often need the advice of experts during the planning phase. Many retainer fees also specify the number of hours the firm will spend on an account each month. Any additional work is billed at normal hourly rates. Out-of-pocket expenses are usually billed separately.
- **Fixed project fee.** The public relations firm agrees to do a specific project, such as an annual report, a newsletter, or a special event, for a fixed fee. For example,

on the job INSIGHTS

Your Choice: A Corporation or a PR Firm?

Recent college graduates often ponder the pros and cons of joining a corporate department or going to work for a public relations firm. The following summarizes some of the pluses and minuses:

PR FIRM: BREADTH OF EXPERIENCE	CORPORATE PR: DEPTH OF EXPERIENCE
Jobs as administrative assistant or assistant account executive often considered entry-level for college grads.	Jobs more difficult to find without experience; duties more narrowly focused.
Variety. Usually work with several clients and projects at same time.	Sometimes little variety at entry level.
Possibility of rapid advancement.	Growth sometimes limited unless you are willing to switch employers.
Fast-paced, exciting.	Can be slower-paced.
Seldom see the impact of your work for a client; removed from "action."	Heavy involvement with executive staff; see impact almost instantly. You are an important component in the "big picture."
Abilities get honed and polished. (This is where a mentor really helps.) High emphasis on tactical skills, production of materials.	Same "client" all the time. Advantage: Get to know organization really well. Disadvantage: Can become boring.
Networking with other professionals leads to better job opportunities.	Sometimes so involved in your work, you don't have time for networking.
Learn other skills, such as how to do presentations and budgets and establish deadlines.	Strength in all areas expected. Not a lot of time for coaching by peers.
Intense daily pressure on billable hours, high productivity. Some firms are real "sweatshops."	Less intense daily pressure; more emphasis on accomplishing longer-term results.
Somewhat high employment turnover.	Less turnover.
Budgets and resources can be limited.	More resources usually available.
Salary traditionally low at entry level.	Salaries tend to be higher.
Insurance, medical benefits can be minimal.	Benefits usually good, sometimes excellent.
Little opportunity for profit sharing, stock options.	More opportunities available.

a counseling firm may maintain a client's online newsroom for $75,000 annually. The fixed fee is the least popular among public relations firms because it is difficult to predict all work and expenses in advance. Many clients, however, like fixed fees for a specific project because it is easier to budget and there are no "surprises."

A fourth method not widely used is to charge clients on the basis of successful media placements. PRServe, for example, charges a flat rate of $425 to $750 for each story that the firm places on behalf of a client. The vast majority of public relations firms and media outlets, however, consider the concept somewhat unprofessional and even unethical. Public relations firms say it negates the whole concept of counseling and reduces the concept of public relations to simply a publicity function. It's also a poor business model because revenue is based on the independent decisions of editors to run a story. Media also bristle at the thought of publicists getting paid on the basis of an editor's independent judgment to run an article. TechCrunch, according to *O'Dwyer's Newsletter*, banned pitches from PRServe after finding out that the firm was getting paid on basis of placements.

The primary basis of the three standard methods—the basic hourly fee, the retainer fee, and the fixed project fee—is to estimate the number of hours that a particular project will take to plan, execute, and evaluate. The first method—the basic hourly fee—is the most flexible and most widely used among large firms. It is preferred by public relations people because they are paid for the exact number of hours spent on a project and because it is the only sound way that a fee can be determined intelligently. The retainer fee and the fixed project fee are based on an estimate of how many hours it will take to service a client.

A number of variables are considered when a public relations firm estimates the cost of a program. These may include the size and duration of the project, the geographical locations involved, the number of personnel assigned to the project, and the type of client. A major variable, of course, is billing the use of the firm's personnel to a client at the proper hourly rate.

The standard industry practice is for account executives to achieve 90 percent billable hours and generate revenue equal to three times their salary. This multiple allows the firm to pay for such overhead expenses as office space, equipment, insurance, supplies, utilities, and even some potted plants. Of course, the object is to also make a net profit of 15 to 20 percent before taxes. Thus, the billing rate of a senior account executive could easily reach $200+ per hour, which one study by an executive search firm found was about the national average.

The primary income of a public relations firm comes from the selling of staff time, but some additional income results from markups on photocopying, travel expenses, and materials provided by vendors such as graphic designers. The standard markup in the trade is between 15 and 20 percent.

Summary

Public Relations Departments

- Most organizations have a public relations department, which is often called *corporate communications*.
- Organizations, depending on their culture and management, structure the public relations function in various ways.
- Public relations professionals often serve at the tactical level, but others are counselors to the top executive and have a major role in policy making.
- In management theory, public relations is a staff function rather than a line function.

Public Relations Firms

- Public relations firms come in all sizes, are found worldwide, and provide a variety of services.
- Many large, international firms are part of giant communication conglomerates.
- The advantages of using outside firms include versatility and extensive resources.
- Revenues primarily come from charging a basic hourly fee, plus out-of-pocket expenses.

Case Activity Planning a Career in Public Relations

You will graduate from college in several months and plan on pursuing a career in public relations. After applying for a number of positions, you receive two job offers.

One is with a national chain of pizza parlors. The corporate communications department has about 20 professionals, and it is customary for beginners to start in employee relations and write articles for the company's website and intranet. Later, with more experience, you might be assigned to do marketing communications or work in a specialized area such as investor relations, governmental affairs, or even community relations.

The second job offer is from a local office of a large, national public relations firm. You would begin as an assistant account executive and work on several accounts, including a chain of fast-food restaurants and a manufacturer of computer keyboards. The starting pay is about the same, but the pizza chain offers better health and pension benefits. Taking into consideration the pros and cons of working for public relations firms versus corporations, what job would best fit your abilities and preferences? Explain your reasons.

Questions For Review and Discussion

1. How have the role and function of public relations departments changed in recent years?
2. In what ways do the structure and culture of an organization affect the role and influence of the public relations department?
3. What are the top five activities of a public relations department, according to a survey by CCI?
4. What are the key responsibility areas of a PR manager working in an organization?
5. What is the difference between a line function and a staff function? To which function does public relations belong, and why?
6. Why is a compulsory-advisory role within an organization a good role for a public relations department to have?
7. Read the job description for a public relations specialist (page 129) and the job description for an account executive at a public relations firm (page 142). In what ways are they similar in terms of qualifications and skills required? How are they different?
8. What four areas in an organization have the potential for friction with the public relations department?
9. How and why is the PR department relevant to other departments, such as human resources, marketing, and legal, in an organization?
10. Why would an organization that has an internal public relations department also retain a public relations consultancy?
11. What are the four largest communications conglomerates in the world?
12. How important is international business to American public relations firms?
13. What were IBM's four objectives during the globally celebration of its hundredth birthday?
14. If you were offered a job in the public relations department of an organization and a public relations consultancy with almost similar pay and perks, which would you choose and why?

Media Resources

Agency business report (2012, May). *PRWeek*, 22–82.

Armitage, C., & Samson, D. (2012, May). Should clients be more understanding about potential account conflicts? *PRWeek*, 15.

Chan, A., & Geller, B. (2013, March). Is the traditional PR agency structure broken in the age of digital comms? *PRWeek*, 23.

Gallicano, T., Curtin, P., & Mattews, K. (2012). I Love What I Do, but…A relationship management survey of millennial generation public relations agency employees. *Journal of Public Relations Research, 24*, 222–242.

Gingerich, J. (2012, June). Membership, revenues surge for global PR networks. *O'Dwyer's PR Report*, 14–18.

Howell, A. (2012, January 27). 14 essentials for PR newbies. Retrieved from www.prdaily.com

Meng, J., Berger, B., & Gower, K. (2012). A test of excellent leadership in public relations: Key qualities, valuable sources, and distinctive leadership perceptions. *Journal of Public Relations Research, 24*, 18–36.

Salerno, D. (2012, July). Time is money: How to improve your agency's profitability. *Public Relations Tactics*, 16.

Shearman, S. (2013, April). Essential guide: Independent agency networks. *PRWeek*, 38–39.

5 chapter

The Role and Scope of Research in Public Relations

After reading this chapter, you will be able to:

- Understand the importance of research in public relations planning
- Conduct online and database research
- Organize a focus group
- Design a scientific survey
- Write a survey questionnaire
- Determine the best method of reaching respondents
- Conduct basic Web and social media analytics

The Importance of Research

Public relations professionals in today's world embrace research as an integral part of strategic communication campaign development. Beginning with the research phase, effective public relations includes four essential steps: (1) research, (2) planning, (3) communication, and (4) measurement. In this chapter, an award-winning campaign that celebrates 25 years of hospitality at DoubleTree Hotels will be introduced and this will provide continuity through the process. The nationwide campaign by Ketchum for DoubleTree produces formative **research**, thorough **planning**, complete **communication** efforts, and precise **evaluation** of results, all working together to develop a complete communication program.

Research gets the process started. It provides the information required to understand the needs of publics and to develop powerful messages. Planning, the process of setting goals and objectives and determining ways to meet them, is referred to as the central function of management. Communication is related to message strategy—making a message more appealing and persuasive to the public. Measurement (or evaluation) is becoming increasingly important in the public relations profession. Executives justifiably demand accountability from public relations practitioners. Measurement techniques provide a means for demonstrating to management that public relations is achieving objectives and contributing in a meaningful way to the organization.

Defining the Research Role

In basic terms, research is a form of careful listening. Broom and Dozier, in their book *Using Research in Public Relations*, say, "Research is the controlled, objective, and systematic gathering of information for the purpose of describing and understanding." Two standards are commonly considered for this listening process: validity and reliability.

Put simply, validity is achieved when research measures what it purports to measure. Reliability is achieved when very similar results are obtained if a study is repeated. For example, we cannot use a thermometer to gauge wind speed because it measures temperature, not wind speed. Similarly, a popularity poll for President Obama should not be used to gauge support for American foreign policy. An expensive thermometer will give consistent and stable measurements of temperature no matter how many times the temperature is read, making it highly reliable. But it is still not a valid measure of wind speed. In the same way, if the popularity poll were to be repeated, the study would be reliable if the results are consistent and stable. But those reliable results do not measure what people think of foreign policy.

Measure what you claim to measure and do it so well that others can repeat your work.

A public relations research aphorism

Determining the Research Role and Scope

Before any public relations program can be undertaken, information must be gathered and data must be collected and interpreted. Only by performing this first step can an organization begin to make policy decisions and map out strategies for effective communication programs. This research often becomes the basis for evaluating the program once it has been completed. The results of an evaluation can lead to greater accountability and credibility with upper management. (See Chapter 8 for details.)

Various types of research can be used to accomplish an organization's objectives and meet its need for information. What type of research to use really depends on the particular subject and situation. As always, time and budget are major considerations, as is the perceived importance of the situation. Consequently, many questions should be asked and answered before formulating a research project:

- What is the problem?
- What kind of information is needed?
- How will the results of the research be used?
- What specific public (or publics) should be researched? (See profile of Juggler 2.0 in the chapter Casebook on page 174.)
- Should the organization do the research in-house or hire an outside consultant?
- How will the research data be analyzed, reported, or applied?
- How soon will the results be needed?
- How much will the research cost?

> Research gives a context in which to talk about the product.
>
> *Lisa Eggerton, SVP and head of consumer practice, RSCG Magnet*

The answers to these questions will help the public relations person determine the extent and nature of the research needed. In some cases, informal research may be appropriate because of its low cost or the need for immediate information. In other cases, a random scientific survey may be used, despite its costs and time requirement, because a large retailer such as Wal-Mart or Home Depot wants to know how a community might vote on a referendum to approve the construction of a "big-box" store. The pros and cons of each research method will be discussed later in the chapter. A consensus of opinion now holds that the best public relations practice is research-driven and that results of that work earn influence for public relations as a key management function.

Using Research

Research is a multipronged tool that is involved in virtually every phase of a communications program. In general, studies show that public relations departments spend about 3 to 5 percent of their budget on research. Some experts contend that it should be 10 percent. With the rise of digital analytics and social media monitoring, covered in this chapter, the ratio may increase in the future. Public relations professionals use research in the following ways:

- **To achieve credibility with management.** Executives want facts, not guesses and hunches. The inclusion of public relations personnel in an organization's policy and decision making, according to the findings of IABCs research on excellence in communication management, is strongly correlated with their ability to do research and relate their findings to the organization's objectives.

- **To define audiences and segment publics.** Detailed information about the demographics, lifestyles, characteristics, and consumption patterns of audiences helps to ensure that messages reach the proper audiences. Hyojung Park, an assistant professor at Louisiana State University, developed a semantic map of blogs and discussion groups addressing the role of dogs in homes with autism spectrum disorder. Health specialists in human–animal interaction on her team received a clear signal from the conversational patterns in hundreds of thousands of words that dogs mainly helped the families. Selecting the right breeds and providing training were recommended. For another example, see DoubleTree's targeted audiences in the Casebook on page 154.

■ **To formulate strategy.** Much money can be spent pursuing the wrong strategies. Officials of the New Hampshire paper industry, given the bad press about logging and waterway pollution, thought a campaign was needed to tell the public what it was doing to reduce pollution. An opinion survey of 800 state residents by a public relations firm, however, indicated that the public was already generally satisfied with the industry's efforts. Consequently, the new strategy focused on reinforcing positive themes such as worker safety, employment, and environmental responsibility.

■ **To test messages.** Research is often used to determine what particular message is most salient with the target audience. According to one focus group study for a campaign to encourage carpooling, the message that resonated the most with commuters was saving time and money, not air quality or environmental concerns. Consequently, the campaign emphasized how many minutes could be cut from an average commute by using carpool lanes and the annual savings in gasoline, insurance, and car maintenance.

■ **To help management keep in touch.** In a mass society, top management is increasingly isolated from the concerns of employees, customers, and other important publics. Research helps bridge the gap by periodically surveying key publics about problems and concerns. This feedback is a "reality check" for top executives and often leads to better policies and communication strategies.

■ **To prevent crises.** An estimated 90 percent of organizational crises are caused by internal operational problems rather than by unexpected natural disasters. Research can often uncover trouble spots and public concerns before they become page-one news. (See the section on issues management in Chapter 10.) Analyzing complaints made to a toll-free number or monitoring Internet chat rooms and blogs can often tip off an organization that it should act before an emerging problem or issue becomes a serious threat that attracts widespread media attention and public opprobrium.

■ **To monitor the competition.** Savvy organizations keep track of what the competition is doing. Competition monitoring can be done using surveys that ask consumers to comment on competing products, content analysis of the competition's media coverage, and reviews of industry reports in trade journals. Digital monitoring using Google Alerts, for example, delivers news content alerts based on selected search terms. Similar print news tracking is possible with Reddit, the "internet's front page" and for broadcast news with Critical Mention.

Google Alerts monitors a developing news story or keeps the professional current on a competitor or industry. Similarly, RSS (Real Simple Syndication) feeds provide timely updates from favored websites such as online news sites or aggregate feeds from many sites into one place on the professional's home page. Such research helps an organization shape its marketing and communication strategies to counter a competitor's strengths and capitalize on its weaknesses.

> We recommend that between 5 and 10% of your budget should be spent on measurement. Doesn't it make sense to spend that much to find out if the other 90–95% isn't doing anything for you?
>
> *Katie Paine, CEO of KD Paine and Partners*

■ **To sway public opinion.** Facts and figures, compiled from a variety of primary and secondary sources, can change public opinion. A coalition called Ohioans for Responsible Health

Information opposed a cancer labeling bill on thousands of products. The coalition commissioned research on the economic impact of such legislation on consumers and major industries. The research, which was used as the basis of the grassroots campaign, caused the defeat of the ballot measure, with a 78 percent "no" vote.

- **To generate publicity.** Polls and surveys can generate publicity for an organization. Indeed, many surveys seem to be designed with publicity in mind. Simmons Mattress once polled people to find out how many sleep in the nude. Jello-O-Pudding, capitalizing on media and public interest in the prediction that the Mayan calendar forecast the end of the world on December 21, 2012, received considerable brand publicity by reporting the results of a commissioned national survey about Americans' perceptions of the forthcoming apocalypse. While only 4 percent actually believed the world would end, 82 percent said they would "party like there was no tomorrow."

News organizations are drawn to releases that include research findings that add some substance and interest to stories. This holds true for major national surveys, but at least as much for interesting, "tid-bites" such as those about the iconic DoubleTree cookie, which is shown on page 154. Although public relations is a management function, it often includes creative, playful elements that add verve to the work.

- **To measure success.** The bottom line of any public relations program is whether the time and money spent accomplished the stated objective. As one of its many programs to boost brand awareness, Doritos snack chips pioneered the use of consumer-created content by airing Super Bowl commercials created by fans. Doritos sales for the week after the Super Bowl increased by 16 percent over the same week the previous year.

As the four public relations process chapters in this text will demonstrate, even the humble cookie requires thorough **research**, careful and detailed **planning**, creative **communication** in traditional and social media, ending with thorough **evaluation** of the entire effort. The award-winning Ketchum Public Relations Cookie CAREavan for DoubleTree Hotels made good use of background research to publicize the celebration of hospitality at DoubleTree Hotels (Figure 5.1).

A Variety of Research Techniques

When the term *research* is used, people tend to think of *quantitative research*, which uses scientific surveys and complex statistical tabulations. In public relations, however, research techniques can also be as simple as gathering available data and information. Although the distinctions between different types of research are not absolute, Table 5.1 helps to sort out some of the options selected by public relations professionals.

In fact, a survey of practitioners by Walter K. Lindenmann, former senior vice president and director of research for Ketchum, found that three-fourths of the respondents described their research techniques as casual and informal rather than scientific and precise, tending to be qualitative, secondary analysis.

This technique is called *secondary research*, because it uses existing information in books, magazine articles, electronic databases, and so on. In contrast, *primary research* uses new and original information that is generated through a research project and is directed to answer a specific question.

Figure 5.1 **Research for the Humble Cookie**

CONTACT:
DoubleTree by Hilton Global Brand Public Relations

The Cookie by DoubleTree:
More Than 230 Million Warm Welcomes
Proudly Served Around the World

2011 Marks the 25th Anniversary of the Beloved Sweet Treat

DoubleTree by Hilton hotels have built a reputation on a sweet treat that keeps leisure and business travelers coming back for more – its oven-fresh chocolate chip cookie which is presented to each guest at check-in. In what has become a refreshing welcome to travelers for 25 years, the Cookie by DoubleTree has played a starring role in differentiating the brand's delivery of hospitality from its competition.

Following are a few **"tid-bites"** about this hospitality icon:

- Doubletree by Hilton gives out approximately **60,000 chocolate chip cookies each day**. That's more than **21,000,000 warm welcomes annually**!
- DoubleTree by Hilton began giving out chocolate chip cookies in the **1980s**, when many hotels across the country used them as treats for VIPs.
- In 1986, the same secret recipe for today's chocolate chip cookie welcome at all DoubleTree by Hilton hotels around the world was created
- Nashville-based Christie Cookie Company currently holds the brand's secret recipe, which ensures that **the same, delicious cookie is delivered consistently at every Doubletree by Hilton hotel and resort**.
- Every Doubletree by Hilton chocolate chip cookie is **baked fresh daily** at each hotel.
- Each cookie weighs more than **2 ounces** and has an average of **20** chocolate chips.
- The Christie Cookie Company uses more than **750,000** pounds of chocolate chips each year for Doubletree by Hilton's cookies
- In June 2002, Doubletree by Hilton presented its **100,000,000th** cookie!
- To date, more than **230,000,000** cookies have been served to delighted guests and customers
- More than **1,000,000 chocolate chip cookies have been donated** by Doubletree by Hilton hotels to celebrate and thank deserving members of the community from doctors and nurses to police and firefighters as well as non-profit groups such as food banks and homeless shelters.
- From the United Kingdom to Canada and Tanzania to China, the signature chocolate chip cookie welcome is **presented to travelers at more than 250 Doubletree locations around the world.**

###

May 2011

Table 5.1 **Qualitative and Quantitative versus Primary and Secondary Research**

	QUALITATIVE RESEARCH: Non-numerical research to seek insights	QUANTITATIVE RESEARCH: Numerically based research with larger samples of respondents
PRIMARY Data collected by the professional	Professional conducts interviews or focus groups	Professional conducts large national survey
SECONDARY Data collected previously by others	Professional carefully reads news coverage or transcripts	Professional analyzes statistical data from General Social Survey

Table 5.2 Qualitative versus Quantitative Research

QUALITATIVE RESEARCH	QUANTITATIVE RESEARCH
"Soft" data	"Hard" data
Usually uses open-ended questions, unstructured	Usually uses close-ended questions, requires forced choices, highly structured
Exploratory in nature; probing, fishing-expedition type of research	Descriptive or explanatory type of research
Usually valid, but not reliable	Usually valid and reliable
Rarely projectable to larger audiences	Usually projectable to larger audiences
Generally uses nonrandom samples	Generally uses random samples
Examples: Focus groups; one-on-one, in-depth interviews; observation; participation; role-playing studies; convenience polling; social media participation	Examples: Telephone polls, mailed surveys, mall intercept studies, face-to-face interviews, shared cost, or omnibus studies; panel studies; digital analytics

Another way of categorizing research is by distinguishing between *qualitative* and *quantitative* research. Lindenmann's determinations of the basic differences between qualitative and quantitative research appear in Table 5.2. In general, qualitative research affords the researcher rich insights and understanding of a situation or a target public, but seldom uses numerical data. It also provides "red flags" or warnings when strong or adverse responses occur. These responses may not be generalizable, but they may provide the practitioner with an early warning. Quantitative research is often more expensive and complicated, but it gives the researcher greater ability to generalize to large populations. If enormous amounts of money are to be spent on a national campaign, an investment in quantitative research may be appropriate.

The following sections briefly describe the three broad, and somewhat overlapping, approaches to research. They are: (1) secondary research, (2) qualitative research, and (3) quantitative research based on scientific sampling.

For public relations research to provide support and assistance to the strategic planning and program development process, a mix of both qualitative and quantitative research is preferable.

Walter K. Lindenmann, specialist in public relations research and measurement

Secondary Research

When a public relations professional analyzes data of any sort—whether numerical or textual in nature—that was originally collected by someone else, it is considered secondary research. Techniques range from archival research in an organization's files to reference books, computer databases, online searches, and digital analytics of websites and social media platforms.

Online Databases

Reference books, academic journals, and trade publications are increasingly found online either for a fee or free through nearly every city or university library. Online databases such as LexisNexis contain abstracts or full text of thousands, or even millions, of articles.

on the job

SOCIAL MEDIA IN ACTION

New Brunswick Targets Audiences Using Google Analytics

The Canadian province of New Brunswick sought to increase visits by tourists. Tourism New Brunswick teamed up with T4G, a Google Analytics certified digital marketing agency, to develop a strategic plan based on website analysis. (The sidebar provides the key components of the successful summer campaign—"New Brunswick Finds.") By achieving a 58% increase in customer inquiries, the digital analytics helped drive a strong tourism season in a short, intense time period for this Northern destination. T4G was agile, measuring in real time what was working or not regarding website and campaign components, with changes implemented on-the-fly.

The previous year, Tourism New Brunswick and T4G launched a website full of New Brunswick trip ideas to support the summer campaign—"New Brunswick Finds."

The primary goal was to increase engagement for two target audience segments with activities and experiences that suited their interests:

1. "No-Hassle Travelers": Those looking for quick and easy summer getaway vacation ideas.
2. "Cultural Explorers/Authentic Experiencers": Those looking for natural wonder and authentic cultural experiences.

Tourism New Brunswick and T4G wanted to use Web analytics to evaluate the site's performance and to influence decisions for the ongoing campaign as well as future campaigns.

T4G used several of Google Analytics' features to accomplish crucial tasks for Tourism New Brunswick:

1. Campaign Tracking to learn which links were bringing the most relevant and engaged traffic to the website. For example, a link placed by Tourism New Brunswick on a travel review website might bring people from all over the world to the "New Brunswick Finds" website. But if analysis found that the site visits did not predict weekend bookings in the Province, then the effort and expense of placing the link was not justified. The campaign could then focus its campaign efforts on media, social media, and online sites that drove more promising prospects to the website for "New Brunswick Finds."
2. Google Event Tracking to analyze behavior on the New Brunswick website itself. Such analysis of what are called the landing pages, the web location to which a link directs the visitor, focused on how the website performs once visitors arrive at the site. Analysis included counts of numerous behaviors of visitors on the site, but probably the most important one was the "Make an Enquiry" form. Enquiries often become visits and that was the main point of the campaign.
3. Website Optimizer to test online activity on the tourism

T4G was crucial in the success of the "New Brunswick Finds" campaign. Their knowledge and expertise in Google Analytics allowed us to make quick decisions and appropriate changes required to meet the customers' expectation."

Carol Alderdice, Manager Web Technology, New Brunswick Department of Culture, Tourism and Healthy Living

campaign landing page. The test determined that the original landing page had lots of links to click on, some leading deeper into the site and some taking visitors off the site altogether. Based on analysis, a new landing page design gave visitors only two options, one button for the No-Hassle target market and one button for Cultural Travelers. The focus was on simplicity and funneling users to relevant content. Each of the two audience segments would see clear calls to action for simple vacations or cultural experiences, respectively. The result was an 11.4 percent decrease in bounce rate—loss of visitors from the site.

These combined insights informed an overhaul of Tourism New Brunswick's main tourism website, which launched in the spring of 2012. Moving forward, analytics will help T4G continually optimize the users' online experience and deliver additional performance improvements to Tourism New Brunswick's campaign for weekend visits to New Brunswick.

Source: Google Analytics website and T4G Agency website

Some common reference sources used by public relations professionals include the *Statistical Abstract of the United States* (http://www.census.gov/compendia/statab/), which summarizes census information; the Gallup Poll (http://poll.gallup.com/), which provides an index of public opinion on a variety of issues; and *Simmons Study Media and Markets*, an extensive annual survey of households on their product usage by brand and exposure to various media.

The World Wide Web

The Internet is a powerful research tool for the public relations practitioner. Any number of corporations, nonprofits, trade groups, special interest groups, foundations, universities, think tanks, and government agencies post reams of data on their websites. In addition, archival information such as policy statements, annual financial reports, speeches of key executives, issues of company magazines and newsletters, and a media resource center are often available for perusal. An Internet search engine can help inform public relations campaign development by making a wealth of data immediately available.

Helpful sites for public relations professionals:

- *Statistical Abstract of the United States:* http://www.census.gov/compendia/statab/
- Bureau of Labor Statistics: www.bls.gov
- Environmental News Network: www.enn.com
- A list of home pages of various public relations firms: www.prfirms.org
- International Association of Business Communicators (IABC): www.iabc.com
- Public Relations Society of America (PRSA): www.prsa.org

- Business Wire (hyperlinks to corporate home pages): http://www.businesswire.com/portal/site/home/
- PR Newswire: http://www.prnewswire.com/
- Vanderbilt Television News Archive: www.tvnews.vanderbilt.edu/
- Google Trends search pattern service: www.Google.com/trends

Qualitative Research

A great deal of public relations research is qualitative, relying less on numbers and statistics and more on interpretation of text such as editorial pages or focus group transcripts for themes or insights; such research is good for probing attitudes and perceptions, assessing penetration of messages, and testing the clarity and effectiveness of materials. This section explores five qualitative research techniques: (1) content analysis, (2) interviews, (3) focus groups, (4) copy testing, and (5) ethnographic techniques.

Content Analysis

Content analysis is the systematic and objective counting or categorizing of information. In public relations, content analysis is often used to measure the amount of media coverage and the nature of that coverage. This research method ranges from relatively informal to quite scientific in terms of random sampling and establishing specific subject categories.

Professionals regularly analyze news stories about an organization to document themes and general conclusions about media coverage that might signal important issues needing attention. See Chapter 10 for a discussion of issues management. Content analysis can help to determine whether a need exists for additional public relations efforts.

By analyzing the media coverage given to an organization's competitors, a public relations professional can learn about the competition's marketing strategies, strengths, and weaknesses. The results often help shape an organization's marketing, advertising, and public relations programs to gain a bigger share of media attention.

At a basic level, a researcher can assemble news clips and count the number of column inches or minutes of broadcast time. Don Stacks, University of Miami professor and author of *Primer of Public Relations Research*, writes that content analysis "is particularly appropriate for the analysis of documents, speeches, media releases, video content and scripts, interviews, and focus groups. The key to content analysis is that it is done objectively . . ., and content is treated systematically. . . ."

Meaningful content analysis that enables public relations departments to plan responsive communication should include factors such as (1) the percentage of favorable, neutral, and negative mentions about the company or its product or service; (2) the overall tone of the article or broadcast mention; and (3) the percentage of articles that contain key message points that the organization wants to communicate. Dr. David Michaelson of Echo Research noted at a recent Measurement Summit sponsored by the Institute for Public Relations that his clients worldwide do care about favorability, but frequently are at least as concerned with accuracy, regardless of the tone of the news coverage. Presence of a company's key messages goes a long way toward the judgment that coverage is indeed accurate.

Because Internet chat groups and blogs, as well as letters and phone calls to an organization, provide good feedback about problems with the organization's policies and services, they can be vital sources of current opinion about performance and reputation. A pattern of blog postings, letters, and phone calls pointing out a problem is often evidence that the organization needs to address the situation. A number of companies, such as Carma International, Cymfony, and VMS, can slice and dice media data in any number of ways for their clients. Research firm KD Paine and Partners delivers content analysis on a custom-designed web page for the client. Called a *Dashboard*, clients can see at a glance how they are being covered in traditional and new media.

Public Opinion Survey

Interviews, often conducted by researchers on the street or in shopping malls, help public relations practitioners target audiences they wish to reach and to shape their messages.

Interviews

As with content analysis, interviews can be conducted in several different ways. Almost everyone talks to colleagues on a daily basis and calls other organizations to gather information. In fact, public relations personnel faced with solving a particular problem often "interview" other public relations professionals for ideas and suggestions. Increasingly, interviews of varying levels of formality are conducted online using chat or Skype-style technologies.

If information is needed on public opinions and attitudes, many public relations firms will conduct short interviews with people in a shopping mall or at a meeting. This kind of interview is called an *intercept interview*, because people are literally intercepted in public places and asked their opinions. It is also called a *convenience poll* because it's relatively convenient to stand in a mall and talk to people.

The intercept interview is considered by researchers to be highly unscientific and unreliable, but it does give an organization some sense of current thinking or exposure to certain key messages. For example, a health group wanted to find out whether the public was actually receiving and retaining crucial aspects of its message. To gather such information, intercept interviews were conducted with 300 adults at six malls. Both unaided and aided recall questions were asked, to assess the overall impact of the publicity.

Intercept interviews last only two to five minutes. At other times, the best approach is to do in-depth interviews to get more comprehensive information. Major fund-raising projects by charitable groups, for example, often require in-depth interviews of community and business opinion leaders. The success of any major fund drive, those seeking $500,000 or more, depends on the support of key leaders and wealthy individuals.

Focus Groups

A good alternative to individual interviews is the *focus group*. The focus group technique is widely used in advertising, marketing, and public relations to help identify attitudes and motivations of important publics. Another purpose of focus groups is to formulate or pretest message themes and communication strategies before launching a full campaign.

on the job

A MULTICULTURAL WORLD

Reaching a Diverse Audience about Electric Rates

How do you reach an audience when almost 40 percent of your audience is illiterate, 20 percent live below the poverty line, and many speak a language other than English? That's exactly what Dittus Communications faced—not in a developing nation, but in Washington, D.C.

The challenge was legislation passed by the city council that deregulated electricity so that residents could choose service from several competing suppliers instead of just one company having a monopoly. A Customer Education Advisory Board—a partnership of government, local utility, and consumer advocacy groups—was formed and given the assignment of implementing a two-year public education campaign to inform D.C. residents about their electricity supply choices.

Dittus Communications started with a literature search to gain information about the demographic profile of D.C. residents. Personal interviews were then conducted with city officials and leaders of local nonprofit and faith-based organizations to gain insight into the best ways to reach the population. One key finding was that messages had to be simple and direct, and feature one fact at a time. It was also necessary to have multiple communication tools that could be customized for hard-to-reach audiences. To reach the illiterate audience, for example, radio announcements and talks at community and faith-based organizations were used.

Ongoing research tracking the residents' awareness of electricity choices found that women were more interested in the topic than men, so additional female models were used in the campaign's advertising. Ultimately, the award-winning campaign helped increase resident confidence about making electricity choices. Almost 45 percent of the population felt more capable of decision making than when the effort had begun.

This more in-depth approach is called *purposive interviewing*, because the interviewees are carefully selected based on their expertise, influence, or leadership in the community. For example, the Greater Durham, North Carolina, chamber of commerce interviewed 50 "movers and shakers" to determine support for an extensive image-building and economic development program.

Focus groups usually consist of 8 to 12 people who represent the characteristics of the target audience, such as employees, consumers, or community residents. During the session, a trained facilitator uses nondirective interviewing techniques that encourage group members to talk freely about a topic or give candid reactions to suggested message themes. The setting is usually a conference room, and the discussion is informal. A focus group may last one or two hours, depending on the subject matter.

A focus group, by definition, is an informal research procedure that develops qualitative information rather than hard data. Results should not be summarized by percentages or even projected onto an entire population because this accords a level of precision not supported by the method. See Table 5.3 for precautions on discussing the results of a focus group.

Nevertheless, focus groups are useful in identifying the range of attitudes and opinions among the participants. For example, the opinion of several focus group participants that a proposed slogan or logo is off-color and in bad taste may not be generalizable to large populations, but it raises a red flag that communication staff should go back to the

Table 5.3 **Words of Caution for Discussing Focus Group Results**

FREQUENT MISTAKE	EXPLANATION OF THE CAUTION
Talking like a number cruncher	The general principle is to embrace the insightful and richly explanatory findings of qualitative research and avoid dressing up findings within quantitative terms.
False precision	Don't mix quantitative terms with qualitative research. This creates a false precision that is not the point of sound qualitative research methods. For example, for qualitative work, one does not draw a sample and certainly is not concerned with a random sample. In fact, sometimes a qualitative researcher actually learns the most from unrepresentative, exceptional persons.
Avoid generalizing to large publics	Don't conduct focus groups as though they represent large populations or demographic groups. For example, beginners will hold separate focus groups for men and women, then compare the findings to generalize about gender differences. A dozen focus group members cannot represent all women or men. But you may get valuable insights about how women think, for example, and keep in mind how best to relate to them.
Numerical breakdowns make no sense	Do not use counts or percentages for findings from interviews or focus groups. For example, if one interviews ten people and two of them give a certain opinion, one should not imply that 20% of all citizens would answer that way. Say that some people think this, some think that—and strive to better understand why they think the way they do.

drawing board. Such insights can help an organization structure its messages or, on another level, formulate hypotheses and questions for a quantitative research survey.

Increasingly, focus groups are being conducted online. The technique can be as simple as posing a question to a chat or interest group online. Researchers are also using more formal selection processes to invite far-flung participants to meet in a prearranged virtual space. In the coming years, techniques and services will be well developed for cost-effective, online focus group research.

Although highly informal, Domino's Pizza conducted an online focus group regarding its bold move to completely change the recipe for its pizza—crust, cheese, and sauce. In national taste tests, Domino's inhabited the basement with Chuck E. Cheese. Domino's canvassed food bloggers and tweeters to respond in real time as they tasted the new pizza and to comment live on Domino's website about the new formula. This daring move reflected Domino's confidence in the new recipe as it conducted an online focus group with the whole world watching. Opportunities for publicity and for brand advertising related to the recipe change made the uncontrolled research process a gamble worth taking.

Copy Testing

All too often, organizations fail to communicate effectively because they produce and distribute materials that the target audience can't understand. In many cases, the material is written above the educational level of the audience. To avoid this problem, representatives of the target audience should be asked to read or view the material in draft form before it is mass-produced and distributed. This can be done one on one or in a small-group setting.

In health public relations, readability is crucial to enhancing health literacy so that individuals can make smart health decisions. A brochure about employee medical benefits or pension plans, for example, should be pretested with rank-and-file employees for readability. Executives and lawyers who must approve the copy may understand the material, but a worker with a high school education might find the material difficult to follow.

Another approach to determine the degree of difficulty of the material is to apply a readability formula to the draft copy. Fog, Flesch Reading Ease, and similar techniques relate the number of words and syllables per sentence or passage with reading level. Highly complex sentences and multisyllabic words require an audience with a college education. One readily available software tool for assessing readability is Microsoft Word.

Two examples of how to test copy using Internet sources are Web surveys and Wikis. Web survey systems such as Survey Artisan (www.surveyartisan.com) allow attachment of video or photo files that can be critiqued by a target audience across many locations. A less sophisticated but equally effective way to test copy is simply to attach the copy to an e-mail and provide a link to an online survey. Similarly, photos or videos can be tested through secure Flickr or YouTube sharing communities. A Wiki is a website that allows users to easily edit content; these sites provide a way for clients or audience members to critique and correct copy, essentially turning audience members into copy collaborators or crowd source editors.

Ethnographic Techniques

Public relations often takes a page from anthropology to conduct research. One technique is observation of individual or group behavior. One director of public relations, for example, wanted to know how effective bulletin boards were in terms of informing employees in an industrial plant, so he stationed staff near bulletin boards to record how many employees actually stopped and read something off the board. In another situation, a public relations representative sat in a coffee house for most of one day to gain insights about the types of customers who came in, how much they spent, and how long they stayed.

On occasion, role-playing can be helpful for gaining insights into the strengths and weaknesses of an organization. One public relations professional with a college as a client had his daughter and several other young adults in the area apply to the university just to see how the college compared with others in handling prospective students. He also got feedback from his daughter about how well she was treated in the process.

Quantitative Research

The research techniques discussed thus far can provide good insights to public relations personnel and help them formulate effective programs. Many involve a thoughtful review of existing materials or careful listening in one form or another to small numbers of individuals. Increasingly, however, public relations professionals need to conduct polls and surveys using highly precise, scientific sampling methods. Such sampling is based on two important factors: randomness to ensure that the subject pool is not biased and a large number of respondents to ensure that results can be generalized to the entire population being studied.

Random Sampling

Effective polls and surveys require a random sample. In statistics, this means that everyone in the targeted audience (as defined by the researcher) has an equal or known chance of being selected for the survey. This is also called a probability sample.

In contrast, a nonprobability survey is not random at all. Improper sampling can lead to misleading results. The most precise random sample is generated from lists that have the name of every person in the target audience. This is simple if the researcher is conducting a random survey of an organization's employees or members, because the researcher can randomly select, for example, every 25th name on a list. To avoid patterns in the lists based on rank or employee category, the researcher should choose large intervals between selected names so that he or she makes numerous passes through the list. Computerized lists often allow for random selection of names to be generated in a list.

> Opinion and experience are still important, and we want to be data-informed rather than data driven, but the orientation clearly needs to shift more strongly toward data and facts.
>
> *Don Bartholomew, Senior Vice President, Ketchum, in* PRNews

The distinction between probability and nonprobability samples can be illustrated with two different approaches to Web-based surveys. When ESPN invites viewers of *Sports Central* to vote among five NFL teams as the best bet to win the Super Bowl, the response can be enormous—but is unscientific. For one thing, fans of a team can vote repeatedly.

By contrast, a doctoral student at the University of Missouri obtained the membership list of the Health Academy of PRSA. She then randomly drew a sample of members, assigned a unique identification number to each respondent to allow only one visit to the website, and e-mailed them an invitation to complete the Web-based survey. Respondents had an equal and known chance of being included, making the results of the survey representative of Health Academy members. The point is that Web-based surveys run the gamut from trivial popularity polls to rigorously drawn surveys of important respondents.

Another common method to ensure representation is to draw a random sample that matches the statistical characteristics of the audience. This is called quota sampling. Human resource departments usually have breakdowns of employees by job classification, and it is relatively easy to proportion a sample accordingly. For example, if 42 percent of a company's employees work on the assembly line, then 42 percent of the sample should be assembly-line workers. A quota sample can be drawn on any number of demographic factors—age, sex, religion, race, income—depending on the purpose of the survey.

Random sampling becomes more difficult when comprehensive lists are not available. In those cases, researchers surveying the general population often use telephone directories or customer lists to select respondents at random. A more rigorous technique employs random, computerized generation of telephone numbers; this process ensures that new, unlisted, and even cell phone numbers are included in the sample.

Sample Size

In any probability study, sample size is always a big question. National polling firms usually sample 1,000 to 1,500 people and get a highly accurate idea of what the U.S. adult population is thinking. The average national poll samples 1,500 people, and the margin of error is within three percentage points 95 percent of the time. In other words, 19 out of 20 times the same questionnaire is administered, the results should be within the same 3 percentage points and reflect the whole population accurately.

In public relations, the primary purpose of poll data is to get indications of attitudes and opinions, not to predict elections. Therefore, it is not usually necessary or practical to do a scientific sampling of 1,500 people. A sample of 250 to 500 will

on the job

ETHICS

Sex and Alcohol: The AMA's News Release

The American Medical Association (AMA) wanted to call public attention to the issue of "risky" behavior by college students during spring break. The AMA's strategy was to commission a survey of female college students so that it would have some "facts" to demonstrate the seriousness of the issue.

The resulting news release stated that its survey of 644 college women and graduates aged 17 to 35 showed troubling findings about drinking habits on spring break trips. For instance, 92 percent of respondents said it was easy to get alcohol on these trips. The news release also stated, "One in five respondents regretted the sexual activity they engaged in during spring break, and 12 percent felt forced or pressured into sex." Because of the topic, which included sex, the Associated Press moved the story and many media outlets reported the survey results.

What the news release didn't say was that the survey was less than scientific. It was an online survey in which respondents self-selected themselves to participate. In other words, the survey was not a random or representative sample of female college students. The news release also didn't mention that a quarter of the respondents had never gone on a spring break trip, so their opinions were actually secondhand impressions or perceptions of what occurs during spring break.

Carl Bialik, who writes a column for the *Wall Street Journal* titled "The Numbers Guy," called the AMA about the validity of the survey. He was told by an AMA spokesperson, "We used the poll mostly to bring national attention to the issue." What do you think of this answer? Was the news release misleading? Do you think sending out news releases reporting survey results based on nonscientific research methods is ethical? The news release did accomplish the objective of getting "national attention," so does the end justify the means?

give relatively accurate data—with a 5 or 6 percent variance—that will help determine general public attitudes and opinions. A sample of about 100 people, accurately drawn according to probability guidelines, will include about a 10 percent margin of error.

Reporting the results of such surveys often raises some ethical issues. See the Ethics box above.

Questionnaire Construction

Although correct sampling is important in gaining accurate results, pollsters generally acknowledge that sampling error may be far less important than the errors that result from the wording and order of questions in a survey and even the timing of a survey.

Carefully Consider Wording

Wording the questions on a questionnaire is a time-consuming process, and it is not unusual for a questionnaire to go through multiple drafts to achieve maximum clarity. The question "Is it a good idea to limit alcohol consumption on college campuses?" differs from "Do you think campus alcohol prohibitions will curtail drinking on campus?" On first glance, the two questions seem to be asking the same thing.

On closer examination, however, one realizes that a respondent could easily answer "yes" to the first question and "no" to the second.

The first question asks whether limiting student drinking is a good idea. The second asks whether people think it will curtail drinking. A third question that might elicit a different response would be "Do you think that a policy curtailing drinking on campus would work?" Thus, the questions emphasize three different aspects of the problem.

Avoid Loaded Questions

Some organizations engage in what is called *advocacy research*. They send out surveys with questions that use highly charged words to elicit an emotional reaction from the respondent. Such questions are considered "loaded" because they are intentionally skewed to generate a predictable response. Such surveys often are done in the arena of politics and public policy debate.

Public relations practitioners have a professional obligation to avoid using the rubric of "surveys" if the objective is really advocacy research. Such "surveys" are misleading and tarnish the reputation of legitimate survey research.

Consider Timing and Context

Responses to survey questions are influenced by events, and this should be taken into consideration when reviewing the results of a survey. Consequently, polls and surveys should be conducted when the organization isn't in the news or connected to a significant event that may influence public opinion. In a neutral context, therefore, a more valid survey can be conducted about an organization's reputation, products, or services.

Avoid the Politically Correct Answer

Another problem with questionnaire design involves questions that tend to elicit the "correct" response. This is also called a *courtesy bias*. In such a situation, respondents often choose answers that they think are the "politically correct" answers that the sponsor of the survey wants to hear or that reflect favorably on them as good workers or citizens. For example, surveys show that more than 80 percent of Americans consider themselves "environmentalists." As skeptics point out, however, would anyone admit that he or she is not concerned about the environment?

Give a Range of Possible Answers

Answer categories also can skew a questionnaire. It is important that the provided answer choices cover a range of opinions. Several years ago, a national polling organization asked the question "How much confidence do you have in business corporations?" but provided only the following answer categories: (a) a great deal, (b) only some, and (c) none at all. A large gap exists between "a great deal" and the next category, "only some."

Use Scaled Answer Sets

In general, "yes or no" questions are not very good for examining respondents' perceptions and attitudes. An answer of "yes" or "no" provides little feedback on the strength or weakness of a respondent's opinion. A question such as "Do you agree

on the job INSIGHTS

Questionnaire Guidelines

The following are some general guidelines for the construction of questionnaires:

- Determine the type of information that is needed and in what detail.
- State the objectives of the survey in writing.
- Decide which group(s) will receive the questionnaire.

For rigorous online surveys, send links to the scientifically selected sample.

- Decide on the size of the sample.
- State the purpose of the survey and guarantee anonymity.
- Use closed-end (multiple-choice) answers as often as possible. Respondents find it easier and less time-consuming to select answers than to compose their own.
- Design the questionnaire in such a way that answers can be easily coded for statistical analysis.
- Strive to make the questionnaire fewer than 25 questions. Long questionnaires put people off and reduce the number of responses.
- Use categories when asking questions about education, age, and income. People are more willing to answer when a range is given. For example, "What best describes your age? (a) Under 25, (b) 26 to 40," and so on.
- Use simple, familiar words. Readability should be appropriate for the group being sampled.
- Avoid ambiguous words and phrases that may confuse the respondents.
- Remember to consider the context and placement of questions. A question earlier in the questionnaire might influence the response to a later question.
- Provide space at the end of the questionnaire for respondents' comments. This allows them to provide additional information that may not have been covered in the main body of the questionnaire.
- Pretest the questions with representatives of the target audience for understanding and possible bias. Their feedback will help improve the final draft.

with the company's policy of requiring drug testing for all new employees?" can be answered by "yes" or "no," but more useful information would be obtained by setting up a Likert-type scale—(a) strongly agree, (b) agree, (c) undecided, (d) disagree, and (e) strongly disagree. These types of answers enable the surveyor to measure the depth of feeling among respondents and may serve as guidelines for management in making major changes or just fine-tuning the existing policy. The advantage of numeric scales is that medians (half above, half below) and means (average) can be calculated. See the Insights box above that gives questionnaire guidelines.

How to Reach Respondents

A questionnaire is only as good as the delivery system that gets it to respondents. This section presents the pros and cons of (1) mail questionnaires, (2) telephone surveys, (3) personal interviews, (4) omnibus surveys, and (5) Web and e-mail surveys.

Mailed Questionnaires

Questionnaires may be distributed in a variety of settings. They may be handed out at a manufacturing plant, at a county fair, or even in a bank lobby. Historically, most survey questionnaires were mailed to respondents to control costs and to ensure that the right person got the survey. With care, these advantages can be achieved with e-mail and Web-based survey-collection techniques. Because practitioners find the Internet approach convenient and quicker, mailed questionnaires are used less often than in the recent past.

Mailed questionnaires suffer from low response rates, as low as 1 to 2 percent when mailed to the general public. Better response is garnered when an organization is known and trusted by the survey subjects, but may increase only to 20 to 30 percent. These response rates threaten the generalizability of the results. To increase response rates, researchers should keep the following suggestions in mind:

- Include a stamped, self-addressed return envelope.
- Personally sign a note explaining the importance of the survey.
- Provide an incentive.
- Use first-class mail.
- Mail a reminder postcard.
- Do a second mailing.

Telephone Surveys

Surveys by telephone, particularly those that are locally based, are used extensively by research firms. The telephone survey has four major advantages: (1) the feedback is immediate, (2) the telephone is a more personal form of communication, (3) it's less intrusive than interviewers going door to door, and (4) the response rate, if the survey is short and handled by skilled phone interviewers, can regularly reach 60 percent.

The major disadvantage of telephone surveys is the difficulty in getting access to telephone numbers. In many urban areas, one-third to one-half of all numbers are unlisted. The greater challenge is the shift away from landline telephone service in homes to individual cell phones within the residence. Because cell phones are portable, area codes no longer reflect place of residence, which can be crucial for surveys intended only for current residents of a geographical area, such as voters in a state election. Fortunately, researchers can use a computer program or sampling service to generate random phone numbers that will include unlisted numbers and cell numbers.

Another barrier is convincing respondents that a legitimate poll or survey is being taken. Historically, salespeople, and even charitable organizations, attempted to sell goods or get donations by posing as researchers. Today, citizens are protected by "do-not-call" laws that block marketing solicitations. Genuine public opinion surveys are not blocked by the do-not-call registration so that citizens can be confident that the survey is genuine.

Personal Interviews

The personal interview is the most expensive form of research because it requires trained staff and travel. If travel within a city is involved, a trained interviewer may

Online surveys are easier and less intrusive than a phone call.

Giselle Lederman, survey methodologist for Zoomerang

be able to interview only 8 to 10 people a day, and salaries and transportation costs make it expensive. Considerable advance work is required to select and arrange interview appointments. Such interviews, taking 20 minutes to an hour, are usually much more intensive and representative than the mall-intercept interviews that occur when an interviewer stops mall shoppers to record a few quick answers on a clipboard.

Omnibus or Piggyback Surveys

The word *omnibus* means something that serves several purposes. In survey research, it means that an organization buys one or two questions in a national survey conducted by a national polling firm such as Gallup or Harris. For example, General Mills may place one or two questions in a large, professionally conducted survey that asks respondents what professional athlete they most admire, as a way to find new endorsers for its breakfast foods. In the same survey, the American Cancer Society may place a question to find out what percentage of women know the common symptoms of ovarian cancer. If awareness is low, such a finding shows that a public information campaign is needed.

Web and E-Mail Surveys

The newest way to reach respondents is through the Internet. One such method is to post a questionnaire on an organization's website and ask visitors to complete it online. The advantage of this is that once the visitor completes the survey, his or her response is immediately available and the results can be added to a running tabulation of results.

A classic example of an online survey is one that Church & Dwight, the maker of Trojan Condoms, conducted before it launched its new Elexa line of condoms and sexual health products, including a vibrating ring targeting women. The online survey, aimed at women ages 18 to 59, was conducted to understand "women's sexual journeys." The responses enabled the company to position the new product line through a research report called the "Elexa Study of Women and Desire," which, of course, generated a great deal of media coverage.

As *PRWeek* pointed out, "What lifestyle reporter doesn't want to know that 'American women want great sex.' " The survey found, for example, that "84% of women agree that a good sex life is part of a healthy life," and "76% say that, at the request of a partner, they have tried something new sexually that they have enjoyed." Cassandra Johnson, a product manager for Elexa, told *PRWeek*, "We were expecting that the research would help refine the voice of the campaign and key messages, and give us something thought-provoking to say to the media and to women about female sexuality."

Because the survey employed a convenience sample consisting of those who visited the site and volunteered to respond, the generalizability of results is suspect. But as "main event research" intended to be newsworthy and stimulating, the research was a great success.

The major disadvantage of a Web survey is that it is difficult to know the exact characteristics of the respondents, because a website is accessible to virtually anyone with a computer and an Internet connection. It is also very important to prevent repeated participation by the same respondent by identifying the unique identifying number of the computer (called the IP address) and allowing only one submission. One of the biggest problems for online surveys is the low response rate due to the impersonal nature of the survey and the ease of exiting the survey's website with a single mouse click. For this reason, many online surveys begin with the most crucial questions.

Advances in the sampling process for Internet surveys enable researchers to reach specific respondents using a list of known respondents. This could be a list of National Rifle Association members or employees of a multinational company or any other sampling list that includes e-mail addresses. Organizations can compile e-mail lists of clients or customers or purchase e-mail address lists from a variety of sources. Full-service Web survey companies target populations, collect responses, and deliver data to the client. One of the most innovative is Google (http://www.google.com/insights/consumersurveys/home). The costs of such surveys can be low if an online survey service such as www.freeonlinesurveys.com—more of a do-it-yourself service—is used. Zoomerang (www.zoomerang.com) and Harris Interactive recruit and maintain pools of respondents to fit profiles that clients want to survey. Gender, income, and political persuasion are examples of characteristics that can be selected for Web survey purposes.

As in all research methods, there are advantages and disadvantages of using Web and e-mail surveys. The three major advantages are that (1) large samples are generated in a short amount of time, (2) they are more economical than even mailed questionnaires or phone interviews, and (3) data can be analyzed continually. The three major disadvantages are: (1) respondents are often self-selected, (2) there is no control over the size of the sample or selection of respondents, and (3) probability sampling is not achievable when a survey is simply made available on a website to all visitors.

Digital Analytics for Public Relations

Given the explosion in Web and social media as communication tools in public relations, an overview of the emerging tools and methods for doing research in online settings is essential. Learning ways to analyze what people are saying and thinking in places such as Twitter, the "blogosphere" for online opinion writing, Facebook postings, the web pages of virtually any organization in the world, and emerging communication platforms such as Pinterest and Instagram can provide a sound basis for planning and implementing communication programs.

The rise of digital strategies and tactics has led to a shift from more traditional archival and library work to a suite of research tools that this section groups together as digital analytics for public relations. Digital analytics will be presented in three sections to help organize the many emerging research tools and research strategies made possible in the digital age.

You can see where users enter and exit, what paths they follow, and where they come from in the first place . . . to break your site into specific components, establishing which are most effective and which need work.

Rob Toledo, Ragan's PR Daily

Web Analytics

The first section will provide an overview and some of the basic research methods used to help organizations make sense of their Web traffic and the impact of their websites on key publics. This is the most fully developed type of online research.

Social Media Monitoring Tools

The second section presents an overview of methods and services that can help an organization develop metrics to provide strategic information about social media efforts and plans.

Social Media Participatory Research

The third section introduces the idea that organizations should participate in social media as a qualitative research process that might also simply be called *listening* carefully to key audiences in virtual social settings.

Web Analytics

Web analytics provides information about the number of visitors to a website and the number of page views. It helps gauge traffic and popularity trends which is useful for setting measurable objectives and for improving the effectiveness of a website. Of equal importance, Web analytics applications help organizations measure the results of traditional print or broadcast campaigns. Analysts can estimate how traffic to a website changes after the launch of a new campaign as well as identify which campaign components are driving the most valuable Web traffic for the organization.

Web analytic procedures can be applied to **on-site** web pages maintained by an organization and **off-site** web pages maintained by others.

1. Off-site analytics enables the public relations professional to hear what others are saying on their sites and how big their audiences are. Knowing about the opportunities on other sites, as well as current knowledge and attitudes "out there," can help design a website that attracts visitors.

Figure 5.2 The Engagor Dashboard Summarizes Social Media Mentions

The Engagor Dashboard shows, at a glance, the number of mentions on sites such as Twitter and Facebook about the company or organization being represented in the social media environment. Such data can be essential in reports to a client about the impact of blogging, tweeting, or posting to Facebook for a cause or a product.

Dashboard source for permissions: http://engagor.com/features/social-media-dashboard

2. On-site Web analytics measure visitors' behavior once they are on the organization's website. The analysis tells the professional what causes visitors to stay on-site (drivers) and what causes desirable behavior on the site (conversions). Because conversions focus on the ultimate goals and objectives of the entire organization, conversions are the ultimate Web metric. Here are some public relations conversions that Web analytics captures:

- Donate to the organization
- Volunteer
- Purchase
- Comment favorably on the website

On-site Web analytics measures the performance of a website in a competitive environment where many organizations vie for the attention and loyalty of visitors. This process of assessing how a site ranks compared to its peers can help to improve a web site or the online audience response to a campaign.

Social Media Monitoring Tools

Social media analytics is the practice of gathering data from blogs and social media platforms. The most common use of social media analytics is to mine customer sentiment in order to support marketing and customer service activities. For example, a company may track how customers react to its offer of free supplies of heart medicine to low income persons.

The first step in a social media analytics initiative is to determine which goals the data analysis will benefit. Typical objectives include:

- Increasing revenues
- Tracking and managing issues
- Developing content that tracks trends in thinking and fashion (called memes)
- Increasing awareness of the organization's mission
- Improving public opinion of a particular cause or organization

Once the business goals have been identified, key performance indicators (KPIs) in social media environments can be defined. For example, customer engagement might be measured by the number of followers for a Twitter account and number of retweets and mentions of a company's name.

Services and apps help to tame the enormous amounts of social media content generated every day on the Internet. In addition to text analysis, many social media tools will harvest and store results in forms such as the report in Figure 5.2. Dashboards enable the public relations person to act on what is learned and to make concise reports to management.

A whole new and evolving vocabulary has arisen around the monitoring and analysis of social media. Some of the most important terms in public relations research about social media are:

share of voice (visibility)

for example, the National Rifle Association and gun control activists vie for voice-share in the ongoing discourse about guns buzz (comment analysis)

comments on news stories about Pope Francis trended vastly in favor of the humble Pontiff

sentiment (positive–negative valence of conversation)

tracking in blogs and discussion space such as Twitter are particularly important for strategy development and planning

mindshare (trends in news and comment)

Reddit's ranking of content by its users and Google Trends' calculations of Internet volume about topics help gauge what is on people's minds

meme (evolving ideas)

services identify memes that can shape message strategy to resonate with the current fashion in thought

Figure 5.3 BuzzStream for Social Media Monitoring

One of the best ways to grasp the process of social media monitoring is to go to social media monitoring sites such as BuzzStream and take a tour. The features depicted in the screenshot of BuzzStream focus on identifying social influencers for a given topic that can then be targeted by the public relations professional.

Table 5.4 Contribution of Web/Social Analytics and Social Media Monitoring to Public Relations Research

This table presents each of the uses of research in public relations covered on pages 151–153. Brief notes and popular tools are presented to help beginners get started with Web and Social analytics, as well as social media participation in public relations.

USES OF RESEARCH (PAGES 151–153)	WEB ANALYTIC AND SOCIAL MEDIA RESEARCH TOOLS
Credibility with Management	Large datasets and extensive textual analysis of comments and online discussion offer management real value from PR researchers.
Audience Segmentation	Google Analytics and BuzzStream not only identify key audiences but seamlessly provide action steps within their software systems.
Strategy Formulation	Web analytics and social media monitoring ensure evidence-based solutions to measurable problems and objectives.
Message Testing	Social media monitoring and participation afford wonderful test environments for determining how well messages will be received.
Management Reality Check	Dashboard screenshots combined with vivid quotes from social networks provide management alerts that are both credible and compelling.
Crisis Prevention	Online tools enable environmental scanning and issue tracking in real time with quantifiable measurement of trends in sentiment.
Competition Monitoring	Web analytics can give extensive, even exhaustive, documentation of what competitors are doing online and how those efforts are performing with key audiences.
Public Opinion Influence	Social media participation can serve to equip an organization with opportunities to engage in discourse that shapes media agendas and public opinion.
Publicity Generation	Traditional media increasingly follow what happens on websites and social media platforms, especially during viral events.
Success Measurement	Unprecedented amounts of data as well as exhibits of pages and social media posts enable precise assessments of success.

Social Media Participatory Research

Qualitative researchers and experienced public relations professionals know that one of the best ways to understand people—what they think, how they feel, how they get by from day-to-day, what they believe about current events—is participant observation. Engaging in conversations and discussions with key audiences and influencers can provide insights that would be difficult to obtain through large data analysis. This "walking around research" often happens now in virtual communities where people of all ages and demographics spend time online.

The following rather absorbing activities can actually be part of a day's work in public relations:

- Tweeting and following influential tweeters
- Pinning and viewing pins on Pinterest
- Watching and posting Youtube or Vimeo videos
- Reading blogs
- Reviewing comments on news stories and opinion pieces relevant to the client's business
- Tracking what people consider important or good current reading on Reddit
- Monitoring activity in Facebook groups that impact one's business

PRCasebook

Research Provides Foundation for Cookie Campaign

Ketchum Public Relations' award-winning campaign to celebrate 20 years of hospitality symbolized by the DoubleTree cookie was built on a broad and solid research foundation.

Targeting an Audience. One of the key contributions of research was to clearly identify and then flesh out characteristics of a key target audience. Ketchum employed a Simmons research audience profile called JUGGLER 2.0. This customer base, comprising 23 percent of all Americans, balances a family orientation with career ambition. Jugglers like to travel and have reasonable income to do so, but not necessarily at premium hotels.

Social media play a moderate role in the lives of these busy working parents. The target is not edgy Millennials, but people with kids who want a homey hotel experience. The cookie symbolizes this hospitality for parents and children alike.

Research for Campaign Publicity. A second major use of research by Ketchum can be called "main event" research. The agency commissioned a survey by its research division that gathered further intelligence for campaign planning, but was mainly an opportunity to garner media coverage and social media buzz. Reporters, bloggers, and commentators all avidly use substantive and interesting research results to strengthen stories or to pose a story angle.

Although research can be expensive to commission or to carry out, it does generate media interest when well done. In the provisional budget for the DoubleTree Cookie Campaign, two options were offered to garner media coverage: (1) a celebrity spokesperson or (2) a consumer survey. The celebrity lost out to the survey as a reliable and cost-effective means of contacting media about story ideas and telling audiences to think of DoubleTree Hotels as hospitable places to stay.

In subsequent chapters, the research foundation of the Doubletree campaign will provide a sound basis for planning the campaign, for developing messages and tactics on the road as part of the communication program by Ketchum staff, and for evaluating the campaign in progress and after its conclusion.

For example, the Health Communication Research Center (HCRC) in the Missouri School of Journalism discovered a potential problem while providing health public relations services for a grassroots social action group called Tobacco Free Missouri (TFM). An HCRC staffer participating in a discussion on the TFM site discovered that marketers were posting favorable comments and suggestions about electronic cigarettes. Because the product also poses health risks much like other tobacco products, staff developed a strategy for dealing with the interlopers. Fortunately, the marketers moved on before HCRC was forced to engage with them online.

Participatory research is not a license to spend hours dabbling online at work. But purposeful social media activity does offer an intuitive sense of what the climate is like for a client as well as a subtle understanding of the thinking among key stakeholders who can impact an organization.

Summary

The Importance of Research
Research is the basic groundwork of any public relations program. It involves the gathering and interpretation of information. Research is used in every phase of a communications program.

Secondary Research
Secondary research often begins by doing archival research, which reviews an organization's data on sales, profile of customers, and so on. Another source is information from library and online databases. Search engines such as Google and Bing allow practically everyone to find information and statistics on the Internet and the World Wide Web.

Qualitative Research
The value of this technique is that it gains insights into how individuals behave, think, and make decisions. It's also used to ascertain whether key messages were communicated by the media. The primary techniques are: (1) content analysis, (2) interviews, (3) focus groups, (4) copy testing, and (5) ethnographic observation and role-playing.

Quantitative Research
This kind of research demands statistical rigor and proper sampling procedures so that information will be representative of the general population. Random sampling gives everyone in the target audience the chance to be in the sample. Sample size determines the margin of error in the statistical findings.

Questionnaire Construction
Many factors are considered when designing a questionnaire, including wording, biased questions, politically correct answers, and answer categories. Guidelines include clearly deciding what you want to find out, keeping the questionnaire relatively short, defining the target audience, and selecting the appropriate sample size.

How to Reach Respondents
Survey respondents may be reached by mail, telephone, personal interviews, and omnibus surveys. Increasingly, surveys are being done via the Web and e-mail, as well as services such as Google Consumer Surveys.

Digital Analytics and Social Media Monitoring
Over the past five years, many methods, systems, and software tools have emerged to measure where people go, how long they stay, and what they do on websites. Similar tools help us know details of the social interaction of millions of people worldwide on Facebook, Twitter, and other virtual gathering places.

Case Activity Conducting Research about Rumors in Real Time

The board of directors of Hi-Loft Golf Clubs, International, was split down the middle about how to deal with supposed rumors that the company was filing for bankruptcy. Although the U.S. economic collapse had severely stressed the company's resources, Hi-Loft had actually come through stronger than expected. And yet, the 6,000 employees seemed to be stricken by fear of job losses.

Some board members argued that the worries would take care of themselves with time. They counseled to avoid making the issue any bigger by publicly addressing it. Others disagreed. The public relations director was brought in to provide a recommendation. Because she had started a social media monitoring process earlier in the year, she reported to the board that some quick visits to social media sites as well as buzz analysis indicated the company had a serious problem. She stated, "Employee morale is indeed very low and perception sometimes creates reality."

After her substantive briefing, Hi-Loft's board voted to take the bankruptcy rumor head on with a communication campaign targeting employees, community leaders, and investors.

As a recently trained public relations graduate, you are placed in charge of tracking the social media and Web impact of this campaign for a report at the board's semi-annual meeting in six months. You have a week to lay out your quantitative and qualitative methods for determining success of the campaign to restore confidence in the future of Hi-Loft. Draft a short memo of research recommendations.

Questions For Review and Discussion

1. Why is research important in accomplishing an organization's goals?
2. Research is said to be "a form of listening." What is its role in public relations?
3. Identify at least five ways that research is used in public relations.
4. What is secondary data research? How is it different or similar to primary research?
5. List at least five informal research methods.
6. What are online databases? How are they used by public relations professionals?
7. How can the Internet and World Wide Web be used as research tools?
8. What is the procedure for organizing and conducting a focus group? What are the pros and cons of using focus groups?
9. What is an intercept interview?
10. What is the difference between probability (random) and nonprobability samples?
11. Define content analysis and its relevance in public relations.
12. Describe three practical uses of Web analytics and social media monitoring.
13. Identify at least five guidelines that should be followed when preparing a questionnaire.
14. What are the pros and cons of each of the following: mail questionnaires, telephone surveys, personal interviews, piggyback surveys, and Web surveys?
15. Why is it important to analyze an organization's own website for drivers and conversions?

Media Resources

Bowen, S., Gilfeather, J., & Rawlins, B. (March 7, 2012). *Ethical Standards and Guidelines for Public Relations Research and Measurement*. Approved by IPR Measurement Commission, Retrieved from http://www.instituteforpr.org/topics/ethical-standards-and-guidelines-for-public-relations-research-and-measurement/

Duhé, S. (2012). A thematic analysis of thirty years of public relations literature addressing the potential and pitfalls of new media. In S. Duhé (Ed.), *New media and public relations* (2nd ed., pp. xiii–xxvi). New York: Peter Lang.

Moran, R., & Ryan, T. (2012, June). Are focus groups still an effective method to gauge consumer insight? *PRWeek*, 27.

Paine, K. D. (2011). *Measure what matters: Online tools for understanding customers, social media, engagement, and key relationships*. New York: Wiley.

Stacks, D. W. (2010). *Primer of public relations research*. New York, NY: Guilford Press.

Stansberry, K. (2011). Mapping mommy bloggers: Using online social network analysis to study publics. *PRism* *8*(2), 1–14.

Toledo, R. (2013). A Beginner's Guide to Google Analytics. *Ragan's PR Daily*, April 24, 2013.

chapter 6

The Public Relations Process

After reading this chapter, you will be able to:

- Understand the value of the planning process
- Identify the elements of a plan
- Describe two approaches to planning
- Provide a rationale for including each element of a plan
- Describe the essentials of each element of a plan

The Value of Planning

A program plan is the formal, written presentation of your research findings and program recommendations for strategy, tactics, and evaluation.

Ronald Smith, author of Strategic Planning for Public Relations

The second step of the public relations process, following research, is program planning. In the RACE acronym mentioned in Chapter 1, this step was labeled "Action" because the organization starts making plans to do something about an issue or situation. Before any public relations activity can be implemented, it is essential that considerable thought be given to what should be done and in what sequence to accomplish the organization's objectives.

A good public relations program hinges on an effective strategy to support the organization's business, marketing, and communication objectives. Jim Lukaszewski, a veteran public relations counselor, adds, "Strategy is a unique mixture of mental energy, injected into an organization through communication, which results in behavior that achieves organizational objectives."

In other words, public relations planning should be strategic. As Glen Broom and David Dozier say in their text Using Public Relations Research, "Strategic planning is deciding where you want to be in the future (the goal) and how to get there (the strategies). It sets the organization's direction proactively, avoiding 'drift' and routine repetition of activities." A practitioner must think about a situation, analyze what can be done about it, creatively conceptualize the appropriate strategies and tactics, and determine how the results will be measured. Planning also involves the coordination of multiple methods—social media, news releases, special events, web pages, press kits, news conferences, media interviews, brochures, newsletters, speeches, advocacy ads, and so on—to achieve specific results.

Systematic and strategic planning prevents haphazard, ineffective communication. Having a blueprint of what is to be done and how it will be executed makes programs more effective and public relations more valuable to the organization.

Approaches to Planning

Planning is like putting together a jigsaw puzzle. Research, which was discussed in Chapter 5, provides the various pieces. Next, it is necessary to arrange the pieces so that a coherent design, or picture, emerges. The best planning is systematic, that is, gathering information, analyzing it, and creatively applying it for the specific purpose of attaining an objective.

Planning is important because a plan is the instrument used to propose and obtain approvals, a mechanism for monitoring and evaluating and a product that distinguishes true public relations professionals.

Thomas R. Hagley, author of Writing Winning Proposals: PR Cases

Management by Objective

One fundamental approach to planning is a process called management by objectives (MBO). MBO provides focus and direction for formulating strategy to achieve specific organizational objectives. According to Robert E. Simmons, author of Communication Campaign Management, the use of MBO in planning ensures the "production of relevant messages and establishes criteria against which campaign results can be measured."

In their seminal book *Public Relations Management by Objectives*, Norman R. Nager and T. Harrell Allen discuss nine basic MBO steps that can help a practitioner conceptualize everything

on the job
INSIGHTS

Social Media in Action

Planners for the Cookie CAREavan campaign for DoubleTree Hotels knew that social media would be important to the target audience, the Jugglers 2.0 described in Chapter 5. In fact, the socially savvy hotel chain is known for its comprehensive social media training at each of its 250 international properties.

The CAREavan plan included a second online strategy requiring extensive tactical steps from shooting video regularly that was then edited and posted to social spaces such as YouTube. Tour staff captured "Cookie Confessionals," short videos of people sharing when they most need a DoubleTree chocolate chip cookie to brighten their day. A simple video camera and an external microphone to capture the best sound quality were on hand at events along with publicity waiver forms to get the video capture done properly. Videos were shared on the Cookie CAREavan Facebook tab.

To leverage the on-site work, DoubleTree by Hilton's social media agency, Digital Royalty, executed plan components developed by Ketchum and DoubleTree. The contractor was tasked with posting the videos on social media platforms in real time throughout the tour. The strategy was to reach young professionals where they spend time (in social space) using video—the most preferred format for audiences today. The tactics fulfill the strategy through action steps accounted for in the planning process by the client well before the campaign launch. Ketchum and Digital Royalty provided support and training so that the capacity to do social media efficiently was already in place as the national tour unfolded. Preparation and planning, including a strong grounding in social media techniques, assured success for the online component of the CAREavan campaign.

Sources: Silver Anvil and http://thedigitalroyalty.com

from a simple news release to a multifaceted communication program. The steps can serve as a planning checklist that provides the basis for strategic planning.

1. **Client/employer objectives.** What is the purpose of the communication, and how does it promote or achieve the objectives of the organization? A specific objective such as "to make 40% of television buyers aware of the product's #1 *Consumer Reports* rating" is more meaningful than "to make people aware of the product."

2. **Audience/publics.** Who exactly should be reached with the message, and how can that audience help achieve the organization's objectives? What are the characteristics of the audience, and how can demographic information be used to structure the message? The primary audience for a campaign to encourage carpooling consists of people who belong to environmental groups and commute long distances, not the general public.

3. **Audience objectives.** What is it that the audience wants to know, and how can the message be tailored to audience self-interest? Consumers are more interested in how a new tablet computer will increase their productivity than in how it works.

4. **Media channels.** What is the appropriate channel for reaching the audience, and how can multiple channels such as news media, brochures, special events, and Twitter reinforce the message among key publics? A news release or an ad may be good for making consumers aware of a new product, but a posting on a popular consumer website may be better for conveying more credible consumer information about the product.

5. **Media channel objectives.** What is the media gatekeeper looking for in a news angle, and why would a particular publication be interested in the information? A community newspaper is primarily interested in a story with a local angle. A television station is interested in stories that have good visuals and emotional impact.

6. **Sources and questions.** What primary and secondary sources of information are required to provide a factual base for the message? What experts should be interviewed? What archival, secondary, and primary research should be conducted? A quote from a project engineer about a new technology is better than a quote from the marketing vice president. A survey, properly conducted, might be best for media interest if there's an interesting statistic or finding.

7. **Communication strategies.** What environmental factors will affect the dissemination and acceptance of the message? Are the target publics hostile or favorably disposed to the message? What other events or pieces of information negate or reinforce the message? A campaign to conserve water is more salient if there has been a recent drought.

8. **Essence of the message.** What is the planned communication impact on the audience? Is the message designed merely to inform, or is it designed to change attitudes and behaviors? Telling people about the dangers of global climate change is different from telling people what they can do about it.

9. **Nonverbal support.** How can photographs, graphs, films, and artwork clarify and visually enhance the written message? Bar graphs, pie charts, and other infographics are easier to understand than columns of numbers.

An Agency Planning Model

By working through the checklist adapted from Nager and Allen's book, a practitioner has in place the general building blocks for planning. These building blocks serve as background to create a specific plan. Ketchum offers a more business-oriented, competitive set of questions in its "Strategic Planning Model for Public Relations." Its organizational model makes sense to professionals and clients alike, moving both parties toward the clear situation analysis needed to make planning relevant to the client's overall objectives. As Larry Werner, executive vice president of Ketchum, points out, "No longer are we simply in the business of putting press releases out; we're in the business of solving business problems through communications." See the Insights box on page 179 for an example of Cookie CAREavan strategies to promote DoubleTree's reputation for hospitality.

Facts

- **Category facts.** What are recent industry trends?
- **Product/service issues.** What are the significant characteristics of the product, service, or issue?
- **Competitive facts.** Who are the competitors, and what are their competitive strengths, similarities, and differences?
- **Customer facts.** Who uses the product and why?

Goals

- **Business objectives.** What are the company's business objectives? What is the time frame?
- **Role of public relations.** How does public relations fit into the marketing mix?
- **Sources of new business.** What sectors will produce growth?

Audience

- **Target audiences.** Who are the target audiences? What are their "hot" buttons?
- **Current mindset.** How do audiences feel about the product, service, or issue?
- **Desired mindset.** How do we want them to feel?

Key Message

- **Main point.** What one key message must be conveyed to change or reinforce mindsets?

Each of the many planning processes has its strengths and weaknesses. The culture of the organization as well as the wants and needs of upper management will often give a public relations professional the best indication of which planning approach to adopt. For example, executives who take a bottom-line orientation concerning performance will likely prefer the Ketchum approach to strategic planning. These various approaches to planning lead to the next important step—the writing of a strategic public relations plan. The next section explains the elements of such a plan.

While we want to tell the feel-good story, we also realize that media don't necessarily embrace positive story lines . . . employ an angle that speaks to DoubleTree by Hilton's messages, but also embraces . . . distributing 50,000 cookies throughout New York City in one day.

Strategic consideration included in the Ketchum plan for the Cookie CAREavan

Elements of a Program Plan

A public relations program plan identifies what is to be done, why, and how to accomplish it. By preparing such a plan, either as a brief outline or as an extensive document, the practitioner can make certain that all the elements have been properly considered and that everyone involved understands the "big picture."

It is common practice for public relations firms to prepare a program plan for client approval and possible modification before implementing a public relations campaign. At that time, both the public relations firm and the client reach a mutual understanding of the campaign's objectives and how to accomplish them.

Public relations departments of organizations also map out a particular campaign or show the department's plans for the coming year.

Although there can be some variation, public relations plans include eight basic elements:

1. Situation
2. Objectives
3. Audience
4. Strategy
5. Tactics
6. Calendar/timetable
7. Budget
8. Evaluation

The following offers a brief description of the various components of a public relations plan and also gives some examples from campaigns receiving PRSA Silver Anvil awards. In addition, the PR Casebook on page 183 gives a real-world example of how public relations planning can include a blend of traditional events and media coverage to achieve measurable objectives that matter to top management.

Situation

Valid objectives cannot be set without a clear understanding of the situation that led to the conclusion that a public relations program is needed. Three traditional situations often prompt a public relations program: (1) The organization must conduct a remedial program to overcome a problem or negative situation; (2) the organization needs to conduct a specific, one-time project to launch a new product or service; or (3) the organization wants to reinforce an ongoing effort to preserve its reputation and public support.

Monster energy drinks, for example, had to conduct a remedial program after the Food and Drug Administration (FDA) claimed that five people may have died over the past three years after consuming Monster's highly caffeinated drinks. In a more humorous situation, Lululemon had to do a remedial program after reports emerged that its black yoga pants were too sheer and revealing when people bent over, leading to the company being the butt of jokes on late night TV.

Specific, one-time events often lead to public relations programs. IBM, for example, conducted a series of events to celebrate its 100th birthday. One such event was a yearlong volunteerism initiative that involved community service organizations worldwide and generated the participation of more than 80 percent of the company's 400,000 employees. The Beam Company also conducted an extensive public relations and marketing campaign to introduce its new Skinnygirl Margarita product at a yacht club in New York.

In the third situation, program plans are initiated to reinforce corporate reputation or to preserve customer loyalty or public support. Procter and Gamble (P&G) put its enormous family of brands behind a school dropout prevention program named Communities in the Schools (CIS). Mainstream consumers who used a P&G brandSAVER coupon triggered a \$.02 donation to dropout prevention. The coupon program generated \$0.6 million for the charity and bolstered P&G's standing with consumers.

PRCasebook

Chase Sapphire Serves Up Foodie Experiences

A public relations plan contains eight basic elements. The following is an outline of a plan that Chase Bank and its public relations firm, Ketchum, developed to build awareness for its upscale rewards credit card in the affluent portion of the San Francisco market.

Situation

Ketchum grounded the campaign in primary, qualitative research by arranging for Chase executives to spend two days immersed in the San Francisco culture. Neighborhood visits included a tour of hot dining spots, meetings and panel discussions with leaders in arts, food, philanthropy, media, and politics. The executives learned that well-heeled Bay residents take pride in DIY (do-it-yourself) skills, care deeply about charitable causes, and make San Francisco a top foodie city, a place where quality and innovation in food choices are paramount.

A subsequent media audit of food coverage in the Bay area revealed that events sponsored by *Sunset* magazine and San Francisco Chefs were heavily covered by lifestyle reporters. Key story angles for the campaign featured celebrity chefs and the growing food truck trend.

Ketchum identified several key insights to inform the campaign strategy:

- Choose Sunset Weekend and SF Chefs as premier events.
- Embrace DIY-oriented food events and topics.
- Build food–media relationships to drive positive coverage.
- Put real money into community supported charities.

Objectives

Ketchum used several useful types of objectives, including the following:

Awareness Objective: Increase awareness for Chase Sapphire to 60 percent of affluent San Francisco target audience.

Communication Objective: Secure publicity in food and lifestyle outlets showing Sapphire as a facilitator of unique food experiences.

Media Objective: Secure 50 million media impressions (a calculation of the potential total audience for publications or broadcast programs featuring Sapphire in any way).

Target Audience

Sapphire sought the "working affluent" who value quality time more than money and who enjoy new experiences, personal education, and charitable events.

Strategies and Tactics

- **Strategy:** Align with celebrity chefs and local charities to drive visibility for Chase Sapphire as a supporter of unique culinary experiences.
- One **Tactic** was hosting a culinary battle for charity, which entailed special event planning and media hosting.
- **Strategy:** Engage target audience with the city's food truck obsession.
  - Tactics included an eater's choice awards program for food truck contestants and related so cial media conversation.
  - And funding of donations to the local food bank that were commensurate with the awards.

Calendar

The program was developed around selected food events over a six-month span in the Bay area. Initially, the campaign quietly built its credibility in the local food scene by participating in what was already happening in the food scene. Later in the campaign, Chase sponsored its own culinary experiences and events in the community.

Budget

The budget for the campaign was undisclosed.

(continued)

Evaluation

Evaluation was quite substantive because it was based on specific, measurable objectives for participation, media coverage, and increase in card memberships. Results included:

- A 12 percent increase in new Sapphire card applications
- Awareness of the card exceeding the 60 percent target
- The objective of 50 million media impressions for campaign coverage exceeded the objective by 40 percent—70 million

These numbers reflect measurable success that top management can assess objectively for impact on the financial bottom line. For many campaigns, achieving numerical and financial objectives is the ultimate endorsement for the campaign's success.

In a program plan, relevant research often is included as part of the situation analysis. Generally, this involves environmental scanning by closely following local and national news as well as the newer social media participation introduced in Chapter 5. Scanning the external communication environment is a crucial means of recognizing an issue or an opportunity that merits a carefully planned campaign.

Objectives

Once the situation or problem is understood, the next step is to establish objectives for the program. A stated objective should be evaluated by asking: (1) Does it really address the situation? (2) Is it realistic and achievable? (3) Can success be measured in meaningful terms?

It is particularly important that public relations objectives complement and reinforce the organization's objectives. Professor David Dozier of San Diego State University expressed the point well in a Public Relations Review article: "The prudent and strategic selection of public relations goals and objectives linked to organizational survival and growth serves to justify the public relations program as a viable management activity."

Before goals and tactics are drafted, PR directors must thoroughly understand their organization's business plan.

David B. Oates, a Stalwart Communications executive, San Diego

Basically, objectives are either informational or motivational.

Informational Objectives Many public relations plans are designed primarily to expose audiences to information through key message points and to increase awareness of an issue, an event, or a product. The five objectives of public relations activity will be discussed in Chapter 7. The first two of these—message exposure and accurate dissemination of messages—are the most common.

The following are some examples of informational objectives:

- **Mexico Tourism:** "Reset the US media dialogue by proactively engaging a powerful army of advocates to speak on behalf of Mexico . . . ."
- **Best Bones Forever!:** "Increase awareness of . . . about the importance of bone health."
- **P&G's Communities in the Schools (CIS):** "Raise profile and position of CIS in order to increase awareness of the organization and its success."

One difficulty with informational objectives is measuring how well a particular objective has been achieved. Public awareness and the extent of education that takes place are somewhat abstract and difficult to quantify. Some novices try to quantify informational objectives by stating something like "Increase awareness 30 percent."

That's very difficult to prove unless an organization has solid baseline research determining the awareness level of the target audience before the campaign was launched and another scientific sample after the campaign to measure any differences in the audience's knowledge or perceptions.

Another approach that many organizations and public relations firms take is to infer that "awareness" or "education" occurred because many media placements were obtained. In reality, message exposure doesn't necessarily lead to increased public awareness. First the message must be viewed or read and then the audience must actually internalize the message for it to have any real impact on knowledge or attitude, much less on behavior. (See Chapter 7 for more on information processing.)

Motivational Objectives Although changing attitudes and influencing behavior are difficult to accomplish in a public relations campaign, motivational objectives are much easier to measure than informational ones. That's because the former are bottom-line-oriented and based on clearly measurable results that can be quantified. This is true whether the objective is an increase in product sales, a sellout crowd for a theatrical performance, or expanded donations to a charitable agency. The following are some examples of motivational objectives:

- **IBM Service Jam:** "Conduct service projects in majority of 170 countries in which IBM operates."
- **Best Bones Forever!:** "Increase physical activity levels and consumption of foods with calcium and vitamin D."
- **Suave Parading with Style:** "Drive product trial via consumer engagement of new Suave Professionals styling products."

Although many public relations programs specify an increased number or percentage as a target, others don't. That increase, of course, could be minimal and still meet the objective of the campaign. Objective setting is the joint responsibility of the public relations firm and the client. Both sides have to keep in mind that the objectives, as already mentioned, must be realistic, achievable, and measurable in some way. Chapter 8 further discusses measurement and evaluation.

Audience

Public relations programs should be directed toward specific and defined audiences or publics. Although some campaigns are directed to a general public, such instances are the exception. Even the word-of-mouth campaign for Clorox Anywhere bleach, a variant of a common household item, was specifically targeted to moms with children under six who are active in the community.

In other words, public relations practitioners target specific publics within the general public. This is done through market research that can identify key publics by such demographics as age, income, social strata, zip code, education, and existing ownership or consumption of specific products. For example, market research told Suave styling products that Latinas like to share their experiences about products, especially on Facebook where 4 in 5 of Suave's Hispanic target market spend time. In fact, Latinas are one of the fastest growing online demographics in the United States.

This audience for Suave professional hair styling products who like to be "Red Carpet Ready" is featured in the Multicultural World box on page 188, which focuses on style-oriented Latinas.

The following are examples of how other organizations have defined target audiences.

- **Mexico Tourism:** Media influencers, such as travel/tourism reporters; U.S., Canadian, and European consumers; Online advocates such as bloggers and "tweet stars"....
- **Chase Sapphire:** "Working Affluent" who care about food and wine, ... personal growth and charities.
- **Best Bones Forever!:** American girls who all tend to decline in physical activity levels from pre-teen through teen years to the detriment of their bone health. Research found that friendship and mutual encouragement energized girls who were generally blasé about long-term bone health.

Many campaigns have multiple audiences, depending on the objectives of the campaign. An example is the Catholic Basilica of Minneapolis. Its annual fund-raising concert to aid the homeless identified four target audiences:

- Potential concert-goers
- Participating performers
- Local music-scene influencers
- Event volunteers

Some organizations and public relations firms identify the media as a "public." On occasion, in programs that seek media endorsements or try to change how the media report on an organization or an issue, editors and reporters can become a legitimate "public." In general, however, mass media outlets fall in the category of a means to an end, channels to reach defined audiences that need to be informed, persuaded, and motivated.

A thorough understanding of the primary and secondary publics is key to accomplishing a program's objectives. Such knowledge also sharpens selection of appropriate strategies and tactics to reach defined audiences. Cost is a driving force for narrowing the audience; spending large sums to reach members of the general public on matters in which they have no stake or interest is nonproductive and a waste of money.

Strategy

A strategy describes how and why campaign components will achieve objectives. A strategy provides guidelines and key message themes for the overall program, and offers a rationale for the actions and program components that are planned. A single strategy may be outlined or a program may have several strategies, depending on the objectives and the designated audiences.

With the motto "Go big or go home," Doritos made a strategic gamble so daring that Las Vegas bookies accepted bets on whether it would pay off. The company gave fans complete creative control of the brand and dangled a reward so sweet it motivated avid consumer and media engagement. Among the strategies were:

1. Invite America to develop Doritos Super Bowl ads and award the winning creator with $1 million.
2. Implement a two-pronged media outreach approach to simultaneously reach Doritos' core target audience and likely ad competition entrants and maintain ongoing coverage in mainstream news outlets.

Key Messages Public relations plans, as part of the strategy, often contain a listing of key messages that the campaign wants to get across to the target audiences and the media. In the case of Go Red for Women, a national awareness campaign for heart disease in women, the three key messages were:

1. Heart disease is the number-one killer of women.
2. Take the Go Red Heart Checkup to find out your personal risk for heart disease.
3. Spread the national rallying cry to "Share Your Untold Story of the Heart."

In the case of Ketchum's DoubleTree cookie CAREavan campaign, the key messages were as follows:

25th Anniversary of the Cookie. The hotel chain will celebrate the anniversary of its signature chocolate chip cookie by touring various cities and distributing samples through a summer CAREavan tour.

Share the Care. Little things and kindness mean a lot and help contribute to a rewarding hotel experience—the ultimate mission of the chain's 60,000 employees.

Join Us Online. Visit *www.facebook.com/DoubleTree* to enter a sweepstakes and get the latest news and deals on all the properties.

Tactics

Tactics, in contrast to strategies, are the nuts-and-bolts part of the plan. They describe the specific activities that put each strategy into operation and help to achieve the stated objectives. In the public relations field, the implementation of various tactics is

on the job INSIGHTS

A New Frontier for Strategy

One of the tendencies in human nature that is shared among public relations professionals is a blind faith in common sense as well as a tendency to use a "same-old, same-old" approach to strategies.

Both of these are probably wise instincts in general. However, from the perspective of upper management, commonsensical, clichéd counsel on communication strategy may appear less rigorous and less valuable than comparable counsel from legal professionals who bring case law to bear on questions, or counsel from consulting engineers who bring materials science to their recommendations to management. Over the last several decades, a large body of social science research has developed to provide better understanding of how communication works and what effect it has on audiences.

The next frontier for the field of public relations, and for students entering the profession now, should be to embrace theories of communication as a basis for strategy recommendations. (See Chapters 9 and 10 for an introduction to many of the social science breakthroughs that can provide a sound basis for strategy development.)

on the job

A MULTICULTURAL WORLD

Latinas Don't Walk, They Strut: A Celebration of Latin Style

Hispanics have become an important audience for most brands, but it takes special insight to design a public relations program that is culturally relevant to them. This was the challenge that Unilever and its public relations firm, Edelman Worldwide, faced in promoting its Suave Haircare products.

One insight was that Latinas don't just march to their own tune. They strut. They like to look their best in clothes, shoes, and make-up. They also place a great emphasis on their hair, so Suave Haircare and Edelman used this insight to introduce its 175 beauty products to a Hispanic audience with the theme, "Desfilando Contigo con Mas Estilo" (Strutting with you with more styles).

Celebrity stylist Leonardo Rocco and friends.

The strategy for Suave was to position its hair care products as access to achievable "red carpet" beauty by (1) partnering with top Spanish-language media Univision and People en Espanol to build strong onside, online, TV, print, and in-store promotions, (2) using celebrity stylist Leonardo Rocco as an expert voice on the brand, and (3) enlisting "Hispanic America's sweetheart" Blanca Soto to build credibility for the products.

The program had several elements. One was being the official hair sponsor of Premios Juventud (Youth Awards), Univision's top-rated show hosted by Blanca Soto. The major event was when Blanca revealed her fan-voted winning hairstyle, created by Suave stylist Leonardo Rocco. In addition, a number of in-store retail events were held. Social media included real-time beauty advice from Rocco and Blanca on a Facebook page since surveys indicated that 84 percent of Hispanic moms are on Facebook.

The results, which won a PRSA Silver Anvil for excellence in 2012, were impressive.

- Awareness of Suave Haircare increased six-fold, including three editor choice awards for styling products.
- Sales increased almost 13 percent.
- Likes on Facebook increased by 43,000 and 36,000 requested free product coupons.

the most visible part of any plan. Tactics use various methods to reach target audiences with key messages. Chapters 13 through 16 discuss tactical communication tools in greater detail. To help the reader better understand the difference between strategies and tactics, several tactics of the campaign plan to promote Suave Professionals beauty products (see the Intercultural World box) to Latina consumers are nested under the strategy that drove the campaign:

> **Strategy:** Partnering with top Spanish-language media Univision and People en Espanol to build out strong onsite, online, TV, print, and in-store promotions.
>
> **Tactics:** (1) Consumer Engagement—Suave secured the official position as Hair Sponsor of Univision's top-rated award show hosted by rising novella (soap opera) star Blanca Soto. A show highlight was Soto revealing her fan-voted winning hairstyle created by Suave stylist Leonardo Rocco.
>
> (2) Social Media—Facebook page, Belleza Suave, featured Rocco's real-time

Strategy establishes why something is being proposed and why it will achieve the purposes of the campaign. But it is in the tactics that the job gets done.

And a crucial part of detailed planning requires that the "marching orders" or action steps get into the hands of those who will do the work. Ketchum created a toolkit for local DoubleTree hotels to do their own marketing and event promotion consistent with the entire look and scheme of the CAREavan tour. Toolkits prove equally valuable for the people on the ground that may not be trained in public relations as well as the campaign planners who want a safe and coordinated effort by associates who are supportive of the effort.

Conceiving tactics requires a lot of creativity, which is often accomplished through a brainstorming session that can generate any number of ideas from the practical to the impractical. The goal is to generate many ideas that are innovative and unusual, but grounded in the objectives of the program (Table 6.1).

Calendar/Timetable

The next step is to determine a timetable for the campaign or program. Depending on the objectives and complexity of the program plan, a campaign may last less than three months. Other programs may take more than a year to implement all the strategies and tactics required to accomplish program objectives. The following are three aspects of establishing a calendar and timetable for a program.

The Timing of a Campaign Program planning should take into account when key messages are most meaningful to the intended audience. A campaign to encourage carpooling, for example, might be more successful if it follows a major price increase

Table 6.1 **Tactics by Media Category**

A useful way to categorize tactics for disseminating messages is the four categories of media that can be used—paid, earned, shared, or owned. Given here is a simplified version of the planning matrix used by Fleishman Hillard.

	TECHNIQUE	AUDIENCE	INFLUENCE	DESIRED ACTION
Paid	Purchase ads to reach millions	Large media audiences	Ads often discounted as biased sales pitches	Remember message when voting or joining or buying
Earned	Pitch news stories to traditional media	Readers and viewers of news content	Credible coverage, but of both sides of a story	Change or reinforce position on an issue or event
Shared	Participate in social media	Other tweeters, bloggers, Facebookers, etc.	Engaging and personal, but preaching to a choir	Consider input from virtual friends and colleagues
Owned	Mount content on your own websites	Visitors to your websites	Satisfies information needs but pushes your view	Reinforce or even act on prior view of your organization

in gasoline or a government report that traffic congestion has reached gridlock proportions. Continuing news coverage and public concern about an issue or event also trigger public relations campaigns. Some subjects are seasonal. The rock 'n' roll concert series on the grounds of the Minneapolis Basilica takes place in the summer. A similar series in San Diego might be done in any month, but in Minnesota the series needs to happen when temperatures are pleasant. The timing also serves to raise funds that will help the homeless through the winter season to come. Charitable agencies, such as Second Harvest Food Banks, launch special campaigns around Thanksgiving and Christmas, when there is increased interest in helping the unfortunate.

Other kinds of campaigns depend less on environmental or seasonal context. For example, Home Instead Senior Care Service promotes its 40–70 rule year-round (children in their forties need to talk to their parents in their seventies about long-term care year-round). Similarly, the launch of the IBM 100-year anniversary commemorated the beginning of the company, but the celebration was a yearlong, worldwide effort to spur local volunteerism by employees, not a self-congratulatory fest.

on the job ETHICS

Grassroots Environmentalism: Conflict of Interest or a Win-Win?

In response to record-high oil prices that were driving airlines into bankruptcy, a coalition of business and labor groups formed a grassroots campaign against oil speculation in commodity-trading markets. Two weeks of intense strategic planning resulted in a movement called SOS Now (Stop Oil Speculation Now). The plan included impressive tactics:

- Broad coalition building
- Clear, multilingual website
- Airline Frequent Flier Call to Action
- Grassroots advocacy to Congress
- Coalition media toolkit
- Coalition press conference
- Congressional information packets

The campaign succeeded in building congressional interest in regulatory action, resulting in investors pulling $39 billion from commodity markets during the first seven weeks of the campaign. Public opinion polls taken before and during the campaign showed a jump from 6 percent to 50 percent against speculative oil trading. Although planning, execution, and outcomes of the campaign were impressive, several ethical questions need to be considered.

- The SOS campaign was motivated by skyrocketing fuel costs but didn't make it clear that SOS was instigated primarily by the airline industry. In 2012, this "oversight" was addressed through explicit support for airlinesforamerica.org. Is this effort really a grassroots movement? Is it ethical, according to PRSA ethical guidelines, to create what are called false-front organizations? What is needed for such movements to be ethical? Is the more explicitly named airlines group more appropriate?
- Would it be ethical for the American Petroleum Institute (API) to undertake a similar campaign opposing SOS, based on API's conviction that free markets should exist and that the only way to ensure oil exploration and production is healthy oil markets, with strong oil prices responding to supply and demand pressures?
- Environmental activists argue that high fuel prices are good for the environment because they curtail wasteful travel. Would such groups be doing the right thing to argue for oil speculation?

The point may be that in a free society, pluralistic voices often arise on opposing sides of an issue. (See Chapter 10 for explication of the idea of a wrangle of voices in the marketplace of ideas and that there is no single worldview or "truth.") The key may be to work for an organization that one personally believes in, whether, in this case, that is the airline, the petroleum, or the environmental group.

Source: @StopSpeculation on Twitter, 2013

Scheduling of Tactics The second aspect of timing is the scheduling and sequencing of various tactics or activities. A typical pattern is to concentrate the most effort at the beginning of a campaign, when a number of tactics are implemented. The launch phase of a campaign, much like that of a rocket, requires a burst of activity just to break the awareness barrier. After the campaign has achieved orbit, however, less energy and fewer activities are required to maintain momentum.

Public relations campaigns often are the first stage of an integrated marketing communication program. Once public relations has created awareness and customer anticipation of a new product, the second stage may be a marketing and advertising campaign.

Apple serves as a paragon of suspense and anticipation in product development and launch. The iPad, Apple's dominant tablet computer generated thousands of news stories before it was available for purchase. Ads for the device didn't appear until several months after the launch of the new product. Apple kept buzz about the product going by rolling out new versions, dropping prices of earlier versions, and promoting the app store, the nifty applications for the iPad developed by inventive third-party programmers.

Currently, Apple CEO Tim Cook is signaling that an Apple "iWatch" receives serious thought and attention in the company. But in classic Apple form perfected by founder Steve Jobs, the current CEO is coy about a smart watch. "The wrist is interesting," Cook said, noting that it is more natural [than Google's smart eyeglass device]. "You still have to convince people it is worth wearing."

Compiling a Calendar An integral part of timing is advance planning. A video news release (VNR), a press kit, or a brochure often takes weeks or months to prepare. Arrangements for special events also take considerable time. Practitioners must thus take into account the deadlines of publications. Monthly periodicals, for example, frequently need information several months before publication. A popular talk show may book guests three or four months in advance.

Figure 6.1 **A Typical Gantt Chart**

Basic Gantt charts can depict work flow, but tend to be spare in detail. An alternative is a more detailed timeline that includes key action items by month to accomplish the strategy and achieve basic objectives. A good example is an excerpt from Ketchum's DoubleTree Cookie CAREavan shown in Figure 6.2.

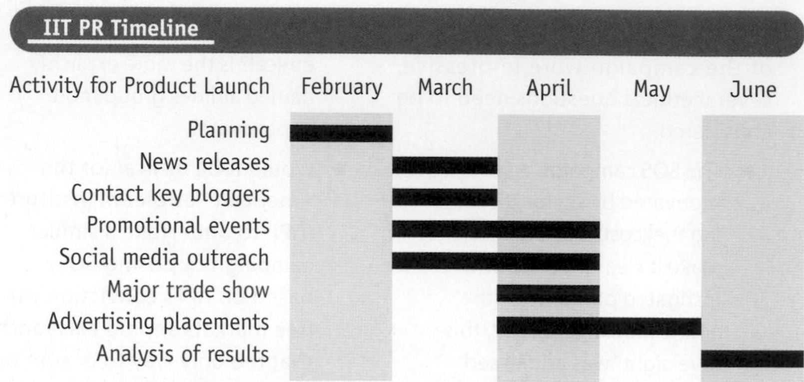

The public relations professional must think ahead to make things happen in the right sequence at the right time. One way to achieve this goal is to compile timelines and charts that list the necessary steps and their required completion dates. Calendars and timelines take various forms. One simple method is to post activities for each day on a large monthly calendar that indicates who has responsibility for a particular task. Gantt charts (see Figure 6.1) are popular for scheduling purposes and can be formatted easily using Microsoft Excel or an Office template.

Budget

No program plan is complete without a budget. Both clients and employers ask, "How much will this program cost?" In many cases, the reverse approach is taken, in which organizations establish an amount they can afford and then ask the public relations staff or firm to write a program plan that reflects the amount allocated.

A budget is often divided into two categories: (1) staff time and (2) out-of-pocket expenses. The latter often goes by the acronym OOP and includes such collateral material as news releases, media kits, brochures, VNRs, transportation, Web programming, and even video production. Staff and administrative time usually takes the lion's share, as much as 70 percent, of any public relations budget. Information about how public relations firms charge fees was presented in Chapter 4.

One method of budgeting is to use two columns. The left column lists the staff cost for writing a pamphlet or compiling a press kit. The right column lists the actual OOP expense for having the pamphlet or press kit designed, printed, and delivered. Internal public relations staffs, whose members are on the payroll, often complete only the OOP expenses. It is good practice to allocate about 10 percent of the budget for contingencies or unexpected costs.

Evaluation

The evaluation element of a plan relates directly back to the stated objectives of the program. As discussed earlier, objectives must be measurable in some way to show clients and employers that the program accomplished its purpose. Consequently, it's important to have a good idea what metrics you will use to evaluate whether the plan's objectives have been met. Again, evaluation criteria should be realistic, credible, and

Figure 6.2 Detailed Planning for Cookie CAREavan Strategies and Tactics

Strategic Approach
Leveraging the 25th anniversary of the cookie and the start of the summer travel season, the DoubleTree Cookie CAREavan will hit the streets in May, bringing the company's legendary chocolate chip cookies to the streets. The mobile tour creates a key moment-in-time to generate buzz with consumers and maintain momentum of the DoubleTree by Hilton story with local and national media on the heels of the DoubleTree by Hilton rebrand announcement.

Why it Works

- Connects the DoubleTree by Hilton brand to bringing humanity to travel
- Leverages the DoubleTree by Hilton story of product, service and growth to tell a consistent story to a diverse group of media
- Creates a consumer engagement story drive awareness among new consumers and take the service message outside of the box
- Utilizes key moments in time to tell a continuous story

Tactical Execution

ACTIVITY	KEY ACTION ITEMS	TIMING

Pre-Launch Logistics	• Secure price estimates for cost of cookie mobile / details for what is included in cost
	• Facilitate contract with truck company
	• Identify markets and specific high-traffic locations or places where people could really use an act of CARE within the markets, such as:
	  • Gas stations
	  • High-traffic business areas (e.g. Wall Street)
	  • Congested roads during rush-hour traffic
	• Determine quantity of cookies needed / cookie bags
	• Secure ANR / RMT company names and price estimates; confirm dates for controlled media opportunities
		March

	• Develop detailed master tour timeline outlining schedule of mobile tour stops, staff schedule, etc. • Determine approach for Hilton HHonors activations	April
	• Secure cookie bags from Diana. P. • Secure cookies	May
Messaging / Media Materials	• Develop messaging for traditional and controlled media • Develop press materials; secure client approvals	March – April

specific. The evaluation section of a program plan should restate the objectives and then name the evaluation methods to be used.

Evaluation of an informational objective often entails a compilation of news clips and an analysis of how often key message points were mentioned. Other methods might be to determine how many brochures were distributed or the estimated number of viewers who saw a VNR. Motivational objectives often are measured and evaluated by increases in sales or market share, by the number of people who called an 800 number for more information, or by benchmark surveys that measure people's perceptions before and after a campaign.

Evaluation and measurement techniques are thoroughly discussed in Chapter 8, with reference to many of the campaigns mentioned in this chapter.

on the job INSIGHTS

The "Big Picture" of Program Planning

The eight elements of a program plan are important for structuring an effective campaign, but the perspective of the "bigger picture" should also be kept in mind. Michael Morley, president of his own consulting firm in New York City, and recipient of PRSA's Atlas Award gave four personal guideposts at the organization's annual convention in San Diego. He said the guideposts "have] served me well over the years when embarking on every public relations initiative." They are:

- The idea is more important than the message.
- The message is more important than the medium.
- The individual is more important than the audience.
- Thinking and acting locally are the only sound building blocks of a global strategy.

Another key part of the "Big Picture" in planning is to get outside one's own view of the world to anticipate how others will react to a message or a complete campaign. Not doing so can allow serious issues to arise. Because the DoubleTree cookie CAREavan was designed to draw attention and crowds, it became a target for opportunists to trumpet a political position. The planners for the Hilton DoubleTree celebration grasped the big picture and prepared for several issues that could be encountered:

- Street protests (labor union issues, bed bugs, ...)
- Food allergy tragedy (nuts in cookies)
- Criticism by environmental activists (fuel consumption for a frivolous national tour)

The Ketchum plan stated how important it would be to prepare for issues that may arise based on experiences from past road tours for other clients. "Approach: When provoked, protesters can be vocal and we will do everything we can to avoid further inciting them. If protesters are calmly and quietly expressing their opinions within a reasonable distance, we do not recommend taking any action.

If protests are allowed, can be seen/heard from the event, and are causing a disturbance we will call the police to report them. If protesters do not have a permit the police can choose to ask them to leave. We will not take matters into our own hands and directly interact with protesters as this may cause tempers to flare. If protests are sizable and extremely loud, catch and will work with Doubletree to determine if it is in our best interest to shut the activities down."

Experience and careful thought lead to detailed and well-considered planning components. In this case, the initial position is to accommodate the protesters, but the plan also acknowledges that staff may need to push back or even pack up to leave protestors with no venue for their activity.

Farsighted planning also led to a careful labeling of the food risk of the cookie for those with nut allergies. Food tragedies are remote, but absolutely heartbreaking when they occur. By doing a risk assessment, the plan forestalled inadvertent walnut consumption and offered an alternative for kids who are allergic to nuts. In addition, the campaign used energy-efficient vehicles to alleviate any possible criticism that the traveling vans were a frivolous waste of fossil fuel.

Chapter 10 will offer a systematic process for dealing with conflict. As you study the lifecycle of an issue in Chapter 10, remember how professionals charged with touring a cookie throughout the United States planned effectively for issues that might arise to besmirch the baked good and especially, its hotel sponsor.

Summary

The Value of Planning

After research is done, the next step in the public relations process is planning a program or campaign to accomplish organizational objectives. Such planning must be strategic, creative, and pay close attention to reaching key audiences. A program's objectives can be purely informational to create awareness, or more motivational to actually increase participation or sales.

Approaches to Planning

One classic approach is the management by objective (MBO) model, which systematically categorizes objectives, communication strategies, audiences, and the essence of the message. Public relations firms often have their own planning model, which often includes market research, demographic segmentation of target audiences, and establishment of key messages.

Elements of a Program Plan

A program plan is either a brief outline or an extensive document identifying what is to be done and how. Public relations firms prepare these for client approval, and there is joint consultation about budgets, strategies, and tactical communication tools. A public relations plan, at minimum, should contain eight elements: situation, objectives, audience, strategy, tactics, calendar or timeline, budget, and evaluation.

Case Activity **A Plan for Fair Trade Mojo**

Fair Trade Mojo, a chain of coffee houses, conducted market research and found that college students would be an excellent audience for its product and services. The research emphasized one challenge: half of the students know what fair trade means, but nearly all (82 percent) agreed/strongly agreed that fair trade deserves their business. To this end, Fair Trade Mojo has contacted your public relations firm and asked you to develop a comprehensive plan that does two things: (1) creates brand awareness, including an understanding of what fair trade coffee is, among college students and (2) increases walk-in business at their local stores in college towns.

Using the eight-point planning outline described in this chapter, write a public relations program for Sunshine Cafe. You should consider a variety of communication tools, including campus events. No money has been allocated for advertising.

Questions **For Review and Discussion**

1. What is program planning? What are its various elements?
2. What is MBO, and how can it be applied to public relations planning?
3. Explain the difference between an informational objective and a motivational objective.
4. Define "audience" from the planning perspective. Why is audience segmentation important?
5. How does the planning process help in knowing the current mindset of the target audience and achieving its desired mindset? Discuss with examples.
6. Why are timing and scheduling so important in a public relations campaign?
7. Why is evaluation of a campaign linked to the program's objectives?

Media Resources

Ashkenas, R. (2013, May 28). Seven strategies for simplifying your organization. *Harvard Business Review Blog Network*. Retrieved from http://blogs.hbr.org/2013/04/change-management-needs-to-cha/

Bartholomew, D. (2010, May 12). *The digitization of research and measurement in public relations*. Retrieved from http://www.socialmediaexplorer.com/online-public-relations/

Dupont, S. (2013, Spring). Building your core strategy: Technology and content converge to drive branded content. *The Strategist*, 22–23.

Golob, A. (2011). Is company-wide training part of your social media strategy? Retrieved from http://thedigitalroyalty.com/2011/

Gregory, A. (2010). *Planning and managing public relations campaigns: A strategic approach*, 3rd ed. Kogan Page Limited, e-books.

Meranus, R. (2013, June 1). Want to make sure your business's name gets heard this year? You need to plan for PR. Retrieved from http://www.entrepreneur.com/article/173460

Nicholson, N., & Beck, A. A., eds. (2012, March). Developing a communication plan. *CW Bulletin*, IABC. Volume 10 Issue 3. Retrieved from http://www.iabc.com/cwb/archive/2012/0312/

Zandt, D. (2013). Three essential components of successful social media campaigns. *Forbes Woman*. Retrieved from http://www.forbes.com/sites/deannazandt/2013/05/22/3-essential-components-of-successful-social-media-campaigns/

Communication Concepts and Practice in Public Relations

chapter 7

After reading this chapter, you will be able to:

- Recognize the components of how audiences receive messages and process them
- Understand the five stages of how individuals adopt a new product or idea
- Understand the role of effective communication in the public relations process
- Identify the characteristics of various media channels
- Be familiar with the communication objectives of a campaign

The Goals of Communication

The third step in the public relations process, after research and planning, is *communication*. This step, also called *execution*, is the most visible part of public relations work.

Implementing the Plan

In a public relations program, as pointed out in Chapter 6, communication is the implementation of a decision, the process and the means by which objectives are achieved. A program's strategies and tactics may take the form of news releases, news conferences, special events, social media such as Facebook and Twitter, speeches, webcasts, rallies, posters, and even word of mouth.

The goals of the communication process are to inform, persuade, motivate, or achieve mutual understanding. To be an effective communicator, a person must have basic knowledge of (1) what constitutes communication and how people receive messages, (2) how people process information and change their perceptions, and (3) what kinds of media and communication tools are most appropriate for a particular message.

Concerning the last point, Kirk Hallahan of Colorado State University notes that today's communication revolution has given public relations professionals a full range of communication tools and media, and the traditional approach of simply obtaining publicity in the mass media—newspapers, magazines, radio, and television—is no longer sufficient, if it ever was. He writes:

> PR program planners need to reexamine their traditional approaches to the practice and think about media broadly and strategically. PR media planners must now address some of the same questions that confront advertisers. What media best meet a program's objectives? How can media be combined to enhance program effectiveness? What media are most efficient to reach key audiences?

Hallahan's concept of an integrated public relations media model, which outlines five categories of media, is shown in Table 7.1. Social media, of course, play a major communication role in today's public relations campaigns. This is illustrated by Table 7.2 that shows highlights of the social media channels used in Ketchum's DoubleTree Cookie CAREavan campaign. Many of these media are also discussed in Chapters 13–16.

A Public Relations Perspective

A number of variables must be considered when planning a message on behalf of an employer or client. Patrick Jackson, who was editor of *pr reporter* and a senior counselor before his death, believed that the communicator should ask whether the proposed message is (1) appropriate, (2) meaningful, (3) memorable, (4) understandable, and (5) believable to the prospective recipient. According to Jackson, "Many a wrongly directed or unnecessary communication has been corrected or dropped by using a screen like this."

In addition to examining the proposed content, a communicator should determine exactly what objective is being sought by means of the communication. James Grunig, professor emeritus of public relations at the University of Maryland, lists five possible objectives for a communicator:

1. ***Message exposure.*** Public relations personnel provide materials to the mass media and disseminate other messages through owned media such as newsletters and the organization's websites. Intended audiences are exposed to the message in various forms.

2. ***Accurate dissemination of the message.*** The basic information, often filtered by journalists, editors, and bloggers, remains intact as it is transmitted through various channels.
3. ***Acceptance of the message.*** Based on its view of reality, the audience not only retains the message, but accepts it as valid.
4. ***Attitude change.*** The audience not only believes the message, but makes a verbal or mental commitment to change behavior as a result of the message.
5. ***Change in overt behavior.*** Members of the audience actually change their current behavior or purchase the product and use it.

Table 7.1 An Integrated Public Relations Media Model

The variety and scope of media and communication tools available to public relations professionals run the spectrum from mass media (public media) to one-on-one communication (interpersonal communication). Here, in chart form, is a concept developed by Professor Kirk Hallahan at Colorado State University.

← Mass Communication
High tech, Perceptually Based,
Low Social Presence, Asynchronous

Personalized Communication →
Low tech, Experientially Based,
High Social Presence, Synchronous

PUBLIC MEDIA	CONTROLLED MEDIA	INTERACTIVE MEDIA	EVENTS	ONE-ON-ONE COMMUNICATIONS
		Key Uses in a Communication Program		
Build awareness; Enhance credibility	Promotion; Provide detailed information	Respond to queries, Exchange information; Engage users	Motivate participants; Reinforce existing beliefs, attitudes	Obtain commitments, Negotiation, resolution of problems.
		Principal Examples of Media		
Publicity/advertising/ advertorials/product placements in Newspapers Magazines Radio Television *Paid advertising* Transit media Out-of-home media (Billboards, posters, electronic displays) Directories Venue signage Movie theater trailers, online video ads	Brochures Newsletters Sponsored magazines Annual reports Books Direct mail Exhibits and displays Point-of-purchase support DVDs/Videobrochures Statement inserts Other collateral or printed ephemera Advertising specialties	E-mail, instant, text and microblog messages E-newsletters, e-zines Web sites, mobile Apps Blogs, podcast, vodcasts Social networking sites Media sharing sites Entertainment and serious games Wikis Forums (chats, groups) Web conferences, webinars, webcasts Electronic public kiosks Automated telephone response systems, audiotext Intranets and extranets in workplaces Paid text/display click-through advertising	Meetings/conferences Speeches/ presentations Government or judicial testimony Trade shows, exhibitions Demonstrations/rallies Sponsored events Observances/ anniversaries Contests/sweepstakes Recognition award programs (Often supported with multi-media presentations)	Personal visits/lobbying Correspondence Telephone calls

(continued)

Table 7.1 **An Integrated Public Relations Media Model (*continued*)**

Comparison of Five Major Media Groups

	PUBLIC MEDIA	CONTROLLED MEDIA	INTERACTIVE MEDIA	EVENTS	ONE-ON-ONE
Social presence, ties to others	Low	Low	Moderate	High	High
Basis for judgments	Perceptual	Perceptual	Perceptual and Experiential	Experiential	Experiential
Personalization of message	None	Limited	Moderate-High	Limited	High
Directionality of communication	One-way	One-way, with potential to include response mechanisms	Potentially two-way	Quasi- two way	Two-way
Synchronicity (Real time v. delayed)	Mostly asynchronous	Asynchronous	Synchronous	Synchronous	Synchronous
Technological sophistication	High	Moderate	High	Moderate	Low
Channel ownership/control	Media organizations	Sponsor	Sponsor or third-party site operator	Event organizers	None
Message selection	Third-parties media editors/producers	Sponsor	Receiver	Presenters and event organizers	Participants
Audience engagement	Low	Low-moderate	Moderate-High	Moderate	High
Reach	High	Low-Moderate	Low-Moderate	Low	Low
Cost per impression	Extremely low	Moderate	Moderate	Moderate	High
Key challenges for use, effectiveness	Competition for attention, media clutter	Design, distribution	Availability, accessibility	Attendance, atmosphere	Empowerment of organization representative, personal dynamics

Grunig says that most public relations experts usually aim for the first two objectives: exposure to the message and accurate dissemination. The last three objectives depend in large part on a mix of variables—predisposition to the message, peer reinforcement, feasibility of the suggested action, and environmental context, to name a few. The first two objectives are easier to accomplish than attitude change (see Chapter 9).

Although the communicator cannot always control the outcome of a message, researchers recognize that effective dissemination is the beginning of the process that leads to opinion change and adoption of products or services. Therefore, it is important to review all components of the communication process.

> To be successful, a message must be received by the intended individual or audience. It must get the audience's attention. It must be understood. It must be believed. It must be remembered. And ultimately, in some fashion, it must be acted upon. Failure to accomplish any of these tasks means the entire message fails. David Therkelsen, executive director of Crisis Connection, Minneapolis.

The communication phase of the public relations process places the emphasis on the audience and what it does with a message. The following sections elaborate on the

Table 7.2 Social Media Tactics for DoubleTree's Cookie Campaign

The Cookie CAREavan social media components illustrate the aphorism: The better the plan, the better the execution.

SOCIAL MEDIA CHANNEL	TACTIC
Twitter	Develop detailed schedule of Twitter updates
	Develop sponsored tweet with hashtag #uneedacookie
	Maintain constant Twitter feed from the cookie mobile for real-time updates
Facebook	Detailed schedule of Facebook updates
	Create Facebook tab with visual map showcasing exact locations and upcoming events for the team
	Maintain buzz with ongoing Facebook updates
Foursquare	Create check-in sites at local market stops for consumers
	Develop branded badge with existing popular Food Truck—"Ziggy's Wagon"
Blogger Relations	Coordinate blogger partnerships
	Hold blogger contests and giveaways
	Ongoing outreach to generate blog posting about the tour

six elements Grunig enumerates: (1) receiving the message, (2) paying attention to the message, (3) understanding the message, (4) believing the message, (5) remembering the message, and (6) acting on the message.

Receiving the Message

There are numerous communication models that explain how a message moves from the sender to the recipient. Some are quite complex, attempting to incorporate an almost infinite number of events, ideas, objects, and people that interact among the message, channel, and receiver.

Five Communication Elements

The evolution of communication models is best illustrated by Figure 7.1. Wilbur Schramm, a pioneer in communication theory, first conceptualized a one-way linear model that shows the five basic elements of source, encoder, signal, decoder, and destination. The model emphasizes that both the source and the receiver continually encode, interpret, decode, transmit, and receive information.

The two additional models developed by Schramm made fundamental points of modern communication theory that make sense to this day:

1. Communication occurs only if both the sender and the receiver have a field of shared experience, such as a common language and similar educational levels.
2. Constant feedback between the source and the receiver occurs in a continual loop.

In the public relations process, communication to internal and external audiences produces feedback that is taken into consideration during research, the first step, and evaluation, the fourth step. In this way, the structure and dissemination of messages are continuously refined for maximum effectiveness.

Figure 7.1 **Schramm's Communication Models**

These three models, formulated by Wilbur Schramm, show the evolution of our thinking about communication toward the current emphasis on an interactive process between a sender and a receiver. Effective communication takes place within a sphere of "shared experience."

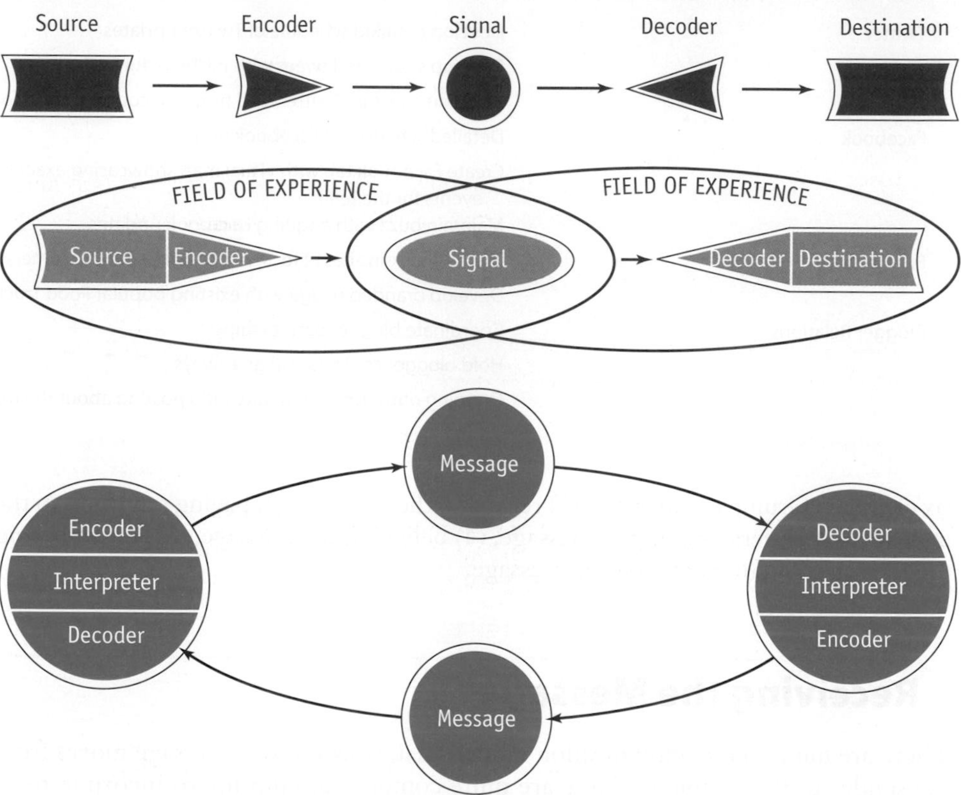

The Importance of Two-Way Communication

The concept of continuous feedback became the foundation for models of two-way communication, usually viewed as more complete and effective communication. One-way communication, from sender to receiver, only disseminates information. Such a monologue is less effective than two-way communication, which establishes a dialogue between the sender and the receiver.

> In the symmetric model, understanding is the principal objective of public relations, rather than persuasion.
>
> *James E. Grunig, professor emeritus, University of Maryland*

Grunig postulates that the ideal public relations model should be *two-way symmetrical* communication, that is, communication balanced between the sender and the receiver. Today's social media networks are a good example of Grunig's two-way symmetrical concept because their focus is on dialogue and engagement between the organization and individuals.

In reality, research shows that most organizations have mixed motives when they engage in two-way communication with targeted audiences. Although they may employ dialogue to obtain a better sense of how they can adjust to the needs of an audience, their motive often is asymmetrical—to convince the audience of their point of view through dialogue and engagement.

The most effective two-way communication, of course, is two people having a face-to-face conversation. Small-group discussion also is effective. In both forms, the message is fortified by gestures, facial expressions, intimacy, tone of voice, and the opportunity for instant feedback. If the listener asks a question or appears puzzled, the speaker has an instant cue and can rephrase the information or amplify a point. It's worth noting that social media give the appearance of face-to-face conversation but still lack key nonverbal cues. Early indications suggest that as Internet capacity increases, more face-to-face exchanges will occur with video chat apps such as Google's Hangouts. Consequently, digital words often have greater impact on receivers and often lead to protracted arguments. See the Social Media in Action box below about Nestlé's dialogue with some irate customers.

Barriers to communication tend to mount as one advances to large-group meetings and, ultimately, to the mass media. Organizational materials can reach millions of people at the same time through traditional media and the Internet, but the psychological and physical distance between sender and receiver is considerably lengthened. Communication is less effective because the audience no longer is involved with the source. No immediate feedback may be possible, and the message may undergo distortion as it is edited and revised by journalists and editors in traditional mass media outlets.

on the job

SOCIAL MEDIA IN ACTION

Nestlé Gets Bruised in Social Media Fight with Greenpeace

According to Andy Beaupre, CEO of Beaupre public relations, Nestlé Foods offers seven important lessons for any company wanting to use social media to engage in meaningful communication with key audiences. Lessons learned clearly also showcase the value of genuine, two-way communication in a world made tiny by the Internet and social media. The case also reinforces recommendations made on page 198 by Dr. James E. Grunig. Beaupre states: "If a company still doesn't 'get' how social media has changed the rules of branding by empowering consumers, look no further than the ongoing Nestlé firestorm."

Nestlé endured a protracted conflict with Greenpeace over Nestlé's persistent use of palm oil in its food products. Greenpeace argued that palm oil is linked to environmental harm, including deforestation, greenhouse gas emissions, and endangered species loss. For a potentially upsetting but powerful video from Greenpeace, go to the site playing the video after Nestlé forced YouTube to pull the piece: http://vimeo.com/10236827.

According to *CNET News*'s blog called *The Social*, Nestlé created a backlash and a "twitstorm" of negative reaction on Facebook and Twitter by taking sharp action against a flood of comments to the Nestlé Facebook page inspired and orchestrated by Greenpeace. Greenpeace encouraged individuals to create satirical slogans using Nestlé food logos as profile photos. Nestlé responded with a sharp warning about copyright violation for altering logos and rude comments to its social media critics as the furor built momentum. Typical responses from the global community, concerned about rain forest habitat and orangutan decimation, included:

> Thanks, you are doing a far better job than we could ever achieve in destroying your brand.

(continued)

It's not okay for people to use altered versions of your logos, but it's okay for you to alter the face of Indonesian rainforests? Wow!

I would like to enjoy my Kit Kats without feeling responsible for rainforest destruction and orangutan deaths.

Writing for *CNET*, Caroline McCarthy summed up the situation with a word of caution for public relations practitioners using social media:

> Putting aside all judgment on who's right and who's wrong in this situation, we are seeing the dark side of the Facebook fan page: what was intended to be an open way for fans to show their support was turned into a billboard of outrage on behalf of critics, and with the company representative in obvious panic over how to tame the mob. It's rare that public opposition will reach a truly uncontrollable level, but when it does, it's ugly. . . . Whether this will be remembered as a single badly mismanaged user backlash or a pratfall of social media marketing in general has yet to be seen.

Beaupre notes that Nestlé was clueless about the power shift enabled by social media and acted in an old-school, authoritarian, "we own the brand" way.

Vital lessons from the Nestlé debacle are offered by Beaupre for professional communicators advising their execs or clients:

1. **Before diving into social media,** make sure key decision makers truly "get" how the game is played. It's not a press release.
2. **Make sure they understand** that tools like Facebook, Twitter, and LinkedIn aren't one-way vehicles (where the brand dominates the message), but an invitation to a never-ending dance with constantly changing partners, some of whom are never your friends.
3. **Don't use social media unless the brand** is willing to take the risk of *jumping off the cliff*, giving up control to customers and consumers who will express their viewpoints, both positive and negative.
4. **If your company or client wants to control the message,** then social media isn't the right choice. Look at how Nestlé tried to tell people not to post their logos. Imposing controls on participants will only incur their wrath.
5. **Creating LinkedIn, Facebook, and Twitter accounts is just the first step.** The goal isn't to Tweet or post, but to build an active community and an authentic two-way relationship based on trust. It's easy to get started in social media, but time-consuming and challenging to remain engaged and build a following.
6. **Remember** that even if your company or client decides not to engage in social media, that won't stop rants, rebellion, and revolution. People will find a way to express themselves and let it be known they're disturbed, upset, confused, or disappointed. The train has left the station—be prepared.
7. **As we've learned from Nestlé** (and many others), people don't want to be scammed, ignored, or mistreated. It *will* come back to bite you. So if your exec or client wants social media to become a positive tool, the brand must be a concerned good listener prepared to take action to correct situations that aren't right.

By the way, Nestlé ultimately dropped the palm oil supplier.

Paying Attention to the Message

Sociologist Harold Lasswell defines the act of communication as "Who says what, in which channel, to whom, with what effect?"

> Who says what, in which channel, to whom, with what effect?
>
> *Sociologist Harold Lasswell*

Although in public relations much emphasis is given to the formation and dissemination of messages, this effort is wasted if the audience pays no attention. The axiom of Walt Seifert, pioneering professor of public relations at Ohio State University, still holds true today: "Dissemination does not equal publication, and publication does not equal absorption and action." In other words, "All who receive it won't publish it, and all who read or hear it won't understand or act upon it."

Some Theoretical Perspectives

Seifert and social psychologists recognize that the majority of an audience at any given time is not particularly interested in a message or in adopting an idea. This doesn't mean, however, that audiences are merely passive receivers of information. Werner Severin and James Tankard, in their text *Communication Theories*, quote one researcher as saying:

> The communicator's audience is not a passive recipient—it cannot be regarded as a lump of clay to be molded by the master propagandist. Rather, the audience is made up of individuals who demand something from the communication to which they are exposed, and who select those that are likely to be useful to them.

This is called the *media uses and gratification theory* of communication. Its basic premise is that the communication process is interactive. The communicator wants to inform and even persuade; the recipient wants to be entertained, informed, or alerted to opportunities that can fulfill individual needs. Later theoretical versions compare uses and gratifications sought with those achieved. This emphasizes that a professional can communicate with an eye toward what is sought by an audience and then assess what the audience felt it achieved by reading or viewing the public relations message.

Audiences come to messages for very different reasons. People use mass media for such purposes as (1) surveillance of the environment to find out what is happening, locally or even globally, that has some impact on them; (2) entertainment and diversion; (3) reinforcement of their opinions and predispositions; and (4) decision making about buying a product or service.

The media uses and gratification theory assumes that people make highly intelligent choices about which messages require their attention and fulfill their needs. If this is true, as research indicates it is, the public relations communicator must tailor messages that focus on getting the audience's attention.

One approach is to understand the mental state of the intended audience. Grunig and Hunt, in *Managing Public Relations*, suggest that communication strategies be designed to attract the attention of two kinds of audiences: those who passively process information and those who actively seek information.

Passive Audiences Individuals in this category pay attention to a message only because it is entertaining and offers a diversion. Passive audiences use communication channels such as billboards or radio spots that they can briefly notice while they are doing something else.

For this reason, passive audiences need messages that have style and creativity. The person must be lured by photos, illustrations, and catchy slogans into processing information. Press agentry, the dramatic picture, the use of celebrities, radio and television announcements, and events featuring entertainment can make passive audiences aware of a message. The objectives of a communication, therefore, are simply exposure to and accurate dissemination of a message. In most public relations campaigns, communications are designed to reach primarily passive audiences. See the PR Casebook on page 207 to get a sense of how unusual and somewhat zany tactics can become in award-winning publicity efforts. The release of "IT in the Toilet" by the upstart 11mark agency documented the frequent use of mobile phones in the bathroom.

Active Audiences A communicator's approach to audiences that actively seek information is different. These people are already interested and engaged, and are in search of more sophisticated, supplemental information. An example is the person who has already determined that further health care reform is needed and begins actively seeking more detailed information by visiting health policy websites and reading in-depth newspaper and magazine articles about single-payer health systems. A person actively seeking information may attend a talk or begin following experts on Twitter who offer useful arguments and links to fellow advocates of a shared policy position.

At any given time, of course, the intended audience has both passive and active information seekers in it. It is important, therefore, that multiple messages and a variety of communication tools be used in a full-fledged information campaign so that both passive and active audiences can be effectively reached.

The Concept of Triggering Events Public relations practitioners should spend more time thinking about what behaviors they are trying to motivate in target publics than about what information they are communicating to those publics. Professionals should build triggering events into their planning to cause people to act on their latent willingness to behave in a certain way.

A triggering event, for example, might be rapid response to a natural disaster such as the H1N1 flu epidemic, which threatened the well-being of millions worldwide. Although this was not planned, it was the catalyst for thousands of people to act on their latent readiness to take care of themselves and their loved ones through frequent hand washing and revised sneezing practices—into the shirt sleeve, not the hand. The H1N1 trigger was a boon to companies selling hand-disinfectant gels. However, a triggering event doesn't have to be a disaster or a crisis; it can also be the launch of a new product such as the iPad or the celebration of 25 years of hospitality symbolized by the humble cookie. In either case, the "event" was the catalyst for people to engage with others about a shared interest.

Other Attention-Getting Concepts

Communicators should think in terms of the five senses: sight, hearing, smell, touch, and taste. Motion media such as television, animation, games, virtual reality, and videos are the most effective and the most popular modes of communication today for an audience expecting a full sensual experience, with 3-D sight, sound, color, movement, and engagement. Radio, on the other hand, relies on only the sense of hearing. Print media, although capable of communicating a large amount of information in great detail, rely only on sight.

Individuals learn through all five senses, but psychologists estimate that 83 percent of learning is accomplished through sight. Hearing accounts for 11 percent. Fifty percent of what individuals retain consists of what they see and hear. For this reason, speakers often use visual aids.

These figures have obvious implications for the public relations practitioner. Any communication strategy should, if possible, include vehicles of communication designed to tap the sense of sight or hearing or a combination of the two. In other words, a variety of communication tools is needed, including news releases, publicity photos, special events, YouTube videos, billboards, newsletters, radio announcements, video news releases, media interviews, and news conferences. This multiple approach not only assists learning and retention, it also provides repetition of a message in a variety of forms that accommodate audience needs.

Other research suggests that audience attention can be engaged if the communicator raises a "need" level first. The idea is to "hook" an audience's attention by

PRCasebook

Mobile on the John: A Public Relations Firm Scores a Royal Flush

It takes creative thinking to develop messages that arouse the interest of the media and the public, but a news release headlined "Three quarters of Americans use their mobile phones in the bathroom" seemed to do the trick for **11mark** public relations firm.

The firm, new in the market, wanted to showcase its capabilities in research, media relations, tech savvy, and graphic design so the staff decided to conduct a survey of 1,000 mobile phone users. The results produced a variety of stats that were somewhat humorous. Nearly 60 percent, for example, text while sitting on the porcelain throne and another 32 percent send e-mails.

The results of the survey, titled "IT in the Toilet," were summarized in a news release and in an infographic (included here) that resulted in almost 500 articles and 200 broadcast placements in such outlets as the *New York Times*, *CBS News*, and the *Huffington Post*. On Twitter, the study results moved around the world in a dozen different languages, while the firm's website traffic increased 3,700 percent during the campaign. The release and infographic were downloaded over 2,000 times, and Facebook and LinkedIn likes also reached the thousands.

The founder of 11mark, Nicole Burdette, told *Bulldog Reporter*, "Research-based campaigns let us share new insights and give something of interest and value to the target audience. Anytime we plan a campaign, we think about WIIFM—'What's in it for me' from an audience perspective. Why would they want to read our content? What do they gain?"

Source: 11mark public relations firm (www.11mark.com)

beginning the message with something that will make its members' lives easier or benefit them in some way. An example is the message from the Census Bureau emphasizing that everyone counts in America and urging people to complete the simple census form so that government resources get distributed fairly. Public relations writers also should be aware that audience attention is highest at the beginning of a message. Thus, it is wise to state the major point at the beginning, give details in the middle, and end with a summary of the message.

Another technique to garner audience attention is to begin a message with a statement that reflects audience values and predispositions. This is called channeling (see Chapter 9). According to social science research, people pay attention to messages that reinforce their predispositions.

Prior knowledge and interest also make people pay more attention to messages. If a message taps current events or issues of public concern already in the news, there is an increased chance that the audience will pay attention.

Understanding the Message

Communication is the act of transmitting information, ideas, and attitudes from one person to another. Communication can take place, however, only if the sender and receiver have a common understanding of the symbols being used. This is Schramm's concept of "field of experience," shown in Figure 7.1 on page 202.

Effective Use of Language

Words are the most common symbols. The degree to which two people understand each other is heavily dependent on their common knowledge of word symbols. Anyone who has traveled abroad can readily attest that very little communication occurs between two people who speak different languages. Even signs translated into English for tourists often lead to some confusing and amusing messages. A brochure for a Japanese hotel, for example, said, "In our hotel, you will be well fed and agreeably drunk. In every room there is a large window offering delightful prospects."

Even if sender and receiver speak the same language and live in the same country, the effectiveness of their communication depends on such factors as education, social class, regional differences, nationality, and cultural background.

Employee communication specialists are particularly aware of such differences as a multicultural workforce becomes the norm for most organizations. One major factor is the impact of a global economy in which multinational organizations employ culturally diverse workforces in the countries where they operate. One study says that 85 percent of new entrants into the American workforce are now white women, immigrants, African Americans, Hispanics, and Asians. For many of these workers, English will be a second language.

These statistical trends will require communicators to be better informed about cultural differences and conflicting values in order to find common ground and build bridges between various groups. At the same time, a major task will be to communicate in clear and simple terms. National studies show that 42 million American adults fall within the lowest category of literacy, with one in eight employees reading at no better than a fourth-grade level. Delivering usable information to these citizens is a challenge and a problem. For example, Health Literacy Missouri (www.healthliteracymissouri.org) points out that errors, confusion, and miscommunication due to low health literacy result in tragic human costs as well as billions of dollars annually.

Writing for Clarity

The nature of the audience and its literacy level are important considerations for any communicator. The key is to produce messages that match, in content and structure, the characteristics of the audience.

The Illinois Public Health Department had the right idea when it commissioned a song in rap-music style as one way to inform low-income, poorly educated groups about the dangers of AIDS. The words and music of the "Condom Rag," however, were offensive to elected officials, who cancelled the song.

This example poses the classic dilemma for the expert communicator: Should the message be produced for supervisors, whose backgrounds and education levels may be totally different from those of the intended audience, or should it be produced with the audience in mind? The obvious answer is the latter, but it is often difficult to convince management of this. One solution is to copy-test all public relations materials on the target audience. This helps convince management—and communicators—that what they like isn't necessarily what the audience wants, needs, or understands.

Another solution is to read widely about your target audience, especially when information sheds light on the wants, needs, values or predispositions of a demographic group. For example, PRSA's *Strategist* recapped valuable insights about the millennial generation, including the following: "McDonalds isn't the only major marketer trying to reach millennials, as brands like Coke and Gatorade and industries from brewers to media companies struggle to understand this group that seems to prefer higher-quality products and lots of choices."

Another approach is to apply readability and comprehension formulas to materials before they are produced and disseminated. Learning theory makes the case: The simpler the piece of writing, the easier it will be for audiences to understand.

The most widely known readability formula is by Rudolph Flesch. Another is by Barr, Jenkins, and Peterson. Both are based on average sentence length and the number of one-syllable words per 100 words. If a randomly selected sample of 100 words contains 4.2 sentences and 142 syllables, it is ranked at about the ninth-grade level. This is the level for which most news releases and daily newspapers strive. In other words, long, complex sentences (more than 19 words) and multisyllabic words (e.g., "compensation" instead of "pay") reduce comprehension for the average reader.

The Cloze procedure, developed by William Taylor, also tests comprehension. The concept comes from the idea of closure, or the human tendency to complete a familiar but incomplete pattern. In the Cloze procedure, copy is tested for comprehension and redundancy by having test subjects read sentences in which words have been removed. The subjects' ability to fill in the missing words determines whether the pattern of words is familiar and people can understand the message.

If these formulas sound like too much work, Microsoft Word has a built-in readability testing function, making it relatively easy to test any message for clarity.

Audience understanding and comprehension can also be increased by applying some of the following concepts.

Use Symbols, Acronyms, and Slogans Clarity and simplicity of message are enhanced by the use of symbols, acronyms, and slogans. Each is a form of shorthand that quickly conceptualizes an idea and travels through extended lines of communication.

The world is full of symbols. Corporate symbols such as the Mercedes Benz star, the Nike swoosh, and the multicolored, now holographic, apple of Apple Computer are known throughout the world. The concept is called *branding*, and corporations invest considerable time and money in public relations to support their names and logos as symbols of quality and service. Audio symbols such as the NFL theme or Windows' musical chord when a computer boots up are recognized, as are colors such as Coca-Cola red or McDonald's gold.

A symbol should be unique, memorable, widely recognized, and appropriate. Organizations spend extensive time and energy searching for unique symbols that convey the essence of what they are or what they hope to become. Considerable amounts of money are then spent on publicizing the symbols and creating meanings for them.

Acronyms are shorthand for conveying information. An acronym is a word formed from the initial letters of other words. The Group Against Smokers' Pollution goes by the acronym GASP; Juvenile Opportunities in Business becomes JOB. And the National Organization for Women has the acronym NOW, which says a great deal about its sense of urgency for change in the status of women in society, especially the workplace.

In many cases, the acronym—because it is short and simple—becomes the common name. The mass media continually use the term *AIDS* instead of *Acquired Immune Deficiency Syndrome*. And *UNESCO* is easier to write and say than *United Nations Educational, Scientific, and Cultural Organization*. A corporation often adopts its acronym as its official, trademarked name. Thus, we now have KFC instead of Kentucky Fried Chicken, and FedEx instead of Federal Express. In the nonprofit sector the American Association of Retired People now uses AARP as its official name.

Slogans help condense a concept and motivate a movement. Presidential candidate Barack Obama's secondary slogan, "Yes we can," was infectious for its optimism. It has been adapted as "Yes we did" since his election to celebrate victories such as passage of health care reform.

> Our business is infested with idiots who try to impress by using pretentious jargon.
>
> *David Ogilvy, a legend in the advertising industry*

Avoid Jargon One source of blocked communication is technical and bureaucratic jargon. Social scientists call it *semantic noise* when such language is delivered to a general audience. Jargon interferes with the message and impedes the receiver's ability to understand it. Reporters and editors reject jargon in news releases or pitches because the average reader or listener doesn't recognize terms that are unique to a particular industry.

Cell phone executives, for example, may talk about "attenuation rates," which means little or nothing to the average person. And even the public relations field has terms that the average person probably doesn't know, such as "mug shot" or "VNR." Work in social media has proliferated many specialized uses of terms such as *buzz* or *sentiment* that should be used with care outside the public relations office.

Avoid Clichés and Hype Words You can ruin the credibility and believability of your message by using exaggerated words and phrases. Companies often describe their products as "first of its kind," "unique," "a major breakthrough," and even "revolutionary," which tends to raise suspicion among journalists and the public.

Factiva, a media-monitoring company, analyzed about 14,000 articles in business publications to compile a chart of frequently used hype words. Leading the list was the term *next generation*. Other most frequently used words, in descending order, were *robust*, *flexible*, *world class*, *easy to use*, and *cutting edge*. A list of other overused hype words in digital news releases is in the Insights box on page 211.

Avoid Euphemisms According to Frank Grazian, founding editor of *Communication Briefings*, a *euphemism* is "an inoffensive word or phrase that is less direct and less distasteful than the one that represents reality."

Public relations personnel should use positive, favorable words to convey a message, but they have an ethical responsibility not to use words that hide information, mislead, or offend. Probably little danger exists in saying a person is *hearing impaired* instead of *deaf*. Some euphemisms can even cause amusement, such as when car mechanics become *automotive internists*, and luxury cars are called *preowned* on the used-car lot.

More dangerous are euphemisms that actually alter the meaning or impact of a word or concept. Writers call this *doublespeak*—words that pretend to communicate but really do not. Governments are famous for doublespeak. In Afghanistan, the U.S. military sometimes describe civilian casualties and destruction as "collateral damage." A government economist once called a recession "a meaningful downturn in aggregate output."

on the job
INSIGHTS

Hit Parade of Overused Words in News Releases

Source: http://www.prnewsonline.com/overusedwordsinfographic/attachment/most-overused-words-pr-infographic/

Corporations also use euphemisms and doublespeak to hide unfavorable news. Reducing the number of employees, for example, is often called *right-sizing*, *skill-mix adjustment*, or *career assignment and relocation*. An airline once called the crash of one of its planes as "the involuntary conversion of a 727."

Using euphemisms to hide or mislead is obviously contrary to professional public relations standards and the public interest. As William Lutz writes in *Public Relations Quarterly*, "Such language breeds suspicion, cynicism, distrust, and, ultimately, hostility."

Avoid Discriminatory Language In today's world, effective communication also means nondiscriminatory communication. Public relations personnel should double-check every message to eliminate undesirable gender, racial, and ethnic connotations. See the Insights box on page 213 about social media divas to explore gender roles in public relations.

With regard to gender, it is unnecessary to write about something as being *man-made* when a word such as *synthetic* or *artificial* is just as good. Companies no longer have *manpower*, but rather *employees*, *personnel*, and *workers*. Most civic organizations have *chairpersons* now, and cities have *firefighters* instead of *firemen* and *police officers* instead of *policemen*. Airlines, of course, have *flight attendants*, not *stewardesses*. It also is considered sexist to write about a woman's physical characteristics or clothing, particularly if similar comments would not be made about a man.

As a general rule, you should not identify any individual by ethnic background or sexual orientation. It may, however, be appropriate in some situations to provide context. It is newsworthy, for example, when a major corporation hires an African American woman to be its CEO. In any case, you should be aware of what terms are acceptable. The term *black*, for example, is widely used and even preferred by a large percentage of the black population, according to the U.S. Bureau of Labor Statistics. A smaller percentage prefers *African American* and *Afro American is considered archaic*. Headlines almost always use *black* because it is short.

Although preferences change, today's writers use *Asian American* or even a more specific designation such as *Chinese American* because Asia has multiple ethnic groups. The term *Oriental* is no longer acceptable in any situation. *Hispanic* is now more acceptable than the politically charged *Spanish-speaking*.

Believing the Message

One key variable in the communication process, discussed further in Chapter 9, is *source credibility*. Do members of the audience perceive the source as knowledgeable and expert on the subject? Do they perceive the source as honest and objective or as representing a special interest? For example, audiences ascribe lower credibility to statements in an advertisement than to the same information contained in a news article, because news articles are selected by media gatekeepers with little vested interest in the product. Hence, the value of favorable news coverage remains high, even in the social media landscape.

Source credibility is a problem for any organizational spokesperson, especially for corporations, because audiences are generally skeptical. In one study conducted for the GCI Group, Opinion Research Corporation found that more than half of Americans surveyed are likely to believe that a large company is probably guilty of some wrongdoing if it is being investigated by a government agency or if a major lawsuit is filed against the company. At the same time, only one-third would trust the statements of a large company.

The problem of source credibility is the main reason that organizations, whenever possible, use respected outside experts or celebrities as representatives to convey their messages.

The *sleeper effect* also influences source credibility. This concept was developed by Carl Hovland, who stated: "There is decreased tendency over time to reject the material presented by an untrustworthy source." In other words, even if organizations are perceived initially as not being very credible sources, people may retain the information and eventually separate the source from the opinion. On the other hand, studies show that audiences register more constant opinion change if they perceive the source to be highly credible in the first place.

A second variable in believability is the *context* of the message. Action (performance) speaks louder than a stack of news releases. A bank may spend thousands of dollars on a promotion campaign with the slogan "Your Friendly Bank—Where Service Counts," but the effort is wasted if public relations efforts do not build a culture of caring among bank employees.

Incompatible rhetoric and actions can be somewhat amusing at times. At a press briefing about the importance of "buying American," the U.S. Chamber of Commerce

on the job INSIGHTS

Are Women Better Communicators Than Men?

The influx of women into the public relations field has been well documented by any number of studies, which has raised some debate among practitioners and social scientists whether women are better communicators than men.

Rosanna Fiske, former chief executive and chairwoman of PRSA, believes more women gravitate to the field because public relations jobs required skills that tend to come by women naturally, such as empathy, listening, and multitasking. In an interview with the *Financial Times*, she continued, "PR is about communication, and women are born communicators. PR is also about relationship building and there is a lot of research in cultural anthropology that this is strength of women."

The rise of social media has also placed a focus on the communication abilities of women. *Bulldog Reporter* once sponsored a conference titled, "Social Media Divas on Digital PR: Top-Ranked Women Online Gurus Reveal 10 Best Social Media and Practices for PR." In Chapter 13, for example, there's an essay by a female manger of social media for a public relations firm.

The Skill Set Needed in the Digital Age

Women are prominent across the public relations field today, but never more so than in the social media and Web development areas of the profession.

So, are women really better communicators than men? It may be worth discussing among both males and females in a classroom setting. The following are some questions to be considered:

- Do you agree or disagree with how Fiske stereotypes the skill set of women?
- Do you think there's really a gender difference in how men and women communicate?
- Would you agree or disagree with the perception that men are better at strategy and women are better at coming up with creative ideas that maximize communication effectiveness?

passed out commemorative coffee mugs marked in small print on the bottom, "Made in China."

Another barrier to the believability of messages is the audience's *predispositions*. This problem brings to mind the old saying, "Don't confuse me with the facts, my mind is already made up." In this case, Leon Festinger's theory of *cognitive dissonance* should be understood. In essence, it says that people will not believe a message contrary to their predispositions unless the communicator can introduce information that causes them to question their beliefs.

Creating Dissonance

The issue of fracking, pumping water and chemicals into the ground, to extract reserves of oil, has caused considerable dissonance among the public. Supporters say it makes the U.S. energy independent; the opposition says the process causes environmental problems such as an increase in earthquakes.

Dissonance can be created in at least three ways. First, make the public aware that circumstances have changed. Both the Bush and Obama administrations emphasize that after the 9/11 attacks on the United States, greater surveillance of people within U.S. borders is necessary. A trade-off must be made between personal privacy for Americans and personal safety from terroristic attacks. Second, give information about new developments. The National Football League acknowledges that equipment and rules must change to protect players from debilitating brain injuries. Nuclear power interests can quote a former leader of Greenpeace and longtime nuclear power critic who now believes carbon-free atomic power can address global climate change.

Involvement is another important predisposition that impacts how audience members process messages. Involvement can be described in simple terms as interest or concern for an issue or a product. Those with a higher level of involvement often process persuasive messages with greater attention to evidence and to logical argument, whereas those with a low level of involvement with the topic are impressed more by incidental cues, such as an attractive spokesperson, humor, or the number of arguments given. The public relations professional can use the involvement concept to devise messages that focus more on "what is said," for high-involvement audiences, and more on "who says it," for low-involvement audiences.

Remembering the Message

For several reasons, many messages prepared by public relations personnel are repeated extensively:

- Repetition is necessary because not all members of the target audience see or hear the message at the same time. Not everyone reads the newspaper on a particular day, watches the same television news program, or regularly reads the same blog.
- Repetition reminds the audience, so there is less chance of a failure to remember the message. If a source has high credibility, repetition prevents erosion of opinion change.
- Repetition helps the audience remember the message itself. Studies have shown that advertising is quickly forgotten if not repeated constantly.
- Repetition can lead to improved learning and increase the chance of penetrating audience indifference or resistance.

Researchers say that repetition, or *redundancy*, also is necessary to offset the "noise" surrounding a message. People often hear or see messages in an environment filled with distractions—a baby crying, the conversations of family members or office staff, a barking dog—or even while daydreaming or thinking of other things.

Consequently, communicators often build repetition into a message. Key points may be mentioned at the beginning and then summarized at the end. If the source is asking the receiver to seek more information, the telephone number or Web address must be repeated several times.

Such precautions also fight *entropy*, which means that messages continually lose information as media channels and people process the information and pass it on to others. In one study about employee communication, for example, it was found that rank-and-file workers got only 20 percent of a message that had passed through four levels of managers.

The key to effective communication and retention of the message is to convey information in a variety of ways, using multiple communication channels. This helps people remember the message as they receive it through different media and extends the message to both passive and active audiences. The distribution of promotional items can also play a role in reinforcing key messages and branding. A good example is the DoubleTree CAREavan that used the following promotional items over a period of months:

Truck. Wrapped in DoubleTree branded design that included key messages, social media account names, and website. Cut-out on side of truck with large-screen monitor played new DoubeTree commercials and property shots.

Banners. Three banners at each event carried key messages and also directed consumers to the campaign's Facebook page.

T-Shirts. Brand ambassadors wore CAREavan T-shirts at all events.

Table. A table skirt with key messages was used at all events.

Cookie bag. Each cookie bag given out was sealed with the CAREavan official sticker that led consumers to the Facebook page and entering the sweepstakes.

> Communicators must have a thorough understanding of their audiences, and they must stay very current with the media being used by those audiences.
>
> *Jerry Swerling, director of the Strategic Public Relations Center at USC Annenberg*

Acting on the Message

The ultimate purpose of any message is to have an effect on the recipient. Public relations personnel communicate messages on behalf of organizations to change perceptions, attitudes, opinions, or behavior in some way. Marketing communication, in particular, has the objective of convincing people to buy goods and services.

The Five-Stage Adoption Process

Getting people to act on a message is not a simple process. In fact, research shows that it can be a somewhat lengthy and complex procedure that depends on a number of intervening influences. One key to understanding how people accept new ideas or products is to analyze the adoption process. The five stages are summarized as follows:

1. **Awareness.** A person becomes aware of an idea or a new product, often by means of an advertisement, a news story in a newspaper, a mention on the nightly news, or a posting in a chat group.
2. **Interest.** The individual seeks more information about the idea or the product, perhaps by ordering a brochure, reading an in-depth article in a newspaper or magazine, or doing a Google search.

3. **Evaluation.** The person evaluates the idea or the product on the basis of how it meets specific needs and wants. Feedback from friends and family is part of this process.
4. **Trial.** Next, the person tries the product or the idea on an experimental basis by using a sample, witnessing a demonstration, or making qualifying statements such as, "I read. . . ."
5. **Adoption.** The individual begins to use the product on a regular basis or integrates the idea into his or her belief system. The "I read . . ." becomes "I think . . ." if peers provide support and reinforcement of the idea.

Figure 7.2 is a more sophisticated concept that describes the five-step adoption process in terms of *knowledge*, *persuasion*, *decision*, *implementation*, and *confirmation*. The *evaluation* stage, for example, is called the *decision* stage in the chart formatted by Everett Rogers in his book *Diffusion of Innovation*. He notes that at least five factors influence a person's evaluation of a product or an idea.

1. **Relative advantage.** The degree to which an innovation is perceived as better than the idea it replaces.
2. **Compatibility.** The degree to which an innovation is perceived as being consistent with the existing values, experiences, and needs of potential adopters.
3. **Complexity.** The degree to which an innovation is perceived as difficult to understand and use.

Figure 7.2 **Adoption Model**

This graph shows the steps through which an individual or other decision-making unit goes in the innovation-decision process from first knowledge of an innovation to the decision to adopt it, followed by implementation of the new idea and confirmation of the new decision.

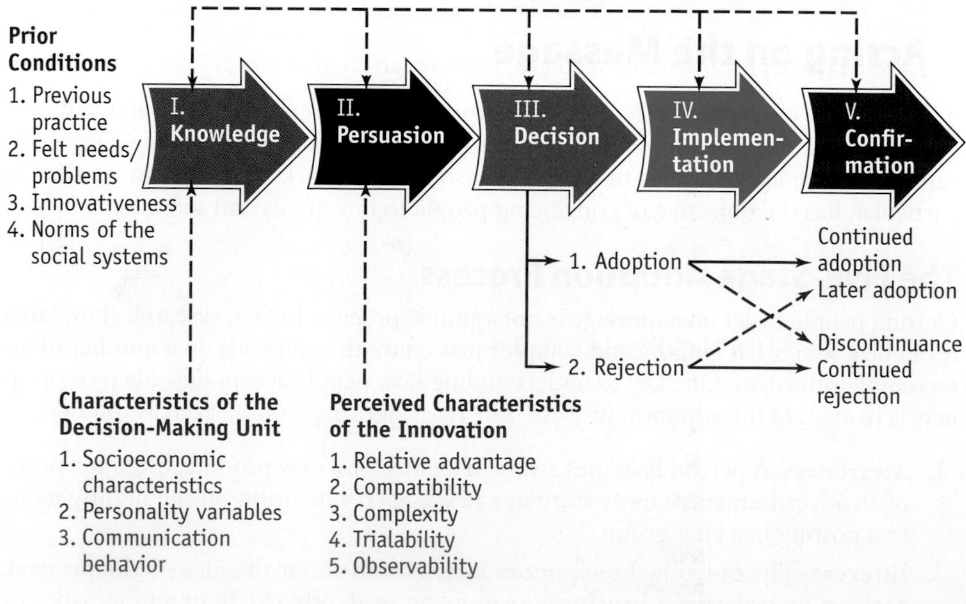

4. **Trialability.** The degree to which an innovation may be experienced on a limited basis.
5. **Observability.** The degree to which the results of an innovation are visible to others.

The communicator should be aware of these factors and attempt to implement communication strategies that will overcome as many of them as possible. Repeating a message in various ways, reducing its complexity, taking into account competing messages, and structuring the message to meet the needs of the audience are ways to do this.

It's also important to understand that a person does not necessarily go through all five stages with any given idea or product. The process may be terminated after any step. In fact, the process is like a large funnel. Although many are made aware of an idea or a product, only a few will ultimately adopt it.

The Time Factor

Another aspect that confuses people is the amount of time needed to adopt a new idea or product. Depending on the individual and the situation, the entire adoption process can take place almost instantly if the result is of minor consequence or requires low-level commitment. Buying a new brand of soft drink or bar of soap is relatively inexpensive and often done on impulse. On the other hand, deciding to buy a new car or vote for a particular candidate may involve an adoption process that takes several weeks or months.

Rogers's research shows that people approach innovation in different ways, depending on their personality traits and the risk involved. There are five levels:

- **Innovators:** Individuals who are venturesome and eager to try new ideas.
- **Early Adopters:** Savvy individuals who keep up with new ideas and new products, often the opinion leaders for their friends and colleagues.
- **Early Majority:** Individuals who take a deliberate, pragmatic approach to adopting ideas.
- **Late Majority:** Individuals who are often skeptical and somewhat resistant but eventually bow to peer pressure.
- **Laggards:** Individuals who are very traditional and the last group to adopt a new idea or product.

Psychographics, discussed in Chapter 9, can often help communicators segment audiences that have "Innovator" or "Early Adopter" characteristics and would be predisposed to adopting new ideas.

How Decisions Are Influenced

Of particular interest to public relations people is the primary source of information at each step in the adoption process.

Awareness Stage Mass media vehicles such as advertising, short news articles, feature stories, and radio and television news announcements are the most influential, with support from electronic word of mouth (eWOM) and websites. A news article or a television announcement makes people aware of an idea, event, or new product.

It's interesting to find that as much time as we spend online, we still prefer a personal recommendation from someone we know and trust.

Chris Haack of Mintel

They also are made aware through such vehicles as direct e-mail, office memos, simple brochures, and online news sites.

Interest Stage There is reliance on mass media vehicles, but individuals actively seek information on the Web and pay attention to longer, in-depth articles. They rely more on detailed brochures, specialized publications, small-group seminars, websites, and meetings to provide details.

Evaluation, Trial, and Adoption Stages Personal experience, group norms, and opinions of family and friends become more influential than mass media. Also influential is personal contact and conversation with individuals who are perceived as credible sources and experts. Feedback, negative or positive, may determine adoption. For this reason, word-of-mouth public relations and viral marketing campaigns can be crucial at this stage.

Word-of-Mouth Campaigns

The influence of peers and colleagues in the adoption process has been known for years. Now, word of mouth (WOM) has been institutionalized by a number of organizations to reach consumers and other audiences through their friends and colleagues. Procter & Gamble (P&G) was an early pioneer in the field. Its Tremor Division, for example, enlisted 225,000 teenagers to tell their friends about brands such as Herbal Essences and Old Spice. P&G has also signed up about 500,000 mothers to receive coupons and sample products, in the hope that these women will tell their friends and colleagues about the products.

The popularity of WOM is based on recent research that reinforces the classic theory of adoption articulated by Everett Rogers and others many years ago. One recent study by Mintel, a research firm, found that even Internet users find that "real friends" are more influential in the decision to buy a product than "online friends." Sixty percent said the source of product recommendations came from friends, relatives, or spouses. Only 10 percent listed a blogger or a chat room as influential in their buying decision. "It's interesting to find that as much time as we spend online, we still prefer a personal recommendation from someone we know and trust," commented Chris Haack of Mintel. One recent study, for example, found that 72 percent of consumers are influenced by their own experience, and another 56 percent by friends and family.

The new strategy for manufacturers is to engage customers to do the talking for them, and then amplify the customer's voice within their own site and through multiple channel marketing strategies.

Sam Ecker, chief marketing officer, Bazaarrvoice

Other studies have found that a key factor in WOM is to identify and reach *opinion leaders*, who are also known as *influentials* or *catalysts*. Opinion leaders and their characteristics are discussed more thoroughly in Chapter 9, but a study by the Keller Fay Group and Manning Selvage & Lee found that conversation catalysts (either online or in person) average about 200 weekly WOM conversations, and a large percentage of these conversations mention various products and brands.

An example of a successful WOM marketing campaign is one by U.K. pet food maker Masterfoods. The company identified 10,000 consumers likely to generate positive WOM reports to others if they liked the product, Whiskas Oh So. These "influencers" were then mailed free samples and coupons to

on the job

INSIGHTS

New and Improved Press Releases Still Achieve Communication Objectives

According to Sheldon Levine, community manager for Marketwire, even in the new media landscape with social media, corporate websites, and advertising managed by public relations firms, the vast majority of companies still issue news releases. Levine argues they are a real-time, effective way to distribute information to shareholders, and the networks are deep, broad, and efficient. But Levine offers some valuable tips for smart use of media releases:

1. More isn't always better.

   Watch out for the fine line between sharing and oversharing. If a reporter views the release as spam, it is the kiss of death for your story. Not only content, but frequency should be limited; as a rule, send only one or two news releases per month. "It's better to distribute a limited number of engaging releases than a steady stream of mediocre content."

2. Know your audience.

   Keep your audience in mind, both the media gatekeepers and the ultimate news consumers. Keep your audience in mind and target the demographics, interests, and media outlets to connect with your target public.

3. Integrate multimedia.

   Just as blog posts that include photos tend to garner more views, adding images, videos, and infographics to your release can make it more memorable and engaging. Even if the video does not get used in a reporter's story, it helps frame the story favorably for him or her.

   In an increasingly immersive and participatory online culture, multimedia in a release may become necessary, but be sure to include a concise description, as well as a link to your website or product information to deepen user engagement.

4. Create a buzz.

   Mobile devices now outsell laptop computers for online use, making social sites like Facebook, Twitter, LinkedIn, Google+, and Pinterest increasingly important for news and information. Not only are the sites serving as news sources, but also as platforms to share and discuss information with others in their network.

5. Take advantage of Search Engine Optimization (SEO).

   Put simply, find a service that allows you to select additional keywords for your digital release that will enhance the visibility of your press release across the Web. Some SEO services offer keyword analyzers that take it one step further by grading a press release's search-engine ranking potential.

6. Use reports to your advantage.

   Data can provide valuable information about the effectiveness of a release in ways that were never possible before the digital age. Many newswires offer analytical metrics regarding the pick-up and impact of the release, which can inform adjustments to communication campaigns as well as substantive evaluation of the effort (see Chapter 8 for more on evaluation).

   Levine concludes that "the press release remains one of the most effective, efficient ways to distribute information. Integrating these best practices into your communication strategy will ensure that you're maximizing the impact of your release and reaching the right people."

Source: PRSA *Tactics*, July 1, 2013.

pass on to family and friends. Sales of the product among those who received WOM recommendations and coupons from their friends were 11 times higher than from consumers who didn't receive any information or coupons from a family member or friend. In other situations, WOM campaigns have raised some ethical concerns. See the Ethics box on page 220.

on the job

ETHICS

eWOM Poses Ethical Challenges

Electronic word-of-mouth (eWOM) tactics are now a major communication tool in marketing and increasingly in public relations campaigns. The basic principle is that friends and peers are more influential than traditional tactics in changing opinions and motivating people to try new products.

Such campaigns, however, have generated some controversy. Some say it's a form of "stealth" communication because the public isn't told that the hired actor or "peer" is being rewarded to spread the word about a product or a social position. Faking WOM endorsements of products or ideas can be done easily with immediate rewards such as coupons or free products from secret sponsors.

A campaign can be developed without disclosing who is actually behind it. Stop Oil Speculation Now fought high oil and fuel prices with aggressive communication about everything except the funders of the campaign—in *PRWeek*'s words, "making it appear to be a true grassroots effort." However, airlines and unions were actually sponsors as part of efforts to save companies and jobs.

What do you think? Do WOM campaigns such as those just described cross the ethical line? The Word of Mouth Marketing Association (www.womma.org), for example, has a code of ethics requiring transparency and full disclosure. Online standards call for transparency regarding the sponsor of a communication, accuracy of information, and protection of confidential information. Although eWOM works well for marketing efforts, it can also be a powerful tool for corporations and activist groups.

- The Tea Party, a conservative movement dedicated to reduced government, gained momentum through its WOM campaign to defeat health care reform. The effort failed, but the large turnouts at protest events were notable.
- In response, a progressive movement called the Coffee Party used a combination of mass media and viral efforts to execute its own eWOM strategies.
- Edelman Public Relations created a blog on behalf of Wal-Mart to counter some of the accusations made by Walmartwatch.com.

> Word of mouth will only work if it's based on a platform of ethics.
>
> *Andy Sernovitz, CEO of the Word of Mouth Marketing Association (WOMMA)*

The PRSA code mentions that public relations firms should disclose "any existing or potential conflicts of interest," but that primarily applies to clients—not eWOM campaigns. If you decided to use eWOM strategies in a public relations program, what ethical guidelines would you adopt? Or do you hold the view that as long as everyone is free to make his or her case in the court of public opinion, little oversight is needed?

Summary

The Goals of Communication

- Communication, also called *execution*, is the third step in the public relations process.
- The five possible objectives in a public relations campaign are (1) message exposure, (2) accurate dissemination of the message, (3) acceptance of the message, (4) attitude change, and (5) change in overt behavior.
- Many campaigns strive to accomplish only the first two objectives: message exposure and accurate dissemination of the message.

- The six components of effective communication for audiences are (1) receiving the message, (2) paying attention to the message, (3) understanding the message, (4) believing the message, (5) remembering the message, and (6) acting on the message.

Receiving the Message

- Most communication models have five basic elements: (1) source, (2) encoder, (3) signal, (4) decoder, and (5) destination.
- Effective communication requires the sender and the receiver to have a field of shared experience.
- Most modern models emphasize communication as a loop process that involves constant feedback and two-way communication.
- The larger the audience, the greater the number of barriers to communication.

Paying Attention to the Message

- Because audiences have different approaches to receiving messages, communicators must tailor the message to get the recipients' attention.
- Messages for passive audiences must have style and creativity, whereas messages for an audience actively seeking information must have more informative content.
- Effective communication of a message requires the use of multiple media channels.

Understanding the Message

- The most basic element of understanding between communicator and audience is a common language. This is becoming a greater issue with the emphasis on multiculturalism.
- Public relations practitioners must consider their audiences and style their language appropriately, taking into consideration literacy levels, clarity and simplicity of language, and avoidance of discriminatory or offensive language.

Believing the Message

- Key variables in believability include source credibility, context, and the audience's predispositions, especially their level of involvement.

Remembering the Message

- Messages are often repeated extensively to reach all members of the target audience and to help them remember and enhance their learning.
- One way to do this is to convey information in several ways, through a variety of channels.

Acting on the Message

- The five steps in the acceptance of new ideas or products are awareness, interest, evaluation, trial, and adoption.
- The adoption process is affected by relative advantage, compatibility, complexity, trialability, and observability.
- The time needed to adopt a new idea or product can be affected by the importance of the decision as well as by the personality of the person receiving the message.
- Word-of-mouth (WOM) campaigns are increasingly being used to take advantage of peer influence in the persuasion process.

Case Activity **A New Campaign to Combat Heart Disease**

The American Heart Association (AHA) has been educating the public about heart disease for a number of years with great success, but has recently found that the level of awareness about how to prevent heart attacks has not increased in the past two years. A new communication campaign is needed to convey key messages through multiple platforms and channels. What strategies and tactics would you recommend, using this chapter as a guideline in terms of (1) tailoring messages to what is described as "passive" audiences, (2) how to make the message relatively simple and easy to understand, (3) reinforcing the message through social media, videos, and even events, and (4) using word-of-mouth—WOM—techniques.

Questions For Review and Discussion

1. What are the five basic elements of a communication model?
2. What is controlled media, and how is it different from mass media?
3. What are the various considerations that a public relations practitioner must keep in mind before using social media for PR mileage?
4. Nestlé learnt its lesson the hard way in its fight with Greenpeace. What are the lessons this case teaches us about using social media?
5. Why is it necessary to use a variety of messages and communication channels in a public relations program?
6. How can symbols, acronyms, and slogans help in public relations communication?
7. What is source credibility? Why is it essential in public relations?
8. Explain the five steps of the adoption process. What are some of the factors that affect the adoption of an idea or product?
9. What is e-WOM? Why are many organizations now using it as a major strategy for marketing and public relations campaigns?

Media Resources

Levine, S. (2013, July). 6 best practices for distributing press releases. Retrieved from http://www.prsa.org/Intelligence/Tactics

McCarthy, C. (2010, March 19). Nestlé mess shows sticky side of Facebook pages. *CNET News, The Social*. Retrieved from http://news.cnet.com

Scudder, V. (2012, October 12). Chick-fil-A under fire: The perils of corporate outspokenness. *The Public Relations Strategist,* 10–12.

Sinkinson, T. (2013, June 27). Pitching research for PR: 11mark's study on mobile habits in the bathroom delivers the agency's royal flush. Retrieved from www.bulldogreporter.com

Swann, P. (2013, June). To serve and protect: How the Boston Police used Twitter after Marathon attacks. *Public Relations Tactics,* 12–13.

Ward, D. (2013, May). A culture of communication: Your most important audience is all around you. *Public Relations Tactics,* 18.

chapter 8

Evaluation and Measurement of Public Relations Programs

After reading this chapter, you will be able to:

Know the key elements of objectives

Understand the purpose of evaluation

Distinguish the measurement of different communication components

The Purpose of Evaluation

> We are talking about an orderly evaluation of our progress in attaining the specific objectives of our public relations plan. We are learning what we did right, what we did wrong, how much progress we've made and, most importantly, how we can do it better next time.
>
> *Frank Wylie, emeritus professor at California State University in Long Beach*

The fourth step of the public relations process is evaluation. It is the measurement of results against established objectives set during the planning process discussed in Chapter 6.

Evaluation involves the systematic assessment of a program, particularly focusing on communication results. It is a means for practitioners to offer accountability to clients—and to themselves. Evaluation provides the opportunity to learn what was done right and what was done wrong, both as a look backward at performance and as a look forward at the improvement of performance.

The desire to do a better job next time is a major reason for evaluating public relations efforts, but another equally important reason is the widespread adoption of the management-by-objectives system by clients and employers of public relations personnel. They want to know whether the money, time, and effort expended on public relations are well spent and contribute to the realization of an organizational objective, such as attendance at an open house, product sales, or increased awareness of obesity in children.

Objectives: A Prerequisite for Evaluation

Before any public relations program can be properly evaluated, it is important to have a clearly established set of measurable objectives. These should be part of the program plan (discussed in Chapter 6), but first some points need to be reviewed.

- Public relations personnel and management should agree on the criteria that will be used to evaluate success in attaining objectives.
- Don't wait until the end of the public relations program to determine how it will be evaluated. Albert L. Schweitzer at Fleishman-Hillard public relations in St. Louis makes the point: "Evaluating impact/results starts in the planning stage. You break down the problem into measurable goals and objectives, then after implementing the program, you measure the results against goals."
- If an objective is informational, measurement techniques must show how successfully information was communicated to target audiences. Such techniques fall under the rubrics of "message dissemination" and "audience exposure," but they do not measure the effect on attitudes or overt behavior and action.
- Motivational objectives are more difficult to accomplish. If the objective is to increase sales or market share, it is important to show that public relations efforts, rather than advertising or other marketing strategies, caused the increase. Or, if the objective is to change attitudes or opinions, research should be done before and after the public relations activity to measure the percentage of change.

> Write the most precise, most results-oriented objectives you can that are realistic, credible, measurable, and compatible with the client's demands on public relations.
>
> *Agency monograph, Ketchum Public Relations*

Although objectives may vary, the following checklist contains the basic evaluation questions that any practitioner should ask:

- Was the activity or program adequately planned?
- Did the recipients of the message understand it?
- How could the program strategy have been more effective?
- Were all primary and secondary audiences reached?
- Was the desired organizational objective achieved?
- What unforeseen circumstances affected the success of the program or activity?
- Did the program or activity fall within the budget set for it?
- What steps can be taken to improve the success of similar future activities?

Current Status of Measurement and Evaluation

Public relations professionals have made considerable progress in evaluation and measurement, the ability to tell clients and employers exactly what has been accomplished. Sophisticated software programs and techniques are being used, including computerized news clip analysis, survey sampling, quasi-experimental designs in which the audience is divided into groups that see different aspects of a public relations campaign, and attempts to correlate efforts directly with sales.

Today, the trend toward more systematic evaluation is well established. Katherine Paine, founder of her own public relations measurement firm, says that the percentage of a public relations budget devoted to measurement and evaluation was about 1 percent in the 1990s, but is now closer to 5 percent. A 2010 study by the USC Annenberg Strategic Public Relations Center found about the same percentage; the average corporation devotes only 4 to 5 percent of its total public relations budget to evaluation and measurement. Advocates say measurement should be at least 10 percent of budget because there is constant pressure on public relations departments to justify their budgets and prove their value to the bottom line.

> If you have not carved off at least 10 percent of your budget to measure your impact, you're flying blind, and you have no way of proving your value.
>
> *Mark Stouse, director of worldwide communications for BMC*

Some practitioners maintain that public relations is more art than science and is thus extremely difficult to measure. Walter K. Lindenmann, a former senior vice president and director of research at Ketchum, takes a more optimistic view. He wrote in *Public Relations Quarterly*: "Let's get something straight right off the bat. First, it is possible to measure public relations effectiveness. . . . Second, measuring public relations effectiveness does not have to be either unbelievably expensive or laboriously time-consuming."

The Institute for Public Relations (www.instituteforpr.org) also takes the view that public relations effectiveness can be systematically evaluated. It has commissioned a notable library of research and guidelines about measurement over the past 20 years, with most papers available free of charge on its website. The institute's slogan captures the essence of its mission: "The science beneath the art of public relations."

Lindenmann suggests that public relations personnel use a mix of evaluation techniques, many adapted from advertising and marketing, to provide more complete evaluation. In addition, he notes that there are at least three levels of measurement and evaluation (see Figure 8.1).

On the most basic level are compilations of message distribution and media placement. The second level, which requires more sophisticated techniques, deals with the

Figure 8.1 **Public Relations Effectiveness Yardstick**

Evaluation goals for public relations programs can be grouped at three levels of measurement, as shown in this chart.

Source: Ketchum, New York, published in *Public Relations Quarterly.*

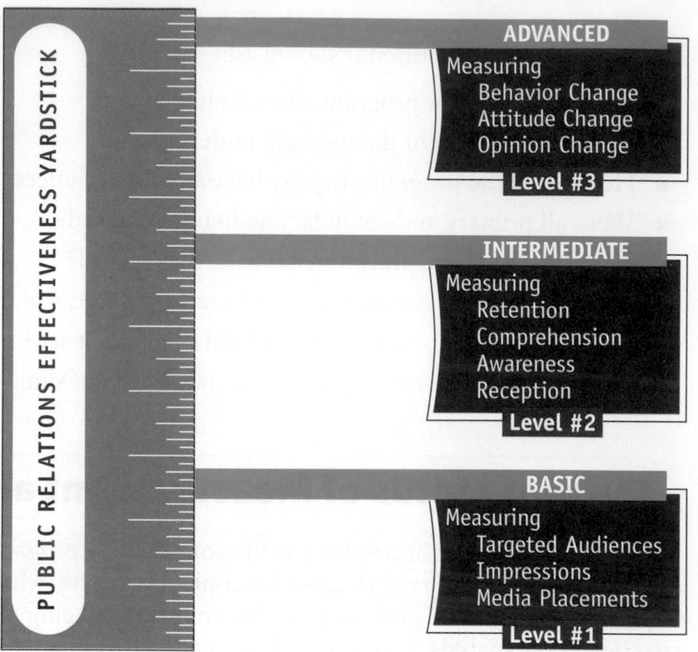

measurement of audience awareness, comprehension, and retention of the message. The most advanced level is the measurement of changes in attitudes, opinions, and behavior.

The following sections outline the most widely used methods for evaluating public relations efforts. These include measurement of (1) production, (2) message exposure, (3) audience awareness, (4) audience attitudes, and (5) audience action. Supplemental activities such as communication audits, readability tests, event evaluation, and split messages also are discussed. In most cases, a skilled practitioner will use a combination of methods to evaluate the effectiveness of a program.

Measurement of Production

One elementary form of evaluation is simply to count how many news releases, feature stories, photos, tweets, guest editorials, blog postings, and the like, are produced in a given period of time. This kind of evaluation is supposed to give management an idea of a staff's productivity and output.

Public relations professionals, however, do not believe that this evaluation is very meaningful, because it emphasizes quantity instead of quality. In most cases, it is more cost effective to write fewer news releases and spend more time on the few that really are newsworthy (see Insights box in Chapter 7 on page 219). It could also be more valuable to the organization for a staff person to spend five weeks working to place an article in the *Wall Street Journal* than to write 29 routine personnel releases.

Closely allied to the production of publicity materials is their distribution. Thus, a public relations department might report, for instance, that a total of 756 news releases were sent to 819 daily newspapers, 250 weeklies, and 137 trade magazines within one year or that 230 messages were posted on the organization's blog. A Centers for Disease Control and Prevention campaign to inform parents about the early symptoms of autism in children, for example, reported that 21,000 resource kits were distributed to health professionals and another 60,000 were distributed to parents.

Measurement of Message Exposure

The most widely practiced form of evaluating public relations programs is the compilation of print and broadcast mentions, often called "clips." The Insights box which follows, for example, shows that both U.S. and European professionals still heavily rely on "clippings." Public relations firms and company departments working primarily on a local basis, for example, often have a staff member scan area newspapers for client or product mentions.

Large companies with regional, national, or even international outreach usually retain monitoring services to scan large numbers of publications and various Internet/social media sites. It is also possible to have services such as Critical Mention monitor television newscasts in major markets as well as local and national talk shows. Web analytics covered in Chapter 5 measures similar exposure metrics for Web and social media.

on the job INSIGHTS

Effectiveness of Measurement Tools

BenchPoint, a measurement firm, conducted a global survey of public relations and communications professionals for the first European Measurement Summit in Berlin. The respondents, coming primarily from Europe and the United States, ranked the effectiveness of the measurement tools they use to monitor the public relations initiatives in their firms and departments. As illustrated in Figure 8.2, respondents ranked "clippings" first in effectiveness but using advertising equivalency ranked eleventh.

Figure 8.2 **Benchpoint's Survey Data**

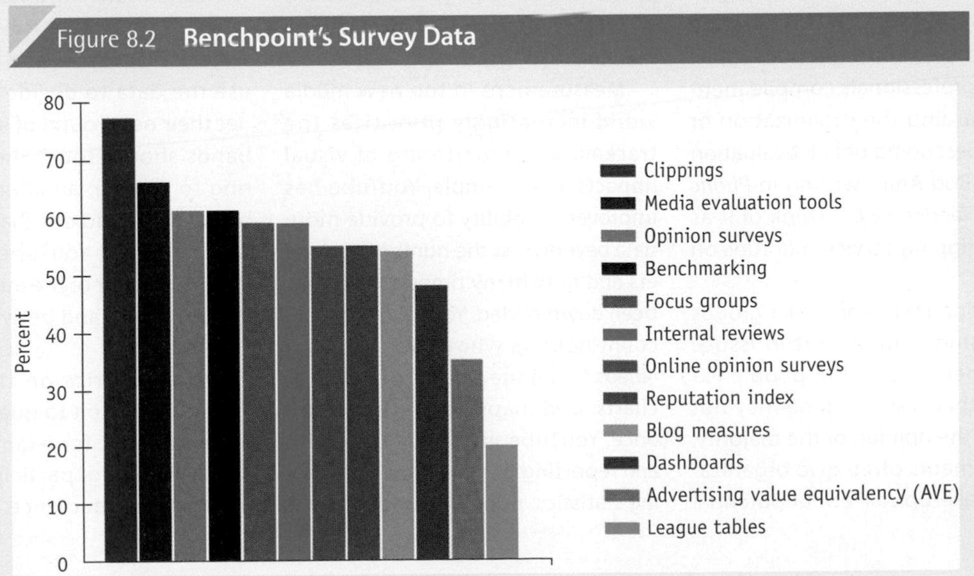

Burrelles/Luce, for example, monitors over 40 million blogs and Internet forums, thousands of Web news sources, over 10,000 daily and nondaily newspapers, magazines, and trade journals, and virtually all TV and cable stations. Another monitoring service, National Aircheck, is able to search almost 8,000 hours of news talk radio each week. Robb Wexler, president of the firm, told *O'Dwyer's PR Report*, "We should be able to tell someone within 10 to 15 minutes where and when they're being talked about."

The result of all this electronic research is the ability for the organization or its public relations firm to do a fairly accurate count of how many traditional and new media stories are generated by the program or campaign. The celebration of Latin style by Suave beauty products featured in Chapter 6, generated a sixfold increase in print coverage of the product line and a 12 percent increase in Hispanic TV ratings over the previous year. The number of media placements, however, is just the first level of assessing the exposure of the message to potential audiences.

on the job INSIGHTS

Measuring Effectiveness on the Web

Blogs, chat groups, and online publications can also be monitored using the metric of visits to a site, but such data are less valuable than the content and tone of what is being said. (See Web Analytics and Social Media Monitoring in Chapter 5 for details on cutting-edge research tools.) Consequently, public relations professionals compile mentions regarding the organization or client. In describing online evaluation research, Rod Amis, writing in *Public Relations Tactics*, says, "Think of it as a digital clipping service that runs on autopilot."

Monitoring blogs and chat groups is increasingly important in issues management. While the people expressing their views online may not represent the opinion of the majority, their comments often give organizations a "wake-up call" about potential problems and issues. Social media monitoring and participation provide direct feedback about what people are thinking, what rumors are circulating about the organization, and how well public relations efforts have performed to manage the trajectory of important issues in vast online communities.

Measurement in the new media world increasingly prioritizes the tracking and monitoring of visual impacts. For example, YouTube has improved its ability to provide more data beyond just the number of viewers and how many times a video has been downloaded. YouTube gives account holders who have uploaded videos to the site a range of statistics, charts, and maps about their audience. YouTube Insight, an analytics and reporting engine, provides viewing statistics, popularity metrics, and demographic information for videos and channels. The data available through Insight include age, gender, and geographic location as well as the identities of the Internet sites that viewers came from and where they went after watching a video.

Tracy Chan told the *Los Angeles Times*, "Marketers and advertisers use the data to decide how to target their next round of ads or where bands should tour." She was referring to Weezer, an alternative rock band that found out that 2.2 million watched their YouTube video, but that 65 percent of the audience were men under 18 and between ages 35 and 45.

Other metrics on the Internet are more difficult to quantify. Social network sites, for example, are all about listening, participating, and engaging the audience, rather than

(continued)

necessarily delivering key messages. Ed Terpening, VP of social media at Wells Fargo, told a Dow Jones seminar, "We care a lot about participation and engagement. That's our No. 1 metric." These communication activities can be evaluated using more qualitative methods such as analysis of themes or breakdown of patterns in the online conversations combined with illustrative quotes for management to get a sense of the social discourse.

One dimension is called the "conversation index," which is the ratio between blog posts and comments. It helps measure whether a blogger is doing a lot of writing with very little response from readers, or whether the audience is engaged and contributing to the conversation. Obviously, blogs that generate a lot of "conversation" are more important to organizations in terms of feedback and dialogue.

Another metric that is somewhat difficult to quantify is the tone of the conversation; is it positive, hostile, or neutral? Some experts say this is too simplistic since it doesn't take into consideration whether someone is being sarcastic. Tone can be misconstrued by analysis that evaluates language too literally. Nevertheless, such information generally helps organizations respond to concerns raised by key publics such as consumers. Other forms of measurement are (1) engagement, such as time spent with the site and whether visitors downloaded materials; (2) word-of-mouth impact; and (3) search engine visibility.

In sum, the ability to measure the effectiveness of social media is continuing to evolve. For example, concepts such as human voice and authenticity of social media offerings are being developed to enhance the value of raw numbers that are so readily found in new media environments by capturing server data. Both new measures challenge public relations professionals to craft messages in new media channels to which audiences can relate.

Right now we are doing a lot of work to mash up social [media] data with business data to get cause and effect . . . . You've got to be able to tie causes to effects, and that is the big challenge right now, what all our clients, and what is frankly hardest to accomplish.

Josh Jones-Dilworth, founder and CEO of Jones-Dilworth, Inc.

Media Impressions

In addition to the number of media placements, public relations departments and firms report how many people may have been exposed to the message. These numbers are referred to as *media impressions*, the potential audience reached by a periodical, a broadcast program, or a website.

If, for example, a story about an organization appears in a local daily that has a circulation of 130,000, the media impressions are 130,000. If another story is published the next day, this counts as 130,000 more impressions. Estimated audiences for radio and television programs, certified by auditing organizations, also are used to compile media impressions. Thus, if there's even a brief mention of a new product or service on *Today*, for example, this might constitute 10 million impressions, if that is the audited size of the audience that regularly watches the program.

Some firms inflate the number of "impressions" by also estimating the number of people who are not actual subscribers, but who may read a newspaper because it is delivered to the office or home. So instead of 130,000 impressions, it would be 520,000 impressions based on the pass-along readership, the estimated additional individuals with access to the newspaper. A regional or national news story can generate millions of impressions by simple multiplication of each placement by the circulation or audience of each medium. The Doritos Super Bowl advertising competition generated more than 600 million impressions. The breakdown, in part, included:

- 25 national print/wire features
- 108 national TV and radio segments
- More than 360 online news stories
- More than 2,200 local TV/radio mentions

Media impressions are commonly used in advertising to document the breadth of penetration of a particular message. Such figures give a rough estimate of how many people are potentially exposed to a message. They don't, however, document how many people actually read or heard the stories and, more importantly, how many absorbed or acted on the information. Other techniques needed for this kind of evaluation are discussed later in this chapter.

Basic Web Analytics

Measuring the reach and effectiveness of messages on the Internet is getting more sophisticated by the month. One cyberspace version of media impressions, used for some years, is the number of people reached via an organization's web page. Each instance of a person accessing a site is called a **hit** or a **visit**. (See Web Analytics in Chapter 5, which details online measurement techniques and the Multicultural World box in this chapter about World Water Day on page 231, which shows some Web and social analytics in action.)

In a national campaign to increase awareness of autism, for example, the Centers for Disease Control and Prevention reported 540,000 unique visitors and more than 50,000 materials downloaded from its website. Even a campaign by the National Potato Board did pretty well. Its Mr. Potato Head site attracted almost 10,000 visitors, who spent an average of 5.5 minutes at the site, reviewing an average of 6.6 pages, about the health benefits of potatoes.

> Targeted outreach affects web traffic. That's the gold standard of how to develop our measurement program.
>
> *Sbonali Burke, VP of media for ASPCA, as quoted in* PRWeek

Additional information about users is often gathered by asking them to answer some demographic questions before they use the site or as they leave it. For best results, offer free software or something similar that must be mailed to users; this entices people to give their names and addresses. Marketers, for example, use this technique to compile databases of potential customers.

Advertising Value Equivalency (AVE)

Another approach, now widely condemned by most national and international professional groups, is to calculate the value of a news story or broadcast mention by comparing it to what the space or time would cost in advertising. In other words, a five-inch article in a trade magazine that charges $200 per column inch for advertising would be worth $1,000 in publicity value. The Doritos Super Bowl campaign, mentioned earlier, claimed that the news coverage was comparable to $40 million in paid advertising.

Some practitioners even take the approach of calculating the cost of advertising for the same amount of space and then multiplying that total three to six times to reflect the common belief that a news story has greater credibility than an advertisement. Several mitigating factors, however, argue against using a multiplier. For one, there is

on the job

A MULTICULTURAL WORLD

YouTube Videos Promote World Water Day

Public relations agency Weber Shandwick (WS) and Population Services International (PSI) combined forces to create a social media campaign that capitalizes on the emotional power of video. World Water Day Viral Video Series set out to open eyes to the heartbreaking reality of water-related disease as a major cause of death worldwide for children.

PSI wanted socially and environmentally conscious Americans to know that unsafe drinking water often leads to sudden death and devastating illness for children in developing countries. The online public service announcement (PSA) video series informed people of the simple, cheap solutions to the problem.

The team knew that the key to generating strong viewership of the online PSA videos was telling a compelling story, so it enlisted Good, an integrated media company, to help build a strong narrative. From here, the team took an unconventional approach and drew upon existing footage from iconic Hollywood moments, including scenes from *Cool Hand Luke* and *Psycho*. In one video, children are seen sliding down a chute of the popular toy Crocodile Mile, but landing in sludgy, contaminated water.

To generate buzz leading up to World Water Day, WS conducted a staggered rollout. Prior to the videos' launch, content editors at YouTube got a sneak peek to stimulate their interest in a home page exclusive. The first four videos were then launched on PSI's partner sites such as YouTube, with promotion of the videos on Facebook and Twitter.

Within 10 days of launching, total video views exceeded 1 million. The video *Transparency* was featured as a YouTube home page exclusive and generated 600,000 views in its first three days. The top-viewed video, *Psycho*, was YouTube's most viewed video in its nonprofit and activism category.

- The viewer feedback showed that the videos raised awareness and interest in helping the cause.
- The cause was good.
- The delivery channel capitalized on the reach of social media.
- And the narrative was compelling.

The tagline under PSI's logo states: "Healthy Lives. Measurable Results." But could the sponsors be certain that money was well spent on public relations based only on the measurement of media exposure and anecdotal praise from viewers? Using the measurement guidelines from this chapter, what would you recommend to PSI that would enhance substantive evaluation of these sorts of communication programs in the future?

Source: PRWeek, www.prweekus.com/awards

> Once you start comparing a PR placement to an ad, that raises a whole spectrum of issues.
>
> *Don Bartholomew, director of research at MWW Group*

no empirical evidence to support any multiple factor. Professor Don Stacks at the University of Miami has conducted several research studies about AVE and concluded, "We failed to find the existence of a multiplier." The Institute for Public Relations (IPR) was even blunter. In a policy paper, IPR called the use of multipliers "unethical, dishonest, and not at all supported by research literature."

Despite such condemnation, many publicists still use AVE and multiplier formulas. News photos of President Obama drinking a Guinness beer during a trip to Ireland, for example, were touted by one UK publicist as being worth $32 million in worldwide publicity for Guinness. Corporate practitioners rationalize the use of AVE because they say it is a form of return on investment (ROI). It shows management that the public relations staff is earning its salary by generating more "income" than it costs to pay their salaries.

Comparing news coverage (called earned media) with advertising, however, is like comparing apples and oranges. One reason why the two can't be compared is the fundamental difference between advertising and publicity. Advertising copy is directly controlled by the organization and can be oriented to specific objectives. The organization also controls the size and placement of the message. News mentions, on the other hand, are determined by media gatekeepers and can be negative, neutral, or positive. In addition, a news release can be edited to the point that key corporate messages are deleted. In other words, the organization can't control size, placement, or content.

The most important concern is that AVEs concentrate on outputs, not outcomes. AVE tends to relegate public relations to a media relations function, which diminishes the role of public relations' strategic counsel to upper management when decisions are made, not just when they are publicized. At the same time, equating publicity with advertising rates for comparable space does not engender good media relations. The technique reinforces the opinion of many media gatekeepers that all news releases are just attempts to get free advertising.

In summary, the **dollar-value** approach to measuring publicity effectiveness is rapidly declining as a metric. Andre Manning, head of global communications for Philips Electronics, told *PRWeek*, "The PR practitioner who says, 'We got 500 hits, which generated 250 impressions with an AVE of $2 million' is a thing of the past." The winning campaigns in PRSA's Silver Anvil awards, for example, rarely used AVE as a major criterion to demonstrate the success of a campaign. Instead, the emphasis is on outcomes such as increased sales, awareness, change in attitudes or behavior, and contribution to overall corporate objectives.

Systematic Tracking

As noted earlier, message exposure traditionally has been measured by sheer bulk. New advances in computer software and databases, however, now make it possible to track media placements in a more sophisticated way.

Systems can now analyze the content of media placements by such variables as market penetration, type of publication, tone of coverage, sources quoted, and mention of key copy points. Ketchum, for example, can build up to 40 variables into its computer program, including the tracking of reporter bylines to determine whether a journalist is predisposed negatively or positively to the client's key messages.

on the job

ETHICS

The New Math: Ad Rates versus News Coverage

You've been hired as an intern at a public relations firm for the summer. One of your duties is to go through recent online issues of trade magazines and "clip" any article in which the name of a client appears. You are then asked to look up advertising rates for these publications and calculate what the comparable space in advertising would cost. The public relations firm routinely triples the ad cost because a news story is more "valuable" than an ad.

The idea, says the account supervisor, is to count entire articles even if the client's name is mentioned only once. "The client is impressed with big numbers," she says, "so count anything you can find, get the actual ad cost, and then triple it." You ask whether you should also try to judge whether the coverage is favorable or not. Your supervisor says that all the client really wants is to be visible—and besides, it takes too much time to decide what is favorable or unfavorable coverage.

Does AVE raise any ethical concerns on your part? Why or why not? How would you handle the assignment? Would you be inclined to suggest to your boss that Weighted Media Equivalency might be worth considering?

Specialty measurement firms such as Vocus, Visible Technologies, and Factiva do extensive analysis for a variety of clients on a number of metrics such as (1) analysis of coverage telling how a company's news coverage compares with that of the competition, (2) share of voice in terms of what percentage of overall coverage about an industry or subject focuses on the client company, (3) tone showing whether the slant of coverage is positive or negative, (4) percentage of time that stories mention key messages, and (5) analysis of what third-party experts, consumers, and bloggers say about the organization. See Figure 8.3 for sample charts compiled with Vocus software about the athletic shoe market for use in this textbook.

Systematic monitoring can provide a baseline to determine whether an organization's publicity efforts paid off in terms of placements and mention of key messages. Essentially, a baseline study is a measurement of audience response (awareness, understanding, or attitudes and opinions) before, during, and after a public relations campaign. Baseline studies can graphically show the percentage difference in measured audience performance as a result of public relations campaign components.

For example, the Johnson & Johnson public service campaign to increase parental awareness of dangers to children in swimming pools used a baseline survey by Harris Interactive before its campaign. Post-campaign research found that awareness of pool-drain hazards increased from 26 to 32 percent.

Another form of analysis compares the number of news releases sent with the number actually published and in what kinds of periodicals. Such analysis often helps a public relations department determine what kinds of publicity are most effective and earn the most ROI. Over time, findings can also indicate what publications tend to use news releases from the organization.

> **The world doesn't need more data. What it needs is analyzed data.**
>
> *Katharine Paine, president of KD Paine & Partners*

Figure 8.3 **Measuring Results in the Athletic Shoe Industry**

Public relations software and research firms are able to capture enormous amounts of data over time, which are then encapsulated in graphics that inform evaluation of measurable objectives. For example, if Nike had set the objective of leading the top four shoe manufacturers in share of media mentions, the Company Mindshare chart would demonstrate success at a glance. If the objective were to hold negative comments to a minimum among bloggers and tweeters, the Social Media by Tone chart would show a small red band of negative comments compared to the large sections of neutral and positive comments.

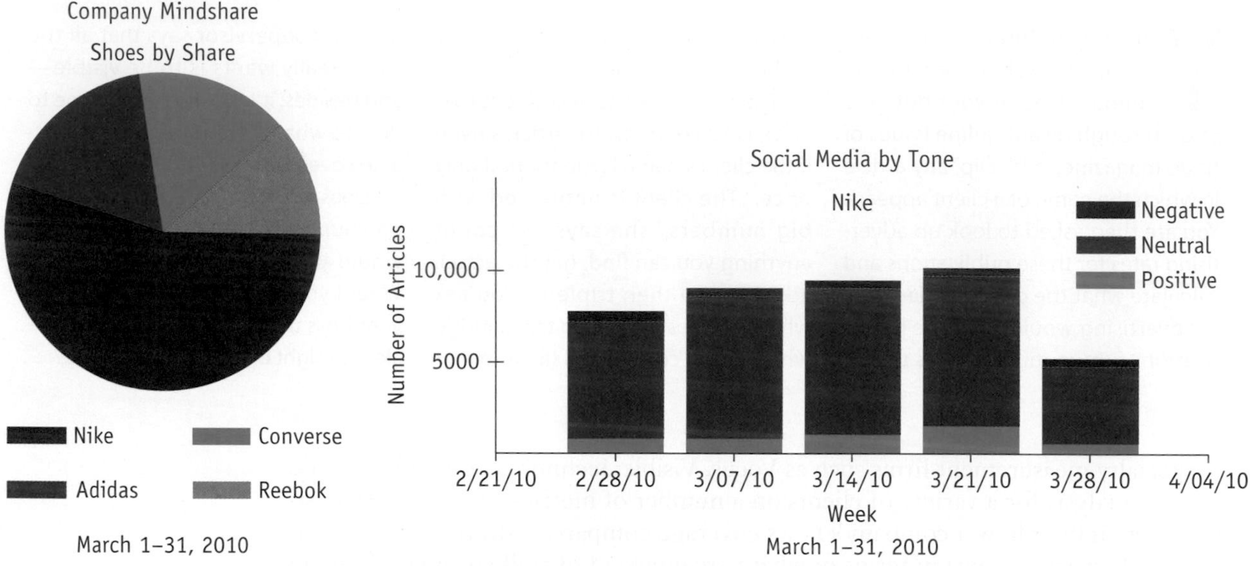

Requests and 800 Numbers

Another measure of media exposure is to compile the number of requests for more information. A story in a newspaper or a company spokesperson on a broadcast often tells people where they can get more information about a subject. In addition, part of Web analytics is how many people download a video or a "brochure" from a website.

In many cases, a toll-free 800 number is provided. Dayton Hudson Corporation, owner of several department store chains, once used a toll-free hotline number as part of its "Child Care Aware" program to help educate parents about quality child care and how to get it. In a six-month period, 19,000 calls were received from people seeking advice and copies of a brochure.

Requests for materials also can show the effectiveness of a public relations program. An information program by the U.S. Centers for Disease Control on AIDS prevention, for example, received nearly 2,000 phone calls on its information hotline after its "Safe Sex" program was broadcast by the Public Broadcasting Service (PBS). In addition, the program and resulting publicity generated 260 requests for videos and 400 requests for "Smart Sex" organization kits.

Return on Investment (ROI)

Another way to evaluate exposure to a message is to determine the cost of reaching each member of the audience. The technique is commonly used in advertising to place costs in perspective. Although a 30-second commercial during the Super Bowl telecast costs millions, advertisers believe it is well worth the price because an audience of more than 100 million is reached for less than a half-cent each.

Cost-effectiveness, as this technique is known, is also used in public relations. *Cost-per-thousand* (CPM) is calculated by taking the cost of the publicity program and dividing it by the total media impressions (discussed earlier). Nike produced a sports video for $50,000, but reached 150,000 high school students, for a per-person cost of 33 cents.

Many professionals also call this ROI, or return on investment. In other words, if an organization spends $500,000 on a campaign that results in a $20 million increase in sales, the ROI is 40 times the cost. Increasingly, public relations professionals are measuring public relations in terms of (1) what sales or revenues are generated, and (2) how much they have saved the company in terms of avoiding a crisis or litigation.

> It was clear to us that you can't go and ask for money . . . unless you can show a return. You can't show a return unless you have measurement.
>
> *Valerie M. Cunningham, VP of corporate marketing for Xerox*

Measurement of Audience Awareness

Thus far, techniques of measuring audience exposure and accurate dissemination have been discussed. A higher level of evaluation is needed to determine whether the audience actually became aware of the message and understood it.

Walter Lindenmann calls this the second level of public relations evaluation. He notes:

> At this level, public relations practitioners measure whether target audience groups actually received the messages directed at them: whether they paid attention to those messages, whether they understood the messages, and whether they have retained those messages in any shape or form.

The tools of survey research are needed to answer such questions. Members of the target audience must be asked about the message and what they remember about it. Public awareness of the organization which sponsors an event is also important. The internationally recognized advocacy group Health Literacy Missouri conducts annual surveys of media in the state to assess awareness of the organization, but, more importantly, of health literacy as a crucial factor in the health and well-being of everyday citizens.

Measuring audience awareness and comprehension with *day-after recall* offers a credible metric for evaluating the impact of a campaign component. Participants are asked to view a specific television program or read a particular news story. The next day, they are interviewed to find out which messages they remember.

Ketchum, on behalf of the California Prune Board, used this technique to determine whether a 15-city media tour was conveying the key message that prunes are a high-fiber food source. Forty women in Detroit considered likely to watch daytime television shows were asked to view a program on which a Prune Board spokesperson appeared. The day after the program, Ketchum asked the women questions about the show, including their knowledge of the fiber content of prunes. Ninety-three percent remembered the Prune Board spokesperson, and 65 percent, on an unaided basis, named prunes as a high-fiber food source.

Measurement of Audience Attitudes

Closely related to audience awareness and understanding of a message are changes in an audience's perceptions and attitudes, which can be evaluated using pre- and post-measurements of attitudes. A number of intervening variables may account for changes in attitude, of course, but statistical analysis of variance can help pinpoint how much the change is attributable to public relations efforts. Advanced evaluation designs can even control for the effect of all the measurement, which has its own impact on audiences.

The insurance company Prudential Financial regularly conducts baseline studies. One survey found that the company scored high in respondent familiarity, but achieved only a 29 percent favorable rating in fulfilling its corporate social responsibilities. As a result, the company launched The Prudential Spirit of Community Awards program, the United States' largest youth-recognition program based exclusively on volunteer community service. The value of the baseline survey is underscored by Frank R. Stansberry, former manager of guest affairs for Coca-Cola, who said, "The only way to determine if communications are making an impact is by pre- and posttest research. The first survey measures the status quo. The second one will demonstrate any change and the direction of that change."

Measurement of Audience Action

The ultimate objective of any public relations effort, as has been pointed out, is to accomplish organizational objectives. As David Dozier of San Diego State University aptly points out, "The outcome of a successful public relations program is not a hefty stack of news stories. . . . Communication is important only in the effects it achieves among publics."

The objective of an amateur theater group is not to get media publicity; the objective is to sell tickets. The objective of an environmental organization such as Greenpeace is not to get publicity on behalf of whales, but to motivate the public to (1) write to elected officials, (2) send donations for preservation efforts, and (3) get protective legislation passed that actually saves whales.

Similarly, the ultimate objective of a company is to sell its products and services, not get 200 million media impressions. See the Insights box which follows for more information about linking sales to measurements. Although the immediate objective of many public relations campaigns is to raise awareness driven by the number of media placements and impressions, such campaigns should be seen in the context of the adoption theory that was described in Chapter 7. In other words, raising awareness and raising interest are the first two steps of the five-step process to ultimately motivate people to adopt an idea, vote for a candidate, use a service, or buy a product.

> The outcome of a successful public relations program is not a hefty stack of news stories. . . . Communication is important only in the effects it achieves among publics.
>
> *Dr. David Dozier, professor, San Diego State University*

Thus, public relations efforts ultimately are evaluated on how they help an organization achieve its objectives. For example, Suave's celebration of Hispanic style tracked increased awareness as mentioned previously, but the campaign also touted the increase in product trial for the Suave Professionals line:

- Sales were lifted by 12.6 percent at 24 test stores.
- Suave Styling Aids sold at a 14.3 percent increase where the campaign's celebrity stylist, Rocco, appeared prior to the television award show.
- Measuring Success: The Cookie Careavan evaluation plan offers a clear example of how components of a campaign are itemized and plans are made in advance for measurement.

PRCasebook

Ketchum's Evaluation of the DoubleTree CAREavan

The four process chapters culminate with evaluation of the research, the plan, and the communication. For the Ketchum Public Relations campaign to celebrate the hospitality of DoubleTree Hotels by Hilton, several components of the national tour serve to showcase key points in this evaluation chapter:

- the importance of setting clear, measurable objectives for the campaign (informational and motivational)
- the role of measurement for social media tactics in contemporary campaigns (buzz, visual impact, spinoff traditional media coverage)
- the measurement of various communication components (from simple awareness to membership decision)

Ketchum used plain language in the objectives section of its plan, describing what success would look like. Overarching goals were brand awareness and brand engagement. Success metrics included the following, with blue annotations to point to particularly notable evaluation measures:

Cookies distributed/attendees at cookie events [an indicator of event participation]

- Media coverage:
  - Overall media impressions [a calculation of potential reader and viewer numbers based on tracking of media coverage and audience for media outlets]
  - Message quality: percentage of key message in resulting impressions [content analysis of the coverage to confirm campaign story was being told]
- Social media buzz:
  - Social Media ROI Score
  - Increase in online ecosystem
  - Terms "Cookie," "CARE," or additional defined terms rank higher in the overall ecosystem
  - Increase in DoubleTree by Hilton (DTbH) Twitter and Facebook followers and "Likes" [a measure of actual communication behavior, moving the campaign beyond mere awareness and understanding to favorable attitude toward the brand]
  - Facebook tab analytics (clicks, engagement, photo submissions, etc.)
- Visits to online platforms (DTbH website, Facebook, Twitter, etc.): Create deeper engagement by driving consumers to online platforms where they can interact with the brand [the use of Web analytics, such as which sites drive visitors and landing page activity to confirm the tour, led to greater engagement with the DoubleTree brand]
- HHonors sign-ups: Educate consumers on HHonors benefits and drive sign-ups through

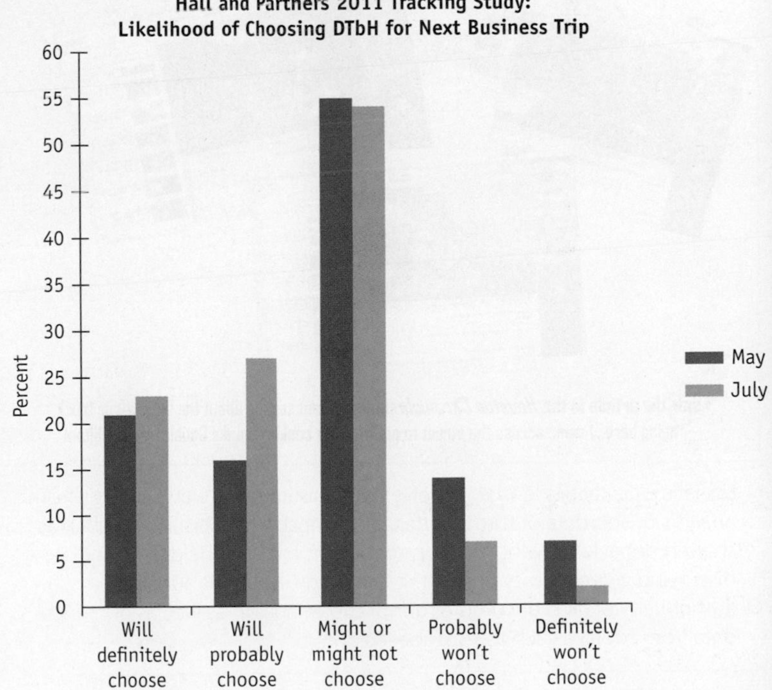

(continued)

event activities and overall messaging. Note that Ketchum will need to work with DTbH to determine the best way to capture CAREavan-driven HHonors sign-ups [although actual behavior such as enrolling in a program is often the trickiest to attribute directly to a campaign, the case is worth making; conversion of tour visitors into members of the Hilton awards program impacts the bottom line for Hilton by increasing likely hotel bookings with the chain]

One of the crucial quantitative evaluation measures of any campaign or public relations program is to provide documentation of how the public relations effort helped the organization achieve its overall objectives. For the Cookie CAREavan for DTbH, the ultimate objective was to increase bookings at the hotels. In the bar graph given next, Ketchum employed a tracking study to present before-and-after statistics about choosing DoubleTree for one's next business trip. The largest and most notable shift in intentions was in the "will probably choose" box, a point that Ketchum would emphasize in presenting results to DoubleTree. To be fully accountable, the evaluation report should also address that among those with low loyalty to DTbH, sentiment fell further. Even so, the focus should be on the larger increase in those likely to choose DoubleTree.

"Cookie Confessionals" YouTube Videos

"I'm taking a cookie back to someone in my office because **she's having a really rough day.**"

"Coming **home** from school and Mom's got them on the counter." --CAREavan visitor about her favorite childhood memory of a chocolate chip cookie.)

"I saw the article in the *Houston Chronicle* entertainment section about the DoubleTree truck being here...I came across the street to get my **free cookie**. Thanks DoubleTree by Hilton!"

Social media tactics lend themselves to measurement, either directly from analysis of app data or through traceable impacts of social media such as sharing behavior. Driving home campaign impact can be done by displaying video activity during the campaign itself. This adds to the authenticity of facts and figures about the campaign as well as numerical data from sources such as YouTube Insights.

The Silver Anvil from the Public Relations Society of America was fully justified by the completeness of the evaluation component of the campaign submission. Professionals in public relations know that numbers and bar graphs matter more than ever before in evaluating campaigns. But evaluation must also tell the compelling, even moving story of how the communication touched people. This narrative is increasingly one that clients want to see, not simply read. Ketchum professionals on the Cookie CAREavan clearly kept in mind the growing trends toward television over print news and the explosion of video documentation on YouTube. The collage of YouTube clips and comments help confirm the success story being told by the hard data by providing lively, emotional examples of what the DoubleTree cookie means to real people.

Measurement of Supplemental Activities

Other forms of measurement can be used in public relations activities. This section discusses (1) communication audits, (2) pilot tests and split messages, (3) meeting and event attendance, and (4) newsletter readership.

Communication Audits

The entire communication activity of an organization should be evaluated at least once a year to make sure that every primary and secondary public is receiving appropriate messages. David Hilton-Barber, a past president of the Public Relations Institute of South Africa (PRISA), once wrote: "The most important reasons for an audit are to help establish communication goals and objectives, to evaluate long-term programs, to identify strengths and weaknesses, and to point up any areas which require increased activity."

A communication audit, as an assessment of an organization's entire communications program, could include the following:

- Analysis of all communication activities
- Informal interviews with rank-and-file employees, middle management, and top executives
- Informal interviews with community leaders, media gatekeepers, consumers, distributors, and other influential persons in the industry

A number of research techniques, as outlined in Chapter 5, can be used during a communication audit, including mail and telephone surveys, focus groups, and so forth. The important point is that the communications of an organization should be analyzed from every possible angle, with the input of as many publics as possible.

Pilot Tests and Split Messages

Evaluation is important even before a public relations effort is launched. If exposure to a message is to be maximized, it is wise to pretest it with a sample group from the targeted audience. Do its members easily understand the message? Do they accept the message? Does the message motivate them to adopt a new idea or product?

A variation of pretesting is the *pilot test*. Before going national with a public relations message, companies often test the message and key copy points in selected cities to learn how the media accept the message and how the public reacts. This approach is quite common in marketing public relations because it limits costs and enables the company to revamp or fine-tune the message for maximum exposure. In the new media landscape, with numerous controlled media such as Web and social media platforms, piloting also allows the company to switch channels of dissemination if the original media channels are not exposing the message to the proper audiences.

The *split-message* approach is common in direct mail and direct e-mail campaigns. Two or three different appeals may be prepared by a charitable organization and sent to different audience segments. The response rate is then monitored (perhaps the amount of donations is totaled) to learn what messages and graphics seemed to be the most effective.

Meeting and Event Attendance

Audience awareness is often evaluated by attendance at an event. The crisis prevention campaign for the Basilica of St. Mary in Minneapolis featured in Chapter 6 proudly documented record-breaking attendance at the two-day fund-raising rock concert.

Such data provide information about the number of people exposed to a message, but don't answer the more crucial question of what the audience took away from the meeting.

Public relations people often get an informal sense of an audience's attitudes by its behavior. A standing ovation, spontaneous applause, complimentary remarks as people leave, and even the expressions on people's faces provide clues as to how a meeting was received. On the other hand, if people are not responsive, if they ask questions about subjects supposedly explained, or if they express doubts or antagonism, the meeting can be considered only partly successful.

Public relations practitioners use a number of informal methods to evaluate the success of a meeting, but they also employ more systematic methods. The most common technique is providing an evaluation sheet for participants to fill out at the end of the meeting. Hiring independent evaluators is money well spent for major conferences or annual meetings.

A simple form asking people to rate such items as location, costs, facilities, and program on a 1 to 5 scale (1 being the best) can be used. Other forms may ask people to rate aspects of a conference or meeting as (1) excellent, (2) good, (3) average, (4) poor, or (5) very poor.

Evaluation forms also determine how people heard about the program and what suggestions they have for future meetings. Another approach is to ask attendees whether they heard or believed the key messages of a spokesperson's presentation and whether they would like to receive any follow-up information from the sponsoring organization.

Newsletter Readership

Editors of newsletters, e-newsletters, and internal communication tools such as company magazines should evaluate readership annually. Such an evaluation can help ascertain (1) reader perceptions, (2) the degree to which stories are balanced, (3) the kinds of stories that have high reader interest, (4) additional topics that should be covered, (5) the credibility of the publication, and (6) the extent to which the newsletter is meeting organizational objectives.

Materials can be evaluated in a number of ways. The methods include (1) content analysis, (2) readership-interest surveys, (3) readership recall of articles actually read, and (4) the use of advisory boards.

Content Analysis Based on a representative sample of past issues, stories may be categorized under general headings such as (1) management announcements, (2) new product developments, (3) new personnel and retirements, (4) features about employees, (5) corporate finances, (6) news of departments and divisions, and (7) job-related information.

Such a systematic analysis will show what percentage of the publication is devoted to each category. It may be found that one division rarely is covered in the employee newsletter or that management pronouncements tend to dominate the entire publication. Given the content-analysis findings, editors have an empirical basis on which to shift the content.

on the job

SOCIAL MEDIA IN ACTION

Chevy at SXSW: Event Success by the Numbers

Event sponsorship is an integral part of a company's business strategy, but each event must also be evaluated in terms of how it enhances the brand and creates new markets for a product or service.

With this in mind, Chevrolet became a sponsor at the annual South by Southwest (SXSW) festival in Austin, Texas, to position itself as an innovative brand among a younger, more hip audience. It was also an opportunity to show off the technology of its newest models, the Cruze and the Volt, through interaction with festival goers.

A number of interactive activities were planned throughout the festival that included (1) using a Chevy shuttle to get around the grounds, (2) organizing a music showcase featuring new performers, (3) sponsoring an outdoor concert, (4) staffing an exhibit booth, (5) having a Tweet-house panel, and (6) hosting a trivia contest. Social media also played a major role in extending awareness of Chevy's participation in the festival.

The SXSW sponsorship was evaluated according to how well the company's three stated objectives were accomplished. The box score is as follows:

Chevy's successful event at SXSW received a PRSA's Silver Anvil award in the category of marketing consumer products.

OBJECTIVE	RESULTS
Enhance the SXSW experience for festival-goers by way of the brand's role	■ Catch a Chevy provided more than 12,000 rides around the festival. ■ More than 7,000 people recharged at the Volt Lounge, using power strips and the space to network and spread SXSW across social channels. ■ Over l6,000 social mentions from festival-goers mentioned Chevy's presence.
Introduce attendees to the brand and new products	■ Social media Web impressions exceeded 53 million. ■ Chevy added more than 37,000 Facebook fans and more than 2,400 followers on Twitter. ■ Content efforts generated more than 25,000 page views through Facebook and SXSW .com/Chevrolet. ■ Chevrolet Foursquare following grew by 3,600—more than 85 percent. ■ More than 150 traditional media placements, including coverage by NBC, Forbes, and USA Today.
Increase positive brand perception	■ More than 75 percent of the attendees strongly identified with the statement, "Chevrolet is heading in the right direction." ■ Almost 85 percent of those polled thought Chevy was a good fit for SXSW, referring to auto maker's innovation and eco-friendly products.

Readership-Interest Surveys The purpose of these surveys is to get feedback about the types of stories employees are most interested in reading. The most common survey method is simply to provide a long list of generic story topics and have employees rate each as (1) important, (2) somewhat important, or (3) not important. The International Association of Business Communicators (IABC) conducted such a survey on behalf of several dozen companies and found that readers were not very interested in "personals" about other employees (birthdays, anniversaries, and the like).

Article Recall One effective readership survey involves trained interviewers asking a sample of employees what they have read in the latest issue of the publication. Employees are shown the publication page by page and asked to indicate which articles they have read. As a check on the tendency of employees to report that they have read everything, interviewers also ask them (1) how much of each article they have read and (2) what the articles were about. The results are then content-analyzed to determine which kinds of articles have the most readership.

Advisory Boards Periodic feedback and evaluation can be provided by organizing an employee advisory board that meets several times a year to discuss the direction and content of the publication. This is a useful technique because it expands the editor's feedback network and elicits comments that employees might be hesitant to tell the editor face-to-face. A variation of the advisory board method is to occasionally invite a sampling of employees to meet and discuss the publication or website.

Summary

The Purpose of Evaluation

- Evaluation is the measurement of results against objectives in the communication plan.
- One major purpose of evaluation is to do a better job of planning future programs.

Objectives: A Prerequisite for Evaluation

- Objectives should be part of any program plan.
- There must be agreed-upon criteria used to evaluate success in obtaining these objectives.

Current Status of Measurement and Evaluation

- Studies indicate that about 4 or 5 percent of a typical public relations budget is allocated to evaluations and measurement.
- On the most basic level, practitioners can measure message distribution and media placements. The second level is measurement of audience awareness, comprehension, and retention. The most advanced level is the measurement of changes in attitudes, opinions, and behaviors.

Measurement of Production

- The most elementary form of measurement is a tabulation of how many news releases, brochures, annual reports, and so on, are distributed in a single year.
- Measurement of production gives management an idea of a staff's productivity and output.

Measurement of Message Exposure

- Several criteria can be used to measure message exposure, including the compilation of media placements in print, broadcast, and Internet media.
- One common method is calculating media impressions—the potential audience reached with a message. Advertising value equivalency, commonly called AVE, is calculated by converting news stories to the cost of a comparable amount of paid space.
- More sophisticated methods include systematic tracking using software and databases to find out such information as tone of coverage, percentage of key messages used, and percentage of coverage related to that of the competition.

- Sometimes, exposure is evaluated by determining how much it costs to reach each member of the target audience.

Measurement of Audience Awareness

- The next level of evaluation is whether the audience became aware of and understood the message.
- Audience awareness can be measured through survey research, which, by having the audience engage in unaided recall, can determine whether the audience understood and remembered the message.

Measurement of Audience Attitudes

- Changes in audience attitudes can be evaluated through a baseline or benchmark study, which measures awareness and opinions before, during, and after a public relations campaign.

Measurement of Audience Action

- Ultimately, public relations campaigns are evaluated based on how they help an organization achieve its objectives through changing audience behavior, whether that involves sales, fund-raising, or the election of a candidate.

Measurement of Supplemental Activities

- A yearly communication audit helps ensure that all publics are receiving appropriate messages. Several techniques, such as pilot tests and split messages, can be used to pretest a public relations effort.
- Meeting and event attendance can be measured both by the number of attendees and by their behavior, which is an indicator of their acceptance of a message.
- Newsletter readership can be evaluated by content analysis, interest surveys, and article recall.

Case Activity **Evaluating the Success of Tourism Promotion**

The Mexico Tourist Board has hired your youth-oriented public relations agency to boost bookings to Mexican resorts for college spring breaks and high school senior trips. A big part of your challenge is to assure parents who often pay the travel bill that Mexico is a safe destination. The bottom-line objective for the tourist board is the increased bookings. The board also wants to dispel the misimpression that drug-gang violence occurs in resort towns. How will you develop a set of evaluation criteria starting with awareness and working through the types of evaluation covered in this chapter to make the case that your campaign offered a good return on investment through significant upticks in flights to Mexico and bookings at beach resorts?

Questions **For Review and Discussion**

1. What is the role of stated objectives in evaluating public relations programs?
2. What are some general types of evaluation questions that a person should ask about a program?
3. List four ways that publicity activity is evaluated. What, if any, are the drawbacks of each one?
4. Do you think news stories about a product or service should be evaluated in terms of comparable advertising costs? Why or why not?
5. What are the various methods used in measuring public relations efforts?
6. How are pilot tests and split messages used to determine the suitability of a message?
7. What are media impressions? How are these measured?
8. What is the relative importance of ROI to a public relations client?
9. What is a communication audit? What should a communication audit ideally include?

Media Resources

Bialik, C. (2010, February 20). Dot-complicated: Measuring traffic on the web. *Wall Street Journal.* Retrieved from http://online.wsj.com

Jeffrey, A., Jeffries-Fox, B., & Rawlins, B. L. (2010). *A new paradigm for media analysis: Weighted media cost* [Monograph]. Retrieved from Institute for Public Relations Research website, www.instituteforpr.org

Lindenmann, W. K. *Guidelines and standards for measuring and evaluating PR effectiveness*. Retrieved from Institute for Public Relations website, www.instituteforpr.com

Paine, K. (2010, February). Six indicators of hope in PR measurement. *The RaganReport*, 19–20.

PR measurement lumbers into the digital age. (2010, March 22). PRNews Online. Retrieved from http://www.prnewsonline.com/topics/measurement/2010/03/22/pr-measurement-lumbers-into-the-digital-age/

Said, L. (2013, July 8). TV Is Americans' Main Source of News: Preferred news source varies by age, education, and politics, among other factors. Gallup Politics. www.gallup.com/poll/163412/americans-main-source-news.aspx

Watson, T. (2013). Advertising value equivalence—PR's orphan metric. *Public Relations Review,* 26(2), 139–146. Special Issue on Public Relations History.

Public Opinion: Role, Scope, and Implications

9 chapter

Oprah Winfrey uses her position as a trusted opinion leader to advance social projects such as the Girl's Leadership Academy in South Africa.

After reading this chapter you will be able to:

Understand the implications of public opinion for public relations

Explain the crucial role of opinion leaders in public discourse

Describe key theories explaining the role of mass media

Understand the pervasive role of persuasion in modern life

Enumerate key factors in persuasion

Identify major considerations in conducting ethical persuasive campaigns

What Is Public Opinion?

Americans talk about public opinion as if it were a monolithic entity overshadowing the entire landscape. Editorial cartoonists humanize it in the form of John or Jane Q. Public, characters who symbolize what people think about any given issue. The reality is that public opinion is somewhat elusive and extremely difficult to measure at any given moment.

In fact, to continue the metaphor, public opinion is a number of monoliths perceived by John and Jane Q. Public, all existing at the same time. Few issues create unanimity of thought among the population, and public opinion on any issue is split in several directions. It also may come as a surprise to note that only a small number of people at any given time take part in public opinion formation on a specific issue. But once people and the media begin to speak of public opinion on an issue as an accomplished fact, it can take on its own momentum. According to Elisabeth Noelle-Neumann's spiral-of-silence theory, public opinion can be an almost tangible force on people's thinking. Noelle-Neumann defines *public opinion* as opinions on controversial issues that one can express in public without isolating oneself. This implies the element of conformity that perceived public opinion can impose on individuals who want to avoid alienation.

There are two reasons for the profound influence of vocal segments of society and public opinion momentum. First, psychologists have found that the public tends to be passive. It is often assumed that a small vocal group represents the attitude of the public, when in reality, it is more accurate to say that the majority of the people are apathetic because an issue doesn't interest or affect them. Thus, "public" opposition to such issues as gay marriage, abortion, and gun control may really be the view of a small but influential number of concerned people.

Second, one issue may engage the attention of one part of the population, whereas another arouses the interest of another segment. Parents, for example, may form public opinion on the need for improved secondary education, whereas senior citizens constitute the bulk of public opinion on the need to fully fund Medicare.

These two examples illustrate the most common definition of *public opinion*: "Public opinion is the sum of individual opinions on an issue affecting those individuals." Another popular definition states: "Public opinion is a collection of views held by persons interested in the subject." Thus, a person unaffected by or uninterested in (and perhaps unaware of) an issue does not contribute to public opinion on the subject.

Inherent in these definitions is the concept of *self-interest.* The following statements appear in public opinion research:

- Public opinion is the collective expression of opinion of many individuals bound into a group by common aims, aspirations, needs, and ideals.
- People who are interested in or who have a vested or self-interest in an issue—or who can be affected by the outcome of the issue—form public opinion on that particular item.
- Psychologically, opinion basically is determined by self-interest. Events, words, or other stimuli affect opinion only insofar as their relationship to self-interest or a general concern is apparent.
- Opinion does not remain aroused for a long period of time unless people feel their self-interest is acutely involved or unless opinion—aroused by words—is sustained by events.
- Once self-interest is involved, opinion is not easily changed.

Studies also emphasize the importance of *events* in the formation of public opinion. Social scientists, for example, have made the following generalizations:

- Opinion is highly sensitive to events that have an impact on the public at large or a particular segment of the public.
- By and large, public opinion does not anticipate events. It only reacts to them.
- Events trigger formation of public opinion. Unless people are aware of an issue, they are not likely to be concerned or have an opinion about it. Awareness and discussion lead to crystallizing of opinions and often a consensus among the public.
- Events of unusual magnitude are likely to swing public opinion temporarily from one extreme to another. Opinion does not stabilize until the implication of the event is seen with some perspective. The terrorist attacks on the World Trade Center and the Pentagon on 9/11 are perhaps the most galvanizing events in recent memory to swing public opinion, including media opinion at the time, regarding external threats to safety and security. The groundswell of militant public opinion probably served as the driving force for the U.S. invasion of Afghanistan and Iraq.

People also have more opinions, and are able to form them more easily, with respect to goals rather than with respect to the methods necessary to reach those goals. For example, according to a Gallup poll, there is fairly strong public opinion for immigration reform. However, there is little agreement on how to do this. One group calls for more government funding to patrol U.S. borders, another endorses requiring employers to check the immigration status of new hires, while others called for a pathway to citizenship for undocumented immigrants living in the United States.

Opinion Leaders as Catalysts

Public opinion on an issue may have its roots in self-interest or in events, but the primary catalyst is public discussion. Only in this way does opinion begin to crystallize to the extent that pollsters can measure it.

Serving as catalysts for the formation of public opinion are people who are knowledgeable and articulate about specific issues. They are called *opinion leaders*. Sociologists describe them as:

1. Highly interested in a subject or issue
2. Better informed on an issue than the average person
3. Avid consumers of mass media
4. Early adopters of new ideas
5. Good organizers who can get other people to take action

Types of Leaders

Sociologists traditionally have defined two types of opinion leaders. First are the *formal opinion leaders*, so called because of their positions as elected officials, presidents of companies, or heads of membership groups. Journalists often ask them for statements when a specific issue relates to their areas of responsibility or concern. People in formal leadership positions also are called *power leaders*.

Public opinion is more cohesive on goals, such as ending obesity, than on the possible solutions to the problem, such as efforts to regulate sales of large-sized sugary soft drinks.

Second are the *informal opinion leaders*, those who have clout with peers because of some special characteristic. They may be role models who are admired and emulated or opinion leaders who can exert peer pressure on others to go along with something. In general, informal opinion leaders exert considerable influence on their peer groups by being highly informed, articulate, and credible on particular issues. Both formal and informal opinion leaders play a major role in the life cycle of public opinion, which is discussed in the Insights box on page 249.

on the job

PITT'S PROJECT

Brad Pitt is a current example of an informal leader who has had a great impact on public opinion regarding issues such as rebuilding New Orleans after Hurricane Katrina. Pitt maintains attention for the plight of New Orleans with regular fund-raisers for his "Make it Right" charity. The focus of a celebrity like Pitt on a project like reconstructing New Orleans' lower 9th ward serves to move public opinion and keep topics on the public agenda. While Pitt's charity is somewhat controversial because critics say sufficient low-income housing was not provided, there is no doubt that it has helped form public opinion.

on the job INSIGHTS

The Life Cycle of Public Opinion

Public opinion and persuasion are important catalysts in the formation of a public issue and its ultimate resolution. The natural evolution of an issue involves five stages:

1. **Definition of the issue.** Activist and special interest groups raise an issue, perhaps a protest about the environmental dangers of extracting oil through fracking or hydraulic fracturing. These groups have no formal power but serve as "agenda stimuli" for the media that cover controversy and conflict. Visual opportunities for television coverage occur when activists hold rallies and demonstrations.

2. **Involvement of opinion leaders.** Through media coverage, the issue is put on the public agenda and people become aware of it. Opinion leaders begin to discuss the issue and perhaps see it as being symbolic of broader environmental issues. According to research in *The Influentials*, a book by Ed Keller and Jon Berry, 10 percent of the population tells the other 90 percent "what to buy, which politicians to support, and where to vacation."

3. **Public awareness.** As public awareness grows, the issue becomes a matter of public discussion and debate, garnering extensive media coverage. The issue is simplified by the media into "them versus us." Suggested solutions tend to be at either end of the spectrum.

4. **Government/regulatory involvement.** Public consensus begins to build for a resolution as government/regulatory involvement occurs. Large groups identify with some side of the issue. Demand grows for government to act.

5. **Resolution.** The resolution stage begins as people with authority (elected officials) draft legislation or interpret existing rules and regulations to make a statement. A decision is made to protect the underground water supplies or to reach a compromise with advocates of fracking. If some groups remain unhappy, however, the cycle may repeat itself.

People seldom make a decision on their own but are influenced by their friends, parents, educators, supervisors, church leaders, physicians, public officials, celebrities, and the media in general when deciding to vote for a president or a city mayor, or to purchase a car or even toothpaste. Public relations professionals attempt to influence these leaders just as they seek to influence the public at large.

For example, those seeking stronger gun control laws requiring universal background checks for gun buyers, the banning of assault weapons, and increased support for mental health treatment make use of statistics about increased gun violence, but they also take advantage of shifting public opinion following tragedies like those in Newtown, Connecticut, where 20 first graders and six adults were killed in December 2012. According to *The Atlantic*, proponents of gun control changed their persuasive strategy in 2013, shifting from referring to their cause as "ending gun violence" rather than "gun control." Politicians like Colorado governor John Hickenlooper and New York City mayor Michael Bloomberg used their opinion leader status in an effort to shift public opinion in favor of stricter gun laws. Bloomberg even founded the group Mayors Against Illegal Guns, which sponsored a Super Bowl ad in some markets.

A survey of 20,000 Americans by the Roper Organization found that only 10 to 12 percent of the general public are opinion leaders. These "influentials," those whom other people seek out for advice, fit the profile of:

1. Being active in the community
2. Having a college degree
3. Earning a relatively high income
4. Regularly reading newspapers and magazines
5. Actively participating in recreational activities
6. Showing environmental concern by recycling

The Flow of Opinion

Many public relations campaigns, particularly those in the public affairs area, concentrate on identifying and reaching key opinion leaders, who are pivotal to the success or failure of an idea or project. In the 1940s, sociologists Elihu Katz and Paul Lazarsfeld discovered the importance of opinion leaders during their study of how people choose candidates in an election. They found that the mass media have minimal influence on electoral choices, but that voters do rely on person-to-person communication with formal and informal opinion leaders.

These findings led to the *two-step flow theory* of communication, a model that remains central to public relations strategy 70 years later. Although later research confirmed that it is really a multiple-step flow, the basic idea remains intact: Public opinion is formed by the views of people who have taken the time to sift information, evaluate it, and form an opinion that they express to others.

The *multiple-step flow model* starts with opinion makers, who derive large amounts of information from the mass media and other sources and then share that information with the "attentive public." The latter are interested in the issue but rely on opinion leaders to provide synthesized information and interpretation. The "inattentive public" is unaware of or uninterested in the issue and remains outside the opinion-formation process. The multiple-step flow theory, however, means that some members of the inattentive public eventually will become interested in or at least aware of the issue.

Another variation of the two-step model is *N-step theory.* Individuals are seldom influenced by only one opinion leader but interact with different leaders around one issue. For example, patients can seek information from their primary-care physician but may also turn to family members when making a medical decision.

Mass media effects are limited by personal influences. Diffusion of innovation theory, discussed in Chapter 7, explains that individuals adopt new ideas or products through the five stages of awareness, interest, trial, evaluation, and adoption. According to Everett Rogers, author of *Diffusion of Innovations*, individuals are often influenced by media in the first two steps, but by friends and family members in the third and fourth steps. And each individual is the decision maker who will adopt a new idea or product and reach the final step.

Author Malcolm Gladwell popularized a version of diffusion in his book *The Tipping Point*. Gladwell noted that what he called "social epidemics" are set in motion by a few people who are set apart by "how sociable they are, or how energetic or knowledgeable or influential among their peers."

The Role of Mass Media

Public relations personnel reach opinion leaders and other key publics via the mass media—radio, television, newspapers, and magazines. The term *mass media*, also called traditional or legacy media when contrasted with digital media, implies that information from a public relations source can be efficiently and rapidly disseminated to literally millions of people.

Although journalists often argue that they rarely use public relations materials, one has only to look at what is covered in the press to see the quote in the local newspaper from the press officer at the sheriff's department, a television news segment on a new computer product, or even the after-game interview with the winning quarterback on ESPN.com. In almost all cases, a public relations source at the organization provided the information or arranged the interview. Indeed, Oscar H. Gandy Jr., of the University of Pennsylvania, said that up to 50 percent of what the media carry comes from public relations sources in the form of "information subsidies." A more recent study by professors and students at the University of Technology in Sydney (UTS) found that 55 percent of the stories in leading Australian dailies come from public relations sources. Researchers Lynne Sallot and Elizabeth Johnson Avery found that one-third of the journalists they surveyed estimated between 60 and 100 percent of news content was influenced by public relations.

> Few professions have so many skilled and talented individuals contributing to the thoughts, actions, and policies of our nation.
>
> *Elizabeth L. Toth and Robert L. Heath, authors of* Rhetorical and Critical Approaches to Public Relations

These scholars have concluded that public relations people—via the mass media—are major players in forming public opinion because they often provide the mass media with the information in the first place. This opinion also is echoed by Elizabeth L. Toth and Robert L. Heath, authors of *Rhetorical and Critical Approaches to Public Relations.* They wrote, "Few professions have so many skilled and talented individuals contributing to the thoughts, actions, and policies of our nation."

To better understand how public relations people inform the public and shape public opinion via the mass media, it is necessary to review briefly several theories about mass media effects.

Agenda-Setting Theory

One of the early theories, pioneered by Max McCombs and Don Shaw, contends that media content sets the agenda for public discussion. People tend to talk about what they see or hear on the evening news or read in the newspaper or a blog. Media, through the selection of stories and headlines, tell the public what to think about, although not necessarily what to think.

Social scientist Joseph Klapper calls this the *limited-effects model* of mass media. He postulates, "Mass media ordinarily does not serve as a necessary and sufficient cause for audience effects, but rather functions among and through a nexus of mediating factors and influence." Such factors may include the way that opinion leaders analyze and interpret the information provided by the mass media.

More recently, Professor Wayne Wanta and others have explored second-level agenda-setting effects, finding evidence that the media not only set an agenda, but also convey a set of attributes about the subject of the news. These positive or

Public relations materials and activities (i.e., news releases, speeches, and newsletters) are major forces shaping the agenda-setting process.

Ji Young Kim and Spiro Kiousis, writing in Journalism & Mass Communications Quarterly

negative attributes are remembered and color public opinion. For example, a steady flow of news stories regarding the inaction of the U.S. Congress to avoid "sequestration" or mandatory budget cuts in 2013 led to a Gallup-reported approval rating of only 13 percent for how Congress was handling its job.

From a public relations standpoint, even getting a subject on the media agenda is an accomplishment that advances organizational goals. Sales of Apple's iPad rose as the media reported its success and the public became aware of this "hot" item. Researchers examine how public relations efforts can build the media agenda, and thus affect public opinion. Research evidence from Patricia Curtin, Qi Qiu, and Spiro Kiousis suggests that public relations effort does contribute to the creation of news media agendas. Agenda-building research continues to explore and empirically document how public relations sets the agenda that the media then adopt, ultimately influencing what audiences think about, if not what they think.

Media-Dependency Theory

Although the agenda-setting function of the media is generally valid, other research indicates that mass media can have a "moderate" or even a "powerful" effect on the formation of opinions and attitudes. When people have no prior information or attitude disposition regarding a subject, the mass media play a role in telling people what to think.

Mass media effects also are increased when people cannot verify information through personal experience or knowledge but are highly dependent on the media for that verification. This tendency is particularly evident in crisis situations, which also often leave reporters and editors dependent on official spokespersons for information as the story breaks. Therefore, if much of this crucial initial information comes from official spokespersons of organizations, it's an opportunity for public relations to shape the tone and content of a story, that is, to put a particular emphasis on the story. In sum, media dependency often occurs when the media are, in turn, quite dependent on public relations sources.

Framing Theory

The term *framing* has a long history in mass media research. Traditionally, framing was related to journalists and how they selected certain facts, themes, treatments, and even words to "frame" a story. According to researchers Julie L. Andsager at the University of Iowa and Angela Powers at Kansas State University, "Mass media scholars have long argued that it is important to understand the ways in which journalistic framing of issues occurs because such framing impacts public understanding and, consequently, policy formation." For example, how media frame the debate over health care and the role of insurance often plays a major role in public perceptions of the problem. See the Ethics box on page 253 about the ethics of framing hydraulic fracturing.

Dietram Scheufele at the University of Wisconsin–Madison suggests there are two types of framing: media framing and audience framing. He argues that framing is a continuous process and that the behavioral, attitudinal, cognitive, and

on the job ETHICS

Framing Fracking: What Is the Truth?

Debates over energy production and consumption always seem to be contentious. One such debate pitted energy producers against environmentalists and sometimes land owners. Each stakeholder in hydraulic fracturing or "fracking" to extract natural gas frames the pros and cons of the process is quite different ways.

Producers argue that natural gas is a relatively clean fuel when compared to coal. Billionaire energy industry insider T. Boone Pickens says he first witnessed fracking in 1952 and after fracking more than 2,000 wells he's convinced that there's absolutely no environmental hazard. "Nobody gives any evidence you're damaging anything," he has declared. Supporters of extracting natural gas through fracking argue that it will lower the price of energy, make the United States more energy independent, and create jobs. According to the Colorado Oil and Gas Conservation Commission, "When properly conducted, modern fracking is a safe, sophisticated, highly engineered and controlled procedure."

But environmental activists argue that fracking endangers underground water supplies with the potential of contaminating drinking water and contributes to air pollution. The group New Yorkers Against Fracking argued, "Fracking has brought rampant environmental and economic problems to rural communities. Accidents and leaks have polluted rivers, streams and drinking water supplies. Regions peppered with drilling rigs have high levels of smog as well as other airborne pollutants, including potential carcinogens. Rural communities face an onslaught of heavy truck traffic—often laden with dangerous chemicals used in drilling—and declining property values."

Rival documentaries tout the pros and cons of fracking. Phelim McAleer in his film *FrackNation* promotes fracking and "uncovers fracking facts suppressed by environmental activists" while Josh Fox in his films *GasLand* and *GasLand II* "embarks on a cross-country odyssey uncovering a trail of secrets, lies and contamination."

Each group frames issues surrounding fracking in ways that support their perspectives. No doubt each believes that their facts are stronger (and more factual) than those of their opponents. But as you can see the frames are remarkably different.

Amidst the frames and counter-frames were signs of progress. Some of the largest companies to use fracking agreed to self-policing in such a way that some environmental groups embraced the move as progress. In March 2013, environmentalists and energy producers announced the Center for Sustainable Shale Development, a group that will certify when energy companies are using commonly agreed upon best standards for natural gas production.

What do you think? Is the energy industry being unjustly criticized? If you were public relations counsel for Shell or Chevron, do you think framing hydraulic fracturing as "safe and sophisticated" is a good strategy for conflict management? Or would you develop a different strategy for justifying the use of the practice? Would you suggest your employer work to meet commonly agreed upon sustainable standards? What frames and conflict management practices would you support?

> … public relations professionals fundamentally operate as frame strategists, who strive to determine how situations, attributes, choices, actions, issues, and the responsibility should be posed to achieve a favorable objective. Framing decisions are perhaps the most important strategic choices made in a public relations effort.
>
> *Kirk Hallahan, Colorado State University*

affective states of individuals are also involved in how they interpret issues. For example, voters in Florida may be less likely to respond favorably to a story about increased school funding than voters in Georgia, which has a younger population and many parents of school-aged children. However, a range of variables, beliefs, and attitudes simultaneously affect how individuals interpret an issue.

Political science Professors Shanto Iyengar and Donald Kinder focus on the media's power to prime people in a more subtle but significant form of persuasive effect. They note how public relations professionals working for political campaigns seek to emphasize considerations that will help voters decide in their favor, often enlisting the expertise of a popular leader, and to downplay the considerations that will hurt their cause or candidate. Ultimately, the goal is to encourage voters to change the basis on which they make decisions about voting rather than to simply change their choices about a given candidate or issue.

Using this approach, supporters of Governor Mitt Romney sought to frame the 2012 presidential election as a referendum on President Obama and the economy rather than on the choice between the two candidates. However, President Obama continued to frame the election as a choice between himself and Romney because polling showed that he was simply more popular than Romney with the American public, regardless of the state of the economy. Each candidate attempted, as all candidates do, to frame the election in terms that favored him.

Conflict Theory

The process of public discourse is often rooted in conflict. Social scientists and legal scholars define conflict as any situation in which two or more individuals, groups, organizations, or communities perceive a divergence of interests. Conflict theory offers insight into differences among individuals or groups and explains conflicting interests, goals, values, or desires. Public opinion often reflects such different, or even conflicting, views, attitudes, and behaviors.

According to conflict resolution scholars Morton Deutsch and Peter Colman, conflict in the public arena does not necessarily yield negative outcomes but creates a constructive process that builds toward consensus. Indeed, conflict or consensus is an actual theme of court opinions, which regulate and help ensure social stability and peaceful change within a democratic society. Conflict itself is an inherent constraint within social structures. Controversies often serve to shape public opinion intensively and extensively. Public relations professionals frequently have the challenging role of trying to minimize or resolve controversy in conflict situations. See the Multicultural World box about the perception of corporations' "authenticity" around the world.

on the job

A MULTICULTURAL WORLD

What Does It Mean to "Be Authentic" around the World?

Global public relations agencies continually grapple with how expectations and experiences combine to address stakeholder wants and needs. An already daunting task is further complicated by political, cultural, and lifestyle traditions that may vary widely between countries within which the agencies practice. To examine this challenge, global PR agency Fleishman-Hillard conducted an "Authenticity Gap Study," which it released in 2013.

"When brand and reputation are not aligned, it creates a gap that damages an organization's credibility and authenticity," Fleishman-Hillard President and CEO Dave Senay told the *Wall Street Journal*. The firm conducted research in the United States, Germany, and China, looking at 20 product categories to determine what behaviors were perceived as most authentic.

According to Marjorie Benzkofer, global leader of the agency's reputation management practice, there are "nine behaviors consumers said were important in shaping their perceptions about a company." Fleishman-Hillard execs believe that when you know where those perceptions lay, you can adjust messages and behaviors to improve the stakeholder experience. Those nine behaviors fall into three broad categories: management behavior, customer benefits, and society outcomes.

Fleishman-Hillard found that four product categories—online shopping, major appliances, tablets and e-readers, and pharmaceuticals—were viewed as most authentic across all three countries. Three categories—vacation and travel, Internet service providers, and wireless carriers—were seen as least authentic across all three countries. China was the most positive of the three countries followed by the United States and then Germany. "There is no such thing as a global market," the agency reported. "Consumer expectations in virtually every one of the 20 categories studied differ from country to country."

So to be authentic around the world, according to the Authenticity Gap Study, a company must be experienced by stakeholders as:

1. Doing the right thing
2. Being consistent in performance
3. Providing credible communications
4. Providing better value than competitors
5. Providing superior customer care
6. Being innovative
7. Treating employees well
8. Having a positive impact on the community
9. Being environmentally conscious

What do you think? Can those nine elements be addressed through public relations activities? If so, how? If not, why not? How does public opinion play a role? If you were the public relations professional in one of the three low-ranking industries, what would you strive to address first? Why?

Maintaining Authenticity

Management Behaviors	Consumer Benefits	Societal Outcomes
• Commit to doing the right thing. • Communicate more frequently and credibly. • Provide consistent and stable financial and operational performance.	• Offer products and services that are of better value. • Take better care of customers. • Innovate new and better products and services.	• Take better care of employees. • Contribute to society in a way that has a better impact on the community. • Take better care of the environment.

At other times public relations practitioners may generate or promote controversy to rouse key publics. "Mayors Against Illegal Guns," for example, decided to employ a long-time tactic of the National Rifle Association (NRA) to create controversy. The NRA is well known for its report cards on politicians' support for gun rights. The Mayors Against Illegal Guns, an organization of 900 mayors announced its intent to issue its own report cards on politicians' support for gun control. CNN reported, "According to the [Mayors'] ratings system, the more often a lawmaker supports tougher gun legislation, the higher score they will receive. With the NRA, the scoring works in the reverse."

Mass media play a role in the unfolding of a conflict and serve to promote public debate by engaging widespread public involvement, a process known as *escalation*. The media may also enable parties to de-escalate the conflict by working out the conflict in public fora. But in an era of 24-hour news, communication between parties via talk shows and endless news segments does more harm than good, as the same arguments are stridently repeated and nonnegotiable positions are formed. The role of the media should instead be to interpret the issue, deliver the position of the opposing party, and even suggest avenues for resolution. A good example is the debate on national gun control, which is outlined in the PR Casebook below.

PRCasebook

Gun Control Advocates and Opponents Work to Shape Public Opinion

Gun control has been a topic of hot debate in the United States ever since 1791 when the Second Amendment to the Constitution provided citizens the right to bear arms. Or so it seems.

In May 2000, at a National Rifle Association convention, actor and then-NRA president Charlton Heston ended a speech by saying, "For the next six months, [Democratic presidential candidate and then-vice president Al Gore] is going to smear you as the enemy. He will slander you as gun-toting, knuckle-dragging, bloodthirsty maniacs who stand in the way of a safer America. Will you remain silent? I will not remain silent." Heston raised a rifle replica and continued, "So, as we set out this year to defeat the divisive forces that would take freedom away, I want to say those fighting words for everyone within the sound of my voice to hear and to heed, and especially for you, *Mr. Gore*: 'From my cold, dead hands!'" Heston was citing a then-popular slogan of the NRA: "I'll give you my gun when you pry it from my cold, dead hands."

Following a December 2012 shooting episode at Sandy Hook Elementary School in Newtown, Connecticut, that killed 20 children and six adults, the factions for and against gun restrictions renewed efforts to shape public opinion. National polls following the shootings showed that more than half of Americans favored the passage of a new federal gun control law. But the rhetoric on both sides of the issue was often heated. Such rhetoric serves to "fire up the base," meaning it reinforces the attitudes of supporters.

The pro-control group Moms Demand Action for Gun Sense in America aired controversial ads showing one child holding an apparently benign object (a kick-ball in one ad) and one holding an assault rifle. The accompanying message was that while dodgeball is banned as too violent, assault rifles are not. On the other side, NRA executive Wayne LaPierre told a convention that gun control activists were "coming after us with a vengeance to destroy us and every ounce of our freedom." Others attempted to develop a commonly accepted solution.

Gun legislation was proposed in the U.S. Senate, but was voted down. A supporter of the legislation, Senator Joe Manchin of West Virginia said the legislation failed because gun owners were afraid that it was the first step toward taking away their weapons. The thinking was this: First they'd be listed as a gun owner on a national registry, then the federal government could confiscate their guns at will. Manchin claimed there was a lot the NRA liked in the legislation. He told *The Atlantic*, "I have never seen something that resonated with so many people in so many parts of society because it made so much sense." He was speaking of the proposed legislation. "When something makes that much sense, you have facts to back you up, and you just have to walk out into your community and explain it."

Other tactics were used to try to bring public opinion to one side of the issue or another: A "Mother's Day Week of Action" was planned by the Brady Campaign to Prevent Gun Violence and other groups. Gun enthusiasts made news by voting with their wallets. Sales of guns increased 39 percent in the first quarter of 2013 for one gun manufacturer, resulting in a backlog of 2.1 million orders. Grieving parents of those killed in Newtown visited politicians and went on television talk shows. Former Alaska governor Sarah Palin told NRA conventioneers, "We're fighting the good fight. A fight for the Constitution. This is a fight for the future of freedom." Mayors Against Illegal Guns bought ads criticizing senators who voted against the proposed legislation. The NRA ran ads opposing background checks. It was hard to see the two parties coming together in compromise. It was easy to see the issue continuing to divide public opinion.

How has public opinion in the case of gun control been informed by interest groups?

In what ways has public opinion been divided on the proposed legislation?

What persuasion techniques have proponents and opponents of gun control used to present their messages?

Conflict is inherent in how a reporter frames most issues. A reporter's story on a conflict can be the sole information available to an audience. For example, an investigative reporter with special access to information about a controversial secret program at the Pentagon may represent the only perspective seen by the public. How that reporter frames the conflict can bias the public in favor of one party, or one solution, over another.

Because the media are so crucial not only in presenting and explaining conflicts but also in keeping them from escalating, it is necessary for the parties and public relations practitioners involved to know how to work effectively with the media. Similarly, the media play a central role when public relations professionals want a conflict to escalate, to bring the issue to the fore.

Conflict, as a component of news, ranges from wars to philosophical differences of opinion. Daily news stories and op-ed pieces include people criticizing government agencies or policies, a company's fraud, or celebrity scandals. All too often, conflict is regarded as more newsworthy than resolution.

The media's inclination to focus on tribulation posing as human interest often creates a conflict with sources. To maintain their credibility as objective judges of information, journalists are primed to conflict as part of their strategic approach to dealing with sources, while public relations practitioners, as advocates for favorable coverage, have a tendency to be accommodative or cooperative with reporters, according to researchers Jae-Hwa Shin and Glen T. Cameron. The relationships between public relations professionals and journalists moves on a continuum from conflict to cooperation.

Public relations professionals should understand journalists' orientation to escalate conflict as a means of maintaining balance and independence. Public relations practitioners should also try to transform conflicts in constructive ways. Rather than reporting only from the perspective of a dominant power such as governments and delivering the ideology of media conglomerates, the public interest can best be served by healthy competition among public relations sources and the media. From this perspective, public relations serves as a social force in the ongoing creation of news and news trends or agendas.

The Dominant View of Public Relations

The dominant view of public relations, in fact, is one of persuasive communication actions performed on behalf of clients. Oscar Gandy Jr. notes that ". . . the primary role of public relations is one of purposeful, self-interested communications." And Edward Bernays, featured in Chapter 2, even called public relations the "engineering" of consent to create "a favorable and positive climate of opinion toward the individual, product, institution or idea which is represented."

To accomplish this goal, public relations personnel use a variety of techniques to reach and influence their audiences. At the same time, persuasion or rhetoric should be considered more than a one-way flow of information, argument, and influence. In the best sense, Toth and Heath say that persuasion should be a dialogue between points of view in the marketplace of public opinion, where any number of persuaders are hawking their wares.

Indeed, persuasion is an integral part of democratic society. It is the freedom of speech used by every individual and organization to influence opinion, understanding, judgment, and action. Consequently, it is important for public relations professionals to master the basic principles of persuasion. See the Insights box which follows for the six basic principles of persuasion.

Uses of Persuasion

Persuasion is used to (1) change or neutralize hostile opinions, (2) crystallize latent opinions and positive attitudes, and (3) conserve favorable opinions.

The most difficult persuasive task is to turn hostile opinions into favorable ones. There is much truth to the adage "Don't confuse me with the facts; my mind is made up." Once people have decided, for instance, that health insurers are making excessive profits or that a nonprofit agency is wasting contributions, they tend to ignore or disbelieve any contradictory information. Everyone, as Walter Lippmann has described, has pictures in his or her head based on an individual perception of reality. People

on the job INSIGHTS

Six Principles of Persuasion

No public relations professional can succeed without mastering the art of persuasion. Robert Cialdini, author of *Influence: Science and Practice*, says there are six basic principles of winning friends and influencing people. The following chart, from a *Harvard Business Review* article, gives the basic principles and an example of each one:

Principle	Example
Liking: People like those who like them.	At Tupperware parties, guests' fondness for their host influences purchase decisions twice as much as regard for the products does.
Reciprocity: People repay in kind.	When the Disabled American Veterans enclosed free personalized address labels in donation-request envelopes, response rates doubled.
Social Proof: People follow the lead of others.	More New York City residents tried returning a lost wallet after learning that other New Yorkers had tried to do so.
Consistency: People fulfill written, public, and voluntary commitments.	Ninety-two percent of residents of an apartment complex who signed a petition supporting a new recreation center later donated to the cause.
Authority: People defer to experts who provide shortcuts requiring specialized information.	A single *New York Times* expert-opinion news story aired on TV generates a 4 percent shift in U.S. public opinion.
Scarcity: People value what's scarce.	Wholesale beef buyers' orders jumped 600 percent when they received information on a possible beef shortage.

generalize from personal experience and what peers tell them in person or through blogs and tweets.

Persuasion is much easier if the message is compatible with a person's general disposition toward a subject. If a person tends to identify Starbucks as a company with a good reputation, he or she may express this feeling by being a loyal customer. Nonprofit agencies usually crystallize the public's latent inclination to help by asking for donations. Both examples illustrate the reason that organizations strive to have a good reputation—it is translated into sales and donations.

The easiest form of persuasion is communication that reinforces favorable opinions. Public relations people, by providing a steady stream of reinforcing messages, keep the reservoir of goodwill in sound condition. More than one organization has survived a major problem because public esteem for it tended to minimize current difficulties. Continual efforts to maintain the reservoir of goodwill are called *preventive public relations*, and it is the most effective type of public relations.

Persuasion in Negotiation

How parties position themselves before negotiations begin can be crucial to how the give-and-take unfolds. Public relations can play a major role in this positioning. Persuasion is an integral component of the public relations effort to bring parties into ultimate agreement. For example, using persuasion to put your organization on an equal footing with a competitor could lead to the realization that the two parties need to talk. In other words, public relations can be used as a tool leading to the alternative dispute resolution (ADR) process. ADR takes place outside the traditional courtroom and has gained acceptance among public relations professionals, the legal profession, and the public at large. ADR is typically much less expensive and often much more efficient than a traditional lawsuit.

"Public relations, based on the contingency theory, can be viewed as a constructive creator of antecedent conditions for alternative dispute resolution," note researchers Bryan Reber, Fritz Cropp, and Glen Cameron. They illustrate this with a case in which public relations and legal professionals worked cooperatively to negotiate the hostile takeover bid of Conrail Inc. by the Norfolk Southern Corporation. Conrail resisted Norfolk Southern's bid, favoring an offer by the CSX Corporation that was considered inferior by Conrail's stockholders.

With the help of a public relations campaign coordinated by Fleishman-Hillard, Norfolk Southern effectively persuaded their target audiences that their offer was superior. The public relations campaign, which helped sway public opinion in Norfolk Southern's favor, facilitated the negotiation process. The three companies reached a mutually beneficial agreement—CSX would purchase Conrail and immediately sell 58 percent of the rail routes and assets to Norfolk Southern.

Formulating Persuasive Messages

Psychologists have found that successful speakers, bloggers, and viral marketers use several persuasion techniques:

- **Yes–yes.** Start with points with which the audience agrees to develop a pattern of "yes" answers. Getting agreement to a basic premise often means that the receiver will agree to the logically developed conclusion.
- **Offer structured choice.** Give choices that force the audience to choose between A and B. College officials may ask audiences, "Do you want to raise taxes or raise tuition?" Political candidates ask, "Do you want more free enterprise or government telling you what to do?"
- **Seek partial commitment.** Get a commitment for some action on the part of the receiver. This leaves the door open for commitment to other parts of the proposal at a later date. "You don't need to decide on the supplemental insurance plan now, but check out this YouTube video to see how major surgery can exhaust typical deductibles. . . ."
- **Ask for more, settle for less.** Submit a complete public relations program to management, but be prepared to compromise by dropping certain parts of the program.

A persuasive speech can either be one-sided or offer several sides of an issue, depending on the audience. One-sided speeches are most effective with persons already favorable to the message, whereas two-sided speeches are most effective with audiences that might be opposed to the message.

By mentioning all sides of the argument, the speaker accomplishes three objectives. First, the speaker is perceived as having objectivity. This translates into increased credibility and makes the audience less suspicious of the speaker's motives. Second, the speaker is treating the audience as mature, intelligent adults. Third,

Using social media and blogs

SOCIAL MEDIA IN ACTION

Changing Nutrition Perceptions about McDonald's

Fast-food chains usually get a bad rap for failing to offer wholesome and nutritious menu choices. McDonald's, however, wanted to change public opinion so it launched a Nutrition Network to highlight its commitment to nutrition.

To localize the message, the company and its public relations firm, MWW, created the McDonald's New York Metro Nutrition Network (MNN) and turned to influential bloggers, a dietician, and social media. One objective was to award local organizations with seed money to fund projects and programs to promote nutrition and responsible eating choices.

A high-profile dietician was selected to tell the brand's story. She gave a number of talks in the New York metro area, answered questions, and provided McDonald's menu items for people to sample. In addition, she provided nutrition tips on the program's website, which was also amplified by McDonald's local Twitter and Facebook platforms.

"Mommy bloggers" were selected for special attention. McDonald's invited them to attend the program's launch event and attend follow-up meetings, which was live-tweeted by McDonald's

The idea of actually meeting with the bloggers offline turned out to be better than just sending them posts online in terms of changing their perceptions. According to Alissa Blate of MWW, "When they learned about the better for you options available at McDonald's restaurants, their perceptions changed."

The results tell the story. The McDonald's program generated more than 100 stories in the traditional media and favorable posts from more than 20 bloggers in the local New York metro market. According to *Ragan's PR Daily*, which awarded the program its annual digital PR and Social Media Award, Blate reported that there was a 2,300 percent increase in social media impressions around McDonald's and nutrition with 99 percent of them considered "favorable." She continued, "Additionally, many local bloggers who had previously written negative posts around McDonald's and its nutritional benefit have begun to praise the brand for its commitment to bringing responsible eating to the forefront."

including counterarguments allows the speaker to control how those arguments are structured. That is, it allows the speaker to frame the opponent's perspective. It also deflates opponents who might challenge the speaker by saying, "But you didn't consider. . . ."

Findings from Persuasion Research

Many of the precepts offered in this chapter come from experience and from some level of common sense. Starting with the Office of War Information (see Chapter 2), researchers have also systematically studied persuasion processes. A number of research studies have contributed to persuasion concepts. Here are some precepts from the text *Public Communication Campaigns*, edited by Ronald E. Rice and William J. Paisley, that can be used in public relations practice:

- Positive appeals are generally more effective than negative appeals for retention of the message and actual compliance.
- Radio and television messages tend to be more persuasive than print, but if the message is complex, better comprehension is achieved through print media.
- Strong emotional appeals and fear arousal are most effective when the audience has minimal concern about or interest in the topic.
- High fear appeals are effective only when a readily available action can be taken to eliminate the threat.
- Logical appeals, using facts and figures, are better for highly educated, sophisticated audiences than strong emotional appeals.
- Altruistic need, like self-interest, can be a strong motivator. Men are more willing to get a physical checkup to protect their families than to protect themselves.
- A celebrity or an attractive model is most effective when the audience has low involvement, the theme is simple, and broadcast channels are used. An exciting spokesperson attracts attention to a message that would otherwise be ignored.

Factors in Persuasive Communication

A number of factors are involved in persuasive communication, and the public relations practitioner should be knowledgeable about each one. The following is a brief discussion of (1) audience analysis, (2) source credibility, (3) appeal to self-interest, (4) clarity of message, (5) timing and context, (6) audience participation, (7) suggestions for action, (8) content and structure of messages.

Audience Analysis

Knowledge of audience characteristics such as beliefs, attitudes, concerns, and lifestyles is an essential part of persuasion. It helps the communicator tailor messages that are salient, answer a felt need, and provide a logical course of action.

Basic demographic information, readily available through census data, can help determine an audience's gender, income level, education, ethnic background, and age groupings. Other data, often prepared by marketing departments, give information on a group's buying habits, disposable income, and ways of spending leisure time. In many cases, the nature of the product or service easily defines the audience along the lines of age, gender, and income.

Another audience-analysis tool is *psychographics.* This method attempts to classify people by lifestyle, attitudes, and beliefs. The Values and Lifestyle Program, popularly known as VALS, was developed by SRI International, a research organization in

Menlo Park, California. VALS groups people into one of eight categories: innovators, thinkers, believers, achievers, strivers, experiencers, makers, and survivors. VALS is routinely used in public relations to help communicators structure persuasive messages to different members of the population. Current audience analysis is moving in new directions. Information-processing research employs everything from brain scans while subjects view messages, to measurement of smile and frown muscle groups, galvanic skin reaction, and heart rate to better understand how messages are processed and what effects different kinds of message strategies have on audiences.

Such audience analysis, coupled with suitably tailored messages in the appropriate media outlets, is the technique of *channeling*. Persuasive messages are more effective when they take into account the audience's lifestyles, beliefs, and concerns.

Source Credibility

A message is more believable to the intended audience if the source has *credibility*. This was Aristotle's concept of *ethos*, mentioned earlier, and it explains why organizations use a variety of spokespeople, depending on the message and the audience.

The National Cattleman's Beef Association, for example, arranged for a grilling expert to author a cookbook, participate in a book tour, and appear on radio and television broadcasts to communicate safe techniques of grilling to ensure that consumers learned that beef should reach a temperature of 160 degrees Fahrenheit. Consumers found the expert highly credible and knowledge of safe beef handling increased measurably. Similarly, a manufacturer of sunscreen lotion used a professor of pharmacology and a past president of the State Pharmacy Board to discuss the scientific merits of sunscreen versus suntan lotions.

The concept of motion media (TV, YouTube, virtual reality, games, animation appearing all around us from giant billboards to smartphones in our pockets) mentioned in Chapter 8 is particularly relevant here with regard to credibility of UGC (user-generated content such as YouTube video and v-logging).

Motion media pose challenges for traditional thinking about source credibility in the new media landscape, where less is known about the source and a more egalitarian approach to sources prevails. Based on an old saying, "Seeing is believing," the veridicality of a message takes on greater importance. As initially introduced by Professor Michael Slater at Ohio State and Professor Donna Rouner at Colorado State, the features of an online story, such as production values and quality of the script, can accord credibility to the source. This process also diminishes the distinction between a news source and a public relations source for a message, because judgments derive from how well done the story is, not who is doing it.

Popularization happens when you get credible third parties to speak for your brand, and that is something PR can do extremely well.

Scott Keogh, chief marketing officer of Audi

The Three Factors Source credibility is based on three factors. One is *expertise*. Does the audience perceive the person as an expert on the subject? Companies, for example, use engineers and scientists to answer news conference questions about how an engineering process works or whether an ingredient in the manufacturing process of a product presents a potential hazard.

The second component is *sincerity*. Does the person come across as believing what he or she is saying? Lady Gaga was accused by People for the Ethical Treatment of Animals (PETA) of being a poor role model when she wore fur coats. Gaga fired back effectively questioning PETA's sincerity when she said she doesn't support "violent, abusive and childish campaigns for any cause." Was PETA sincere or simply attempting to gain attention by stirring controversy with a celebrity?

The third component, which is even more elusive, is *charisma*. Is the individual attractive, self-assured, and articulate, projecting an image of competence and leadership? Expertise is less important than sincerity and charisma if celebrities are used as spokespersons. Their primary purpose is to call attention to the product or service. Another purpose is to associate the celebrity's popularity with the product. This technique is called *transfer*.

Some kinds of celebrities, however, are more persuasive than others. An Adweek Media/Harris poll, for example, found that celebrity business leaders endorsing a product are more persuasive overall than athletes, television stars, and movie stars. Age, however, is a factor. Business leaders are more persuasive with people over 45 years old, while athletes, television stars, and movie stars are more persuasive with people under 45. Former political figures are the least persuasive celebrities among all age groups.

Problems with Celebrities Using celebrities, however, has several possible downsides. One is the increasing number of celebrity endorsements, to the point that the public sometimes can't remember who endorses what. A second problem can be overexposure of a celebrity, such as David Beckham or Beyoncé, who earn millions of dollars annually from multiple products.

A third problem occurs when an endorser's actions undercut the product or service. And when such a popular celebrity as Lance Armstrong falls from grace after an admission of doping in premier events such as the Tour de France, the panic of sponsors, criticism of journalists, and desertion of fans is notable. Celebrities and some of their foibles are further discussed in Chapter 18.

A fourth problem is when a celebrity decides to speak out on controversial public issues and even endorses political candidates. Such actions tend to reduce

Lance Armstrong attempted to resurrect his reputation when he confessed to Oprah on a widely watched television special that he was guilty of doping.

the celebrity's effectiveness as an endorser of products or services because they tend to alienate segments of the consumer public who disagree with their views. One survey, for example, found that a third of the respondents said they would avoid buying products endorsed by celebrities who express political views that they disagree with.

In summary, the use of various sources for credibility depends, in large part, on the type of audience being reached. That is why audience analysis is the first step in formulating persuasive messages. An important component of source credibility, of course, is the concept of trust. The Edelman Trust Barometer, an annual international survey of most trusted industries and spokespersons found that academics or experts are most trusted, followed closely by technical experts within the company, and a person like you. Other research shows that a friend's recommendation is the most trusted.

Appeal to Self-Interest

Self-interest was described during an earlier discussion about the formation of public opinion. Publics become involved in issues or pay attention to messages that appeal to their psychological or economic needs.

Charitable organizations don't sell products, but they do need volunteers and donations. This is accomplished by careful structuring of messages that appeal to self-interest. A Functional Foods project at the University of Missouri promoted special benefits of berries, broccoli, and soy to diet and lifestyle during cancer recovery.

Based on audience research, oncology nurses expressed a lack of knowledge of nutrition and a desire to shape up their own diet and lifestyle. Appeals for these nurses to order an information kit to share with their patients were promoted first and foremost for the nurses' own edification. Evaluation revealed that once the kits were in hand, the nurses regularly shared recommendations about functional foods with patients during chemotherapy.

Self-interest is powerful, but altruism is not dead. Thousands of people give freely of their time and money to charitable organizations, but unless they receive something in return, they will stop their contributions. The "something in return" may be (1) self-esteem, (2) the opportunity to make a contribution to society, (3) recognition from peers and the community, (4) a sense of belonging, (5) ego gratification, or even (6) a tax deduction. Public relations people understand psychological needs and rewards, and that is why there is constant recognition of volunteers in newsletters and at award banquets. (Further discussion of volunteerism appears in Chapter 21.)

Sociologist Harold Lasswell says that people are motivated by eight basic appeals. They are:

- Power
- Respect
- Well-being
- Affection
- Wealth
- Skill
- Enlightenment
- Physical and mental vitality

The challenge for public relations personnel, as creators of persuasive messages, is to tailor information to address these appeals. Social scientists have said that success in persuasion largely depends on accurate assessment of audience needs and self-interests.

Long words are difficult and reduce readability. Keep yours short. *The Wall Street Journal* weighs in at an average of 4.8 characters per word—proving that you can tell complex stories with simple words.

Ann Wylie in Public Relations Tactics

Clarity of Message

Many messages fail because the audience finds the message unnecessarily complex in content or language. The most persuasive messages are direct, simply expressed, and contain only one primary idea.

Public relations personnel should always ask two questions: "Will the audience understand the message?" and "What do I want the audience to do with the message?" Although persuasion theory says that people retain information better and form stronger opinions when they are asked to draw their own conclusions, this doesn't negate the importance of explicitly stating what action an audience should take. Do you want the message recipient to buy a product, visit a showroom, write a member of Congress, make a $10 donation, or something else?

If an explicit request for action is not part of the message, members of the audience may not understand what is expected of them. Public relations firms, when making a presentation to a potential client, always ask at the end of the presentation to be awarded the account.

Timing and Context

A message is more persuasive if environmental factors support the message or if the message is received within the context of other messages and situations with which the individual is familiar. These factors are called *timing* and *context.*

Information from a utility on how to conserve energy is more salient if the consumer has just received the January heating bill. A pamphlet on a new stock offering is more effective if it accompanies an investor's dividend check.

Political candidates are aware of public concerns and avidly read polls to learn what issues are most important to voters. If the polls indicate that violent crime and unemployment are key issues, the candidate begins to use these issues—and to offer his or her proposals—in the campaign.

Timing and context also play an important role in achieving publicity in the mass media. Public relations personnel, as pointed out earlier in the text, should be voracious news consumers to find out what media gatekeepers consider newsworthy. A manufacturer of a locking device for computer files got extensive media coverage about its product simply because its release followed a rash of news stories about thieves gaining access to bank accounts through computers. Media gatekeepers found the product newsworthy within the context of actual news events.

The value of information and its newsworthiness are based on timing and context. Public relations professionals must immerse themselves in news and public affairs to disseminate information at just the right time.

Audience Participation

Practitioners have known for decades that a change in attitude or reinforcement of beliefs is enhanced by audience involvement and participation. With the onset of widespread social media such as YouTube videos produced by individual amateurs, this sort of user-generated content (UGC) can have a beneficial effect on the creator, if not the audience. For example, health campaigns for teenagers that encourage UGC by the teens about health issues and their solutions can strengthen and reinforce positive attitudes toward healthy lifestyles.

Activist groups use participation as a way of helping people actualize their beliefs. Not only do rallies and demonstrations give people a sense of belonging, but the act of participation reinforces their beliefs. The political Tea Party Movement formed in response to Wall Street and automaker bailouts and built its initial momentum through major events that cemented the resolve of members.

Suggestions for Action

A principle of persuasion is that people endorse ideas only if the sponsor proposes an action. Recommendations for action must be clear. Public relations practitioners must not only ask people to conserve energy, for instance, but must also furnish rationale on why and ideas on how to do so.

Content and Structure of Messages

A number of techniques can make a message more persuasive. Writers throughout history have emphasized some information while downplaying or omitting other pieces of information. Thus, they address both the content and the structure of messages.

Expert communicators continue to use a number of devices, including (1) drama, (2) statistics, (3) surveys and polls, (4) examples, (5) testimonials, (6) endorsements, and (7) emotional appeals.

Drama Because everyone likes a good story, the first task of a communicator is to get the audience's attention. This is often called *humanizing* a situation or issue. Relief organizations, in particular, attempt to galvanize public concern and donations through stark images of an individual accompanied by emotionally charged descriptions of the person's suffering.

A more mundane use of drama is the *application story*, sent to the trade press. This is sometimes called the *case study technique*, in which a manufacturer prepares an article on how an individual or a company is successfully using the product.

Statistics People are impressed by statistics. Use of numbers can convey objectivity, size, and importance in a credible way that can influence public opinion. Statistics can also be enlightening when they are related to common things that people understand. In the news release for the largest truck in the world, Caterpillar announced that the bed of the truck is so large that it could haul 4 blue whales, 217 taxicabs, 1,200 grand pianos, and 23,000 Barbie dolls.

Surveys and Polls Airlines and auto manufacturers, in particular, use the results of surveys and polls to show that they are first in "customer satisfaction," "service," and even "leg room" or "cargo space." The most credible surveys are those conducted by independent research organizations, but readers still should read the fine print to see what is being compared and rated.

Examples A statement of opinion can be more persuasive if some examples are given. A school board can often get support for a bond issue by citing examples of how the present facilities are inadequate for student needs. Environmental groups, when they are requesting a city council to establish a greenbelt, tell how other communities have successfully done so. Automakers—going back to Henry Ford—promote the durability of their vehicles by citing their performance on a test track or in a road race.

Testimonials These are usually statements by a person who is a satisfied customer. Testimonials honoring an individual or organization are often given at banquets and other public events.

Endorsements An endorsement, unlike a testimonial, is usually given by celebrities who are paid to say nice things about the organization, product, or service. Organizations such as the American Dental Association and the National Safety Council also endorse products and services.

Media endorsements are unpaid and take the form of editorials, reviews, surveys, and news stories. The most direct endorsement is an editorial supporting a political candidate or a community cause. A more indirect "endorsement" is a published, broadcasted, or posted favorable review of a play, a movie, or a restaurant. The media also produce news stories about new products and services that, because of the media's perceived objectivity, are considered a form of third-party endorsement. The idea is that media coverage bestows legitimacy and newsworthiness on a product or service.

Emotional Appeals Fund-raising letters from nonprofit groups, in particular, use this persuasive device. Appeals to protect animals, for example, often use the emotional appeal of personifying the animal. See the sample letter from the Defenders of Wildlife on page 269.

Emotional appeals are also used in politics. Opponents of gun control, for example, claimed that the government would confiscate firearms after compiling a registry of gun owners.

This kind of emotional appeal is called *fear arousal.* Strong statements like this, however, can alienate the audience and cause them to tune out the message. Research indicates that a moderate fear arousal, accompanied by a relatively easy solution, is more effective. A moderate fear arousal is: "What would happen if your child were thrown through the windshield in an accident?" The message concludes with the suggestion that a baby, for protection and safety, should be placed in a secured infant seat.

Psychologists say the most effective emotional appeal is one coupled with facts and figures. The emotional appeal attracts audience interest, but logical arguments also are needed for the appeal to be persuasive.

The Limits of Persuasion

The discussion on the previous pages examined ways in which an individual can formulate persuasive messages. The ability to use these techniques often leads to charges that public relations practitioners have great power to influence and manipulate people.

In reality, the effectiveness of persuasive techniques is greatly exaggerated. Persuasion is not an exact science, and no surefire way exists to predict that people will be persuaded to believe a message or act on it. If persuasive techniques were as refined as the critics say, all people might be driving the same make of car, using the same soap, and voting for the same political candidate.

Snowflake

Dear Friend,

For polar bear cubs like Snowflake, life starts out as a nearly impossible challenge.

Born with her sister Aurora in the frigid darkness of the Arctic winter, Snowflake weighed only about a pound at birth, the size of a cell phone. For months, she and her sister didn't leave the den where they were born, a small cave that their mother had dug in a snow bank. Helpless, they depended on their mother for the essentials of life — her body warmth and her nutrient-rich milk.

Snowflake and her sister will stay with their mother for more than two years. She will feed them, teach them to hunt, and protect them from predators.

With the fierce maternal protection of her mother, cuddly little Snowflake will grow up to become one of the most awesome animals on Earth.

But now, a looming new threat could cut short the lives of precious little polar bear cubs like Snowflake.

You see, the powerful oil lobby and its political allies in Congress are pushing to open Snowflake's home — the Arctic National Wildlife Refuge — to environmentally destructive oil and gas drilling. The Refuge's coastal plain is America's most important on-shore polar bear nursery, and scientist warn that the habitat destruction, pollution and other impacts of the plan could be deadly to the bears.

That's why I'm asking you to please "adopt" a polar bear cub like Snowflake by joining Defenders of Wildlife today with a contribution of $15 or more.

Defenders of Wildlife is helping lead the fight to save America's greatest wildlife sanctuary for Snowflake and the other wild animals that call it home. But to succeed, we urgently need the help of concerned individuals like you to overcome the enormous money and political clout of the oil lobby.

And we must act now — because politicians are already moving to hand over this unique natural treasure to Big Oil. Congressman Don Young (R-Alaska) — who decorates his office with animal skins — has already introduced legislation to allow drilling. The pristine 19 million-acre Arctic Refuge is the last place in North America where Arctic wildlife is fully protected. And the Refuge's coastal plain, often referred to as "America's Serengeti," is the biological heart of this

(over, please)

Defenders of Wildlife • 1101 Fourteenth Street, N.W. • Room 1400 • Washington, D.C. 20005
www.defenders.org • www.kidsplanet.org

Your continued activism is important. Please call your representatives in Washington to let them know you support the preservation of wildlife and its habitat. You can contact them at 202-224-3121. Thank you.

Persuasion by Direct Mail

An eye-catching opening must persuade the recipient to read on rather than to toss the letter aside. Letters such as this have a strong emotional appeal and often stir a reader's high concern for a particular situation. The plight of the polar bear has become a potent symbol of the effects of global warming.

This doesn't happen because several variables intervene in the flow of persuasive messages. Elihu Katz says the two major intervening variables are selectivity and interpersonal relations; these are consistent with the limited-effects model of mass communication.

For purposes of discussion, the limitations on effective persuasive messages can be listed as (1) lack of message penetration, (2) competing messages, (3) self-selection, and (4) self-perception.

Lack of Message Penetration

The diffusion of messages, despite omnipresent communication technologies, is not pervasive. People don't, of course, watch the same television programs, read the same newspapers, or watch the same YouTube videos. There is also the problem of messages being distorted as they pass through traditional media gatekeepers or get interpreted by tweets, blogs, and other social network interaction. Key message points often are left out or the context of the message is changed.

Competing Messages

In the 1930s, before much was known about the complex process of communication, it was believed that people receive information directly, without any intervening variables. This was called the *bullet theory* or the *hypodermic-needle theory* of communication.

Today, communication experts realize that no message is received in a vacuum. Messages are filtered through a receiver's entire social structure and belief system, which includes the influences of opinion leaders and even acquaintances. Nationality, race, religion, gender, cultural patterns, family, and friends are among the variables that filter and dilute persuasive messages. People receive countless competing and conflicting messages daily. Social scientists say a person usually conforms to the standards of his or her family and friends. Consequently, most people do not believe or act on messages that are contrary to group norms.

Self-Selection

The people most wanted in an audience are often the least likely to be there. Vehement supporters or loyalists frequently ignore information and even facts from the other side. They do so by being selective in the messages they want to hear. They read books, newspaper editorials, blog posts, and magazine articles and view television programs that support their predispositions. This is why social scientists say that the media are more effective in reinforcing existing attitudes than in changing them.

Self-Perception

Self-perception is the context through which messages are interpreted. People will perceive the same information differently, depending on their predispositions and already formulated opinions. In other words, public relations personnel must take into account the axiom "Perception is reality."

The Ethics of Persuasion

Public relations people, by definition, are advocates of their clients and employers. Their emphasis is on persuasive communication to influence a particular public in some way. At the same time, as Chapter 3 points out, public relations practitioners must conduct their activities in an ethical manner.

The use of persuasive techniques, therefore, calls for some additional guidelines. Professor Richard L. Johannesen of Northern Illinois University, writing in Charles Larson's *Persuasion, Reception and Responsibility*, lists the following ethical criteria for using persuasive devices that every public relations professional should keep in mind:

- Do not use false, fabricated, misrepresented, distorted, or irrelevant evidence to support arguments or claims.
- Do not intentionally use specious, unsupported, or illogical reasoning.
- Do not represent yourself as informed or as an "expert" on a subject when you are not.
- Do not use irrelevant appeals to divert attention or scrutiny from the issue at hand. Among the appeals that commonly serve such a purpose are smear attacks on an opponent's character, appeals to hatred and bigotry, innuendo, and "God" or "devil" terms that cause intense but unreflective positive or negative reactions.
- Do not ask your audience to link your idea or proposal to emotion-laden values, motives, or goals to which it actually is not related.
- Do not deceive your audience by concealing your real purpose, your self interest, the group you represent, or your position as an advocate of a viewpoint.
- Do not distort, hide, or misrepresent the number, scope, intensity, or undesirable features or consequences.
- Do not use emotional appeals that lack a supporting basis of evidence or reasoning or that would not be accepted if the audience had the time and opportunity to examine the subject itself.
- Do not oversimplify complex situations into simplistic, two-valued, either/or, polar views or choices.
- Do not pretend certainty when tentativeness and degrees of probability are more accurate.
- Do not advocate something in which you do not believe yourself.

It is clear from the preceding list that a public relations professional should be more than a technician or a "hired gun." Persuasive messages require truth, honesty, and candor for two practical reasons, according to Robert Heath. First, a message is already suspect because it is advanced on behalf of a client or organization. Second, half-truths and misleading information do not serve the best interests of the public or the organization.

Summary

What Is Public Opinion?

- Public opinion can be difficult to measure; there are few if any issues on which the public (which is in fact many publics) can be said to have a unanimous opinion.
- Only a small number of people will have opinions on any given issue.
- Engaging the interest of a public will involve affecting its self-interest. Publics also react strongly to events.

Opinion Leaders as Catalysts

- The primary catalyst in the formation of public opinion is public discussion.
- People who are knowledgeable and articulate on specific issues can be either formal opinion leaders (power leaders) or informal opinion leaders (role models).
- Opinion "flows" from these leaders to the public, often through the mass media.

The Role of Mass Media

- Mass media play a major role in setting the agenda for public discussion and debate.
- People who know little or nothing about a subject depend on mass media for their information and opinions. This is called the media-dependency theory.
- Framing theory describes how both journalists and public relations personnel promote a particular aspect of an issue or controversy.
- Journalists often look for conflict in a story; public relations people strive for accommodation and conflict resolution.

The Dominant View of Public Relations

- The dominant view of public relations is of persuasive communications on behalf of clients.
- Persuasion can be used to change or neutralize hostile opinions, crystallize latent opinions and positive attitudes, and conserve favorable opinions.
- Research studies have established many basic concepts of persuasive communication.

Factors in Persuasive Communication

- Factors involved in persuasion include audience analysis, source credibility, appeal to self-interest, message clarity, timing and context, audience participation, suggestions for action, content and structure of messages, and persuasive speaking.

The Limits of Persuasion

- Limitations on effective persuasion include lack of message penetration, competing messages, self-selection, and self-perception.

The Ethics of Persuasion

- Publics will automatically have a level of suspicion because they know the communicator is promoting a client or organization.
- The interests of that client or organization will not be well served by false or misleading communications.

Case Activity Persuading People to Help Fund-Raise

You have been elected philanthropic chair for your sorority or fraternity. Past fund-raising events have been well attended by your members, but lacked buy-in from alumni and community members. Your organization is planning to host a barbecue picnic during homecoming to raise money for the local Boys and Girls Club.

Your task is to persuade not only students, but also alumni attending homecoming to participate in your fundraiser. What persuasive techniques would you employ to encourage students to attend? What different techniques would you need to use to reach alumni?

Questions For Review and Discussion

1. Public opinion is highly influenced by self-interest and events. What are these concepts?
2. Who are opinion leaders? Why are they so named?
3. What is the role of mass media in shaping and articulating public opinion?
4. What is framing theory? How does it impact public relations?
5. What are the three factors involved in source credibility?
6. What is meant by "audience participation" in persuasion? Give some examples of how audience participation can be used.
7. What are the various factors in persuasive communication?
8. What can limit the effectiveness of persuasion?
9. What are the challenges for PR when public opinion is formed instantly by communities cutting across geographical, social, and economic boundaries in a flat world facilitated by the Internet?

Media Resources

Berger, B. K., & Reber, B. H. (2006). *Gaining influence in public relations: The role of resistance in practice.* Mahwah, NJ: Erlbaum Associates.

Coombs, W. T., & Holladay, S. J. (2012). Fringe public relations: How activism moves critical PR toward the mainstream. *Public Relations Review, 38*(5), 880–887.

Hindman, D. B. (2012). Knowledge gaps, belief gaps, and public opinion about health care reform. *Journalism and Mass Communication Quarterly, 89*(4), 585–605.

Holtz-Bacha, C. & Stromback, J. (2012). *Opinion polls and the media: Reflecting and shaping public opinion.* Houndmills, Basingstoke, Hampshire: Palgrave Macmillan.

Kim, Y., & Kiousis, S. (2012). The role of affect in agenda building for public relations: implications for public relations outcomes. *Journalism & Mass Communications Quarterly, 89*(4), 657–676.

Ladd, J. M. (2012). *Why Americans hate the media and how it matters.* Princeton: Princeton University Press.

Lecheler, S. & de Vreese, C. H. (2012). News framing and public opinion: A mediation analysis of framing effects on political attitudes. *Journalism and Mass Communication Quarterly, 89*(2), 185–204.

Miller, B. M. (2010). Community stakeholders and marketplace advocacy: A model of advocacy, agenda building and industry approval. *Journal of Public Relations Research, 22*(1), 85–112.

Murphy, P. (2010). The intractability of reputation: Media coverage as a complex system in the case of Martha Stewart. *Journal of Public Relations Research, 22*(2), 209–237.

Pasadeos, Y., Berger, B., & Renfro, R. B. (2010). Public relations is a maturing discipline: An update on research networks. *Journal of Public Relations Research, 22*(2), 136–158.

Rotolo, A. (2010, May). Beyond friends and followers: Next steps for social media. *Public Relations Tactics, 17*(5), 9.

chapter 10

Conflict Management and Crisis Communication

After reading this chapter, you will be able to:

- Understand the role of public relations in managing conflict
- Describe the two basic principles of strategic conflict management
- Identify the four phases of the conflict management life cycle
- Understand the issues management process as a key public relations contribution
- Explain the relationship between the conflict stance and the communication strategy
- Identify important steps to deal with a crisis as it occurs
- Define reputation and the role public relations plays in image repair

Strategic Conflict Management

Conflict takes many forms, from warfare between nations to spats between teenagers and their parents. Often, conflicts take place in the marketplace of ideas as opposing groups clash over issues such as gun control, same-sex marriage, and immigration reform, or even where Home Depot or Wal-Mart should build a "big-box" store.

Many of these conflicts fall under the purview of public relations. This means that a public relations professional must develop communication strategies and processes *to influence the course of conflicts to the benefit of the organization and, when possible, to the benefit of the organization's many constituents.* Such use of public relations to influence the course of a conflict, and ultimately a crisis, is called *strategic conflict management.* Its key components are:

- Strategic—for the purpose of achieving particular objectives
- Management—planned, deliberate action
- Competition—striving for the same object, position, or prize as others
- Conflict—sharp disagreements or opposition resulting in a direct, overt threat of attack from another entity

This approach to public relations is more assertive than most definitions, which place an emphasis on building mutually beneficial relationships between the organization and its various stakeholders. Indeed, building relationships is a key objective, but it is only one part of what public relations does for organizations. The management of competition and conflict offers relationship building but also more "muscular" public relations. Olympic swimmer Missy Franklin embodies the preparation, strength, and fair play required to compete against others while maintaining cordial relationships.

The point is that public relations plays a key role in enabling both profit and nonprofit organizations to compete for limited resources (customers, volunteers, employees, donations, grants, etc.) and to engage in healthy, honest conflict with others who hold different views of what is best and right for society. Achieving these sorts of objectives increases the value of public relations to the organization. It is how public relations professionals earn influence, which leads to greater recognition by top management, increased respect in the field, and, ultimately, better-paying, more secure positions for public relations professionals.

Although competition and conflict are closely related to each other, this book makes a distinction between the two terms (see Figure 10.1). *Competition*, a pervasive condition in life, occurs when two or more groups or organizations vie for the same resources. In business, these "resources" can be sales, share of market, contracts, employees, and, ultimately, profits. In the nonprofit sector, the competition might be donations, grants, clients, volunteers, and even political influence.

Conflict, on the other hand, occurs when two groups direct their efforts against each other, devising actions and communication that directly or

Relationship Building

Missy Franklin embodies the view of public relations as strong and competitive in spirit, yet not manipulative or underhanded.

Figure 10.1 **Competition and Conflict**

Competition is inevitable and omnipresent. It occurs when two or more groups or organizations vie for the same resources.

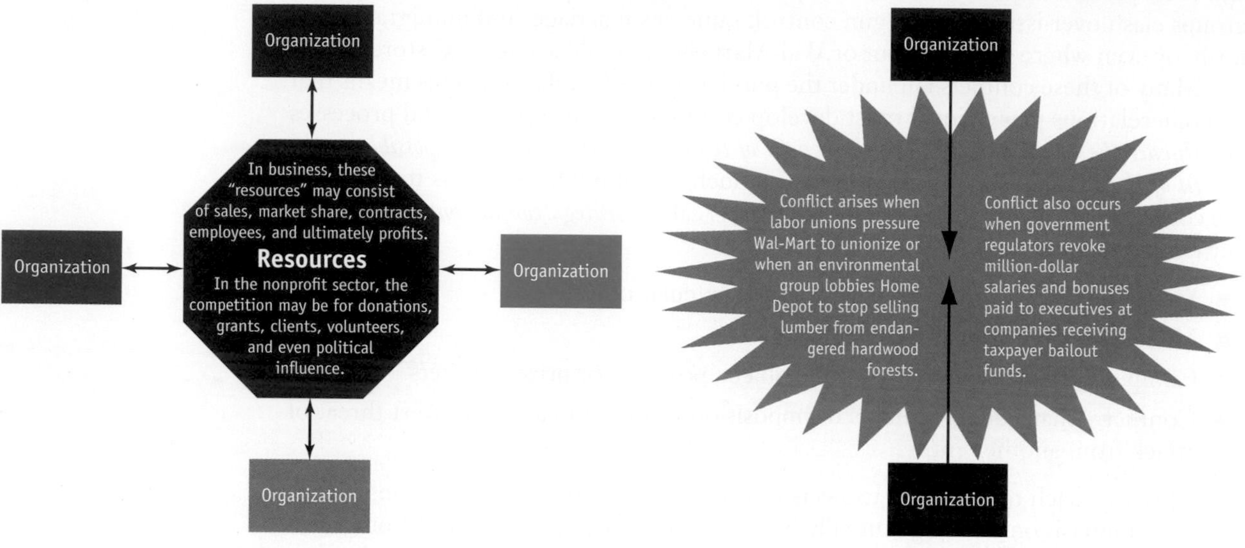

COMPETITION is inevitable and omnipresent. It occurs when two or more groups or organizations vie for the same resources.

CONFLICT occurs when two groups direct their efforts against each other, devising communication and actions that attack.

verbally attack the other group. Conflict arises, for example, when labor unions hold Black Friday pickets to pressure Wal-Mart to unionize, or when Apply the Brakes (ATB), a conservation group concerned about population growth, asks the Sierra Club to clarify its support for a Senate immigration bill. ATB argued that the higher legal immigration levels endorsed by the bill would lead to environmental degradation because of U.S. population growth. It also occurs when government regulators investigate BP's lax standards for fail-safe valves on drilling rigs to prevent deaths and environmental disaster.

Experienced public relations experts, however, are quick to point out that many practitioners will spend most of their professional lives with fairly moderate levels of competition (such as marketing communications) but perhaps have few, if any, situations that involve conflict. For example, the development director for the Nature Conservancy may be competing to get donations for a new program from the same donors who are being approached for donations by the World Wildlife Fund. The two professionals may be friends and perhaps one was actually the mentor of the other. On the other hand, a more heightened level of competition might exist between public relations professionals at Wal-Mart, Target, and Costco, who compete with each other to increase consumer visibility and retail sales.

Most public relations activity and programs, as already noted, deal with competition between organizations for sales and customers. Conflict, in contrast, deals with attacks and confrontations between organizations and various stakeholders or publics. For example, when the Internal Revenue Service (IRS) admitted that it had targeted conservative political groups for extensive review of applications for nonprofit status,

Republicans accused President Obama's administration of misdeeds. President Obama pushed back, firing the head of the IRS and strongly denouncing the activity.

This was met with furor from ordinary citizens suffering from the consequences of the excessive scrutiny of applications for tax-exemption for new political activist organizations. Admittedly, the distinction between competition and conflict is partly a matter of degree, but it is also a matter of focus. In competition, the eye is on the prize—such as sales or political support. In conflict, the eye is on the opposition, on dealing with or initiating threats of some sort or another. In either case, professional practice by this definition is vitally important to organizations. It requires a sense of mission and conviction that:

- Your organization's behavior is honorable and defensible.
- Your organization is ethical.
- Your organization's mission is worthy.
- Your advocacy of the organization has integrity.
- Your organization works at creating mutual benefits whenever possible.

The last point, striving for mutual benefit, is extremely important. It involves balancing the interests of an employer or client against those of a number of stakeholders. Often, professionals are able to accommodate the interests of both the organization and its various publics. By the same token, an organization may not be able to please all of its publics because there are differences in worldview.

Wal-Mart may please labor unions by paying for more employee benefits, but stockholders who believe the increased costs eat into their profits may object. Environmentalists may want to close a coal-burning power plant, but the employees and the local community may be the most avid supporters for keeping the plant open despite its pollution problems. Given competing agendas and issues, the public relations professional will need to look first to the needs of the organization and manage the inevitable conflicts that arise.

The Role of Public Relations in Managing Conflict

The influence of public relations on the course of a conflict can involve reducing conflict, as is often the case in crisis management. At other times, conflict is escalated for activist purposes, such as when antiabortion advocates not only picket health clinics but also assault clients, doctors, and nurses. Other strategies are less dramatic, such as oil industry advocates lobbying to lay a pipeline from Canada to the Gulf coast of Texas, striving to win approval over time from the public—and, ultimately, politicians.

Indeed, conflict management often occurs when a business or industry contends with government regulators or activist groups that seem determined to curtail operations through what the industry considers excessive safety or environmental standards. At the same time, both the regulatory body and the activists engage in their own public relations efforts to make their case against the company.

A good example is the regulation of dolphin parks in India. Amidst a handful of proposals to develop dolphin parks across India as a new, exotic form of entertainment, animal welfare advocates urged the Indian government to intercede. The Animal Welfare Board of India ruled that dolphin parks would violate the country's

Managing Conflict

In cases like the conflict between fast-food restaurants and the activists who are attempting to raise awareness about butchering practices, effective public relations tactics can mitigate the conflict.

1960 Prevention of Cruelty to Animals Act. Park promoters argued that their proposed projects would be educational and entertaining and would in no way inflict cruelty on the dolphins. Animal welfare activists pointed to a 1998 experience with the Dolphin City amusement park in which all the dolphins were dead within six months of their introduction to the park. One activist told the *New York Times*, "The Animal Welfare Board is not promulgating any new legislation. All it is doing is informing the states that [dolphin parks] are in violation of the existing laws of the land." Park proponents countered that they would look for legal ways to move their projects forward. Activists said they would fight any such attempts in court.

Professor Jae-Hwa Shin, at the University of Southern Mississippi, describes this dialogue between multiple parties as the "wrangle in the marketplace of ideas." And much like Olympic skiers striving on the slopes to represent their own interests, this wrangle is inevitable and perfectly acceptable, according to Shin. Sometimes, an organization is able to catch a conflict at an early stage and reduce damage to the organization. However, in other cases, an issue may smolder until it finally becomes a major fire. Cruise lines, like airlines, should be aware of potentially dangerous situations they could face well in advance of a crisis, however it seems they are often taken by surprise, unprepared. Dealing with problems early on is not only more efficient, it is also usually the morally right thing to do. The basic concepts of issue and risk management will be discussed shortly.

on the job

A MULTICULTURAL WORLD

Managing Conflict: Benetton Balances Humanitarian and Business Ideals

Benetton is an Italian clothing company known for its shocking advertisements in support of humanitarian causes. The strategy garners attention and substantial worldwide press coverage, but also holds the retailer to a higher standard of corporate behavior than other clothiers.

The controversial ad campaigns gain attention not only for Benetton but also for a social cause—racism, world hunger, and unemployment to name only a few. One highly publicized example was its 2011 "Unhate" campaign that showed digitally manipulated images of world leaders kissing.

So when Benetton was accused of being one of the brands manufactured in a Bangladesh factory that collapsed killing hundreds, the company faced an unusual problem. Could it be true that the legendary corporate do-gooder was supporting an unsafe sweatshop that paid its workers a minimum wage of $38 a month? Benetton denied the charge.

"In reference to the tragic news on the collapse of the building in Bangladesh, Benetton Group wants to clarify that none of the companies involved are suppliers to Benetton Group or any of its brands," Benetton tweeted the day of the collapse. But evidence quickly contradicted that claim. Clothing with Benetton labels was found in the rubble of the collapsed factory. Pictures of the clothing circulated instantly in the media and online. Benetton's Twitter account was silent for five days.

Benetton then tweeted, "A one-time order was completed and shipped out of one of the manufacturers involved several weeks prior to the accident. Since then, this subcontractor has been removed from our supplier list." The company had been working with a manufacturer named New Wave.

Labor activists criticized the company for profiting from the labor of poor people in a poor country. Scott Nova, executive director of the Worker Rights Consortium, an independent organization that monitors labor rights, told the *Huffington Post*, "If Benetton is serious about preventing future accidents they will sign a binding, enforceable agreement that requires them to pay for the repairs and renovations needed to make their factories safe. They have made no such commitment and given their track record of public dissembling since the collapse, people can be forgiven for not taking them at their word."

Benetton acknowledged its contradictory public statements but blamed the situation on the fact that the company contracts with more than 700 manufacturers in 120 countries. Furthermore, Benetton noted the order from the Bangladesh factory was relatively small—only 200,000 shirts.

Nonetheless, Benetton was faced with harsh criticism. Activists called the wages in Bangladesh "an act of cruelty." Benetton countered that a low wage was better than no wage and that the work provided a means for worker advancement, especially for women. Some companies believed the solution to the ongoing Bangladesh factory problems (there were four workplace catastrophes in quick succession in which workers were killed) was to move production to another country.

Benetton CEO Biagio Chiarolanza told *Huffington Post*, "It's not the solution to go outside from Bangladesh or to think in the future we can leave Bangladesh. I spent some period of my life in this part of the world, and I believe—I really believe—Benetton and other international brands can help these countries improve their condition. But we need a safe and happy working environment and we need to have better conditions."

Action taken by Benetton included getting the message out that it had ended its contract with the supplier months before the factory tragedy, working with the International Labor Organization (ILO) to improve working conditions, and setting up a relief fund for survivors of the collapse. Within weeks, the company released the news that it had signed

(continued)

a five-year Bangladesh Fire and Building Safety Agreement. The release quoted Chiarolanza, "The agreement resulted from a multi-stakeholder approach that involved global retailers and manufacturers, trade unions, the ILO as well as non-governmental organizations. From the beginning, we believed that only this type of collaborative approach could bring effective and sustainable change to the issues faced by the garment industry in Bangladesh."

Benetton weathered the initial criticism by striving to accommodate the demands of brand fans and labor activists. Labor leaders termed the agreement a "huge victory" and something that would "benefit each and every garment worker."

Benetton is known for its controversial social activist campaigns such as the 2011 Unhate ads.

Shirts with the Benetton label were found in the rubble of a collapsed Bangladesh garment factory.

Unfortunately, most conflict situations are not clear-cut in terms of an ideal solution. In many cases, public relations professionals will not be able to accommodate the concerns of an activist group or a particular public because of many other factors, including the survivability of the organization. KFC, for example, is not going out of the fried chicken business in response to People for the Ethical Treatment of Animals (PETA) picketing stores over treatment of chickens. In such cases, public relations professionals have to make tough calls and advocate strictly on behalf of their organization. How they decide what stand to take is the subject of the next section.

Public relations practitioners should understand the . . . challenges of public relations practice by identifying what constraints they have in their activities and recognizing that their professional qualifications are important assets.

Jae-Hwa Shin, University of Southern Mississippi

It Depends—A System for Managing Conflict

A public relations professional or team must determine the stance its organization will take toward each public or stakeholder involved in the conflict situation. Stance then determines strategy—what will be done and why. The stance-driven approach to public relations began with the discovery that virtually all practitioners share an unstated, informal approach to managing conflict and competition: "It depends."

In other words, the stance taken toward publics "depends" on many factors that cause the stance to change in response to changing circumstances. Simply put, the outstanding practitioner monitors for threats, assesses them, arrives at a stance for the organization, and then begins communication efforts from that stance.

Practitioners face a complex set of forces that must be monitored and taken into consideration. One approach is the "threat appraisal" model, which is shown in Figure 10.2. Essentially, a threat to an organization requires an assessment of the

Figure 10.2 Threat Appraisal Model

The public relations practitioner must consider both situational demands and organizational resources.

Source: Jin, Y., & Cameron, G. T. (2007). The effects of threat type and duration on public relations practitioner's cognitive, affective and conative responses to crisis situations. *Journal of Public Relations Research, 19*(3), 256.

demands that threat makes on the organization, as well as what resources are available to deal with the threat. An identified threat, for example, forces the public relations professional to consider two major factors. One is *organizational*. Do you have the knowledge, time, finances, and management commitment to combat the threat? The second is *situational*. How do you assess the severity of the threat to the organization? What effort is required from you? Is it a difficult situation with potential for long duration, or is it a relatively simple matter that can be solved fairly quickly? How much is uncertain about the facts or actual situation? Oftentimes, the public relations professional must base decisions on past experience and instinct.

An example of how the threat appraisal model is used in the real world is how McDonald's reacted when the mayor of Bogota, New Jersey, accused the restaurant chain of racism because it posted a billboard in Spanish to advertise its new iced coffee. He said the company was assuming local Latinos didn't speak English. McDonald's and its public relations firm, MWW Group, had to assess the threat to the company's reputation and how the media and the public (particularly the Hispanic public) would react to the charge of racism.

The appraisal indicated that a response was required, but at a localized level. It based its decision, in part, on researching the background and popularity of the mayor among Hispanics. It found that the mayor himself had distributed Spanish-language campaign materials in the past and that he was not particularly popular in the generally Democratic Hispanic community because he was a Republican.

McDonald's then prepared its store managers in the tri-state area to handle local media inquiries and also immediately sent backgrounders to editors and reporters about its long history of multicultural programs, including extensive annual scholarship grants to Hispanic students. Many media outlets referenced this information in stories about the controversial billboard, and McDonald's received generally positive coverage. Thus, the issue was short-lived and didn't snowball into a national controversy. Sales of iced coffee even increased 22 percent in the greater New York metro area.

It is important to note that organizations assess threat in different ways. Books and films about industries are an example. In the case of the documentary *Food Inc*, which criticized corporate farming, agricultural giant Monsanto developed a website (which it labeled a "fact site") and an employee blog to counter criticisms made in the film. Monsanto said the film demonized farmers and the agricultural system. The company said, "any factual errors in *Food, Inc.* regarding other companies are best addressed by those organizations themselves. It is our responsibility to set the record straight on the film's portrayal of Monsanto."

It Depends: Two Basic Principles

> When a public relations practitioner is involved in a crisis situation, external and long-term threats lead to the most severe consequences.
>
> *Yan Jin, University of Georgia*

The threat appraisal model, assessing the seriousness of the threat and the resources needed to combat it, is common in the practice of strategic public relations. The model illustrates the "it depends" approach, but there are two other principles that are important.

The first principle is that many factors determine the stance or position of an organization when it comes to dealing with conflict and perceived threats against the organization. The second principle is that the public

Figure 10.3 **Contingency Continuum**

This continuum from pure advocacy to pure accommodation forms the foundation for identifying the stance of an organization toward a given public at a given time.

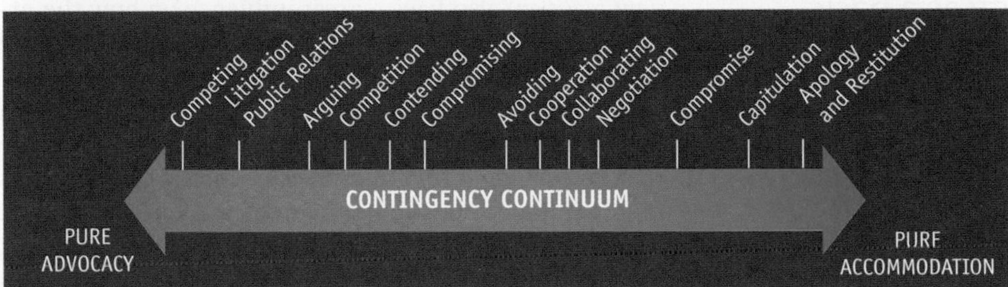

relations stance for dealing with a particular audience or public is dynamic; that is, it changes as events unfold. This is represented by a continuum of stances from pure advocacy to pure accommodation (see Figure 10.3). These two principles, which form the basis of what is called *contingency theory*, are discussed further in the next sections.

A Matrix of Contingency Factors

Through a series of contingency studies, researchers learned that professionals in public relations recognize dozens of forces and factors that can influence the stance on the continuum from advocacy to accommodation. The public relations approach chosen is contingent on the many factors that professionals must take into account when assessing a threat, although only a few factors will present themselves in most situations. Professionals and scholars thus do not need to memorize the 80+ factors found so far; they simply need to keep a watchful eye for what might move the public relations stance. The factors can be grouped into external factors:

- External threats
- Industry-specific environment
- General political/social environment
- External public's characteristics
- The issue under consideration

and internal factors:

- General corporate/organizational characteristics
- Characteristics of the public relations department
- Top management characteristics
- Internal threats
- Personality characteristics of internal, involved persons
- Relationship characteristics

A nationwide survey at the University of Missouri of 1,000 members of the Public Relations Society of America (PRSA) explored what variables affect the stance that public relations professionals take, ranging from more advocacy to more accommodation, with a public regarding an issue in order to accomplish organizational goals.

In times of uncertainty and danger, the organization reverts to denial, ritual, and rigidity and invokes its own version of reality as a basic defense against external evidence or attack.

Professor Astrid Kersten, LaRoche College

The survey found that the expertise and experience of the public relations professional play a major role in formulating the proper strategy for dealing with heated competition or a conflict. By the same token, the values and attitudes of top management (known as the *dominant coalition*) also have a great influence on how the organization responds to conflict and threats. Corporate culture also plays a major role.

In fact, Astrid Kersten of LaRoche College in Pittsburgh wrote in a *Public Relations Review* article that an organization's everyday culture and operations highly influence how organizations respond to conflict. She observes, however, that organizations often aren't very realistic in analyzing situations. She wrote, "Conflict and crisis often reinforces organizational dysfunction."

The Contingency Continuum

The matrix, or list of possible variables, that influences an organization's response is helpful in understanding inputs into the complex decision-making process. Depending on circumstances, the attitudes of top management, and the judgment of public relations professionals, such factors may move the organization toward or away from accommodation of a public.

As mentioned earlier, the range of response can be shown on a continuum from pure advocacy to pure accommodation (see Figure 10.3). Pure advocacy might be described as a hard-nosed stance of completely disagreeing or refuting the arguments, claims, or threats of a competitor or a group concerned about an issue. In pure advocacy the practitioner ignores the requests or demands of the contending public in favor of full-fledged support of your organization's position. Later in the chapter, for example, the conflict management of Pepsi, when it was claimed that used syringes were found in cans of its product, is examined. In this case, Pepsi took the stance that such claims were a hoax and stood 100 percent behind its product, resisting suggestions that a product recall was needed.

The other extreme of the continuum is pure accommodation. In this case, the organization agrees with its critics, changes its policies, makes restitution, and even makes a full public apology for its actions. A good example of pure accommodation is that of natural juice company Odwalla. In this case, after it was found that a problem in production caused food poisoning in customers, it immediately issued a product recall, offered to pay all medical expenses of the victims, and made a full apology to the public.

There are other stances along the continuum that an organization can take. Norfolk Southern railroad, for example, used litigation public relations to shift stockholder opinion concerning an offer to take over Conrail. Following a garment factory collapse that killed more than 1,100 people in Bangladesh, retailer Abercrombie & Fitch moved toward total accommodation of activist demands by signing a legally enforceable plan to improve factory safety in Bangladesh. Gap, on the other hand, took a place closer to the middle of the continuum. It announced the steps it already took to ensure workplace safety, but was not a signatory to the agreement with Abercrombie. Wal-Mart took a position of nearly pure advocacy (denial of a problem) when it denied knowledge that its garments were being manufactured in the collapsed factory, created a black list of Bangladesh manufacturers with which it would not do business, and said it would not sign on to the group agreement. See the Multicultural World box on page 279 for an examination of how Benetton addressed the Bangladesh crisis. Another part of the continuum is compromise; KFC improved conditions of chickens supplied to its stores as a result of complaints by the animal rights group PETA.

The key point about the continuum is that it identifies the stance of an organization toward a given public at a given time. It also shows the dynamism of public relations. In many cases, an organization will initially adopt a pure advocacy stance but, as the situation changes, new information comes to light, and public opinion shifts, the stance will change toward more accommodation. A similar continuum is used to portray how organizations respond to a crisis situation, which is discussed on pages 291–295.

The Conflict Management Life Cycle

To best understand the entire conflict management process, it helps to think of it as a life cycle of a problem or issue that professionals must track. Figure 10.4 shows the *Conflict Management Life Cycle*. The life cycle shows the "big picture" of how to manage a conflict. Strategic conflict management can be divided into four general phases, but keep in mind that the lines between the phases are not absolute and that some techniques overlap in actual practice. Furthermore, in the fast-moving world of public relations, busy practitioners may be actively managing different competitive situations as well as conflicts in each of the four phases simultaneously. To better understand the conflict management life cycle, each phase will be briefly explained.

Proactive Phase

The proactive phase includes activities and thought processes that can prevent a conflict from arising or getting out of hand. The first step in the phase is *environmental scanning*—the constant reading, listening, and watching of current affairs with an eye

Figure 10.4 **Conflict Management Life Cycle**

The cycle of conflict depicts the four phases in conflict management experienced by public relations professionals. Typically, events move through time from left to right along the life cycle. At the end of the cycle, the process begins all over again on the left side of the cycle.

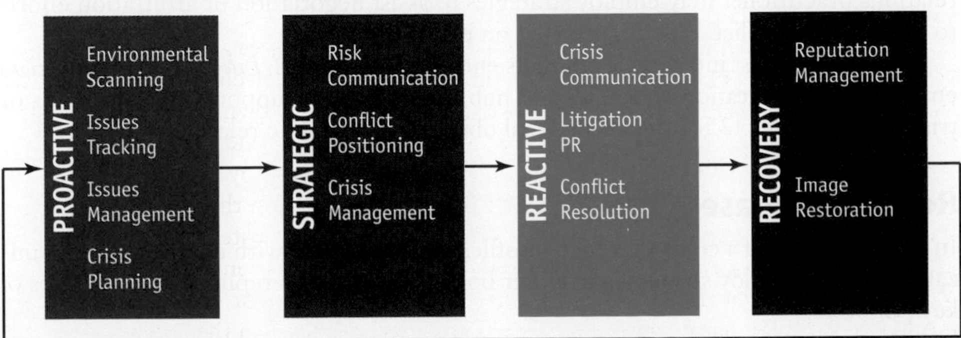

to the organization's interests. As issues emerge, *issues tracking* becomes more focused and systematic through processes such as the daily collection of news stories. *Issues management* occurs when the organization makes behavioral changes or creates strategic plans in ways that address the emerging issue.

In the proactive phase, well-run organizations will also develop a general *crisis plan* as a first step in preparing for the worst—an issue or an event that has escalated to crisis proportions. Also in the proactive phase, an organization can use a strategy called stealing thunder to disclose its crisis before it is discovered by the media or other interested parties. Studies show that stealing thunder enhances credibility of the organization and decreases the perceived severity of the problem. When an organization self-discloses a problem or issue it has two major advantages—stronger credibility is created with stakeholders and the organization has the opportunity to frame the issue rather than reacting to someone else's framing.

Strategic Phase

In the strategic phase, an issue that has become an emerging conflict is identified as needing concerted action by the public relations professional.

Three broad strategies take place in this phase. Through *risk communication*, dangers or threats to people or organizations are conveyed to forestall personal injury, health problems, and environmental damage. This risk communication continues so long as the risk exists or until the risk escalates into a crisis. *Conflict-positioning* strategies enable the organization to position itself favorably in anticipation of actions such as litigation, boycott, adverse legislation, elections, or similar events that will play out in "the court of public opinion." To be prepared for the worst outcome—that is, an issue that resists risk communication efforts and becomes a conflict of crisis proportions—a specific *crisis management plan* is developed for that particular issue.

Reactive Phase

Once the issue or imminent conflict reaches a critical level of impact on the organization, the public relations professional must react to events in the external communication environment as they unfold.

Crisis communications include the implementation of the crisis management plan as well as the hectic, 24/7 efforts to meet the needs of publics such as disaster victims, employees, government officials, and the media. When conflict has emerged but is not careening out of control, *conflict resolution* techniques are used to bring a heated conflict, such as collapsed salary negotiations, to a favorable resolution. The public relations practitioner may employ strategies to assist negotiation or arbitration efforts to resolve the conflict. (See Figure 10.4 on page 285.)

Often, the most intractable conflicts end up in the courts. *Litigation public relations* employs communication strategies and publicity efforts in support of legal actions or trials (see Chapter 12 for details on legal obligations in public relations).

Recovery Phase

In the aftermath of a crisis or a high-profile, heated conflict with a public, the organization should employ strategies to either bolster or repair its reputation in the eyes of key publics.

Reputation management includes systematic research to learn the state of the organization's reputation and then take steps to improve it. As events and conflicts occur, the company responds with actions and communication about those actions. Poorly managed issues, excessive risk imposed on others, and callous responses to a crisis damage an organization's reputation. When this damage is extreme, *image restoration* strategies can help, provided they include genuine change by the organization.

Processes for Managing the Life Cycle

Not only do public relations practitioners face the challenge of addressing different conflicts in different phases of the life cycle, but no sooner do they deal with a conflict than the cyclical process starts over again for that very same issue. Environmental scanning is resumed to ensure that the conflict does not reemerge as an issue. Although challenging, conflict management is not impossible. Systematic processes described in the next sections of this chapter provide guidance and structure for this highly rewarding role played by public relations professionals in managing competition and conflict. Those processes include (1) issues management, (2) risk communication, (3) crisis management, (4) and reputation management.

Issues Management

Essentially, *issues management* is a proactive and systematic approach to (1) predict problems, (2) anticipate threats, (3) minimize surprises, (4) resolve issues, and (5) prevent crises. Martha Lauzen, a professor at San Diego State University, says that effective issues management requires two-way communications, formal environmental scanning, and active sense-making strategies.

Another definition of issues management has been formulated by Coates, Jarratt, and Heinz in their book *Issues Management: How You Can Plan, Organize, and Manage for the Future.* They say, "Issues management is the organized activity of identifying emerging trends, concerns, or issues likely to affect an organization in the next few years and developing a wider and more positive range of organizational responses toward the future."

The basic idea behind issues management is *proactive planning.* Philip Gaunt and Jeff Ollenburger, writing in *Public Relations Review*, say, "Issues management is proactive in that it tries to identify issues and influence decisions regarding them before they have a detrimental effect on a corporation." See the Insights box on page 288 for a matrix on how to evaluate an issue's importance.

Gaunt and Ollenburger contrast this approach with crisis management, which is essentially reactive in nature. They note, "Crisis management tends to be more reactive, dealing with an issue after it becomes public knowledge and affects the company." In other words, active planning and prevention through issues management can often mean the difference between a noncrisis and a crisis, or, as one practitioner put it, the difference between little or no news coverage and a page-one headline. This point is particularly relevant because studies have shown that the majority of organizational crises are self-inflicted, because management ignored early warning signs.

The issue of the looting of antiquities from Cambodia during its 20-year civil war simmered for some time before it finally broke into the headlines after the Metropolitan Museum of Art in New York agreed to return two stolen statues to the Cambodian government. Suddenly, museums in Denver, Cleveland, and Pasadena that held

Cambodian statues in their collections were faced with pressure from news coverage and Cambodian officials to return the artifacts.

Similarly, companies like Benetton and H&M faced harsh criticism from consumer activists following a garment factory fire that killed 112 in Bangladesh in November 2012. With an April 2013 factory collapse that took more than 1,100 workers' lives, the death toll in Bangladesh garment factories exceeded 1,800 since 2005.

All of the publicity and public outrage might have been avoided if museum curators and retail clothiers had paid attention to the concept of issues management.

Public relations counselors W. Howard Chase and Barrie L. Jones were among the first practitioners to specialize in issues management. They defined the process as consisting of five basic steps: (1) issue identification, (2) issue analysis, (3) strategy options, (4) an action plan, and (5) the evaluation of results. The following is a brief description of how these steps could have been used by the garment industry.

Strategy Options

If the company decides that the emerging issue is potentially damaging, the next step is to consider what to do about it. One option might be to set higher standards for foreign contractors seeking the company's business. Another option: Work with human

on the job

INSIGHTS

The Issues Management Process

Public relations counselors W. Howard Chase and Barrie L. Jones were among the first practitioners to specialize in issues management. They defined the process as consisting of five basic steps:

Step 1. Issue Identification
Organizations should track the alternative press, mainstream media, online chat groups, and the newsletters of activist groups to learn which issues and concerns are being discussed. Of particular importance is establishing a trend line of coverage.

Step 2. Issue Analysis
Once an emerging issue has been identified, the next step is to assess its potential impact on and threat to the organization. Another consideration is to determine whether the organization is vulnerable on the issue.

Step 3. Strategy Options
If the company decides that the emerging issue is potentially damaging, it must then consider what to do about it. The pros and cons of each option are weighed against what is most practical and economical for the company.

Step 4. Action Plan
Once a specific policy (stance) has been decided on, the fourth step is to communicate it to all interested publics.

Step 5. Evaluation
With the new policy in place and communicated, the final step is to evaluate the results. Has news coverage been positive? Is the company being positioned as an industry leader? Have public perceptions of the company and the industry improved? If the company has acted soon enough, perhaps the greatest measurement of success is avoiding the media coverage that occurs when a problem becomes a crisis.

rights groups to monitor possible violations in foreign factories that produce the company's products. A third option might be to establish a new policy that would ensure that Third World workers' work environment is safe. The pros and cons of each option are weighed against what is most practical and economical for the company.

Action Plan

Once a specific policy has been decided on, the fourth step is to communicate it to all interested publics. These may include consumers, the U.S. Department of Labor, labor unions and worker activist groups, company employees, and the financial community. The action may be an opportunity to use the new policy as a marketing tool among consumers who make buying decisions based on a company's level of social responsibility.

Evaluation

With the new policy in place and communicated, the final step is to evaluate the results. Has news coverage been positive? Have activist groups called off product boycotts? Have the working conditions in the factories improved? Is the company being positioned as an industry leader? Have public perceptions of the company and the industry improved? If the company has acted soon enough, perhaps the greatest measurement of success is having avoided the media coverage that occurs if the problem becomes a crisis.

Conflict Positioning and Risk Communication

Following issues management is conflict positioning. Any verbal or written exchange that attempts to communicate information that positions the organization favorably regarding competition or an anticipated conflict is called *conflict positioning*. Ideally, the public relations professional is not only communicating in a way that positions the organization favorably in the face of competition and imminent conflict, but is also influencing the actual behavior of the organization favorably. For example, facing enormous financial losses and the need to lay off thousands of employees, General Motors announced that it was freezing executive salaries. Doing so reduced the level of criticism for the employee layoffs that followed.

Often, a public relations professional can engage in communication that may reduce risk for affected publics and for his or her employer. Communication regarding risk to public health and safety and the environment are particularly important roles for public relations professionals. (See Chapter 21, "Public Relations in Non-Profit, Health, and Education Sectors," for more on health communication as an important risk communication field in public relations.) The risk may be naturally occurring, such as undertows and riptides on beaches that require warning signs and flyers in hotel rooms. Or the risk may be associated with a product, such as over-the-counter drugs or a baby crib.

Organizations, including large corporations, increasingly engage in risk communication to inform the public of risks such as those surrounding food products, chemical spills, radioactive waste disposal, or the placement of drug-abuse treatment centers or halfway houses in neighborhoods. These issues deserve public notice in fairness to the general populace. Such risks may also result in expensive lawsuits, restrictive legislation, consumer boycotts, and public debate if organizations fail to disclose potential hazards. As is often the case, doing the right thing in conflict management is also the least disruptive to the offending organization in the long run.

Product recalls, in particular, require doing the "right thing." Toy manufacturers often recall products because it is discovered that some part of the toy may break off and cause a choking hazard for children. However some manufacturers are *forced* to recall products. The Food and Drug Administration (FDA) threatened a mandatory recall of pet treats because traces of salmonella were found on the treats. The mere threat from the FDA nudged the manufacturer to "voluntarily" withdraw the products.

Risk communication can minimize adverse effects on publics, but it also often reduces risk—of lawsuits, of damaged morale in the organization, and of diminished reputation—to the organization itself. When risk communication fails, however, the organization often faces a crisis.

Variables Affecting Risk Perceptions

Risk communication researchers have identified several variables that affect public perceptions:

- Risks voluntarily taken tend to be accepted. Smokers have more control over their health situation, for example, than airline passengers do over their safety.
- The more complex a situation, the higher the perception of risk. Disposal of radioactive wastes is more difficult to understand than the dangers of texting while driving.
- Familiarity breeds confidence. If the public understands the problem and its factors, it perceives less risk.
- Perception of risk increases when the messages of experts conflict.
- The severity of consequences affects risk perceptions. There is a difference between having a stomachache and getting cancer.

Suzanne Zoda, writing on risk communication in *Communication World*, gives some suggestions to communicators:

- Begin early and initiate a dialogue with publics that might be affected. Do not wait until the opposition marshals its forces. Vital to establishing trust is early contact with anyone who may be concerned or affected.
- Actively solicit and identify people's concerns. Informal discussions, surveys, interviews, and focus groups are effective in evaluating issues and identifying outrage factors.
- Recognize the public as a legitimate partner in the process. Engage interested groups in two-way communication and involve key opinion leaders.
- Address issues of concern, even if they do not directly pertain to the project.
- Anticipate and prepare for hostility. To defuse a situation, use a conflict resolution approach. Identify areas of agreement and work toward common ground.
- Understand the needs of the news media. Provide accurate, timely information and respond promptly to requests.
- Always be honest, even when it hurts.

Crisis Management

In public relations, high-profile events such as accidents, terrorist attacks, disease pandemics, and natural disasters can dwarf even the best conflict positioning and risk management strategies. This is when crisis management takes over. The conflict management process, which includes ongoing issues management and risk communication efforts, is severely tested in crisis situations in which a high degree of uncertainty exists.

Unfortunately, even the most thoughtfully designed conflict management process cannot have a plan in place for every situation. Sometimes, in spite of risk communication to prevent an issue from becoming a major problem, that issue grows into a crisis right before the professional's eyes. At such times, verifiable information about what is happening or has happened may be lacking. This causes people to become more active seekers of information and, as research suggests, more dependent on the media for information to satisfy the human desire for closure.

A crisis situation, in other words, puts a great deal of pressure on organizations to respond with accurate, complete information as quickly as possible. How an organization responds in the first 24 hours, experts say, often determines whether the situation remains an "incident" or becomes a full-blown crisis.

What Is a Crisis?

Kathleen Fearn-Banks, in her book *Crisis Communications: A Casebook Approach*, writes, "A crisis is a major occurrence with a potentially negative outcome affecting the organization, company, or industry, as well as its publics, products, services, or good name."

In other words, an organizational crisis can constitute any number of situations. A *PRWeek* article makes the point:

> Imagine one of these scenarios happening to your company: a product recall; a plane crash; a very public sexual harassment suit; a gunman holding hostages in your office; an *E. coli* bacteria contamination scare; a market crash, along with the worth of your company stock; a labor union strike; a hospital malpractice suit...

Often, management tends to minimize or deny there's a crisis. However, there is a crisis if the organization's stakeholders—customers, vendors, employees, or even local community leaders—perceive the situation to be a crisis. Airline manufacturer Boeing said its new 787 aircraft was no more trouble-prone than any other new airliner. But when Japan and All Nippon Airlines grounded the twenty-four 787s in their fleets, the problem could no longer be denied. There were problems with the planes' lithium-ion batteries, including catching fire. Eventually the U.S. Federal Aviation Administration grounded all 787s and Boeing set to work to identify and rectify the problem. Crises are not always unexpected. In 2011, the Institute for Crisis Management (www.crisisexperts.com) found that only 39 percent of business crises are unexpected. And 16 percent are what the institute calls "smoldering" crises, in which an organization is aware of a potential business disruption long before the public finds out about it. The study also found that management—or in some cases, mismanagement—causes 50 percent of the crises. Employees accounted for another 32 percent of the crises. In fact, a study by Weber Shandwick public relations with KRC Research found that the top three triggers for a crisis are (1) financial irregularities, (2) unethical behavior, and (3) executive misconduct.

A Lack of Crisis Planning

A study, by Steven Fink, found that 89 percent of the chief executive officers of Fortune 500 companies reported that a business crisis was almost inevitable; however, 50 percent admitted that they did not have a crisis management plan.

This situation has caused Kenneth Myers, a crisis consultant, to write, "If economics is the dismal science, then contingency planning is the abysmal science." As academics Donald Chisholm and Martin Landry have noted, "When people believe that because nothing has gone wrong, nothing will go wrong, they court disaster. There is noise in every system and every design. If this fact is ignored, nature soon reminds us of our folly."

> A quick response is an active response because it tries to fill the vacuum with facts. A slow response allows others to fill the vacuum with speculation and misinformation. But others could be ill-informed or could use the opportunity to attack the organization.
>
> *Timothy Coombs, author of* Ongoing Crisis Communications: Planning, Managing, and Responding

Many "smoldering" crises could be prevented if professionals used more environmental scanning and issues management leading to the development of a strategic management plan. A common crisis planning technique is rating both the "probability" of a particular crisis and its "impact" on the organization. A fire at a Mattel toy factory, for example, would probably receive a "2" rating for probability, and a similar score for impact because the company has multiple suppliers. On the other hand, the probability of unsafe products might be a "3" but rank as a "5" in terms of impact on the company because public trust would be eroded and sales would drop.

on the job

SOCIAL MEDIA IN ACTION

Social Media Plays Crucial Role after Tornado

A crisis caused by nature can come up suddenly and without warning. That was the case when a tornado hit the world headquarters of Spirit AeroSystems in Wichita, Kansas. The strong winds tore up the roof, damaged equipment, and knocked out the company's IT Server that ordinarily would be used in a crisis to update the media and the public on the situation.

The Plan

An AeroSystems team, under the direction of the VP of communications, immediately switched to a communication plan that relied heavily on social media to get messages and updates out quickly to workers, investors, financial markets, customers, and the public. The following social media were used:

Twitter: The team used Twitter to communicate with employees, investment banks, and the news media. One tweet: "Spirit is suspending operations due to damage—employees should not report to work tomorrow unless called. Grateful all are accounted for."

Flickr: To counter a possible drop in stock price, the team chartered a

The Spirit AeroSystems manufacturing building was destroyed in a 2012 Wichita, Kansas, tornado.

helicopter and hired a photographer to take pictures of the tornado damage. The photos were then posted on the company's Flickr site.

YouTube: Spirit's videographers made two- and three-minute videos for stakeholders, updating them on the recovery every 24 hours.

Gmail and Google: The communications team used Gmail to tell stakeholders about media briefings and respond to inquiries. Google Docs hosted employee FAQs and posts of return-to-work information and instructions for managers.

In addition, the company conducted its first press briefings to distribute employee safety, reporting, and time-keeping information just 12 hours after the tornado hit. By mid-week, Spirit had conducted two site tours of the damage for the news media and government officials, held customer conference calls, and sent employees direct e-mails to keep them updated.

The Results

- One week after the disaster, 11,000 employees returned to work. Social media and mass media messages kept absenteeism to a minimum.
- The stock price went down just 1 percent, partly as a result of a proactive information campaign.
- Spirit's largest customers publicly complimented the company for its rapid recovery.
- The traditional media praised the company for its rapid communication and transparency.
- *Ragan's PR Daily* awarded the company its annual social media prize in "best crisis communications" for 2012.

How to Communicate during a Crisis

Many professionals and books offer good checklists on what to do during a crisis. Figure 10.5 offers a compilation of good suggestions:

Strategies for Responding to Crises

The chart in Figure 10.5 offers sound, practical advice, but recent research has shown that organizations don't respond to a crisis in the same way. Indeed, Timothy Coombs postulates that an organization's response may vary on a continuum from defensive to accommodative, which is similar to the contingency continuum explained on page 284. Here is Coombs's list of crisis communication strategies that an organization may use:

- **Attack the accuser.** The party that claims a crisis exists is confronted and its logic and facts are faulted. Sometimes a lawsuit is threatened.
- **Denial.** The organization explains that there is no crisis.
- **Excuse.** The organization minimizes its responsibility for the crisis. Any intention to do harm is denied, and the organization says that it had no control over the events that led to the crisis. This strategy is often used when there is a natural disaster or product tampering.

Figure 10.5 **How to Communicate in a Crisis**

Many professionals offer good advice on what to do during a crisis. Here's a compilation of good suggestions.

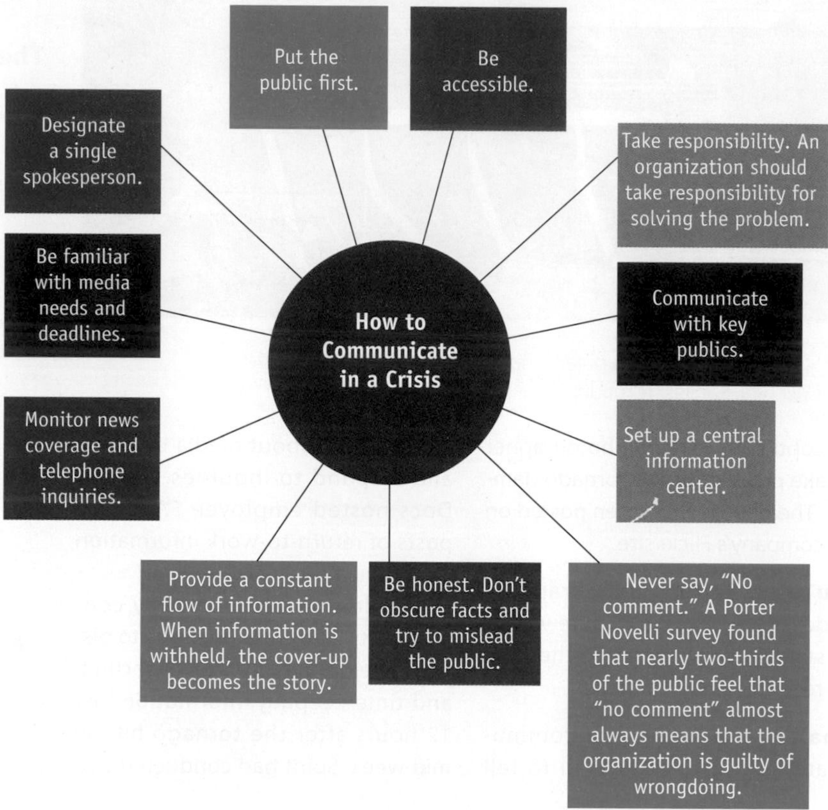

- **Justification.** Crisis is minimized with a statement that no serious damage or injuries resulted. Sometimes, the blame is shifted to the victims, as in the case of the iPhone 4. Consumers complained that when held a certain way their new iPhones had problems with reception. Initially, Apple's response was to tell consumers they were holding the phone wrong.
- **Ingratiation.** Actions are taken to appease the publics involved. Consumers who complain are given coupons, or the organization makes a donation to a charitable organization. Burlington Industries, for example, gave a large donation to the Humane Society after the discovery that it had imported coats from China with fur collars containing dog fur instead of coyote fur.
- **Corrective action.** Steps are taken to repair the damage from the crisis and to prevent it from happening again.
- **Full apology.** The organization takes responsibility and asks forgiveness. Some compensation of money or aid is often included.

The Coombs typology gives options for crisis communication management that depend on the situation and the stance taken by the organization. He notes that organizations do have to consider more accommodative strategies (ingratiation, corrective action, full apology) if defensive strategies (attack accuser, denial, excuse) are not effective. The more accommodative strategies not only meet immediate crisis communication demands but can help subsequently in repairing an organization's reputation or restoring previous sales levels. He says, "Accommodative strategies emphasize image repair, which is what is needed as image damage worsens. Defensive strategies, such as denial or minimizing, logically become less effective as organizations are viewed as more responsible for the crisis."

Often, however, an organization doesn't adopt an accommodative strategy because of corporate culture and other constraints included in the contingency theory of the conflict management matrix. Organizations do not, and sometimes cannot, engage in two-way communication and accommodative strategies when confronted with a crisis or conflict with a given public. Some variables proscribing accommodation, according to Cameron, include: (1) management's moral conviction that the public is wrong; (2) moral neutrality when two contending publics want the organization to take sides on a policy issue; (3) legal constraints; (4) regulatory constraints such as the FTC or SEC; (5) prohibition by senior management against an accommodative stance; and (6) possible conflict between departments of the organization on what strategies to adopt.

In some cases, the contingency theory contends that the ideal of mutual understanding and accommodation doesn't occur because both sides have staked out highly rigid positions and are not willing to compromise their strong moral positions. For example, it is unlikely that the pro-life and pro-choice forces will ever achieve mutual understanding and accommodation. At other times, conflict is a natural state between competing interests, such as oil interests seeking offshore exploration and environmental groups seeking to block that exploration. Frequently, one's stance and strategies for conflict management entail assessment and balancing of many factors.

It is important to emphasize that not all successful crisis communication strategies are accommodative. Pepsi-Cola was able to mount an effective defensive crisis communication strategy and avoid a recall when a hoax of nationwide proportions created an intense but short-lived crisis for the soft-drink company.

Reputation Management

Reputation is defined as the collective representation of an organization's past performance that describes the firm's ability to deliver valued outcomes to multiple stakeholders. Put in plain terms, reputation is the track record of an organization in the public's mind.

Public relations scholar Lisa Lyon makes the point that reputation, unlike corporate image, is owned by the public. Reputation isn't formed by packaging or slogans. Rather, a good reputation is created and destroyed by everything an organization does, from the way it manages employees to the way it handles conflicts with outside constituents.

The Three Foundations of Reputation

Reputation scholars offer three foundations of reputation: (1) economic performance, (2) social responsiveness, and (3) the ability to deliver valuable outcomes to stakeholders. Public relations plays a role in all three foundations, but professionals who manage conflict effectively will especially enhance the latter two foundations of reputation. The social responsiveness of an organization results from careful issue tracking and effective positioning of the organization. It is further enhanced when risk communication is compelling and persuasive. The ability to make valuable contributions to stakeholders who depend on the organization results in part from fending off threats to the organization that would impair its mission.

Research techniques called *reputation audits* can be used to assess and monitor an organization's reputation. These can be as basic as *Fortune* magazine's list of "Most Admired Companies" (money.cnn.com/magazines/fortune/most-admired/) to rigorous global reputation measures, such as the Reputation Quotient offered by the Reputation Institute (www.reputationinstitute.com) in conjunction with Harris Interactive. Of particular interest to public relations professionals is the Media Reputation Index (MRI), which measures the effects of media coverage on corporate reputations. Working with Delahaye Medialink, the project documents the important role of media in reputation management. This relationship is depicted in Figure 10.6.

In addition to tracking and dealing proactively with issues, conveying risks to publics, and managing crises as they arise, public relations practitioners also will be faced with the need to apologize when all efforts to manage conflict have fallen short. The future trust and credibility of the organization are at stake in how well this recovery phase of conflict management is handled.

The frequent platitude in post-crisis communication is that practitioners should acknowledge failings, apologize, and then put the events in the past as quickly as possible. Warren Buffett, in an interview with CNBC about how a company should deal with a crisis, offered this succinct variation on the stealing thunder strategy: "Get it right; Get it fast; Get it out; and Get it over." Of course, such an approach works best when one has a reputation for integrity and vast charitable generosity such as Mr. Buffett enjoys. What is clear, regardless of track record, is that public relations professionals earn respect by overcoming management's human inclination to obfuscate and stonewall. Stealing thunder rather than letting media break the news does frequently work to advantage.

Get it right;
Get it fast;
Get it out; and
Get it over.

Warren Buffett, CEO of Berkshire Hathaway

However, Lyon has found that apology is not always effective because of the hypocrisy factor. When an organization has a questionable track record (i.e., a bad reputation), the apology may be viewed as insincere and hypocritical. Coombs suggests a relational approach, which assumes that crises are episodes within a larger stakeholder–organization relationship. Applying the contingency theory, considering how stakeholders perceive the situation can help communicators determine which strategy is best to rebuild the stakeholder–organization relationship and restore the organization's reputation.

Image Restoration

Reputation repair and recovery is a long-term process, and the fourth phase in the conflict management life cycle is called the recovery phase. Research by Burson-Marsteller public relations, for example, found that it takes about three years for an organization to recover from a crisis that damaged its reputation. A survey of 685 business influentials also found that quickly disclosing the details of a scandal or

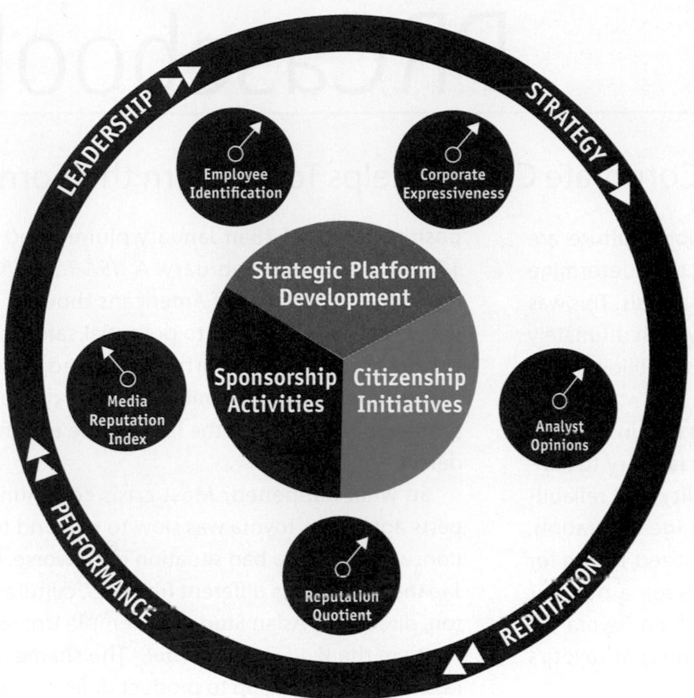

Figure 10.6 The Role of Media in Reputation Management

This diagram shows many of the forces affecting corporate reputation, most notably, how media coverage and performance of an organization impact its reputation and, in return, how reputation influences the health of the organization.

corporate misstep should be management's number-one strategy as it begins the process of restoring its reputation.

Other strategies used by executives to recover reputation are, in descending order, (1) make progress/recovery visible, (2) analyze what went wrong, (3) improve governance structure, (4) make the CEO and leadership accessible to the media, (5) fire employees involved in the problem, (6) commit to high corporate citizenship standards, (7) carefully review ethics policies, (8) hire outside auditors for internal audits, and (9) issue an apology from the CEO.

Professor William Benoit of Ohio State University offers a more academic model, with five general strategies for image restoration and a number of substrategies, adding to the options available to the public relations professional when the worst of a crisis has passed:

1. Denial
   - Simple denial—Your organization did not do what it is accused of.
   - Shift the blame—Someone else did it.
2. Evade responsibility
   - Provocation—Your organization was provoked.
   - Defeasibility—Your organization was unable to avoid its actions.
   - Accident—The bad events were an accident.
   - Good intentions—Good intentions went awry.

PRCasebook

Changing Corporate Culture Helps Toyota Turn the Corner

Corporate culture, and even a nation's culture, are among the important variables that determine how an organization responds to a crisis. This was clearly illustrated in the case of Toyota, which ultimately had to recall 9 million cars, including 3.2 million in the United States, because of safety defects.

The company had its first annual net loss in 60 years in 2009. And in a matter of weeks from January to February 2010, Toyota's reputation for quality and reliability hit rock bottom when media coverage saturation, the blogosphere, and politicians all criticized Toyota for not telling consumers that there had been a number of incidents in which the gas pedal stuck on Toyota vehicles. A poll by YouGov Brandindex found that Toyota's positive rating of 28 in January plummeted to a minus 17.1 rating by mid-February. A *USA Today*/Gallup poll found that 55 percent of Americans thought Toyota had failed to respond quickly to potential safety defects. The U.S. Transportation Department agreed, ultimately fining the company $16.4 million for not disclosing safety problems earlier. It was the largest fine ever for a vehicle defect.

PRWeek produced an extensive feature about Toyota's communications plan and its comeback.

So what happened? Most crisis communication experts agree that Toyota was slow to respond to the situation, which made a bad situation even worse. In addition, Japanese culture is different from U.S. culture. Jeff Kingston, director of Asian Studies at Temple University Japan, wrote in the *Wall Street Journal*, "The shame and embarrassment of owning up to product defects in a nation obsessed with craftsmanship and quality raises the bar on disclosure and assuming responsibility. And a high status company like Toyota has much to lose since its corporate face is at stake."

It was in this cultural environment that the president of Toyota, Akio Toyoda, finally gave a news conference a month after the recall had dominated most of the American and European media. The classic approach in crisis communication, if the company is at fault, is to immediately apologize, but Toyoda failed to meet this criterion because he made an apology late in the game and didn't actually take responsibility for the problem. Furthermore, at the news conference Toyoda only read a statement and refused to answer reporter questions. Members of the international press reacted angrily.

As if this wasn't enough, after the recall and heavy fines Toyota faced more problems, though not of its own making. In 2011 an earthquake and tsunami damaged its manufacturing plants in Japan.

Fast-forward to 2013. Toyota once again was the top automaker in the world. In fall 2012, Toyota introduced a new campaign with the slogan, "Let's Go Places," which replaced the "Moving Forward" tagline that had been in place since 2004. And the company embraced a new way of thinking and communicating. VP of marketing Jack Hollis told *PRWeek*, "In my heart of hearts, I believe we have to get away from words such as consumer and customer. We're evolving and the message needs to talk to guests. And when you talk to guests, you talk to them differently than consumers."

Toyota is now striving to interact with its "guests." The company encouraged brand fans to post photos of themselves on Twitter or Instagram with the hashtag #wishgranted. A winner was selected to be featured in the Toyota 2013 Super Bowl commercial. And every month Toyota hosts activities aimed at getting consumers to tell the company what "Let's Go Places" means to them.

Julie Hamp became chief communication officer for Toyota, North America, in 2012. She told *PRWeek* that the communications team was focusing on three themes: storytelling, thought leadership, and field communications. In an attempt to create a more open and transparent communications culture, Toyota is embracing not only traditional media, but also digital and social media. VP Hollis told *PRWeek* that integration of communications was the new key. "It's about trying to equalize all of them and leverage all three pieces, earned, owned, and shared, as well as paid."

The shift in communications culture seemed to help the automaker. Toyota was the best-selling automaker worldwide in 2012 and remained on top as of the first quarter of 2013, beating GM and Volkswagen. "Toyota will probably keep the top spot this year," Kentaro Hayashi, an analyst at Tachibana Securities Co., told *Bloomberg*.

3. Reduce offensiveness
   - Bolstering—Refer to the organization's clean record and good reputation.
   - Minimization—Reduce the magnitude of negative feelings.
   - Differentiation—Distinguish the act from other similar, but more offensive, acts.
   - Transcendence—Justify the act by placing it in a more favorable context.
   - Attack the accuser—Reduce the credibility of the accusations.
   - Compensation—Reduce the perceived severity of the injury.
4. Corrective action—Ensure the prevention or correction of the action.
5. Mortification—Offer a profuse apology.

Benoit's typology for image restoration is somewhat similar to Coombs's list on pages 293–294 about how organizations should respond to a crisis. Both scholars outline a response continuum from defensive (denial and evasion) to accommodation (corrective action and apology).

The image restoration strategy that an organization chooses depends a great deal on the situation, or on what has already been described as the "It depends" concept. If an organization is truly innocent, a simple denial and presentation of the facts is a good strategy. However, not many situations are clear-cut. Consequently, a more common strategy is acknowledging the issue, but making it clear that the situation was an accident or the result of a decision with unintended consequences. Benoit calls this the *strategy of evading responsibility*. Benoit lists six response strategies for *reducing offensiveness*—all the way from bolstering by telling the public about the organization's good record to compensating the victims. Ultimately, the most accommodative response is a complete apology from the organization to the public and its various stakeholders.

The Benoit and Coombs continuums give a tool chest of possible strategies for dealing with a crisis or beginning image restoration, but it should be noted that a strategy or a combination of strategies may not necessarily restore reputation. A great deal depends on the perceptions of the public and other stakeholders. Do they find the explanation credible? Do they believe the organization is telling the truth? Do they think the organization is acting in the public interest? In many cases, an organization may start out with a defensive strategy, only to find that the situation ultimately demands corrective action or an apology before its reputation can be restored.

Déjà Vu—All Over Again

Empirical evidence from Benoit's work is ongoing, but it appears that image restoration can be an effective final stage in the conflict management process. But to paraphrase Yogi Berra, conflict management is like déjà vu all over again. The best organizations, led by the best public relations professionals, will strive to improve their performance by starting once again along the left side of the conflict management life cycle on page 285 with tasks such as environmental scanning and issues tracking. Issues that are deemed important receive attention for crisis planning and risk communication. When preventive measures fail, the crisis must be handled with the best interests of all parties held in a delicate balance. Reputation then must be given due attention. At all times, the goal is to change organizational behavior in ways that minimize damaging conflict, for the sake of not only the organization, but also its many stakeholders.

Indeed, the true value of public relations and the highest professionalism require that students today also embrace their roles as managers of competition and conflict. Outstanding and successful public relations professionals must serve as more than communication technicians carrying out the tactics of organizing events, writing news releases, handling news conferences, and pitching stories to journalists. They also must take on the responsibilities of managing conflict and weathering the inevitable crises that all organizations face at one time or another.

Summary

Strategic Conflict Management

- By defining public relations as strategic management of competition and conflict, a fresh and vigorous approach to public relations is envisioned. Public relations is positioned to earn influence within organizations by focusing on achieving objectives.

The Role of Public Relations in Managing Conflict

- Some of the most crucial roles played by public relations professionals involve the strategic management of conflict. The contingency theory argues for a dynamic and multifaceted approach to dealing with conflict in the field.

The Conflict Management Life Cycle

- Strategic conflict management can be broadly divided into four phases, with specific techniques and functions falling into each phase. The life cycle emphasizes that conflict management is ongoing and cyclical in nature.

Issues Management

- Issues management is a proactive and systematic approach to predicting problems, anticipating threats, minimizing surprises, resolving issues, and preventing crises. The five steps in the issues management process are issue identification, issue analysis, strategy options, an action plan, and the evaluation of results.

Conflict Positioning and Risk Communication

- Risk communication attempts to convey information regarding risk to public health and safety and the environment. It involves more than the dissemination of accurate information. The communicator must begin early, identify and address the public's concerns, recognize the public as a legitimate partner, anticipate hostility, respond to the needs of the news media, and always be honest.

Crisis Management

- The communications process is severely tested in crisis situations, which can take many forms. A common problem is the lack of crisis management plans even when a crisis is "smoldering."

Reputation Management

- One of an organization's most valuable assets is its reputation. This asset is impacted by how the organization deals with conflict, particularly those crises that generate significant media attention. Using research to monitor reputation and making realistic responses after crises have passed can minimize damage to an organization's reputation. More important, returning to the proactive phase of conflict management to improve organizational performance will ultimately improve the organization's reputation.

Case Activity Unlikely Coalitions Fight New York over Soda Ban

New York Mayor Michael Bloomberg railed against sugary soft drinks and the New York City board of health banned large servings. A New York Supreme Court Justice later invalidated the regulation. The city government faced unlikely foes in this case.

Hispanic and African American civil rights groups, health advocacy organizations, and small businesses opposed the ban. Some filed briefs to support overturning the ban. They claimed it was discriminatory, paternalistic, and ineffective, according to the *New York Times*. The newspaper investigated the relationship between the civil rights and advocacy groups and the soft drink industry. It reported that groups, including the National Hispana Leadership Institute, the National Association for the Advancement of Colored People, the National Puerto Rican Coalition and the National Hispanic Medical Association, had benefited from millions of dollars given by the soft drink industry to sponsor conferences, scholarships, and financial literacy classes.

"A lot of these organizations have particular niches that they use to service the communities," Gus K. West told the *Times*. West is president of the Hispanic Institute, a policy advocacy organization that supports tighter regulation of sugary drinks. "And they're getting funded by the soda industry. They're taking the money and looking the other way on obesity, diabetes, heart disease. They look the other way or issue statements that have no teeth or don't go after the industry."

Pepsico denied any link between charitable giving and public policy. Katelyn Jackson, a spokeswoman for Coca-Cola, told the *Times*, "The suggestion that our community

philanthropic efforts are motivated by something other than good-will is grossly inaccurate and ignores our history of true partnership for well over a century." In fact, Coca-Cola introduced an antiobesity campaign that called for nutritional labeling and a pledge to stop advertising targeting children.

Soft drink executives said that black and Hispanic nonprofit groups were helpful partners in contesting unwanted regulations and taxes. "It's important to have all impacted parties out there so we can educate lawmakers and the media about the impact bans would have on our business," Christopher Gindlesperger, a spokesman for the American Beverage Association, told the *Times*.

What do you think of the soft drink industry's stance or position? Review the concepts given in this chapter of how organizations deal with conflict. If you were public relations counsel for Pepsi or Coca-Cola, what would you recommend regarding this conflict?

Questions For Review and Discussion

1. Why does it help a public relations department to be aware of contingency factors in the organization? Discuss with examples.
2. What are the five steps in the issues management process?
3. How can effective issues management prevent organizational crises?
4. What crisis communication strategies did Benetton use following the collapse of a garment manufacturing plant in Bangladesh? Which strategies did you think were most effective? Why?
5. What is the conflict management life cycle? What are its various phases?
6. How can PR use social media effectively in the event of a natural disaster?
7. How does self-disclosure of an issue or stealing thunder potentially benefit an organization?
8. Provide an example from the current news to illustrate each of Coombs's seven crisis response strategies.
9. What are the three foundations of reputation? How does each one contribute to building and maintaining a positive reputation?

Media Resources

Coombs, W. T. (2012). *Ongoing crisis communication (3rd ed.).* Thousand Oaks, CA: Sage.

Jin, Y., Pang, A., & Cameron, G. T. (2012). Toward a publics-driven, emotion-based conceptualization in crisis communication: Unearthing dominant emotions in multi-staged testing of the Integrated Crisis Mapping (ICM) Model. *Journal of Public Relations Research, 24*(3), 266–298.

Kim, S., & Liu, B. F. (2012). Are all crises opportunities? A comparison of how corporate and government organizations responded to the 2009 flu pandemic. *Journal of Public Relations Research, 24*(1), 69–85.

Liu, B. F., Jin, Y., Briones, R., & Kuch, B. (2012). Managing turbulence in the blogosphere: Evaluating the blog-mediated crisis communication model with the American Red Cross. *Journal of Public Relations Research, 24*(4), 353–370.

Passariello, C., & Banjo, S. (2013, May 14). Benetton, Mango agree to Bangladesh safety pact. *Wall Street Journal.* Retrieved from www.wsj.com.

Rosenbloom, S. (2013, May 12). Cruise mishaps: How normal are they? *New York Times,* TR4.

Scudder, V. (2012, Fall). Chick-fil-A under fire: The perils of corporate outspokenness. *The Strategist*, 30–31.

Sisco, H. F. (2012). Nonprofit in crisis: An examination of the applicability of Situational Crisis Communication Theory *Journal of Public Relations Research, 24*(1), 1–17.

Sohn, Y. J., & Lariscy, R.A. (2012). Resource-based crisis management: The important role of the CEO's reputation. *Journal of Public Relations Research, 24*(4), 318–337.

Stein, Lindsay (2013, April). Toyota hits top gear. *PRWeek*, 30–32.

chapter 11

Audiences

After reading this chapter, you will be able to:

Learn about public relations campaigns directed to specific audiences

Understand the characteristics of various age and lifestyle groups

Understand the diversity of audiences in the United States

Gain insights on how to communicate with diverse audiences

Be familiar with the cultural values of Hispanic, black, and Asian audiences

A Multicultural Nation

If the audience on which public relations practitioners focus their messages were a monolithic whole, their work would be far easier—and far less stimulating. The audience, in fact, is just the opposite: It is a complex intermingling of groups with diverse cultural, ethnic, religious, and economic attributes that public relations professionals must understand and deal with every day.

Indeed, diversity is the most significant aspect of the mass audience in the United States. Today minorities constitute a third of the U.S. population, and the U.S. Census Bureau projects that they will constitute the majority of the total population by 2042. There are also major differences in geography, history, and economy among regions of the sprawling country; rural populations in the Midwest have different attitudes than residents in the heavily populated Eastern seaboard cities. Yet people in the two areas do have national interests in common. Ethnicity, generational differences, and socioeconomic status also shape the audience segments that public relations practitioners must address when planning a program or campaign.

For example, the American Heart Association (AHA) provides resources aimed at African American and Latino populations that reflect differences in culture for each that impact compliance with diet and lifestyle to ensure a healthy heart. The Power to End Stroke movement targets African Americans with a strategy to increase a sense of self-efficacy or personal empowerment over one's own health outcomes. Soul Food Recipes, an AHA-supported publication, facilitates healthy eating habits that reduce the risk of stroke.

Many product launches and other public relations campaigns also target specific audiences. McDonald's, for example, promoted its new McCafé espresso-based drinks to the African American community in Chicago. In another campaign, the fast-food chain sponsored a traveling exhibit with Latin music artifacts that led up to its sponsorship of the Latin Grammy Awards in Houston. Allstate Insurance kicked off a "Give Back" day on Martin Luther King's birthday to encourage more volunteerism in the black community. And Subaru reached out to the Asian community in the San Francisco Bay area by partnering with the Asian Foundation to encourage Asian Americans to get tested for Hepatitis B, a condition for which the group is at high risk.

Such ethnic campaigns, however, are only one aspect of reaching diverse audiences. Public relations campaigns are also designed to reach specific audiences that are defined by age, gender, income, and lifestyle. Technology is often used to segment the mass audience and compile related valuable information about target audiences. Geographic and social statistics found in Census Bureau reports provide a rich foundation. Much of these data can be broken down by census tract and zip code. Data on automobile registrations, voter registrations, sales figures, mailing lists, and church and organization membership also can be merged into computer databases.

The increasing sophistication of Internet analytics and the retrieval of "big data" from the websites that individuals visit also tell marketers a great deal about a person's interests, educational level, political orientation, and buying patterns. Such data can also enable public relations efforts to be more efficient and effective in reaching diverse audiences, but they also require greater cultural literacy among public relations professionals to plan campaigns that are tailored to specific audiences and their particular lifestyles.

> Targeting multicultural audiences with dedicated campaigns around cultural expression multiplies the entry points and opportunities for brands to establish meaningful connections that ultimately lead to sales.
>
> *Armando Azarloza, president of the Axis Agency in* PRWeek

An integral part of this planning is understanding what media channels are most appropriate for reaching a particular public.

The following sections will explore these aspects by providing information about (1) ethnically diverse audiences, (2) age group audiences, and (3) gender/lifestyle audiences.

Reaching Ethnic Audiences

Historically, the United States has welcomed millions of immigrants and assimilated them into the cultural mainstream. They bring a bubbling mixture of personal values, habits, and perceptions that are absorbed slowly, sometimes reluctantly. The question of assimilation somewhat pertains to all immigrant groups, whether they are from Ireland, Poland, Cuba, or the Philippines. It also pertains to two minorities that have a long history in the United States: African Americans and Native Americans. This diversity is a great strength of the United States, but also a source of friction and, at times, negative stereotyping.

Recently, the easily identifiable ethnic groups—primarily Hispanics, African Americans, and Asian Americans—have been growing faster than the general population, with nonwhite ethnic groups now comprising a majority in some states, including California, Texas, Hawaii, New Mexico, and the District of Columbia (D.C.). According to the U.S. Census Bureau, whites are already a minority in 22 of the country's 100 largest urban areas.

Hispanics and African Americans now constitute about 16 percent and 13 percent of the U.S. population, respectively, for a total of 28 percent. The population of Asian Americans is also experiencing major growth to a record 18.2 million in 2012, or about 5.8 percent of the U.S. population. According to the Census Bureau, even greater changes will occur by 2050. Today, one out of every four babies born in the United States is Hispanic that helps account for the projection that Hispanics will comprise nearly 30 percent of the U.S. population in future years. (See Figure 11.1.)

Figure 11.1 **Projected Demographic Shifts in the U.S. Population: 2010 to 2050**

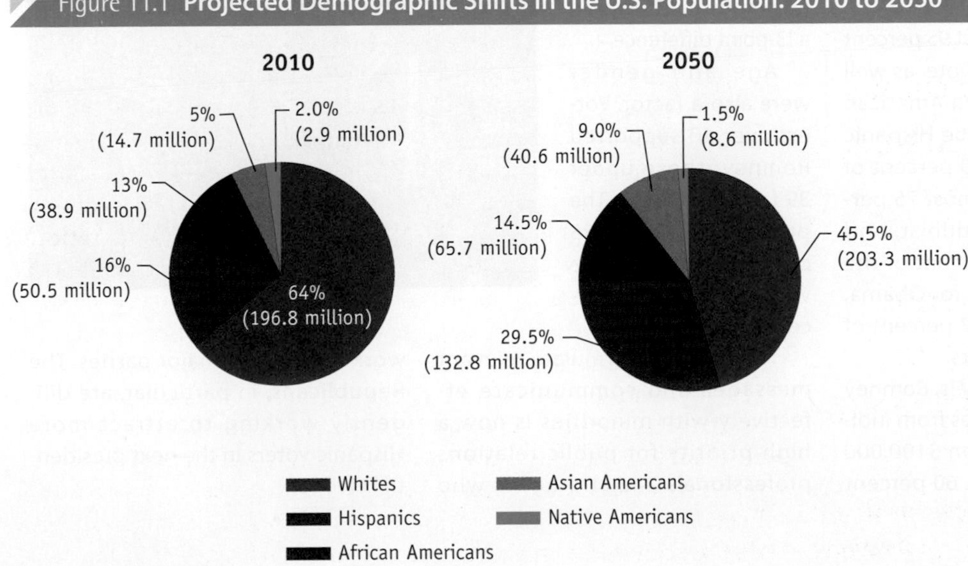

Source: U.S. Census Bureau.

Such statistics place a strong focus on diversity and multiculturalism in the workplace (internal publics) as well as how public relations and marketing experts communicate with these groups as citizens and consumers. The stakes are high. In terms of buying power, significant amounts of money are involved. By 2015, the purchasing power of Hispanics will reach $1.5 trillion and the buying power of African Americans will be $l.1 trillion. Asian Americans, the racial group with the highest percentage of college graduates, currently have about $725 billion in buying power, but Nielsen research projects the figure to be at least $1 trillion by 2017, which is equal to the l8th largest economy in the world. Another major trend is the growing influence of minorities on elections, which is highlighted in the Insights box below.

on the job INSIGHTS

Minorities Assure Obama's Election

The changing demographics of the United States played a major role in the 2012 presidential election as the nation becomes majority/minority electorate. Mitt Romney did well among white voters with nearly 60 percent voting for him, but Obama carried minorities by a large margin. On average, Obama got 80 percent of the minority vote.

Obama received almost 95 percent of the African American vote, as well as 73 percent of the Asian American vote and 71 percent of the Hispanic vote. He also received 50 percent of the Catholic vote and almost 75 percent of the Muslim, Buddhist, and Jewish vote. Even 70 percent of the nonreligious voters went for Obama. Romney, however, got 57 percent of the white protestant voters.

In terms of income levels, Romney got 54 percent of the votes from individuals making more than $100,000 annually, but Obama got 60 percent of the voters who made less than $50,000 a year. Both candidates evenly split the vote from college graduates, but Obama got a larger percentage of votes from people with a graduate degree—55 percent vs. Romney with 42 percent, a l3-point difference.

Age and gender were also a factor. Voters over 40 supported Romney; those under 39 favored Obama. The president also got 55 percent of the female vote, but only 45 percent of the male vote.

The ability to formulate relevant messages and communicate effectively with minorities is now a high priority for public relations professionals and strategists who work for the two major parties. The Republicans, in particular, are diligently working to attract more Hispanic voters in the next presidential election.

Hispanics

The Hispanic/Latino population is the largest ethnic group in the United States. There were about 54 million in 2013, according to the Advertising Research Foundation. By 2050, the U.S. Census Bureau estimates that the Hispanic population will be more than 130 million. As a result, public relations campaigns are increasingly focused on reaching this important buying public.

Colgate, for example, has targeted mothers in its "El Mes de la Salud Cucal" campaign to promote oral health because the company recognized the importance of maternal influence in Hispanic culture. Heineken's recent "Demuestra Quein Eres" ("Give Yourself a Good Name") Mural Arts Series tapped into Latino cultural pride and male emphasis on establishing reputation. Even Harley-Davidson now has a website just for its Hispanic enthusiasts, www.harley-davidson.com/haristras, and has produced a video, "Harlistras," to celebrate Harley riders with Hispanic roots.

It's simplistic, however, to think of the Hispanic public as a single entity. First, they represent the heritage of more than 20 nations, ranging from Spain to Mexico, the Caribbean, and South America. On a national basis, about two-thirds of the Hispanic population is of Mexican heritage but Florida and New York have larger numbers of Hispanics from the Caribbean and South America. Each national group has its own set of values, traditions, beliefs, foods, festivals, consumer patterns, and even differences in speaking Spanish. A public relations campaign directed to Cuban Americans in Florida, for example, would be somewhat different from one directed to Latinos living in Texas and Arizona.

With more than 50 million people and $1 trillion in purchasing power, Hispanics are not the market of the future—they are the market of now.

John Echeveste, partner in VPE Public Relations in PRWeek

In general, market research indicates that Hispanics prefer ads and other informational materials in Spanish over English, although the younger generation is more comfortable with English. More than 90 percent of Hispanic youth, for example, are bilingual. Spanish-language media, however, have dramatically increased in recent years. There are now almost 2,500 unique U.S. Hispanic media outlets, including more than 1,200 print publications, more than 1,000 television and radio outlets, 200 Internet-only outlets, and 20 AP-style wire services and news syndicates. Univision, primarily aimed at audiences of Mexican origin, is still the largest Hispanic network, but is getting increased competition from NBC's Telemundo and the Fox network's Spanish language MundoFox.

Radio is an especially important way to reach this ethnic group. Surveys show that the average Hispanic person listens to the radio 26 to 30 hours a week, about 13 percent more than the general population. The Spanish-language station in Los Angeles, KLVE-FM, has a larger audience than any other station in southern California. Indeed, the Pew Hispanic Center found that nearly all Hispanics (91 percent) have access to Spanish-language television stations at home and that even highly assimilated Latinos (46 percent) watch Spanish-language programming. The Pew study concludes that Spanish-language TV is an opportunity to reach across the assimilation spectrum.

Hispanic audiences, particularly the younger generation, have also turned to online sources. In fact, Matthew Robson of Morgan Stanley bank states, "There is no statistical difference between Hispanic youth and the general youth population in relation to their heavy use of social media like Facebook." As a result, the use of social marketing and networks among Latinos has expanded. For example, American Airlines used Twitter and Facebook to promote its AA Advantage program to Hispanic

on the job

SOCIAL MEDIA IN ACTION

Pampers Makes Every Hispanic Baby Special

Procter & Gamble (P&G) is well aware of the potential for its Pampers brand among Hispanic women. Demographic research indicates that about half of Hispanic women in the United States are moms and two-thirds of them have children between the ages of 2 and 11. In addition, one out of every four babies born in the United States is of Hispanic heritage.

With this data in mind, P&G commissioned public relations firm Citizen Paine to launch an integrated campaign in Los Angeles where more than 50 percent of its population is Hispanic. The strategy was to link Pampers with the belief that every baby is a little miracle to be celebrated, supported, and protected.

Barbara Bermudo, a Univision journalist and mother, who was widely respected in the Hispanic community, was selected as the celebrity spokesperson. She was the campaign's honorary "madrina" (godmother) who made personal appearances at Hispanic community events, served as spokesperson for traditional media and influential bloggers, and also wrote a blog series about her experience as a mother and giving tips about parenthood.

In addition, P&G launched a Facebook Pampers Latino page to encourage conversations with Hispanic fans. The page was a forum for moms interested in receiving baby care information and connecting with other parents. It also was the vehicle for mothers to submit their own "miracle" stories and enter a sweepstakes contest to win a $5,000 scholarship for their baby. A third function of the Facebook page was to show the progress on the painting of a mural on a building that honored babies of Hispanic heritage.

The result was widespread coverage in the general and Hispanic media, including posts by influential Hispanic bloggers. In addition, the Pampers Latino Facebook page generated more than 30,000 fan "likes." The campaign received a Silver Anvil award in multicultural public relations from the Public Relations Society of America.

audiences in the United States. Fleishman-Hillard is working with the Boy Scouts of the United States to create bilingual social media components on *Scouting.org* to "reintroduce Scouting to America."

It is important, however, to understand that traditional and online media need more than news releases and features translated into Spanish. The messages must also be relevant to the audience, with themes important to the audience, such as family, education, and health. This point is made by John Echeveste, partner in VPE Public Relations, who wrote in *PR Week*, "Effectively speaking the language of Hispanics means using cultural cues and passion points that have relevance to the market and tactically executing in a way that makes most sense depending on factors including the target's age, level of acculturation, lifestyle, and media consumption preferences."

African Americans

The largest racial minority in the United States is African Americans because Hispanics are considered an ethnic group. There are now more than 43 million African Americans, according to a 2012 research report by Nielsen, which is 13.7 percent of the American population , and they have the longest history in the United States as a minority group. But they are not necessarily a homogeneous group.

on the job

A MULTICULTURAL WORLD

Pepsi Sponsors Global Latin Music Concert

Spanish singer and song-writer Alejandro Sanz is widely known for his talent and is the recipient of 15 Latin Grammy Awards, plus three Grammys. That's why Pepsi's U.S. Hispanic and Latin American marketing teams chose him to be a lead sponsor for a concert by Sanz that was live-streamed to 19 nations, including the United States.

The concert was made possible by using digital media company Terra that reaches a monthly audience of 100 million through TVs, PCs, tablets, smartphones, and other mobile devices. Mobile accessibility was particularly important to Pepsi because U.S. Hispanic and Latin American consumers are avid users of mobile devices. The concert in HD was offered in English, Spanish, and Portuguese.

Pepsi promoted the concert on its Spanish and English language site, MiPepsi, as well as MiPepsi's Facebook and Twitter pages. Sanz also promoted the concert to his 7.7 million Twitter followers and 2.4 million Facebook fans. In addition, Pepsi used social media to promote a sweepstakes in 12 Latin American countries. The grand prize was a VIP trip package for two to attend the live Sanz concert in Miami and meet the singer. To enter, consumers sent a tweet to @TerraMusicalUS, explaining why they wanted to see Sanz live, using the hashtag #DondelHayPepsi HayMusica.

The concert was part of Pepsi's overall campaign "Viva Hoy," which is a translation of the brand's new "Live for Now" marketing and public relations platform. The Hispanic market is important to Pepsi because of Hispanic population growth trends. Market research also shows that Latino consumption of carbonated soft drinks is higher than average.

One distinction is their geographical origin. One group are citizens whose African relatives were first brought to this country in the 1800s as slaves. A second, more recent group are blacks with Hispanic or Caribbean origin, who tend to self-identify as Hispanic. The terms "African American" and "black" are often used interchangeably in marketing and public relations contexts. In fact, the Nielsen research found that 44 percent preferred "black" and 43 percent preferred "African American." And 11 percent did not care.

In terms of income, the number of black households with $75,000+ income has risen to about 2.5 million. "The world is now a different place for the affluent African American demographic," said Len Burnett, cofounder of specialty magazine *Uptown*. "Luxury brands understand the importance of niche shoppers with disposable income and Uptown delivers them efficiently." Other marketing research found that affluent blacks are more likely than other consumers to spend money on fashionable dress, toiletries, cosmetics, and cruise vacations. See the Insights box on page 310 about Royal Caribbean's outreach to the black community.

on the job

INSIGHTS

Art Connects Cruise Ship Line with African Americans

African Americans are traveling in greater numbers and the competition for their business is intense. Royal Caribbean International, working with Fleishman-Hillard public relations, decided on a cause-marketing strategy that would benefit the local community.

The format was a free, live art auction series held on docked cruise ships in Los Angeles, Baltimore, and Miami. It showcased art donated by nationally acclaimed African American artists, and all proceeds supported summer art programs for African American teens in those cities.

The auctions generated more than $20,000 for local art programs and, at the same time, generated extensive coverage in the African American media. In terms of establishing brand awareness, 95 percent of the attendees said they were likely to take a Royal Caribbean cruise. Other African American groups also have inquired about holding charitable events aboard the ships.

Cause Marketing

Royal Caribbean's art auctions to benefit local art programs for black teenagers proved to be a successful opportunity to increase its African American market share and build brand loyalty.

Public relations professionals, however, need to ensure that programs and product packaging don't reinforce negative stereotypes. A good example of racial insensitivity was the traditional figure of Aunt Jemima on packages of Quaker Oats food products. Her image was widely regarded in the black community as a patronizing stereotype. To change this perception, Quaker Oats cooperated with the National Council of Negro Women to honor outstanding African American women in local communities, who then competed for a national award. At the local award breakfasts, all food served was Aunt Jemima brands, and Quaker Oats officials participated in the programs.

The black media are less extensive than Hispanic media. Two possible reasons are that African Americans have a longer history in the United States and that English is their native language. Currently, there are only about 175 black newspapers in the United States, but the Black Entertainment Television Network has a large national audience, as do such magazines as *Ebony* and *Essence*. Business Wire's "Black PR Wire" lists more than a thousand black-owned publications and journalists.

The survey research firm Nielsen also notes that African Americans are the heaviest TV consumers, watching almost seven hours a day vs. five hours average for all U.S. households. They also use more voice minutes on their mobile phones than other groups, about 1,300 minutes a month. Although there is no language problem, most experts recommend that organizations should still advertise and do media placement in black media because over 90 percent of the respondents in the Nielsen survey said they believe black media is more relevant to them. Another 80 percent say products featured or advertised in black media is more relevant to them.

Asian Americans

There are now more than 18 million Asian Americans in the United States, according to a 2012 Nielsen report titled "The State of the Asian American Consumer." In addition, they are the most affluent and well-cducated multicultural group. The median family income, for example, is $66,000—28 percent higher than the total median U.S. income. In terms of higher education, 50 percent of Asian Americans over age 25 have undergraduate degrees compared to only 28 percent of the U.S. population. See the chart in the Insights box below for comparisons with other ethnic and racial groups.

Asian Americans, however, are just as diverse as Hispanics. There are 17 major Asian groups in the United States, but the four major groups are the Chinese (22 percent), Asian Indian (19 percent), Filipino (18 percent), and the Vietnamese

on the job

INSIGHTS

The Diversity of Education and Income

The following graphs reflect U.S. Census data showing the percentage of college graduates and the median household income of the four major ethnic and racial groups in the United States.

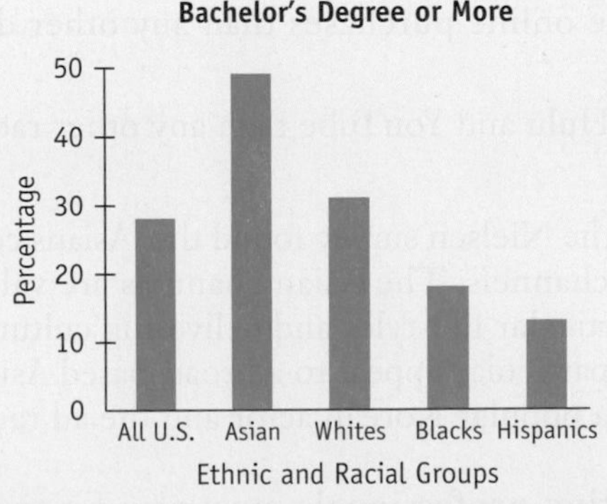

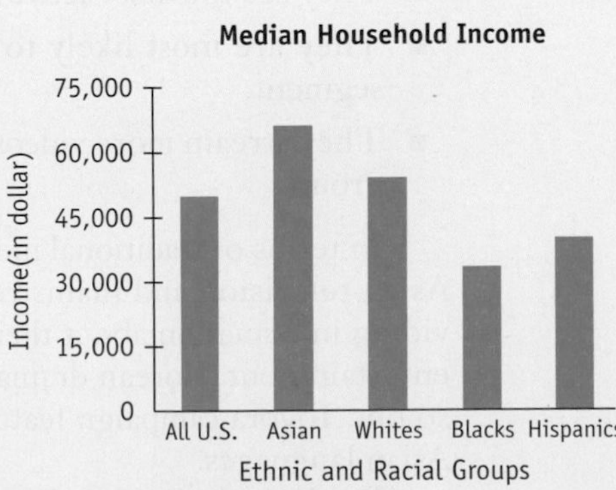

Source: Graphs based on U.S. Census Bureau, *Current Population Survey, 2010 Annual Social and Economic Supplement.*

(11 percent). Each group, of course, has its own language and culture. India, with a population of more than 1 billion, is a totally different culture from that of Thailand or China. There are even generational differences within each group. The lifestyles, values, and interests of fourth-generation Korean Americans in Los Angeles are dramatically different from first-generation Koreans who have recently arrived in the United States.

Thus, the practitioner must define the audience with particular care and sensitivity, taking into account the cultural and ethnic self-identity of many target audience segments. Citizens of Indian descent, for example, often prefer to call themselves Indian or Indo Americans because of their long history as a major civilization. Indian Americans prefer English to receive information because of India's British colonial past but public relations professionals should use cultural cues such as a few Hindi words, music, or images.

The Asian American media, because of language diversity and culture, has dramatically increased in recent years. According to Nielson, there are more than 400 print publications, 136 TV channels, 140 radio stations, and 550 digital platforms catering to the Asian American audience. For example, KTSF-TV in San Francisco has a local newscast in Cantonese every night that has an audience of 23,000. Using such media is important for conducting marketing and public relations campaigns because, as Nielson reports, "It is imperative to utilize the Asian-language and/or Asian-culture media to convey culturally tailored messages that can resonate with the Asian American audience."

Asian Americans, in particular, can be reached via digital media. According to the Nielsen survey, "When compared with other multicultural segments, Asian Americans more frequently utilize multiple digital screens to view programming and video." Some statistics:

- They average 80 hours a month surfing the Internet and view 3,600 web pages, that is 1,000 pages higher than any other demographic group.
- They have 70 percent smartphone penetration and the highest usage of any group.
- Adoption of tablets is higher than any other group.
- They have more accessibility to broadband at home than any other group.
- They visit computer and consumer electronics websites more often than any other group.
- They are the most active demographic segment on social networks.
- They are most likely to make online purchases than any other demographic segment.
- They stream more videos on Hulu and YouTube than any other racial or ethnic group.

In terms of traditional media, the Nielsen survey found that Asians consume both Asian television and mainstream channels. The Asian channels are valued for providing information about their particular lifestyles and delivering culturally relevant entertainment. Korean dramas in particular appeal to a broad-based Asian audience; so one Toyota campaign featured a popular Korean actor and the ad ran in multiple Asian languages.

Public relations and marketing professionals must also be aware of some common traits among all Asian Americans. One is the emphasis on family and traditions. This is further explored in the following Insights Box, but the Nielsen report adds, "Asian Americans enjoy being a part of activities and traditions celebrating their ethnicity, and like to expose their children to their ethnic backgrounds."

on the job

INSIGHTS

Communicating with Multicultural Groups

Although the sensitive communicator needs to take into consideration the differences in nationality, language, generations, and cultural values, there are some general guidelines. Fernando Figueredo, head of the multicultural practice for Porter Novelli, says there are some unique characteristics shared by the top three minority groups—Hispanics, African Americans, and Asian Americans.

"Minorities outpace their counterparts with social media but this doesn't mean that you'll reach a 65-year-old Filipino on Twitter. Meet your audiences where they already are." Carolina Madrid, diversity chair of PRSA's New Professionals Section, writing in *Public Relations Tactics*.

Figueredo, writing in *The Strategist*, says, "These include a deep family network with a strong mother or father figure, music, food, religion, and strong bonds between friends and family." He also says that multicultural consumers tend to be more loyal to brands that make an attempt to reach them in ways that are culturally relevant. He continues, "Whether through advertising, in-store promotions, or special festivals and events, reaching consumers in their culture has a strong impact on new and repeat purchases."

A strong community relations program is one way to effectively reach ethnic audiences. Indeed, many major corporations such as McDonald's, Coke, and Pepsi have spent considerable money and time developing community-based programs. In terms of product promotion, Estee Lauder developed a marketing campaign using models from France, Puerto Rico, and China to promote a new product line for various skin tones and ethnicities. See also the Insights box on page 310 on an African American art auction sponsored by Royal Caribbean Cruises.

State Farm is a good example of a company tailoring public relations programs for specific audiences. To reach Hispanics, the insurance company partnered with the Univision network on Web novellas that feature messages about being there for friends and family. For Asian Americans, the company provided online video contests through social media. For the black community, it promoted "The 50 Million Pound Challenge" with fitness expert Dr. Ian Smith as the spokesperson. A website and blogs were used to build an online community.

Other companies, such as Allstate and American Airlines, have sponsored community-based events during the Asian Lunar New Year celebration that is significant for many Asian cultures. Figueredo gives five basic concepts that should be considered when developing a communications campaign for multicultural consumers:

1. Organize a team with an inherent understanding of the customs and values of the various demographic groups you are trying to reach.
2. Understand that consumers of diverse cultural backgrounds respond better to messages that are culturally relevant.
3. Remember that consumers of diverse cultural backgrounds are extremely loyal and once your products and services become part of their lives, there is a very good chance you will keep them.
4. Use the primary language of the audience. A large portion of your target audience prefers to communicate in their primary language, even if they also have strong English skills.
5. Use spokespersons that represent the audience. The spokesperson must be a good communicator and be sensitive to the issues that are important to the audience.

Although this book has emphasized the three major minority groups, it should be noted that there are any number of other ethnic communities in the United States that add to the diversity of the population. The *Gale Directory*, for example, lists publications in 48 languages other than English. For more information on multicultural media consumption, Nielsen has compiled a number of studies (www.Nielson.com). Another good source is the Pew Research Center (www.pewresearch.com) for a variety of surveys on multicultural lifestyles and attitudes on various social issues.

Reaching Diverse Age Groups

As the demographic makeup of the United States continues to change, three major age groups deserve special attention. They are youth and young adults, baby boomers, and seniors. The following is a brief snapshot of each group.

The Millennial Generation

Individuals born between 1980 and 1995 are called the Millennial Generation because many of them entered the workforce at the start of the 21st century. In 2013, for example, the oldest in this generation was 33 and many of them had already become parents with established careers. At the youngest end of the spectrum are 18-year-olds just entering college. This diverse age group constitute about 20 percent of the U.S. population. Worldwide, the *World Fact Book* reports that there are 1 billion millennials.

Because they are such voracious consumers of digital media, some pundits have labeled today's Millennials the *E-Generation*. Indeed, they are the first generation to grow up as digital "natives," who have grown up with computers, cell phones, the Internet, and social networking sites. Communicating with these tech-savvy individuals takes a great deal of creativity and a thorough knowledge of how to effectively engage them.

A number of research studies have probed the attitudes and characteristics of the Millennial generation to gain insights that would help public relations and marketing professionals better understand this audience. One such study was done by Scarborough, a consumer research and lifestyle firm (*www.scarborough.com*). Titled "Millennials. OMG: Getting Inside the Millennial Mind," some of its findings include the following:

> Today, Millennials spend just over 82 minutes a day on social networking activities—32 minutes longer per day than the average adult. It is an ingrained part of their lives that has become even more prevalent with the continued advancements in wireless technology.
>
> *Scarborough Research survey*

- 80 percent want brands to entertain them.
- 65 percent like to compare prices across different sites before purchasing something online.
- 62 percent recycle glass, plastic, or paper.
- 40 percent agree that a celebrity endorsement influences them to buy a product.
- 46 percent agree that they are more likely to buy a brand that supports a charity.
- 53 percent are more likely than all U.S. adults to believe that social media sites are very important for finding information.

- 44 percent get their news via the Internet, compared to only 24 percent who read a daily newspaper.
- 49 percent are more likely than all generations to identify as Hispanic.
- 51 percent use their mobile phones to do social networking on Facebook, Twitter, etc.
- 90 percent do text messaging.

According to the report, "By understanding Millennial attitudes—what motivates them and makes them tick—marketers and advertisers can craft a more intuitive marketing mix to appeal to this young audience."

Teenagers

The younger brothers and sisters of the Millennials are today's teenagers who are even more addicted to wireless communication. Research by Nielsen Company shows that the average mobile teen racks up about 3,000 text messages a month. In addition, the Pew Research Center found that (1) 95 percent of teenagers use a cell phone, (2) 75 percent have posted a profile to a social networking site, and (3) 20 percent have posted a video of themselves online. The Fortino Group (Pittsburgh) projects that today's teenagers will spend one-third of their lives online and exhibit some of the following characteristics that public relations professionals will need to consider in terms of effectively communicating with them. They will:

- Spend equal time interacting with friends online and in person.
- Make initial contact online before dating and marriage.
- Spend more time online than in interaction with parents by tenfold.
- Be more reserved in social skills.
- Be more skeptical about online identities such as chat participants.
- Be intolerant of print forms, slow application processes, or archaic systems.

Another major impact will be in the workplace. A Deloitte Teen Ethics survey found that 60 percent of teenagers probably would not take a job with an employer who restricted their ability to access networking sites during working hours. Many employers, however, say that such restrictions are necessary due to concern about work productivity, spreading rumors about coworkers, and leaking proprietary information.

Baby Boomers

This age group, born between 1946 and 1964, represents the tidal wave of Americans born after World War II, when thousands of GIs returned home and started raising families. Today, as a large percentage of these men and women begin to add a "6" to their birthdays, they comprise a market of 78 million people, or about 24 percent of the U.S. population. They have about $3 trillion in buying power, include many of the country's current business and political leaders, and are active users of the Internet.

Baby boomers, particularly those born in the 1960s, grew up in an age of prosperity and continue to have few qualms about spending on consumer goods instead of saving for retirement, although the economic recession of 2009 changed some of their

> Baby boomers are the wealthiest, best educated, and most sophisticated purchasers, which is why a unique marketing approach is required.
>
> *Denise Vitola, SVP of MSL Group in* PRWeek

spending habits. Despite such setbacks, the McKinsey Global Institute estimates that by 2015, Boomers will control almost 60 percent of the nation's net worth and consume about 40 percent of the nation's products and services. Because of their wealth and numbers, many corporations and nonprofit groups have taken a keen interest in reaching this market. Toyota, for example, has promoted its Highlander by tailoring communications to baby boomers who now have "empty nests" because their children are in college or have already established their own careers. One ad, for example, emphasizes the message "For your newfound freedom."

The oldest boomers turned 65 in 2011 and for the next 20 years, 19,000 people a day will turn 65 according to the Pew Research Center. They are starting to share many of the same concerns as their immediate elders, the seniors, who will be discussed next. In other words, they are naturally concerned about health care, insurance, retirement planning, personal investing, and other issues. But it should also be remembered that about 60 percent of the beer and carbonated beverages in the country are purchased by boomers. Companies such as Procter & Gamble and L'Oreal Paris are also seeing the demand for new products that cater to mature adults who lead active lifestyles and want to look vibrant and healthy, not necessarily younger.

Baby boomers, as a result of growing up in the 1960s and 1970s, also tend to be more involved in social causes. Catherine Welker of Strauss Radio Strategies told *PRWeek*, "Many are parents, voters, retirees, and potentially have disposable income. This is a generation most likely to get involved in a cause." It's also a generation that actively surfs the Internet for information on goods and services. Cruise ship lines, for example, have developed extensive websites to reach Boomers who have the disposable income for extensive travel.

Seniors

This group frequently is defined as men and women 65 years or older, although some sociologists and marketing experts, including the American Association of Retired Persons (AARP), include everyone over age 50. However, a typical 50-year-old in good health and working full-time usually doesn't quite see himself or herself as a "senior."

Medical advances have improved life expectancy to the point that today, almost 36.3 million Americans are age 65 or older (12 percent of the population), according to the U.S. Census Bureau. A heavy upsurge in the senior population occurred in 2011, when the post–World War II baby boomers began to reach age 65. These older citizens form an important opinion group and a consumer market with special interests.

When appealing to seniors, public relations people should try to ignore the stereotypes of "old folks" so often depicted in the movies and television. A large percentage of seniors today, thanks to advances in health care, are active citizens who regularly do volunteer work, work out at the gym, attend cultural events, and do extensive travel. The older generation is just as diverse in their interests, financial status, and lifestyle as any other age group. Public relations practitioners should consider these characteristics of seniors:

- With the perspective of long experience, they often are less easily convinced than young adults, demand value in the things they buy, and pay little attention to fads.
- They vote in greater numbers than their juniors and are more intense readers of newspapers and magazines. Retirees also watch television heavily.

- They form an excellent source of volunteers for social, health, and cultural organizations because they have time and often are looking for something to do.
- They are extremely health-conscious, out of self-interest, and want to know about medical developments. A Census Bureau study showed that most people over age 65 say they are in good health; not until their mid-80s do they frequently need assistance in daily living.

Financially, the elderly are better off than the stereotypes suggest. The poverty rate among older Americans (9.8 percent) is slightly below that of the population at large (12.5 percent). The Census Bureau found that people ages 65 to 74 have more discretionary income than any other group, with median assets of $108,885. A large percentage owns their own homes without a mortgage, and they hold 70 percent of the country's assets.

Although they are poor customers for household goods, they eat out frequently and do much gift buying. They travel frequently. In fact, seniors account for about 80 percent of commercial vacation travel, especially cruises. All public relations personnel working in the restaurant, travel, and tourism industries should be particularly cognizant of this audience and how to effectively communicate with them. Even toy companies find seniors a lucrative market because grandparents tend to spoil their grandchildren.

In terms of media consumption, seniors do spend 30 percent more time watching TV and 25 percent more time reading a daily newspaper than the average U.S. adult, according to the Center for Media Research. But they are also becoming more active on the Internet; almost 20 million regularly go online to check their e-mail, download maps, check the weather, and pay bills. Facebook even reports that the fastest-growing demographic for new members is the over-55 group, as seniors connect with their children and grandchildren.

An increasing number of seniors now live in retirement communities and many companies reach them by organizing events around a brand or service. Seniors are often looking for new experiences and social engagement so an event that offers some entertainment and information in the club house or recreation room is a good strategy.

Gender/Lifestyle Audiences

Women

Diversity also includes gender. Women of all nationalities and ethnic groups have always been an important audience for retailers and manufacturers of consumer goods.

Indeed, Ketchum communications makes the point, "Today's women hold an overwhelming share of consumer purchasing influence, making more than 80 percent of household purchase decisions. . . ." According to a Nielsen report in 2013, estimates on female purchasing power varies from $5 trillion to $15 trillion annually and trends indicate that women will control two-thirds of the consumer wealth in the United States over the next decade. Given these statistics, it is no surprise that women are also emerging as "influentials" in a variety of campaigns for a spectrum of companies.

The Ketchum research, conducted by the University of Southern California's Annenberg Strategic Public Relations Centre, also found that women aged 25 to 54 are not only "super consumers" but are much faster than men to embrace some new media, such as social networking sites, and also to use corporate websites.

on the job

SOCIAL MEDIA IN ACTION

Potty Humor for Moms

Flushable fact #58: About 4 percent of our days are spent using a toilet. This tidbit of information was one of many "facts" offered by Clorox, a maker of cleaning products, as part of a social media campaign to reach moms.

The company created a social media hub, Clorox Lounge, that featured contests, giveaways, coupons, and comic relief for moms during their "potty breaks." The inspiration for the campaign came from survey data that found 75 percent of Americans use their mobile devices while sitting on the toilet. The website, according to Clorox, offered moms who might seek a few minutes of privacy some light entertainment.

The campaign was built on a pre-existing Facebook page, *Ode to the Commode*, which had almost 200,000 "likes" and included humorous pictures, infographics on potty-related topics, and conversations between consumers on such topics as the merits of toilet seat covers. The site was promoted on various social media sites and blogs, interviews on national TV shows, and print placements in such publications as *People* and *OK! Weekly*. Within three months, 10,000 "moms" became registered users on *The CloroxLounge.com* site.

A Weber Shandwick and KRC Research study in 2013, for example, found that females who use social networking sites exceed that of men (75 percent vs. 63 percent). The study also found that women spend an average of 12 hours a week using social media.

Other research studies have identified a segment called "supermoms" in terms of opinion leadership and word-of-mouth influence. These women, about 5 percent of mothers, have such characteristics as (1) at least 75 friends with whom they keep in touch, (2) regularly give their friends advice on what to buy and restaurants to try, and (3) participate in online chats and discussions. Given these data, companies such as Procter & Gamble have used these supermoms to find out their opinions and also to have them sample new products, with the idea that their word-of-mouth influence will motivate other women to buy the product.

Companies have also been paying attention to what have been called "mommy bloggers." Campbell Soup Company, for example, invited 11 mom bloggers to corporate headquarters to start a dialogue about the company's policies and products. Other companies, such as Graco, have also engaged in dialogue with mom bloggers and even started their own mommy blogs and branded Twitter accounts.

The LGBT Community

The gay, lesbian, bisexual, and transgender community is a diverse demographic estimated to be between 9 and 16 million Americans, depending on various studies extrapolating data from the U.S. Census Bureau and other demographic data. Its estimated purchasing power is about $750 billion, according to *Packaged Facts*, so companies have begun to offer domestic partnership benefits and reach out to gay online sites and various publications. The Internet is a good way to reach this community;

some studies have indicated that they are the most wired and technologically oriented groups in the country with about 80 percent online.

General Motors was a leader in such programs, but such corporations as Marriott, Disney, and Starbucks have also been active in promoting same-sex employee benefits and reaching out to the LGBT community. Starbucks, for example, even endorsed gay marriage legislation in Washington State despite an effort by the National Organization for Marriage urging a boycott of the coffee giant. Such boycotts, however, have never succeeded. According to Andy Bagnall, VP of Prime Access, "There has never been a successful boycott due to supporting or marketing to gay consumers." See the Casebook on page 320 about Ben & Jerry's celebrating same-sex marriage legislation in Vermont.

> Corporate America has learned that it's a smart business decision to engage in LGBT consumers because they are known to be very loyal to companies that support their community.
>
> *Rich Ferraro, VP of communications for the Gay and Lesbian Alliance Against Defamation (GLAAD) in* PRWeek

The Greater Philadelphia Tourism Marketing Corporation (GPTMC) tapped into gay buying power when it decided to launch a "Get Your History Straight and Your Nightlife Gay" campaign in order to generate more tourism for the city. It produced a 36-page trip planner for gays. Gay and lesbian media and travel professionals were contacted, news releases were sent to gay/lesbian publications, and two familiarization trips for journalists were conducted.

The campaign got widespread coverage in the gay and mainstream press, including the *Daily Show with Jon Stewart*. The campaign's website usage increased 1,000 percent, and more than 1,000 hotel packages were sold. Media targeted to gay and lesbian consumers have grown over the last two decades. Magazines such as *Out* and *Advocate*, and the cable network Logo, focus exclusively on gay themes. Mainstream television shows featuring gay themes, such as ABC's *Modern Family* and the film *Brokeback Mountain*, have attracted gay and straight audiences alike.

Gays also are being incorporated into mainstream commercials. Unilever, for example, hired three actors to play a girl's best gay friends in a campaign to introduce Sunsilk shampoo to the United States. They were positioned as style experts who wrote advice columns in magazines such as *Cosmopolitan* diagnosing consumers' hair problems.

It's important, however, to realize that the LGBT market is not "one size fits all." Laurie Phillips, writing in *Public Relations Tactics*, points out that the "population is composed of individuals representing all ages, gender identities and expressions, racial and ethnic categories and various abilities." She adds, "Therefore, messaging used to reach l8–34 gay males should vary from messaging used to reach 35–54 lesbians just as cultural differences should also dictate the verbiage and media outlets used to target various segments within the broader LGBTQ population."

Religious Groups

The United States is predominantly a Christian nation, but there is a great deal of diversity among various religious groups. Catholics constitute the largest single group, with about 70 million followers, making the United States the fourth largest Catholic nation in the world. Other large denominations include the Southern Baptist Convention, with 16 million members, and the United Methodist Church, with 8 million followers. There are, however, other major religions represented. For instance, there are about 6.5 million Jews and about 6 million Muslims living in the United States.

PRCasebook

Ben & Jerry's Celebrates Same-Sex Marriage

Vermont is the home of the iconic ice-cream maker, Ben & Jerry's, and is also the fourth state to legalize gay and lesbian marriage. Many companies would avoid any comment on the highly politicized issue, but Ben & Jerry's saw it as a great opportunity to reinforce the company's commitment to social justice and equality for all people.

It engaged Cone/Cone public relations to launch a traditional and social media campaign to accomplish three objectives: (1) raise awareness throughout the nation about Ben & Jerry's commitment to social justice, (2) encourage consumers to support marriage equality, and (3) reinforce the Ben & Jerry's brand. The "Hubby Hubby" campaign was based in Vermont but was designed to reach a national audience.

The following strategies and tactics were used:

- Established a partnership with Freedom to Marry, a nonprofit group, to provide consumers with a resource and call-to-action to sign its online Marriage Resolution.
- A national announcement renaming its "Chubby Hubby" flavor to "Hubby Hubby" for the month of September in celebration of the Vermont legislation on September 1.
- Broadcast interviews with all local Vermont network affiliates.
- Extensive media relations outreach to targeted gay community and mainstream print, online, and broadcast outlets.
- Two Ben & Jerry's vans with signage "Just Marriage" traveled to cities throughout Vermont and provided samples of "Hubby Hubby" to celebrate the legislation with locals.
- Development of a special "Hubby Hubby" sundae in its Vermont stores and special signage about the flavor and its nonprofit partner, Just Marriage.

- Digital distribution of information via Ben & Jerry's "Chunkspelunker" e-mail newsletter and online database.
- Campaign posts via Facebook and Twitter.

The results were impressive and received a Silver Anvil excellent award from the Public Relations Society of America (PRSA).

- The campaign reached a wide national audience through mentions on "The Jay Leno Show," "The Late Show with David Letterman," and Perezi-Hilton .com, among many others.
- Overwhelming majority (86 percent) of coverage was rated positive or neutral.
- Interviews with every major network (ABC, NBC, CBS, FOX, and CNN).
- More than I5, 000 visitors to FreedomtoMarry.org within the first week, a 720 percent increase.
- Received 3,250 Facebook "likes" and 580 comments.
- More than 35,000 relevant tweets in the first two weeks and more than 11,000 consumer blog posts.
- Chubby Hubby sales increased almost 5 percent.

Christian Evangelicals Members of religious groups express a great deal of diversity in terms of attitudes and opinions about a variety of topics, but a highly visible element is the evangelical Christian right. In general, they have strong opinions about preserving traditional family values, supporting prayer in public schools, and voting for conservative politicians. They typically are opposed to civil rights for gays and lesbians, sex education in the schools, and abortion. Such groups also express themselves by calling for boycotts of companies who have benefits for same-sex partners or make donations to Planned Parenthood. Disney theme parks and cruise ships, for example, have also generated their wrath by providing same-sex partner benefits and offering gay marriage packages.

The Jewish Community This group has a high demographic profile in comparison to the general population. More than half of all Jewish adults have a college degree and more than a third of Jewish households earn more than $75,000 annually. Jews have a long history of fighting against discrimination of any kind, and tend to be more liberal on social issues. They strongly supported the civil rights movement in the 1960s and tend to vote for Democratic Party candidates.

The Jewish community also has a reputation for being well organized, active in political fund-raising, and influential on pending legislation. The American Israel Public Affairs Committee (AIPAC), for example, is considered one of the most powerful lobbying groups in Washington, D.C. It has a record of successfully promoting legislation in favor of Israel and allocating extensive military aid to the country. Another Jewish group, J Street, is more liberal and actively supports a two-state solution between Israel and the Palestinians.

The Muslim Community The United States has the most diverse Muslim population in the world, which now numbers more than 6 million individuals. There is a stereotype that all Muslims come from the Middle East, but the reality is that Muslims represent a variety of ethnic groups and come from a variety of nations, including those in Asia, Europe, and parts of Africa. In fact, Indonesia's 242 million population makes it the largest Muslim country in the world.

American Muslims are an attractive market because their purchasing power is estimated between $125 billion and more than $200 billion. In addition, research by the American Islamic Conference shows that the percentage of affluent American Muslim households earning more than $100,000 annually is nearly equal to general population households. This has led a number of companies to reach the Muslim population through tailored promotions and offering Halal foods that contain no pork or alcohol.

> It's a multi-faith, inter-ethnic multicultural group—it's not homogeneous. It's multi-faith in that multiple sects within Islam exist in America.
>
> *John Pinna, director of government and international relations for the American Islamic Congress,* in PRWeek

Best Buy, for example, now wishes its Muslim customers "Happy Eid-al-Adha" in its store displays and promotions, Whole Foods now regularly stocks Halal-certified products, and McDonald's even offers Halal chicken McNuggets in the Detroit area where there is a large Muslim population. Western Union focused a public relations campaign around the celebration of Ramadan by sponsoring a "Fly Home" contest for customers from the Middle East and Pakistan. "Ramadan is one of the key sending periods for our customers," explains Maher Kayali, marketing manager for Western Union.

Despite such efforts, a survey by Ogilvy Noor found that 98 percent of American Muslims feel U.S. Brands don't actively reach out to them. Part of the problem is continuing negative stereotypes by segments of the American population about Muslims and Islam. See the Ethics box on page 322 about the backlash that Lowe's received for being a sponsor of the reality TV show *All-American Muslim*.

on the job ETHICS

Lowe's Stumbles on Sponsorship of All-American Muslim

It sounded like a good idea. Lowe's, like many companies, wanted to reach out to the Muslim community so it signed up to be a sponsor of a TLC show, *All-American Muslim*, that showed the daily life of a family living in Michigan. That's the good news. The bad news is that the building supply chain cancelled its advertising after a conservative Christian group, the Florida Family Association, objected to the program.

Lowe's announced on its Facebook page that it was pulling its ads because the show had become a "lightning rod." Its decision, however, generated its own controversy and an avalanche of reader comments, both from individuals who criticized the decision and those who supported it. Many of the in-favor comments fell in the realm of hate speech and Lowe's did nothing to delete the anti-Muslim tirades, claiming "respect for the transparency of social media." This, in turn, outraged civil rights groups that called for a boycott of Lowe's.

This incident raises some ethical dilemmas. Does cancelling its sponsorship also reflect the company's lack of commitment to diversity and inclusion? Would it have been more ethical for Lowe's to stand by their initial decision to sponsor the show and not cave-in to pressure from the Florida Family Association (FFA)? Did Lowe's have an ethical obligation to delete hate speech from its Facebook page, or would that violate the idea of "free speech"? If you were public relations counsel for Lowe's, what advice would you give Lowe's?

In sum, public relations professionals must be attuned to the sensitivities of religious groups and be prepared to engage in conflict management. How would you handle, for example, a threat by a conservative Christian group to boycott your company's products because the company offers same-sex health benefits to employees? Or what would you do to ensure that Jewish employees can fully participate in Passover and other Holy Days? How would you accommodate Muslim employees who, as part of their religion, pray to Mecca five times a day? It is an increasingly diverse marketplace in which public relations staffs must walk a tightrope in attempting to serve varied and often conflicting religious audiences.

The Disability Community

There are almost 60 million people in the United States that have some disability. Many require a wheel chair for mobility, but others are deaf, blind, or have some level of learning, behavioral, or speech disability. Many recognize they are disabled, but others—such as aging baby boomers—are often in denial that their hearing, eyesight, or mobility is gradually diminishing.

Companies and other groups should be sensitive to their needs and how to effectively communicate with them. Often, one feels uncomfortable around a person with a disability. As Barbara Bianchi-Kai, a specialist in disability marketing, writes in *The Strategist*, "We're afraid of offending the person through our actions or our language choices."

She goes on to say that it's okay to use the word *deaf* instead of *hearing impaired*, but that it's more proper to use *mobility impaired* or *physically disabled*. It's not OK to ever use *handicapped* or even worse, *crippled*. Special Olympics has also led a successful campaign to "End the R-Word" because "retard" or "retarded" are demeaning to many highly intelligent and accomplished individuals who may also have some behavioral or speech disability.

As in any communication, language and the medium are key elements. Many deaf people, for example, use American Sign Language (ASL) as their first language. If you can't communicate in ASL, it's best to produce brochures, newsletters, and specialized web pages that are graphics-heavy and text-light. Sight-impaired individuals, on the other hand, not only require bold graphics but at least 18-point type in all printed materials.

Bianchi-Kai says the best medium to reach a variety of disability groups at the same time is television. Closed-captioning makes television accessible to deaf people, and those with speech or mobility disabilities are also easily reached.

The crafting of key messages is important. Many people, particularly those who are aging, don't know or are unwilling to admit that they have a disability such as hearing loss. For such audiences, the message has to be about innovation and making life easier instead of about buying a hearing aid out of necessity.

Summary

A Multicultural Nation

- Audiences are not monolithic. They are a complex mingling of groups with diverse cultural, ethnic, religious, and economic attributes.
- The demographics of the United States are becoming more multicultural. Minorities, by 2050, will constitute the majority of the U.S. population.
- Through technology and research, it's now possible to segment audiences a number of ways that help the public relations communicator understand the characteristics of the audience and how to best communicate with them.
- Public relations professionals will need to be more culturally literate to understand and communicate with diverse audiences.

Reaching Ethnic Audiences

- The three major ethnic groups in the country are Hispanics, African Americans, and Asian Americans.
- There is a great deal of diversity within a particular ethnic or racial group, depending on country of origin, language, educational levels, and income.
- Each group has its own cultural values that must be understood by professional communicators.
- In general, the various ethnic groups are strongly family-oriented and community-minded.
- The ethnic media in the country are rapidly developing, and there are many Spanish-speaking media outlets.
- In conducting campaigns for the Hispanic audience, Spanish is often the preferred language even though the younger generation is increasingly bilingual.

Reaching Diverse Age Groups

- Audiences are generational and each has different values, interests, and needs.
- Public relations practitioners must understand the millennial generation as well as the coming tidal wave of baby boomers reaching retirement. Baby boomers and seniors tend to be relatively affluent and constitute the majority of the travel and tourism business.
- Each group, however, prefers to receive information via different media channels.
- Although youths prefer information online and via cell phones, traditional media such as newspapers and television are still popular with seniors.

Gender/Lifestyle Audiences

- Women are a major and influential audience. They constitute about 60 percent of the workforce, spend most of the family's disposable income, and are more heavily involved in social networking, including blogging.
- The LGBT community is relatively affluent and well educated, and marketing/public relations programs are increasingly directed to them.
- Religious groups run the spectrum from conservative to liberal. The Christian Right is highly vocal, but the Jewish and Muslim communities are somewhat more affluent and represent major purchasing power for goods and services.
- Communicating with the disability community requires sensitivity and specialized tactics such as brochures with large type or captioning on videos.

Case Activity A Campaign to Increase Student Diversity

A state university in the Midwest wants to increase the number of students from multicultural backgrounds. Surveys show that Native Americans, African American, Hispanic, and Asian American students are under-represented in terms of reflecting the state's percentage of minorities in the general population.

University officials want to reach minority high school students in neighborhoods and schools that have a high concentration of these under-represented groups. The campaign would have the theme "Make College Part of Your Future" and provide students and their parents information about the advantages of going to college.

Your public relations firm is awarded a $350,000 contract for a year-long program. The campaign objectives are threefold:

- Encourage students and parents to consider college and take steps to apply.
- Generate understanding that higher education is the key to a good job.
- Convince students and parents to seek more information and visit the campus.

This campaign is not a "one size fits all" situation. What strategies and tactics would you do to effectively reach all of these under-represented groups?

Questions For Review and Discussion

1. Public relations practitioners are cautioned not to think of audiences as monolithic, but as very diverse. Why?
2. How can technology be used to segment audiences?
3. Differences of class, ethnicity, and creed are a fact of life in many countries. What guidelines can PR use towards achieving "unity in diversity"?
4. In your view, have social networking sites helped in cutting across artificial boundaries based on class, color, and ethnicity? How?
5. What reasons would you ascribe to President Barack Obama's popularity across various ethnic groups during his presidential campaign?
6. Divide audiences based on various demographic characteristics.
7. What strategies in your view does PR need in order to reach out to audiences belonging to religious minorities?
8. What are the challenges for PR if audiences are generational, each with exclusive values, interests and needs? Discuss.
9. What are some characteristics of Millennials, also called the E-Generation?
10. What is the baby boomer generation, and what are some of this group's characteristics?
11. Why is the senior audience so important? What are some characteristics of this audience?
12. Why are women considered an important audience for public relations and marketing personnel?
13. What are some characteristics of the gay/lesbian community?
14. In what ways can religious conservatives impact a company's policies and product sales?

Media Resources

Armstrong, S. & others (2012, March). How can multicultural outreach blend heritage and mainstream influences? *PRWeek*, 51–52.

King, N. (2012, November 8). Demographic shifts upend former election landscape. *Wall Street Journal*, A1, 7.

Lazarus, N. (2013, March 20). Ten Trends in Marketing to Latinos. Retrieved from www.mediabistro.com

Lewis, T. (2012, June). Affluent and untapped: Muslim Americans. *PRWeek*, 35–39.

Lights, Camera, Accion! Media companies are piling into the Hispanic market. (2012, December 15). *The Economist*, 68.

Madrid, C. (2012, March). Five tips for multicultural communications. *Public Relations Tactics*, 6.

Nielsen, H. (2013, October). The Value of Diversity and Inclusion. *Public Relations Tactics*, 14.

O'Brien, T. (2013, October). Disability Inclusiveness: It's About How We Do It. Pubic Relations Tactics, 15.

OMG: Getting Inside the Millennial Mind (2012, December). Retrieved from www.scarborough.com

Perez, E. (2012, June). Spanglish Generation: evolution of the Hispanic market. *O'Dwyer's PR Report*, 24.

Phillips, L. (2012, July). Steps for reaching an LGBTQ audience. *Public Relations Tactics*, 6.

Sammons, K. (2012, June). The challenges of minority healthcare communications. *O'Dwyer's PR Report*, 26.

Siegel, L. (2012, October 27–28). Rise of the Tiger Nation (Asian Americans). *Wall Street Journal*, C1–2

Skrilo, L. (2013, June). When multicultural marketing turns into a PR crisis. *O'Dwyer's PR Report*, 32–33.

State of the Asian American Consumer (2012, Quarter 3). Retrieved from www.nielsen.com

Stein, L. (2012, February). Outreach efforts mature to appeal to an older audience. *PRWeek*, 14.

Stein, L. (2012, October). Brands leverage policies and social for LGBT engagement. *PRWeek*, 14.

The lust for Latino lucre: How Americans firms are chasing the elusive Hispanic dollar. (2013, May 11). Economist, 63.

Toth, E. L. (2009). Diversity and public relations practice: Essential knowledge project. Retrieved from *Institute for Public Relations website*: www.instituteforpr.org

Villa, J. (2013, June). Major changes sweeping through Hispanic market. *O'Dwyer's PR Report*, 31.

Zeitzer, D. (2013, February). Why language matters when writing about people with disabilities. *Public Relations Tactics*, 8.

chapter 12

Laws and Applications

After reading this chapter, you will be able to:

Identify which government agencies regulate the commercial speech used by public relations professionals

Explain how public relations professionals can work effectively with lawyers

Describe what public relations professionals need to know about defamation, employee and privacy rights, copyright, and trademark laws

Understand the key issues surrounding freedom of speech and public relations

A Sampling of Legal Problems

The law and its many ramifications are somewhat abstract to the average person. Many people may have difficulty imagining exactly how public relations personnel can run afoul of the law or generate a lawsuit simply by communicating information. The following are just a few of the many ways that public relations practitioners can get in legal hot water:

- Cosmetic surgery company Lifestyle Lift paid a $300,000 settlement to the New York State Attorney General's office after being accused of having employees post fake consumer reviews online.
- LeVar Burton sued Child's Play Communications for $10,000 for failing to adequately represent the actor in the roll-out of his "Reading Rainbow" app for the iPad. When Burton discovered the PR agency was using his likeness on their website to promote their services, he filed another lawsuit, this time for $50,000.
- The Federal Trade Commission (FTC) ruled that two video news releases from King Pharmaceuticals were "false and misleading" because they omitted mention of the risks associated with a painkiller drug and presented misleading claims.
- American Apparel paid a $5 million settlement to film director Woody Allen for using his image in an advertising campaign and other promotional literature without his permission.
- Papa John's Pizza was hit with a $250 million class action suit charging it sent customers promotional text messages without receiving opt-in permission from the consumers. The pizza chain agreed to settle for $16.5 million.
- Koch Industries filed a lawsuit when Internet pranksters affiliated with Youth for Climate Truth issued a news release attributed to the conglomerate suggesting that Koch Industries had changed its position on climate change research and advocacy. Koch sued for "damages for the cost of responding to the fake release, trademark infringement, cybersquatting and legal expenses in pursuing the pranksters," according to *Suffolk Media Law* journal.

These examples provide some idea of the legal pitfalls that a public relations person may encounter. Many of the charges were eventually dismissed or settled out of court, but the organizations paid dearly for the adverse publicity and the expense of defending themselves.

Public relations personnel are charged with winning legal cases in the "court of public opinion." The prospect of litigation, as just illustrated, can appear from about anywhere. For instance, in a diverse world, public relations practitioners need to be fully aware and sensitive to cultural and religious traditions. See the Multicultural World box on page 328 for more discussion on this issue.

A public relations person can be named a coconspirator with other organizational officials if he or she:

- Participates in an illegal action such as bribing a government official or covering up information of vital interest to public health and safety.
- Counsels and guides the policy behind an illegal action.
- Takes a major personal part in the illegal action.

on the job

A MULTICULTURAL WORLD

MillerCoors Faces Controversy in a Long-Held Sponsorship

For seven years MillerCoors had been a primary sponsor of the Puerto Rican Day Parade in New York City. The parade is a major cultural event, drawing 80,000 participants and 2 million spectators and providing high visibility for Miller Coors within the Latino community. But in 2013, the brewer ran into public relations and potential legal trouble.

MillerCoors, producer of Coors Light beer, produced special packaging for the light beer. The cans featured a circular logo of the Puerto Rican flag shaped as an apple accompanied by the words "National Puerto Rican Day Parade, Inc." The logo was reviewed and approved by the parade organizers—National Puerto Rican Day Parade.

But selling beer by associating it with a national emblem backfired. City Councilwoman Melissa Mark-Viverito told the *New York Times*, "The flag is a symbol of a nation, of a culture, and slapping it on a can of beer is disrespectful and trivializes a community and its contributions." A Puerto Rican activist organization sent a letter of objection to MilllerCoors and coordinated a protest at a Coors distribution center.

MillerCoors responded quickly distributing letters and statements to the media and to the activists. The company also quit making and distributing the cans. MillerCoors Chief Public Affairs and Communications Officer Nehl Horton wrote: "We apologize if the graphics on our promotional packaging inadvertently offended you or any other members of the Puerto Rican community."

Dealing with the public outcry wasn't the only problem that MillerCoors faced. The New York attorney general Eric Schneiderman contacted MillerCoors and the National Puerto Rican Day Parade organization requesting full disclosure of the financial relationship between the entities.

Do you think MillerCoors handled the controversy well? Why or why not?

What potential legal issues do you see?

How could the brewer have avoided the cultural misstep?

- Helps establish a "front group" whereby the connection to the public relations firm or its clients is kept hidden.
- Cooperates in any other way to further an illegal action.

These five concepts also apply to public relations firms that create, produce, and distribute materials on behalf of clients. The courts have ruled on more than one occasion that public relations firms cannot hide behind the defense of "the client told me to do it." Public relations firms have a legal responsibility to practice "due diligence" in the type of information and documentation supplied by a client. Regulatory agencies such as the FTC (Federal Trade Commission) have the power under the Lanham Act to file charges against public relations firms that distribute false and misleading information.

Libel and Defamation

Traditionally, *libel* was a printed falsehood and *slander* was an oral statement that was false. Today, as a practical matter, there is little difference in the two, and the courts often use *defamation* as a collective term.

Essentially, defamation is any false statement about a person (or organization) that creates public hatred, contempt, or ridicule, or inflicts injury on reputation. A person filing a defamation suit usually must prove that:

- the false statement was communicated to others through print, broadcast, or electronic means;
- the person was identified or is identifiable;
- there is actual injury in the form of money losses, loss of reputation, or mental suffering; and
- the person making the statement was malicious or negligent.

In general, private citizens have more success winning defamation suits than do public figures or corporations. With public figures—government officials, entertainers, political candidates, and other newsworthy personalities—there is the extra test of whether the libelous statements were made with actual malice (*New York Times v. Sullivan*).

Corporations, to some degree, also are considered "public figures" by the courts for several reasons: (1) They engage in advertising and promotion offering products and services to the public, (2) they are often involved in matters of public controversy and public policy, and (3) they have some degree of access to the media—through regular advertising and news releases—that enables them to respond to and rebut defamatory charges made against them.

Avoiding Libel Suits

Libel suits can be filed against organizational officials who make libelous accusations during a media interview, send out news releases that make false statements, or injure someone's reputation. For example, suits have been filed for calling a news reporter "a pimp for all environmental groups." Such language, although highly quotable and colorful, can provoke legal retaliation. Accurate information, and a delicate choice of words, must be used in all news releases.

Another potentially dangerous practice is making unflattering comments about the competition's products. Although comparative advertising is the norm in the United States, a company must walk a narrow line between comparison and "trade libel," or "product disparagement." Statements should be truthful, with factual evidence and scientific demonstration available to substantiate them. Companies often charge competitors with overstepping the boundary between "puffery" and "factual representation."

An organization can offer the opinion that a particular product or service is the "best" or "a revolutionary development" if the context clearly shows that the communication is a statement of opinion attributed to someone. Then it is classified as "puffery" and doesn't require factual evidence.

Don Sneed, Tim Wulfemeyer, and Harry Stonecipher, in a *Public Relations Review* article, say that a news release should be written to indicate clearly statements of opinion and statements of fact. They suggest that:

1. opinion statements be accompanied by the facts on which the opinions are based;
2. statements of opinion be clearly labeled as such; and
3. the context of the language surrounding the expression of opinion be reviewed for possible legal implications.

The Fair Comment Defense

Organizations can do much to ensure that their communications avoid materials that could lead to potential lawsuits. By the same token, organizations are somewhat limited in their ability to use legal measures to defend themselves against criticism.

Executives are often incensed when an environmental group includes their corporation on its annual "dirty dozen" polluters or similar lists. Executives are also unhappy when a consumer affairs blogger flatly calls the product a "rip-off."

A corporate reputation may be damaged and product sales may go down, but a defamation case is difficult to win because, as previously mentioned, the accuser must prove actual malice. Also operating is the concept of *fair comment and criticism*.

This defense is used by theater and music critics when they lambaste a play or concert. Fair comment also means that when companies and individuals voluntarily display their wares to the public for sale or consumption, they have no real recourse against criticism done with honest purpose and lack of malicious intent.

A utility company in Indiana, for example, once tried to sue a citizen who had written a letter to a newspaper criticizing the utility for seeking a rate hike. The judge threw the suit out of court, stating that the rate increase was a "matter of public interest and concern" even if the letter writer didn't have all the facts straight.

Invasion of Privacy

An area of law that particularly applies to employees of an organization is *invasion of privacy*. Public relations staff must be particularly sensitive to the issue of privacy in at least four areas:

- Employee communication
- Photo releases
- Product publicity and advertising
- Media inquiries about employees

Employee Communication

It is no longer true, if it ever was, that an organization has an unlimited right to publicize the activities of its employees. In fact, Morton J. Simon, a Philadelphia lawyer and author of *Public Relations Law*, writes, "It should not be assumed that a person's status as an employee waives his right to privacy." Simon correctly points out that a company newsletter or magazine does not enjoy the same First Amendment protection that the news media enjoy when they claim "newsworthiness" and "public interest."

This distinction does not impede the effectiveness of newsletters, but it does indicate that editors should try to keep employee stories organization-oriented. Indeed, most lawsuits and complaints are generated by "personals columns" that may invade the privacy of employees. Although a mention that Mary Worth is now a great-grandmother may sound completely innocent, she may consider the information a violation of her privacy. The situation may be further compounded into possible defamation by "cutesy" comments on social media such as Facebook.

In sum, one should avoid anything that might embarrass or subject an employee to ridicule by fellow employees. Here are some guidelines to remember when writing about employee activities:

- Keep the focus on organization-related activities.
- Have employees submit "personals" in writing.
- Double-check all information for accuracy.
- Ask: "Will this embarrass anyone or cause someone to be the butt of jokes?"
- Don't rely on secondhand information; confirm the facts with the person involved.
- Don't include racial or ethnic designations of employees in any articles.

Photo Releases

An organization must have a signed release on file if it wants to use the photographs or comments of its employees and other individuals in product publicity, sales brochures, and advertising. In a new book on public relations law, Parkinson and Parkinson offer straightforward advice about contracts that apply to photo releases: a contract is not binding without some form of compensation. Therefore, an added precaution is to give some financial compensation to make a more binding contract. A second principle is that amicable relationships can change, increasing the importance of clarity and documentation, although not necessarily in legal language. According to Michael and L. Marie Parkinson, authors of *Public Relations Law: A Supplemental Text*, the courts require only that agreements be understandable and do-able for each side.

Public relations departments, in addition, should take the precaution of (1) storing all photographs electronically, (2) dating them, and (3) giving the context of the situation. This precludes the use of old photos that could embarrass employees or subject them to ridicule. In other cases, it precludes using photographs of persons who are no longer employed with the company or have died. This method also helps to make certain that a photo taken for the employee newsletter isn't used in an advertisement. If a photo of an employee or customer is used in product publicity, sales brochures, or advertisements, the standard practice is to obtain a signed release.

Product Publicity and Advertising

The National Football League (NFL) unfortunately learned the basics of photo releases the hard way. The NFL was sued by a group of retired players because the League continued to use the former players' names and images. Six players filed the class action lawsuit in which they accused the NFL of using retired players' identities in films and highlight reels to market the League. The NFL settled the lawsuit by setting up a $42 million fund to help retired players with medical expenses and other issues related to the transition out of their playing careers. The League also paid $8 million in legal costs. "The retired players who created these glory days . . . have gone almost completely uncompensated for this use of their identities," the plaintiffs argued. This action is called *misappropriation of personality*. Jerry Della Femina, an advertising executive, succinctly makes the point: Get permission. "If I used my mother in an ad," he said, "I'd get her permission—and I almost trust her 100 percent."

Media Inquiries about Employees

Because press inquiries have the potential to invade an employee's right of privacy, public relations personnel should follow basic guidelines as to what information will be provided on the employee's behalf.

In general, employers should give a news reporter only basic information.

Do Provide:

1. confirmation that the person is an employee,
2. the person's title and job description, and
3. date of beginning employment, or, if applicable, date of termination.

Do Not Provide Employee's:

1. salary,
2. home address,
3. marital status,
4. number of children,
5. organizational memberships, or
6. job performance.

Here we try to correct some misconceptions about journalists' legal rights, because often journalists try to use those "rights" to coerce information or access from public relations practitioners.

Parkinson and Parkinson, Public Relations Law: A Supplemental Text

If a reporter does seek any of this information because of the nature of the story, several principles should be followed. First, as Parkinson and Parkinson clearly establish in their public relations law text, the rights of reporters are often exaggerated to mythic levels, partly by the journalists themselves. In fact, reporters have no greater rights to private information than any other citizen. Second, because the information is private, it should be provided by the employee through arrangement with the public relations person. What the employee chooses to tell the reporter is not then the company's responsibility.

If an organization uses biographical sheets, it is important that they be dated, kept current, and used by permission of the employee. A sheet compiled by an employee five years previously may be hopelessly out of date. This is also true of file photographs taken at the time of a person's employment.

Although employee privacy remains an important consideration, the trend is toward increased monitoring of employee e-mail by employers, who are concerned about being held liable if an employee posts a racial slur, engages in sexual harassment online, or even transmits sexually explicit jokes that might cause another employee to perceive the workplace as a "hostile" environment. In other words, everyone should assume that any e-mails he or she writes at work are subject to monitoring and that he or she can be fired if the e-mails violate company policy. Further complicating this issue is the fact that government employees may have their e-mails made public if some interested party files a Freedom of Information

Act (FOIA) request. E-mails produced by a public employee on a government-owned computer are considered requestable documents under the FOIA.

Other important, and sometimes controversial, aspects of employee free speech include the tension between whistle-blowing and protection of an organization's trade secrets. State and federal laws generally protect the right of employees to "blow the whistle" if an organization is guilty of illegal activity, but the protections are limited and the requirements for the whistle-blower are quite specific. Whistle-blowing can occur in corporate, nonprofit, and government organizations. For example, an employee might blow the whistle on his or her organization by reporting to the Environmental Protection Agency (EPA) about the illegal release of a toxic substance from a manufacturing plant.

Copyright Law

Should a news release be copyrighted? How about a corporate annual report? Can a *New Yorker* cartoon be used in the company magazine without permission? What about reprinting an article from *Fortune* magazine and distributing it to the company's sales staff? Are government reports copyrighted? What about posting a video clip from Comedy Central on the Internet? What constitutes copyright infringement?

These are some of the bothersome questions that a public relations professional should be able to answer. Knowledge of copyright law is important from two perspectives: (1) what organizational materials should be copyrighted and (2) how to utilize the copyrighted materials of others correctly.

In very simple terms, *copyright* means protection of a creative work from unauthorized use. A section of the U.S. copyright law of 1978 states: "Copyright protection subsists . . . in the original works of authorship fixed in any tangible medium of expression now known or later developed." The word *authorship* is defined in seven categories: (1) literary works; (2) musical works; (3) dramatic works; (4) pantomimes and choreographic works; (5) pictorial, graphic, or sculptural works; (6) motion pictures; and (7) sound recordings. The word *fixed* means that the work is sufficiently permanent or stable to permit it to be perceived, reproduced, or otherwise communicated.

The shield of copyright protection was weakened somewhat in 1991, when the U.S. Supreme Court ruled unanimously that directories, computer databases, and other compilations of facts may be copied and republished unless they display "some minimum degree of creativity." The Court stated, "Raw facts may be copied at will."

Thus a copyright does not protect ideas, only the specific ways in which those ideas are expressed. An idea for promoting a product, for example, cannot be copyrighted—but brochures, drawings, news features, animated cartoons, display booths, photographs, recordings, videotapes, corporate symbols, slogans, and the like, that express a particular idea can be copyrighted.

Because much money, effort, time, and creative talent are spent on developing organizational materials, obtaining copyright protection for them is important. By copyrighting materials, a company can prevent its competitors from capitalizing on its creative work or producing a facsimile brochure that may mislead the public.

The law presumes that material produced in some tangible form is copyrighted from the moment it is created. This presumption of copyright is often sufficient to discourage unauthorized use, and the writer or creator of the material has some legal protection if he or she can prove that the material was created before another person claims having created it. A more formal step, providing full legal protection, is official registration of the copyrighted work within three months after its creation. This process consists of depositing two copies of the manuscript (it is not necessary that it has been published), recording, or artwork with the Copyright Office of the Library of Congress. Registration is not a condition of copyright protection, but it is a prerequisite to an infringement action against unauthorized use by others. The Copyright Term Extension Act, passed in 1998 and reaffirmed by the U.S. Supreme Court (*Eldred v. Ashcroft*) in 2003, protects original material for the life of the creator plus 70 years for individual works and 95 years from publication for copyrights held by corporations.

Fair Use versus Infringement

Public relations people are in the business of gathering information from a variety of sources, so it is important to know where fair use ends and infringement begins.

Fair use means that part of a copyrighted article may be quoted directly, but the quoted material must be brief in relation to the length of the original work. It may be, for example, only one paragraph of a 750-word article and up to 300 words in a long article or book chapter. Complete attribution of the source must be given regardless of the length of the quotation. If the passage is quoted verbatim, quote marks must be used.

It is important to note, however, that the concept of fair use has distinct limitations if part of the copyrighted material is to be used in advertisements and promotional brochures. In this case, permission is required. It also is important for the original source to approve the context in which the quote is used. A quote out of context often runs into legal trouble if it implies endorsement of a product or service.

The copyright law does allow limited copying of a work for fair use such as criticism, comment, or research. However, in recent years, the courts have considerably narrowed the concept of "fair use" when multiple copies of a copyrighted work are involved.

News and entertainment website BuzzFeed faced a lawsuit seeking $3.6 million by photographer Kai Eiselein. The photographer claimed a picture he posted on Flickr of a soccer player heading a ball was captured and used without his permission by BuzzFeed in a feature titled, "The 30 Funniest Header Faces." He contacted BuzzFeed and asked the site to take down the photo they were using without permission. BuzzFeed took it down, but by that time Eiselein claimed the image had already gone viral. The damage was done.

Legal experts suggested that the photographer likely would not win a multimillion dollar verdict. But *Forbes* magazine opined at the time, "Of course, it's best to avoid a fight over fair use in the first place. Companies like BuzzFeed would be better served by steering clear of images that aren't either in the public domain or easily licensable."

The ready availability of unlicensed content through online and social media sources has only served to further muddy the legal waters surrounding copyright infringement and fair use. Distribution of more mainstream copyrighted work can be arranged for a fee with the copyright holder or often by paying a royalty fee to the Copyright Clearance Center (www.copyright.com), which has been established to represent a large number of publishers.

Government documents (city, county, state, and federal) are in the public domain and cannot be copyrighted. Public relations personnel, under the fair use doctrine, can freely use quotations and statistics from a government document, but care must be exercised to ensure that the material is in context and not misleading. The most common problem occurs when an organization uses a government report as a form of endorsement for its services or products. An airline, for example, might cite a government study showing that it provides the most service to customers, but neglect to state the basis of comparison or other factors.

Photography and Artwork

The copyright law makes it clear that freelance and commercial photographers retain ownership of their work. In other words, a customer who buys a copyrighted photo owns the item itself, but not the right to make additional copies. That right remains with the photographer unless transferred in writing.

In a further extension of this right, the duplication of copyrighted photos is also illegal. This was established in a 1990 U.S. Federal District Court case in which the Professional Photographers of America (PPofA) sued a nationwide photofinishing firm for ignoring copyright notices on pictures sent for additional copies. Photoshop edits and other manipulations of original artwork can also violate copyright provisions.

Freelance photographers generally charge for a picture on the basis of its use. If it is used only once, perhaps for an employee newsletter, the fee is low. If, however, the company wants to use the picture in the corporate annual report or on the company calendar, the fee may be considerably higher. Consequently, it is important for a public relations person to tell the photographer exactly how the picture will be used.

Arrangements and fees then can be determined for (1) one-time use, (2) unlimited use, or (3) the payment of royalties every time the picture is used. As noted above, the availability of photographs—both professional and amateur—online has only served to further complicate these issues. Another example is a lawsuit filed by photographer Robert Caplin against Mario Armando Lavandeira, Jr. (better known as Perez Hilton). Caplin accused Lavandeira of using 14 of his photos on the perezhilton.com website without authorization. The safest way to treat use of photographs is to pay for their use unless they are in the public domain.

The Rights of Freelance Writers

In the *Reid* case (*Community for Creative Nonviolence v. Reid*), the U.S. Supreme Court in 1989 set a lasting precedent that writers retain ownership of their work and that purchasers of it gain merely a "license" to reproduce the copyrighted work.

Prior to this ruling, the common practice was to assume that commissioned articles are "work for hire" and that the purchaser owns the copyright. In other words, a magazine could reproduce the article in any number of ways and even sell it to another publication without the writer's permission.

Under the *Reid* interpretation, ownership of a writer's work is subject to negotiation and contractual agreement. Writers may agree to assign all copyright rights to the work they have been hired to do or they may give permission only for a specific one-time use.

In a related matter, freelance writers are pressing for additional compensation if an organization puts their work on CD-ROM, online databases, or the Web. Writers won a major victory when the Supreme Court (*New York Times v. Tasini*) ruled that publishers, by making articles accessible through electronic databases, infringe the copyrights of freelance contributors.

Public relations firms and corporate public relations departments are responsible for ensuring compliance with the copyright law. This means that all agreements with a freelance writer must be in writing, the use of the material must be clearly stated, and fair exchange of value must be made. Ideally, public relations personnel should negotiate multiple rights or even complete ownership of the copyright.

Copyright Issues on the Internet

The Internet and World Wide Web raise distinct issues about the protection of intellectual property. Two issues regarding copyright are (1) the downloading of copyrighted material and (2) the unauthorized uploading of such material.

The Downloading of Material In general, the same rules apply to cyberspace as to more earthbound methods of expressing and disseminating ideas. Original materials in digital form are still protected by copyright, a precedent first established with legal language delivered by telegraph early in the last century. The fair use limits for materials found on the Internet are essentially the same as the fair use of materials disseminated by any other means.

Related to this is the use of news articles and features that are sent via e-mail or the Web to the clients of clipping services. An organization may use such clips to track its publicity efforts, but it can't distribute the article on its own website or intranet without permission and a royalty payment to the publication where the article appeared.

The Uploading of Material In many cases, owners of copyrighted material have uploaded various kinds of information with the intention of making it freely available. Examples include software, games, and even entire books. The problem comes, however, when third parties upload copyrighted material without permission. Consequently, copyright holders are increasingly patrolling the Internet to stop the unauthorized use of material.

A good example is Google Books. The online behemoth Google expressed its intention to scan and make available online every book in the world. In 2005, the Authors Guild filed a class action lawsuit against Google. The Guild argued that the scanning project was a violation of copyright and it sought a $125 million legal settlement. As the case wends its way through the court system, the United States Court of Appeals for the Second Circuit ruled that a lower court had to consider the fair use issues cited in the case before determining whether the class action suit could move forward.

Another example is Viacom, which constantly monitors such sites as Google's YouTube for unauthorized postings of video clips from its various television programs. Under the 1998 Digital Millennium Copyright Act, Internet businesses such as YouTube are immune from liability for material posted by its users, but are required to take down any infringing material after it is notified by the copyright owner. In one year alone, YouTube removed 230,000 clips at the request of Viacom. The posting of illegal video clips continues to dog the industry, causing a great deal of lobbying for more protective legislation and even major lawsuits.

Copyright Guidelines

A number of points have been discussed about copyright. A public relations person should keep the following in mind:

- Ideas cannot be copyrighted, but the expression of those ideas can be.
- Major public relations materials (brochures, annual reports, videotapes, motion pictures, position papers, and the like) should be copyrighted, if only to prevent unauthorized use by competitors.

- Despite the concept of fair use, any copyrighted material intended directly to advance the sales and profits of an organization should not be used unless permission is given.
- Copyrighted material should not be taken out of context, particularly if it implies endorsement of the organization's services or products.
- Quantity reprints of an article should be ordered from the publisher.
- Permission is required to use segments of television programs or motion pictures.
- Permission must be obtained to use segments of popular songs (written verses or sound recordings) from a recording company.
- Photographers and freelance writers retain the rights to their works. Permission and fees must be negotiated to use works for purposes other than originally agreed on.
- Photographs of current celebrities or those who are now deceased cannot be used for promotion and publicity purposes without permission.
- Permission is required to reprint cartoon characters, such as Snoopy or Garfield. In addition, cartoons and other artwork or illustrations in a publication are copyrighted.
- Government documents are not copyrighted, but caution is necessary if the material is used in a way that implies endorsement of products or services.
- Private letters, or excerpts from them, cannot be published or used in sales and publicity materials without the permission of the letter writer.
- Original material posted on the Internet and the World Wide Web has copyright protection.
- The copyrighted material of others should not be posted on the Internet unless specific permission is granted.

Trademark Law

What do the names Diet Coke, iTunes, Kindle, eBay, Academy Awards, and even Coco Chanel have in common? They are all registered trademarks protected by law.

A *trademark* is a word, symbol, or slogan, used singly or in combination, that identifies a product's origin. According to Susan L. Cohen, writing in *Editor & Publisher*'s annual trademark supplement, "It also serves as an indicator of quality, a kind of shorthand for consumers to use in recognizing goods in a complex marketplace." Research indicates, for example, that 53 percent of Americans say brand quality takes precedence over price considerations, making brand identity crucial to commercial success.

The concept of a trademark is nothing new. The ancient Egyptians carved marks into the stones of the pyramids, and the craftsmen of the Middle Ages used guild marks to identify the source and quality of products. What is new, however, is the proliferation of trademarks and service marks in modern society. Coca-Cola may be the world's most recognized trademark, according to some studies, but it is only 1 of over 1 million active trademarks registered with the Federal Patent and Trademark Office (FPTO). About 40,000 trademarks are registered worldwide each year, according to the World Intellectual Property Association (WIPA).

Protecting Valuable Trademarks

The Chrysler corporation has for years placed trademark advertisements to protect the name "Jeep."

Sports logos and team uniforms constitute one of the largest categories of registered trademarks. A *licensing fee* must be paid before anyone can use logos for commercial products and promotions. *The Licensing Letter* is a trade publication that reports on licensing issues. Recently it announced that Major League Baseball (MLB) pocketed \$2.75 billion, the NFL earned \$2.7 billion, the National Basketball Association (NBA) earned \$1.75 billion, and the National Hockey League (NHL) made \$630 million just selling licensed merchandise, and the sale of college and university trademarked goods is rapidly approaching that mark.

The Collegiate Licensing Company (CLC) represents 200 universities in their licensing agreements. CLC estimates that licensed university products earn about \$4.6 billion annually. The University of Texas at Austin, the University of Alabama, and the University of Kentucky topped the list of CLC's highest earning clients. After winning the NCAA men's basketball championship in 2012, Kentucky earned \$6.7 million from licensed products. Schools license everything from beer mugs to T-shirts. The penalty for not paying a licensing fee is steep. The NFL and federal investigators collaborated in a months-long investigation they called "Project Red Zone" leading up to the Super Bowl. They confiscated more than \$17 million in bogus goods and filed criminal charges against dozens of offending vendors. They also closed down more than 300 websites selling unlicensed goods ranging from jerseys to caps to jackets. An array of confiscated items is shown in the photograph on page 339.

Because brand identity is so valuable, a major clothing company took an equally aggressive approach against a whimsical startup making a play on its brand name and logo. South Butt was a small company formed as a spoof on the North Face outdoor clothing brand. With the logo inverted, the new company's name, South Butt, became quite apt as the logo took on an abstract resemblance to that lower anatomical part. North Face threatened and then filed suit, boosting the spoof into a viable company through the viral response of supporters to a South Butt Facebook page.

Confiscated counterfeit merchandise like this from Super Bowl XLVII in New Orleans is often displayed by law enforcement at news conferences.

An out-of-court settlement was reached and the South Butt company reformed as The Butt Face. North Face was no more enamored with that parody and again filed suit. This time the litigation ended less amicably. *Courthouse News Service* reported that in a consent judgment the South Butt founders "agreed to abandon their trademark application for 'The Butt Face,' cease sales of products, silence all social media promotions and take down YouTube videos." They were also fined $65,000, which decreased by $1,000 for every month they continued complying with the terms of the judgment.

The Protection of Trademarks

There are three basic guidelines regarding the use of trademarks:

- Trademarks are proper adjectives and should be capitalized and followed by a generic noun or phrase (e.g., *Kleenex tissues* or *Rollerblade skates*).
- Trademarks should not be pluralized or used in the possessive form. Saying, "American Express's credit card" is improper.
- Trademarks are never verbs. Saying, "The client FedExed the package" violates the rule.

Organizations adamantly insist on the proper use of their trademarks in order to avoid the problem of the name or slogan becoming generic. Or, to put it another way, a brand name becomes a common noun through general public use. Some trade names that have become generic include *aspirin*, *thermos*, *cornflakes*, *nylon*, *cellophane*, and *yo-yo*. This means that any company can use these names to describe a product.

Organizations take the step of designating brand names and slogans with various marks. The registered trademark symbol is a superscript, small capital "R" in a circle: ®. "Registered in U.S. Patent and Trademark Office" and "Reg. U.S. Pat. Off." may also be used. A "TM" in small capital letters indicates a trademark that isn't registered. It represents a company's common-law claim to a right of trademark or a trademark for which registration is pending. For example, 3M™ Post-it® Notes.

A *service mark* is like a trademark, but it designates a service rather than a product, or is a logo. An "SM" in small capitals in a circle—(SM)—is the symbol for a registered service mark. If registration is pending, the "SM" should be used without the circle.

These symbols are used in advertising, product labeling, news releases, company brochures, and so on, to let the public and competitors know that a name, slogan, or symbol is protected by law. Chrysler regularly runs trademark ads to protect the "Jeep" brand from becoming a generic term for sports utility or other off-road vehicles.

Public relations practitioners play an important role in protecting the trademarks of their clients. They safeguard trademarks and respect other organizational trademarks in the following ways:

- Ensure that company trademarks are capitalized and used properly in all organizational literature and graphics. Lax supervision can cause loss of trademark protection.
- Distribute trademark brochures to editors and reporters and place advertisements in trade publications designating names to be capitalized.
- Educate employees as to what the organization's trademarks are and how to use them correctly.
- Monitor the mass media to make certain that trademarks are used correctly. If they are not, send a gentle reminder.
- Check publications to ensure that other organizations are not infringing on a registered trademark. If they are, the company legal department should protest with letters and threats of possible lawsuits.
- Make sure the trademark is actually being used. The Trademark Act does not permit an organization to hold a name in reserve.
- Ensure that the trademarks of other organizations are correctly used and properly noted.
- Avoid the use of trademarked symbols or cartoon figures in promotional materials without the explicit permission of their owner. In some cases, to be discussed, a licensing fee is required.

The Problem of Trademark Infringement

Today, in a marketplace populated with thousands of businesses and organizations, finding a trademark not already in use is extremely difficult. The task is even more frustrating if a company wants to use a trademark on an international level.

The complexity of finding a new name, coupled with the attempts of many to capitalize on an already known trade name, has spawned a number of lawsuits and complaints claiming trademark infringement. An example is when sportswear retailer Under Armour filed a lawsuit against rival Nike alleging the latter had used Under Armour's trademarked phrase "I Will" in advertising. The Nike tagline in question was "I will protect my home court." Organizations often claim that their registered trademarks are being improperly exploited by others for commercial gain. In many cases, conflicts are settled out of court; in others, the courts have to weigh the evidence and make a decision based on the following:

- Has the defendant used a name as a way of capitalizing on the reputation of another organization's trademark—and does the defendant benefit from the original organization's investment in popularizing its trademark?

- Is there an intent (real or otherwise) to create confusion in the public's mind? Is there an intent to imply a connection between the defendant's product and the item identified by trademark?
- How similar are the two organizations? Are they providing the same kinds of products or services?
- Has the original organization actively protected the trademark by publicizing it and by actually continuing to use it in connection with its products or services?
- Is the trademark unique? A company with a trademark that simply describes a common product might be in trouble.

Misappropriation of Personality

A form of trademark infringement also can result from the unauthorized use of well-known entertainers, professional athletes, and other public figures in an organization's publicity and advertising materials. A photo of a rock or movie star may make a company's advertising campaign more interesting, but the courts call it "misappropriation of personality" if permission and licensing fees have not been negotiated.

Deceased celebrities also are protected. To use a likeness or actual photo of a personality such as Elvis Presley, Marilyn Monroe, or Michael Jackson, the user must pay a licensing fee to an agent representing the family, studio, or estate of the deceased. The estate of Marilyn Monroe sold the licensing rights to her image to a Canadian marketing firm for an estimated $20 million to $30 million. The Presley estate, almost 30 years after his death, is still the "King," with about $50 million in income annually. Similar to the Monroe business deal, Presley's estate sold an 85 percent stake in his licensing rights to CKX, Inc., an entertainment conglomerate, for $100 million. Even boxing legend Muhammad Ali made a deal with CKX, Inc. The company paid the boxer $50 million for the rights to license his name and likeness. According to the *Wall Street Journal*, Ali's name and image currently generate about $4 million to $7 million annually in licensing fees and endorsements.

The *Guardian* newspaper reported that U.S. revenue generated by dead celebrities is $2.25 billion. Not all of that is from licensing, of course. But when it comes to protecting the value of a dead celebrity (or "delebs" as the *Guardian* dubbed them) heirs can be aggressive. The Albert Einstein estate, which makes millions from the licensing rights to Baby Einstein products, sued General Motors when the automaker ran an ad showing Einstein's head superimposed on a sexy, nude torso. The courts found, however, that the image was in the public domain giving GM the right to use it. In another example, every evening the sidekick of late night talk show host Johnny Carson introduced the comedian with the phrase "Here's Johnny." So the Carson heirs went to court to stop the marketing of a portable toilet under the moniker "Here's Johnny." In this case, the courts upheld the rights of the estate and issued an injunction to end the marketing campaign.

The legal doctrine is the *right of publicity*, which gives entertainers, athletes, and other celebrities the sole ability to cash in on their fame. The legal right is loosely akin to a trademark or copyright, and many states have made it a commercial asset that can be inherited by a celebrity's descendents. Legal protection also extends to the use of "sound-alikes" and "look-alikes."

Regulations by Government Agencies

The promotion of products and services, whether through advertising, product publicity, or other techniques, is not protected by the First Amendment. Instead, the courts have traditionally ruled that such activities fall under the doctrine of commercial speech. This means that messages can be regulated by the state in the interest of public health, safety, and consumer protection.

Consequently, the states and the federal government have passed legislation that regulates commercial speech and even restricts it if standards of disclosure, truth, and accuracy are violated. One consequence was the banning of cigarette advertising on television in the 1960s. A more difficult legal question is whether government can completely ban the advertising or promotion of a legally sold product such as cigarettes or alcohol.

Public relations personnel involved in product publicity and the distribution of financial information should be aware of guidelines established by major government agencies such as the Federal Trade Commission (FTC), the Securities and Exchange Commission (SEC), and even the Federal Communications Commission (FCC).

Federal Trade Commission

The Federal Trade Commission has jurisdiction to determine that advertisements are not deceptive or misleading. Public relations personnel should also know that the Commission has jurisdiction over product news releases and other forms of product publicity, such as videos and brochures. The FTC makes it clear that its purview also includes social media such as blogs:

"FTC guidelines state that businesses and reviewers will be liable for any false statements made about a product. If a blogger receives a free sample of skin cream that claims to cure his eczema, for example, the company and the blogger could be held liable for false advertising." See the Social Media in Action box about the celebrity endorsements on page 343 for an example of this questionable behavior.

In the eyes of the FTC, both advertisements and product publicity materials are vehicles of commercial trade—and therefore are subject to regulation. In fact, Section 43(a) of the Lanham Act makes it clear that anyone, including public relations personnel, is subject to liability if that person participates in the making or dissemination of a false and misleading representation in any advertising or promotional material. This includes advertising and public relations firms, which also can be held liable for writing, producing, and distributing product publicity materials on behalf of clients.

An example of an FTC complaint is the one filed against Kellogg for claiming that its Frosted Mini-Wheats were "clinically shown to improve kids' attentiveness by nearly 20%." The Commission charged that the claim was deceptive and Kellogg pulled the ads. The cereal maker also faced a class action lawsuit by consumers, which it eventually settled for $4 million. It also agreed to stick to statements such as: "Clinical studies have shown that kids who eat a filling breakfast like Frosted Mini-Wheats have an 11 percent better attentiveness in school than kids who skip breakfast."

A Campbell Soup case raises an important aspect of FTC guidelines. The soup company claimed that because its soups were low in fat and cholesterol, they were helpful in fighting heart disease. What Campbell Soup didn't say was that the high sodium in the soup could actually increase the risk of heart disease. Although a publicized fact may be accurate in itself, FTC staff also considers the context or "net impression received by the consumers." In Campbell's case, advertising copywriters and publicists ignored the information about high sodium, which placed an entirely new perspective on the health benefits of the soup.

Hollywood's abuse of endorsements and testimonials to publicize its films also has attracted the scrutiny of the FTC. It was discovered that Sony Pictures had concocted quotes from a fictitious movie critic to publicize four of its films. And 20th Century Fox admitted that it had hired actors to appear in "man on the street" commercials to portray unpaid moviegoers.

Recently, the FTC has been focusing on the marketing of food and beverages to children. The agency subpoenaed 44 food marketers, asking for detailed reports on how much they spend promoting their products to children and adolescents to determine whether more federal regulations might be required.

FTC investigators are always on the lookout for unsubstantiated claims and various forms of misleading or deceptive information. Some of the words in promotional materials that trigger FTC interest are *authentic, certified, cure, custom-made, germ-free, natural, unbreakable, perfect, first-class, exclusive,* and *reliable*.

The FTC also has established guidelines for "green" marketing and the use of "low-carb" in advertisements and publicity materials for food products. The FTC has ruled that anyone who endorses a product, including celebrities and bloggers, must make explicit the compensation received from companies. The FTC guidelines also state that businesses and reviewers (including bloggers) may be held liable for any false statements about a product.

on the job

SOCIAL MEDIA IN ACTION

The FTC Tackles Undisclosed Celebrity Social Media Endorsements

The Federal Trade Commission is attempting to rein in celebrities who are paid thousands of dollars to endorse products through the celebrities' social media outlets. In 2013, the FTC issued a revised set of social media disclosure guidelines. The last time the federal regulatory body issued such guidelines was 2000. A lot has happened in the online and social media landscape since then.

Broadly the guidelines include:

1. The regulations apply to anyone and any medium (now existing or yet to be developed).
2. Disclosures must be made regardless of platform. Using the excuse that a medium doesn't support disclosure is not acceptable.
3. If a medium doesn't allow for disclosure (e.g., a limited number of characters provides a challenge), then perhaps the medium isn't appropriate. The FTC says that preceding a promotional tweet with the word "Ad:" or "Sponsored:" would be sufficient compliance.
4. Disclosures have to be clear and conspicuous. Disclosures should be of the same size as the message and in the same

(continued)

format. They should be close to the promotional information so the consumer doesn't have to search for them.

5. It's not good enough to just link to disclosures. They must accompany the message.

The complete guide is available at "www.ftc.gov/os/2013/03/130312dotcomdisclosures.pdf".

But FTC regulations are not laws and so celebrities and sponsors often try to skirt the rules. Even after the revised regulations were broadly announced, sponsored content continues to appear. The *Huffington Post* estimated that Kim Kardashian earned about $20,000 when she posted a TwitPic of herself using EOS lip balm for her 17.9 million followers in May following the March FTC announcement. Miley Cyrus tweeted a supportive statement about BlackJet to her 12 million Twitter followers. BlackJet admitted to the *New York Times* that the star "was given some consideration for her tweet." Justin Bieber's 40 million followers received a tweet preceding Mother's Day that included a reference to 1-800-Flowers. When fans thought a tweet from comedian Michael Ian Black referring to Dos Equis' Legend of You app was suspicious, they called him on it and he admitted in a subsequent tweet that he was paid "thousands of dollars to run it."

The *New York Times* reported, "The F.T.C. declined to comment on any particular instances where celebrities have posted about companies with which they have financial relationships. The agency did say there are 'open investigations' into companies that have broken federal rules."

What do you think? Is it ethical for celebrities to pair with brands to promote products or services via the celebrities' Twitter or Facebook or Vine accounts? Are the FTC's rules unreasonable? Would preceding a tweet with the words "Ad:" or "Sponsored:" spoil the effectiveness of the endorsement? Why or why not? Are celebrity endorsements on television different than on social media? If so, how?

The following general guidelines, adapted from FTC regulations, should be taken into account when writing product publicity materials:

- Make sure the information is accurate and can be substantiated.
- Stick to the facts. Don't "hype" the product or service by using flowery, nonspecific adjectives and ambiguous claims.
- Make sure celebrities or others who endorse the product actually use it. They should not say anything about the product's properties that cannot be substantiated.
- Watch the language. Don't say "independent research study" when the research was done by the organization's staff.
- Provide proper context for statements and statistics attributed to government agencies. They don't endorse products.
- Describe tests and surveys in sufficient detail so that the consumer understands what was tested and under what conditions.
- Remember that a product is not "new" if only the packaging has been changed or the product is more than six months old.
- When comparing products or services with a competitor's, make certain you can substantiate your claims.
- Avoid misleading and deceptive product demonstrations.

Companies found in violation of FTC guidelines are usually given the opportunity to sign a consent decree. This means that the company admits no wrongdoing but agrees to change its advertising and publicity claims. Companies may also be fined by the FTC or ordered to engage in corrective advertising and publicity.

Securities and Exchange Commission

The megamergers and the IPOs (initial public offerings) of many new companies has made the Securities and Exchange Commission (SEC) a common name in the business world. Such complex and enormous deals have also made the practice of investor relations increasingly important. This federal agency closely monitors the financial affairs of publicly traded companies and protects the interests of stockholders.

SEC guidelines on public disclosure and insider trading are particularly relevant to corporate public relations staff members, who must meet those federal requirements. The distribution of misleading information or failure to make a timely disclosure of material information may be the basis of liability under the SEC code. A company may even be liable if, while it satisfies regulations by getting information out, it conveys crucial information in a vague way or buries it deep in the news release.

A classic example is Enron, the now defunct Houston-based energy company that became a household word overnight when it became the largest single corporate failure in U.S. history. The company management was charged with a number of SEC violations, including the distribution of misleading news releases about its finances. According to congressional testimony, the company issued a quarterly earnings news release that falsely led investors to believe the company was "on track" to meet strong earnings growth in 2002. Three months later, the company was bankrupt. Later, in criminal trials, Enron's head of investor relations, Mark Koenig, received 18 months for aiding and abetting securities fraud.

The SEC has volumes of regulations, but the three concepts most pertinent to public relations personnel are as follows:

1. **Full information must be given on anything that might materially affect the company's stock.** This includes such things as (1) dividends or their deletion, (2) annual and quarterly earnings, (3) stock splits, (4) mergers or takeovers, (5) major management changes, (6) major product developments, (7) expansion plans, (8) change of business purpose, (9) defaults, (10) proxy materials, (11) disposition of major assets, (12) purchase of own stock, and (13) announcements of major contracts or orders.

2. **Timely disclosure is essential.** A company must act promptly (within minutes or a few hours) to dispel or confirm rumors that result in unusual market activity or market variations. The most common ways of dispensing such financial information are through electronic news release services, contacting the major international news services (Dow Jones Wire), and bulk e-mails.

3. **Insider trading is illegal.** Company officials, including public relations staffs and outside counsel, cannot use inside information to buy and sell company stock. The landmark case on insider trading occurred in 1965, when Texas Gulf Sulphur executives used inside information about an ore strike in Canada to buy stock while at the same time issuing a news release downplaying rumors that a rich find had been made.

The courts are increasingly applying the *mosaic doctrine* to financial information. Maureen Rubin, an attorney and professor at California State University, Northridge, explains that a court may examine all information released by a company, including news releases, to determine whether, taken as a whole, they create an "overall misleading" impression. One such case was *Cytryn v. Cook* (1990), in which a U.S. District Court ruled that the proper test of a company's adequate financial disclosure is not the literal truth of each positive statement, but the overall misleading impression that the statements combine to create in the eyes of potential investors.

As a result of such cases, investor relations personnel must also avoid such practices as:

- Unrealistic sales and earnings reports
- Glowing descriptions of products in the experimental stage
- Announcements of possible mergers or takeovers that are only in the speculation stage
- Free trips for business reporters and offers of stock to financial analysts and editors of financial newsletters

- Omission of unfavorable news and developments
- Leaks of information to selected outsiders and financial columnists
- Dissemination of false rumors about a competitor's financial health

The SEC also has regulations supporting the use of "plain English" in prospectuses and other financial documents. Companies and financial firms are supposed to make information understandable to the average investor by removing sentences littered with lawyerisms such as *aforementioned*, *hereby*, *therewith*, *whereas*, and *hereinafter*. The cover page, summary, and risk factor sections of prospectuses must be clear, concise, and understandable. A SEC booklet gives helpful writing hints such as (1) make sentences short; (2) use *we* and *our*, *you* and *your*; and (3) say it with an active verb. More information about SEC guidelines can be accessed from its website: www.sec.gov/

Fair Disclosure Regulation In 2000, the SEC issued another regulation related to fair disclosure, known as Reg FD. Although regulations already existed regarding "material disclosure" of information that could affect the price of stock, the new regulation expands the concept by requiring publicly traded companies to broadly disseminate "material" information via a news release, webcast, or SEC filing. According to the SEC, Reg FD is intended to ensure that *all* investors—not just brokerage firms and analysts—receive financial information from a company at the same time.

Sarbanes–Oxley Act The Sarbanes–Oxley Act was made law in 2002 as a result of the Enron and Worldcom financial scandals. Although the Enron scandal alone cost investors an estimated $90 billion, the devastation was dwarfed by the 2009 collapse of banks, market valuation, and real estate prices. Largely due to regulatory failings combined with ruthless speculation akin to betting, the Act failed to protect consumers. For public relations and investor relations professionals, the admonition that ignorance is no excuse before the law should be the operating principle.

Federal Communications Commission

The FCC historically licensed radio and television stations, allocating frequencies and ensuring that the public airwaves are used in the public interest. Increasingly, the Commission oversees Internet policy. FCC actions directly impact public relations personnel who distribute video news releases (VNRs) on behalf of employers and clients and public relations professionals who facilitate viral spread of copyrighted material on the Web.

The controversy about proper *source attribution* of VNRs by television stations was somewhat discussed in Chapter 3, but political debate still continues about the FCC's ruling that broadcasters must disclose to viewers the origin of video news releases produced by the government or corporations when the material runs on the public airways. The agency didn't specify what form such disclosure should take, but broadcasters argued that the FCC was curtailing their First Amendment rights.

FCC Commissioner Jonathan Edelstein disagreed, saying the issue is not one of free speech, but of identifying who is actually speaking. He told the *Washington Post*, "We have a responsibility to tell broadcasters they have to let people know where the material is coming from. Viewers are hoodwinked into thinking it's really a news story when it might be from the government or a big corporation trying to influence the way they think."

Both the broadcast and the public relations industries have joined together to call for voluntary controls and disclosure instead of "government intrusion" into the news process. Both industries have also adopted codes of practice (discussed in Chapter 3). Fines have also been levied by the FCC in terms of enforcing regulations concerning indecency on the airwaves. The triggering event was Janet Jackson's "wardrobe malfunction" at the 2004 Super Bowl halftime show when Justin Timberlake ripped off a piece of her black leather top, exposing her right breast for an instant. The "malfunction," of course, garnered more media coverage and public discussion than the game itself. The FCC, however, was not amused; it levied a $550,000 fine on CBS television (a division of Viacom) for airing the incident.

Increasingly, the Internet has become not only a major channel for delivery of content, but also a point of contention as a utility. The FCC has consistently supported Net neutrality. In 2010, the FCC passed a Net neutrality rule that essentially requires all Internet service providers to treat all websites equally. Providers are not allowed to speed up or slow down access to certain websites based on whether the websites have paid a fee to the provider. In 2012, Verizon filed a suit against the FCC to overturn the rule.

Other Federal Regulatory Agencies

Although the FTC and the SEC are the major federal agencies concerned with the content of advertising and publicity materials, public relations professionals should be familiar with the guidelines of two other major agencies: the Food and Drug Administration (FDA) and the Equal Employment Opportunity Commission (EEOC).

The Food and Drug Administration

The FDA oversees the advertising and promotion of prescription drugs, over-the-counter medicines, and cosmetics. Under the federal Food, Drug, and Cosmetic Act, any "person" (which includes advertising and public relations firms) who "causes the misbranding" of products through the dissemination of false and misleading information may be liable.

The FDA has specific guidelines for video, audio, and print news releases on health care topics. First, the release must provide "fair balance" by telling consumers about the risks as well as the benefits of the drug or treatment. Second, the writer must be clear about the limitations of a particular drug or treatment, for example, that it may not help people with certain conditions. Third, a news release or media kit should be accompanied by supplementary product sheets or brochures that give full prescribing information. On television, these rules result in the often-parodied, rapid-fire recitation of caveats and side effects of an advertised drug.

Because prescription drugs have major FDA curbs on advertising and promotion, the drug companies try to sidestep the regulations by publicizing diseases, creating patient advocate groups, and enlisting celebrity spokespersons. In 2012 pharmaceutical company GlaxoSmithKline was accused by the federal government of hiring experts including celebrity physician Dr. Drew Pinsky to promote drug uses that were not approved by the FDA.

The government accusation was buoyed by evidence including an invoice from a public relations firm that had arranged for "Dr. Drew" to make media appearances on behalf of GSK. *Forbes* reported, "A note from the PR firm . . . says: 'During the fifteen-minute segment, Dr. Pinsky communicated key campaign messages.' The spot is almost a textbook for the way drug companies have used speakers to promote medicines." GlaxoSmithKline settled the case paying a fine of $3 billion.

Equal Employment Opportunity Commission

Diversity in the workplace has dramatically increased in recent years, and the EEOC is charged with ensuring that workers are not discriminated against on the basis of their religion, ethnic background, gender, or even their English skills.

Employers, for example, need to accommodate the religious needs of their employees. For example, Muslims pray five times a day and have attire prescribed by their religion, and Jews must also be allowed to be absent from the workplace on various Holy days. At the same time, EEOC guidelines also call for employers to ensure that employees don't express their religious views at work or impose their beliefs on others. In other words, a company's policy about harassment also needs to include wording about religion.

For example, Abercrombie & Fitch clothing retailer faced a $40 million lawsuit for refusing to hire a Muslim applicant for a sales associate position because the applicant intended to wear a head scarf, which the manager said violated the store's "Look Policy." In a similar situation, a judge fined Abercrombie & Fitch $20,000 for firing a Muslim teenager on the same grounds. Abercrombie & Fitch consistently adheres to its view that the associates are part of the advertising and image of the store, which overrides liberties that are protected outside the work environment.

> Employers must understand that discriminatory English-only rules can hurt productivity, morale, and ultimately their bottom line.
>
> *Kimberlie Ryan, Denver attorney*

The EEOC also gets involved in the contentious issue of language. Federal law doesn't prevent employers from requiring workers to speak only English if it is justified by business necessity or safety concerns, but a blanket policy of English-only can get an employer in trouble if it forbids workers to speak another language during breaks, or if the language spoken doesn't make a difference in the performance of the job.

English-only advocates argue that multilingualism in the workplace encourages newcomers to retain their own language and that English speakers feel slighted when fellow workers talk to each other in their native language. On the other hand, Denver attorney Kimberlie Ryan told the *Wall Street Journal*, "This is not about whether people should learn English; it's about not using language as a weapon of harassment."

Being sensitive to the diversity of the workplace, plus a thorough understanding of EEOC guidelines, are requirements for anyone working in employee communications. Public relations personnel often work closely with human resources to offer workshops and educational materials on diversity to educate employees to be more tolerant and understanding of each other. It is much cheaper than a series of lawsuits charging discrimination.

Corporate Speech

The First Amendment to the U.S. Constitution guarantees "freedom of speech," but exactly what speech is protected has been defined by the courts over the past 200 years, and is still being interpreted today. However, there is a well-established doctrine that commercial speech doesn't have the same First Amendment protection as other forms of speech.

Essentially, the government may regulate advertising that is

- false,
- misleading,
- deceptive, or
- promotes unlawful goods and services.

The courts also have ruled that product news releases, brochures, and other promotional vehicles intended to sell a product or service constitute commercial speech.

Another area, however, is what is termed corporate speech. Robert Kerr, author of *The Rights of Corporate Speech: Mobil Oil and the Legal Development of the Voice of Big Business*, defines corporate speech as "media efforts by corporations that seek to affect political outcomes or social climate—in contrast with 'commercial speech,' which promotes products or services." The courts, for the most part, have upheld the right of corporations and other organizations to express their views on public policy, proposed legislation, and a host of other issues that may be of societal or corporate concern. Organizations traditionally did so through op-ed articles, letters to the editor, postings on their website, and even news releases.

Nike's Free Speech Battle

The Supreme Court became involved with corporate free speech in 2003 when it was petitioned by Nike, the shoe and sports clothes manufacturer, to redress a California Supreme Court decision that had ruled that the company's efforts to explain its labor policies abroad were basically "garden variety commercial speech." The ruling seemed to equate public relations speech about a policy issue with commercial advertising.

The case, *Nike v. Kasky*, raised the thorny question of how to deal with the blurred lines that often separate "free speech" and "commercial speech." Marc Kasky, an activist, had sued Nike, claiming that the company had made false and misleading statements that constituted unlawful and deceptive business practices. Nike, on the other hand, claimed that it had the right to express its views and defend itself against allegations by activist groups that it operated sweatshop factories in Asia and paid subpar wages.

The U.S. Supreme Court, however, was less certain about the "commercial" nature of Nike's public relations campaign. It did not make a decision and sent the case back to the California courts where the case was settled out of court.

> Because the commercial message (buy our shoes) was mixed with a political message (our political opponents are wrong), and was presented outside a traditional advertising medium, it should have been treated as fully protected.
>
> *Eugene Volokh, professor of law at UCLA, in a* Wall Street Journal *op-ed*

Employee Speech

A progressive organization encourages employee comments and even criticisms. Many employee newspapers and e-bulletin boards carry letters to the editor because they breed a healthy atmosphere of two-way communication and make company publications more credible. However, organizations are increasingly setting guidelines and monitoring what employees say online. The following is a discussion of employee e-mail, surfing the Internet, and blogging.

Employee E-Mail

The monitoring of employee e-mail by management is well established. A survey by Forrester Consulting for Proofpoint, a maker of e-mail security products, found that almost 50 percent of large companies audit outbound e-mail by their employees. In fact, 38 percent of large U.S. companies surveyed by Proofpoint said they employ staff to read or analyze outgoing e-mail.

A number of court decisions have reinforced the right of employers to read employees' e-mail. However a company must be clear about its e-mail monitoring policies. A New Jersey appeals court ruled that a home-health worker who sent e-mail via personal account had every reason to believe her e-mail was private. Still, the *Wall Street Journal* reported, "Employees often assume their communications on personal e-mail accounts should stay private even if they are using work-issued computers or smart phones. But in most instances when using a work device, e-mails of all kinds are captured on a server and can be retrieved by an employer."

Employers are increasingly monitoring employee e-mail for two reasons. First, they are concerned about being held liable if an employee posts a racial slur, engages in sexual harassment online, or even transmits sexually explicit jokes that would cause another employee to feel that the workplace is a "hostile" environment. Second, companies are concerned about employee e-mails that may include information that the organization considers proprietary, such as trade secrets, marketing plans, and development of new products, which would give the competition an advantage. In other words, you should assume that any e-mails you write at work are subject to monitoring and that you can be fired if you violate company guidelines.

Surfing the Internet

Employees should also be careful about using the Internet at work. According to a survey by the American Management Association (AMA), more than 75 percent of American employers monitor personal Web surfing at work. And more than 25 percent of these companies have fired someone for doing it. Other studies, of course, show that Web surfing at work for personal reasons is done by the majority of employees—and many even think of using the Internet in the same context as using the lowly telephone.

Employers, for their part, are concerned about the loss of productivity when employees sit at their desks watching YouTube videos or updating their Facebook pages. Potential liability, however, is another big factor. Companies can and do get sued for what their employees do online. Office workers accessing porn sites, instant messaging smutty and racial jokes, and posting dubious photos and comments to Facebook invite lawsuits when other workers are offended and file complaints with the EEOC.

Employee Blogs

Many organizations now encourage employees to have a blog, as a way of fostering discussion on the Internet and getting informal feedback from the public. In some large companies, even top executives have a blog. In most cases, the blog prominently features their association with the business and gives information (and images) about the employer. As John Elasser, editor of *Public Relations Tactics*, says, "Some of that content may be innocuous; other types may be embarrassing or come back to haunt the company in litigation."

Consequently, it is important for a business to have a clear policy that provides guidelines for what rank-and-file employees, as well as executives, can say or not say on their blogs or in a posting on another blog. The public relations staff often prepares general guidelines and trains employees about such matters.

Liability for Sponsored Events

Public relations personnel often focus on the planning and logistics of events. Consequently, they must also take steps to protect their organizations from liability and possible lawsuits associated with those activities.

Plant tours, open houses, and other events should not be undertaken lightly. They require detailed planning by the public relations staff to guarantee the safety and comfort of visitors. Consideration must be given to such factors as possible work disruptions as groups pass through the plant, safety, and the amount of staffing required. Many events call for special logistical planning by the public relations staff. Such precautions will generate goodwill and limit the company's liability. It should be noted, however, that a plaintiff can still collect if negligence on the part of the company can be proved.

Liability insurance is a necessity when any public event is planned because accidents can occur that might result in lawsuits charging the sponsoring organization with negligence. Organizations can purchase comprehensive insurance to cover a variety of events or a specific event. The need for liability insurance also applies to charitable organizations when they sponsor fund-raising events such as a 10K run. Participants should sign a release form that protects the organization against liability in case of an accident. Promotional events that use public streets and parks also need permits from the appropriate city departments. For more information about event management, see Chapter 16, "Event Management."

on the job

INSIGHTS

Are Conversations Between Public Relations Pros and Their Clients Legally Protected?

Public relations practitioners frequently work with lawyers to protect an employer or client. Conversations between lawyers and their clients are legally protected; they are confidential and cannot be introduced as evidence in a legal action. But generally, conversations between public relations practitioners and their clients are not protected. There are some exceptions.

Lawyer Cayce Myers, a PR doctoral student at the University of Georgia, writing for the Institute of Public Relations, outlined four considerations in determining whether conversations between public relations practitioners and their clients are protected by attorney–client privilege.

1. Who hired the public relations practitioner? Myers wrote that if the PR counsel is hired by legal counsel, the likelihood of attorney–client privilege is greater because it could be argued that the practitioner was a member of the legal team and part of the legal strategy.
2. How involved is the public relations practitioner in the actual legal strategy? According to Myers, "Courts extending the privilege to PR practitioners look at the relationships between practitioners and attorneys and the role practitioners play within litigation."
3. When are public relations professionals involved? If the public relations practitioner is working with the client during the actual litigation, there is a stronger argument to be made for extending attorney–client privilege to public relations, Myers wrote.
4. Where is the public relations practitioner based? If the public relations pro is an in-house practitioner, that is, he or she is working within the corporation rather than being hired from an outside agency, the courts are more likely to extend privilege. Myers wrote, "This is because courts view the internal corporate relationships as an environment where communications, legal, and other departments work in a close relationship with each other."

It is essential to understand that attorney–client privilege never automatically applies to relationships between a public relations practitioner and her or his employer as it does between an attorney and her or his client. However, the four questions above can help assess the potential for such protection.

Source: "Litigation and Public Relations: Four Questions Every Practitioner Should Ask." Retrieved from http://www.instituteforpr.org/2013/03/litigation-and-public-relations-four-questions-every-practitioner-should-ask/

The Attorney/Public Relations Relationship

Litigation is an integral part of today's business environment. In fact, it is estimated that 90 percent of American corporations are dealing with lawsuits at any given time. Indeed, Philip Rudolph, a partner in a Washington, D.C., law firm, is quoted in *PRWeek* as saying, "The bounds of liability are beginning to stretch in ways that traditional lawyering does not address. You see companies being sued by their own customers over the lawful use of a legal product—such as obesity lawsuits brought against McDonald's."

In such an environment, it's important for public relations personnel and lawyers to work together to win not only in the court of law but also in the court of public opinion. Indeed, a survey by Kathy R. Fitzpatrick, a public relations professor at Quinnipiac University, found that almost 85 percent of the public relations respondents said their relationships with legal counsel are either "excellent" or "good." Researchers at the University of Houston and the University of Missouri, in separate studies, also found that lawyers and public relations practitioners report cooperative relationships. Winning in the court of public opinion is the responsibility of the public relations professional, and such work is the practice of "litigation public relations." Winning in the court of law, of course, is the responsibility of the lawyer. Both professions are looking out for the interests of their employer.

The cooperation between lawyers and public relations counsel has been strengthened in recent years by court rulings that conversations between the two can be considered attorney–client privilege if certain conditions are met. For example, U.S. District Court Judge Lewis Kaplan in New York ruled that attorney–client privilege exists if the following five conditions are met. In addition, each point must be checked off, says Kaplan, before the next point can be considered: "(1) confidential communications . . . (2) between lawyers and PR consultants . . . (3) hired by the lawyers to assist them in dealing with the media in cases such as this . . . (4) that are made for the giving or receiving of advice . . . (5) directed at handling the client's legal problems are protected by the attorney–client privilege." Other legal experts, however, say that attorney–client privilege is better protected if outside legal counsel actually employs a litigation public relations firm as a consultant instead of using internal public relations staff.

PRSA's *Tactics* suggests six "keys to winning in the court of law—and public opinion." They are:

- Make carefully planned public comment in the earliest stages of a crisis or legal issue.
- Understand the perspective of lawyers and allow them to review statements when an organization is facing or involved in litigation.
- Guard against providing information to the other side of the legal case.
- Counsel and coach the legal team.
- Build support from other interested parties, such as industry associations or chambers of commerce.
- Develop a litigation communication team before you need it.

To review how Coca-Cola is countering legal and regulatory actions, see the PR Casebook on page 354.

PRCasebook

Coca-Cola Fights Legal Battles on Regulatory and Consumer Fronts

Beverage makers have been under attack for years, dodging accusations that their products contribute to obesity. Global beverage producer Coca-Cola has faced litigation in recent years related to alleged deceptive marketing.

On the regulatory side, Coca-Cola, together with other manufacturers of sugary beverages, has faced bans on the sale of large containers of sugary drinks as well as other government regulations—proposed and enacted. Consumer lawsuits alleged that the beverage makers' various orange juice brands are falsely marketed as "100 percent pure" and that its "Vitaminwater" brand wrongly claims health benefits.

When the beverage giant embarked on an antiobesity campaign it was applauded by supporters and pilloried by opponents. Chris Daniels, writing in *PRWeek*, noted that while media reports characterized the campaign that began in early 2013 as "manipulative" and "disingenuous," public relations experts thought the cola company was overdue in engaging directly as a partner in the fight against obesity.

Coca-Cola ran two advertisements—one an extended two-minute ad ran during cable news shows, a second 30-second ad ran during the season premiere of *American Idol*. According to the *New York Times*, the longer ad was aimed at policy makers while the second was aimed at consumers in general. The ads acknowledge links between the company's products and obesity, but note that calorie consumption should be paired with appropriate exercise. The shorter ad emphasized, "the calories in a can of soda and offer[ed] ideas about how to work them off, like walking the dog for 25 minutes, doing a victory dance or even laughing," according to the *Times*.

While Coca-Cola took on the obesity and regulatory issues head-on, it was more circumspect in communicating about the legal actions. It is not uncommon that corporations will say little, if anything, publicly about potential or ongoing legal actions. This is because anything that is said could end up as evidence in the courtroom. So when different judges ruled that cases regarding labeling of orange juice and Vitaminwater could proceed, corporate spokespersons made very measured responses.

In the case of Vitaminwater, the plaintiffs were a health-advocacy group called the Center for Science in the Public Interest. They wanted to prevent Coca-Cola from making claims on its labels that link the product to increased eye health and an improved immune system. In the juice case, which included labels on brands such as Simply Orange, Minute Maid Premium, and Minute Maid Pure Squeezed, consumers brought the lawsuit alleging that the labels that claim the products are "100 percent pure squeezed" are false. In fact, the Bloomberg news organization reported that the plaintiffs claimed the products are actually "chemically flavored, heavily processed, designed and modified and is not '100% pure squeezed,' 'simply orange,' 'pure' or 'natural.'"

Did the beverage producer make the right decision in taking on obesity and allowing its products to be linked to obesity?

Does the ad as described strike you as helpful or distracting? Why?

How would you respond to accusations that your product's labeling was misleading at best and false at worst?

Summary

A Sampling of Legal Problems

- There are a number of ways that a public relations practitioner may get caught up in a lawsuit or a case with a government regulatory agency.
- Practitioners may also be held legally liable if they provide advice or support the illegal activity of a client.

Libel and Defamation

- Libel and slander are often collectively referred to as *defamation*.
- Defamation involves a false and malicious (or at least negligent) communication with an identifiable subject who is injured by loss of money, by loss of reputation, or through mental suffering.
- Libel suits can be avoided through the careful use of language.
- Some offensive communications, such as negative reviews by a theater critic, fall under the "fair comment" defense.

Invasion of Privacy

- When publishing newsletters, companies cannot assume that a person waives his or her right to privacy just because of his or her status as an employee.
- Companies must get written permission to publish photos or use employees in advertising materials, and they must be cautious in releasing personal information about employees to the media.

Copyright Law

- *Copyright* is the protection of creative work from unauthorized use.
- Published works are by definition copyrighted, and permission must be obtained to reprint such material.
- The "fair use" doctrine allows limited quotation, as in a book review.
- Unless a company has a specific contract with a freelance writer, photographer, or artist to produce work that will be exclusively owned by that company (a situation called "work for hire"), the freelancer owns his or her work.
- New copyright issues have been raised by the popularity of the Internet and the ease of downloading, uploading, and disseminating images and information.

Trademark Law

- A *trademark* is a word, symbol, or slogan identifying a product's origin that can be registered with the U.S. Patent and Trademark Office.
- Trademarks are always capitalized and used as adjectives rather than nouns or verbs.
- Companies vigorously protect trademarks to prevent their becoming common nouns.
- One form of trademark infringement may be "misappropriation of personality," the use of a celebrity's name or image for advertising purposes without permission.

Regulations by Government Agencies

- Commercial speech is regulated by the government in the interest of public health and safety, and consumer protection.
- Regulating agencies include the Federal Trade Commission (FTC), the Securities and Exchange Commission (SEC), the Federal Communications Commission (FCC), the Food and Drug Administration (FDA), and the Equal Employment Opportunity Commission (EEOC).

Corporate Speech

- Organizations have the right to express their opinions and views about a number of public issues.
- Federal election rules now allow direct corporate support of candidates for office.
- However, there is still some blurring of lines between what is considered "commercial speech" and "free speech," as illustrated by the *Nike* case.

Employee Speech

- Employees are limited in expressing their opinions within the corporate environment.
- Employee e-mail and surfing the Internet are subject to monitoring.
- Employees can be fired (or former employees sued) for revealing trade secrets or harassing fellow employees.

Liability for Sponsored Events

- Plant tours, open houses, and other promotional events raise liability issues concerning safety and security.
- Liability insurance is a necessity.
- Permits may be required for the use of public streets and parks and for serving food and liquor.

The Attorney/Public Relations Relationship

- A cooperative relationship must exist between public relations personnel and legal counsel to handle today's challenges.

- Both groups should report to the same top executive and be represented on key committees.
- Public relations practitioners should also be aware of legal concepts and regulatory guidelines and receive briefings from the legal staff on impending developments.
- A new practice area is litigation public relations.

Case Activity Should Employees' Social Media Activities Be Controlled?

The ever-increasing reach of digital and social media demands examination by all employers. When an employee posts a Facebook entry grousing about her workplace, should the organization be concerned? How about when an employee tweets excitedly about a new product yet to be introduced to consumers? To handle such thorny issues, most organizations should have digital and social media policies.

Your company is committed to protecting its employees' rights to free speech, but it is also aware that there can be legal repercussions to uncontrolled social media activity. As a communication law and social media expert, what issues would you advise management to consider in developing a digital and social media policy for employees? Write a brief memo outlining issues to examine and justify their inclusion on such a list. To get started, search online for social media and blogging policies.

Questions For Review and Discussion

1. Define defamation according to the relevant laws in your county, state, or province. How is libel different from slander?
2. What are the defenses of libel?
3. What information can you provide when the media call about an employee?
4. Is it essential to formally copyright all public relations materials? Why or why not?
5. What rights do freelance photographers and writers have regarding ownership of their works?
6. "An idea can't be copyrighted, but the expression of those ideas can be." Explain this statement.
7. Under what circumstances can a PR professional be named a co-conspirator with other officials?
8. What should public relations people know about the regulations of the Federal Trade Commission? The Securities and Exchange Commission?
9. What challenges does PR have to grapple with in the Internet age?
10. What is privilege from a legal perspective? When, if ever, might it apply to public relations counsel?

Media Resources

Bilton, N. (2013, June 9). Disruptions: Celebrities' product plugs on social media draw scrutiny. *The New York Times*. Retrieved from bits.blogs.nytimes.com

Bradford, H. (2012, July 3). Dr. Drew allegedly paid $275,000 to illegally promote GlaxoSmithKline drugs. *The Huffington Post*. Retrieved from www.huffingtonpost.com

Burke, M. (2013, February 21). Under Armour files lawsuit against Nike for trademark infringement. *Forbes*. Retrieved from www.forbes.com

Daniels, C. (2013, January 25). Communicators applaud Coke joining obesity debate. *PRWeek*. Retrieved from www.prweekus.com

Gower, K. K. (2008). *Legal and ethical considerations for public relations*. Long Grove, IL: Waveland Press.

Heathfield, S. M. (2013). Blogging and social media policy sample. Retrieved from humanresources.about.com

Moore, R. L., Maye, C., & Collins, E. L. (2010). *Advertising and public relations law*. New York: Routledge.

Myers, C. (2013, March 25). Litigation and public relations: Four questions every practitioner should ask. Retrieved from www.instituteforpr.org

Parkinson, M. G., & Parkinson, L. M. (2009). *Public relations law: A supplemental text*. New York: Taylor & Francis.

Reber, B., Gower, K., & Robinson, J. (2006). The Internet and litigation public relations. *Journal of Public Relations Research, 18*(1), 23–44.

Internet and Social Media: Role & Scope in Public Relations

chapter 13

After reading this chapter, you will be able to:

Understand why the Internet is a communications revolution

Organize and design an effective website

Be familiar with the mechanics of doing a webcast

Use social media and networking as public relations tactics

Understand the rapid growth and potential of mobile-enabled content

The Internet: Pervasive in Our Lives

The Internet and social media networks are now dominant in almost everyone's lives, and it's hard to imagine daily life without it. It's even difficult to realize that today's popular social networks such as Facebook, YouTube, and Twitter didn't even exist 10 years ago. Indeed, the Internet is truly a revolutionary concept that radically transformed a media system that had been in place since Gutenberg invented the printing press in the 1400s.

> Armed with digital cameras, camera phones, handheld video cameras, podcasts, blogs, and social networks, we've entered the era of citizen journalism and user-generated content.
>
> *Brian Solis and Deirdre Breakenridge, authors of* Putting the Public Back in Public Relations

For 500 years, mass media dominated the world's landscape. They had the characteristics of being (1) centralized/top-down, (2) costly in terms of being published, (3) staffed by professional gatekeepers known as editors and publishers, and (4) mostly one-way communication with limited feedback channels.

Thanks to the Internet, there are now two spheres of influence, which are constantly interacting with each other. CooperKatz & Company calls them (1) the mediasphere and (2) the blogosphere. The new media system has the characteristics of (1) widespread broadband; (2) cheap/free, easy-to-use online publishing tools; (3) new distribution channels; (4) mobile devices, such as camera phones; and (5) new advertising paradigms. For the first time in history, a medium, the Internet, has literally caused the democratization of information around the world. See Figure 13.1 for a breakdown by region of the world's 2.4 billion users. More recently, the International Telecommunications Union (ITU)

Figure 13.1 Internet Users Around the World

More than a third of the world's population (7 billion) are now using the Internet and the development of mobile broadband is rapidly increasing the numbers of users in Asia, Africa, and the Middle East.

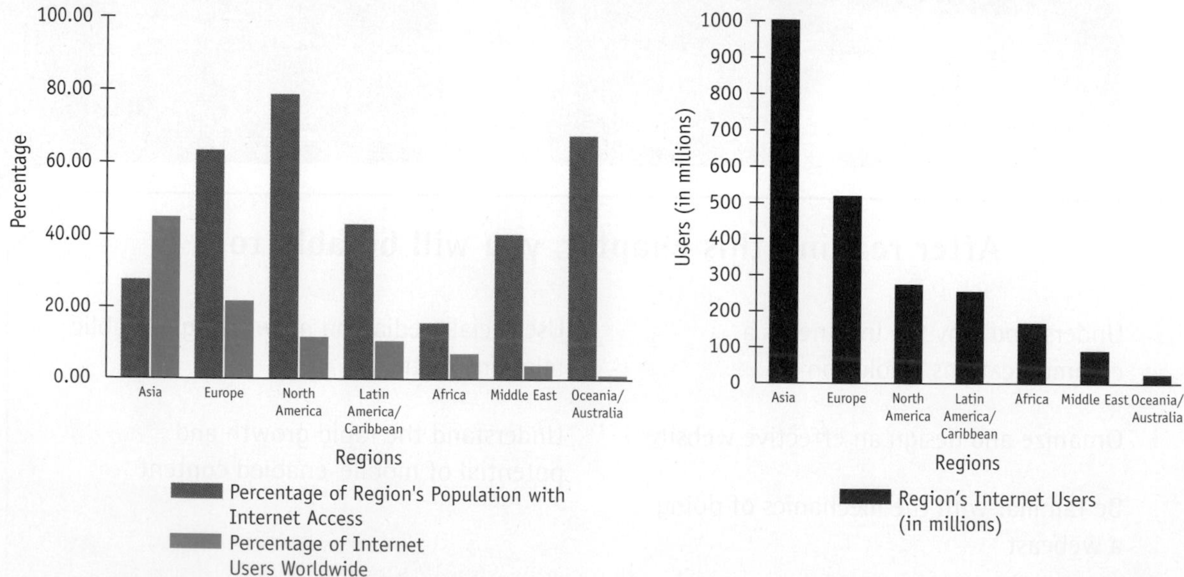

Source: Adapted from www.internetworldstats.com (June 2012)

reported that 2.7 billion people were now online—almost 40 percent of the world's population.

The Internet, first created as a tool for academic researchers in the 1960s, came into widespread public use in the 1990s, and the rest is history. Indeed, the worldwide adoption of the Internet has taken less time than the growth of any other mass medium. Marc Newman, general manager of Medialink Dallas, says, "Whereas it took nearly 40 years before there were 50 million listeners of radio and 13 years until television reached an audience of 50 million, a mere four years passed before 50 million users were logging on to the Internet since it became widely available."

The growth of the Internet and social media networks continues at an astounding rate. The established ones keep expanding, and newer networks such as Pinterest and Instagram become overnight sensations. Consequently, any figures published today regarding digital media are already out of date. Yet some stats and projections are worth noting as a reference point.

- There will be 3 billion Internet users worldwide by 2016, more than 40 percent of the world's population.
- Almost 70 percent of the U.S. population will be using smartphones by 2017. Currently, users spend an average of more than two hours daily on their devices.
- U.S. consumers send and receive more than 6 billion text messages every day.
- About 2.8 million e-mails are sent every second, and an average office worker spends about 13 hours a week using e-mail.
- There are more than 700,000 apps in each of the Google Android and Apple stores.
- Facebook, launched in 2004, now has more than 1 billion users worldwide or one out of every seven people on the planet.
- There are 10.5 million photos uploaded to Facebook every hour.
- About 48 hours of video are uploaded to YouTube every hour.
- More than 140 million people spend an average of four hours a week watching video online.
- Twitter, launched in 2006, has almost 300 million active users worldwide, and about 400 million tweets are sent every day.
- Two million searches are done on Google every minute.
- Instagram, launched in 2010, surpassed 1 billion photos uploaded, by the end of 2012.
- Wikipedia, if made into a book, would be 2.25 million pages.

The World Wide Web

The exponential growth of the World Wide Web is due, in large part, to browsers such as Internet Explorer and search engines such as Google, which have made the World Wide Web accessible to literally billions of people. Here are some characteristics of the Web that enable public relations people to do a better job of distributing a variety of messages:

- Information can be updated quickly without having to reprint brochures and other materials. This is an important element when it comes to major news events and dealing with a crisis.

- Web allows interactivity; viewers can ask questions about products or services, download information of value to them, and let the organization know what they think.
- Online readers can dig deeper into subjects that interest them by linking to information provided on other sites, in other articles, and in other sources.
- A great amount of material can be posted. There is no space or time limitation.
- It is a cost-effective way to disseminate information on a global basis to the public and journalists.
- You can reach niche markets and audiences directly without messages being filtered through traditional mass media gatekeepers (editors).
- The media and other users can access details about your organization 24 hours a day from anywhere in the world.

Nobody cares about your products and services. They care about themselves and solving problems. Your online content needs to be less egotistical and more helpful.

David Meerman Scott, author of The New Rules of Marketing and PR.

From a public relations standpoint, a website is literally a distribution system in cyberspace. Organizations, for example, use their websites to market products and services and post news releases, corporate backgrounders, product information, position papers, and even photos of key executives or plant locations. The public, as well as media personnel, can access the information, download selected materials into their computers, and even print out hard copies. Websites have also become more interactive, giving public relations professionals' valuable feedback from consumers and the general public. In many cases, an organization's website is hyperlinked to other web pages and information sources. A user can thus jump immediately to a related website by clicking the mouse on various icons. Business Wire's website, for example, links to the home pages of various organizations that use its distribution services.

Various surveys indicate that journalists also extensively use websites to retrieve current news releases and other materials. A survey by Cision and Don Bates of George Washington University, for example, found that corporate websites are ranked number one by journalists as a research tool.

In sum, the Web has become a major source of information for journalists. According to *NetMarketing*, companies are sending out fewer media kits and getting fewer phone inquiries as a result of putting material on websites. As Rick Rudman, president of Capital Hill Software, told *PR Tactics*, "The days of just posting press releases on your website are gone. Today, journalists, investors, all audiences expect to find media kits, photos, annual reports, and multimedia presentations about your organization at your press center."

Marketing communications is also a common objective of organizational websites. All companies, from mom-and-pop businesses to multinational corporations, have websites to sell products and services directly to the public. Public relations firms, for example, often have extensive websites to promote their services by profiling their expertise and providing case studies of campaigns for clients. See the Insights on page 361 for examples of how organizations are using their websites.

Other marketing approaches might be page links where potential customers can learn about the organization and its approach to producing environmental friendly, "green" products. Web pages with a strong marketing emphasis may have several main sections, such as (1) information about the organization and its reputation for

on the job INSIGHTS

Ways That Organizations Use Their Websites

Organizations use their websites in different ways. Here's a sampling:

- Red Bull's website emphasizes it sponsorship of sporting events and provides extensive stories, photos, and videos that enhance its brand image among active, athletic consumers. The site is shown below.
- Rutherford Hill Winery in California uses its website to give a video tour of the winery.
- L. L. Bean has a website that gives a history of the company, shows how it hand-sews its shoes, and lists attractions at 900 state and national parks.
- Westchester Medical Center posts a virtual encyclopedia of disease and health care information that is freely available to the public. The site also establishes the medical center as a premier medical facility by describing its multiple clinics and medical services.
- IBM devotes segments of its website to its activities on various continents. One segment on Africa, for example, provides pdfs of case studies and short video clips.

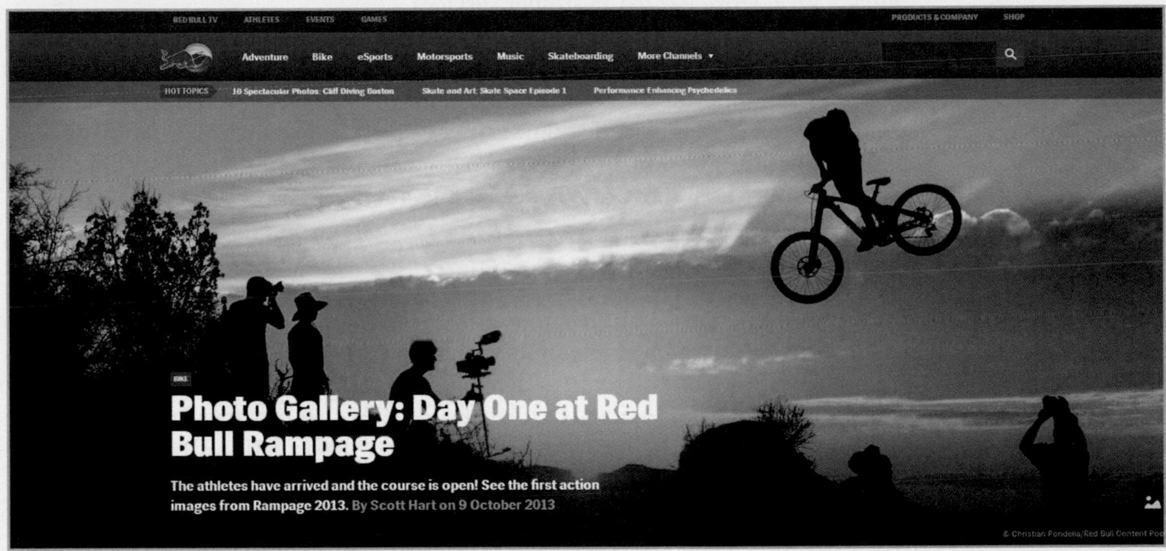

service and reliability, (2) a list of product lines, (3) technical support available to customers, (4) information on how to order products or services, and (5) a list of the various services available.

A preliminary step before creating any web page is to understand the potential audience and their particular needs. Are they accessing the website to find a particular product? Are they primarily investors who are looking for financial information? Or are they looking for employment information? Are they likely to download the material and save documents in print form? Focus groups, personal interviews, and surveys

> As more people use the Internet to search for information, a user's first impression of a website can determine whether that user forms a favorable or unfavorable view of that organization.
>
> *Dr. Hong Sheng, Missouri University of Science and Technology*

often answer these questions and help the company design a user-friendly site.

The San Diego Convention Center, for example, redesigned its website by forming a customer advisory board of 28 clients that used the facility. Focus groups were held to determine what clients wanted to see in an updated website. According to *PRWeek*, "The Customer Advisory Board feedback enabled SDCC to jettison a great deal of the clutter that plagues many sites and focus on exactly what the target audience wanted. Gone was dense copy and hard-to-navigate pages, replaced by hot links to key portions of the site."

Indeed, paying attention to the needs of the audience helps a company decide exactly what links to list on the home page. Starbucks (www.starbucks.com) has a somewhat affluent audience that is digital natives so its site provides instant links to its profiles on Facebook, Twitter, and YouTube. There's also a section "Newest Blog Posts." The page changes almost daily with a new lead story such as "April Is the Global Month of Service." There are also thumbnail photos highlighting four or five other major stories about new products. At the bottom of the page are subject links such as About Us (including a newsroom), Career Center (working for Starbucks), Online Community (a list of social network profiles), and Quick Links (store locator, customer service).

Forrester Research says there are four main reasons why visitors return to a particular website. First and foremost is high-quality content. Then, in descending order, is ease of use, quick downloads, and frequent updates. It's important for a website to be attractive and well-designed. First-time users take less than two-tenths of a second to form a first impression and decide whether they will continue, according to a study at the Missouri University of Science and Technology.

Making a Website Interactive

A unique characteristic of the Internet and the World Wide Web, which traditional mass media do not offer, is interactivity between the sender and the receiver.

One aspect of interactivity is the "pull" concept. The Web represents the "pull" concept because the user actively searches for sites that can answer specific questions. At the website itself, the user also actively "pulls" information from the various links that are provided. In other words, the user is constantly interacting with the site and "pulling" the information most relevant to him or her. The user thus has total control over what information to call up and how deep to delve into a subject.

In contrast, the concept of "push" is that of information delivered to the user without active participation. Traditional mass media—radio, TV, newspapers, and magazines—are illustrative of the "push" concept, as are news releases that are automatically sent to the media. Another dimension of interactivity is a person's ability to engage in a dialogue with an organization. Many websites, for example, encourage questions and feedback by giving an e-mail address that the user can click on to send a message.

Unfortunately, the ideas of being "interactive" and encouraging feedback are more buzzwords than reality on many websites. A 2012 study by McKinsey & Company, for example, found that most Fortune 500 companies were behind the curve. Half of them didn't provide Twitter or Facebook links on their home page, and 90 percent didn't bother to provide an e-mail address.

Providing an e-mail address or another way of contacting the organization is a good strategy but tends to damage a corporation's reputation and credibility if it doesn't respond to a consumer query in a timely manner. Reporter Thomas E. Weber of the *Wall Street Journal* wrote a somewhat humorous article about his experience. He e-mailed two dozen major corporate websites and reported "Nine never responded. Two took three weeks to transmit a reply, while others sent stock responses that failed to address the query. Only three companies adequately answered within a day."

Managing the Website

An organizational website must serve multiple audiences. Consequently, the overall responsibility of managing the website should lie with the corporate communications department, which is concerned about the needs of multiple stakeholders. One survey of corporate communications and public relations executives by the Institute for Public Relations, for example, found that 70 percent of the respondents believed that an organization's communications/public relations function should manage and control all content on the website.

The reality, however, is that a successful website takes the input and knowledge of several departments. Information technology (IT), for example, has the technical expertise to create a website. In addition, marketing also plays a major role to ensure that the website includes information and links enabling the purchase of products and services. Consequently, the practical solution is a team approach, where representatives from various departments collaborate.

The advantage of cross-functional teams is that various members bring different strengths to the table. IT can provide the technical know-how, public relations can share expertise on the formation of messages for various audiences, and marketing can communicate the consumer services available through the site. Even human resources, as a team member, can contribute ideas on how to facilitate and process employment inquiries.

Webcasts

A website is enhanced and supplemented by using webcasts. Indeed, webcasting has become more common as bandwidth has increased and technology has evolved. In fact, one survey found that more than 90 percent of public companies use webcasts for everything from employee training to briefings for financial analysts and news conferences launching a new product. One big advantage is that webcasts save time and money because they eliminate the cost of travel for participants.

A good example of a media-oriented webcast is the one hosted by the Chocolate Manufacturers Association (CMA) and its public relations firm, Fleishman-Hillard. The CMA sponsored a chocolate-tasting webcast for food writers around the country, who also received a "tasting kit" before the event. They could taste various chocolates as they viewed the webcast, which featured experts on chocolate. By having a webcast, the organization doubled attendance from the previous year.

A variation of the webcast is live streaming, the broadcasting of live video content over the Internet. An event such as a concert, a fashion show, or even a demonstration can be live streamed in much the same way as a webcast, but conducting "chats" is a popular second use. Kevin Foley, owner of KEF Media Associates, writes in *O'Dwyer's Report*, "Chats are streaming video conversations between spokesperson(s) and audience hosted on a web site, micro site, Facebook account, YouTube channel, or a similar platform." Webcasts tend to be for specific, invited audiences such as financial analysts or journalists, but chats are more open to almost anyone on a social network who wants to click in and participate.

Podcasts

The term "podcast" comes from "pod" as in Apple's iPod and "cast" as in "broadcast," meaning to transmit for general and public use. It is somewhat like a webcast but designed to be distributed over the Internet using syndication feeds (RSS) for playback to computers, MP3 players, iPods, and even smartphones.

Many podcasts are audio only, but video podcasts are also on smartphones, websites, YouTube, and other social networking sites. The three major advantages of podcasts for distributing messages are (1) cost-effectiveness, (2) the ability of users to access material on a 24/7 basis, and (3) portability. For example, a person can listen to an audio podcast while driving to work, walking down a mountain trail, or even while gardening. Simply put, podcasts have many of the same advantages as traditional radio.

Organizations use podcasts for a variety of purposes. These may include (1) news about the company, (2) in-depth interviews with executives and other experts, (3) features giving consumer tips about the use of products and services, and (4) training materials for employees. Some examples:

- Whirlpool produces a podcast series titled "American Family." Topics range from advice and discussions about traveling with kids, weight loss, stroke in women, and even snowmobile safety. The idea is to build customer loyalty and connect with women, the primary audience of Whirlpool.
- Purina, the maker of pet food, has a podcast series that gives advice to pet owners. The series' introduction on the company's website gives the essence of its content: "Is it unusual for a cat to use the toilet? Is your dog bored out of its skull? Can cats and dogs suffer from heart attacks? Get answers to these questions and more in season two of Animal Advice, where veterinarians field questions from pet lovers like you." See the Purina podcast illustration.
- Disneyland has podcasts as part of its global campaign to generate interest in the park. The content includes interesting facts about the park's history, current attractions, and in-depth interviews with employees about their work at the park.
- The University of Pennsylvania's Wharton School produces podcasts that primarily feature insights from professors at the business school regarding current trends and issues.
- Greater Rochester Enterprise repackages its hour-long "Eyes on the Future" radio broadcasts as podcasts for area business people and accessing anytime.

Podcasts

Companies such as Purina are increasingly using podcasts to reach audiences about pet care and, of course, their products.

A podcast should not be an infomercial or the recording of an executive's speech. Like radio, a podcast must be informal, be conversational, and have useful practical information of value to the consumer. Here are some other tips about podcast content: (1) Keep it to less than 15 minutes, (2) use several stories or segments, (3) don't use a script, (4) create an RSS feed, and (5) produce new podcasts on a weekly basis.

Blogs: Everyone Is a Journalist

Blogs, dating back to 1998, have now become mainstream media in terms of numbers and influence. In the beginning, they were called *weblogs* because they were websites maintained by individuals who wanted to post their commentary and opinions on various topics. Today, the abbreviated term "blog" is commonly used.

Although the vast majority of blogs are still the province of individuals who post their diaries and personal opinions, they are now widely recognized by public relations personnel as an extremely cost-effective way to reach large numbers of people. The format and mechanics of blogs make them attractive for several reasons:

- Almost anyone can create a blog with open-source software. A blog is as ideal for a small business as it is for a large company.
- There are virtually no start-up costs.
- The format and writing are informal, which can give an organization a friendly, youthful human face.
- Links can be made to other blogs and web pages.
- Readers can post comments directly on the blog.
- Material can be updated and changed instantly.
- Extensive uses of syndication technologies allow aggregation of information from hundreds of blogs at once. An organization can immediately assess what customers and various publics are saying about it.
- Blogs give an organization an outlet to participate in the online dialogue already going on in other blogs and message boards.
- They allow organizations to post their own points of view unfettered by the editing process of the traditional media.
- A blog(s) on organizational websites dramatically increases indexing by Google and other search engines.

Susan Balcom Walton, writing in *Public Relations Tactics*, says organizations enter the blogosphere for four reasons:

- To achieve real-time communication with key stakeholders
- To enable passionate, knowledgeable people (employees, executives, customers) to talk about the organization, its products, and its services
- To foster conversation among audiences with an affinity for or connection with the organization
- To facilitate more interactive communication and encourage audience feedback
- To dramatically increase the indexing by Google and other search engines

Public relations writers are usually involved in three kinds of blogs: (1) corporate or organizational blogs, (2) employee blogs, and (3) third-party blogs.

Organizational Blogs A corporate blog, unlike an employee blog, is usually written by an executive and represents the official voice of the organization. In many cases, someone in the public relations department actually writes the blog for the executive. Some corporate blogs are now even being outsourced to public relations firms, but some critics say this is a guaranteed way to ensure that the blog is artificial and full of "execu-babble."

Larry Genkin, publisher of *Blogger and Podcaster* magazine, gives a good description of what a corporate blog should be. He says:

> In its best incarnation, corporations will use blogs to become more transparent to their customers, partners, and internally. By encouraging employees to speak their minds, companies will be able to demonstrate their heart and character. Not an easy trick for a faceless entity. This will facilitate stronger relationships and act as "grease in the gears" of a business operation.

An example is how Southwest Airlines uses its blog, "Nuts About Southwest." Posts on the blog may come from the blog's editorial team, employees, or even airline customers. Content comes from the CEO, baggage handlers, and customers who mention an interesting experience on Twitter and even YouTube videos. The blog's editors constantly look for content on Southwest's intranet, e-mails, and other social networking sites. The team contacts the employees and customers to flesh out a story for details and even video clips and then packages them for the blog. One blog post, for example, featured a marriage proposal on a Southwest flight. The blog is further amplified through the airline's 1.3 million Twitter followers and more than 3 million Facebook users who see links to each post.

Employee Blogs Many organizations also encourage their employees to blog on behalf of the organization. Sun Microsystems, for example, has more than 4,000 employee blogs, or about 15 percent of its workforce. More than half of them, according to the company, are "super-technical" and "project-oriented," which appeal only to fellow computer programmers and engineers. Others, such as those written by the CEO as well as managers in human resources and marketing, are more general in subject matter.

Companies, however, do need to establish some guidelines for employee blogs and how they comment on social network sites. Cisco, for example, tells employees, "If you comment on any aspect of the company's business . . . you must clearly identify yourself as a Cisco employee in your postings and include a disclaimer that the views are your own and not those of Cisco." See the following Ethics box for more guidelines.

Third-Party Blogs Organizations, in addition to operating their own blogs and providing guidelines for employee blogs, must monitor and respond to the postings on other blog sites. The products and services of organizations are particularly vulnerable to attack and criticism by bloggers, and an unfavorable mention is often multiplied by links to other blogs and search engine indexing.

Dell, for example, experienced the wrath of bloggers about its customer service, which caused sales to decline, but the company learned a good lesson. Today, according to the *New York Times*, "It's nearly impossible to find a story or blog entry about Dell that isn't accompanied by a comment from the company." Comcast, a cable giant, also gets its share of consumer complaints on blogs, but it also has stepped

on the job ETHICS

The Rules of Social Engagement

Companies increasingly are adopting policies to instruct employees on the appropriate use of blogs and social networking sites on the job. The goal, of course, is to ensure that the organization isn't embarrassed by an employee making "stupid remarks" or that proprietary information is disclosed.

The Gap, for example, provides social media guidelines and training to its 134,000 employees, saying "These guidelines are important—because if you don't follow them a few things could happen; your posts can get deleted, we could lose customers and investors, we could get in trouble, or, worse of all, you could even lose your job. . . . So do the right thing, stick to the guidelines."

Consequently, employees have an ethical responsibility to their employers and to themselves to follow some basic guidelines. Brian Solis, author of several books on social media, has posted 25 employee guidelines (http://www.briansolis.com), including some of the following:

- Ensure that you honor copyrights and promote fair use of content
- Protect confidential and proprietary information
- Don't trash the competition; focus on points of differentiation and value
- Take accountability for your actions and offer no excuses
- Always disclose your identity and affiliation in any posts about your employer or client
- Practice self-restraint; don't get into a shouting match
- Keep things conversational as they apply to portraying and reinforcing the personality and value of your brand and the brand you represent

up its Internet monitoring and has customer service representatives follow up with anyone who posts a complaint.

It's now common practice for organizations to establish relationships with the most relevant and influential bloggers who are talking about the company. Rick Wion, interactive media director of Golin Harris, told Susan Walton in *Public Relations Tactics*, "Treat them the same as you would any other journalist. In most cases, they will appreciate the recognition. By providing materials directly in a manner that is helpful to bloggers, you can build positive relationships quickly."

A good example is how Weber Shandwick works with about 20 influential food bloggers on behalf of its food industry clients. The public relations firm regularly monitors their posts to find out what the bloggers are saying and which hot-button issues they are discussing. This, in turn, allows the firm to build relationships with the bloggers and offer information that they can use in their blogs. Janet Helm, director of the food and nutrition practice at Weber Shandwick, told *PRWeek*, "They are an influential source, and we can't leave them out of the marketing mix."

Wikis: Saving Trees

Interaction between individuals working on a particular project is facilitated by what are known as Wikis. Basically, Wikis are a collection of web pages that enable anyone who accesses them to provide input and even modify their content.

Ward Cunningham, coauthor of *The Wiki Way: Quick Collaboration on the Web*, gives the essence of Wikis:

- They invite all users to edit any page within the website using a basic Web browser.
- They promote meaningful topic associations among different pages.
- They involve visitors in an ongoing process of creation and collaboration.

General Motors, for example, created a Wiki site for its employees and customers as part of its centennial celebration. The site encouraged individuals to contribute first-person experiences—via stories, images, video, and audio—related to the company's history. The advantage of the Wiki was that individuals could comment on other contributions, correct inaccurate information, and even add supplemental information regarding their experiences and viewpoints.

Wikis and collaboration is a space we and many people in the industry are using now as opposed to just sticking to dry e-mail.

Jorand Chanofsky, CEO of Fusion Public Relations

Wikis also are used by public relations departments and firms to keep employees and clients up-to-date on schedules and plans for executing campaigns. Joel Postman, EVP of Eastwick Communications, told *Ragan.com* that the firm's Wiki "allows almost everyone in the agency to set up a well-organized, attractive, customized workspace for any number of tasks.

The Tsunami of Social Media

Using social media has become the number one activity on the Web. One study by *Creativa.com* found that 40 percent of its respondents said they socialize more online than they do face-to-face. In addition, an Experian Hitwise survey in 2013 found that 27 percent of the time Americans spend online is devoted to social media. And one-third of all adults under 30 years obtain their news from social networks.

Collectively, the social media—including blogs, social networks, RSS feeds, podcasts, wikis, reviews, bulletin boards, and newsgroups—have the power to support or destroy a brand or reputation. Transparency is the key; but it's risky business and requires a new mindset and toolkit.

Markovsky Company

Thus, the term "social media" has now entered the mainstream as what Paul Rand of Ketchum communications calls "one of the most dramatic, if not revolutions, in history." David Bowen, writing in the *Financial Times*, adds, "Social networks are all about a shift from vertical to horizontal communications on the Web." More to the point, this social media conversation is not organized, not controlled, and not on message. Instead, the conversation is vibrant, emergent, fun, compelling, and full of insights. Social media is also a place where a single posting can go viral in a matter of hours and reach millions of people around the world, as in the logo for marriage equality shown on page 369. Some experts have even called social networks the world's largest focus group (Figure 13.2).

The tidal wave of social networks, which exploded in 2007, has also changed the landscape of public relations in three ways:

- Listening and two-way dialogue are the basis of today's practice. According to the Institute for Public Relations (IPR), "Social media has provided an opportunity to truly put

on the job

SOCIAL MEDIA IN ACTION

Marriage Equality Symbol Goes Viral

A simple red box with two pink bars in the middle doesn't sound like much, but it became a viral social media sensation within 24 hours.

The symbol was launched by the Human Rights Campaign (HRC) in April 2013 as the U.S. Supreme Court started to hear arguments about the right of same-sex couples to marry. HRC, as the nation's largest LGBT civil rights organization, wanted to show support for marriage equality by changing its traditional blue and yellow symbol to red in its profile image on Facebook, Twitter, Instagram, Tumblr, and Pinterest. The idea caught on, and millions of individuals also replaced their profile image with the red box symbolizing equality to show their support for marriage equality.

"Red is a symbol for love, and that's what marriage is all about," HRC spokesperson Charlie Joughin explained to *MSNBC.com*. "We wanted to give people an opportunity to show their support for marriage equality in a public and visible way."

The symbol was further promoted and displayed by public officials, celebrities, and even companies. A number of U.S. Senators changed their Facebook profile image and celebrities from Beyoncé to George Takei shared the symbol with all their followers. In addition, Bud Light put the symbol on its beer cans, Martha Stewart incorporated it into a red velvet cake, and GroupOn posted a video showing dozens of employees wearing red shirts. In fact, the social media campaign also encouraged a million Facebook users to wear red on the day that the Supreme Court started to hear the legal briefs.

The symbol also gained popularity because it generated dozens of iterations. Many individuals superimposed the equal sign over personal photos or integrated it with other images. The popular TV shows *True Blood* even shared a version of the photo with vampire fangs as part of the equal sign.

With the social media a sea of red, traditional media also picked up the story and amplified it throughout the 50 states and the world. Not bad for a simple red box.

Figure 13.2 **The Use of Social Media Sites by Online Adults**

There is an increasing number of social networking sites, and this chart shows the relative popularity of the major sites in terms of usage. The largest percentage of social media users are between 18 and 29 years, followed by the 30–49 age group. The primary users of Facebook tend to be women, aged 18–29 years.

Source: Pew Research Center, 2013.

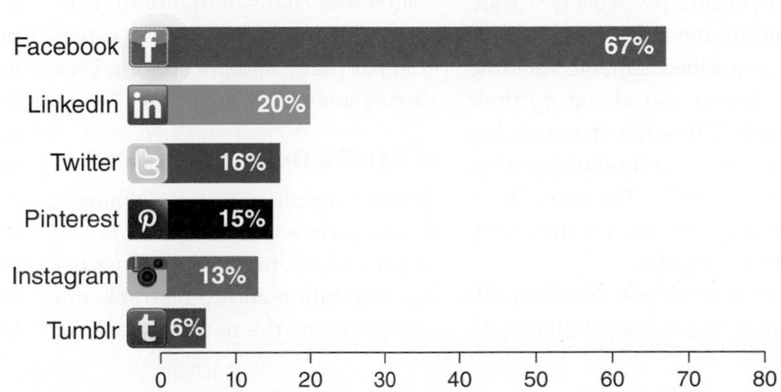

the public back into public relations by providing a mechanism for organizations to engage in real-time, one-on-one conversations with stakeholders."

- Organizations must perform and behave because society expects greater transparency and accountability. Communication must be more authentic and credible.
- Social media is now fully integrated as a major tactic in almost every public relations program or campaign. Public relations firms and departments are now hiring individuals who are specialists in social media and digital media management. See the Insights box below about the life of a social media manager.

The following sections provide a snapshot of today's most popular social media and how they are being integrated as an essential strategy in almost every public relations program and campaign. There is a discussion of (1) Facebook, (2) Twitter, (3) LinkedIn, (4) YouTube, (5) Flickr, (6) Instagram, and (7) Pinterest.

Facebook: King of the Social Networks

There are multiple online social networking communities, including the business-oriented LinkedIn, but MySpace and Facebook established early leads in popularity. Facebook, in 2013, was the most popular site, with more than 1 billion users worldwide, of which 70 percent are outside the United States.

With such numbers, Facebook is clearly the most visited social network in the United States, with more than 150 million visitors daily. In addition, visitors spend almost seven hours a month on the site, according to *Ragan's PR Daily*, compared to its nearest rivals Tumblr and Pinterest, where visitors spend only 1.5 hours a month.

on the job

INSIGHTS

Some Misconceptions About Being a Social Media Manager

By Michelle Kraker

Today, businesses of every size are realizing the importance of having a qualified, capable, full-time staff engaging and elevating their social media presence. However, because this role is still relatively new, some people think the job is best suited for a young intern or their tech-savvy granddaughter.

But let me tell you from experience, social media is a tough gig. It's a vital role that's demanding, constantly changing, and often a career that has many misconceptions. Let's discuss some of them, shall we?

It Can Be Done by Anyone

There's a specific skillset and dramatic learning curve. Techniques are key when it comes to managing your online reputation and to be frank, not everyone has the natural knack for communicating your messaging appropriately. The social media manager is responding to customer service questions, setting the tone and personality for your brand, and curating content that your followers will resonate with. If the person you hired is not immersed in the industry you're targeting, chances are you're going to get a whole lot of inspirational quotes and Internet memes for content.

All We Do Is "Play" on Social Media All Day

There's always "that person" who will ask you what you do for a living and if you reply that you work in social media, they sometimes say (or think), "So are you just playing on Facebook and Twitter all day?" And after I imagine myself pouring hot grease on them, I calmly tell them about how social media management requires a tremendous amount of strategy in order to yield a positive ROI. A social media manager's performance should be measured with inbound marketing analytics from campaigns, content, and engagement.

Integration with the company's overall marketing strategy should be an intricate part of the goals and objectives. Identifying and nurturing leads should be among the primary goals of social media strategy, and the sharpest brands are working to find ways to identify and reward their brand evangelists.

That Our Job Stops at the End of the Workday

Wouldn't that be nice! Alas, there is no 9 to 5 in the social mediasphere. A social media manager is expected to be "always on." There are constant notifications up on my iPhone. Between customer service questions on Twitter, thoughtful comments that need responses on Facebook, and notifications on LinkedIn, there really is no down time. And don't even get me started on

Michelle Kraker

Instagram. It's a common theme among my family and friends that I instagram, like, everything. The perfect shot, the right angle, the perfect crop, the artistic photo filler, the compelling caption and just the right hashtag. I probably put more thought into my Instagram account than I do what I'm making for dinner.

It's a Job with No Pressure

Social media managers are tasked with building out the personality and reach of the brand, yet some professionals don't value the role. It's our responsibility to stay up to date on social topics, trends, changes, and tools. Our strategies and platforms are always changing, being added to, and growing in influence. We're putting out fires where there's a fire and even shaping perceptions about brands that need to repair their online reputation.

Our Mistakes Are the Biggest Mistakes

Forget the pen; the send button is mightier than the sword. Every email you send goes right to the recipient. Every tweet I send goes to tens of thousands of people. It's critiqued, talked about, torn apart, praised, or shared. For most of you, your completed tasks go straight to your boss—whereas mine go to several different clients across hundreds of networks. Just about every day you hear about a social media manager that gets fired for posting the wrong post or tweeting the wrong tweet.

Don't think for a second that this article is all about "woe is me" attitude when it comes to my job. I do this because I love it. I love the pressure. I love the pace, and I love the reward of engaging people online.

Michelle Kraker is the CEO and founder of SOHO, The Social House, in Nashville, TN. She attended Olivet Nazarene University and has worked in the ever-changing landscape of Social Media Marketing for more than 10 years. She has utilized marketing tactics to help enhance the personality, content, and reach of many major brands. Despite the variety of social networks, stilettos are still Michelle's favorite platform.

According to Nielsen research, almost 20 percent of time spent online via personal computer is on Facebook. A profile of Facebook is given in Figure 13.3.

The popularity Facebook has been noted by advertising, marketing, and public relations professionals. *Advertising Age's* top 100 advertisers, for example, have Facebook pages, and they see the site as an excellent opportunity to make "friends" in several ways. A survey of executives by TNS Media Intelligence/Cymfony, for example, found that marketing and public relations personnel believe networking sites are vital for (1) gaining consumer insights, (2) building brand awareness, and (3) creating customer loyalty.

Figure 13.3 A Snapshot of Facebook in 2013

Facebook in 2013

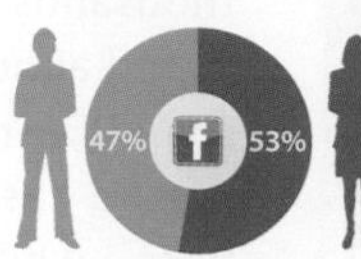

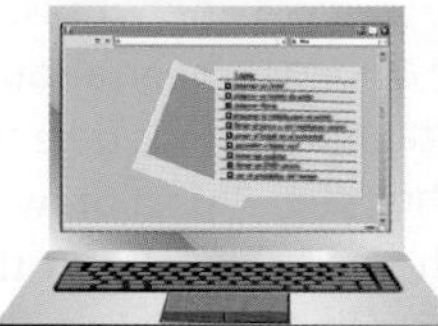

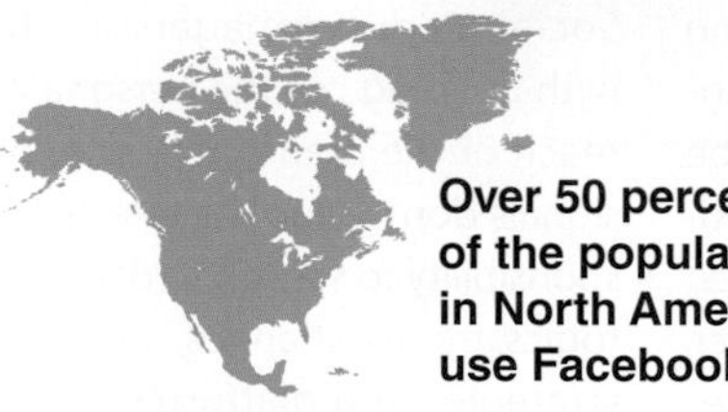

> We use tools based on their strengths, and each of the entries in the social media space offers its own strengths and weaknesses, possibilities and limitations.
>
> *Shel Holtz, social media guru at an IABC workshop*

Accomplishing these objectives, however, takes a great deal of thought and creativity because the public relations professional must shape messages that are relevant and interesting to the company's "friends." This often requires techniques such as humor, short video clips, music, contests, and audience participation.

A good example is Yoplait. It grew its Facebook "likes" by 800,000 in one year by decreasing the number of product promotions and hiring a social media manager known to its Facebook users as "Yoplait Sara." She became the personality of the brand by drawing on the aspects of her personal and family life in Minnesota and weaving in Yoplait references. She, for example, talked about her latest garden project that, of course, includes nurturing seedling plants in Yoplait containers. Yoplait also restructured the page by

Figure 13.4 **The Top 10 Organizations with Facebook and Twitter Followers**

Facebook	77 million
Coca-Cola	51 million
MTV	42 million
Disney	39 million
Starbucks	35 million
Converse	33 million
Red Bull	31 million
McDonald's	23 million
Snaptu	22 million
Wal-Mart	21 million

Source: Top-Business-Degrees.net and *Ragan's PR Daily* News Feed.

changing product-centered tabs with more consumer friendly topics such as "Feeling Good," "Looking Good," and "photos."

Coors has also expanded its traditional advertising and product publicity to embrace social networking sites. One initiative on Facebook enabled visitors (those aged at least 21 years, of course) to send friends a "Code Blue" alert inviting them to meet up for a Coors Light. They could even use Facebook maps to direct their buddies to the nearest bar. Aaron, one of Coors' almost 2,000 fans, gave the site five stars: "This app is epic. I used it to set up my birthday party and it was so easy to invite everyone." Another example of an excellent Facebook page is Springfield Clinic, which is shown on the next page.

Springfield Clinic in Illinois has a Facebook page that encourages consumers to interact with the page. The clinic posts a new article every morning that deals with such topics as the latest medical news, background information on current event in the health industry, and new scientific studies. It was named the best Facebook page in 2012 by *Ragan's PR Daily*.

Twitter: Saying It in 144 Characters

Twitter, a social networking and microblogging site launched in 2006, had about 300 million active users worldwide by its seventh birthday. It has grown rapidly if the number of tweets sent daily is any indication; it was 50 million a day in 2010 but had reached 400 million daily by 2013. In addition, about 85 percent of the world's largest corporations now have one or more Twitter accounts to issue micro news releases, give updates of an evolving situation or crisis, pitch a journalist about a story, or to offer discounts on goods and services.

Twitter is Web based, so its major advantage over texting is that posts are now indexed by Google and readily available to anyone with Internet access. Twitter, as it matures, is getting more robust. A tweet can now provide easy links to documents, websites, photos, and videos. In 2013, the site began to introduce new apps such as Vine that allows a user to post a six-second video. McDonald's, for example, used Vine to promote its new menu item, Fish McBites. There is also convergence with mobile apps. One creative use was Tweet-a-Beer at the Southwest by Southwest Interactive

Festival (SXSW), which enabled users to buy someone a beer via Twitter. The idea was the brainchild of Waggener Edstrom, a public relations firm that wanted to show off its digital capabilities.

The following are some examples of how organizations and their public relations staffs use Twitter:

- Qwest Communications, a telecommunications company, uses @TalkToQwest to handle customer questions, concerns, and complaints.
- The Nuclear Energy Institute (NEI) used tweets to give 24/7 updates on the situation in Japan's nuclear plants after the 2011 tsunami.
- Both the Israeli Defense Force and the Hamas military use tweets to communicate their viewpoint to foreign government officials and the public.
- The Phoenix Suns, as well as other professional teams, uses team and player tweets to update fans and build brand loyalty.

- Krazy Glue conducted a contest (#KrazyBigFix), asking users to submit photos and videos of how they used the product to repair something.
- Burson-Marsteller writes promotional tweets on behalf of Kim Kardashian who is the paid celebrity spokesperson for the frozen dessert firm, Millions of Milkshakes. See the following Insights about Justin Bieber's 37 million followers.
- Many organizations (as well as individuals) expressed shock and sympathy via Twitter after the act of terrorism at the Boston Marathon in 2013.

Public relations professionals who use Twitter, however, should be aware of some basic guidelines. They include:

- **Think outside the box.** Use Twitter to create ways to engage the public, make the organization stand out, and bring awareness to the brand.
- **Tell a story.** An interesting story about a product is better than a pitch to buy the product. Coca-Cola got massive re-tweets by just posting "When you open a Coke, 12,067 bubbles are born. Happy Birthday, bubbles!"
- **Avoid bulletin board syndrome.** Don't just post announcements and links. Instead, use Twitter to engage in a conversation with your followers.
- **Don't be a "twammer."** Limit the number of tweets that you post. Post only important and relevant information.

on the job INSIGHTS

Does Justin Bieber Really Have 37 Million Followers?

Probably not. *SocialBakers*, a social media analytics company, found that the likes of Justin Bieber, Lady Gaga, and Katy Perry are all followed by tens of millions of fake accounts. In fact, it was found by *digitspy.co.uk* that 45 percent of Bieber's followers are fake accounts, while many of the other top Twitter users also had high percentages of dubious accounts following them.

It's not uncommon for musicians and other entertainers, according to *bbc.co.uk*, to buy YouTube views, Twitter followers, and Facebook likes in order to promote themselves and increase their online social status. It's possible, for example, to buy 10,000 YouTube views for less than $50 and thousands of Twitter followers for about the same amount. The companies selling these services set up fake accounts and then post to them automatically using computer software. A variety of IP addresses are used to avoid detection by major social networks that strive to delete all fake accounts.

- **Update on a daily basis.** Although you should not post excessive tweets, it is a good idea to tweet about something once a day. It keeps your name in front of your followers.
- **Use Twitter in a crisis.** Twitter is an ideal form of communication when there is a crisis or fast-breaking news. It is one of the first steps an organization should take to provide up-to-the-minute details—or reactions—to a crisis. See the box on Spirit AeroSystems in Chapter 10.
- **Think twice before posting.** An inappropriate tweet can cause major problems for you or an employer. A Ketchum executive, visiting client FedEx in Memphis, tweeted, "I'm in one of those towns where I scratch my head and say, I would die if I had to live here." FedEx officials were not amused, and Ketchum had to quickly issue an apology to save the account.

LinkedIn: The Professional Network

This social networking website primarily connects individuals in professional occupations. It has about 200 million users from around the world, but about half of them live in the United States.

The site works on several levels. First, it allows individuals to connect with other professionals in their occupational field or area of interest. There are also more than 1 million interest groups, including several hundred in the public relations field that individuals can join to get information and exchange ideas.

On a second level, LinkedIn has become a major resource for finding a job and advancing career opportunities. It's a site where users post their profiles, their updated résumés, and even recommendations from work colleagues and former employers. Users can search for a job in several ways. They can search by job position (e.g., account executive for a public relations firm), or they can also research the hundreds of organizations that have pages on LinkedIn to find out about the organization and what jobs are currently available. LinkedIn also enables the individual to apply online for the job. One note of caution: Employers often look at the user's LinkedIn profile and the submitted résumé to see if they match.

YouTube: King of Video Clips

YouTube is the second most popular search engine site after Google and gets more than 4 billion views a day. According to data from Nielsen, more than 150 million people watch online videos an average of four hours in a typical week. In terms of sites, the *Socially Aware Blog* says that in a single month, YouTube averages 3 hours compared to Hulu and Tudou with 2.5 hours. Of course, Netflix is the feature film king with 10 hours monthly.

The popularity of video is not lost on organizations who want to reach and influence audiences. David Murdico, writing in *Ragan's PR Daily* (www.prdaily.com), cites some statistics from various sources:

- Videos have appeared in almost 70 percent of the top 100 search listings on Google in 2012.
- Almost 180 million Americans watch 33 billion online content videos in an average month for an average of 17.4 hours per viewer.
- More than 80 percent of companies use online video content in their marketing programs.

- People share video 12 times more than links and text posts combined.
- Users share 700 YouTube videos on Twitter each minute.
- Photos and videos drive the most engagement on Facebook's top 10 brand pages.
- More than 60 percent of consumers in one survey will spend at least two minutes watching a video about a product.
- Consumers are much more likely to buy a product after seeing a video than those who do not.
- Online video is now 50 percent of all traffic on smartphones.

Most videos are posted by individuals, but organizations have also established their own YouTube channels and have upgraded their websites to include more video content as part of their marketing and public relations outreach. Research firms such as Nielsen/NetRatings have found that the 35 to 64 age group constitutes about 50 percent of YouTube's audience. Another large audience is college students; research shows that 95 percent of them regularly view videos online.

About 48 hours of video are uploaded to YouTube every minute of the day so public relations professionals must be creative thinkers and produce engaging content. As Murdico writes, "Everyone is watching video. You need to be making ads, promos, branded entertainment, Web series, video blogs, funny viral videos, videos of your cat, your dog, your cat riding your dog—whatever style and format that best reaches your customers."

Humor and parody are often used to attract viewers. H&R Block, for example, used a fictional oddball character to talk about the joys of online tax preparation and spoof popular YouTube shorts such as the precision treadmill routine team. Smirnoff launched a new iced tea malt beverage on YouTube showing three blond men in polo shirts at a yacht club rapping lines such as "Straight outta Cape Cod, we are keepin' it real." It worked because the parody of fashionable white men rapping isn't typical rap imagery.

> Embrace online video and watch how creative, genuine, and cool content becomes incredibly viral. Words can carry the message just so far, but video is an opportunity to showcase the product while entertaining viewers.
>
> *Brian Solis and Deirdre Breakenridge, authors of* Putting the Public Back in Public Relations

However, not all YouTube videos have to be humorous and entertaining in order to be successful. The United Steelworkers, during a strike against Goodyear Tire & Rubber Co., posted a 30-second video spot on YouTube that showed a photo montage of auto accidents. As a sport-utility vehicle flips over, a question appears on-screen: "What tires do you plan to buy?"

Less startling but just as effective is a series of videos by Cisco Systems about cities of the future such as Songdo, South Korea. The video series was distributed on its YouTube channel, the company's online newsroom, Facebook, Twitter, and LinkedIn. The videos had more than 61,000 views and were shared more than 100,000 times via social channels. It's not exactly a "Gangnam Style" viral video with 1 billion views, but Cisco did position itself as an innovative technology company with a vision for the future. YouTube also played a role in the Department of Energy's Decathlon, which is highlighted on page 378.

On occasion, a YouTube video posted by a third party can do considerable damage to a corporate reputation. United Airlines found this out after refusing to compensate Canadian musician Dave Carroll, when baggage handlers broke his guitar. He composed a video song, "United Breaks Guitars," and posted it on YouTube. It became a hit and was played more than 3.5 million times over the next several months.

PRCasebook

Social Media Fuel a Solar Decathlon

The U.S. Department of Energy (DOE) wanted to promote energy-efficient housing, but how do you design a public relations campaign to make the message newsworthy and mentioned on social media networks?

The answer is a Solar Decathlon that involves a biennial competition between college teams from the United States and abroad to build the most attractive, energy-efficient, and affordable house. Instead of just submitting a model or a blueprint, however, the teams actually design and build model homes that are exhibited in a single location over a two-week period. The 2011 competition, for example, was held on the National Mall in Washington, D.C.

Not everybody, of course, could visit Washington to tour the houses so DOE and its public relations firm, Stratacomm, took a variety of steps to ensure that the public and Solar Decathlon fans from around the world could experience the competition online.

- The college teams were encouraged to have their own Facebook pages, blogs, and YouTube videos to tell about their house project and tell their own personal stories.
- More than 1,000 posts appeared on Facebook, Twitter, YouTube, and Flickr in the eight months before the live house display in Washington, D.C.
- QR codes and Foursquare check-ins were introduced throughout the solar village.
- TweetChats and media webcasts were organized to let online audiences see and talk to student contestants and DOE representatives.
- Captioned photos were posted daily in Facebook, Flickr, newswires, and the DOE website, *Solardecathalon.gov*.
- Student teams were asked to shoot video and create computer-animated walkthroughs of their houses.

- An overview video and an online virtual tour of each house were posted to DOE's YouTube channel and its website.
- An online newsroom was established, and a media guide featuring tips for reporters on what to cover was made available.

Thanks to the extensive social media outreach, the Solar Decathlon achieved considerable visibility and engagement.

- Facebook users increased 289 to 7,700 percent. Facebook referred 25,900 visits to *Solardecathalon.gov*.
- Twitter followers increased 588 to 5,300 percent.
- There were almost 500,000 views of Solar Decathlon's YouTube channel.
- Views of photos on Flickr tripled to 500,000.
- Many student teams built their own YouTube, Flickr, and blog sites to further increase public awareness of the competition and promote energy-efficient housing.
- Website traffic during the two-week event generated 1.2 million page views.
- QR codes received almost 9,000 scans.

This success garnered even more publicity when it became a smash hit on iTunes, and Carroll made guest appearances on every major television network. All this, of course, ignited a firestorm on social networks as hundreds of individuals also shared their unsatisfactory experiences with United.

In another incident, two bored employees of a Domino's Pizza franchise in North Carolina decided to post on YouTube a video of them making a truly obnoxious sandwich that violated all health standards. The video went viral, and it took some weeks for the company to restore its reputation for serving quality food.

Flickr and Instagram: Sharing Photos

The popularity of YouTube has also led organizations to increase the use of photos and infographics to attract and engage audiences. A study by HubSpot, for example, found that 300 million photos were being uploaded on Facebook every day in early 2013, a 20 percent increase over the previous year. The study also found that photo posts attracted 104 percent more comments than the average post.

Studies indicate that 65 percent of Americans are visual learners, so public relations professionals are increasingly using visuals to communicate key messages. As Scott Signore, CEO of Matter Communications, writes in *O'Dwyer's Report*, "Visual storytelling helps clients tell their story better, and in turn do better business." The two major photo-sharing sites are Flickr and Instagram, which are described here.

Flickr. If YouTube is the king of video, Flickr is the queen of photo sharing by virtue of its age and inventory of photos. The site was launched in 2004 and acquired by Yahoo a year later. It hosts about 6 billion photos and has more than 50 million registered users, according to Wikipedia. For smartphone users, there's even an official Flickr app.

Ann Smarty, writing in the *Ragan Report*, says, "It is a place for people to show off their work, and it's probably the most popular photo site on the Web. It has plenty of professional portfolios, amateur albums, and even a Creative Commons item you can use freely for personal or commercial purposes—with proper credit, of course." In other words, public relations professionals use Flickr in two ways:

first, to find photos and even video clips they can use on an employer's website and social network pages, and second, to make photos available for possible use by other bloggers and individuals who post photos on their sites. Organizations may also post photos in more than 60 user groups that help gain visibility for the organization.

Brands of all flavors see higher engagement with their customers when they deploy visual content across their marketing disciplines, from social and public relations, to website content and even static materials like annual reports.

Scott Signore, CEO of Matter Communications

Flickr discourages photos that are too commercial in terms of displaying a product or service, but there are more creative ways for organizations to use Flickr. The Monterey Aquarium, for example, encourages the posting of photos taken by visitors at the facility. It even sponsored a photo contest in connection with World Ocean Day. The aquarium's public relations staff also monitor blogs, and if someone posts a good photo from an exhibit, they ask the individual to also post it on the Flickr site. Ken Peterson, communications director, told *Ragan.com*, "We've let some people know that we're interested in using their photos on the aquarium Web site or in other vehicles. That creates great word of mouth, since the photographer will likely tell his or her friends to visit the aquarium Web site—or Flickr group—and see the photo on display."

Instagram If Flickr is the father of photo-sharing sites, the ambitious son is Instagram that was launched in 2010. Acquired by Facebook in 2012, it rapidly grew to more than 100 million registered users the following year.

The primary selling point is that it enables users to take pictures on their smartphones, apply digital filters to them, and then share them on a variety of social networks such as Facebook or Twitter. In fact, one survey by *All Things D* found that smartphone users were spending more time on Instagram than on Twitter and noted "This is indicative of a broader shift toward visual content in digital space."

From a public relations standpoint, various brands are opening accounts to post photos, videos, and infographics that can be easily accessed by the public via smartphones, tablets, and regular PCs. Although Instagram started out as a mobile application, it has also added web-based profiles, expanding the service to the larger-screen Web. The top brands on the site in early 2013 were MTV (1.14 million followers), Starbucks (1.1 million followers), and Nike (880,000 followers). According to Cotton Delo, writing in *Advertising Age*, brands are ". . . intrigued by the prospect of having a place to showcase their content in one place and possibly to direct users there from other media."

Pinterest

A close cousin of Flickr and Instagram is Pinterest. It's a photo-sharing site, launched in 2010, for both companies and individuals, but also includes a wider variety of content such as infographics and even recipes that can be easily "pinned" by individuals to their websites, blogs, and social media profiles.

The travel, fashion, and food industries in particular have ample opportunity for visual content, but a number of organizations now use Pinterest because it's highly integrated with social networking sites such as Facebook and Twitter. In addition, the various topic boards and brand pages can be easily accessed via a Pinterest app available on iPhones and Android devices.

The following are some examples of how organizations are using Pinterest:

- Fashion designer Oscar de la Renta "live-pinned" photographs about a bridal show, which was re-pinned by hundreds of fans.
- Whole Foods created several Pinterest boards with such topics as urban farming and do-it-yourself projects using household items. The grocery store chain has also posted recipes that have driven traffic to its website, WholeFoodsMarket.com.
- The National Wildlife Association has more than 20 boards on Pinterest, including its "Shop NWF," "#Squirrels4Good," and "Wild Crafts & Recipes." See the following NWF page.
- Beauty product line Elizabeth Arden supported its longtime charity partner Look Good Feel Better through a campaign, Pin It to Give It, in which each "re-pin" generated one product donation to cancer patients.

> Pinterest is a place for people to share photos, bookmark images, comment on posts and generate conversation around a visual centerpiece.
>
> *Amy Jacques, writing in* PR Tactics

The following are some tips for public relations specialists using Pinterest:

- Use only high-quality photos that are creative and interesting because the site is all about "eye candy."
- Write short 20-word descriptions of the photo or infographic because they are the most re-pinnable.
- Data and survey statistics should be made highly visual through the use of colorful, well-designed infographics.

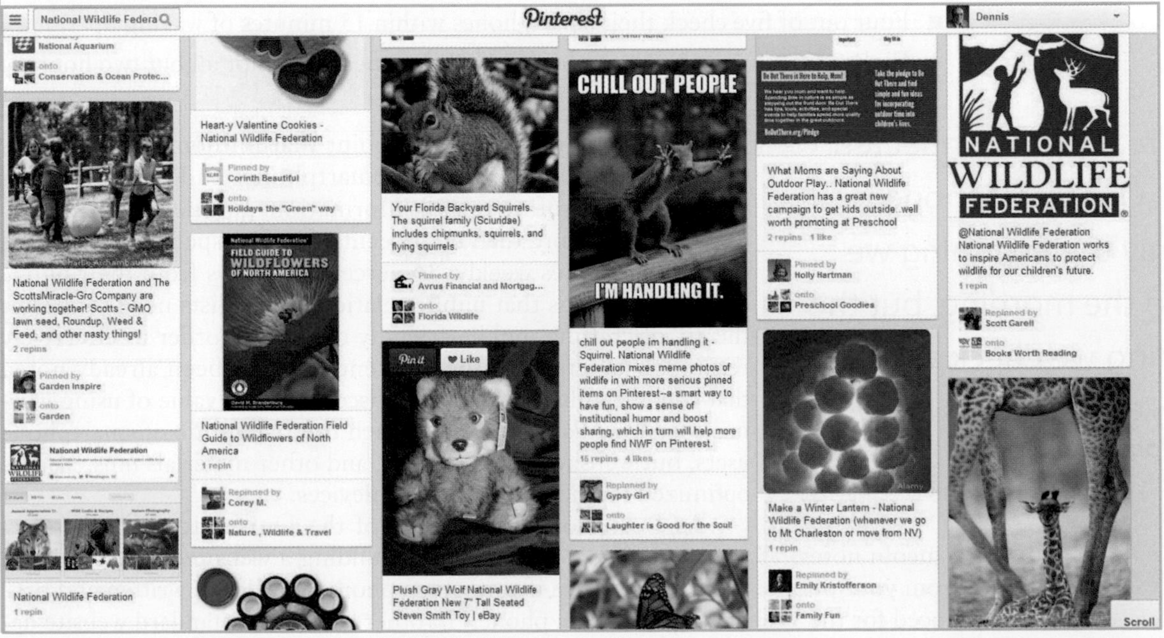

The National Wildlife Federation (NWF) has a number of boards on Pinterest that display high-quality photos and illustrations. Such boards are a virtual store front for the organization. In addition, NWF photos can be found on topic boards such as "wild animals."

- Publish your Pinterest activity on the organization's Facebook timeline.
- Tweet your pins to draw Twitter users to your profile.
- Add Pinterest "follow" buttons to the organization's blogs and websites.

Pinterest, by early 2013, had about 50 million registered users and continued to show major growth. The site is particularly popular with women; the company says about 85 percent of its users worldwide in 2012 were women.

The Rising Tide of Mobile-Enabled Content

The tsunami of social media is also a major contributor to the rising tide of mobile-enabled content. Indeed, most studies show that smartphones and tablets have now replaced PCs as the most common device for Web access. On a global basis, research firm Strategy Analytics reports there is now 1 billion smartphone users, or one out of every seven people in the world. And the firm projects that another billion will be using smartphones by 2015.

In sum, access to the world of information and social interaction is rapidly becoming available in everyone's pocket. Indeed, the ITU reported in 2013 that mobile penetration around the world has reached almost 100 percent. There are 6.8 billion subscribers among the world's 7.1 billion population, a number achieved in part by many people and organizations having multiple accounts.

In the United States, ComScore reports that there are almost 135 million smartphone users, or about 45 percent of the population, but the percentage will increase to 70 percent by 2017. Indeed, smartphones are already pervasive in most people's lives. A study by IDC Research revealed some the following findings:

- Smartphone users, aged 18 to 44, spend more than two hours daily communicating and using social media on their devices.
- Four out of five check their smartphones within 15 minutes of waking up.
- Eighty percent of users have their phone on or near them for all but two hours of their waking day.

> We're really in a connected world. Our smartphone is not only the first thing we turn to the morning, but the last thing we check at night.
>
> *Mary Gorges, creative communications manager at Cisco Systems, writing in the* Ragan Report.

Such findings amplify the point that millions of consumers (and journalists) now use their smartphones and tablets as their primary source of news and information. In one Pew Research Center study, more than 60 percent of U.S. respondents get news from their phones weekly; 36 percent get news from their phone daily. This means that public relations specialists need to master the art of crafting mobile-friendly content in order to effectively reach consumers and other audiences. It has been already noted that organizations have already discovered the value of using various social media networks to reach the rising tide of smartphone users, but websites, news releases, and other materials must also be optimized for viewing on mobile devices.

As Professor Gary Kebbel of the University of Nebraska–Lincoln notes, "You don't create a mobile site by building a website and accessing it from your phone. You lose audience if your story, photo, or video is written and produced for the Web, and viewed on a phone." In other words, the standard website designed for viewing on a PC screen needs to be supplemented by a mobile version that is much shorter and contains only the information that a person on the go would like to see. This approach is also applicable to news releases. McCormick & Company, for example, prepares news releases and recipes for standard Web distribution, but also re-formats them into short, narrow columns that fit a smartphone screen.

Organizations are also actively producing apps and using QR codes specifically designed for smartphones and tablets, which will be discussed next.

An Ocean of Apps

Back in the old days, the basic cell phone was a relatively simple device. It enabled people to call their friends from practically any location or even to send them a text message. Today's smartphone is less of a telephone than a small computer that allow users to download videos, surf the Internet at will, receive e-mails, post comments on blogs, and receive an extensive array of mobile-enabled content. In other nations, mobile phones are being used as virtual credit cards to pay bills and withdraw cash, as files that store a person's medical records, and even as a form of money that allows users to make a purchase by waving the phone over a scanner.

Making all this happen are various computer applications, which are now just called "Apps." In fact, research by the analytics firm Flurry found that U.S. consumers now spend an average of 2 hours and 38 minutes per day on smartphones and tablets, but 80 percent of that time is spent using various apps. Given the results, Flurry titled its research report, "It's an App World. The Web Just Lives in It." According to the study, the 10 most popular apps categories on smartphones are in descending order:

- E-mail
- Web browsing
- Facebook
- Maps/directions
- Games
- General search
- Share/post photos
- Read news, sports
- Local search
- Watch TV/Video

The number of apps keeps multiplying. In mid-2013, there were about 700,000 apps available for downloading at each of the Apple stores and Google Android stores. One estimate says that about 40 billion apps are downloaded worldwide every year. Increasingly, public relations professionals are using apps to reach audiences and provide information that they can use. In general, the best app advances a brand by providing useful, objective information without being too commercial. A good example is Kraft's Food Assistant app that provides a variety of recipes that, of course, include Kraft products. The app is available on iPhone, Android tablets, and Kindle Fire.

An app, as in the case of Kraft, must reinforce the brand in terms of informing or entertaining its key customers. Akron Children's Hospital, for example, created an app titled "Care4Kids," which helped parents find locations, contact the hospital, and get essential care tips for their children. Kendall-Jackson winery, on the other hand, needed to expand its market to the 25 to 40 age group so it developed a mobile app, "K-J Recommends" that paired wines—not necessarily with food—but with mood, social situations, and even the color of the table setting.

On a more entertaining side, the pet food manufacturer, Friskies, offered a "Catify App" in which users could use cat templates and insert their own facial photo to see themselves in cat form. Friskies also offers a variety of apps for cats and humans, including a game, "You vs. Cat." See the box below about how Singapore created an iPhone app for Chinese tourists.

When creating an app for your organization, remember the following tips:

- Make sure the app is simple to use, meets the needs of consumers, and is original.
- Provide content that empowers the user to interact with the app.
- Publicize the app through social networking and mainstream media.

Quick response codes, known as QR codes, are two-dimensional matrix bar codes that serve as URLs to connect mobile users with an organization's website and any number of apps. The idea is that the consumer or a journalist can easily access additional information in the form of articles, videos, and photos about an organization, a product, or even an event.

The ability to readily access and download information is particularly attractive to journalists who are often out of the office. Consequently, media relations specialists often embed QR codes in flyers, media kits, annual reports, brochures, and news

on the job

A MULTICULTURAL WORLD

Adidas, Singapore Campaigns Tap Social Media

Social media are often used to reach specific audiences. An Adidas campaign was focused on female teenagers around the world, and Singapore wanted to increase the number of Chinese visitors.

Adidas

Adidas, the maker of running shoes and other athletic gear, launched an effort to get young women around the world engaged with the brand by having them share their athletic pursuits with each other. The central hub was www.adidas.com/mygirls that also provided linkage to Twitter and Instagram. The website provided Adidas-themed news, information about products, style trends, and how to get involved in community events.

There was also a series of videos at the MyGirls.Adidas.com site in which girls of various nations talked about the challenge of athletic training and dealing with local social taboos. One video, for example, was about a team of female boxers in Amman, Jordan. One boxer said, "I don't care if it's for boys or for girls."

Singapore

Chinese tourists were the focus of the Singapore Tourism Board (STB) in an effort to engage them via social media. The major tactic was to encourage potential Chinese tourists to interact with Singapore's official ambassador Stephanie Sun on China's equivalent of Twitter, Sina Weibo.

MSL Group, the STB's public relations firm, made the campaign interactive by asking users to design their own travel plans and upload Singapore shopping experiences and travelogues to www.yoursingapore.com. This tactic was so successful that an iPhone app was created to showcase user-generated content in the form of a travel guidebook.

The campaign, in part, helped generate a record-breaking 1.1 million Chinese tourists to Singapore in a single year. Singapore's social media fans increased to almost 190,000, and almost 100 articles and features were published or broadcast about Singapore as an attractive destination for tourists instead of just being a stop-over city.

QR Codes: Rich Content a Scan Away

releases, and even pitch to journalists via a tweet or an e-mail. By scanning a QR code on a mobile-enabled device, both journalists and consumers can access a variety of content, including videos, photos, and additional background information.

QR codes can be used in a variety of ways, and some organizations are quite innovative in their use. The Sandy Springs (Georgia) fire department, for example, conducted a campaign to get more citizens trained in CPR so it embedded a QR code on business cards that were given out at meetings, school visits, and other speaking engagements. The QR code enabled individuals to access video and guidelines on how to recognize and treat sudden cardiac arrest. Deputy Fire Chief Dennis Ham told *Ragan.com*, "We've leveraged that technology to educate 10,000 people in Sandy Springs in CPR."

The city of Cupertino (California) has even placed QR codes on the trees in its parks so visitors, using an Apple app, can get information about the name and background of a particular tree. And the Sonoma County Transit Authority (California) has a large QR sign outside the local airport so travelers can check local bus schedules. In another application, Heinz Ketchup put QR codes on its bottles to promote the Wounded Warrior Project. For each scan that prompts a user to send a thank you note to military service personnel, Heinz donates $1 to Wounded Warrior. In this way, more than $200,000 was raised.

Magazine ads and articles also have embedded QR codes so readers can easily access information and visual content. QR codes played a major role, for example, in a Gillette campaign for a new razor designed to remove hair from all parts of a man's body. The ad, of course, featured model Kate Upton in a swim suit sitting on a beach lounge chair with the caption, "How does Kate Upton like her man's body styled?" In the thought bubble was a QR code that took the reader to a short video of Upton answering such questions as "How important is it for a guy to groom down there?" She answers "very important."

Texting: Not Sexy but Pervasive

A new breed of apps such as WhatsApp or Kik is gaining popularity as new messaging systems, but SMS, like e-mail, is still an effective public relations strategy.

Nonprofits, in particular, have effectively used text messaging for providing information and fund-raising. Lifeline, a British nonprofit that provides drug and alcohol services, sends a weekly inspirational quote via text message that has helped the agency maintain regular contact with its clients. A texting program also raised millions for Haiti earthquake relief by enabling Americans to dial 90999 and automatically donate $10 to the Red Cross that was billed to their cell phone accounts. Other health agencies, such as Planned Parenthood, have successfully used SMS to communicate one-on-one with teenagers who text questions relating to sexual health.

Summary

The Internet: Pervasive in Our Lives

- The worldwide adoption of the Internet and the World Wide Web has taken less time than the adoption of any other mass medium in history.
- The Internet is the first major revolution in communication since the invention of the printing press.
- The Internet has democratized information in the respect that nearly anyone can now send and receive vast amounts of information without journalists or editors serving as gatekeepers and mediators of that content.

The World Wide Web

- The new media, including the Web, have unique characteristics. These include (1) easy updating of material, (2) instant distribution of information, (3) an infinite amount of space for information, and (4) the ability to interact with the audience.
- A website is the organization's digital front door; it must be well designed.
- Webcasts are now used for news conferences, briefing financial analysts, and training employees.
- Podcasts, readily available on mobile-enabled devices, can be either audio or video.
- Blogs are used by organizations, employees, and others to provide information and opinion in a more informal way.

The Tsunami of Social Media

- Social media provides public relations professionals with the opportunity to participate in social networking sites to get feedback and build relationships.
- Facebook is the largest social network in the world with more than 1 billion users.
- Flickr and Instagram are photo-sharing sites, with a large number of users.
- Pinterest allows individuals and organizations to "pin" photos and other infographics that can be "re-pinned" by consumers on their own social media sites.
- The success of YouTube and other sites such as Instagram shows the strong trend toward highly visual content on the Internet.

The Rising Tide of Mobile-Enabled Content

- Smartphones and mobile-enabled tablets are now the major devices for accessing the Internet and the social media networks.
- It is estimated that 2 billion people in the world will have smartphones by 2017.
- Individuals using smartphones spend most of their time accessing various apps such as e-mail or Facebook.
- QR codes can be used in a variety of ways to allow mobile-enabled users to access more information and visual content about an organization or a product.

Case Activity **A Social Media Campaign for Yogurt Program**

Happy Valley Yogurt distributes its products nationally and has about 25 percent of the market. It makes a variety of flavors, and about 80 percent of its sales come from individual packages of eight ounces. The company has done the standard marketing, advertising, and public relations activities, but your public relations staff believe sales could increase with the use of social networking sites such as Facebook, Twitter, YouTube, Instagram, and Pinterest. Prepare a proposal to management showing how Happy Valley can tap social media for fun and profit. You need to consider the special characteristics of these sites and what kind of content would be appropriate.

Questions **For Review and Discussion**

1. In what ways has the Internet completely revolutionized a media system that goes back to Gutenberg in the 1400s?
2. What are the basic rules of social media engagement?
3. What are some characteristics of the Web that make it possible for public relations people to do a better job of distributing information?
4. Why is it important for an organization to have a website?
5. One example of Web interactivity is the "pull" and "push" concepts. What's the difference between the two terms?
6. What's the difference between a podcast and a webcast?
7. How can a PR professional use a webcast to organize a news conference and also brief journalists?
8. How can an organization use Facebook as part of its public relations strategy?
9. What are the challenges for PR when the company has an active Facebook presence?
10. In what ways is a blogger different or similar to a journalist?
11. Organizations now have their own YouTube channels. Visit three sites and write a critique of what you found in terms of content. What grade would you give the channel?
12. What are the major differences between Instagram and Pinterest? Which site do you think would have the best value in a public relations campaign for a cookie company?
13. Apps are designed for use on smartphones and mobile-enabled devices. What kind of app would you develop for the cookie company?
14. What is a QR code? Give an example of how you would use one in a public relations campaign.

Media Resources

Allen, K. (2013, March 6). Mind-boggling facts about one day on the Internet. Retrieved from www.ragan.com

Becker, S. (2012, July). Are bloggers vital to the media mix and how do PR pros build good relationships? *PRWeek*, 51–52.

Brown, M. (2013, April 9). Four things to know about having a social media career. Retrieved from www.ragan.com

Careaga, A. (2012, May). Study: First impressions of a website form in less than a second. *The Ragan Report*, 30–31.

Caro, T. (2012, June). How can Pinterest, Instagram, and such platforms raise brands' consumer profile? *PRWeek*, 51–52.

Corbin, J. (2012, October). How can brands, agencies, and developers create apps that will satisfy customers? *PRWeek*, 51–52.

Esco, K. (2012, May). Whenever, Wherever: The continuing evolution of mobile. *Public Relations Tactics*, 14.

Floating Facebook: The Value of Friendship (2012, February 4). *The Economist*, 23–25.

Gorges, M. (2013, March). Why employee communications may be mobile in two years. *The Ragan Report*, 12.

Jacques, A. (2012, May). Parlaying Pinterest: What you need to know about using a virtual pinboard. *Public Relations Tactics*, 10.

Mallon, S. (2012, August). Seven reasons corporate websites are so boring (and how to fix them). *The Ragan Report*, 31–32.

Malnik, J. (2013, April 10). QR codes: The biggest missed opportunity? Retrieved from www.ragan.com

Murdico, D. (2013, April 12). Twelve great benefits of video monitoring. Retrieved from www.ragan.com

Piombino, K. (2013, March 7). Infographic: Ten ways to get more followers on Pinterest. Retrieved from www.ragan.com

Piombino, K. (2013, April 9). Infographic: An inside look at companies' social media teams. Retrieved from www.ragan.com

Royse, M. (2013, February 19). The A to Z guide to social media. Retrieved from www.ragan.com

Sebastian, M. (2012, September 26). Tweets that will incite a PR firestorm. Retrieved from www.ragan.com

Sebastian, M. (2013, March 29). Eye-opening stats reveal the extent of our smartphone dependency. Retrieved from www.ragan.com

Smarty, A. (2012, October). Five ways to increase your brand's visibility on Flickr. *The Ragan Report*, 8–9.

Wilson, M. (2012, August). Kraft removes app's price tag—and downloads triple. *The Ragan Report*, 21–22.

chapter 14

Media Relations Management: Print Media

After reading this chapter, you will be able to:

- Write a standard or multimedia news release
- Recognize the components of a good publicity photo
- Prepare media kits, media advisories, and fact sheets
- Use proven techniques to "pitch" a story to a journalist
- Understand the structure of an organization's online newsroom
- Organize media interviews, news conferences, and media tours

The Importance of Mass Media

The mass media—newspapers, magazines, radio, and television—are still pervasive mediums in the age of the Internet and social media. According to the World Association of Newspapers and News Publishers (WAN-IFRA), more than half of the world's adult population read a newspaper—more than 2.5 billion in print and more than 600 million in digital form. That, says the association, represents more readers and users of the mass media than the total global users of the Internet.

In another study by the Pew Research Center, more than 70 percent of U.S. adults follow local news, and newspapers are by far the source they rely on for local information. The Newspaper Association of America (NAA) has also found in its surveys that four out of five adults said they had read a print edition while two-thirds had accessed newspaper content digitally. Television viewing is also pervasive; more people, particularly individuals over age 40 years, spend more time watching TV on a daily basis than surf the Internet and social media networks. This is further discussed in Chapter 15.

The traditional mass media also has the advantage of being perceived as a trusted source of information. Research by Harris Interactive, for example, have found that 69 percent of baby boomers trust television, 72 percent trust radio, and 72 percent trust newspapers. This compares with only 27 percent trusting a tweet and 33 percent trusting a post on Facebook or a professional networking site.

There's also a symbiotic relationship between traditional media and social networks. Although journalists from mass media often get breaking news tips from social networks, bloggers in particular heavily rely on traditional media. Richard Davis, a fellow at the Shorenstein Center at Brigham Young University cites one survey of blog content that found nearly 70 percent of blog posts included sources from a traditional news outlet such as the *New York Times*, the Associated Press, or the *Washington Post*.

Consequently, public relations personnel continue to spend considerable time and energy preparing materials and working with traditional media because of its outreach, trustworthiness, and being amplified by social networks. Messages take a variety of forms, but the news release, commonly called a *press release*, is still a major tactic in the public relations toolkit.

The News Release

The basic news release has been around for centuries in various shapes and forms. Chapter 2 mentioned that the Rosetta Stone of ancient Egypt was basically a publicity release touting a pharaoh's accomplishments. Today's basic version of the news release, commonly referred to as a *press release*, is reputed to go back more than a century, when Ivy Lee wrote one for the Pennsylvania Railroad in 1906.

Indeed, the news release continues to be the most commonly used public relations tactic, although the Internet and social media have changed its basic purpose and format. Some social media gurus have even pronounced the death of the news release. Fuat Kircaali, CEO and publisher of SYS-CON Media, flatly states, "The press release business already belongs to the Stone Age."

But, as Mark Twain is reported to have said, "The news of my death is highly exaggerated." A survey by Oriella PR Network, for example, found that 75 percent of journalists found e-mailed news releases were still useful, assuming the content was "high quality and well targeted." Another survey by Arketi Group of business journalists found that 92 percent of the respondents use news releases for story ideas. "Traditional tools won't go away," says Lauren Fernandez, marketing director of American Mensa. She told *Ragan.com*, "I can't say that something is new and shiny and I'm going to forget everything else. I don't think news releases are dead; most effective brands are using both."

The traditional media rely on basic news releases for two reasons. First, the reality of mass communications today is that reporters and editors spend most of their time processing information, not gathering it. Second, no media enterprise has enough staff to cover every single event in the community. Consequently, a lot of the more routine news in a newspaper is processed from news releases written by public relations practitioners. As one editor of a major daily once said, public relations people are the newspaper's "unpaid reporters."

It must be remembered, however, that a news release is not advertising, which is "paid" media. Instead, a news story based on information provided in a news release is referred to as "earned" media because editors make the ultimate decision whether a news release meets the journalistic standard of being newsworthy.

Planning a News Release

Before writing any news release, several questions should be answered to give the release direction and purpose. A planning worksheet should be used to answer the following questions:

- What is the key message? This should be expressed in one sentence.
- Who is the primary audience for the release? Is it journalists in traditional media, bloggers, or consumers looking for information via a search engine?
- What does the target audience gain from the product or service? What are the potential benefits and rewards?
- What objective does the release serve? Is it to increase product sales, enhance the organization's reputation, or increase attendance at an event?
- Is a news release the best format for the information?

These planning questions should also include an ethical component. See the Ethics box on page 404.

The Basic Online News Release

The traditional news release, going back a century, was a double-spaced document that was distributed to only newspapers and trade publications. Today, the vast majority of news releases are single-spaced and readily available to almost everyone via e-mail, via electronic news services, or from an organization's online newsroom. The content and organization of a news release haven't changed much over the years, but the basic structure tends to be more concise and streamlined to accommodate reading and viewing it online. An example is a news release distributed by BusinessWire for Montana State University, which is shown in Figure 14.1. The following are some guidelines for writing an online news release:

- Use single spacing.
- Keep the news release to 200 words or less.
- Use the inverted pyramid approach, in which the most important information is first, followed by less important details.

- The top line should give the name of the organization and perhaps its logo.
- The second line should give the date (e.g., November 9, 2014).
- The third line should be the headline in boldface with a slightly larger font than the text. This often serves as the subject line in an e-mail, so it should give the key message in 20 words or less. It's also important to include a key word or phrase for search engine optimization (SEO).
- Provide the city of origination at the start of the lead paragraph (e.g., Chicago).
- Write a succinct lead of only two or three sentences that gives the essence of the news release.
- Write only two or three short sentences in each of the five paragraphs.
- Use bulleted points to convey key points.
- Use a pull quote as part of the news release. This is a quote highlighted in a box that gives a major point about the release.
- Provide links in the news release so that readers can easily click on sites that provide related information.
- The last paragraph should provide basic information about the organization.
- The release should end with the name, telephone number, and e-mail address of the public relations contact person.
- Never send a release as an attachment. Journalists, because of possible virus attacks, rarely open attachments.

Online releases distributed on a global basis need special sensitivity, as outlined in the following Multicultural World box.

Figure 14.1 Online News Release

This news release, distributed by BusinessWire, shows the standard format of today's digital news releases. Releases may include a downloadable photo, as shown below and include links to social media networks for further distribution and sharing.

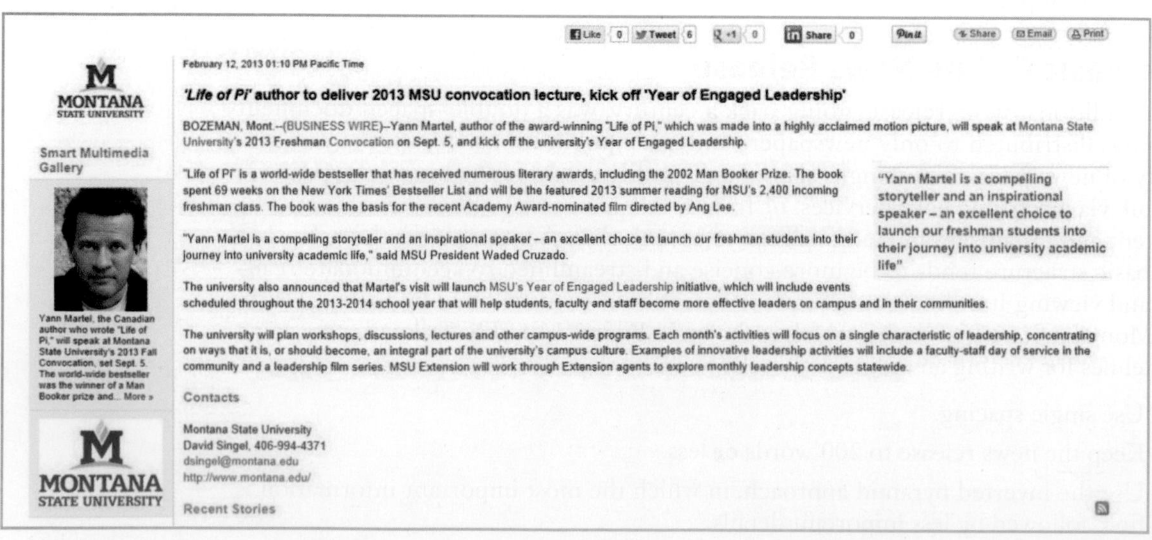

Like 0 Tweet 6 +1 0 Share 0 Pin it Share Email Print

MONTANA STATE UNIVERSITY

Smart Multimedia Gallery

Yann Martel, the Canadian author who wrote "Life of Pi," will speak at Montana State University's 2013 Fall Convocation, set Sept. 5. The world-wide bestseller was the winner of a Man Booker prize and... More »

February 12, 2013 01:10 PM Pacific Time

***'Life of Pi'* author to deliver 2013 MSU convocation lecture, kick off 'Year of Engaged Leadership'**

BOZEMAN, Mont.--(BUSINESS WIRE)--Yann Martel, author of the award-winning "Life of Pi," which was made into a highly acclaimed motion picture, will speak at Montana State University's 2013 Freshman Convocation on Sept. 5, and kick off the university's Year of Engaged Leadership.

"Life of Pi" is a world-wide bestseller that has received numerous literary awards, including the 2002 Man Booker Prize. The book spent 69 weeks on the New York Times' Bestseller List and will be the featured 2013 summer reading for MSU's 2,400 incoming freshman class. The book was the basis for the recent Academy Award-nominated film directed by Ang Lee.

"Yann Martel is a compelling storyteller and an inspirational speaker – an excellent choice to launch our freshman students into their journey into university academic life"

"Yann Martel is a compelling storyteller and an inspirational speaker – an excellent choice to launch our freshman students into their journey into university academic life," said MSU President Waded Cruzado.

The university also announced that Martel's visit will launch MSU's Year of Engaged Leadership initiative, which will include events scheduled throughout the 2013-2014 school year that will help students, faculty and staff become more effective leaders on campus and in their communities.

The university will plan workshops, discussions, lectures and other campus-wide programs. Each month's activities will focus on a single characteristic of leadership, concentrating on ways that it is, or should become, an integral part of the university's campus culture. Examples of innovative leadership activities will include a faculty-staff day of service in the community and a leadership film series. MSU Extension will work through Extension agents to explore monthly leadership concepts statewide.

Contacts

Montana State University
David Singel, 406-994-4371
dsingel@montana.edu
http://www.montana.edu/

MONTANA STATE UNIVERSITY

Recent Stories

on the job

A MULTICULTURAL WORLD

Sensitivity Required for Global News Releases

News releases are now distributed internationally, but there are cultural differences, sensitive political issues, and language differences that must be taken into consideration.

In terms of cultural differences, news releases are perceived differently in various nations. In Latin America, for example, editors are highly suspicious of news releases that describe new products or services as "best," "world-class," or even "cutting edge." In Russia, editors are highly skeptical of anything coming from a U.S. source and won't be interested unless the release is highly oriented to Russia. "Asian general media is more tolerant of technical releases than are Europeans or Latin Americans," according to Colleen Pizarev, PR Newswire's VP of international distribution.

Political issues are another pitfall. The writer of a news release for the Chinese press, for example, should avoid making any mention of such hot topics as human rights, dissent, freedom, or Taiwan, or even referring to the company's commitment to corporate social responsibility (CSR). By the same token, a company sending a news release to the Taiwanese media must be careful not to mention anything about its business in China. Another aspect about China is that it has a highly regulated system and all news stories must follow government guidelines. In other words, news releases can't be distributed directly to media; they first must go through official channels.

Language is another consideration. News releases should be translated into the national language of the country. Figure 14.2, for example,

Figure 14.2 A News Release Available in Multiple Languages

Global companies often make news releases available in various languages. This release by Viber Corporation and distributed by BusinessWire is available in 13 languages. The Japanese version is shown below.

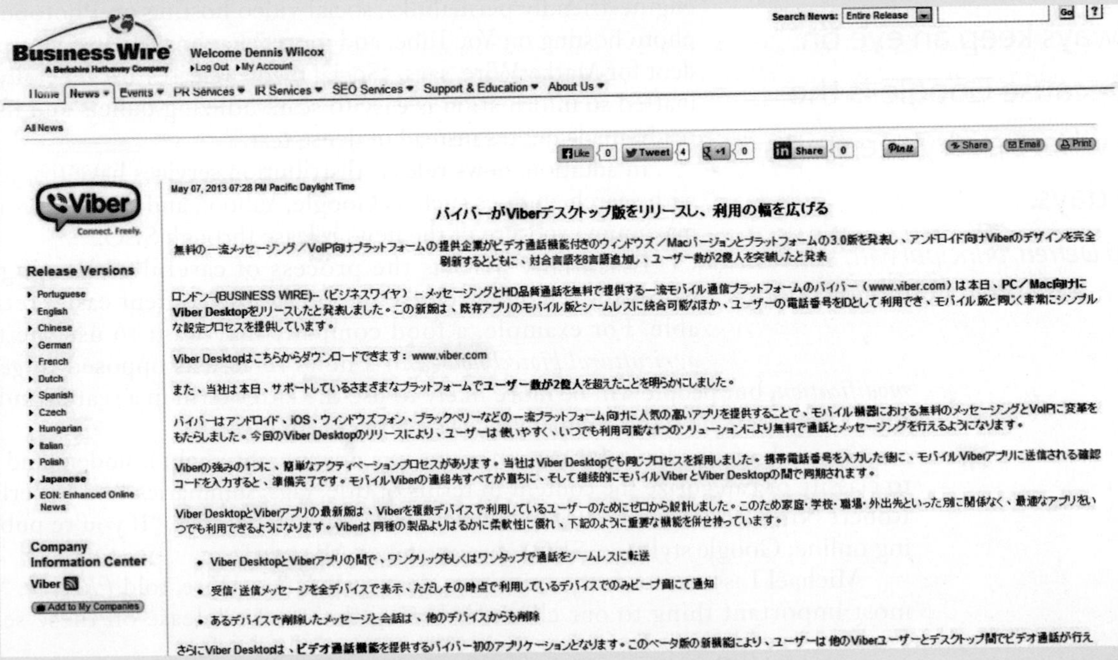

BusinessWire
A Berkshire Hathaway Company
Welcome Dennis Wilcox
Log Out My Account
Search News: Entire Release Go ?
Home | News | Events | PR Services | IR Services | SEO Services | Support & Education | About Us

All News

Like 0 | Tweet 4 | +1 0 | Share 0 | Pin it | Share | Email | Print

Viber
Connect. Freely.

Release Versions
- Portuguese
- English
- Chinese
- German
- French
- Dutch
- Spanish
- Czech
- Hungarian
- Italian
- Polish
- **Japanese**
- EON: Enhanced Online News

Company Information Center
Viber
Add to My Companies

May 07, 2013 07:28 PM Pacific Daylight Time

バイバーがViberデスクトップ版をリリースし、利用の幅を広げる

無料の一流メッセージング／VoIP向けプラットフォームの提供企業がビデオ通話機能付きのウィンドウズ／Macバージョンとプラットフォームの3.0版を発表し、アンドロイド向けViberのデザインを完全刷新するとともに、対合言語を8言語追加し、ユーザー数が2億人を突破したと発表

ロンドン--(BUSINESS WIRE)-- (ビジネスワイヤ) －メッセージングとHD品質通話を無料で提供する一流モバイル通信プラットフォームのバイバー (www.viber.com) は本日、**PC／Mac向けにViber Desktop**をリリースしたと発表しました。この新版は、既存アプリのモバイル版とシームレスに統合可能なほか、ユーザーの電話番号をIDとして利用でき、モバイル版と同じく非常にシンプルな設定プロセスを提供しています。

Viber Desktopはこちらからダウンロードできます：www.viber.com

また、当社は本日、サポートしているさまざまなプラットフォームで**ユーザー数が2億人**を超えたことを明らかにしました。

バイバーはアンドロイド、iOS、ウィンドウズフォン、ブラックベリーなどの一流プラットフォーム向けに人気の高いアプリを提供することで、モバイル機器における無料のメッセージングとVoIPに変革をもたらしました。今回のViber Desktopのリリースにより、ユーザーは使いやすく、いつでも利用可能な1つのソリューションにより無料で通話とメッセージングを行えるようになります。

Viberの強みの1つに、簡単なアクティベーションプロセスがあります。当社はViber Desktopでも同じプロセスを採用しました。携帯電話番号を入力した後に、モバイルViberアプリに送信される確認コードを入力すると、準備完了です。モバイルViberの連絡先すべてが直ちに、そして継続的にモバイルViberとViber Desktopの間で同期されます。

Viber DesktopとViberアプリの最新版は、Viberを複数デバイスで利用しているユーザーのためにゼロから設計しました。このため家庭・学校・職場・外出先といった別に関係なく、最適なアプリをいつでも利用できるようになります。Viberは同種の製品よりはるかに柔軟性に優れ、下記のように重要な機能を併せ持っています。

- Viber DesktopとViberアプリの間で、ワンクリックもしくはワンタップで通話をシームレスに転送
- 受信・送信メッセージを全デバイスで表示、ただしその時点で利用しているデバイスでのみビープ音にて通知
- あるデバイスで削除したメッセージと会話は、他のデバイスからも削除

さらにViber Desktopは、**ビデオ通話機能**を提供するバイバー初のアプリケーションとなります。このベータ版の新機能により、ユーザーは他のViberユーザーとデスクトップ間でビデオ通話が行え

(continued)

shows a news release in Japanese but is also available in 12 other languages. In India, English is widely used, but many organizations also translate news releases into Hindi if they are sending the release to regional and local publications. In Singapore, it's best to have news releases in Chinese and English. Although China now uses simplified Chinese throughout the country, one should be aware that traditional Chinese is still used in Taiwan, Hong Kong, and Macau.

Even English-speaking nations have differences in terms of spelling. A news release in the United Kingdom or Australia, for example, should use the Queen's English. This means "organisation" instead of "organization," and "honours" instead of "honors."

Global public relations firms, with offices in many nations, often serve their clients by having local staff write, translate, and distribute media materials. One key factor, according to *PRWeek* reporter Tanya Lewis, is to adapt a global release by providing local contacts and including quotes from local representatives of the company. Lewis also advises, "Don't use phrases/words that would cause confusion when translated." The number "six," for example, is better than "half dozen."

The Multimedia News Release

The major change in the evolution of the humble news release is the multimedia release, which has also been dubbed the "smart media release" (SMR) and even the *social media news release* by others. These releases, pioneered by the major electronic distribution services such as Business Wire, PR Newswire, PRWeb, and MarketWire, now make it possible to embed a news release with high-resolution photos/graphics, video, and audio components. The components of the modern multimedia news release are shown in Figure 14.3 on page 395.

From press materials to the blog posts that we recommend our clients write, we always keep an eye on SEO because Google is the place where everyone starts these days.

Todd Defren, principal with Boston-based Shift Communications

MarketWire, for example, has a number of social media links embedded in its news releases. According to Craig McGuire, writing in *PRWeek*, "The service includes social bookmarks and tags, news channel distribution, audio headline summaries, search-engine-friendly permalinks, social video hosting on Photobucket, photo hosting on YouTube, and more." Paolina Milana, vice president for MarketWire, says, "Social media releases are generally formatted so information is easy to scan, utilizing bullets and lists of ready-made quotes instead of dense text."

In addition, news release distribution services have teamed up with search engines such as Google, Yahoo!, and Bing to promote maximum exposure of the news release through SEO.

Essentially SEO is the process of carefully selecting key words for the news release that make the content easily retrievable. For example, a food company may want to use the term *agricultural biotechnology* in a news release as opposed to *genetic modification*, but people will be more likely to use the latter term in a search and will thus completely miss the company's news release.

A search engine looks for certain terms in a document to help it understand how to classify or categorize the content in terms of title, tags, summaries, and hyperlinks. Robert Niles, writing in *OJR: The Online Journalism Review*, adds, "If you're publishing online, Google style (i.e. SEO) always trumps AP style."

Michael Lissauer, executive vice president of Business Wire, told *PRWeek*, "The most important thing to our clients is seeing their news release on these search

Figure 14.3 The Components of a Social Media News Release

Shift Communications has pioneered the development of the social media news release that can be used across a variety of platforms, including traditional media, websites, and social media networks. It is also indexed by search engines such as Google for access by consumers.

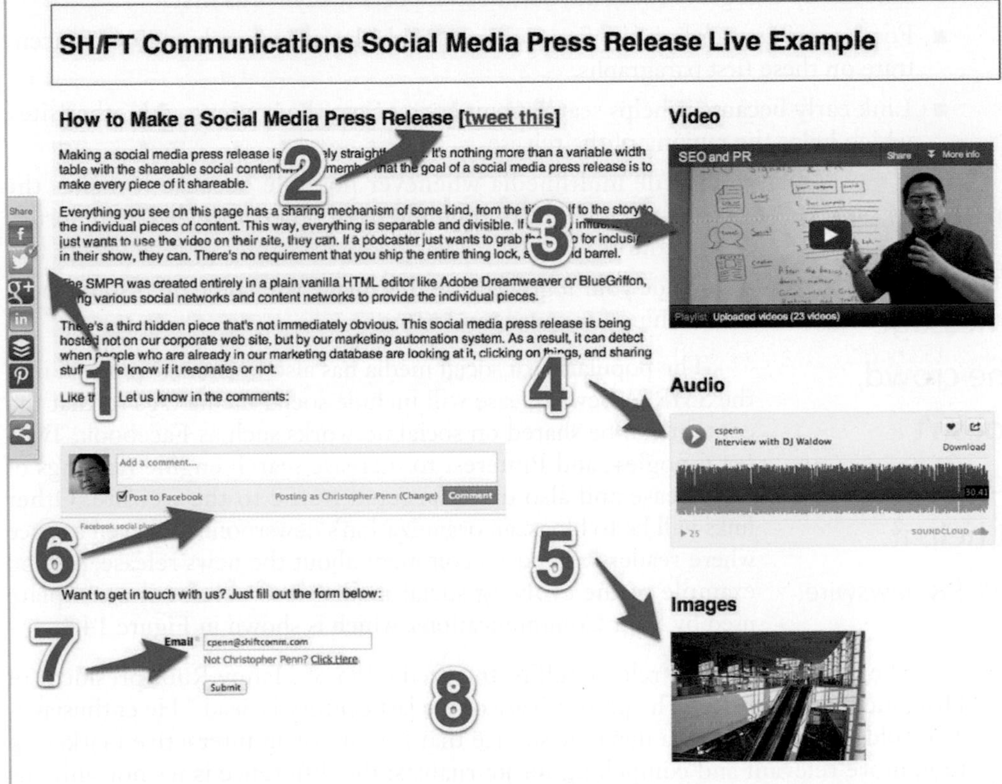

Key to Numbers

1. Simple sharing buttons to share the news release on various networks.
2. Headlines less than 55 characters so they can be easily tweeted and reshared. Such headlines are also more mobile friendly.
3. YouTube video added for several reasons: (1) large audience, (2) player is fully mobile compatible on many platforms and devices, and (3) every social network recognizes YouTube URLs.
4. Mobile-friendly sharable audio.
5. Photo gallery set available on Flickr or another photo platform.
6. Social comment link for discussions using common plugins such as Facebook.
7. Selected contact information—how journalists or consumers can contact the organization via LinkedIn, Twitter, Facebook, or even e-mail.
8. Tracking data—invisible in the release but gives analytics on how many accessed the news release and whether they shared it.

engines. They know consumers go there. If they write a news release effectively, they can bypass the gatekeepers, the journalists, who always had the opportunity of interpreting the release how they wanted." Business Wire has several suggestions for optimizing a news release:

- Write a concise clear headline under 22 words to ensure that the news release is indexed by Google News. Put your most important keywords first.
- Focus your keywords in the first two paragraphs because search engines concentrate on these first paragraphs.
- Link early because it helps search engines associate the content with other sites, which helps the ranking of the release.
- Include multimedia whenever possible because it makes the release stand out from hundreds of others received by reporters and editors.
- Include your logo because this image will come up if someone is searching for your brand name.

> No matter how much technology you employ to help make your message stand out from the crowd, if the message doesn't resonate, the photos, links, and videos won't help it.
>
> *Michael Pranikoff*, PR Newswire

The popularity of social media has also been incorporated into the SMR. A news release will include social media tags so that the content can be shared on social networks such as Facebook, Twitter, Google+, and Pinterest to increase search engine rankings of the release and also drive targeted traffic to the website. Other links will be to blogs, an organization's newsroom, and even a space where readers can post a comment about the news release. A good example of the evolving social media news release is a template used by Shift Communications, which is shown in Figure 14.3.

The multimedia news release fulfills the prediction of Manny Ruiz, president of Hispanic PR Wire, that "The press release of the last century is dead." He enthusiastically adds, "In its place is a dynamic service that is more of an interactive marketing tool, more relevant and compelling for journalists; the difference is it's not only for journalists."

This may be true, but it's still worth remembering that the vast majority of news releases, even those carried by the electronic distribution services such as Business Wire, are still basic releases about mundane activities such as quarterly earnings that don't require photos, videos, and audio components. An increasing number of product news releases do include embedded photos, but more elaborate multimedia releases remain a fraction of the total market because of cost. On the other hand, the number and variety of channels receiving news releases have expanded considerably beyond traditional media outlets.

Publicity Photos and Infographics

The cliché is that a picture is worth a thousand words. For this reason, news releases are often accompanied by a photo, either sent as an attachment or embedded in the release. It may be as basic as a head-and-shoulder picture (often called a *mug shot*) of a person named in the release. New product news releases often include a photo of the product in an attractive setting. See the publicity photo at the right that was distributed by Samsung.

Studies show that more people "read" photographs than read articles. The Advertising Research Foundation found that three to four times as many people notice an average one-column photograph as read an average news story. In another study, Wayne Wanta of the University of Missouri found that articles accompanied by photographs are perceived as significantly more important than those without photographs. In addition, PR Newswire data show that a news release with a photo receives 1.8 times more views. See Figure 14.4 for the multiples of viewers if video and downloadable files are also added.

Like news releases, publicity photos are not published or posted unless they appeal to media gatekeepers who choose the content. Although professional photographers should always be hired to take the photos, public relations practitioners should supervise their work and select the photos that are best suited for media use. Here are some additional suggestions:

Samsung Publicity Photo

Product publicity photos must be creative and interesting. A television set isn't very exciting by itself, but several attractive South Korean models around it cause more attention. This photo, distributed by Samsung Electronics, announced its new 3-D high-definition television to the world.

Quality Photos must have good contrast and sharp detail so that they are reproduced in a variety of formats, including grainy newsprint. Digital photography is the norm, and, in many cases, editors download high-resolution photos (at least 300 dpi) from an organization's online newsroom.

> The bar has been raised because of digital imagery. For that reason alone, same-old same-old is just not cutting it anymore—and that goes for grip-and-grin. There's always a more visually interesting way to show something than the cliché.
>
> *Suzanne Salvo of Salvo Photography in* Ragan.com

Subject Matter A variety of subjects can be used for publicity photos. Trade magazines, weekly newspapers, and organizational newsletters often use the standard "grip-and-grin" photo of a person receiving an award or the CEO shaking hands with a visiting dignitary. Such photos, however, are rarely used by large dailies or major online news sites.

Composition The best photos are uncluttered. Photo experts recommend (1) tight shots with minimum background; (2) an emphasis on detail, not whole scenes; and (3) limiting wasted space by reducing gaps between individuals or objects. At times, context also is important. Environmental portraits show the subject of the photo in a person's normal surroundings—for example, a research scientist in a lab.

Action Too many photos are static, with nothing happening except someone looking at the camera. It's better to show people doing something—talking, gesturing, laughing, running, or operating a machine. Action makes the photo interesting. The exception is the standard "mug" shot that is often included in a personnel release.

Scale Another way to add interest is to use scale. Apple, for example, might illustrate its newest iPod by having someone hold the device while surrounded by large stacks of CDs, to show how much music can be stored on it.

Figure 14.4 **News Releases with Visuals Get More Attention**

Web analytics by PR Newswire has shown that news releases with a photo get 1.8 times more viewers, but a news release with both a photo and a video clip generates 7.4 times more viewers. Copyright © PR Newswire 2013.

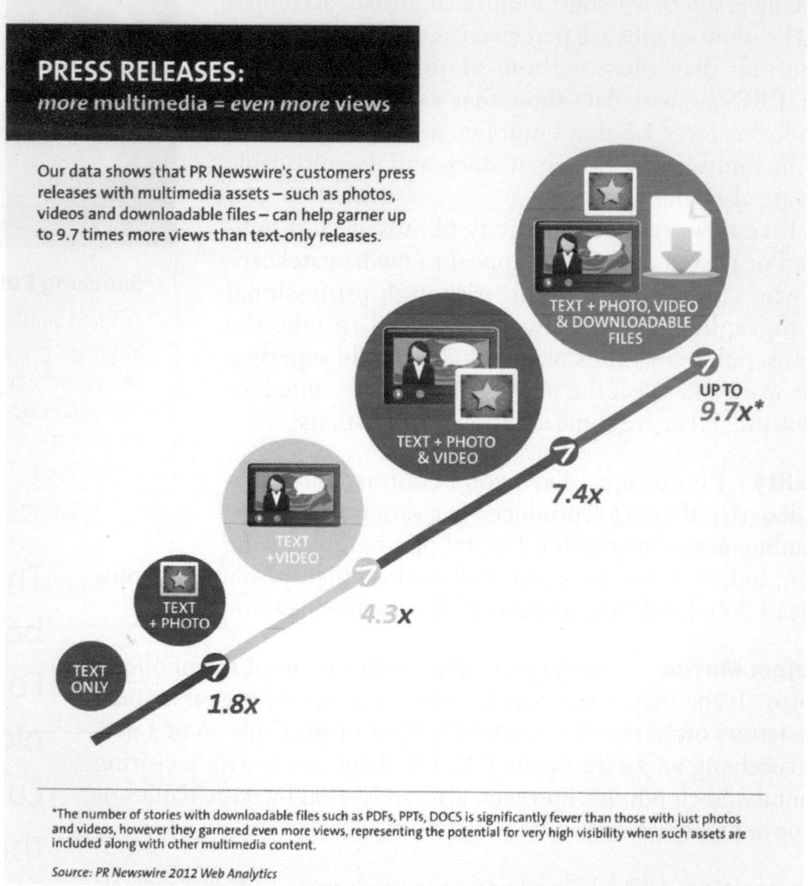

Camera Angle Interesting angles can make the subject of a photo more compelling. Some common methods are shooting upward at a tall building to make it look even taller or shooting an aerial shot to give the viewer an unusual perspective.

Lighting Professional photographers use a variety of lighting techniques to ensure that the subject is portrayed, quite literally, in the best light. Product photos, for example, always have the light on the product, and the background is usually dark or almost invisible.

Color Today, publicity photos are digital and in color. Daily newspapers, for example, regularly use color publicity photos in the food, business, sports, and travel sections. The most common distribution method is the downloadable file, but organizations also make DVDs and flash drives available upon request.

Infographics

Photos are highly visual, but so are colorful charts and other graphic displays of information and facts. The digital revolution and the increasing sophistication of software such as Adobe's Creative Suite has led to a major boom in the creation of what is called *infographics*. Surveys indicate that most people are visual learners, so more effective communication is accomplished by placing facts and statistics in a highly visual graphic context. Consequently, public relations professionals need to always think about how information can be converted to easy-to-read visuals.

Facts and figures in regular text may be pretty boring, but take on new life if presented in a highly readable, colorful chart. The traditional "infographic" is the colored bar or pie chart, which is still widely used, but creative graphic designers can take almost any information and convert it to a colorful infographic. The technique, for example, is often used to distill survey results into digestible information. A good example is how IBM created infographics to highlight the results of a survey on mobile computing, which is shown in Figure 14.5.

Danny Ashton, writing in *Ragan's PR Daily*, gives several reasons why news releases should include photos and infographics:

- **People are visual.** Reporters spend three seconds on average deciding whether to read or delete a news release, and visuals increase the chances of a reporter taking the time to read it. In one survey, 80 percent of reporters said photos and infographics increase the odds of a news release being used.
- **Visuals help with a story.** People tend to remember facts and figures presented in an interesting, visual way instead of just reading a bunch of numbers or percentages.

Figure 14.5 **Infographics Generate More Interest**

Statistics in text format provide the information, but don't generate the same attention as a colorful infographic.

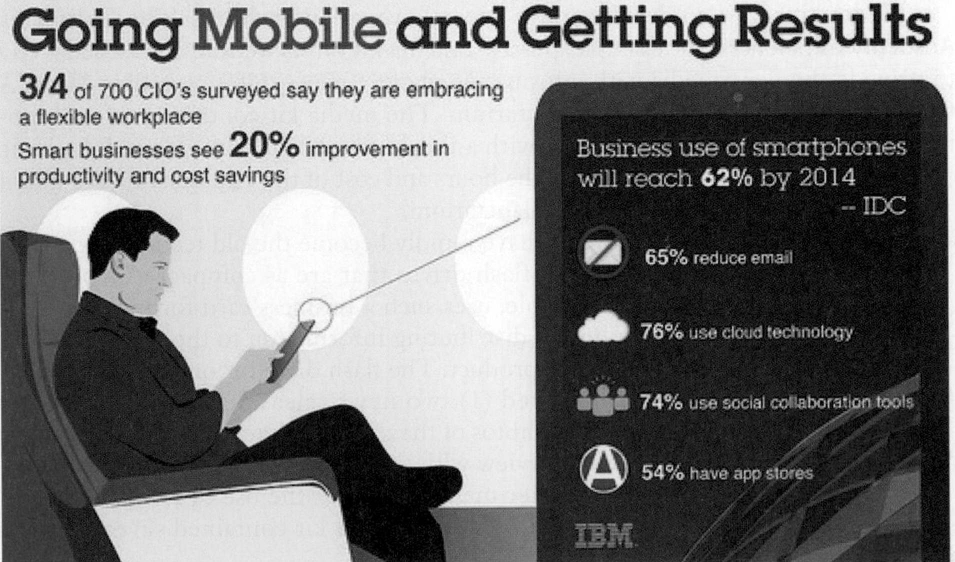

- **Visuals are more shareable.** People love sharing images on their social media networks.
- **Visual elements have more distribution power.** Key messages in infographic format can be distributed via sites such as Pinterest.

Media Kits

A media kit, often called a *press kit*, is often used to combine news releases, publicity photos, and even video clips about a particular event, an issue, or a new product. The purpose is to give editors and reporters a variety of information that makes it easier for them to write about the topic. In some ways, the traditional media kit is the print version of today's multimedia news release.

The traditional media kit for many years was a 9X12 folder with inside pockets. The contents usually consisted of such items as (1) a basic news release; (2) a news feature about the product or service; (3) a fact sheet about the product, organization, or event; (4) photos; (5) bios of the spokesperson or chief executives; (6) a basic brochure; and (7) contact information such as e-mail addresses, phone numbers, and website URLs.

Although the printed media kit, like the traditional news release, is not dead and is still produced by many organizations for journalists who prefer it, today's standard is the digital media kit that is made available on an organization's online newsroom, a CD, or a flash drive. The basic online media kit of SanDisk, for example, includes the following: (1) product photos, (2) executive officer's photos, (3) trademark information, (4) industry association links, (5) product brochures, and (6) video clips showing the capabilities of its SD cards and other products.

Another approach is taken by IBM. Its press kits are usually an aggregation of information about a particular topic. A media kit on IBM's expansion into Africa, for example, features a variety of news releases, video interviews with government officials and business executives, and infographics that document its expansion in terms of mobile computing. See the infographic in Figure 14.5 showing how IBM packages the results of research surveys in an attractive format.

Media kits are also developed for special events and exhibits. The California Academy of Sciences, for example, posted a media kit on its website and issued a CD to provide the news media with information about a new exhibit regarding "Life: A Cosmic Story" at its Morrison Planetarium. The media kit contained (1) 16 high-resolution photos, (2) a video trailer with a link to more YouTube videos, (3) a basic news release about the hours and cost of the exhibit, and (4) a bio of the director of the planetarium.

CDs, however, have rapidly become the old technology that is now replaced with flash drives that are as compact as a business card. HP, for example, uses such a business card format as a cost-effective method of distributing information to the public and the media about a new product. The flash drive for one new computer, for example, featured (1) two news releases, (2) a fact and spec sheet, (3) multiple photos of the new computer from various angles, and (4) a video interview with the chief designer describing the innovations. In another media kit about the use of HP products in the film *Sex in the City 2*, the media kit contained several scenes from the movie.

> The days of a thousand press kits are gone. Instead, well-designed online press kits can have an ongoing shelf life with constantly updated content.
>
> *Tom Bucktold of* Business Wire

Cost savings for the organization is a big factor. Patrick Pharris, founder of Electronic Media Communications, gave *PR News* a good example. The company developed an Internet media kit for a client that included eight documents, five photos, and a PR Newswire distribution for $4,000, instead of four times that amount for a printed media kit. HP, for a trade show, also used an e-kit that saved the company about $20,000 in printing costs.

Honoring the needs of various publications, however, should always be considered. Sarah Rogers of M45 Marketing Services in Freeport, Illinois, says she needs to consider the smaller newspapers in Illinois and elsewhere. She told *Ragan.com*, "In terms of sending out a media kit, I include paper and electronic versions of everything."

Mat Releases

A variation of the traditional news release is what is called the *mat feature release*. They were originally called *mat* because they were sent in mat form, ready for the printing press. Today, these materials are distributed in a variety of formats for use in newspapers, magazines, blogs, and online news or lifestyle sites.

The format is somewhat different from the traditional news release because a feature angle is used instead of a lead that gives a key message. Mat releases also are in the format of a standing column headline such as *Healthy Eating*, *Cooking Corner*, or *Vacations of a Lifetime*.

The concept is geared toward providing helpful consumer information and tips about a variety of subjects in an informative way with only a brief mention of the nonprofit or corporation that has distributed the release via firms such as Family Features (www.familyfeatures.com) and the North American Precis Syndicate (NAPA; www.napsinfo.com). These features, which are now called *brand journalism* or *content marketing*, show up in thousands of weekly newspapers and many dailies in the food, travel, fashion, automotive, and business sections. For example, a recipe feature titled "Chicken and Rice: Always a Winning Combination" distributed by NAPS for Rice-a-Roni generated more than 1,400 newspaper articles in 40 states, with a total readership of 75 million.

Another approach is a regular column that features an expert. Nestlé, for example, distributes a column via Family Features called "Mix It Up With Jenny." The column, under the byline of Jenny Harper, who is identified as a senior culinary specialist for the Nestlé Test Kitchens, offers seasonal recipes that, of course, include ingredients made by Nestlé. One column, distributed in the spring to daily and weekly newspapers, discussed desserts that can be prepared quickly for graduation parties.

A more sophisticated feature is a full-page, color layout that a newspaper can select and publish with no cost. Family Features has pioneered this concept, and a good example is the full-color page about watermelon as a summer treat, which is shown on page 402. This entire feature, offered free to newspapers, was paid for by the Watermelon Promotion Board. Because the feature makes only a passing reference to the sponsor, the entire piece reads like a feature page actually prepared by the newspaper. Indeed, media usually use these features without telling the audience that the content, layout, and graphics were prepared by a vendor such as Family Features on behalf of an organization or association promoting the use of its products and services. The practice is a good example of how the public relations industry subsidizes the media by providing free content as many publications continue to do cost-cutting by reducing news staffs.

See the related box on page 404 about the ethics of "sponsored" content.

Media Alerts and Fact Sheets

On occasion, the public relations staff will send a memo to reporters and editors about a news conference or upcoming event that they may wish to cover. Such memos also are used to let the media know about an interview opportunity with a visiting dignitary or celebrity or what photo and video possibilities are available. A *media alert* is also referred to as a *media advisory*. Media alerts may also be sent with an accompanying news release.

The most common format for media alerts is short, bulleted items rather than long paragraphs. A typical one-page advisory might contain the following elements: a one-line headline, a brief paragraph outlining the story idea or event, some of journalism's five Ws and H, and whom to contact for more information. A basic media advisory about an AIDS march and rally is shown in Figure 14.6.

Sample Mat Release

An innovative approach to the standard mat news release is an entire newspaper page written and designed around a particular theme. This release, distributed by Family Features Editorial Syndicate on behalf of the Watermelon Promotion Board, uses the theme of summer to tell consumers how to select a good melon and enjoy it in several recipes.

Americana Basket

ALL-AMERICAN
Summer Flavor

Choosing a Watermelon

Star Cake

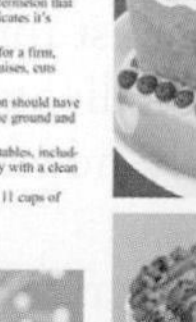

Watermelon Almond Tart

Quick Watermelon Cubes

Patriotic Petit Fours

Red, White and Blue Watermelon Sundaes

09542: All-American Summer Flavor
All materials courtesy of: National Watermelon Promotion Board
To order, download at www.FamilyFeatures.com or contact
Media Communications at support@familyfeatures.com or 1-888-824-3337

Two Kinds of Fact Sheets

Fact sheets are another useful public relations tool. There are two kinds: The first one is basically a summary sheet about the characteristics of a new product that serves as a quick reference for a journalist writing a story. A one-page product fact sheet for Philips Norelco's new Bodygroom shaver, for example, provided such information as (1) ability to remove hair anywhere on the body, (2) chromium steel trimmer blades, (3) three interchangeable attachment combs, (4) 50 minutes of cordless trimming time, and (5) full two-year warranty.

Product fact sheets are often distributed as part of a media kit or with a news release to give supplemental information about a new product.

A second kind of fact sheet, often called a *corporate profile*, is a one-page summary in bulleted list format that gives the basic facts about an organization or a company. It may use headings that provide (1) the organization's full name, (2) products or services offered, (3) the organization's annual revenues, (4) the number of employees, (5) the names and

Figure 14.6 **Media Advisory—A March and Rally for AIDS Prevention**

Media advisories notify reporters in advance about special events and what dignitaries will be attending. They give the basic details of date and time, plus video opportunities, so that media organizations can assign staff to cover the event.

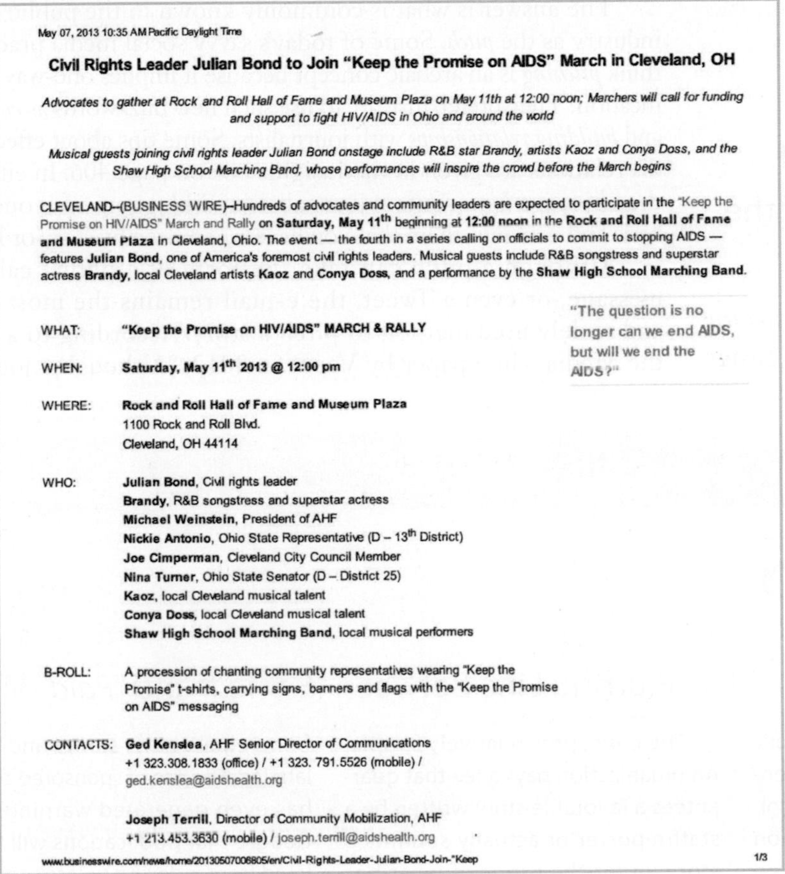

May 07, 2013 10:35 AM Pacific Daylight Time

Civil Rights Leader Julian Bond to Join "Keep the Promise on AIDS" March in Cleveland, OH

Advocates to gather at Rock and Roll Hall of Fame and Museum Plaza on May 11th at 12:00 noon; Marchers will call for funding and support to fight HIV/AIDS in Ohio and around the world

Musical guests joining civil rights leader Julian Bond onstage include R&B star Brandy, artists Kaoz and Conya Doss, and the Shaw High School Marching Band, whose performances will inspire the crowd before the March begins

CLEVELAND--(BUSINESS WIRE)--Hundreds of advocates and community leaders are expected to participate in the "Keep the Promise on HIV/AIDS" March and Rally on **Saturday, May 11th** beginning at **12:00 noon** in the **Rock and Roll Hall of Fame and Museum Plaza** in Cleveland, Ohio. The event — the fourth in a series calling on officials to commit to stopping AIDS — features **Julian Bond**, one of America's foremost civil rights leaders. Musical guests include R&B songstress and superstar actress **Brandy**, local Cleveland artists **Kaoz** and **Conya Doss**, and a performance by the **Shaw High School Marching Band**.

"The question is no longer can we end AIDS, but will we end the AIDS?"

WHAT: **"Keep the Promise on HIV/AIDS" MARCH & RALLY**

WHEN: **Saturday, May 11th 2013 @ 12:00 pm**

WHERE: **Rock and Roll Hall of Fame and Museum Plaza**
1100 Rock and Roll Blvd.
Cleveland, OH 44114

WHO: **Julian Bond**, Civil rights leader
Brandy, R&B songstress and superstar actress
Michael Weinstein, President of AHF
Nickie Antonio, Ohio State Representative (D – 13th District)
Joe Cimperman, Cleveland City Council Member
Nina Turner, Ohio State Senator (D – District 25)
Kaoz, local Cleveland musical talent
Conya Doss, local Cleveland musical talent
Shaw High School Marching Band, local musical performers

B-ROLL: A procession of chanting community representatives wearing "Keep the Promise" t-shirts, carrying signs, banners and flags with the "Keep the Promise on AIDS" messaging

CONTACTS: **Ged Kenslea**, AHF Senior Director of Communications
+1 323.308.1833 (office) / +1 323. 791.5526 (mobile) /
ged.kenslea@aidshealth.org

Joseph Terrill, Director of Community Mobilization, AHF
+1 213.453.3630 (mobile) / joseph.terrill@aidshealth.org

www.businesswire.com/news/home/20130507006805/en/Civil-Rights-Leader-Julian-Bond-Join-"Keep 1/3

one-paragraph biographies of top executives, (6) the markets served, (7) its position in the industry, and (8) any other pertinent details.

The basic corporate profile for Best Buy, for example, starts with a paragraph about the extent of its operations, its annual revenues, the number of employees, its annual philanthropy to community groups, and its environmental policy. Bullet items follow, giving one-line information on headquarters' address and telephone number; the company's website and stock symbol; the CEO's name; and the name, phone number, and e-mail of the major public relations contact person.

The purpose of a corporate profile is the same as that of the product fact sheet. It provides reporters with a "crib sheet" so that they can verify basic facts, such as the organization's annual revenues or even its product lines, when they are writing a story. Corporate profiles are readily available on news release distribution sites such as Business Wire or on the organization's website in its newsroom link.

The Art of Pitching a Story

Getting the attention of media gatekeepers is difficult because they receive literally thousands of news releases and media kits every week. So, the major question is how to get your story noticed among a dense forest of news releases.

> Now it's a better age between journalists and PR. There's an absence of friction, and PR is part of the data stream.
>
> *David Carr, media columnist for the* New York Times

The answer is what is commonly known in the public relations industry as the *pitch*. Some of today's savvy social media practitioners think *pitching* is an archaic concept because it implies one-way communication. They prefer, instead, to use such new buzzwords as *engagement* and *building relationships* with journalists. Some tips about effective media relations are given in the Insights box on page 406. In either case, the objective is to contact journalists and bloggers on a one-to-one basis and convince them that you have a newsworthy story or idea.

Although a pitch can take the form of a phone call, a text message, or even a Tweet, the e-mail remains the most popular and widely used method to pitch a story. According to a State of the Media white paper by Vocus in 2012, "Although a journalist's

on the job

ETHICS

The Blurring Line Between "*Earned*" and "*Paid*" Media

A major objective of most public relations campaigns is to generate coverage in the news columns of newspapers or a mention on the 6 P.M. news hour. This is referred to in the industry as *earned* media because editors and reporters, using their independent judgment, consider the information newsworthy.

The full-page ad or the 60-second commercial, in contrast, is called *paid* media because organizations create the ad and "rent" space in media outlets to publish or broadcast it. Advertising has been the major source of revenue for traditional media, but the Internet and the increasing fragmentation of the mass audience have led many publications to experience a major decline in ad revenue. As a result, many media outlets have turned to "sponsored" content to generate income.

The concept is relatively simple. An organization pays a fee that guarantees a favorable story written by a staff reporter or actually submits a story under the rubric of what has been called *brand journalism* or *content marketing*. Newspapers have traditionally used sponsored content in special insert sections about autos and real estate, but the line between "paid" and "earned" media seems to be blurring in ways that raises some ethical concerns.

Online sites such as *Mashable* or *Tech Crunch*, for example, accept payment in return for writing stories that are circulated as staff-written. Other online news sites, for a fee, will embed links to products and services in news stories. *Forbes*, *Atlantic*, and the *Huffington Post* also run sponsored content, but the stories are separated from regular news stories and clearly labeled. The rise of sponsored content has even generated warnings from Google that publications will be deleted from indexing unless sponsored content is clearly separated from regular news coverage.

The issue of sponsored content raises some ethical questions for both public relations and media personnel in terms of transparency and credibility. Is it a good strategy, for example, for public relations personnel to pay for the placement of articles about their products and services that appear to be legitimate news stories in content and format? And what exactly is the ethical responsibility of media that publish sponsored content? Should readers and listeners be clearly informed that an article is sponsored?

medium preference for receiving pitches varies, several polls and surveys have found that the majority of reporters still favor email." The report continues, "Social media is a good way to get to know reporters, but it's not the most preferred way to pitch."

Blogger Mark Evans advises, "When you're reaching out to a reporter or blogger, it's the two or three introductory paragraphs in an email that play a crucial role in whether they will be intrigued or hit the delete button. If you can capture their attention, they might read the news release to get some more information but in most cases, a reporter or blogger will call or email you to get more information or set up an interview."

Another blogger, David M. Scott, writing in www.webinknow.com, offered what he considers the single most important pitching tip: "Don't pitch your product. Most journalists don't care about products. Instead, tell us how your organization solves problems for customers."

Here are some other basic guidelines for pitching by e-mail:

- Use a succinct subject line that tells the editor what you have to offer; don't try to be cute or gimmicky.
- Get to the point. Present your major point or idea in the first paragraph.
- Keep the message brief, one screen at the most.
- Don't include attachments. Many reporters, due to the possibility of virus attacks, never open attachments unless they requested them and know the source.
- Provide links to photos and other background materials as needed.
- Don't send "blast" e-mails to large numbers of editors. E-mail systems are set up to filter messages with multiple recipients in the "To" and "BCC" fields, a sure sign of spam.
- Send tailored e-mail pitches to specific reporters and editors; the pitch should be relevant to their beats and publications.
- Regularly check the names in your e-mail database to remove redundant recipients.
- Give editors the option of getting off your e-mail list; this will ensure that your list is targeted to those who are interested.
- Establish a relationship. As one reporter said, "The best e-mails come from people I know; I delete e-mails from PR people or agencies I don't recognize."

Pitching is a fine art, however, and public relations personnel must first do some basic research about the publication or broadcast that they want to contact. It's important to know the kinds of stories that a publication usually publishes or what kinds of guests appear on a particular talk show. Knowing a journalist's beat and the kinds of stories he or she has written in the past is also helpful. In addition, reporters are always looking for a topical news hook. The media, for example, express great interest in trends and health issues, so it's also a good idea to relate a particular product or service with something that is already identified as a public concern or a trending topic A good example of a successful pitch that resulted in a front page story on *USA Today* is discussed in the PR Casebook on page 407.

> Media relations specialists should not send out a pitch without knowing the reporters and publications in advance.
>
> *David B. Oates, strategy and planning manager of ContentOne*

The best pitches show a lot of creativity and are successful in grabbing the editor's attention. *Ragan's Media Relations Report* gives some opening lines that generated media interest and resulted in stories:

- "How many students does it take to change a light bulb?" (A pitch about a residence hall maintenance program operated by students on financial aid)

- "The Man Who Will End iPod Whiplash." (A story about a Sun Microsystems engineer who came up with a new technique for searching for music online)
- "Wearing Prada Can Be the Devil for Your Spine." (A story about a hospital that found many of the patients came for spinal therapy were women suffering neck and back pain from lugging around oversized purses.)

on the job INSIGHTS

Media Relations: How to Get a Date with a Reporter

Working with the media and dating have a lot in common. Jeremy Porter provided "Dating Advice for PR Pros" on *http://blog.journalistics.com*. The following is a summary of his key points.

The Best Pickup Line Is a Basic Introduction

There are many cheesy pickup lines in dating circles, but the most effective pickup line is "Hello, my name is . . .". In media relations, you should also skip the clever opening line and just let the reporter know who you are and why you are calling.

Don't Seem Too Desperate

Don't give the impression that you're begging for a date, or for the reporter to write a story. You need to create genuine interest and bring something to the relationship. "Avoid being too needy, it doesn't work in either scenario."

Don't Be a Player

"Dates and journalists like exclusivity. If you're playing the field, the other party will lose interest."

Stop Trying to Hook Up

"Don't expect to get everything you want on the first date. If it's the first time you're talking to a journalist, don't expect them to write about the story the first time." Porter continues, "Just like dating . . . invest the time and energy in building your relationships and you'll get more out of it."

Don't Underestimate Confidence and Humor

"Two of the most attractive qualities in a potential partner are confidence and humor. If you doubt yourself, or come across as boring . . . you're not going to get a second date."

Have a Game Plan

"Don't ask for a date and then have no game plan. The same holds true for PR—have a plan. If a journalist agrees to talk to you, make the best use of their time."

Dress to Impress

In dating and media relations, don't dress like a slob. Written and visual materials provided to a journalist should also be accurate, professional, and impressive. If they aren't, your chances of a second "date" are not good.

Have a Friend Set You Up

Use a mutual friend to "set you up" for a date or with a journalist. A mutual friend can introduce you to a journalist through LinkedIn, Facebook, or Twitter.

Follow Up Is Key to the Second Date

"If you want to build a relationship, you need to follow up after the first date." In the case of a journalist, provide any additional information and ensure that he or she has your contact information.

Manners Matter

"Say please and thank you, be polite. Manners matter in this day and age, and people notice whether or not you have them."

Porter concludes his somewhat tongue-in-cheek advice, "I've seen plenty of desperate people try too hard to win the love and affection of a popular journalist, only to be left sitting alone on Saturday night with no press mentions to speak of. People are people, whether you're trying to date them or get them interested in a story you're pitching."

PRCasebook

A Successful Pitch Pays Dividends

The American Institute for Cancer Research (AICR) had some pretty impressive statistics about cancer, including the fact that excess body fat is responsible for at least 100,000 new cases of cancer every year. The challenge, however, was to get extensive media coverage and raise public awareness.

AICR's public relations firm, MS&L, gave some thought to this and considered having a news conference in Washington, D.C. A better idea, however, was to get a high-profile story in a major publication that would set the agenda for other news outlets. The decision was made to pitch *USA Today*, which has a national readership of 2 million.

USA Today reporter Nanci Hellmich had covered AICR research before, so she was offered the first opportunity to write a story about tying obesity to breast, kidney, and other cancers. Obesity was already in the news, so the essential message was boiled down to three words: Fat equals cancer. MS&L staffers provided basic information and also arranged for Hellmich to interview a leading cancer expert at the University of Colorado.

The resulting story ran on the front page of *USA Today* above the fold (prime space) and did indeed trigger widespread follow-up coverage. The AICR report and statistics, for example, were mentioned in more than 340 radio and television broadcasts, including those of CNN, FOX, NBC, CBS, and ABC.

There were three essential aspects of this successful pitch: (1) MS&L targeted a leading national publication; (2) it contacted a reporter who was already familiar with AICR's work and had written other major health-related stories; and (3) the popular topic of obesity was used as a news hook, which attracted extensive media interest.

on the job

INSIGHTS

Working with "Citizen" Journalists

The most important thing a publicist can do before pitching a blogger is to carefully read his or her blog. In order to begin a conversation with a blogger—and it should be viewed as a conversation, rather than a pitch—it is vital that you are well acquainted with the blogger's opinions and interests. Text 100, a public relations firm, conducted an international survey of 450 bloggers, and the following are some of its findings:

- Blogs have become an influential, mainstream communication channel.
- The most preferred means of contact is via e-mail. Instant messaging is the least welcome.
- Computers, technology, and the Internet are the subjects most blogged about by the respondents.
- Preferred content is news and reviews of new products, opinionated comments, and interviews with key people. Corporate news announcements are of least interest.
- Photographs are the most frequently used content, although many also use video streaming, charts, and graphs. Video and audio podcasts are rarely used.
- Elements of multimedia releases are frequently used.
- Corporate websites and RSS feeds are the most frequently used sources of content.

Tapping into Media Queries

Not all pitches have to be what salespeople term *cold calls*. On many occasions, journalists are seeking information and names of people to interview for a particular story. One of the oldest services that match reporter queries with public relations sources is ProfNet (www.prnewswire.com/profnet), which is operated by PR Newswire. It offers a direct way for journalists to post a query asking for information on a story they are writing, or to find an expert in an organization whom they can interview. ProfNet estimates that between 100 and 200 journalists access the site daily.

ProfNet is available only on a subscription basis, but Help a Reporter Out (HARO), owned by Vocus, is a free service (www.helpareporter.com). It operates in much the same way as ProfNet and claims on its website that it puts 30,000 reporters and bloggers in contact with 100,000 news sources.

Distributing Media Materials

News releases, photos, media kits, and a host of other media materials can be distributed by five major methods: (1) first-class mail, (2) fax, (3) e-mail, (4) electronic wire services, and (5) online newsrooms. The capabilities of e-mail are well known, so this section will focus on two major distribution methods used today, electronic news services and online newsrooms.

Electronic News Services

Most corporations now use an electronic wire service to distribute news releases, photos, and advisories. This is particularly true for financial information that must be released, according to SEC guidelines, to multiple media outlets at exactly the same time.

The two major newswires are Business Wire (www.businesswire.com) and PR Newswire (www.prnewswire.com). Each organization transmits about 25,000 news releases monthly to daily newspapers, broadcast stations, ethnic media, financial networks, and online news services. Other specialty electronic news services include PRWeb, MarketWire, Hispanic PRWire, USAsian Wire, and Black PRWire.

No paper is involved; the release is automatically entered into the appropriate databases and search engines, which can be accessed not only by editors and reporters throughout the world but also by the general public. Editors select releases that are newsworthy to them, write a headline, and then push another key to have it automatically set for publishing or broadcast. Of course, they can easily hit the delete key, too.

Wire services are making the news release more sophisticated. Business Wire, for example, now has "smart" news releases that have already been discussed. According to Craig McGuire, writing in *PRWeek*, "BusinessWire can convert a traditional news release into a search-engine optimized page of Web content that includes photos, graphics, video and multimedia, logo branding, keyword links, formatting, and social media tags." This is best illustrated by Figure 14.7, which shows the various components of a news release from Business Wire.

National distribution of a "smart" release with one photo costs about $1,200, but a complete "smart" page with multiple pictures and files, and distribution to mobile platforms worldwide, can cost up to $3,000. On the other hand, a text-only news release transmitted to all major media in the United States is about $750. If the public relations person wants to cover the entire planet (100 nations and 21 languages), it's about $9,000. Business Wire also offers mobile news releases, which, it says, "makes your news available in multiple languages worldwide, across multiple platforms, including BlackBerry and Droid." In sum, electronic news services provide a cost-effective way to directly reach thousands of media across the nation and even the globe with a single click.

Online Newsrooms

"An online pressroom is the media's front door to the company," writes *PRWeek* reporter Sherri Deatherage Green. Most major organizations have a pressroom or a newsroom as part of their website. With a few clicks, journalists can access everything from the organization's executive profiles to the most recent news releases. They also can download high-resolution photos and graphics, videos, and background materials such as position papers and annual reports.

An organization often informs journalists via e-mail that a particular item is available on the company's site. Because there are virtually millions of web pages, extra effort must be made to ensure that reporters are aware of the website and what's on it. A good online newsroom, at minimum, should have (1) current and archived news releases; (2) the names, phone numbers, and direct e-mail addresses of public relations contacts; (3) photographs; (4) product information; and (5) an opportunity for journalists to sign up for a daily RSS feed if they regularly cover that particular company or industry.

An online pressroom is the media's front door to the company.

Sherri Deatherage Green, reporter for PRWeek

Figure 14.7 Business Wire News Release

The modern news release, distributed via electronic news services, is now embedded with links to photo galleries, social media sites, and other websites. This graphic was prepared by Business Wire in San Francisco exclusively for this textbook.

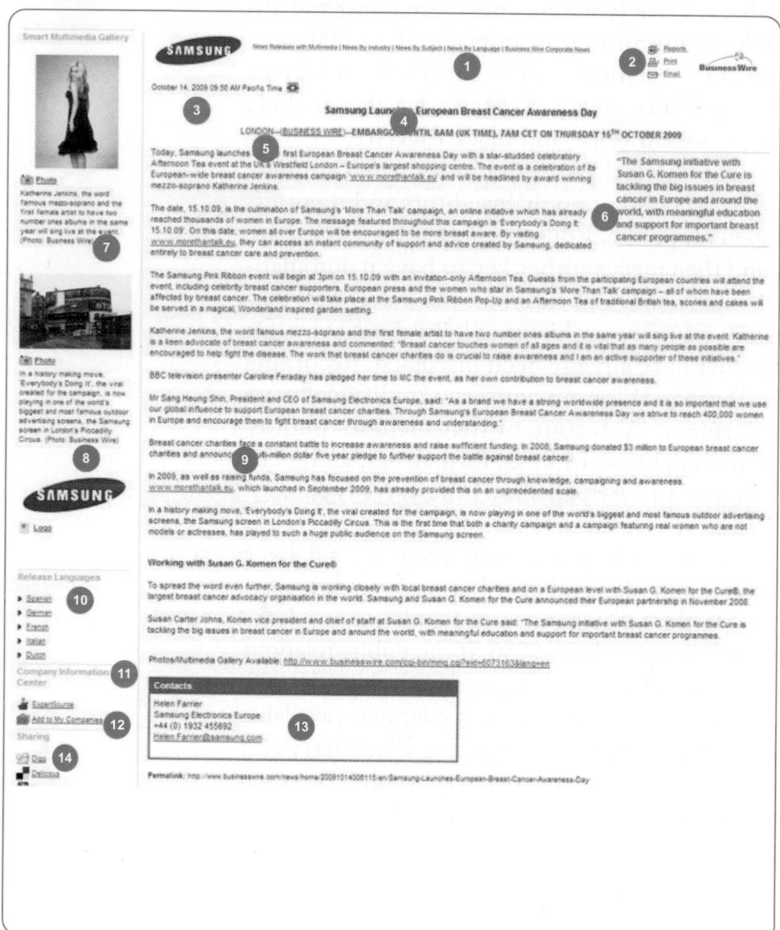

News Releases with Multimedia | News By Industry | News By Subject | News By Language | Business Wire Corporate News

Reports
Print
Email

October 14, 2009 09:56 AM Pacific Time

Samsung Laun European Breast Cancer Awareness Day

LONDON--(BUSINESS WIRE)--EMBARGO NTIL 8AM (UK TIME), 7AM CET ON THURSDAY 15TH OCTOBER 2009

Today, Samsung launches first European Breast Cancer Awareness Day with a star-studded celebratory Afternoon Tea event at the UK's Westfield London – Europe's largest shopping centre. The event is a celebration of its European-wide breast cancer awareness campaign www.morethantalk.eu/ and will be headlined by award winning mezzo-soprano Katherine Jenkins.

The date, 15.10.09, is the culmination of Samsung's 'More Than Talk' campaign, an online initiative which has already reached thousands of women in Europe. The message featured throughout this campaign is 'Everybody's Doing It 15.10.09'. On this date, women all over Europe will be encouraged to be more breast aware. By visiting www.morethantalk.eu, they can access an instant community of support and advice created by Samsung, dedicated entirely to breast cancer care and prevention.

"The Samsung initiative with Susan G. Komen for the Cure is tackling the big issues in breast cancer in Europe and around the world, with meaningful education and support for important breast cancer programmes."

The Samsung Pink Ribbon event will begin at 3pm on 15.10.09 with an invitation-only Afternoon Tea. Guests from the participating European countries will attend the event, including celebrity breast cancer supporters, European press and the women who star in Samsung's 'More Than Talk' campaign – all of whom have been affected by breast cancer. The celebration will take place at the Samsung Pink Ribbon Pop-Up and an Afternoon Tea of traditional British tea, scones and cakes will be served in a magical, Wonderland inspired garden setting.

Katherine Jenkins, the word famous mezzo-soprano and the first female artist to have two number ones albums in the same year will sing live at the event. Katherine is a keen advocate of breast cancer awareness and commented: "Breast cancer touches women of all ages and it is vital that as many people as possible are encouraged to help fight the disease. The work that breast cancer charities do is crucial to raise awareness and I am an active supporter of these initiatives."

BBC television presenter Caroline Feraday has pledged her time to MC the event, as her own contribution to breast cancer awareness.

Mr Sang Heung Shin, President and CEO of Samsung Electronics Europe, said: "As a brand we have a strong worldwide presence and it is so important that we use our global influence to support European breast cancer charities. Through Samsung's European Breast Cancer Awareness Day we strive to reach 400,000 women in Europe and encourage them to fight breast cancer through awareness and understanding."

Breast cancer charities face a constant battle to increase awareness and raise sufficient funding. In 2008, Samsung donated $3 million to European breast cancer charities and announc ulti-million dollar five year pledge to further support the battle against breast cancer.

In 2009, as well as raising funds, Samsung has focused on the prevention of breast cancer through knowledge, campaigning and awareness. www.morethantalk.eu, which launched in September 2009, has already provided this on an unprecedented scale.

In a history making move, 'Everybody's Doing It', the viral created for the campaign, is now playing in one of the world's biggest and most famous outdoor advertising screens, the Samsung screen in London's Piccadilly Circus. This is the first time that both a charity campaign and a campaign featuring real women who are not models or actresses, has played to such a huge public audience on the Samsung screen.

Working with Susan G. Komen for the Cure®

To spread the word even further, Samsung is working closely with local breast cancer charities and on a European level with Susan G. Komen for the Cure®, the largest breast cancer advocacy organisation in the world. Samsung and Susan G. Komen for the Cure announced their European partnership in November 2008.

Susan Carter Johns, Komen vice president and chief of staff at Susan G. Komen for the Cure said: "The Samsung initiative with Susan G. Komen for the Cure is tackling the big issues in breast cancer in Europe and around the world, with meaningful education and support for important breast cancer programmes.

Photos/Multimedia Gallery Available:

Contacts
Helen Farrier
Samsung Electronics Europe
+44 (0) 1932 455692
Helen.Farrier@samsung.com

Permalink:

Release Languages
- Spanish
- German
- French
- Italian
- Dutch

Company Information Center
ExpertSource
Add to My Companies

Sharing
Digg
Delicious

1. NewsTrak reports provide valuable audience and web visibility.

2. Convenient links for readers to forward or print multimedia release.

3. Time and date stamp identify when release was transmitted.

4. Headline and dateline provide key reference information.

5. Business Wire source means your news originates from the most accurate commercial wire in the country.

6. Quotables refresh with quoted material in your press release, alerting search engines to new content and helping your search engine ranking.

7. Smart Multimedia Gallery provides one-click access to high- and low-res photos, streaming audio and video, and other publication- and webready multimedia.

8. Downloadable logo provides added branding and links to company's website.

9. XHTML formatting and distribution allow for centered and stylized headlines, embedded hyperlinks, bold, italic and underlined text, bulleted lists, wider earnings tables and other features that increase the attractiveness of your release and help optimize for search engines.

10. Business Wire supports news delivery in dozens of languages worldwide.

11. Company Information Center provides quick links to stock quotes, Company Profile, experts, news archives and more.

12. Track breaking news with the My Companies feature.

13. Contact information includes live email link for media and investor inquiries.

14. Social media icons allow easy bookmarking and sharing among web-users including consumers, journalists and bloggers.

The newest trend in online newsrooms is the posting of feature stories that goes beyond just reporting news about the organization's products and services. Instead, topics and trends that interest a wider audience are used under the rubric of what is called *brand journalism*. The Red Bull site, shown on page 411, is an excellent example. Cisco Systems has also revamped its newsroom along the lines of producing feature content and has even staffed its online newsroom with former journalists. In the first week of its operation, the newsroom received 90,000 visits from 189 different nations.

In today's 24/7 news cycle, it's important that a company keep its online newsroom up-to-date by posting news and features on a daily basis. Reporters, in particular, regularly access online newsrooms when seeking information about an organization. Indeed, a survey conducted by TEKGROUP found that 98 percent of journalists thought it was important for a company to have an online newsroom, and

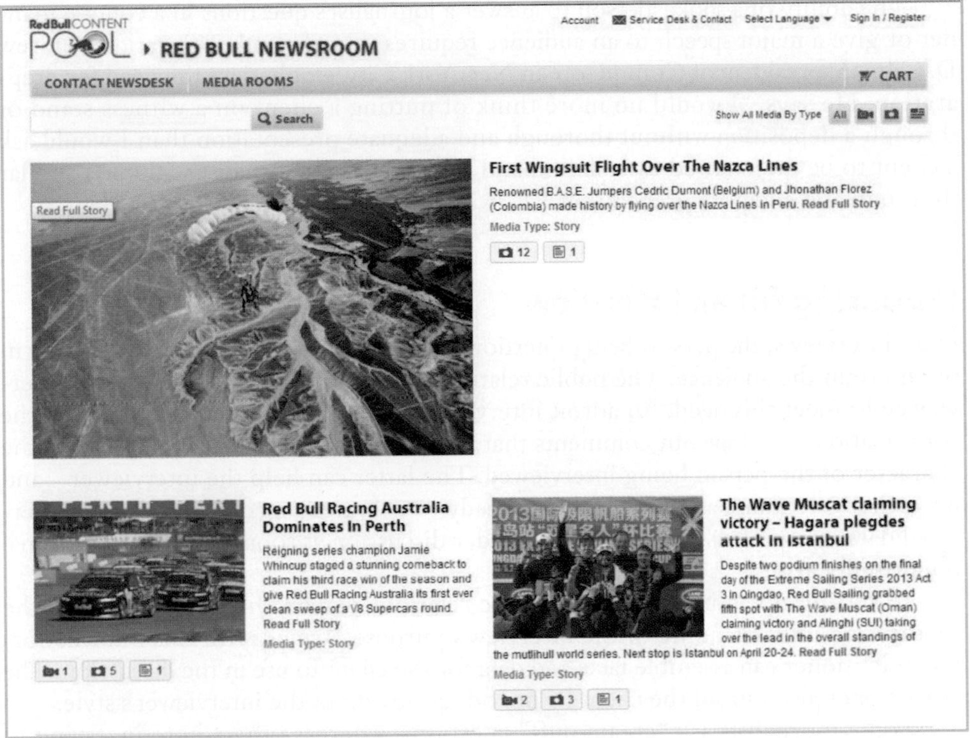

Red Bull's Online Newsroom (www.redbullcontentpool.com)

Journalists and bloggers rely on company online newsrooms to get up-to-date news about the organization. The Red Bull content pool is well designed and emphasizes feature stories about various sports and culture events created by the company. The online newsroom also includes a variety of materials including news releases, graphics photos, and videos.

that almost 30 percent of the journalists surveyed visit a corporate newsroom at least once a week.

Surveys have also found that journalists go first to an organization's website for information in the case of a crisis. It's also important for updates on a current situation or crisis be posted practically on an hourly basis. Any material posted on the website should be more than just copies of printed materials. They must be reformatted and offer short summaries, extensive links, and strong visual elements. All documents, however, should have a "printer-friendly" version available.

Media Interviews

Not all outreach to traditional media requires the preparation of news releases or other materials. Indeed, a great deal of media coverage is generated by reporters calling an organization's spokesperson or working through the public relations department to arrange an interview with an executive or expert.

The ability of a spokesperson to answer a journalist's questions in a concise manner or give a major speech to an audience requires thought and preparation. Andrew D. Gilman, president of CommCore in New York City, emphasizes the need for preparation. He says, "I would no more think of putting a client on a witness stand or through a deposition without thorough and adequate presentation than I would ask a client to be interviewed by a skillful and well-prepared journalist without a similar thorough and adequate preparation."

Preparing for an Interview

In all interviews, the person being questioned should say something that will inform or entertain the audience. The public relations practitioner should prepare the interviewee to meet this need. An adroit interviewer attempts to develop a theme in the conversation—to draw out comments that make a discernible point or illuminate the character of the person being interviewed. The latter can help the interviewer—and his or her own cause as well—by being ready to volunteer specific information, personal data, or opinions about the cause under discussion as soon as the conversational opportunity arises.

In setting up an interview, the public relations person should obtain from the reporter an understanding of the interview's purpose. Armed with this information, the practitioner can assemble facts and data for the client to use in the discussion. The practitioner also can aid the client by providing tips about the interviewer's style.

Some journalists ask "cream puff" questions, whereas others bore in, trying to force the interviewee into unplanned admissions or embarrassment. Thus, it is especially important to be well acquainted with the interviewer's style, whether the interviewer is someone from a local newspaper, a TV reporter, or a *Wall Street Journal* columnist. Short, direct answers delivered without hesitation help a person project an image of strength and credibility. These types of answers also provide more accurate quotes or broadcast soundbites, which the media value.

The Print Interview

An interview with a newspaper reporter may last about an hour and take place perhaps at lunch or over coffee in an informal setting. The result of this person-to-person talk may be a published story of perhaps 400 to 600 words. The interviewer weaves bits from the conversation together in direct and indirect quotation form, works in background material, and perhaps injects personal observations about the interviewee. The latter has no control over what is published, beyond the self-control he or she exercises in answering the reporter's questions. Neither the person being interviewed nor a public relations representative should ask to approve an interview story before it is published. Such requests are rebuffed automatically as a form of censorship.

Magazine interviews usually explore the subject in greater depth than those in newspapers, because the writer may have more space available. Most magazine interviews have the same format as those in newspapers. Others appear in question-and-answer form. These require prolonged, taped questioning of the interviewee by one or more writers and editors. During in-depth interviews, the interviewee should answer the questions, but refrain from going off on tangents.

Radio and television interviews will be covered in the next chapter.

News Conferences

A more formal approach to a media interview is the *news conference*, which is often referred to as a *press conference*. A news conference makes possible quick, widespread dissemination of a person's comments and opinions to a number of reporters at the same time. It avoids the time-consuming task of presenting the information to the news outlets individually and ensures that the intensely competitive newspapers and electronic media hear the news simultaneously. Increasingly, bloggers that cover the particular industry are also invited to attend a news conference. Trade shows are a popular venue for news conferences and media interviews. See the box below about Samsung's launch of the Galaxy Note.

Most news conferences are positive in intent and project the host's plans or point of view. A corporation may hold a news conference to unveil a new product whose manufacture will create many new jobs, or a civic leader may do so to reveal the goals and plans for a countywide charity fund drive he or she will head. Such news conferences should be carefully planned and scheduled well in advance under the most favorable circumstances.

Public relations specialists also must deal frequently with unanticipated, controversial situations, such as a business firm, an association, or a politician becoming embroiled in a difficulty that is at best embarrassing, and possibly incriminating. Press and public demand an explanation. A bare-bones printed statement will not be

on the job

SOCIAL MEDIA IN ACTION

Samsung Smartphone Has Media's Number

Competing with Apple's iPhone for media attention is a challenge for competitors, but Samsung was able to break through with its new Galaxy Note mobile phone that received widespread media coverage.

Samsung and its public relations firm, MWW, launched a year-long campaign to convince consumers that the device's larger screen (one-inch larger than the iPhone) was a better option among smartphones. The Galaxy Note was also positioned as the first smartphone designed for content creation by including a stylus that enabled users to write and draw on the screen.

In order to capitalize on this feature, Samsung partnered with caricature artists, Urban Daddy, *Fashion Week*, and game-maker Rovio (which created the popular Angry Birds) for a series of events to showcase the smartphone's precision. The major event was the Consumer Electronics Show (CES) in Las Vegas where the Galaxy Note was introduced and demonstrated to the print and broadcast media.

In addition to getting coverage on Internet news sites and social media networks, MWW also got the cover of *USA Today* and scored coverage in several monthly magazines, including *Marie Claire*, *Harper's Bazaar*, and *Teen Vogue*. Overall, the campaign generated more than 19,000 media placements in what public relations and marketing personnel call *earned media*.

In terms of sales, the campaign helped Samsung sell 10 million Galaxy Notes in the first year.

The campaign also received *Ragan's PR Daily* grand prize in the category of media relations.

enough to satisfy the clamor and may draw greater press scrutiny of the stonewalling organization.

A well-prepared spokesperson may be able to achieve a measure of understanding and sympathy by issuing a carefully composed statement when the news conference opens.

No matter how trying the circumstances, the person holding the news conference should create an atmosphere of cooperation and project a sincere intent to be helpful. The worst thing he or she can do is to appear resentful of the questioning. In addition, the person never should succumb to a display of bad temper. A good strategy is to admit that the situation is bad and stress that the organization is doing everything in its power to correct it. The approach is described by Professor Timothy Coombs at the University of Central Florida as the "mortification" strategy, which was discussed in Chapter 10.

Most news conferences are planned in advance, but they can also be somewhat spontaneous. Such a situation might involve the recipient of a Nobel Prize meeting reporters right after the award is announced, or an Olympic athlete who has just won a gold medal and is breathlessly describing his or her feelings. Celebrities, in particular, give a lot of impromptu news conferences to announce everything from a divorce to a new multimillion-dollar contract. The other type is the regularly scheduled conference held by a public official at stated times, even when there is nothing special to announce. Usually this is called a *briefing*—the daily State Department briefing, for example.

Planning and Conducting a News Conference

First comes the question "Should we hold a news conference or not?" Frequently the answer should be "No!" The essential element of a news conference is news. If reporters and camera crews are summoned to a conference and receive information of minor news value to their readers or listeners, they go away disgusted. Their valuable time has been wasted—and it is valuable. In other words, public relations professionals should realistically assess whether the information can just as effectively be distributed through a news release or media kit.

What hour is best? This depends on the local media situation. If the city has only an afternoon newspaper, 9:30 or 10 A.M. is good, because this gives a reporter time to write a story before the midday deadline. If the city's newspaper publishes in the morning, 2 P.M. is a suitable hour. Early afternoon is also good for local television stations because they then have time to prepare a story for the 6 P.M. newscast.

Bulldog Reporter, a West Coast public relations newsletter, suggests the following checklist for public relations staff organizing a news conference:

- Select a convenient location, one that is fairly easy for news representatives to reach with minimal travel time.
- Set the date and time. A time between midmorning and midafternoon is good. Friday afternoons are deadly, as are days before holidays.
- Distribute a media advisory about the upcoming news conference when appropriate. This depends on the importance of the event.
- Write a statement for the spokesperson to give at the conference and make sure that he or she understands and rehearses it. In addition, rehearse the entire conference.
- Try to anticipate questions so that the spokesperson can readily answer difficult queries. Problem/solution rehearsals prepare the spokesperson.

- Prepare a media kit. This should include a brief fact sheet with names and titles of participants, a basic news release, and basic support materials.
- Prepare visual materials as necessary. These may include slides, photos, posters, or even a short video.
- Make advance arrangements for the room. Be sure that there are enough chairs and leave a center aisle for photographers. If a lectern is used, make certain that it is large enough to accommodate multiple microphones.
- Arrive 30 to 60 minutes early to double-check arrangements. Test the microphones, arrange name tags for invited guests, and distribute background materials.

A practitioner should take particular care to arrange the room in such a way that photographers and TV crews do not obstruct reporters. Some find it good policy for the speaker to remain after the news conference ends and make brief on-camera statements for the broadcast media or even a blogger. A final problem in managing a news conference is knowing when to end it. The public relations representative serving as backstage watchdog should avoid cutting off the questioning prematurely. A moment will come, however, when the reporters run out of fresh questions. This is the time to step forward and say something like, "I'm sorry, but I know some of you have deadlines to make. So we have time for just two more questions."

Online News Conferences

The previous section focused on news conferences in a specific location, but many of the guidelines also apply to online news conferences. Many news conferences today are interactive webcasts so that journalists and bloggers around the world can participate.

Attendance is often better because journalists can view and even ask questions while sitting at their desks. In fact, if a news conference is for reporters across the country who are covering a particular industry, a webcast with company officials speaking to reporters via the Internet is not only more cost efficient but also more effective. Webcasts, including their use as news conferences, were discussed in Chapter 13.

Media Tours and Press Parties

The purpose of the typical news conference is to transmit information and opinion from the organization to the news media in a businesslike, time-efficient manner. Often, however, an organization wishes to brief the media or get to know journalists and editors on a more personal basis. There are two approaches for doing this. One is the media tour and the other is the dinner or cocktail party. Both require intense attention to every possible detail and an ability to juggle multiple logistics.

Media Tours

There are three kinds of media tours. The most common is a trip, often disparagingly called a *junket*, during which editors and reporters are invited to inspect a company's manufacturing facilities in several cities, ride an inaugural flight of a new air route, or watch previews of the television network programs for the fall season in Hollywood or New York. The host usually picks up the tab for transporting, feeding, and housing the reporters. Many publications, however, insist on paying transportation and housing to avoid any potential conflict of interest. In either case, the public relations staff should give reporters the option of being paid guests of the organization or paying for their own transportation and housing.

A variation of the media tour is the *familiarization trip*. *Fam trips*, as they are called, are offered to travel writers and editors by the tourism industry (see Chapter 18). Convention and visitor bureaus, as well as major resorts, pay all expenses in the hope that the writers will report favorably on their experiences. Travel articles in magazines and newspapers usually result from a reporter's fam trip.

In the third kind of media tour, which is widely used in high-technology industries, the organization's executives travel to key cities to talk with selected editors; for example, top Apple Computer executives toured the East Coast to talk with key magazine editors and demonstrate the capabilities of the new Apple iPad. Depending on editors' preferences, the executives may visit a publication and give a background briefing to key editors, or a hotel conference room may be set up so that the traveling executives may talk with editors from several publications at the same time.

Press Parties

This gathering may be a luncheon, a dinner, or a cocktail party. Whatever form the party takes, standard practice is for the host to rise at the end of the socializing period and make the "pitch." This may be the launch of a new product, a brief policy statement followed by a question-and-answer period, or merely a soft-sell thank-you to the guests for coming and giving the host an opportunity to know them better. Guests usually are given packets of information, either when they arrive or as they leave. Parties giving the press a preview of an art exhibit, a new headquarters building, and so forth are widely used.

The advantages to the host of a press party can be substantial under proper circumstances. During conversation over food or drink, officials of the host organization become acquainted with the media people who write, edit, broadcast, or blog about them. Although the benefit from the host's point of view is difficult to measure immediately, the party opens the channels of communication.

Also, if the host has an important policy position to present, the assumption—not necessarily correct—is that editors and reporters will be more receptive after a social hour. However, the host who expects food and drink to buy favorable press coverage may receive an unpleasant surprise. Conscientious reporters and editors will not be swayed by a free drink and a plate of prime rib followed by baked Alaska. In their view, they have already given something to the host by setting aside a part of their day for the party. They accept invitations to press parties because they wish to develop potential news contacts within the host's organization and to learn more about its officials.

Gifts in the form of a pen, note pad, or a sample of a new product are often given to reporters attending a press party, but anything costing more than a token amount should be avoided. Some large newspapers will not even permit their staffs to accept token gifts, as discussed in Chapter 3.

Summary

The Importance of Mass Media

- The mass media continue to be major distribution platforms for public relations materials.
- Newspapers, radio, and television are still more trusted as a source of information than tweets or Facebook.
- Public relations personnel spend considerable time and energy producing content and working with mass media.

The News Release

- The news release is the most commonly used public relations tactic.
- News releases are sent to journalists and editors for possible use in news columns, and they are the source for a large percentage of articles that are published.
- News releases must be accurate, informative, and written in journalistic style.
- Online news releases are similar to traditional news releases, but the format is condensed and single spacing is used. Most widely distributed news releases are now sent by e-mail or posted on organizational online newsrooms.
- Multimedia news releases harness the capabilities of the Internet and social media by embedding photos, video, links, social tags, and so on, into the basic news release.

Publicity Photos and Infographics

- Publicity photos often accompany news releases to make a story more appealing.
- Photos and infographics can increase the usage and sharing of a news release.
- Photos must be high resolution and well composed.
- A photo can be made more interesting by manipulating the camera angle and lighting and by showing scale and action.
- Color photos are now commonly used in most publications.
- Infographics are now extensively used to communicate facts and figures in a highly visual way.

Media Kits

- A media kit, or press kit, was traditionally a folder containing news releases, photos, fact sheets, and features about a new product, event, or other newsworthy projects undertaken by an organization.
- Digital media kits are now commonly used and are produced on CD, e-mailed, or placed on organizational websites.

Mat Releases

- A mat release is a form of news release that primarily has a feature angle instead of hard news. Mat releases provide consumer information and tips in an objective manner, with only a brief reference to the client that is distributing the information via a distribution firm such as Family Features.
- These canned features appear in the food, travel, automotive, and business sections of a newspaper.

Media Alerts and Fact Sheets

- Advisories, or alerts, let journalists know about an upcoming event such as a news conference or photo or interview opportunities.
- Fact sheets give the five Ws and H of an event in outline form. Fact sheets also can be used to provide background of an executive, a product, or an organization.

The Art of Pitching a Story

- Public relations personnel "pitch" journalists and editors with story ideas about their employer or client.
- Such pitches are usually e-mailed, but can also be a text message or even a tweet.
- A good pitch is based on research and a creative idea that will appeal to the journalist or editor.

Distributing Media Materials

- Electronic news services such as Business Wire provide an efficient way to distribute news releases around the world.
- Online newsrooms are often part of an organization's website. They allow the media and the public to access news releases, photos, videos, and other public relations materials.

Media Interviews

- Journalists often seek interviews with sources, and the role of the public relations person is to facilitate their requests.
- Public relations personnel often do media training to ensure that sources give competent media interviews.

News Conferences

- Such events should be held rarely and only when there is major news or intense media interest.
- Public relations personnel are usually in charge of logistics and arrangements for news conferences.
- Online news conferences are popular because journalists in different locations can easily attend.

Media Tours and Press Parties

- Company executives often go on a media tour to visit editors in various locations and discuss a new product, such as the iPad.
- Press parties are primarily social events that allow an organization's executives to meet journalists and develop working relationships.

Case Activity **Promoting the Opening of a New Library**

A new university library will open next month. The $100 million building is an eight-story wonder of glass and steel beams designed by the famous architectural firm BK Skinner and Associates. The library has over 125 commissioned works of art and 2,500 Internet plug-ins for students and their laptops. In addition, the library has several computer labs for students and meeting rooms for university and community organizations. And, in a special coup, author J. K. Rowling of *Harry Potter* fame will be the guest of honor at the official opening.

Write an online news release about the new library and its planned grand opening. Second, write an e-mail pitch letter to the local media encouraging them to do feature stories about the new library in advance of the opening. Third, write a media alert letting the media know that J. K. Rowling will be available for interviews on a particular day. Include appropriate quotations and information that you deem necessary.

Questions **For Review and Discussion**

1. Is mass media still the major distributor of PR news among audiences? Discuss.
2. What are the basic components of an online news release?
3. Multimedia is often referred to as smart media release. Why?
4. What is SEO, and why is it important?
5. Why is it a good idea to include a photograph or an infographic with a news release? What are the six aspects of a good publicity photo?
6. What is a mat release? How is it different from a regular news release?
7. What's the difference between a media advisory and a fact sheet?
8. In what way is a digital media kit different or similar to the traditional media kit? What do they contain?
9. Before pitching a story to a journalist or editor, why is it a good idea to first do some basic research on the individual or the publication?
10. Why is media training of a spokesperson recommended before organizing a media interview?
11. When should a news conference be organized?
12. How should you prepare for a media interview?
13. What are the mechanics of organizing a news conference?
14. What's the difference between a media tour and a press party?

Media Resources

Barks, E. (2013, March). How to alienate reporters: Forbidden phrases to forgo during interviews. *Public Relations Tactics*, 13.

Falkow, S. (2012, August). Study: Multimedia press releases get 77 percent more views than text only. *RaganReport,* 14.

Hanson, A. (2013, May 6). Six elements your online newsroom must have. Retrieved from www.ragan.com

Infographics are becoming a major story in journalism (2012, June). *PRWeek,* 21.

Jonas, T. & Guarnaccia, T. (2013, April). Is the press release dead or does it still hold relevance in today's world? *PRWeek*, 23.

Junker, D. (2012, February). A picture is worth a thousand words: The importance of writing strong captions. *Public Relations Tactics*, 16.

Luttrell, R. (2013, March). Press pass: 5 questions to ask when writing news releases. *Public Relations Tactics,* 14.

McCarthy, A. (2012, December 31). Editor shares important dos and don'ts of pitching. Retrieved from www.ragan.com

Porter, J. (2013, January 2). How to prepare for press interviews. Retrieved from Journalistics (jporter@journalistics.com).

Sebastian, M. (2012, November 29). Press releases with visuals boost views by nearly tenfold. Retrieved from Ragan's Daily Headlines www.ragan.com

Wilcox, D. & Reber, B. (2013). *Public relations writing & media techniques* (7th ed.). Boston, MA: Pearson.

Wilson, M. (2012, July 2). 25 guidelines for great visual communication. Retrieved from www.ragan.com

chapter 15

Media Relations Management: Electronic Media

After reading this chapter, you will be able to:

Know the procedure for booking a guest on a talk show

Understand the strategy of product placement on television shows

Write radio news releases and video news releases

Prepare public service announcements (PSAs) for broadcast

Understand the components of radio media tours and satellite media tours

The Reach of Radio and Television

Radio and television are important channels of communications for public relations specialists because they reach the vast majority of the American public on a daily basis. Radio reaches 92 percent of the American population and, according to Arbitron, listening by persons 12 or older, is a medium of 2.5 hours a day. The reach of television is even higher. It reaches 95 percent of the population on a daily basis for longer periods of time.

According to Nielsen Media Research, an average American watchs almost 147 hours of television a month, or about 4.9 hours a day. Television also remains the number one news and information source for Americans of all age groups, especially for individuals 65 years and older. In contrast, Nielsen says an average American spends less than 30 hours a month on the Internet.

> Radio's power comes from its accessibility. People can listen to radio in almost any location—at home, the car, or work—and it remains a free medium for listeners.
>
> *David Beasley, marketing manager at News Generation, a public relations firm specializing in radio*

Both radio and television continue to thrive in the Internet Age for three reasons. First, radio and television content has expanded to other digital platforms. More than 40 million people, for example, listen to the radio weekly via the Internet, satellite radio, or iPod/MP3 players. Television programs are also widely downloaded to computers and smartphones. Second, broadcast media generate larger audiences for a particular program or event than any other single media or Internet platform. The 2013 Super Bowl, for example, attracted 108 million viewers. Other television programs, such as *American Idol* and *Dancing With the Stars*, continue to generate a weekly audience of about 18 million and 15 million, respectively.

The third reason is that radio and television are what the *Economist* describes as "an inherently lazy form of entertainment." Listening to either medium is a passive form of activity and doesn't require much work on the part of the individual. Radio is readily available in the home, in the car, and even at work by turning a switch. Radio also has the ability to reach niche audiences, whether they are housewives, baby boomers, or Hispanics. See also the Insights box on page 422 about Hispanic broadcast media. Both media also easily accommodate multitasking; a person can text, Tweet, and do a number of other tasks while listening to a radio or watching television.

Tapping broadcast media for public relations purposes, however, requires a special perspective. Practitioners must constantly think about producing messages in audio and visual terms. This chapter discusses the various tactics used by public relations personnel to distribute information via radio and television, and to secure opportunities for their clients and employers to appear on a variety of broadcast shows.

Radio

The following sections will discuss (1) audio news releases, (2) radio public service announcements, and (3) radio media tours. A section toward the end of the chapter will discuss general guidelines for pitching broadcast outlets and arranging guest appearances on both radio and television talk shows.

Audio News Releases

Radio news releases in the industry are called *audio news releases*, or ANRs. They differ in three ways from online news releases, which were discussed in the last chapter. The most important difference is that a radio news release is written for the ear.

on the job

A MULTICULTURAL WORLD

Broadcast Media Has Large Hispanic Audience

Radio and television are particularly good communication channels for the Hispanic audience. First, in terms of Hispanic media, there are now about 600 Spanish-language radio stations and 75 Hispanic television stations in the United States. In addition, Univision is now the fifth largest network in the country.

Second, research studies show that the Hispanic audience outpaces the general population in terms of listeners and viewers. Hispanics, for example, average 24 hours a week listening to the radio, and one out of every three radio stations in the top 10 media markets is Hispanic. In terms of television, Hispanics daily view an average of one hour more than non-Hispanic whites. Seventy percent watch both English and Spanish programs.

This means that the full range of radio and television tactics, such as news releases, PSAs, media tours, and video news releases (VNRs), should be prepared with the Hispanic audience in mind. However, more is involved than simply translating an English version of the same material into Spanish. As a monograph from Medialink says, "A direct translation from English to Spanish, in many cases, simply does not make sense from a grammatical and syntax perspective." Instead, a public relations professional should practically start from scratch and have translations done by someone completely fluent in Spanish.

> Make sure that PSAs are scripted, reviewed, and voiced by fluent native Spanish speakers.
>
> *Raul Martinez, Strauss Radio Strategies*

Radio and television media tours, called RMTs and SMTs, have their own special requirements. It is important to have a Hispanic spokesperson who speaks Spanish as his or her native language.

Although speaking Spanish is the common denominator, it's also important to have spokespersons who appeal to different age groups. A good example is television PSAs prepared by Strauss Radio Strategies on behalf of the Hispanic Heritage Awards Foundation (HHAF). Celebrity spokespersons included Gloria Estefan, Carlos Ponce, and Jon Secada. In terms of pitching radio and television stations, a public relations person fluent in both English and Spanish is highly recommended.

The emphasis is on strong, short sentences that average about 10 words and can be easily understood by a listener.

A second difference is that an ANR is more concise and to the point. Instead of a news release that may run several hundred words, a standard one-minute ANR is about 125 words. The timing is vital, because broadcasters must fit their message into a rigid time frame that is measured down to the second.

The third difference is writing style. An online news release is more formal and uses standard English grammar and punctuation. Sentences often contain dependent and independent clauses. In a radio release, a more conversational style is used. In such a style, partial or incomplete sentences are OK. The following are some guidelines from the Broadcast News Network on how to write a radio news release:

- Time is money in radio. Stories should be no longer than 60 seconds. Stories without actualities (soundbites) should be 30 seconds or less.
- The only way to time your story is to read it out loud, slowly.
- Convey your message with the smallest possible number of words and facts.
- A radio news release is not an advertisement; it is not a sales promotion piece. A radio news release is journalism—spoken.
- Announcers punctuate with their stories; not all sentences need verbs or subjects.
- Releases should be conversational. Use simple words and avoid legal-speak.
- After writing a radio news release, try to shorten every sentence.
- Never start a story with a name or a vital piece of information. While listeners are trying to figure out the person speaking and the subject matter, they don't pay attention to the specific information.

Format A radio news release can be sent to stations for announcers to read, but the most effective approach is to provide a radio station with a recording of someone with a good radio voice reading the entire announcement. The person doing the reading may not be identified by name. This, in the trade, is called an *actuality*.

A second approach is to have an announcer and also include what is called a *soundbite* from a satisfied customer or a company spokesperson. This approach is better than a straight announcement because the message comes from a "real person" rather than from a nameless announcer. This type of announcement is also more acceptable to radio stations, because the station's staff can elect to use the whole recorded announcement or take the role of the announcer and use just the soundbite.

An example of an effective ANR was the one produced for the American Psychological Association (APA). The APA, using the firm News Generation, got soundbites from a number of researchers presenting papers on topical issues at its national convention. One soundbite, for example, was about the differences in how men and women hear and smell. A number of radio stations used the ANR, reaching a potential audience of 20 million.

Production and Delivery Every ANR starts with a carefully written and accurately timed script. The next step is to record the words. When recording, it is imperative to control the quality of the sound. A few large organizations have complete recording studios, and some hire radio station employees as consultants; but most organizations use a professional recording and distribution service such as Strauss Media Strategies or KEF Media.

These services have state-of-the-art equipment and skilled personnel who can take a script, edit it, record it at the proper sound levels, and package it for distribution to broadcast outlets via telephone, CDs, MP3 format, and Web servers, and even through such networks as ABC and CNN radio.

Radio stations, like newspapers, have preferences about how they want to receive news releases. One survey by DWJ Television found that almost 75 percent of the radio news directors prefer to receive actualities by phone. This is particularly true for late breaking news events in the station's service area. When a forest fire threatened vineyards in California's Napa Valley, a large winery contacted local stations and offered an ANR with a soundbite from the winery's president telling everyone that the grape harvest would not be affected. About 50 stations were called, and 40 accepted the ANR for broadcast use.

Use of ANRs Producing ANRs is somewhat of a bargain compared with producing materials for television. Ford Motor Company, for example, spent less than $5,000 for national distribution of a news release on battery recycling as part of Earth Day activities. More than 600 radio stations picked up the ANR, and about 5 million people were reached.

Despite their cost-effectiveness, ANRs should not be sent to every station. Stations have particular demographics. A release about the benefits of vitamin supplements for senior citizens isn't of much interest to a station specializing in hip-hop. Various media databases such as Cision and Burrelles help practitioners select the right stations for their ANRs.

The use of ANRs is popular with radio stations. Thom Moon, director of operations at Duncan's American Radio Quarterly, told *PRWeek* that he thinks the major reason for this is the consolidation of ownership in radio broadcasting, which has resulted in cost-cutting and fewer news personnel.

Jack Trammell, president of VNR-1 Communications, echoed this thought. He told *PR reporter*, "They're telling us they're being forced to do more with less. As long as radio releases are well produced and stories don't appear to be blatant commercials, newsrooms are inclined to use them." *Public Relations Tactics* gives some additional tips from Trammell:

- **Timeliness.** Stories should be timed to correspond with annual seasons, governmental rulings, new laws, social trends, and so on.
- **Localization.** Newsrooms emphasize local news. A national release should be relevant to a local audience. Reporters are always looking for the "local angle."
- **Humanization.** Stories should show how real people are involved or affected. Impressive statistics mean nothing to audiences without a human angle.
- **Visual appeal.** Successful stories provide vibrant, compelling soundbites that not only subtly promote but also illustrate and explain.

Radio PSAs

Public relations personnel working for nonprofit organizations often prepare *public service announcements* (PSAs) for radio stations.

A PSA is defined by the FCC as an unpaid announcement that promotes the programs of government or voluntary agencies or that serves the public interest. In general, as part of their responsibility to serve the public interest, radio and television stations provide airtime to charitable and civic organizations to make the public aware of and educate them about such topics as heart disease, obesity, and safe driving.

In PSAs, speak to the common man . . . . Make it as simple as possible.

Christiana Arbesu, VP of production, MultiVu

Format and Production Radio PSAs are written in uppercase and double-spaced. Their length can be 60, 30, 20, 15, or 10 seconds. And, unlike radio news releases, the standard practice is to submit multiple PSAs on the same subject in various lengths. To prepare PSAs in various lengths, the writer should use the following guidelines setting margins for a 60-space line:

2 lines = 10 seconds (about 25 words)
5 lines = 20 seconds (about 45 words)
8 lines = 30 seconds (about 65 words)
16 lines = 60 seconds (about 125 words)

The idea is to give the station flexibility in using a PSA of a particular length to fill a specific time slot. DWJ Television explains, "Some stations air PSAs in a way that relates length to time of play, for example, placing one length in their early news shows and another in the late news shows. Supplying both lengths allows a campaign to be heard by those who only listen to one of these shows." See the following Insights box for an example of two lengths used in a radio PSA.

Adding Sound The basic audio news release or radio PSA is a person reading a script. That's OK, but adding sound and other voices can make a radio PSA more interesting. Many PSAs use background music to add a dramatic touch or create a particular mood. Sound effects also work. A PSA for the National Heart, Lung, and Blood Institute, for example, used the sound of a stock car engine as an analogy to the idea that good air flow in a person's lungs is just as important as good air flow to an engine. Another common approach is to have the voices of several people in the PSA as in the following example:

Kid 1: Eat your fruits and veggies.
Kid 2: Brush your teeth.

on the job INSIGHTS

Radio PSAs Should Have Varying Lengths

The following is a basic PSA, produced by the Field Museum in Chicago that shows how the same topic can be treated in various lengths:

10 Seconds

Maps can tell us both where and who we are. The Field Museum's exhibition, "Maps: Finding Our Place in the World," allows visitors to take a look at some of the most historically valuable maps ever created. For more information, visit www.fieldmuseum.org

30 Seconds

Maps can tell us both where and who we are. The Field Museum's exhibition, "Maps: Finding Our Place in the World," allows visitors to take a look at some of the most historically valuable maps ever created. Besides direction, maps can also give us clues on how people, nations, governments, or organizations viewed their worlds. Through contemporary, historical, flat, or three-dimensional maps, the exhibition will explore a variety of themes, ranging from the history of maps to the map maker's political, cultural, or spiritual worldview. For more information, call (312) 922-9410 or visit www.fieldmuseum.org

Kid 3: Put on a coat; it's cold outside.
Kid 4: Did you finish your homework?
Kid 5: Wash your hands before you eat.

Announcer: So, mom, have you heard about MRSA? Methicillin-resistant *Staphylococcus aureus* is a type of staph bacteria that is resistant to certain antibiotics and may cause skin and other infections. The good news is, the earlier it's caught and treated, the better the outcome. So, if anyone in your family develops a bump that looks red, swollen, full of pus—or just plain infected—cover it with a bandage and contact a healthcare professional—especially if there's also a fever.

For more information, call 1-800-CDC-INFO or visit *cdc.gov/MRSA*, that's cdc.gov/MRSA.

A message from the U.S. Department of Health and Human Services' Centers for Disease Control and Prevention.

Delivery PSAs can be distributed in four ways: (1) mailing a script to the station's public service director, (2) sending a CD with announcements of varying lengths, (3) providing an 800 number, or (4) providing downloads from a sponsoring organization's Web server. The Advertising Council (www.adcouncil.org), for example, provides radio and television PSAs on its website for a number of national nonprofit campaigns. The Centers for Disease Control (www.cdc.gov) also provides PSAs for broadcast media on a variety of health subjects.

Use of Radio PSAs Almost any topic or issue can be the subject of a PSA. Stations, however, seem to be more receptive to particular topics. A survey of radio station public affairs directors by West Glen Communications, a producer of PSAs, found that local community issues and events are most likely to receive airtime, followed by children's issues. About 70 percent of the Advertising Council's PSA campaigns, for example, now address issues that affect children, from asthma and obesity to underage drinking.

The major downside for nonprofits using PSAs is that stations don't usually run them in prime time. According to surveys by West Glen, a large percentage of PSAs are run after midnight. As a result, many nonprofits often negotiate with local radio stations to pay a discounted advertising rate in order to ensure broadcast time during the day.

Radio Media Tours

Another public relations tactic is the *radio media tour* (RMT). Essentially, a spokesperson from a central location conducts a series of around-the-country, one-on-one interviews with several radio stations. A public relations representative prebooks telephone interviews with DJs, news directors, or talk show hosts around the country, and the personalities simply give interviews over the phone that can be broadcast live or recorded for later use.

A major multinational pharmaceutical concern, Schering-Plough, used an RMT to point out that most smokers in the United States fail to recognize the warning signs of chronic bronchitis. (Of course, the company makes a drug for such a condition.) The RMT was picked up by 88 stations, with a total audience of more than 2.8 million. The RMT was part of a campaign that also used a *satellite media tour* (SMT) for television stations. SMTs are discussed in the next section.

However, public relations practitioners setting up an RMT need to do their homework. As Richard Strauss, president of Strauss Radio Strategies, told *PRWeek*, "It's not enough just to know the show exists. Listen to the show, understand the format, read the host's bio, and know past guests to gain some kind of familiarity." Another guideline is to tie the RMT to an event, premiere, holiday, or current news that links to the listening audience. "For example, seat-belt safety campaigns are most effective around Thanksgiving and the Fourth of July, when Americans take to the roads in record numbers," says Curtis Gill of News Generation, a firm that arranges RMTs for clients.

Timing is also a consideration. Most interviews are on morning talk shows between the hours of 8 A.M. and noon. This means that the spokesperson, either an expert or a known celebrity, must be prepared to give early morning interviews to cover all the time zones. Other experts also give the tip that an organization should select a spokesperson with some endurance—he or she might be giving one interview after another for three or four hours.

Television

Television is a powerful and influential medium because it taps both sight and sound. It's also pervasive in American society and occupies more of an average American's time than any other medium, including the Internet. Consequently, public relations specialists work very hard to harness this medium in most public relations campaigns.

There are several approaches for getting an organization's news and viewpoints on television. They are:

- Send a standard news release. If the news director thinks the topic is newsworthy, the item may become a brief, 10-second mention by the news announcer. A news release may also prompt the assignment editor to think about a visual treatment and assign the topic to a reporter and a camera crew to conduct an on-camera interview or get additional video.
- Send a media alert or advisory informing the assignment editor about a particular event or occasion that would lend itself to video coverage. Media alerts, which were discussed in Chapter 14, can be sent via e-mail, Twitter, fax, or even express mail.
- Make a pitch by phone or e-mail to the assignment editor to have the station do a particular story. The art of making a pitch to a television news editor is to emphasize the visual aspects of the story.
- Produce a *video news release* (VNR) package that, like an ANR, is formatted for immediate use, with a minimum of effort by station personnel. The alternative, now commonly used, is to offer B-roll material, which will be explained shortly.
- Conduct a satellite media tour (SMT) in which a spokesperson can be interviewed by multiple stations at separate times.

- Arrange for your spokesperson to appear on a television talk or magazine show.
- Do product placement in television entertainment shows.

Several of these approaches will be explored in the rest of the chapter.

Today's VNRs are much more than just broadcast placement tools. They are being targeted to a variety of audiences through Web syndication, strategic placements in broadcast, cable, and site-based media in retail outlets and hospitals.

Tim Bahr, managing director of MultiVu, a broadcast production firm

Video News Releases

Large organizations seeking enhanced recognition for their names, products, services, and causes are the primary clients for VNRs. The production of VNRs can be more easily justified if there is potential for national distribution and multiple pickups by television stations and cable systems. Increasingly, costs are also justified because a VNR package can be reformatted for an organization's website, be part of a multimedia news release, and be posted on an organization's YouTube channel.

A typical 90-second VNR, says one producer, costs a minimum of $20,000 to $50,000 for production and distribution. Costs vary, however, depending on the number of location shots, the number of special effects, the use of celebrities, and the number of staff required to produce a high-quality tape that meets broadcast standards.

Because of the cost, a public relations department or firm must carefully analyze the news potential of the information and consider whether the topic lends itself to a fast-paced, action-oriented visual presentation. A VNR should not be produced if it contains only talking heads, charts, and graphs. Another aspect to consider is whether the topic will still be current by the time the video is produced. On average, it takes four to six weeks to script, produce, and distribute a high-quality VNR. In a crisis situation or for a fast-breaking news event, however, a VNR can be produced in a matter of hours or days.

Format The traditional VNR package is like a media kit prepared for print publications, which was discussed in the last chapter. It has various components that provide the television journalist with everything he or she needs to produce a television news story. According to MultiVu, a production firm, this includes the following:

- Ninety-second news report with voiceover narration on an audio channel separate from that containing soundbites and natural sound.
- A B-roll. This is the video only, without narration, giving a television station maximum flexibility to add its own narration or use just a portion of the video as part of a news segment.
- Clear identification of the video source.
- Script, spokespeople information, media contacts, extra soundbites, and story background information provided electronically.

Conceptualizing and writing a VNR storyboard is somewhat complicated because the writer has to visualize the scene, much like a playwright or screenwriter. In fact, a script for a VNR usually includes two columns. The left column lists the visual components, and the right column outlines the audio elements, such as the anchor lead-in, narration, and a list of any soundbites. See the following excerpt of a script prepared by the College of American Pathologists.

Video	Audio
Soundbite: Nora Bowers/Cervical Cancer Survivor	"When I was diagnosed with cervical cancer, I was scared, I was overwhelmed, and my immediate reaction was worst case."
B-roll of Nora doing activities at her home	37-year-old Nora Bowers, a teacher and mother of two, was diagnosed with cervical cancer in her late twenties, requiring her and her family to make prompt decisions regarding her health.
Soundbite: Nora Bowers	"After I received my diagnosis of cervical cancer I was overwhelmed with research that I was doing, that my family was doing . . . . I didn't know which information I could trust or believe in, and I didn't know what to do."
B-roll of a pathologist performing cervical cancer tests in laboratory	Pathologists, the physicians who actually identify and diagnose cervical cancer and other diseases, recognize this.

Production Although public relations writers can handle the job of writing a rough draft of a VNR script, the final scripting and production of a VNR is another matter. The entire process is highly technical, requiring trained professionals and sophisticated equipment.

Consequently, public relations departments and firms usually outsource production to a firm specializing in scripting and producing VNR and video packages. Public relations personnel, however, usually serve as liaison and give the producer an outline of what the VNR is supposed to accomplish. The public relations person also will work with the producer to line up location shots, props, and the individuals who will be featured. The following are some tips about the production of VNRs and video packages that best meet the needs of television news directors:

- Give television news directors maximum flexibility in editing the material using their own anchors or announcers.
- Produce the video package with news footage in mind. Keep soundbites short and to the point. Avoid commercial-like shots with sophisticated effects.
- Never superimpose your own written information on the actual videotape. Television news departments usually generate their own written notes in their own typeface and style.
- Never use a stand-up reporter. Stations do not want a reporter who is not on their own staff appearing in their newscast.
- Provide television stations with a local angle. This can be done by sending supplemental facts and figures that reflect the local situation.
- Good graphics, including animation, are a plus. Stations are attracted to artwork that shows things in a clear, concise manner.

The New "Normal": B-Roll Packaging

It has been mentioned that a VNR package should always include two or three minutes of B-roll, which contain additional soundbites and video that television news staffs can use for repackaging the story. In fact, a Nielsen Media Research survey of 130 television news directors found that 70 percent wanted a VNR with B-roll attached. Today, most television news directors want B-roll or video packages instead of fully scripted VNRs.

Consequently, video production firms now produce a variety of video packages on behalf of clients. Such packages provide plenty of video files and soundbites, but are not formally scripted into a complete story. This allows television news staffs to easily pick and choose material to produce their own stories.

One example of a B-roll, or video package, was done by KEF Media (www.kefmedia.com) about Coca-Cola moving its secret recipe to a bank vault in its museum at corporate headquarters in Atlanta. This was done with much fanfare, showing the box with the secret recipe being placed in the vault by Coke executives at a news conference. KEF also provided television stations with video clips of short statements by company spokesperson about the secret recipe that was been used for more than a century. The event and video excerpts were picked up by multiple television stations and the major networks.

Bader TV News, a production company based in New York, also produced a B-roll package on behalf of Shell about a college competition to create vehicles that would get exceptional gasoline mileage. VNRs and B-roll packages are also distributed to television stations via satellite, sent to Internet news sites, and posted on an organization's website and YouTube channel. Chapter 13 describes some of the platforms that are used for widespread distribution of organizational videos.

Television PSAs

Television stations, like radio stations, use PSAs on behalf of governmental agencies, community organizations, and charitable groups. In fact, a survey by News Broadcast Network found that a typical television station runs an average of 137 PSAs per week as part of its commitment to public service.

Many of the guidelines for radio PSAs, which were discussed previously, apply to television PSAs. They must be short, to the point, and professionally produced. Television is different, however, in that both audio and visual elements must be present. Even a simple PSA consisting of the announcer reading text must be accompanied by a photo or artwork that is shown on the screen at the same time. A good example is the sample 30-second television PSA from Rotary International shown on page 432.

Another approach is to have a spokesperson, such as a celebrity, talk directly into the camera for 30 seconds. In the trade, such a PSA is known as a *talking head.* This means that the format is relatively simple, involving just one person speaking to the camera. Ogilvy Public Relations Worldwide, for example, produced PSAs for the Centers for Disease Control and Prevention to build awareness about preventative colorectal cancer screenings. The PSAs featured celebrities such as Katie Couric and Morgan Freeman, both with personal ties to the cancer.

A more complex approach is to involve action and a number of scenes to give the PSA more movement and visual appeal. Good examples are two video PSAs distributed by the American Academy of Ophthalmology that is highlighted in the following PRCasebook.

PRCasebook

Video PSA Warns About Use of Decorative Contact Lenses

Although decorative contact lenses are popular among Twilight, Lady Gaga, and Avatar fans, the American Academy of Ophthalmology wanted to warn people that nonprescription decorative contacts can cause blindness.

The organization's public relations and marketing team produced two "This is your brain on drugs" video PSAs. A 30-second video was for teens, and a 90-second video was for parents. The team then sent news releases to all major media with links to the two PSAs and supplemented the videos with the following:

- Created Q&As and talking points for spokespeople and developed FAQs for media
- Drafted social media posts to doctors and Academy staff to use on Twitter and Facebook pages
- Produced downloadable posters for doctor's offices
- Created a promotional tool kit for doctors that included news release templates, social media posts, and a PowerPoint presentation for community groups
- Wrote Facebook and Yahoo ad campaigns targeted at teens

- Posted decorative lens-focused information on the Academy's Facebook and Twitter pages

As a result, visits to the Academy's *EyeSmart* website increased more than 50 percent. Media coverage was also extensive. More than 1,500 stories appeared in the print media, and there were 100 television segments. An RMT secured 40 radio interviews that aired almost 200 times. The campaign was named by *Ragan's PR Daily* as the best public service announcement of 2012.

Satellite Media Tours

The television equivalent of the radio media tour is the *satellite media tour* (SMT). Essentially, an SMT is a series of prebooked, one-on-one interviews from a fixed location (usually a television studio) via satellite with a series of television journalists or talk show hosts. Interviews via satellite are regularly seen on a number of network news shows, including *CNN News* and PBS's *NewsHour*.

The SMT concept started several decades ago when companies began to put their CEOs in front of television cameras. The public relations staff would line up reporters in advance to interview the spokesperson via satellite feed during allocated time frames of one to five minutes. This way, journalists could personally interview a CEO in New York even if they were based in San Francisco or Chicago. For busy CEOs, the SMT was a time-efficient way to give interviews.

Today, the SMT is a staple of the public relations and television industries. In fact, a survey by West Glen Communications found that nearly 85 percent of the nation's television stations participate in satellite tours.

The easiest way to do an SMT is to simply make the spokesperson available for an interview at a designated time. Celebrities are always popular, but an organization

Sample Television PSA

Rotary International distributes a variety of television PSAs on CD format to television stations and cable operators. This is the storyboard for one PSA.

also can use articulate industry experts. In general, the spokesperson sits in a chair or at a desk in front of a television camera. Viewers usually see the local news anchor asking questions and the spokesperson on a large screen, via satellite or even Skype, answering them in much the same way that anchors talk to reporters at the scene of an event.

Another popular approach to SMTs is to get out of the television studio and do them on location. When the National Pork Producers Council wanted to promote outdoor winter grilling, its public relations staff hired a team from Broadcast News Network to fire up an outdoor grill in Aspen, Colorado, and put a celebrity chef in a parka to give interviews, via satellite, while he cooked several pork recipes. Habitat for Humanity, on the other hand, used one of its home building sites for an SMT. The Insights box on page 433 gives some guidelines for planning an SMT.

News Feeds

A variation on the SMT is a news feed that provides video and soundbites of an event to television stations across the country via satellite or through webcasts. The news feed may be live from the event as it is taking place (real time), or it could be video shot at the event, edited, and then made available as a package.

In either case, the sponsoring organization hires a production firm to record the event. Major fashion shows, which take place in New York or Europe, often arrange for video feeds to media outlets around the world. Major auctions also send video feeds to media outlets and even gatherings of interested buyers.

DWJ Television, for example, was hired by Christie's to cover the auction of 56 outfits worn by women at Academy Award ceremonies. Stations could air the entire auction or simply make a video clip for use in later newscasts. News feeds also are regularly used when the president gives a news conference or a company makes a major announcement at a news conference or trade show.

on the job INSIGHTS

Guidelines for a Satellite Media Tour

Television stations get hundreds of opportunities to participate in satellite media tours (SMT), and anecdotal evidence indicates that four out of five pitched SMTs don't get aired. You can increase the odds if you follow these "do's" and "don'ts" compiled by *PRWeek*:

Do

- Include a relevant angle for the stations in every market you pitch.
- Use an interesting, visually appealing background or set. It often makes the difference between your SMT getting on the air and not getting on the air.
- Get stations involved by sending items that will help them perform and promote the interview.
- Respect producers' wishes when they tell you they will get back to you. Incessant follow-up will only annoy those whom you are trying to convince.
- Localize your SMT. If local audiences aren't going to be interested, neither will the producers airing the story be interested.
- Be clear in your pitch. Provide producers with the who, what, when, and why right away.
- Use credible, knowledgeable spokespersons who project confidence and are personable.

Don't

- Let the SMT become a commercial. If producers think there is the possibility of too many product mentions, they won't book it.
- Be dishonest with producers about the content of your SMT.
- Pitch your SMT to more than one producer at a station.
- Be conservative with the amount of talent. A boring medical SMT will pack more punch if you include a patient along with the doctor.
- Surprise the producer. Newscasts are planned to the minute, and unexpected events (spokesperson cancels) will not be appreciated.

Segments on News Programs Not all television coverage is the result of VNRs, SMTs, or news feeds. Public relations experts also work directly with television news directors to facilitate the development of a particular news segment or feature. Burson-Marsteller (B-M), for example, worked with the producers of *ABC World News with Diane Sawyer* to develop a story on a new insomnia drug, Intermezzo, made by Purdue Pharma. ABC News had reported on insomnia issues in the past, so B-M staffer worked with the show's producers by offering an exclusive on the new drug. FDA approval of the drug was the news hook, and B-M provided video clips of the manufacturing process that ended up in a two-minute segment.

Guest Appearances

Thus far, this chapter has concentrated on how to prepare and generate timely material for newscasts and PSAs. This section focuses on how to get spokespersons on talk and magazine shows. In such situations, the public relations person's contact is no longer the news department, but the directors and producers of various programs. The most valuable communication tools in reaching these people are the telephone and the persuasive pitch, which will be discussed shortly.

Before contacting directors and producers, however, it is necessary for the public relations staffs to do their homework. They must be totally familiar with a show's format and content, as well as the type of audience that it reaches. Media databases, such as Cision, are available that give key information about specific programs, such as the names and addresses of producers, the program format, audience demographics, and the purpose of the show.

A second approach, and one that is highly recommended, is to actually watch the program and study the format. In the case of a talk or interview show, what is the style of the moderator or host? What kinds of topics are discussed? How important is the personality or prominence of the guest? How long is the show or its segments? Does the show lend itself to product demonstrations or other visual aids? The answers to such questions will help determine whether the show is appropriate for the chosen spokesperson and how to tailor a pitch letter to achieve maximum results.

The possibilities for public relations people to have their clients interviewed on the air are immense. The current popularity of talk shows, on both local stations and syndicated satellite networks, provides many opportunities for on-air appearances in which the guest expresses opinions and answers call-in questions. A successful radio or television show guest appearance has three requirements:

1. **Preparation.** Guests should know what key message should be emphasized.
2. **Concise speech.** Guests should answer questions and make statements precisely and briefly. They shouldn't hold forth in excessive detail or drag in extraneous material. Responses should be kept to 30 seconds or less, because seconds count on the air: The interviewer must conduct the program under severe time restrictions.
3. **Relaxation.** "Mic fright" is a common ailment for which no automatic cure exists. It will diminish, however, if the guest concentrates on talking to the interviewer in a casual, person-to-person manner and forgets the audience as much as possible. Guests should speak up firmly; the control room can cut down their volume if necessary.

A public relations advisor can help the guest on all of these points. Answers to anticipated questions may be worked out and polished during a mock interview in which the practitioner plays the role of broadcaster. A recording or videotape of a practice session will help the prospective guest to correct weaknesses.

All too often, the hosts on talk shows know little about their guests for the day's broadcast. The public relations advisor can compensate for this difficulty by, in advance, sending the host a fact sheet summarizing the important information and listing questions the broadcaster might wish to ask. On network shows such as David Letterman's, nationally syndicated talk shows, and local programs on metropolitan stations, support staffs do the preliminary work with guests. Interviewers on hundreds of smaller local television and radio stations, however, lack such staffs. They may go on the air almost "cold" unless provided with volunteered information.

Talk Shows

Radio and television talk shows have been a staple of broadcasting for many years. KABC in Los Angeles started the trend in 1960, when it became the first radio station in the country to convert to an all-news-and-talk format. Today, more than

1,110 radio stations have adopted this format. Stations that play music also may include talk shows as part of their programming. In fact, it is estimated that there are now more than 4,000 radio talk shows in the United States.

The same growth applies to television. Phil Donahue began his show in 1967. Today, there are more than 20 nationally syndicated talk shows and a countless number of locally produced talk shows. For many years, the number-one syndicated daytime talk show was *The Oprah Winfrey Show*, which attracted about 8 million viewers on a daily basis. On the network level, three shows are the Holy Grail for publicists: NBC's *Today*, ABC's *Good Morning America*, and CBS's *Early Show*. Collectively, these three shows draw about 14 million viewers between 7 and 9 A.M. every weekday. Other popular venues, particularly for entertainers promoting their most recent film or album, are *The Tonight Show* and the *Late Show*.

> We expect our spokespersons to be able to put the products in a newsworthy context and answer unexpected questions.
>
> *Michael Friedman, EVP of DWJ Television*

The advantage of talk shows is the opportunity to have viewers see and hear the organization's spokesperson without the filter of journalists and editors interpreting and deciding what is newsworthy. Another advantage is the ability to be on the program longer than the traditional 30-second soundbite in a news program. Gresham Strigel, a senior producer, shared his thoughts with *Bulldog Reporter*, a media placement newsletter, about the ideal guest from the media's perspective:

- Guests should be personable and approachable when producers conduct preinterviews on the phone. They should also be forthright but not aggressive. "If you're wishy-washy, non-committed, or stilted, you're not going much further."
- Guests should have strong opinions. "We don't call certain people back because they have been trained not to say anything. The stronger your position is, and the higher up it is, the more media attention you're going to get. Nobody likes guests who play it safe."
- Guests should be passionate about the subject. "We don't want people who are robotic—who just spit out facts. If you convey passion about what you're talking about, you jump off the screen."
- Guests should be able to debate without getting personal or mean-spirited. "Smile . . . . Audiences like to see someone who is comfortable on-screen—someone who is happy to be there."
- Guests should have engaging, outgoing personalities. "Talking heads and ivory-tower types don't do well on television. They're better suited for print, where their personality—or lack of it—can't turn audiences off."

Magazine Shows

The term *magazine* refers to a television program format that is based on a variety of video segments in much the same way that print magazines have a variety of articles. These shows may have a guest related to the feature that's being shown, but the main focus is on a video story that may run from 3 to 10 minutes. At the network level, CBS's *60 Minutes* is an example of a magazine program.

Many human-interest magazine shows are produced at the local level. A sampling of magazine shows in one large city featured such subjects as a one-pound baby who survived, a treatment for anorexia nervosa, a couple who started a successful cookie company, remedies for back pain, tips on dog training, a black-belt karate expert, blue-collar job stress, and the work habits of a successful author.

Most, if not all, of these features came about as the result of someone making a pitch to the show's producers. Such pitches, which are further discussed shortly, must convince a show's producer that not only does the proposed guest have an interesting story, but there are also opportunities for video illustration of the story. The objective of the segments, at least from the perspective of the people featured, is exposure and the generation of new business. The tips on dog training, for example, featured a local breeder who also operated a dog obedience school. The karate expert ran a martial arts academy, and even the story of the one-pound baby was placed by a local hospital touting its infant-care specialty.

Pitching a Guest Appearance

The rules for pitching a radio or television talk show are the same as those for pitching a print publication, which was discussed in the last chapter. The public relations staff has to do their homework, be creative, and be succinct. An e-mail has to have a good subject line, and a telephone call has to tell the story in 30 seconds or less.

When thinking about booking a spokesperson on a local or syndicated talk show, here's a checklist of questions to consider:

> What I love is a catchy subject line for your e-mail pitch. That's the key. It can't be some long sentence with a lot of details.
>
> *Dina Bair, reporter on WGN, Chicago*

- Is the topic newsworthy? Does it have a new angle on something already in the news?
- Is the topic timely? Is it tied to some lifestyle or cultural trend?
- Is the information useful to viewers? How-to and consumer tips are popular.
- Does the spokesperson have viewer appeal? A celebrity may be acceptable, but there must be a natural tie-in with the organization and the topic to be discussed.
- Can the spokesperson stay on track and give succinct, concise statements? The spokesperson must stay focused and make sure that the key messages are mentioned.
- Can the spokesperson refrain from getting too commercial? Talk show hosts don't want guests who sound like an advertisement.

The contact for a talk show may be the executive producer or assistant producer of the show. If it is a network or nationally syndicated show, the contact person may have the title of *talent coordinator* or *talent executive*. Whatever the title, these people are known in the broadcasting industry as *bookers* because they are responsible for booking a constant supply of timely guests for the show. To this end, about 4,000 radio/television producers also read the *Radio/TV Interview Report*, a twice-monthly online magazine published by Bradley Communications Corp., to find guests who are listed by public relations firms and other organizations.

One common approach to placing a guest is to call the booker, briefly outline the qualifications of the proposed speaker, and state why this person would be a timely guest. Publicists also can send an e-mail telling the booker the story angle, why it's relevant to the show's audience, and why the proposed speaker is qualified to talk on the subject. Each show, however, has different preferences on how to be contacted. The production team of the *Daily Show with Jon Stewart*, for example, prefers to receive pitches by regular mail. *The Early Show* on CBS prefers e-mail.

In many cases, the booker will ask for video clips of the spokesperson on previous television shows or newspaper clips relating to press interviews. It's important to be honest about the experience and personality of the spokesperson so that the booker isn't disappointed and the public relations professional retains his or her credibility for another day.

In recent years, there has been controversy over guests who are invited because they are celebrities and have large audience appeal but who, once they get on the show, endorse various products or are paid advocates of special interests. See the Ethics box on page 438. In general, talk shows book guests three to four weeks in advance. Unless a topic or a person is extremely timely or controversial, it is rare for a person to be booked on one or two day's notice. Public relations strategists must keep this in mind as part of overall campaign planning.

Product Placements

Television's dramas and comedy shows, as well as the film industry, are good vehicles for promoting a company's products and services. It is not a coincidence that the hero of a detective series drives a Ford Fusion or that the heroine is seen boarding a United Airlines flight.

Such product placements, sometimes called *plugs*, are often negotiated by product publicists and talent agencies. This is really nothing new. *IPRA Frontline* reports, "In the early 1900s, Henry Ford had an affinity for Hollywood and perhaps it is no coincidence that his Model T's were the predominant vehicle appearing in the first motion pictures of the era."

Product placements, however, came of age with the movie *E.T.* in the early 1980s. The story goes that M&M Candies made a classic marketing mistake by not allowing the film to use M&M's as the prominently displayed trail of candy that the young hero uses to lure his big eyed friend home. Instead, Hershey's Reese's Pieces jumped at the chance, and the rest is history. Sales of Reese's Pieces skyrocketed, and even today, more than 20 years after the film's debut, the candy and *E.T.* remain forever linked in popular culture and in the minds of a whole generation of *E.T.* fans.

Since E.T. went home, product placements have proliferated in television shows and movies. Shows such as *American Idol* have recently been at the forefront of integrating products into television and have even changed the landscape of product placements by charging hefty fees for manufacturers to have their products featured.

Viewers of *American Idol* are quite familiar with product placement. Coca-Cola, for example, places branded cups in front of the judges. The world-famous Coca-Cola logo is prominently displayed as are soda bubbles. But it's not only Coke that gets into the *American Idol* product placement act. Cingular phones and text-messaging were featured on the program as was a new CD by Kenny Rogers.

In other series, clothing manufacturers and other retailers are particularly active in product placements because studies show that today's youth get most of their fashion ideas from watching television shows. This is why Buffy the Vampire Slayer wore jeans from The Gap and James Bond wore Tom Ford suites in *Skyfall*.

on the job

ETHICS

Should Television Guests Reveal Their Sponsors?

Actress Lauren Bacall, appearing on NBC's *Today*, talked about a dear friend who had gone blind from an eye disease and urged the audience to see their doctors to be tested for it. She also mentioned a drug, Visudyne, that was a new treatment for the disease.

Meanwhile, over at ABC's *Good Morning America*, actress Kathleen Turner was telling Diane Sawyer about her battle with rheumatoid arthritis and mentioned that a drug, Enbrel, helped ease the pain. A month later, Olympic gold medal skater Peggy Fleming appeared on the show to talk about cholesterol and heart disease. Near the beginning of the interview, Fleming said, "My doctor has put me on Lipitor and my cholesterol has dropped considerably."

What the viewing audience didn't know was that each of these celebrities was being paid a hefty fee by a drug company to mention its product in prime time. Spokespersons being paid to advocate a particular cause have also come under criticism. A report in *The Nation*, for example, said that numerous lobbyists and public relations experts have appeared on CNN, *Fox News*, MSNBC, and CNBC to promote the financial and political interests of an unidentified client. Fairness and Accuracy in Media (FAIR) believes broadcasters have an obligation to their audience to ensure that guests and their clients or employers are properly identified.

Do you agree? Is it only an ethics problem for broadcasters, or should public relations professionals be also concerned about the public's right to know the affiliations and special interests of spokespersons who are being placed. Should the public know that Peggy Fleming is appearing as an endorser of a product or that a political pundit is also on the payroll of a defense contractor or a health care insurance company?

Another opportunity for product exposure on television is game shows. *The Price Is Right*, for example, uses a variety of products as prizes for its contestants. In one episode, for example, the prize was a tent, a camp table and chairs, and lanterns. It was a great product placement that cost Coleman less than $200.

Branded product placements, of course, are prevalent in the movie industry. Indeed, one industry expert says brands are now funding as much as 25 percent of high-profile films such as *The Great Gatsby*. The film is a virtual fashion show for Prada, Tiffney & Co., and Brooks Brothers. Automakers are also active in product placements on television and the movies. GM cars, for about $3 million, got a starring role in *Transformers*. Public relations specialists should always be alert to opportunities for publicity on television programs and upcoming movies. If a company's service or product lends itself to a particular program, the normal procedure is to contact the show's producers directly or through an agent who specializes in matching the company products with the show's needs.

In some cases, it's a matter of mutual benefit. A television series or a film needs a resort location, for example, so a resort makes an offer to house and feed the cast in exchange for being featured on the program. At other times, it's a matter of whether Pepsi or Coke is used in the scene, and there's often a negotiated fee. A 20-second product placement in *Desperate Housewives*, at the height of its popularity, went for $400,000—about the same cost as a 30-second commercial shown during the commercial breaks. Such fees place product placement more in the category of advertising and marketing than in the category of public relations.

Issues Placement

A logical extension of product placements is convincing popular television programs to write an issue or cause into their plotlines. Writers for issue-oriented shows such as *CSI*, *ER*, and *Law & Order* are constantly bombarded with requests from a variety of nonprofit and special-interest groups.

The National Campaign to Prevent Teen Pregnancy, for example, works very hard to get the issue of teen pregnancy placed into television programming. The WB's *Seventh Heaven* included an episode in which the Camden family supported Sandy as she went into labor. In another situation, the Lewy Body Dementia Association worked with Starz Network's series, *Boss*, to tell the public about the degenerative brain disorder after the lead character, portrayed by actor Kelsey Grammer, was diagnosed with the disease.

The idea is to educate the public about a social issue or a health problem in an entertaining way. Someone once said, "It's like hiding the aspirin in the ice cream." Even the federal government works with popular television programs to write scripts that deal with the dangers and prevention of drug abuse. All of this has not escaped the notice of the drug companies; they seek opportunities for getting their products mentioned in plotlines, too.

The flip side of asking scriptwriters to include material is asking them to give a more balanced portrayal of an issue. The health care industry, for example, is concerned about balance in such programs as *ER*. The popular program deals with a variety of health issues, and, in many cases, health maintenance organizations (HMOs) are portrayed in an unfavorable light. Even the American Bar Association gets upset about the portrayal of lawyers in some series. Consequently, these organizations often meet with the program's scriptwriters to educate them about the facts so that the program is more balanced.

Ultimately, however, the programs are designed as entertainment. Scriptwriters, like newspaper editors, make their own evaluations and judgments.

DJs and Media-Sponsored Events

Another form of product placement is agreements with radio stations to promote a product or event as part of their programming. The most common example is a concert promoter giving DJs 10 tickets to a "hot" concert, which are then awarded as prizes to listeners who answer a question or call within 30 seconds.

A nonprofit group sponsoring a fund-raising festival also may make arrangements for a radio station (or television station) to cosponsor an event as part of the station's own promotional activities. This means that the station will actively promote the festival on the air through PSAs and DJ chatter between songs. The arrangement also may call for a popular DJ to broadcast live from the festival and give away T-shirts with the station's logo on them. This, too, is good promotion for the festival and the radio station, because it attracts people to the event.

The station's director of promotions or marketing often is in charge of deciding what civic events to sponsor with other groups. The station will usually agree to a certain number of promotional spots in exchange for being listed in the organization's news releases, programs, print advertising, and event banners as a sponsor of the event.

Stations will not necessarily promote or cosponsor every event. They must be convinced that their involvement will benefit the station in terms of greater public exposure, increased audience, and improved market position. Events and promotions are discussed in the next chapter.

on the job

SOCIAL MEDIA IN ACTION

Brand Journalism Extends the Reach of Television

The placement of stories on television stations and cable networks continues to be a major tactic in the tool box of a public relations professional, but organizations have also become publishers and distributors of their own content.

The concept is called *brand journalism* and *content marketing*. The idea is to create video stories in a journalistic format that will inform, entertain, and educate consumers about a product or a brand by emphasizing story telling instead of making a promotional pitch. The revolution of the Internet and the pervasive use of social media mean that organizations today are less reliant on traditional media for the effective distribution of product and brand information to audiences.

Red Bull (www.redbull.com), for example, has fully embraced brand journalism by having a website formatted as a virtual magazine with stories that appeal to its major demographic, young people with active lifestyles such as surfing, skiing, and extreme sports. Coca-Cola has also revamped its web page (www.coca-colacompany.com) into a colorful virtual magazine with articles that cover a variety of topics. Some stories posted on particular day were (1) news designs in office furniture, (2) a review of books on big data, and (3) a behind-the-scenes look at a new Coke product. There's also a daily question for readers and a bar graph showing the vote. In another application, Home Depot has posted numerous videos on how to repair things around the house, such as a toilet, or install kitchen cabinet, which in turn generates sales of its hardware and building supplies.

The Internet and social media offer several advantages over traditional media such as radio and television:

- A story segment on television appears only once. Stories posted on a digital site can be archived and is instantly searchable.
- A story on an organization's website can be easily shared through social media, such as Facebook, Twitter, YouTube, and Pinterest.
- Online stories can embed hyperlinks to more information and immediately send a reader directly to an organization's home page or even a site to buy the product.
- A story online can also include video, a gallery of photos, a slide show, and even a colorful infographic.
- Video features can be posted immediately, instead of waiting for the 6 or 10 P.M. newscast.
- An online story can be easily shared with family and friends with the flick of a button.

Summary

The Reach of Radio and Television

- In today's society, radio and television reach the vast majority of people on a daily basis.
- An average American spends about 147 hours a month watching television, which is more than the time spent with any other medium, including the Internet.

Radio

- Radio releases, unlike those for print media, must be written for the ear and should be no longer than 60 seconds.
- A popular format is the audio news release (ANR), which includes an announcer and a quote (soundbite) from a spokesperson.
- Public service announcements (PSAs) are distributed by nonprofit organizations that wish to inform and educate the public about health issues or upcoming civic events.
- PSAs should be written in various lengths to give maximum flexibility for broadcast use.
- A radio media tour (RMT) involves a spokesperson being interviewed from a central location by journalists across the country. Each journalist is able to conduct a one-on-one interview for several minutes.

Television

- The video news release (VNR) is produced in a format that television stations can easily use or edit based on their needs.
- VNRs are relatively expensive to produce, but they have great potential for reaching large audiences through television stations, websites, or even YouTube channels.
- B-rolls, the compilation of video clips and soundbites, are increasingly preferred by television news departments.
- Television PSAs must have audio and visual elements.
- Satellite media tours (SMTs) allow television newscasters to interview a spokesperson on a one-to-one basis.

- With a news feed, an organization arranges for coverage of a particular event, and television stations across the country can watch it in "real time" or receive an edited version of it for later use.

Guest Appearances

- Public relations personnel often book spokespersons on radio and television talk shows. The guest must have a good personality, be knowledgeable, and give short, concise answers.
- Booking a guest on a talk or magazine show requires a creative pitch to get a producer's attention.

Product Placements

- Companies are increasingly making deals with producers to get their products featured on television shows or movies. Nonprofit organizations also lobby to have scripts mention key health messages and deal with various social issues.
- Radio and television stations often cosponsor a civic event with an organization, which leads to increased visibility for the station and the civic organization.

Case Activity **Getting Broadcast Time for Peanut Butter**

Jif has been making peanut butter for 50 years, but this basic product isn't exactly newsworthy. Jif, however, has an idea about generating media attention by publicizing a creative peanut butter sandwich contest for children. The idea is that cooking is linked to fostering creativity among children, so the contest also encourages parents to invite their kids into the kitchen to spend some quality time together. The child chef with the winning peanut butter sandwich will receive a $25,000 college scholarship; runners-up will receive smaller scholarships.

Your public relations firm is retained to come up with some ideas for broadcast publicity and story placement. One goal is to get on a national network show such as the *Today* show. Other tactics include (1) producing a B-roll package for distribution to television stations, (2) doing a satellite media tour (SMT), and (3) getting some product placement of Jif on some television entertainment shows. Write a memo outlining your pitch to the *Today* show. In addition, give your detailed ideas about producing a B-roll and an SMT, and getting a jar of Jif on a popular television program.

Questions **For Review and Discussion**

1. Why should public relations personnel consider radio and television as major tools in reaching the public?
2. Radio news releases must be tightly written. What's the general guideline for the number of lines and words in a 30-second news release? What other guidelines should be kept in mind when writing a radio news release?
3. How does an audio news release (ANR) differ from a standard news release?
4. What are the various approaches for getting an organization's point of view on television?
5. What is a public service announcement (PSA)?
6. What is the advantage of a radio media tour (RMT) or a satellite media tour (SMT) to the organization and journalists? Are there any disadvantages?
7. What are some guidelines for a successful SMT?
8. List four ways that an organization can get its news and viewpoints on local television.
9. What are the format and characteristics of a video news release (VNR)?
10. What is a B-roll? Why is it increasingly used?
11. What's a news feed, and how is it used in public relations?
12. What makes an ideal radio or television talk show guest/spokesperson?
13. What is meant by product placements in a television program?
14. How can a PR professional attract a producer's attention in booking a guest for a talk show?
15. Is brand journalism an ethical PR practice?

Media Resources

Apgood, S. (2013, April). How to make B-roll and interviews for TV news. *O'Dwyer's PR Report*, 29.

Caan, J. (2012, November 20). How to pitch morning news shows. Retrieved from *Ragan's Daily News Feed*, www.ragan.com

Caplan, A. (2013, April). New broadcast strategies for PR pros. *O'Dwyer's PR Report*, 30.

Greene, L. (2013, May 4, 5). A great deal of Gatsby: The new film version of Fitzgerald's novel is overflowing with luxury brands. *Financial Times*, 12.

Hardwick, J. (2013, January 2). Four things every video needs to succeed. Retrieved from *Ragan's Daily Headlines,* www.ragan.com

Mance, H. (2012, June 21). Online is expanding but TV is still king. *Financial Times*, 2.

Sass, E. (2012, June 12). Time Spent on Facebook Lags TV. Retrieved from MediaPost, www.mediapost.com

Ward, D. (2012, October). Insomnia story on ABC shows wake-up call for new drug. *PRWeek*, 20.

Wilcox, D. & Reber, B. (2013). Writing for radio and television. [Chapter 9 of] *Public relations writing & media techniques*. Boston, MA: Pearson.

Wilson, M. (2013, February 15). What effect does TV's receding influence have on brands? Retrieved from *Ragan's Daily Headlines*, www.ragan.com

chapter 16

Event Management

After reading this chapter, you will be able to:

- Know the logistics of organizing a meeting
- Plan a banquet, reception, or cocktail party
- Organize an open house, exhibit, or plant tour
- Understand the multiple aspects of organizing a convention
- Recognize the basic elements of a trade show
- Think creatively about promotional events that will attract attention

A World Filled with Events

Meetings and events are vital public relations tools. Their greatest value is that they let the audience participate, face to face, in real time. In this era of digital communication and information overload, there is still a basic human need to gather, socialize, and be part of a group activity.

Individuals attending a meeting or event use all five of their senses—hearing, sight, touch, smell, and taste—so they become more emotionally involved in the process. Marketing and public relations professionals, for example, often use events to foster more brand awareness and loyalty.

> Events deliver face time between consumers and brands. They also introduce consumers to new products.
>
> *Yung Moon, associate publisher of* Self *magazine, as reported in* PRWeek

Meetings and events, of course, come in all shapes and sizes. A committee meeting of a civic club or an office staff meeting may include only four or five people. Corporate seminars may be for 50 to 250 people. At the other end of the scale is a trade show such as the Consumer Electronics Show (CES) in Las Vegas, which attracts 150,000 attendees over a three-day period. Annual membership conferences, such as that of the Public Relations Society of America (PRSA) or the International Association of Business Communicators (IABC), attract more than 2,000 attendees. The travel research firm PhoCusWright estimates that spending on U.S. corporate meetings is almost $80 billion annually.

Effective meetings and events, however, don't just happen. Detailed planning and logistics are essential to ensure that defined objectives are achieved, whether the public relations specialist is organizing a banquet, an open house, a national conference, or a trade show. Do you have what it takes? See the Insights box on page 446 that gives a job listing for an events manager.

Group Meetings

Having a meeting seems to be part of the human DNA. There are literally thousands of civic clubs, professional societies, trade associations, and hobby groups that have meetings that attract millions of people every year. In addition, many of these organizations sponsor workshops, seminars, and symposia on a regular basis.

Planning

The size and purpose of the meeting dictate the plan. Every plan must consider these questions: How many people will attend? Who will attend? When and where will the meeting be held? How long will it last? Who will speak? What topics will be covered? What facilities will be needed? Who will run it? What is its purpose? How do we get people to attend? A checklist for planning a club meeting is on page 448.

Location If the meeting is to be held on the premises of the organization, it's often necessary to reserve the room in advance with the person responsible for scheduling the room. Many firms have rooms that are made available to nonprofit groups or to employees who are hosting a meeting. A meeting in a hotel or restaurant usually requires making arrangements with the catering manager.

on the job INSIGHTS

A Job Listing for an Events Manager

Many students express an interest in event planning as a career, but being an event manager for a consumer product requires multiple skills and a variety of responsibilities. The following is an excerpt from a job posting on LinkedIn by Paramount Farms, a Los Angeles–based producer of several food brands.

Responsibilities

The Events Manager will manage and execute a consumer event program that helps build awareness for our product portfolio. The primary responsibility will be to manage a partnership with a national sports franchise consisting of over 300 events. The secondary responsibility will include management of other events including sports, entertainment, lifestyle, and epicurean properties. Events will take place in all major markets nationwide.

- Manage the promotional and administrative duties associated with the planning and implementation of sponsored special events that promote messages to targeted audiences, increase brand awareness, and drive sales.
- Create an events calendar leveraging events across different aspects of business (PR, consumer promotions, retail tie-ins, online, etc.) and assist in developing event marketing department strategies
- Identify and negotiate sponsorship and promotional opportunities and evaluate incoming sponsorship proposals
- Manage all aspects of event planning including budgets, timelines, collateral, signage, and legal review as needed
- Coordinate all event logistics on site, on-site set up of events, representation of brands, event break down, and analysis follow-up
- Develop and maintain relationships with corporate partners, vendors, and suppliers
- Develop event recap/evaluation PowerPoint template that will be used to evaluate performance at each event

Desired Skills & Experience

- Bachelor's degree, 3–5 years minimum experience in related field, and live in Los Angeles
- Experience in sports and/or event marketing, promotions
- Excellent project management skills with the ability to multi-task and work in a fast-paced environment are a must
- Experience overseeing event production/coordination and a thorough knowledge of event marketing logistics
- Strong communication and presentation skills.
- Strong interpersonal skills. Personable and professional attitude that lends itself to interacting with multiple contacts in various industries and everyday consumers
- Ability for attention to detail and adherence to deadlines, budgets
- High energy level is essential
- Creative thinker able to bring a product to life at an event
- Must be able to work non-traditional hours; many events occur at night or on weekends.
- Working knowledge of MS Office programs and social media (Facebook, Pinterest, and Twitter)

The meeting room must be the right size for the expected audience. If it is too large, the audience will feel that the meeting has failed to draw the expected attendance. If it is too small, the audience will be uncomfortable. Most hotels have a number of meeting rooms ranging in size from small to very large. Having selected

PRCasebook

Solid Promotional Strategy Makes Picasso a Hit in Seattle

All events, in order to be successful, require extensive promotion. This was crucial for the Seattle Art Museum that planned to host a major exhibition of Picasso's work on loan from the Musée National in Paris. Such an exhibition, however, posed a major challenge for the museum's public relations two-person staff to promote the exhibition to ensure that it would generate attendance and revenue.

The public relations staff began its assignment by doing some research. They first conducted an online survey of museum members to find out what key messages would be of most audience interest. The two most salient key messages were high interest in an exhibition that would display Picasso's life work and that this exhibition was a rare opportunity for citizens of the Northwest. Ten months before the exhibition, the public relations staff developed a plan that included the following:

- An in-depth Picasso media kit that included key images for the show
- Meeting with key organizations such as the Seattle Convention and Visitors Bureau, Seattle Chamber of Commerce, the mayor's office, and downtown association to discuss partnerships.
- Key messaging and media training for spokespeople
- Pre-promotional website and video with "Picasso is Coming" messages for presentations, media coverage, and social media.
- Tools (i.e., Picasso logo) and presentation materials for partners to build awareness among their own constituencies
- Strategic event and speakers bureau rollout plan

Seven months before the exhibition, the public relations staff organized a "Picasso in Seattle" luncheon for the media, VIPS, and community partners that featured the mayor of Seattle highlighting the importance of the show and its potential economic impact on the community. Four months before the show, a reception was held for 150 leaders in the hospitality and retail industries. Two months out, online initiatives were started with a Picasso website and social networking campaign. A press review was held at the opening that generated ongoing media coverage, and various "Picasso" events such as cooking demonstrations, Picasso art classes for kids, and tours for the blind kept the buzz going throughout the four-month exhibition.

All the promotional planning paid off in terms of meeting and exceeding the objectives of the campaign:

Total attendance was 405,000, setting a new record as the most highly attended exhibition in the history of the museum.

- New members, as the result of the exhibition, increased by 22,000.
- The show generated $66 million in economic impact to Washington State, including $23 million in King County.
- Media coverage was 123 million impressions, including ABC News, *Wall Street Journal*, and local media outlets.
- Facebook increased by 7,000 new fans and Twitter increased by 5,000 new followers.
- The campaign received PRSA's Silver Anvil Award for Excellence in events sponsored by a nonprofit organization.

on the job

INSIGHTS

How to Plan a Meeting

Every meeting requires its own specialized checklist, but here is a general "to do" list for a local dinner meeting of a service club or a professional association.

In Advance

- What is the purpose of the meeting?
- What date and time are best for maximum attendance?
- What size audience do you realistically expect?
- Select restaurant facility at least four to six weeks in advance.
- Confirm in writing the following: date, time, menu, cocktails, seating plan, number of guaranteed reservations, and projected costs.
- Enlist speaker four to six weeks in advance. If speaker is in high demand, make arrangements several months in advance. Discuss nature of talk, projected length, and whether audiovisual equipment will be needed.
- Publicize the meeting to the membership and other interested parties. This should be done a minimum of three weeks in advance. Provide complete information on speaker, date, time, location, meal costs, and reservation procedure.
- Organize a phone committee to call members or do an e-mail blast 72 hours before the event if reservations are lagging. A reminder phone call or e-mail is often helpful in gaining last-minute reservations.

On the Meeting Day

- Get a final count on reservations, and make an educated guess as to how many people might arrive at the door without a reservation.
- Check speaker's travel plans and last-minute questions or requirements.
- Give catering manager revised final count for meal service. In many instances, this might have to be done 24 to 72 hours in advance of the meeting day.
- Check room arrangements one to two hours in advance of the meeting. Have enough tables been set up? Are tables arranged correctly for the meeting? Does the microphone system work?
- Prepare a timetable for the evening's events. For example, cocktails may be scheduled from 6:15 to 7 P.M., with registration going on at the same time. Dinner from 7 to 8 P.M., followed by 10 minutes of announcements. At 8:10 P.M., the speaker will have 20 minutes to talk, followed by an additional 10 minutes for questions. Your organizational leaders, as well as the serving staff, should be aware of this schedule.
- Set up a registration table just inside or outside the door. A typed list of reservations should be available, as well as name tags, meal tickets, and a cash box for making change. Personnel at the registration table should be briefed and in place at least 30 minutes before the announced time.
- Decide on a seating plan for the head table, organize place cards, and tell VIPs as they arrive where they will be sitting.
- Designate three or four members of the organization as a hospitality committee to meet and greet newcomers and guests.

After the Meeting

- Settle accounts with the restaurant or indicate where an itemized bill should be mailed.
- Check the room to make sure no one forgot briefcases, handbags, eyeglasses, or other belongings.
- Send thank-you notes to the speaker and any committee members who helped plan or host the meeting.
- Prepare a summary of the speaker's comments for the organization's newsletter and, if appropriate, send a news release to local media.

a room, the public relations professional must make sure that the audience can find it. The name of the meeting and the name of the room should be registered on the hotel or restaurant's schedule of events for a particular day.

Seating A variety of seating arrangements can be used, depending on the purpose of the meeting. A monthly club meeting, for example, often features a luncheon or dinner. In this case, attendees are usually seated at round tables of six or eight, where they first have a meal and then listen to a speaker.

Seminars, designed primarily for listening, usually have what is called "theater" seating, in which rows of seats are set up facing the speakers. Such meetings may be held in theaters or auditoriums.

A workshop or a small seminar, on the other hand, may use what is called "lunch-room" seating, which has long tables with chairs on one side so that attendees can take notes or set up laptop computers. WiFi access should also be considered. A monitor is often used to display tweets and comments from the audience.

Occasionally, large meetings are broken into discussion groups. Typically, the audience starts in one large room, where a speaker gives information and states a problem. The audience then moves into another room, or set of rooms, where round tables seating 8 or 10 people are available. A discussion leader is designated for each table. After the problem has been discussed, the leaders gather the opinions and the audience returns to the first room, where reports from each group are given to the entire assembly.

Facilities A small meeting may not need much in the way of facilities, whereas a large and formal one may require a considerable amount of equipment and furnishings. Following are things that should be considered—and supplied if needed. The public relations person should check everything one or two hours before the meeting.

- **Meeting identification.** Is it posted on the bulletin board near the building entrance? Are directional signs needed?
- **Lighting.** Is it adequate? Can it be controlled? Where are the controls? Who will handle them?
- **Charts.** Are they readable? Is the easel adequate? Who will handle the charts?
- **Screen or monitors.** Are they large enough for the size of the audience?
- **Microphones, projectors, and video equipment.** Are they hooked up and working? Who should be contacted at the facility if there are technical difficulties?
- **Seating and tables.** Are there enough seats for the audience expected? Are they arranged properly for a clear view of the stage or podium?
- **Wiring.** For all electrical equipment, can wires be kicked loose or trip someone?
- **Speaker's podium.** Is it positioned properly? What about a reading light?
- **Water and glasses.** For speakers? For audience?
- **Audience and speaker aids.** Are there programs or agendas? Will there be notepaper, pencils, and handout materials?
- **Name tags.** For speakers? For all attendees?

Invitations For clubs, an announcement in the newsletter, a flyer, or an e-mail should be adequate. For external groups—people who are not required to attend but whose presence is desired—invitations via the mail or e-mail are necessary.

They should go out early enough for people to fit the meeting into their schedules—three to six weeks is a common lead time.

The invitation should tell the time, day, date, place (including the name of the room), purpose, highlights of the program (including names of speakers), and a way for the person to RSVP. This may be a telephone number, an e-mail address, a reply card to mail back to the event's organizers, or even the Web address of an online registration service that handles everything from making the reservation to processing the credit card information to pay for the event. Using an online reservation service is discussed further in the section on conferences and conventions. A map showing the location and parking facilities is advisable if the facility is not widely known.

Registration

If everyone knows everyone else, registration and identification can be highly informal, but if the group is large, it is customary to have a registration desk or table at the entrance of the room. Here the names of arrivals are checked against lists of individuals who said they would attend. Many clubs that have name badges for members now have bar codes embedded so a simple scan compiles a list of those attending.

Greeting A representative of the sponsoring organization should be at the entrance of the room. If the number attending is not large, a personal welcome is in order. This isn't possible when hundreds of people are expected, but the chairperson should greet the audience in his or her opening remarks.

Name Tags Name tags are a good idea at almost any meeting. The public relations person should use label-making software to prepare name tags for everyone with advance reservations. Names should be printed in bold, large block letters so that they can be read easily from a distance of four feet. If the person's affiliation is used, this can appear in smaller bold letters.

For people showing up without advance registration, felt-tip pens can be made available to create on-the-spot name tags. However, a nice touch is to designate one person at the registration desk to make these tags so that they look neat and consistent. Another approach is to use a software program and print out name tags. Most tags are self-adhesive. Plastic badges with clamps or a chain are popular for large meetings such as conventions.

Program

At any meeting, the word *program* has two meanings. It is what goes on at the meeting, and it is also the printed listing of what goes on.

The meeting must have a purpose. To serve that purpose, it is necessary to have a chairperson who controls and directs the meeting, introduces the speakers, and keeps discussions from wandering. It is also necessary to have speakers who will inform, persuade, or motivate the listeners.

The printed program that is handed out to the audience in a workshop or seminar tells them what is going to happen, when, and where. It lists all the speakers, the time they will speak, coffee breaks, lunch breaks, and any other facts attendees should know about the meeting. Because speakers may have last-minute changes in their plans, the programs should not be printed until the last possible moment.

Speakers Select speakers several months in advance, if possible. They should be chosen because of their expertise, their crowd-drawing capacity, and their speaking ability. It is a good idea to listen to any prospective speaker before tendering an invitation, or at least to discuss the intention with someone who has heard the person speak before. Many prominent people are simply not effective speakers.

When a speaker has agreed to give a talk, it is essential to make sure that the speaker has all the information he or she needs to prepare remarks and get to the meeting. A thorough briefing will do much to ensure that the speaker will deliver a relevant talk and meet the expectations of the meeting's organizers.

Meals Club meetings and workshops often occur at a mealtime. In fact, many meetings include breakfast, lunch, or dinner.

Early morning breakfast meetings have the advantage of attracting people who cannot take the time during the day to attend such functions. A full breakfast, served buffet style, is a popular choice because it allows everyone to select what he or she normally eats for breakfast. People attending a half-day or full-day workshop often partake of a self-serve continental breakfast—rolls, juice, and coffee—during the registration period just prior to the start of the meeting.

Luncheons are either sit-down affairs with a fixed menu or a buffet. A 30- to 45-minute cocktail period may precede a luncheon, usually during registration as guests arrive. A good schedule for a typical luncheon is registration at 11:30 A.M., luncheon at 12 noon, and adjournment at 1:30. In rare instances, the adjournment can be as late as 2 P.M., but it should never be later than that.

Dinner meetings are handled in much the same way as luncheons. A typical schedule is registration and cocktails at 6 P.M., dinner at 7 P.M., speaker at 8 P.M., and adjournment between 8:30 and 9 P.M. A speaker should limit his or her remarks to 20 or 30 minutes; after that, attendees get restless.

The public relations person will need to have an accurate count of people who will attend a meal function. The hotel or restaurant facility will need a count at least 24 hours in advance to prepare the food and set up table service. The standard practice is for the organization to guarantee a certain number of meals, plus or minus 10 percent. If fewer than what is guaranteed show up, the organization still pays for the meals.

Banquets

Banquets, by definition, are fairly large and formal functions held to honor an individual, raise money for a charitable organization, or celebrate an event such as an organization's anniversary. Because they are in the category of a "special" event, they require a well-designed invitation package that is mailed to prospective guests. Following is a sample invitation.

A banquet may have 100 or 1,000 people in attendance, and staging a successful one takes a great deal of planning. The budget, in particular, needs close attention. A banquet coordinator has to consider such factors as (1) food, (2) room rental, (3) bartenders, (4) decorations and table centerpieces, (5) audiovisual requirements, (6) speaker fees, (7) entertainment, (8) photographers, (9) invitations, (10) tickets, and (11) marketing and promotion. Major fund-raising galas have additional logistics in terms of generating attendance and donations. A behind-the-scenes look at a fund-raising event is highlighted in the Insights box on page 453.

Sample Invitation

Attractive, well-designed invitations are necessary for banquets and other "special" occasions. Reply cards must be attached, often with a self-addressed envelope, so that attendees can register their names, meal preferences, and credit card information. This invitation was prepared by History San José for an event to honor individuals for their service and contributions to the community.

All these components, of course, must be factored into establishing the per-ticket cost of the event. The attendees are paying $75 to $100 not just for the traditional rubber chicken dinner but for the total cost of staging the event. If the purpose is to raise money for a worthy charitable organization or political candidate, tickets might go for $100 to $250. The actual price, of course, depends on how fancy the banquet is and how much the organization is paying for the speaker. See the Insights box on page 453 for a checklist on how to prepare a budget for a special event.

A well-known personality as a banquet speaker usually helps ticket sales, but it can also be a major expense in the budget. Karen Kendig, president of the Speaker's Network, told *PR Tactics* that the going rate is $3,000 to $10,000 for "bread and butter," business-type talks, $15,000 and up for entertainment celebrities, and $50,000 to $60,000 for well-known politicians. A number of firms, such as the Washington Speaker's Bureau and the Harry Walker Agency, represent celebrity speakers.

Such fees cannot be fully absorbed into the cost of an individual ticket, so in addition to sending out individual invitations, there usually is a committee that personally asks corporations and other businesses to underwrite the event and buy a table for employees, clients, or friends. A corporate table of eight, for example, may go for $25,000 or more, depending on the prestige and purpose of the event. Many local organizations, to minimize speaker cost and maximize fund-raising for a good cause, avoid outside speakers and use a prominent local person, such as the CEO of a major company, to give an address. At other times, the event is primarily a dinner dance and no speaker is necessary.

on the job INSIGHTS

Making a Budget for a Banquet

All events have two sides of the ledger: costs and revenues. It is important to prepare a detailed budget so that you know exactly how much an event will cost. This will enable you to also figure out how much you will need to charge so that you at least break even. Here are some items that you need to consider:

Facilities

Rental of meeting or reception rooms

Set up of podiums, microphones, audiovisual equipment

Food Service

Number of meals to be served

Cost per person

Gratuities

Refreshments for breaks

Bartenders for cocktail hours

Wine, liquor, soft drinks

Decorations

Table decorations

Direction signs

Design and Printing

Invitations

Programs

Tickets

Name tags

Promotional flyers

Postage

Postage for invitations

Mailing house charges

Recognition Items

Awards, plaques, trophies

Engraving

Framing

Calligraphy

Miscellaneous

VIP travel and expenses

Speaker fees

Security

Transportation

Buses

Vans

Parking

Entertainment

Fees

Publicity

Advertising

News releases

Banners

Postage

Office Expenses

Phones

Supplies

Complimentary tickets

Staff travel and expenses

Data processing

Working with Catering Managers

When organizing a banquet, the public relations staff usually contacts the catering or banquet manager of the restaurant or hotel at least three or four months before the event. He or she will discuss menus, room facilities, availability of space, and a host of other items to determine exactly what the banquet needs.

Hotels and restaurants have special menus for banquets, which are often subject to some negotiation. If the banquet will be held during the week, for example, the restaurant or hotel might be willing to give more favorable rates because weeknights aren't ordinarily booked. However, if the organization insists on having a banquet on a Friday or Saturday night—which is the most popular time—it can expect to pay full rates.

A banquet usually has a fixed menu, but a vegetarian dish should be available to those who request it. In general, a popular choice for a meat entree is beef, chicken, or fish. Offering two entrees requires the extra work of providing coded tickets for the waiters, and the hotel or restaurant may charge more for the meal. The public relations specialist should get the catering manager's advice before ordering multiple entrees.

When figuring food costs, many amateur planners forget about tax and gratuity, which can add 25 percent or more to any final bill. That $25 chicken dinner on the menu is really $30.75 if tax and gratuity add up to 23 percent. In addition, there are corkage fees if the planner provides the liquor or wine. In many establishments, corkage fees are set rather high to discourage people from bringing their own refreshment. At one banquet, for example, the organizers thought it was a great coup to have the wine donated, only to find out that the hotel charged a corkage fee of $20 per bottle.

Logistics and Timing

Organizing a banquet requires considerable logistics, timing, and teamwork. First, it's necessary to establish a timeline for the entire process—from contacting catering managers to sending out invitations and lining up a speaker. Second, a detailed timeline for the several days or day of the event is also needed to ensure that everything is in place. A third timeline is needed for the event itself so that it begins and ends at a reasonable time. A good example of a banquet timeline is shown in Figure 16.1.

In addition, the public relations planner needs to work out the logistics to ensure that registration lines are kept to a minimum and everyone is assigned to a table. Table numbers must be highly visible. If the group is particularly large (1,000 or more), it's a good idea to provide a large seating chart so that people can locate where their seats are. Another, more personalized approach is to have staff inside the hall directing people to their seats.

Post-event evaluation is also needed to assess the success and effectiveness of the efforts. See the Insights box on page 456.

Receptions and Cocktail Parties

A short cocktail hour, as mentioned previously, can precede the start of a club's luncheon or dinner. It can also be part of a reception. Its purpose is to have people socialize; it also is a cost-effective way to celebrate an organization's or an individual's achievement, to introduce a new chief executive to the employees and the community, or simply to allow college alumni to get together.

In any event, the focus should be on interaction, not speeches. If there is a ceremony or speech, it should last a maximum of 5 to 10 minutes.

A reception lasts up to two hours, and the typical layout is a large room where most people stand instead of sit. This facilitates social interaction and allows people to move freely around the room. Such gatherings, like any other event, require advance planning and logistics.

> Don't make a lengthy presentation part of an event. You'll lose the attendees' attention.
>
> *Erica Iacono, reporter for* PRWeek

CONSERVATION AWARDS BANQUET
JW MARRIOTT HOTEL
WASHINGTON, DC
WEDNESDAY, MAY 13

Crew Agenda

3:30 – 5:00 p.m.	Program agenda review–participants and staff only. Live run-through of C. Ghylin's remarks. (Grand Ballroom)
5:00 – 6:00	Private pre-reception for honorees, judges, staff. Honoree photo session including E. Zern and J. Sullivan. (Suite 1231)
6:30 – 7:15	Greetings and reception, open bar. Photo opportunities available. (Grand Ballroom Foyer)
7:15 – 7:30	Close bar, enter Grand Ballroom.
7:30 – 7:35	C. Ghylin: Welcome and opening remarks.
7:30 – 8:20	Dinner served.
8:20 – 8:25	C. Ghylin: Introduces special guests at head table, introduces E. Zern.
8:25 – 8:30	E. Zern: Welcome, honoree toast, introduces judges, completes remarks.
8:30 – 8:35	C. Ghylin: Introduces J. Sullivan.
8:35 – 8:45	J. Sullivan: Remarks.
8:45 – 8:50	C. Ghylin: Introduces slide presentation.
8:50 – 9:25	Slide presentation. (C. Ghylin remains at podium) (a) Introduces/explains honoree category; (b) Comments on professionals. Introduces/explains honoree category. (c) Comments on citizens. Introduces/explains organizations' honoree category.
9:25 – 9:40	C. Ghylin: Comments on organizations. Invites J. Sullivan and E. Zern for plaque presentation. Plaque presentation.
9:40 – 9:45	C. Ghylin: Final remarks.
9:45 p.m	America the Beautiful.

Figure 16.1
Event Timeline

The compilation of a timeline, and going over it with the master of ceremonies, helps keep the event on schedule.

It is important, for example, that food be served in the form of appetizers, sandwiches, cheese trays, nuts, and chips. People get hungry, and food helps offset some effects of drinking. The bar is the centerpiece of any reception, but there should be plenty of nonalcoholic beverages available, too. Urns of coffee, punch, and tea should be readily available in other locations around the room.

Such precautions will limit the organizer's liability if someone does get drunk and is involved in an accident on the way home. Liability can also be limited if there is a *no-host bar*, which means that guests buy their own drinks.

Most receptions, however, have a *hosted bar*, meaning that drinks are free. This is particularly true when a corporation is hosting the cocktail party or reception for journalists, customers, or community leaders. In every case, it is important that bartenders be trained to spot individuals who appear to be under the influence of alcohol and to politely suggest a nonalcoholic alternative.

Organizations also try to control the level of drinking by offering only beer or wine instead of hard liquor. Still others issue one or two free drink tickets to arriving

on the job INSIGHTS

Asking the Right Questions After an Event

Post-event analysis is important to determine the success of an event from the standpoint of what worked, and what lessons can be learned for planning the next event. The following diagnostic chart, compiled by Bruce Jeffries-Fox of measurement firm KD Paine and Partners, provides a good starting point.

EVENT COMPONENT	DIAGNOSTIC QUESTIONS
Publicity	Did the event receive substantial coverage among your target public? Was the coverage of your event accurate? Did the coverage contain your key messages? Was the coverage favorable? Was the coverage cited by survey respondents as a substantial source of awareness of your event?
The event experience	Did adequate numbers of people attend your event? Were your event's attendees aware of your sponsorship? Did attendees enjoy the event?
Influence on attitudes, perceptions, purchase intent, etc.	Did your event have a positive impact on these? Were there any unexpected negative impacts?
The event as a whole	Was your event cost effective? Did your event take up more resources than expected? Did your event have positive impacts that you hadn't anticipated?

guests, with the understanding that they will need to pay for additional drinks. This also limits the cost of the reception for the organizers.

A reception, like a meal function, requires the planner to talk with the catering manager to order the finger food and decide how many bartenders are needed. As a rule of thumb, there should be one bartender per 75 people. For large events, bars are situated in several locations around the room to disperse the crowd and shorten lines.

It is also important to find out how the facility will bill for beverages consumed. If the arrangement is by the bottle, bartenders have a tendency to be very generous in pouring drinks because more empty bottles mean higher profits for the caterer.

Starting a cocktail party is easy—just open the bar at the announced time. Closing a party is not so easy. The invitation should give a definite time for the reception to end, but the planner should not assume that people will be ready to leave at the stated ending time. Toward the end of the cocktail party, particularly if the crowd is in a celebratory mood, a vocal announcement may be needed. The smoothest tactic is to say, "The bar will close in 10 minutes." This gives guests a chance to get one more drink. It's also important to ensure that the bartender closes the bar at the designated ending time of the cocktail party.

Open Houses and Plant Tours

Open houses and plant tours are conducted primarily to develop favorable public opinion about an organization. Generally, they are planned to show the facilities where the organization does its work and, in plant tours, how the work is done. A factory might have a plant tour to show how it turns raw materials into finished products. A hospital open house could show its emergency facilities, diagnostic equipment, operating rooms, and patient rooms.

Open houses are customarily one-day affairs. Attendance is usually by invitation, but in other instances, the event is announced in the general media, and anyone who chooses to attend may do so. This is particularly relevant when there is an open house to view a traveling exhibit of some kind.

Many plants offer daily tours on a regular schedule while the plant is in operation. These tours are most common among producers of consumer goods such as beer, wine, food products, clothing, and small appliances. These daily tours are geared to handle only a few people at any one time, whereas open houses generally have a large number of guests, and normal operations are thus not feasible during the tour.

Since the purpose of an open house or a plant tour is to create favorable opinion about the organization, the tour must be carefully planned, thoroughly explained, and smoothly conducted. The visitors must understand what they are seeing. This requires careful routing, control to prevent congestion, signs, and guides. All employees should understand the purpose of the event and be thoroughly coached in their duties.

The following are major factors to consider in planning an open house:

- **Day and hour.** The time must be convenient for both the organization and the guests.
- **Guests.** These may be families of employees, customers, representatives of the community, suppliers and competitors, reporters, or others whose goodwill is desirable.
- **Publicity and invitations.** These materials should be distributed at least a month before the event.
- **Vehicles.** Parking must be available, and there should be a map on the invitation showing how to get there and where to park.
- **Reception.** A representative of the organization should meet and greet all arriving guests. If guests are important people, they should meet the top officials of the organization.
- **Focal point of activity.** An area should be designated for exhibits, product demonstrations, or even entertainment acts for children and adults.
- **Restrooms.** If a large crowd is expected, portable toilets should be arranged to supplement the regular facilities.
- **Safety.** Hazards should be conspicuously marked and well lighted. Dangerous equipment should be barricaded.
- **Routing.** Routes should be well marked and logical (in a factory, the route should go from raw materials through production steps to the finished product). A map should be given to each visitor if the route is long or complicated.

- **Guides.** Tours should be led by trained guides who have a thorough knowledge of the organization and can explain in detail what visitors are seeing on the tour.
- **Explanation.** Signs, charts, and diagrams may be necessary at any point to supplement the words of the guides. The guides must be coached to say exactly what the public should be told. Many experts can't explain what they do, so a prepared explanation is necessary.
- **Housekeeping and attire.** The premises should be as clean as possible. Attire should be clean and appropriate. A punch press operator doesn't wear a necktie, but his overalls need not be greasy.
- **Emergencies.** Accidents or illness may occur. All employees should know what to do and how to request appropriate medical assistance.

Conventions

A convention is a series of meetings, usually spread over two or more days. Its purpose is to gather and exchange information, meet other people with similar interests, discuss and act on common problems, and enjoy recreation and social interchange.

Most conventions are held by national membership groups and trade associations. Because the membership is widespread, a convention is nearly always "out of town" for many attendees, so convention arrangements must give consideration to this.

Planning

It is necessary to begin planning far in advance of the actual event. Planning for even the smallest convention should start months before the scheduled date; for large national conventions, it may begin several years ahead and require hundreds or thousands of hours of work. The main components in planning a convention are (1) timing, (2) location, (3) facilities, (4) exhibits, (5) program, (6) recreation, (7) attendance, and (8) administration.

Timing The time of the convention must be convenient for the people who are expected to attend. Avoid peak work periods. Summer vacation is appropriate for educators, and after harvest is suitable for farmers. Preholiday periods are bad for retailers, and mid-winter is probably a poor time in the northern states but may be very good in the South. Here, as in every other area dealing with the public, it is imperative to know the audience and to plan for their convenience.

Location As real estate agents say, location, location, location. A national convention can be anywhere in the country, but one in Fairbanks, Alaska, is unlikely to be successful; yet one in Honolulu or New Orleans could be a great success because the glamour of the location would outweigh the cost and time of travel. Many organizations rotate their conventions from one part of the state, region, or country to another to equalize travel burdens.

Another factor in choosing a location is availability of accommodations. There must be enough rooms to house the attendees and enough meeting rooms of the right size. Timing enters into this, because many such accommodations are booked months or even years in advance. Large cities usually have large convention facilities and numerous hotels, but early reservations are necessary for such popular cities as San Francisco, New York, New Orleans, San Diego, and Las Vegas. The premier location for large conventions and trade shows is Las Vegas, which has a total of 140,000 hotel rooms. Once a tentative location has been selected, the planner must find out if the convention can be handled at the time chosen. Early action on this can forestall later changes. The planner must be sure to get a definite price on guest rooms as well as meeting rooms.

Small conventions are often held in resorts, but accessibility is a factor. If the visitors have to change airlines several times or if the location is hard to reach by automobile, the locale's glamour may fail to compensate for the inconvenience.

Facilities For every meeting of the convention, it is necessary to have a room of the right size and the equipment needed for whatever is to go on in that room. The convention might start with a general meeting in a large ballroom, where seating is theater fashion and the equipment consists of a public address system and a speaker's platform with large video monitors. After opening remarks, the convention might break into smaller groups that meet in different rooms set up for different speakers.

One speaker may require a computer projector; another may need a whiteboard or an easel for charts; still another may need Internet access. In one room the seating may be around conference tables; another may have theater seating. To get everything right, the planner must know in advance exactly what the speaker needs, who is going to participate, and when.

The Exhibit Area for a Book Expo

Conventions attract millions of attendees every year who belong to professional groups, trade groups, nonprofits, and a host of hobby-activity organizations.

Exhibits The makers and sellers of supplies that are used by people attending conventions frequently want to show their wares. This means that the convention manager must provide space suitable for that purpose. Most large convention centers have facilities that can accommodate anything from books to bulldozers. There is a charge for the use of these rooms, and the exhibitors pay for the space they use.

The exhibit hall may be in the hotel where the convention is being held or in a separate building. For example, McCormick Place is an enormous building on the Chicago lakefront. It is an easy taxi trip from the Loop, where conventions are usually based and where the visitors sleep. Eating facilities, ranging from hot dog stands to elaborate dining rooms, can be found in almost any such building. Exhibits will be covered in more detail when trade shows are discussed.

Program

A convention program usually has a basic theme. Aside from transacting the necessary organizational business, most of the speeches and other sessions will be devoted to various aspects of the theme. Themes can range from the specific "New Developments in AIDS Research" to the more general "Quality Management and Productivity." Some groups use an even broader theme such as "Connections" or "At the Crossroads."

With a theme chosen, the developer of the program looks for prominent speakers who have something significant to say on a particular topic. In addition, there may be a need for discussions, workshops, and other sessions focusing on particular aspects of the general theme.

The printed program for the convention is the schedule, which tells exactly when every session will be, what room it will be in, and who will speak on what subject. Large conventions often schedule different sessions at the same time. Attendees then choose which session they prefer.

Ideally, the program schedule should be small enough to fit in a pocket or a handbag. Large programs may look impressive, but they are cumbersome to hold on to and easy to misplace. One compromise is to give attendees a large program, which contains paid advertising, at registration but to also include a tear-out "crib" sheet that summarizes the time and location of the major presentations. If the convention is on multiple floors of a hotel or convention center, it's also a good idea to provide a floor plan so that attendees can easily find the various meeting rooms. Printing of the program should be delayed until the last possible moment because last-minute changes and speaker defaults are common. Increasingly popular is placing the entire program on an app that people can access on their smartphones.

Recreation and Entertainment This is a feature of practically all conventions and may range from informal get-togethers to formal dances. Cocktail parties, golf tournaments, sightseeing tours, and free time are among the possibilities. Sometimes recreational events are planned to coincide with regular program sessions, for spouses and delegates who would rather relax than listen to a speaker. Evening receptions and dinners at interesting venues such as an art gallery or museum are often planned for both attendees and their significant others.

Attendance Getting people to attend a convention requires two things: (1) an appealing program and (2) a concerted effort to persuade members to attend.

Announcements and invitations should go out several months in advance, to allow attendees to make their individual arrangements. A second and even a third mailing often are sent in the weeks preceding the convention. Reply cards should be provided, accompanied by hotel reservation forms. Many corporations and organizations now use specialty firms such as *cvent* that prepare digital invitations and provide event management tools. See the Social Media in Action box below about using Web-based invitation services.

Administration Managing a convention is a strenuous job. The organization staff is likely to see very little of the program and few delegates. Among the things that must be done are arranging for buses to convey delegates from the airport to the convention (if it is in a remote location) and to take delegates on tours. Meeting speakers and getting them to the right place at the right time is another task.

People arriving at the convention headquarters must be met, registered, and provided with all the essentials (name tags, programs, and any other needed materials). Special arrangements should be made for the media. A small convention may interest only a few people from trade publications, but larger conventions may draw attention from the major media. In this case, a newsroom should be set up with telephones, fax machines, Internet access, and other needed equipment. Newsrooms are further discussed in the next section, on trade shows.

on the job

SOCIAL MEDIA IN ACTION

Making Reservations on the Web

The digital age has made event planning more precise. A number of companies now offer event planners the ability to send invitations via the Internet and to also track the response rate.

E-mail invitations are used for any number of organizational meetings and corporate events, including college students having a party to celebrate their 21st birthday. E-mail invitations, according to *cvent* (www.cvent.com), a firm offering such services, should have eye-catching graphics, an effective subject line, and relevant content such as the five Ws and H.

Most individuals just concern themselves with generating a list of Yes, No, and Maybe answers, but clubs and professional or trade groups often bundle the e-mail invitation with software that enables attendees to pay registration fees online, reserve a hotel room, and even book a flight. According to *cvent*, event planners can achieve up to three times the standard response rate by integrating e-mail, direct mail, and phone calling campaigns.

Meeting planners like the capabilities of software programs and online systems that allow them to manage an entire event. StarCite and *cvent*, for example, offer a variety of meeting management services—from gathering hotel bids to sending electronic invitations and tracking registrations online. Software can even compile data on the reasons individuals aren't coming to the event—which may help in planning future meetings. Other management tools allow groups to track the flow of registrations. If registrations are lagging, it's a signal to send another round of e-mails and direct mail to bolster attendance. You can even track attendance at various sessions.

Trade Shows

Trade shows are the ultimate marketing event. According to *Tradeshow Week* magazine, about 6,000 trade shows are held annually in the United States. They range in size from more than 100,000 attendees to those in very specialized industries, which attract only several thousand people. It is estimated that about 65 million people attend trade shows on an annual basis.

The CES, sponsored by the Consumer Electronics Association, illustrates the power and influence of a trade show. The show, open only to industry professionals, attracts 150,000 attendees and 5,000 journalists to the Las Vegas Convention Center every January. Almost 3,000 companies show their new consumer products, taking up about 2 million square feet of exhibit space. Some new products introduced at the 2014 show were smartwatches, 3D printers, curved high-definition TVs, and the latest advances in driver-less cars.

Exhibit Booths

Although food and entertainment costs are high, the major expense at a trade show is the exhibit booth. At national trade shows, it is not unusual for a basic booth to start at $50,000, including design, construction, transportation, and space rental fees. Larger, more elaborate booths can easily cost between $500,000 and $1 million.

Any booth or exhibit should be designed for maximum visibility. Experts say booths have about 10 seconds to attract a visitor as he or she walks down an aisle of booths. Consequently, companies try to out dazzle each other in booth designs. An HP exhibit booth at a trade show in Geneva, for example, contained 56 tons of steel and 20 tons of glass, and 1,000 meters of neon.

Not every company has the resources of HP, but here are some points to keep in mind for planning an exhibit booth:

- Select the appropriate trade shows that have the best potential for developing contacts and generating future sales.
- Start planning and developing the exhibit 6 to 12 months in advance. Exhibit designers and builders need time to develop a booth.
- Make the display or booth visually attractive. Use bright colors, large signs, and working models of products.
- Think about putting action in the display. Have a video or slide presentation running all the time.
- Use involvement techniques. Have a contest or raffle in which visitors can win a prize. An exhibitor at one show even offered free foot massages.
- Give people an opportunity to operate equipment or do something.
- Have knowledgeable, personable representatives on duty to answer questions and collect visitor business cards for follow-up.
- Offer useful souvenirs. A key chain, a shopping bag, a luggage tag, a flash drive, or even a copy of a popular newspaper or magazine will attract traffic.
- Promote your exhibit in advance. Send announcements to potential customers and media kits to selected journalists four to six weeks before the trade show.

Most organizations feel that the large investment in a booth at a trade show is worthwhile for two reasons. First, a trade show facilitates one-on-one communication

Trade Shows Attract Millions of People
They provide an opportunity to see new products from a number of companies, generate sales leads, and attract media coverage. The CES in Las Vegas attracts 150,000 industry professionals and 5,000 journalists every January.

with potential customers and helps generate sales leads. It also attracts many journalists, so it is easier and more efficient to provide press materials, arrange one-on-one interviews, and demonstrate what makes the product worth a story. Second, a booth allows an exhibitor to demonstrate how its products differ from the competition. This is more effective than just sending prospects a color brochure. It also is more cost-effective than making individual sales calls.

Hospitality Suites

Hospitality suites are an adjunct to the exhibit booth. Organizations use them to entertain key prospects, give more in-depth presentations, and talk about business deals.

The idea is that serious customers will stay in a hospitality suite long enough to hear an entire presentation, whereas they are likely to stop at an exhibit hall booth for only a few minutes. Although goodwill can be gained from free concerts and cocktail parties, the primary purpose of a hospitality suite is to generate leads that ultimately result in product sales.

Pressrooms and Media Relations

Large numbers of journalists usually cover national trade show, so a pressroom is necessary to facilitate their work. It's a central location where various exhibitors distribute media kits (usually in digital form) and other information to journalists. Pressrooms typically have phone, fax, and Internet for reporters to file stories.

For people to pay attention at a trade show, you need real news.

David Rich, SVP of the George P. Johnson marketing company, as reported in PRWeek

An important task of company public relations staffs is to personally contact reporters several weeks before a trade show to offer product briefings and one-on-one interviews with key executives. The competition is intense, so the staff members have to be creative in pitching ideas and showing why their client's products or services merit the journalist's time when multiple other companies are also pitching them.

A survey by Access Communications, for example, found that more than 90 percent of journalists assigned to a trade show want to hear about the company and product news before the show even starts. In other words, the media relations work starts before the show; it continues throughout the show, and then the public relations specialist has to do follow-up with reporters to provide additional information.

Sarah Skerik, director of trade show markets for *PR Newswire*, provides some additional tips for working with the media during a trade show:

- Plan major product announcements to coincide with the show.
- Include the name of the trade show in your news releases so that journalists searching databases can log on using the show as a keyword.
- Include your booth number in all releases and announcements.
- Make it easy for journalists to track down key spokespeople and experts connected with your product by including cell phone, pager, and e-mail addresses in your materials.
- Have your spokespeople trained to make brief presentations and equip them with answers to the most likely asked questions.
- Consider a looped video to run in the booth with copies available to the media.
- Provide photos that show the product in use, in production, or in development.
- Provide online corporate logos, product photos, executive profiles, media kits, and PowerPoint presentations to those journalists who cannot attend or who prefer to lighten their suitcase by having everything in digital format.
- Keep hard copies of news releases, fact sheets, and brochures at the booth and in the pressroom.

Promotional Events

Promotional events are planned primarily to promote a product, increase organizational visibility, make friends, and raise money for a charitable cause. There is also the category of corporate event sponsorship, which is highlighted in the Insights box on page 468.

The one essential skill for organizing promotional events is creativity. There are multiple "ho hum" events that compete for media attention and even attendance in every city, so it behooves the public relations professional to come up with something "different" that creates buzz and interest. A sampling of different, creative events is on page 467.

Grand openings of stores or hotels, however, can be pretty dull and generate a collective yawn from almost every journalist in town, let alone all the chamber of commerce types that attend such functions. So how do public relations professionals come up with something new and different instead of the same old thing? First, they throw out the old idea of having a ribbon cutting. Second, they start thinking about a theme or idea that fits the situation and is out of the ordinary.

It's ordinary, for example, to boost Florida tourism in northern cities during the winter months, but the Fort Lauderdale Convention & Visitor's Bureau took a more creative approach. Its event, on the streets of New York, Toronto, and London, was to have swimsuits encased in blocks of ice with the theme "Defrost Your Swimsuit." Branded ice scrappers were given out to pedestrians to chip away at the ice blocks while beach music played in the background. A smartphone app was provided, and various contests that engaged people. The result was more than 100 media placements and probably a number of people who decided to defrost their own swimsuit and head to Florida.

Events bring you face-to-face with your customer and can often serve as qualifying tools in reaching decision makers. Most often, the individuals that attend events are there by choice.

Jennifer Collins, Event Planning Group, as quoted in PRWeek

Using Celebrities to Attract Attendance

Hiring a celebrity or "personality," as they are called in the trade, is not exactly the most creative solution to every situation, but it's a time-honored way to increase the odds that the media will cover the event, because "prominence" is considered a basic news value.

The creative part is figuring out what "personality" fits the particular product or situation. A national conference on climate change attracted attendees because Al Gore was a major speaker. Unilver, on the other hand, wanted to reach a Hispanic audience through a series of events promoting its Suave and Caress brands, so the company tapped celebrity stylist Leonardo Rocco and popular singer Blanca Soto to give hair and beauty advice to women attending the events. See Chapter 6 for a summary of this campaign.

One source for finding celebrities for promotional events is Celebrity Source (www.celebritysource.com). It matches requests with the 4,500 names in its database and handles all the details of negotiating fees, expenses, and transportation logistics for the organization. The value of a firm such as Celebrity Source or Celebrity Access (www.celebrityaccess.com) is that they have regular contact with celebrities' business agents and publicists. An organization trying to figure out whom to contact for a particular celebrity, let alone how to contact that person, may have less success.

Celebrity Source, on its website, gives some tips on what the firm needs to know in order to select the right celebrity for the event. The following is a good checklist if an organization is thinking about using a celebrity:

- What exactly do you want the celebrity to do?
- Who do you want to appeal to by having a celebrity? Is it the public, the media, or the sponsors?
- What do you want to accomplish by having a celebrity participate? Sell tickets or add glamour?
- What are the demographics of your audience or attendees?
- What is your budget?
- What is the maximum that you're willing to spend for the right celebrity?

- Are you prepared to pay for first-class expenses for the celebrity and at least one staff person?
- Do you have access to any perks or gifts that will help motivate the celebrity to say "yes"?

A personality, however, can be a major budget item. Stars Justin Timberlake and Jennifer Lopez typically charge $100,000 for an appearance. At the $50,000 level, a planner can book basketball player Charles Barkley, actor Angela Bassett, or tennis star Anna Kournikova. If the budget isn't big enough for that, the planner has to make do with what the business calls the "up and coming" or the "down and going." A star of a popular television program can be booked for $10,000, and a soap opera star gets about $5,000 to $10,000 for an appearance. Such fees are the primary reason events using celebrities are usually underwritten by corporations.

Planning and Logistics

Promotional events that attract large crowds require the same planning as an open house. The public relations specialist should be concerned about traffic flow, adequate restroom facilities, signage, and security. Professionally trained security personnel should also be arranged to handle crowd control, protect celebrities or government officials from being hassled, and make sure no disruptions occur to mar the event.

Liability insurance is a necessity, too. Any public event sponsored by an organization should be insured, just in case there is an accident and a subsequent lawsuit charging negligence. If the organization doesn't already have a blanket liability policy, the planner should get one for the event.

Security at public events is a significant aspect that should get as much attention as lighting, sound, or signage.

Matt Glass, managing partner at Eventage, as reported in PRWeek

A case in point was a parade in 2012 for veterans in Midland, Texas, where event organizers planned a parade route over a railroad crossing. They didn't notify the railroad or take other precautions. An oncoming train hit one of the floats killing four veterans and injured a score of others.

Charitable organizations also need liability insurance if they are sponsoring a fundraising event. This is particularly relevant if the organization has an event that requires physical exertion, such as a 10-K run, a bicycle race, or even a hot-air balloon race.

Participants should sign a release form that protects the organization if someone suffers a heart attack or other kind of accident. One organization, which was sponsoring a 5-K "fun run," had the participants sign a statement that read in part: "I know that a road race is a potentially hazardous activity . . . . I assume all risk associated with running in this event, including, but not limited to, falls, contact with other participants, the effects of the weather, including high heat/or humidity, traffic and the conditions of the road."

Events that use public streets and parks also need permits from various city departments. If the organization is sponsoring a run, the public relations person needs to get a permit from the police or public safety department to block off streets and also hire off-duty police to handle traffic control. Permits for the Avon Walk for Breast Cancer, for example, are arranged months in advance because there are many requests for "runs" and many cities have imposed a limit on how many will be permitted each year.

on the job

A MULTICULTURAL WORLD

Beer, Rum, Vibrators, and Garlic: The World of Promotional Events

The planning and implementation of events is a major public relations and marketing tool of almost every organization that has a product, a cause, or even an issue. Event planners spend a great deal of time and energy thinking up creative ways to attract attendees that help generate additional online and traditional media coverage. The following is a snapshot of several kinds of promotional events, all of which involve extensive planning and logistics.

Belgrade Beer Fest

A major event that promotes Serbia as a nation worth visiting is the Belgrade Beer Fest (www.belgradebeerfest.com) that attracts 500,000 visitors over a five-day period to drink 50 different brands of beer and listen to popular bands from the Balkans. Planning for the annual event is a year-round process in terms of signing contracts with bands, negotiating with breweries for exhibit space, vetting food vendors, preparing promotional materials and news releases, and dealing with such logistics as the number of portable potties needed for all those beer drinkers.

The fest, also popular with locals as a form of entertainment in the hot days of August, celebrated its l0th anniversary in 2012 with more than one million liters of beer consumed. Promotion of the event is through stories in the traditional media and in the social media such as Facebook, Twitter, Instagram, and YouTube. Dejan Grastic, general manager of the Belgrade Cultural Network (BCN) and sponsor of the beer fest, says, "The fest takes a lot of diligence and hard work, but it really helps Serbia's image as a tourist destination."

Bacardi Rum

Anniversaries can also generate promotional events. Bacardi, for example, celebrated its 150th birthday by teaming up with *Rolling Stone* to sponsor a consumer event called "Bacardi Bash: 150 Years of Rocking the Party," which was held in Indianapolis the night before the Super Bowl. More than 1,500 attended the event, which featured various rooms with themes from different eras, such as the 1920s. Music acts such as Gym Class Heroes and celebrities such as *Mad Men's* Jon Hamm were also part of the party that generated coverage in *USA Today*, *USWeekly*, and the entertainment show *Access Hollywood*.

Other events were rolled out during the anniversary year, which supplemented Bacardi's 150th anniversary advertising campaign and its outreach on social media such as Facebook, YouTube, and Twitter.

Trojan Pleasure Carts

Creating an event to promote vibrators takes a lot of creative thinking, but Trojan Brand came up with an idea that was named the promotional event of the year by *PRWeek*. The idea

(continued)

was to give away 10,000 vibrators from "Trojan Pleasure Carts" in New York's Times Square. The carts resembled Manhattan's classic hot dog carts in what *PRWeek* described as "Getcha Vibes Here! Trojan Vibrations Takes Pleasure Out of the Bedroom and Into the Streets of New York." As one *PRWeek* judge said, "I loved the carts. There was no way media weren't going to cover it." Indeed, the event got an exclusive story in the *New York Times* and coverage in 15 international markets. About 90 percent of the coverage included pleasure messages tied to Trojan. Not bad for a campaign with an $80,000 budget.

Gilroy Garlic Festival

The farming community of Gilroy, California, is primarily known as the major producer of garlic in the United States and that, in turn, spawned the idea of having an annual Garlic Festival where everything from garlic fries to garlic ice cream would be served. Today, more than 100,000 people attend from as far away as Asia and Europe for three days of cook-off competitions, sample food prepared by celebrity chefs, and enjoy the smell of everything garlic. A community non-profit group sponsors the festival and, in the past 35 years, has raised more than $9 million for local charitable groups. An army of local volunteers staff the festival and oversee the consumption of about 2.5 tons of garlic, 10,000 loaves of French bread, 10,000 pounds of fries, 2,700 pounds of sausages, 5,000 pounds of squid, and 4,000 pounds of prawns.

A food event such as a chili cook-off or a German fest requires permits from the public health department and, if liquor will be served, a permit from the state alcohol board. If the event is held inside a building, a permit is often required from the fire inspector.

The public relations planner must also deal with the logistics of arranging cleanup, providing basic services such as water and medical aid, registering craft and food vendors, and posting signs. Promotion of an event can often be accomplished by having a radio or TV station or local newspaper cosponsor the event, which was discussed in Chapter 15.

on the job INSIGHTS

Corporate Sponsorships: Another Kind of Event

Many corporations, in order to cut through the media clutter and establish brand identity, sponsor any number of events that, in turn, are covered by the media. In North America alone, about $10 billion is spent by corporations to sponsor various events. According to the *Economist*, about two-thirds of this total is sponsorship fees for sporting events. Pepsi's sponsorship of the NFL, for example, is valued at about $900 million.

The FIFA World Cup and the Olympics are the world leaders in corporate sponsorships. Companies such as Coca-Cola, General Electric, Visa, and Samsung are among the top 12 official sponsors of the Olympics. In fact, Coca-Cola has been an official sponsor since 1928 and marked its 81st anniversary of sponsorship at the London Olympics in 2012. The International Olympics Committee, in the three years before London, secured $1 billion in corporate sponsorships. The 2014 World Cup in Brazil will generate more than twice that amount in corporate sponsorships.

It is recommended that for each dollar spent in sponsorship, the sponsor spend twice that much to leverage the sponsorship, and that is true no matter how large or small the project.

Rodger Roeser, writing in KD Paine's Measurement Standard *online newsletter*

If your employer or client is thinking about sponsoring an event, here are some guidelines you should apply:

- Can the company afford to fulfill the obligation? The sponsorship fee is just the starting point. Count on doubling it to have an adequate marketing and public relations campaign to publicize the event and your particular event.
- Is the event or organization compatible with the company's values and mission statement?
- Does the event reach the organization's primary audiences?
- Are the event organizers experienced and professional?
- Will the field representatives be able to use the event as a platform for increasing sales?
- Does the event give the organization a chance to develop new contracts and business opportunities?
- Can you make a multiple-year sponsorship contract that will reinforce brand identity on a regular, consistent basis?
- Is there an opportunity to get employees involved and raise their morale?
- Is the event compatible with the personality of the organization or its products?
- Can you do trade-offs of products and in-kind services to help defray the costs?

Summary

A World Filled with Events

- Events and meetings are important tools of public relations because they reach people on a one-to-one basis, and attendees are more involved because events involve the five senses.
- Events and meetings don't just happen. They must be planned with attention to every detail. Nothing should be left to chance.

Group Meetings

- Club meetings and workshops require attention to such factors as time, location, seating, facilities, invitations, name tags, menu, speakers, registration, and costs.

Banquets

- Banquets are more formal affairs that require extensive advance planning.
- In addition to the factors necessary for a group meeting, decorations, entertainment, audiovisual facilities, speaker fees, and seating charts must be considered.

Receptions and Cocktail Parties

- Cocktail parties and receptions require precautions about the amount of alcohol consumed and the availability of food and nonalcoholic drinks. Possible liability is an important consideration, too.

Open Houses and Plant Tours

- Open houses and plant tours require meticulous planning and routing, careful handling of visitors, and thorough training of all personnel who will be in contact with the visitors.

Conventions

- Conventions require the skills of professional managers who can juggle multiple events and meetings over a period of several days.
- A convention may include large meetings, cocktail parties, receptions, tours, and banquets.

Trade Shows

- Trade shows are the ultimate marketing events and attract millions of attendees annually. Exhibit booths may cost from $50,000 to $1 million.

Promotional Events

- Creative thinking is absolutely necessary for planning a promotional event that will attract attendance and media coverage.
- A celebrity at a promotional event will attract crowds and media attention, but appearance fees can be costly.
- A promotional event may be a "grand opening" of a facility, an event to announce a new product, or a 10-K run sponsored by a charitable organization. It is important to consider such factors as city permits, security, and liability insurance.

Case Activity Plan an Event

Lucite, a manufacturer of high-priced handbags, is celebrating its 75th anniversary. What events would you plan to celebrate this milestone that would also generate more media visibility for the brand? An alternative assignment is to prepare a detailed outline of what must be done to plan a banquet for your university's School of Business annual awards banquet that is targeted to current students and alumni. The outline should include a timeline or calendar of what must be done by specific dates.

Questions For Review and Discussion

1. Why are meetings and events a vital public relations tool even in the digital age of texting and social media?
2. Name at least four factors that must be considered in planning a meeting for a group.
3. What are the key responsibilities of an event manager?
4. What skills should an event manager bring on board to be successful?
5. Draw a checklist for a luncheon meeting with the key vendors of an organization.
6. What is the recommended length of time for a reception or cocktail party?
7. What questions should you ask a catering manager when planning an event?
8. What is an open house? Why is it significant for an organization?
9. What are the components of planning a convention?
10. A booth at a trade show requires some thought. What would you do to attract visitors?
11. What are the pros and cons of using a celebrity as part of a promotional event?
12. Why is it important to consider security and liability issues for a promotional event?
13. What kinds of questions should be asked after an event to determine its success?

Media Resources

Benson, D. (2012, summer). IBM celebrates 100 years. *The Strategist*, 26–27.

Blitz, R. (2012, November 2). Reputations at stake when Fifa's circus comes to town. *Financial Times*, 2.

Daniels, C. (2013, January). Growing battle for coverage intensifies at electronics show. *PRWeek*, 20.

Kortekaas, V. (2012, November 2). Top brands and rights owners take a more savvy approach to sponsorships. *Financial Times*, 3.

McPherson, S. (2010, January). A 12-month guide: How to enhance your company's trade show performance. *Public Relations Tactics*, 14.

Sher, I. (2013, January 9). In Vegas glitz, product busts lurk. *Wall Street Journal*, B8.

Smith, R. (2013, October 10). Let's get this gala started: Event designers aim for art with party décor in the age of Instagram. *Wall Street Journal*, D1, 3.

Stein, L. (2012, June). Bacardi brings consumers to the party for 150th anniversary. *PRWeek*, 15.

Communicating Corporate Affairs

chapter 17

After reading this chapter, you will be able to:

Describe the role of public relations in corporations

Explain how media relations contributes to the success of corporations

Understand the crucial roles of the customer, the investor, and the employee in the corporate communication program

Describe the main supportive functions of public relations for corporate marketing efforts

Explain the environmental relations process

Define corporate philanthropy and the part public relations plays in corporate giving

Today's Modern Corporation

Today, many corporations are global. International conglomerates control subsidiary companies that often produce a grab bag of seemingly unrelated products under the same corporate banner. These companies deal with a number of governments at many levels. Their operations affect the environment, control the employment of thousands, and impact the financial and social well-being of millions.

Although such corporations make up a tiny proportion of all companies, corporations are often associated with powerful conglomerates. The large size of these corporations, however, also brings remoteness. A corporation has a "face" because its products, logo, and brand are readily visible in advertising and billboards from Azerbaijan to Zimbabwe and all the nations in between. However, the average consumer really can't comprehend organizations such as Wal-mart, with $469 billion in worldwide sales and 2.2 million employees globally, or Exxon/Mobil, with $482 billion in global sales and 76,900 employees. These figures boggle the mind, and they represent more than the combined gross national product (GNP) of many nations.

Ordinary citizens become distrustful of the power, influence, and credibility of such giant corporations, often transferring their mistrust to business in general. When U.S. gasoline prices rise rapidly, for example, suspicion spreads that "Big Oil" has conspired to gouge the public—a distrust that the oil companies never fully allay. Major corporate financial scandals in recent years and the misdeeds of corporate executives also take their toll on the public's trust. See the PR Casebook on page 473 about Wal-mart struggles to earn credibility regarding its response to accusations of bribery and lax oversight of vendors.

Ken Cohen, VP of public and government affairs for ExxonMobil, explains the difficulty facing energy companies. His point of view and the trials he faces could be applied to many global corporations. Cohen told *PRWeek*, "The biggest challenge ExxonMobil and the industry face is that people don't know a lot about us."

Diverse Wal-mart Publics

Large corporations need to balance their responsibilities to their stockholders with the worldwide public perceptions.

He noted that it's the job of public relations to keep consumers educated about how global companies function and what they contribute to society. "ExxonMobil contributed $72 billion to the U.S. economy through activities including taxes, salaries, returns to our investors and payments to other businesses and industries," he explained. He also noted that employees volunteered more than 700,000 hours in community service and the company's foundation contributed $278 million to charitable causes. Cohen's communication exemplifies how industries must constantly work to tell their side of any story.

Cohen also noted in a *PRWeek* interview, "One of the challenges is that we have a very vocal and well-funded group

PRCasebook

Wal-mart Scandal Highlights Role of Investor Activists

Wal-mart often seems to have to take it on the chin from several publics at the same time. Community activists shout their opposition to what they call the local-retailer killing behemoth coming to town.

Employees file class action suits accusing the retailer of sex discrimination. Union leaders coordinate pickets to protest wages and benefits. Perhaps all that is to be expected by such a global giant of a company. But you can always count on your shareholders to support you. Right?

Well, maybe not always. In 2012, reports trickled out about a bribery scandal involving Wal-mart executives in Mexico. The accusations were that Wal-mart executives bribed local government officials in Mexico to speed up zoning permissions to build new stores. The *New York Times* reported that the "retail giant fueled growth with bribes." The newspaper reported that when Wal-mart investigators arrived in Mexico they "found a paper trail of hundreds of suspect payments totaling more than $24 million." But the evidence was allegedly downplayed by executives in Wal-mart corporate headquarters in Bentonville, Arkansas. Shareholders began to protest—figuratively and literally.

At the company's 2012 annual shareholders meeting, investors protested what they saw as Wal-mart board's lack of corrective action following the bribery allegations. *Forbes* reported, "Very vocal groups are calling for real change in Wal-mart leadership." Following the shareholders' meeting in 2012, *Businessweek* reported, "Wal-mart final shareholder vote for its board of directors showed unprecedented dissent against key executives and board members . . . in the wake of allegations of bribery in Mexico."

When shares owned by family members and company insiders are excluded, shareholder ire came to light. Thirty-two percent of non-insider-held shares were voted to oust CEO Mike Duke and board member Christopher Williams; 31 percent voted against company chairman Robson Walton; and about 38 percent voted against former CEO and board member Lee Scott. This was unusual because in past years board members were re-elected with near unanimity. "With descendants of Wal-mart founder owning about 50 percent of Wal-mart shares, activist shareholders had little chance of voting out board members," *Businessweek* reported. All board members retained their seats.

Following the 2012 shareholders' vote a Wal-mart spokesman said of the vote, "obviously a substantial majority of our shareholders supported their election." CEO Duke told investors at the meeting, "Let me be clear: Wal-mart is committed to compliance and integrity everywhere we operate. I want to personally assure you, we're doing everything we can to get to the bottom of this matter."

Fast forward a year. When the 2013 shareholders' meeting rolled along, Wal-mart investors had new concerns.

Wal-mart CEO Duke at the 2013 shareholders' meeting.

(continued)

While they were still upset about the ongoing bribery investigations, which had widened to include Brazil, China, and India, there were new problems. Wal-mart, together with other retailers, was accused of not adequately monitoring its suppliers.

The accusations came following tragic fires and a building collapse in which hundreds of Bangladeshi garment workers were killed (see PR Casebook in Chapter 12). Pension funds and other institutional investors, which hold hundreds of millions of dollars in Wal-mart shares, voiced their dissatisfaction with the board action (or perceived inaction) on several fronts. Anne Simpson, an investment manager for large pension fund Calpers, told the *New York Times*, "We're extremely concerned about Wal-mart monitoring on its supply chain—the fires and deaths in Bangladesh, and other concerns about supply-chain issues in the U.S."

The *Los Angeles Times* reported that for its 2013 shareholders' meeting Wal-mart received temporary restraining orders against protesters. The newspaper quoted the restraining order. Select protesters were prohibited from "entering onto or inside Wal-mart private property in the State of Arkansas to engage in activities such as picketing, patrolling, parading, demonstrations 'flash mobs,' handbilling solicitation, and manager confrontations."

The board of directors recommended that shareholders vote against signing onto an agreement to monitor fire and building safety in its outsourced manufacturing plants. CEO Duke assured shareholders, "You operate with integrity, our company was founded on integrity. For Wal-mart, compliance is an absolute. Make no mistake about it, we will do the right thing."

Some shareholders were unimpressed. Institutional Shareholder Services, a shareholder advisory firm said investors "remain in the dark as to the nature and extent of the alleged violations," according to the *New York Times*.

Do you think Wal-mart is working with its investors in a good way? Why or why not?

Why should shareholders be given a voice in corporate business?

Are the tactics of restraining orders and statements by the CEO appropriate responses to shareholder concerns? Why or why not?

of adversaries. Their objective is to get up every day and criticize what we do and convince policymakers that action is needed to restrict the operations of firms such as ExxonMobil. We have to find the right tone and way of engaging someone who has an entirely different point of view."

Public relations professionals representing government, consumers, and corporations wrangle about what is an acceptable level of risk and catastrophe in cases such as the 2011 BP *Deepwater Horizon* oil spill in the Gulf of Mexico. Corporate leaders such as Cohen confirm that corporations can never let up in their efforts to manage what they do in the best interests of all the publics they serve—from investors to consumers to employees to community members and beyond. It is the task of the corporate public relations practitioner to bring some perspective about the scale and complexity of what corporations do to deliver what consumers demand worldwide.

This is a constant challenge. A longitudinal study by Gallup showed that in 2013, 31 percent of Americans said they had "very little" confidence in big business. Twenty years earlier, 28 percent said they had very little confidence. But 40 years earlier, in 1973, only 20 percent said they had very little confidence in big business. Chevron, for the past several years, has tried to change negative public perceptions with a series of ads that "agrees" with many of the public concerns about big business. See one of Chevron's ads on page 475.

The Reputation Institute reported that 60 percent of respondents to its 2012 RepTrak® 100 Study weren't sure that companies are good corporate citizens. Four percent said that companies could "absolutely not be trusted." PR firm Edelman conducts an annual global study on trust. In 2013, Edelman reported that only 18 percent of survey respondents trusted business leaders to tell the truth regardless of how "complex or unpopular" it may be. And a similarly modest 19 percent said they trust business leaders to make ethical and moral decisions.

Public perceptions of greed and corporate misdeeds are reinforced by stories in the media and activists. For example, corporate greed was blamed in many media stories when hundreds of workers were killed in manufacturing plant fires and building collapses in Bangladesh. An activist group calling itself United Students Against Sweatshops used its website to urge people to "sign our petition to the three largest brands in Bangladesh—Wal-mart, the Gap, and H&M—demanding that they stop allowing garment workers to be murdered. . . . [W]e ask you to join us in observing a day of mourning for garment workers who have been killed by corporate greed and negligence." Such strong language from activist groups only underscores the frequent direction of public opinion regarding corporations.

Corporate public relations practitioners face a delicate balance between arguing for realism and making lame excuses on behalf of their companies. Realistically, huge enterprises that make and do things will also make huge mistakes—spills, worker injuries, and the evils of fraud and price abuse. Society rightfully requires corporate communicators and media to expose illegal and incompetent dealings, but with some consideration of how hard corporations of all sorts strive to provide the best value they can, not only for profit but also from a need to have a worthy purpose in life.

Some corporations, such as Chevron, run image ads to identify with concerns of key publics.

The Role of Public Relations

The extensive negative publicity about corporations and business in general over the past several years has made it imperative that companies make a special effort to regain public credibility and trust. Thus, the concept of *corporate social responsibility* (CSR) is now high on the priority list of executives and their public relations staffs, who are charged with improving the reputation and citizenship of their employers. The Reputation Institute supports this goal with research indicating that 42 percent of a company's reputation derives from perceived corporate citizenship, sound governance, and quality as a workplace.

Indeed, the public relations professional regularly takes steps to outline a plan of action for rebuilding public trust in business. "These are people who deal with trust issues all the time," says James Murphy, global managing director of communication

> One of the challenges is that we have a very vocal and well-funded group of adversaries. Their objective is to get up every day and criticize what we do and convince policymakers that action is needed to restrict the operations of firms such as ExxonMobil. We have to find the right tone and way of engaging someone who has an entirely different point of view.
>
> *Ken Cohen, VP of public and government affairs for ExxonMobil*

for Accenture. "Therefore, we're in a good position to address them." American businesses and their leaders need to act in three main areas:

1. adopt ethical principles,
2. pursue transparency and disclosure, and
3. make trust a fundamental precept of corporate governance.

See the Insights box on page 477 for survey evidence of the alarming problem of lack of trust in corporate leaders.

The importance of public relations in CSR is explained by Jack Bergen, then senior vice president of marketing and communication for Siemens Corporation. He told *PRWeek*:

> We are the eyes and ears of an organization. The best way to be socially responsible is to have your eyes and ears trained on all the stakeholders, to know what they want and need from the company. These are classic public affairs issues and the idea that they should be handled by anyone else would show a lack of understanding.

A number of strategies and tactics can be used to implement CSR, which involves corporate performance as well as effective communication. One of the more important roles of the public relations executive is counseling the CEO.

The public relations executive serves as a link between the chief executive and the realities of public opinion in the marketplace and the organization, according to Mark Schumann, global communication practice leader with Tower Perrin. He told an international IABC conference that CEOs are often "disconnected" and surrounded by other executives who simply agree with whatever the CEO says. Schumann believes corporate public relations professionals should be the "playwright and director, but we also need to be the toughest critics" to ensure that the CEO comes across as concerned and involved with employees and customers. As critics, public relations professionals often hold a mirror up for the top leadership to see an unwelcome but valuable view of themselves and their performance.

> Communication is good training for the vision, strategic thinking, and leadership that executive decision-makers are called upon to provide. I have come to think of myself as a generalist, with a strong focus in communications.
>
> *Bill Novelli, CEO, AARP*

Increasingly, corporations have added a position within the C-Suite. Joining the CEO (chief executive officer), COO (chief operating officer), and CMO (chief marketing officer) is the CRO (chief reputation officer), according to *PRWeek* in a special "Reputation Issue."

But 74 percent of CROs told the Reputation Institute in 2013 that they were not ready for what has been dubbed "the reputation economy." Corporations seek a better reputation for a variety of reasons. First, responsible business practices ward off increased government regulation. Demonstrating what can happen when companies fail to police themselves, the U.S. Congress passed new laws regarding accounting practices and disclosure as a result of major financial scandals during the first decade of the century.

Second, there is the matter of employee morale; companies with good policies and a good reputation tend to have less employee turnover. A good corporate reputation also favorably affects the bottom line. For example, a survey of executives by the Center for Corporate Citizenship and the Hitachi Foundation found that 82 percent of the respondents believe that good corporate citizenship contributes to meeting the organization's financial objectives. In addition, 53 percent say corporate citizenship is important to their customers.

on the job INSIGHTS

Study Finds Trust in Leaders Is Low

Fewer than one in five people believe that business or governmental leaders will tell the truth when faced with a difficult issue, according to the 2013 Edelman Trust Barometer study.

Richard Edelman, president and CEO of Edelman, said, "We're clearly experiencing a crisis in leadership. Business and governmental leaders must change their management approach and become more inclusive by seeking the input of employees, consumers, activists and experts such as academics, and adapting to their feedback. They must also pass the test of radical transparency."

Each year, Edelman does a global study to examine trust. The 2013 study showed that trust in business to do the right thing was 50 percent, but trust in business leaders to tell the truth was only 18 percent. The study also showed that academics, technical experts, and people we perceive to be "like us" are almost twice as trusted as a business executive or government official.

The Edelman report showed that lack of trust in banks and financial institutions is driven by "poor performance" and "perception of unethical behavior." Nongovernmental organizations (NGOs) are the most trusted institutions. NGOs posted trust levels above 50 percent in 23 of 26 countries in which the study was conducted. In a press release Edelman noted, "Among the general population, mainstream media and online search (both at 58 percent) are the most trusted sources of information."

Being a good corporate citizen is an admirable goal, but corporations also face a number of pressures and counterpressures when making decisions and forming policies. General Electric, one of the world's largest corporations, with a market value of about $240 billion, once outlined four key factors that have to be considered at all times when making a decision:

- **Political.** How do government regulations and other pressures affect the decision?
- **Technological.** Do we have the engineering knowledge to accomplish the goal?
- **Social.** What is our responsibility to society?
- **Economic.** Will we make a profit?

The following sections discuss various facets of today's modern corporation and the activities that require the expertise and counsel of public relations professionals.

Media Relations

The media are a major source of public information and perceptions about the business world and individual companies. News about corporate behavior often isn't all that favorable.

Major financial scandals and other negative coverage can cause a corporation's reputation to plummet. Disney jumped from the 17th most reputable company in 2012 to the 1st most reputable in 2013, largely based on improved perceptions of the company's governance. A Disney spokesperson told *Forbes*, "As one of the world's best known companies, we continually strive to earn the respect of our consumers, our employees and our shareholders not only for what we achieve, but for how we do it. A great reputation is a reflection of the quality and integrity of a company's people and products."

However, such volatility leads corporate executives to be defensive about how journalists cover their business, because they feel that too much emphasis has been given to corporate misdeeds and exaggeration of impacts on the environment and workforce even when companies devote effort to minimizing emissions, spills, and accidents. From the corporate perspective, you make mistakes only when you are doing things; the more you do, the greater the risk of criticism.

Many corporate executives have several ongoing complaints about media coverage: inaccuracy, incomplete coverage, inadequate research and preparation for interviews, and an antibusiness bias. One survey by the American Press Institute found that one-third of the CEOs polled are dissatisfied with the business news they find in their local newspapers, a sentiment that is not exclusive to the business sector. (See the PR Casebook in Chapter 19 on page 521 for more on BP, President Obama, and media pressure.)

Business editors and reporters respond that often they cannot publish or broadcast thorough, evenhanded stories about business because many company executives, uncooperative and wary, erect barriers against them. Writers complain about their inability to obtain direct access to decision-making executives, which forces them to rely on news releases that don't contain the information they need. Journalists assert, too, that some business leaders don't understand the concept of balanced coverage and assume that any story involving unfavorable news about their company is intentionally biased.

Public relations practitioners serving businesses stand in the middle. They must interpret their companies and clients to the media, while showing their chief executive and other high officials how open, friendly media relations can serve their interests. One major interest that executives have is corporate reputation, and this is often tarnished or enhanced by the type of media coverage that an organization receives.

Savvy public relations professionals understand that business reporters often don't have adequate business preparation. For this reason, they spend a great deal of time and energy providing background to brief reporters on the business operations of their clients and employers. It's one way of ensuring that coverage will be more accurate and thorough.

Communicating through traditional media continues to be a major activity of corporate communications departments, but the advent of the Internet and social media has also given corporations more opportunities to communicate in a way that is less formal and more conversational. Table 17.1 gives the percentage of *Fortune* 500 using various social media in 2013.

Table 17.1 Corporate Use of Social Media

PLATFORM	NO. OF COMPANIES	PERCENTAGE (%)	TOP THREE INDUSTRIES BY USAGE
Blogs	171	34	Telecommunications, specialty retailers, food consumer products
Twitter	387	77	Commercial banks, food consumer products, specialty retailers
Facebook	348	70	Specialty retailers, telecommunications, aerospace and defense
YouTube	359	69	N/A

Based on *2013* Fortune *500 Are Bullish on Social Media: Big Companies Get Excited About Google+, Instagram, Foursquare and Pinterest*. Research conducted by Nora Ganim Barnes, Ph.D., Ava M. Lescault, MBA, and Stephanie Wright.

Customer Relations

Customer service, in many respects, is the front line of public relations. A single incident, or a series of incidents, can severely damage a company's reputation and erode public trust in its products and services. Customer satisfaction is important because of word of mouth. A person who has a bad experience, surveys indicate, shares his or her story with an average of 17 people, whereas a person with a good experience will tell an average of 11 people.

Digital and social media, however, have considerably changed the math. Today, a dissatisfied customer is capable of informing thousands, or even millions, of people in just one posting. According to the *New York Times*, corporations have become less accommodative of malcontents repeatedly posting comments on the Internet. Instead, companies are filing defamation suits against such individuals. Free speech advocates, on the other hand, call such lawsuits a SLAPP (Strategic Lawsuit Against Public Participation).

One example is pressure put on global chocolate makers Mondelez International, Mars, and Nestle. Oxfam, a human rights organization, coordinated a petition drive and an online campaign to urge the chocolate companies to rectify hunger, poverty, and unequal pay for women cocoa farmers. The petition was signed by more than 100,000 consumers. According to Oxfam, "The companies also faced a growing stream of comments on Facebook and Twitter urging them to act." Commitments by the three companies, which account for 40 percent of the global chocolate industry, included signing onto the United Nations Women's Empowerment Principles. Further illustrating the problem, *Pittsburgh Post-Gazette* reporter Teresa Lindeman wrote:

> Companies that consider ignoring tales of dissatisfied customers might want to take a look at a study released yesterday by the Wharton School of the University of Pennsylvania. Researchers there found that more than 50 percent of Americans said they wouldn't go to a store if a friend had a bad shopping experience there. Even worse, when someone has a problem, it gets embellished with every retelling, and pretty soon that store has a really, really big problem.

Product recalls, in particular, test the patience of consumers and bring into question the credibility of the entire company as far as its ability to provide safe and quality products. Toy maker Mattel had to recall more than 20 million toys because figures of famous icons such as Barbie, Elmo, and Dora the Explorer were tainted with lead paint used by Chinese subcontractors. Mattel vacillated initially, but soon took responsibility for quality control. Over time, this move reassured consumers, enabling Mattel to begin rebuilding its reputation. For more insight on how to handle a product recall, see the PR Casebook about Toyota in Chapter 10 on page 298.

Traditionally, customer service has been separate from the communication or public relations function in a company. Bob Seltzer, a leader in Ruder Finn's marketing practice, told *PRWeek*, "I defy anyone to explain the wisdom of this. How a company talks to its customers is among, if not the, most critical communication it has."

> How a company talks to its customers is among, if not the, most critical communication it has.
>
> *Bob Seltzer, marketing expert at Ruder Finn*

Increasingly, however, corporations are realizing that customer relations serves as a telltale public relations barometer. Many public relations departments now regularly monitor customer feedback in a variety of ways to determine what policies and communication strategies need to be revised. One common method is

Managing Conflict
The astute public relations practitioner must keep a watchful eye on the mood of the public while building diverse markets. Controversy over immigration policies, for example, affects multiple publics. Diverse groups raise concerns about how policies may affect them.

to monitor customer queries to the organization's website. Indeed, most companies have a "contacting us" link on their websites. Another method is the content analysis of phone calls to the customer service center.

This sharing of information is valuable from the standpoint of getting public relations professionals involved in active listening so that they can strategize on what steps a company should take to ensure a good reputation among customers. As Andy Hopson, CEO of Burson-Marsteller's northeast region, told *PRWeek*, "Ignoring complaints can ultimately damage a company's reputation."

Public relations professionals also pay attention to consumer surveys. One such mechanism is the American Customer Satisfaction Index, which is the definitive benchmark of how buyers feel about what business is selling to them. The index, which has been tracking customer satisfaction for 230 companies in 43 industries for years, has found that a company offering the lowest prices may not necessarily get the highest satisfaction rating.

Reaching Diverse Markets

The United States is becoming more diverse every year, which is now being recognized by corporate marketing and communication departments. As racial and ethnic minorities continue to increase in number and become more affluent, they will constitute a larger share of the consumer marketplace. A quick perusal of job announcements in trade publications tells the story. Increasingly, agencies are hiring positions such as SVP of multicultural communications and VP of multicultural marketing. See also Chapter 11 about diverse audiences.

According to Maria Rodriguez, president of Vanguard Communications, "Each year, the number of U.S. minority groups increases, as do the diverse perspectives among them. Simply put, diversity in itself is diverse. It is a mistake to assume that a traditionally described minority group—Asian Americans, for example—will respond to messages and ideas as one homogeneous block. Each audience slice represents a different set of cultural beliefs, historical backgrounds, geographical considerations, and current living circumstances."

Jimmy Lee, SVP of marketing and communications at BBCN Bank wrote in *PRWeek*, "Even though Asians only represent 5% of the [U.S.] population, the buying power of the community exceeds $700 billion, a number that is estimated to grow to $1 trillion by 2017. If Asian Americans were a country, by sheer buying power, they would be among the top 20 leading economies in the world."

As with many initiatives in public relations, there are two sides to most arguments. Efforts to address the issue of illegal immigration are met with criticism from many perspectives. In state and federal legislative discussions about addressing illegal immigration, those who feel illegal immigration is out of control support strong

on the job

SOCIAL MEDIA IN PRACTICE

Duke Energy Uses Social Media to Tell Its Story

When Superstorm Sandy hit the Eastern Seaboard in October 2012, Charlotte, N.C.-based Duke Energy was poised to respond. While most of its customers were safe, Duke sent thousands of employees to help with power restoration. Taking pride in its employees and its response, Duke wanted to tell its story. And it employed social media to do so.

Greg Efthimiou wrote in *The Strategist*, "Instead of relying on traditional media to repackage our material and localize the Sandy story, we opted to tell the story ourselves via content created by social media-savvy corporate communications staffer Lee Freedman, and shared it via blogs and Twitter." Freedman was embedded with a somewhat skeptical line crew.

The line crew chief reported that Freedman quickly earned the workers' trust. Supervisor Doug Akins said that it became clear that the objective of the social media campaign was "to understand what we were doing and how we were doing it, and then communicate that back to employees and the public." Freedman told *The Strategist*, "During downtime, I would go truck to truck and hold up my iPhone to line workers in the utility trucks so they could see the tweets of support and encouragement we received in response to my blogs and tweets." Such distant and dramatic support buoyed the spirits of the crews.

In addition to serving as both an employee and a customer relations tactic, Duke used the social media campaign as a media relations effort for traditional media. The Associated Press, *Wall Street Journal*, *Charlotte Business Journal*, and Charlotte CBS affiliate WBTV all used Freedman-generated material. "Using Twitter to show and tell our story was invaluable," Freedman said. "I was able to tweet our work locations so the media could find us. I also sent out photos of our work environments underneath streets, sidewalks and buildings—areas where journalists just could not access."

Duke Energy leveraged social media to meet the needs of internal and external publics.

Adapted from "Power Play: Duke Energy's Social Media Strategy Highlights Superstorm Sandy Heroics," by Greg Efthimiou, in *The Strategist*, Winter 2012, pp. 16–18.

enforcement laws. They freely criticize bilingual efforts in education and marketing as pandering to illegal immigration.

Members of the Hispanic community have their own issues with public communications, claiming that special marketing programs, offers, and appeals are often merely token gestures. Clearly, public relations is strategic conflict management much of the time, and the astute professional keeps a vigilant eye on seemingly innocent, positive communication programs that may stir controversy.

Consumer Activism

A dissatisfied customer can often be mollified by prompt and courteous attention to his or her complaint or even by an offer from the company to replace the item or provide some discount coupons toward future purchases. A more serious and complex threat to corporate reputation, which can also affect sales, is consumer activists who demand changes in corporate policies.

Tyson Foods, a major American producer of meat and poultry products, was accused of inhumane treatment of animals by various animal rights groups, such as the

People for the Ethical Treatment of Animals (PETA). The corporate response was to establish an office of animal well-being to assure retailers and consumers that it takes humane animal handling seriously.

The people from PETA are not going to be satisfied unless we go out of business, but there are consumers less radical than PETA who are still concerned about animal-handling practices.

Ed Nicholson, Tyson Foods spokesperson

Ed Nicholson, Tyson's director of media and community relations, told *PRWeek*, "The people from PETA are not going to be satisfied unless we go out of business, but there are consumers less radical than PETA who are still concerned about animal-handling practices." The new wellness office, headed by a veterinarian, will oversee audits of animal-handling practices and make them available to customers on request.

KFC also has been targeted by PETA and other animal rights groups, whose efforts have received extensive media publicity. The charges of inhumane animal treatment and how chickens are slaughtered can and do affect consumer buying decisions, especially when activists are outside a franchise wearing T-shirts that say, "KFC Tortures Animals." In such a situation, the public relations staff has the difficult job of defending the company against what it believes are unfounded allegations and to simultaneously assure the public that KFC's policies do provide for the humane slaughter of its chickens. The public relations professional also represents the external communication climate to management in a way that calls for redoubled efforts to do what is right.

Consequently, when it came to light that a KFC subcontractor was mistreating chickens, the company immediately called the abuse by workers appalling and told the subcontractor to clean up its act—or lose its contract. In this instance, because of the company's quick response, the media were able to include KFC's response in the story about the abuses, which were documented on videotape.

Coca-Cola also has reputation problems. Some activist groups charged the giant bottler with contributing to childhood obesity by selling its products in schools. Karl Bjorhus, director of health and nutrition communication for the bottler, told *PRWeek*, "We have been listening and trying to understand what people's concerns are." As a result, the company partnered with the American Beverage Association and the Alliance for a Healthier Generation to voluntarily shift to lower-calorie and healthier beverages in school vending machines.

Another activist group had other concerns. One campaign, Stop Killer Coke, claimed that Coca-Cola was using paramilitary thugs in Colombia to intimidate workers and prevent unionization. The company said the charges were "false and outrageous," but that didn't stop the campaign's organizers from spreading the word to colleges, high schools, and unions. As a result, at least six colleges booted Coke beverages off their campuses, and several food co-ops decided to stop selling Coke products. In such a situation, even false allegations can affect the sales of a product.

At the strategic level, a company weighs the potential impact of the charges or allegations on potential customer reaction and possible effect on sales before deciding on a course of action. This threat appraisal concept was discussed in Chapter 10. Activist consumer groups are a major challenge to the public relations staff of an organization. Do you accommodate? Do you stonewall? Do you change policy? Issues management is fully presented in Chapter 10, but here are some general guidelines from Douglas Quenqua on how to be proactive, which appeared in *PRWeek*:

Do

- Work with groups who are more interested in solutions than getting publicity.
- Offer transparency. Activists who feel you're not open aren't likely to keep dealing with you.
- Turn their suggestions into action. Activists want results.

Don't

- Get emotional when dealing with advocacy groups.
- Agree to work with anyone making threats.
- Expect immediate results. Working with adversaries takes patience—establishing trust takes time.

Consumer Boycotts

The *boycott*—a refusal to buy the products or services of an offending company—has a long history and is a widely used publicity tool of the consumer movement. A survey by Cone Communications and Echo Research showed that 9 out of 10 consumers say they would boycott a company if they found out the company was engaging in irresponsible behavior.

Britain's *OK!* magazine earned a consumer backlash when, one day after the Duchess of Cambridge Kate Middleton gave birth to her son and England's heir apparent, it published a cover promoting an "exclusive duchess and diet shape-up plan." Women across the United Kingdom called for a boycott of the magazine, describing the front cover as "tasteless," a "disgrace," and "vile."

According to U.K. newspaper *The Independent*, the magazine's parent company Northern & Shell quickly released this statement: "Kate is one of the great beauties of our age and *OK!* readers love her. Like the rest of the world, we were very moved by her radiance as she and William introduced the Prince of Cambridge to the world. We would not dream of being critical of her appearance. If that was misunderstood on our cover it was not intended." Boycott averted.

PETA once announced that consumers should boycott Safeway until it improved conditions for farm animals. At Safeway's annual stockholders' meeting activists planned to unfurl a banner saying, "Safeway means animal cruelty." It had, as *PRWeek* says, "all the makings of a PR person's worst nightmare."

Safeway, however, headed off a boycott by negotiating. Just days before the annual meeting, the company's public affairs staff began working with PETA and quickly announced new standards for monitoring the conditions at its meat suppliers. Instead of a protest, PETA supporters showed up at the annual meeting with a large "Thank You" sign for entering stockholders. In addition, PETA ended its 20-state boycott of the chain.

The success of consumer boycotts is mixed. Various activist groups have boycotted Procter & Gamble (P&G) for years, but without much effect, because the company makes so many products under separate brand names that consumers can't keep track of everything P&G makes. A single product name can sometimes be more vulnerable to a boycott than a large company that markets its goods and services under multiple brand names.

Activists point out that a boycott doesn't have to be 100 percent effective in order for it to change corporate policies. Even a 5 percent drop in sales will often cause corporations to rethink their policies and modes of operation. Nike got serious

on the job INSIGHTS

Boycotts Come From All Directions

When boycotts are aimed at corporations, they most often originate with consumers. But there are other sources of boycotts, too. They can rise out of tensions or disagreements between countries or among companies.

Chinese activists protested Japan's governmental policies by boycotting Japanese automakers.

Disputes between countries can sometimes boil into boycotts. When China and Japan were engaged in conflict over control of islands claimed by both countries, Chinese officials urged a boycott of Japanese automakers. The boycott was effective. A headline from *Business Insider* tells the story: "Chinese Boycott May Be More Costly for Japan Than The Tsunami."

Even Chinese who already owned Japanese cars were afraid to drive them, fearing attacks on themselves and their cars by Chinese patriots. China's Passenger Car Association predicted that sales of Japanese-branded cars would fall by 22 percent as sales of German vehicles would rise by 22.5 percent. Japanese cars had held the number one spot among foreign automakers in China from 2005 until the boycott began in late 2012.

The strength of the boycott began to abate. During the Shanghai Auto Show in April 2013, Japanese automakers attempted to regain the support of Chinese consumers. Takanobu Ito, president of Honda Motor Co., told the Associated Press, "It's not that all Chinese people dislike our cars. There is no mistake that we want to contribute to Chinese society. We just have to keep at it."

When Facebook was accused of allowing antiwomen hate speech on its pages, activists urged advertisers to boycott the social media giant. The group Women, Action, and the Media sent an open letter to Facebook urging it to act against "groups, pages and images that explicitly condone or encourage rape or domestic violence or suggest that they are something to laugh or boast about." Within hours, 60,000 tweets and 224,000 signatures to an online petition supported the boycott. Five thousand e-mails were sent to Facebook advertisers. Companies listened. Some like Nissan withdrew advertising, others like Dove, Zappos, and American Express issued statements noting the Facebook problem and assuring consumers they did not condone violence against women.

"We thought that advertisers would be the most effective way of getting Facebook's attention," Jaclyn Friedman, executive director Women, Action, and the Media, told the *New York Times*. "We had no idea that it would blow up this big. I think people have been frustrated with this issue for so long and feeling like they had no way for Facebook to pay attention to them. As consumers we do have a lot of power."

Facebook admitted that its systems to identify and eliminate hate speech had failed. The company promised to review its systems and update its training of employees around the issue.

about sweatshop conditions abroad only after activist groups caused its stock and sales to drop. Nike was losing market share, so it decided to formulate new policies for its subcontractors abroad and become active in a global alliance of manufacturers to monitor working conditions in overseas factories.

Employee Relations

Employees have been called an organization's "ambassadors." Consequently, the public relations department, often working with the human resources department, concentrates on communicating with employees just as vigorously as it concentrates on delivering the corporate story to the outside world. A workplace that respects its management, has pride in its products, and believes it is being treated fairly is a key factor to corporate success.

Surveys indicate, however, that the success of communication efforts varies widely among organizations. According to a survey of 32,000 workers worldwide by Towers Watson, 26 percent are disengaged. Only 58 percent believe their organization conducts business activities with honesty and integrity. Earlier studies have shown that 20 percent of workers believe their organization does not tell them the truth. In its 2012 report, Towers Watson noted, "It's essential for organizations and their leaders to have a clear understanding of what matters to employees, and why and how that affects their productivity and behavior on the job."

The extensive media coverage of corporate scandals also has taken its toll in terms of employee perceptions. A Fleishman-Hillard survey of workers, for example, found that 80 percent believe that greed is driving corporate scandals. The majority also agree that corporations care more about stock value than customers' needs. On the plus side, however, more than 70 percent of the respondents think the information they receive from their employer is "adequate" to "very comprehensive."

The value of credible and trustworthy communication cannot be overestimated. Mark Schumann of Towers Perrin told *Public Relations Tactics*, "Regardless of the topic, an organization will find it difficult to motivate, engage, and retain their most talented employees if their messages are not believed."

A good example of successful corporate policies that build employee loyalty is the annual survey by *Working Mother* magazine that compiles a list of the 100 best companies for working mothers. A comparison of these 100 best companies with other organizations shows the following:

- 100 percent of the 100 best companies offer telecommuting, versus 57 percent of companies nationwide.
- 100 percent of the 100 best offer paid maternity leave, versus 16 percent nationwide.
- 98 percent of the 100 best offer health screening programs, versus 45 percent nationwide.
- 96 percent of the 100 best offer on-site seasonal flu vaccinations, versus 61 percent nationwide.
- 93 percent of the 100 best offer nutrition counseling, versus 20 percent nationwide.

Many employee issues must be addressed by a company, and public relations professionals often are involved in counseling not only what policies should be created but also how they should be implemented and communicated. One such issue is health and medical benefits. Company information about benefits should be written in plain English instead of legalese so that employees thoroughly understand what is covered. If there is a change in a health plan, the company must spend time and effort, often through small-group meetings, to explain the changes and why they are necessary.

Another issue is sexual harassment. This worries both employees and management for both legal and ethical reasons. The U.S. Supreme Court ruled in *Monitor Savings Bank v. Vinson* (1986) that a company may be held liable in sexual harassment suits even if management is unaware of the problem and has a general policy condemning any form of verbal or nonverbal behavior that causes employees to feel "uncomfortable" or consider the workplace a "hostile environment."

Organizations, to protect themselves from liability and the unfavorable publicity of a lawsuit, not only must have a policy, they must also clearly communicate the policy to employees and conduct workshops to ensure that everyone thoroughly understands what might be considered sexual harassment. See the discussion in Chapter 12 about a company's legal rights to monitor employee e-mails.

Layoffs

Layoffs present a major public relations challenge to an organization, especially during economic downturns when layoffs are a common event. Julia Hood, a former editor of *PRWeek*, says it best: "The way in which a company handles job reductions can have a significant impact on its reputation, its share price, and its ongoing ability to recruit and maintain good staff. And that presents a major challenge for communication departments."

Although human resource (HR) departments are most often involved in layoffs, it's also a situation in which the expertise of the public relations department is harnessed to ensure employee understanding and support. One cardinal rule is that a layoff is never announced to the media before employees are first informed. Another cardinal rule is that employees should be informed in person by their immediate supervisor; the storied "pink slip" or an e-mail message is unacceptable. Employees who are being retained should also be called in by their immediate supervisor to let them know their status.

> The way in which a company handles job reductions can have a significant impact on its reputation, its share price, and its ongoing ability to recruit and maintain good staff. And that presents a major challenge for communication departments.
>
> *Julia Hood, former editor of* PRWeek

The rumor mill works overtime when there is uncertainty among employees about their job security, so it's also important for the company to publicly announce the layoffs and the impact as quickly as possible. Companies should be very forthright and upfront about layoffs; this is not the time to issue vague statements and "maybes" that just fuel the rumor mill.

Companies that are interested in their reputation and employee trust also make every effort to cushion the layoff by implementing various programs. IBM, for example, announced it would spend about $1 billion on severance and other costs related to shrinking its workforce in 2013. Based on that dollar figure, experts estimated the company would reduce its workforce by 6,000 to 8,000 people. IBM didn't announce a number. Sometimes companies offer employees the option of "voluntary separation" in exchange for one year's pay and a percentage of their annual bonus. Others offer outplacement services, the use of office space, and other programs. Such programs do much to retain employee goodwill even as workers are being laid off. And in recent years, employee communicators have paid more attention to sadness and depression among the survivors of layoffs who feel guilty about their good fortune.

Investor Relations

Another major component of keeping a company's health and wealth is communicating with shareholders and prospective investors. *Investor relations* (IR) is at the center of that process.

The goal of investor relations is to combine the disciplines of communication and finance to accurately portray a company's prospects from an investment standpoint. Some key audiences are financial analysts, individual and institutional investors, shareholders, prospective shareholders, and the financial media. Increasingly, employees are an important public, too, because they have stock options and 401 retirement plans.

Individuals who specialize in investor or financial relations, according to salary surveys, are the highest-paid professionals in the public relations field. One reason for this is that they must be very knowledgeable about finance and a myriad of regulations set down by the SEC on initial public offerings (IPOs) of corporate stock, mergers, accounting requirements, the contents of quarterly financial reports, and public disclosure of information. A company going public for the first time, for example, is required by the SEC to observe a "quiet period" in which company executives do not talk about the offering to analysts or the press so that they don't "hype" the stock.

Google's initial public offering of its stock on the New York Stock Exchange had to be delayed because CEO and founder Marc Benioff had made some comments about the stock offering in a major magazine interview during the SEC's mandated "quiet period." The foul-up gave Google a rocky start in terms of positioning its stock and building a good impression among Wall Street analysts. See Chapter 12 for more information about the SEC.

Investor relations staff must be very comfortable with numbers, as they primarily communicate with institutional investors, individual investors, stockbrokers, and financial analysts. They are also sources of information for the financial press such as the *Wall Street Journal*, *Barron's*, *Bloomburg.com*, and the *Financial Times*. In their jobs, they make many presentations, conduct field trips for analysts and portfolio managers, analyze stockholder demographics, oversee corporate annual reports, and prepare materials for potential investors.

Marketing Communication

Many companies use the tools and tactics of public relations to support the marketing and sales objectives of their business. This is called *marketing communication* or *marketing public relations*.

Thomas L. Harris, author of *A Marketer's Guide to Public Relations*, defines marketing public relations (MPR) as "The process of planning, executing, and evaluating programs that encourage purchase and consumer satisfaction through credible communication of information and impressions that identify companies and their products with the needs, wants, concerns, and interests of consumers."

In many cases, marketing public relations is coordinated with a company's messages in advertising, marketing, direct mail, and promotion. This has led to the concept of *integrated marketing communication* (IMC), in which companies manage all sources of information about a product or service in order to ensure maximum message penetration. This approach was first discussed in Chapter 1 as a major concept in today's modern public relations practice.

In an integrated program, for example, public relations activities are often geared toward obtaining early awareness and credibility for a product. Publicity in the form of news stories builds credibility, excitement in the marketplace, and consumer anticipation. These messages make audiences more receptive to advertising and promotions about the product in the later phases of the campaign. Indeed, there is a growing body of support that public relations is the foundation for branding and positioning a product or service.

Product Publicity

As the cost and clutter of advertising have mounted dramatically, companies have found that creative product publicity is a cost-effective way of reaching potential customers. See Chapter 14 for more on product publicity and branding. Even mundane household products, if presented properly, can be newsworthy and catch media attention.

In Dallas, Sfuzzi Uptown restaurant earned press coverage when Sean Lowe of ABC's *The Bachelor* appeared on Valentine's Day for a meet and greet. Philadelphia-based Wawa convenience stores sponsored "The Wawa Welcome America! Festival" in Philadelphia on July 4, 2013. It got media coverage when it gave away 15,000 hoagies on its 21st annual Wawa Hoagie Day, which was part of the festival.

Product publicity can be generated in other ways. *Food & Wine* magazine sponsored a survey to determine the sexiest foods; Old Bay Seasoning sponsors shrimp-eating contests; Briggs & Stratton, which makes small engines for lawnmowers, compiles an annual top 10 list of beautiful lawns; Hershey Foods set a Guinness record by producing the world's largest Kiss—a chocolate candy that weighed several tons.

The newest trend is "brand journalism," also known as "content marketing." The idea is that organizations should produce stories and features that are written in a journalistic style that focuses primarily on information instead of promotion. Red Bull, for example, creates a lot of buzz and brand loyalty for its product by posting feature stories on its website about athletes who do extreme sports. Many stories, of course, also report on sports events that Red Bull sponsors.

Product Placement

Product placement refers to the appearance of a product as part of a movie or television program, thereby helping to promote the brand. The Mercedes-Benz that the characters in the movie drive to the airport, the United Airlines flight that takes them to a destination, the Hilton where they stay, and the Grey Goose vodka martinis they drink in the bar are all examples of product placement.

Increasingly, product placements are the result of fees paid to film studios and television producers. Sometimes, there is a benefit to both parties. For example, when The Gap volunteers to provide the entire wardrobe for a television show, such a deal reduces the cost of production for the producer and at the same time gives the clothing firm high visibility. See Chapter 15 for more information on product placements in broadcast media.

According to Stuart Elliott and Julie Bosman, writing in the *New York Times*, opportunities to promote products inside television shows come in the form of what is called branded entertainment or product integration. They include mentioning brands in lines of dialogue, placing products in scenes so they are visible to viewers, and giving advertisers roles in plots of shows, whether it is a desperate housewife showing off a Buick and a shopping mall or a would-be apprentice trying to sell a new flavor of Crest toothpaste. . . . The goal of branded entertainment is to expose ads to viewers in ways that are more difficult to zip through or zap the traditional commercials. Devices like digital video recorders and iPods are making it easier than ever to avoid or ignore conventional sales pitches.

Cause-Related Marketing

Companies in highly competitive fields, where there is little differentiation among products or services, often strive to stand out and enhance their reputation for CSR by engaging in *cause-related marketing*. In essence, this means that a profit-making company collaborates with a nonprofit organization to advance the latter's cause and, at the same time, increase the former's sales. A good example is Yoplait yogurt, which tells customers that 10 cents will be donated to support breast cancer research for each pink Yoplait lid customers send in.

Companies supporting worthy causes have good customer support. One study, by Cone, found that 83 percent of Americans wish companies would support causes as part of their corporate citizenship. Forty-one percent said they have bought a product because of its association with a cause.

American Express has been a pioneer in cause-related marketing. In 1983, it raised $1.7 million for the restoration of the Statue of Liberty and Ellis Island. More recently, it conducted an award-winning campaign called "Small Business Saturday." The idea was to support small businesses on the Saturday after Thanksgiving. The Friday after Thanksgiving is popularly known as "Black Friday"—the biggest shopping day of the year.

According to Amex marketing executive John Hayes, "Within two weeks of the [Small Business Saturday] initiative being announced, 1.4 million consumers had joined the movement on Facebook." Small retailers saw a 28 percent increase in their revenue that day compared to the previous year. Of course, this also generated more revenue for Amex when customers used their American Express credit cards. Small Business Saturday continues to be a new tradition thanks to American Express' support of the cause.

Selecting a charity or a cause to support involves strategic thinking. A chain of pet care stores, for example, would be better served by sponsoring projects with the Humane Society of America than by contributing a percentage of its sales to the

American Cancer Society. By the same token, a company such as Bristol-Myers Squibb that makes drugs to treat cancer would find a relationship with the American Cancer Society a good fit. Here are some tips for conducting cause-related marketing:

- Look for a cause related to your products or services or that exemplifies a product's quality.
- Consider causes that appeal to your primary customers.
- Choose a charity that doesn't already have multiple sponsors.
- Choose a local organization if the purpose is to build brand awareness for local franchises.
- Don't use cause-related efforts as a tactic to salvage your image after a major scandal; it usually backfires.
- Understand that association with a cause or nonprofit is a long-term commitment.
- Realize that additional budget must be spent to create public awareness and build brand recognition with the cause.

Corporate Sponsorships

A form of cause-related marketing is corporate sponsorship of various activities and events such as concerts, art exhibits, races, and scientific expeditions.

According to IEG, Inc. (www.sponsorship.com), companies annually spend about $20 billion sponsoring activities ranging from NASCAR races, the Kentucky Derby, the Academy Awards, PGA golf tournaments, and even the concert tour of Tim McGraw (sponsored by Pennzoil). In 2013, for example, companies spent $3.76 billion sponsoring motorsports, $1.28 billion sponsoring music events, $849 million sponsoring fairs and festivals and another $708 million sponsoring tennis matches. Many of these events, unlike causes, are money-making operations in their own right, but a large part of the underwriting often comes from sponsorships provided by other corporations.

Sponsored events offer four benefits:

1. They enhance the reputation and image of the sponsoring company through association.
2. They give product brands high visibility among key purchasing publics.
3. They provide a focal point for marketing efforts and sales campaigns.
4. They generate publicity and media coverage.

Sponsorships can be more cost effective than advertising. Speedo, the swimwear manufacturer, sponsors the U.S. Olympic swim team (as well as several other national teams), getting its name before millions of television viewers. At the London Games, Speedo garnered substantial publicity for its new swimwear design. A headline in *The Telegraph* provides an example: "Olympic swimming records set to tumble at London 2012 as Speedo unveils Fastskin3 swimwear system."

Another level of high visibility for corporations is to put their names on stadiums and concert halls. Bank of America agreed to pay $7 million per year to put its name on the Carolina Panthers home stadium in Charlotte, North Carolina, until 2024. Federal Express is paying $7.6 million each year through 2025 for naming rights to FedEx Field, home of the Washington Redskins. In Philadelphia, Lincoln financial

Pepsi Sponsors Beyoncé in $50 Million Deal
A billboard in New York showing a blonde Beyoncé conquering the world one sip at a time is part of a $50 million sponsorship deal that Pepsi has made with the popular singer. In addition to Beyoncé appearing in Pepsi ads and showing up at other Pepsi-sponsored events such as the Super Bowl, the sponsorship also includes a multi-million dollar fund for Beyoncé to spend on her own humanitarian projects. A Pepsi news release called it a "creative content development fund."

group, not exactly a household name, snapped up naming rights for the new stadium for the Eagles pro-football team. The company's reasoning: Its name will become recognized as a major brand by those attending Eagles games and the 10 million fans who watch NFL games at home on television.

On occasion, a company will sponsor an event for the primary purpose of enhancing its reputation among opinion leaders and influential decision makers. Atofina Chemicals, for example, usually sponsored events and advanced science education. Nevertheless, it agreed to sponsor an exhibit of ballet-themed works by Dégas at the Philadelphia Art Museum to highlight the company's history as a Paris-based corporation.

Viral Marketing

Long before the rise of the Internet, professional communicators recognized the value of favorable recommendations and "buzz" about a product or service. For public relations programs, the primary objective has always been to enhance or maintain the reputation of the company or celebrity. Today, thanks to technology, "word of mouth" can be used to generate greater traffic to a website, where both marketing and public relations objectives can be met.

The primary purpose of viral marketing is to stimulate impulse purchases or downloads, but increasingly, pass-it-on techniques on the Web are also intended to help public relations professionals meet goals for reputation management and message dissemination. Generating excitement about the release of a musician's latest CD and touting the opening of a movie are two common ways viral marketing is employed in the entertainment business. See the Insights box on page 481 about Duke Energy's social media efforts.

Viral marketing has adopted a new terminology and some special techniques that take advantage of new technology to stimulate the natural inclination of people to tell others about a good deal, a good service, or a good group. One successful example of viral marketing is Metro Trains of Melbourne, Australia's public service announcement video "Dumb Ways to Die" (dumbwaystodie.com).

A catchy, silly song coupled with animated characters has earned the video 55 million views and counting on YouTube. The object of the PSA was to raise awareness among young adults about the dangers of being careless around the public transit trains. In addition to poking a stick at a grizzly bear, using your private parts as piranha bait, or taking your helmet off in outer space, the catchy music video notes that an equally dumb way to die is by standing on the edge of a train station platform. The public service campaign won the top award in the public relations category at the Cannes Lions Festival of Creativity in 2013.

Another campaign that went viral was Dove's "Real Beauty Sketches." It, too, has garnered 55 million and counting views on YouTube. *AdWeek* described the campaign as "centered on a video in which a criminal sketch artist drew women as they described themselves, and as other people described them. The differences are stark—a potent reminder to women that they're more beautiful than they think." This was an extension of Dove's years-long "Real Beauty" campaign to promote women's positive self-image, as well as the brand's reputation. The Dove "Sketches" campaign also won at the 2013 Cannes Lions Festival. It earned the Titanium Grand Prix, the award festival's highest honor.

Some viral marketing firms devise ways to stimulate the natural spread of recommendations through financial incentives called cohort communication. Going beyond the relatively organic spread of information via tactics such as a "Tell a Friend" feature, viral marketing specialists use more calculated tactics such as careful dissemination of favorable reviews. Software systems track referrals to a website or recommendations sent to friends, with senders chalking up cash or merchandise credits. Recommending a CD to friends might earn the recommender credit or free downloads of music tracks, for example.

Detractors worry that viral marketing is too easily recognizable as commercial manipulation, except among hard-core enthusiasts. Others say that it is deceptive and unethical to facilitate or reward what should be a natural process of trusted friends exchanging tips and links about great deals or great websites. When the music industry, for example, recruits fans to log on to chat rooms and fan websites to hype a band's new album, some liken the process to the questionable practice of "payola" in the radio industry, in which disc jockeys are paid to play certain tracks.

Viral marketing companies argue that the technique will work only when the idea, the movement, or the product earns genuine support from the marketplace. Public relations professionals need to make careful and ethical decisions to decide how best to use the Web to spread messages.

Environmental Relations

Another aspect of corporate responsibility that is gaining momentum is corporate concern for the environment and sustainable resources. The end of the 20th century witnessed major clashes between corporations and activist NGOs about a host of environmental and human rights issues. See Chapter 20 for more on NGOs. The current trend, however, favors cooperation and partnerships among these former adversaries. Many companies, such as Shell, now issue annual corporate responsibility reports and work with environmental groups to clean up the environment, preserve wilderness areas, and restore exploited natural resources.

Measuring environmental sustainability is difficult. An organization called Global 100 (global100.org) provides one model. It examines data from large, global companies and identifies the 100 companies that are successful in practicing "clean capitalism." The criteria for selection to the Global 100 include things such as energy, carbon, water, and waste productivity. In 2013, a Belgian technology company Umicore was named to the top place on the Global 100. Doug Morrow, vice president of research for the magazine *Corporate Knights*, which sponsors the Global 100, said Umicore "squeezes more revenue out of each resource" while generating fewer negative outputs such as greenhouse gases and waste.

Other ways of recognizing the environmental sustainability of corporations are being named to the *Sustainability Yearbook*, recognized by the Ethical Corporation Responsible Business Awards, or even in the *Guardian* Sustainable Business Awards, sponsored by the U.K. *Guardian* newspaper. Of course, public relations plays a role in both providing data to the recognition programs and heralding the news when their company earns such an award.

Other large corporations around the world are forging alliances with various NGOs to preserve the environment, promote human rights, and provide social/medical services. The following are some examples of long-term CSR programs:

- Unilever, the food and consumer products company, is helping to restore a dying river estuary in the Philippines. The campaign is one of several programs in the company's global Water Sustainability Initiative.
- LM Ericsson, a Swedish telecommunication company, has a program called Ericsson Response, which provides and maintains mobile communication equipment and expertise for humanitarian relief operations.
- Merck, the pharmaceutical giant, partnered with the Bill and Melinda Gates Foundation on a five-year AIDS project in Botswana and often sells its drugs at cost in developing nations.

Corporate Philanthropy

Another manifestation of CSR is *corporate philanthropy*, the donation of funds, products, and services to various causes. Donations range from providing uniforms and equipment to a local Little League baseball team to a multimillion-dollar donation to a university for upgrading its programs in science and engineering. In many cases, the organization's public relations department handles corporate charitable giving as part of its responsibilities.

American corporations gave $18 billion in 2012 to a variety of causes. Although there is a common perception that corporate philanthropy provides the lion's share of donations, the actual percentage is very small. Of the total $316 billion given in 2012, only 6 percent was from corporations. The largest amount of money given, 72 percent, was given by individuals. See Chapter 21, on nonprofits, for more information on charitable contributions.

Corporations, of course, have long used philanthropy to demonstrate community goodwill and to polish their reputations as good citizens. There's also evidence that corporate giving is good for business and retaining customers, with 76 percent of Americans claiming to take corporate citizenship into consideration when purchasing products. At the same time, 76 percent believe that companies participate in philanthropic activities to get favorable publicity, and only 24 percent believe corporations are truly committed to the causes they support.

Getting good publicity, no doubt, is a factor in philanthropy, but companies should not view this as the ultimate objective of being charitable. The survey organization Cone says companies should be very careful about bragging about their good deeds, because the public will be skeptical about the motivation. Instead, companies should concentrate on the people they help, and the programs they showcase should be more than "window dressing." The research firm further states, "Never do it for publicity. Do it for building your business, your brand equity, and your stakeholder relations."

It also should be noted that companies don't donate to just anything and everything. The cause must be related to reflect the company's core values and how the company is positioning itself in the marketplace. Coca-Cola, for example, wants to be strongly identified with healthy, active living, so it tapped into the public's support for parks and asked them to vote for their favorite park and win a grant. The top three vote-getting parks received $100,000, $50,000, and $25,000, respectively, to help restore a part of their parks. More than 13 million votes were cast, 38,000 park photos were uploaded, and more than 17,000 videos were viewed online.

This kind of *strategic philanthropy* is defined by Paul Davis Jones and Cary Raymond of IDPR Group as "the long-term socially responsible contribution of dollars, volunteers, products, and expertise to a cause aligned with the strategic business goals of an organization." Such giving, they say, can reap a number of benefits for the corporation, including:

- Strengthened reputation and brand recognition
- Increased media opportunities
- Improved community and government relations
- Facilitation of employee recruitment and retention
- Enhanced marketing
- Access to research and development
- Increased corporate profitability

Corporate philanthropy, despite its potential benefits, does have its limitations. A large grant by a corporation, for example, cannot offset a major financial scandal or the negative publicity of a class-action suit for discrimination of female employees. Philanthropy can't erase public concern about the promotion and marketing of some

on the job

INSIGHTS

Nudist Group Makes Pitch for Corporate Sponsors

The American Association of for Nude Recreation is facing the bare facts; it's extremely difficult to convince companies that they should become sponsors.

The organization, according to the *Wall Street Journal*, thought the time was ripe for sponsorship since there's been a movement toward organic fare, natural foods without preservatives, and a raft of products such as Naked Juice, Near Naked granola, and even naked beer. There's, of course, the natural tie-in to sunscreens. According to reporter Jennifer Maloney, "The response has been skimpy." But E.&J. Gallo Winery did send a case of Naked Grape Wine.

The association, however, believes they have much to offer potential sponsors. The organization has 34,000 fairly affluent members and almost 300 affiliated Nakation sports clubs, resorts, RV campgrounds, and B&Bs. Association executives also think the movement will grow. One survey indicated that 15 percent of Americans like to go skinny-dipping, and 12 percent would like to go to a nude beach. One member, an owner of a nudist resort, also notes, "Nudists are where the gay community was back in the '60s. A lot of people are still in the closet. It's a much bigger market than people realize."

The organization, so far, has one major sponsor. Tilley hats of Toronto seems to be preferred "uniform" of nudists. Alas, even the famous Geico lizard, who's always nude, didn't pick up the opportunity to become a sponsor. The organization's search for sponsors, however, did get plenty of exposure through a front-page story in the *Wall Street Journal*.

Source: Maloney, J. (2013, January 14). Nudists Seek Corporate Sponsor Looking for Greater Exposure. *Wall Street Journal*, 1, 12.

products such as tobacco. Wal-mart, faced with community opposition to "big-box" stores, probably won't change its opponents' minds by giving several million dollars to local schools.

Another downside to corporate philanthropy can arise when special interest groups object to the cause that's being funded. Pro-life groups, for example, often target companies that give grants to Planned Parenthood and ask their supporters to boycott the company's products. According to Paul Holmes in a *PRWeek* column, there's even a Washington, D.C., group called the Capital Research Center that seeks to "end the liberal bias in corporate philanthropy." The group objects to company donations to "antibusiness" charities such as the Sierra Club.

All this leaves corporations somewhat in a quandary about what charities are "safe" and which ones might raise controversy and protests at annual stockholder meetings. There's also the consideration of what special groups are most influential or have the ability to cause headaches for the corporation through boycotts, pickets, and demonstrations. In bottom-line terms, the corporation also thinks about what decision would be best to keep its overall customer base. See the Insights box above about one group's difficulty in getting corporate sponsors.

Despite the possible downsides and controversies, corporate philanthropy is a good tool for enhancing reputation, building relationships with key audiences, and increasing employee and customer loyalty. It also serves the public interest in many ways.

Summary

Today's Modern Corporation

- Giant corporations have operations and customers around the globe.
- The public is often distrustful of these large entities because of their perceived wealth and power.
- Corporate financial scandals in recent years have further eroded public trust.
- Corporations must make special efforts to win back their credibility and the public's trust, and to tell the story of what corporations contribute to quality of life.
- The concept of CSR is high on the list of public relations priorities.
- Public relations plays a role in corporate transparency and ethical principles of conduct to improve corporate governance.

Media Relations

- The public's perception of business comes primarily from the mass media.
- Corporations must build a rapport with business editors and reporters by being accessible, open, and honest about company operations and policies.

Customer Relations

- Customer service, in many ways, is the front line of public relations.
- Customer satisfaction is important for building loyalty and telling others about the product or the reputation of the company.
- Public relations professionals solicit customer feedback as often as possible and act to satisfy customers' needs for communication and service.
- The U.S. population is becoming more diverse.
- Companies are now establishing communication programs, as well as marketing strategies, to serve this growing diverse audience.
- Special interest groups exert pressure on corporations to be socially responsible.
- Companies cannot avoid activist groups; they must engage in dialogue with them to work out differences.
- Consumer boycotts also require public relations expertise to deal effectively with a group's demands.

Employee Relations

- Employees are the "ambassadors" of a company and are the primary source of information about the company.
- Employee morale is important, and a good communication program does much to maintain high productivity and employee retention.
- The cardinal rule of corporate communications is to first talk to employees in person before announcing a layoff to the public.
- Many companies ease the impact of a layoff by providing a severance package.

Investor Relations

- Public relations professionals who work in investor relations must be knowledgeable about communication and finance.
- This highest-paying field in public relations requires extensive knowledge of government regulations.

Marketing Communication

- Companies often take an integrated approach to campaigns, with public relations, marketing, and advertising staffs working together to complement each other's expertise.
- Product publicity and product placement are part of marketing communication.
- Cause-related marketing involves partnerships with nonprofit organizations to promote a particular cause.
- Another aspect of marketing communication is corporate sponsorships.

Environmental Relations

- A new trend line is for corporations and activist organizations to have a dialogue and engage in collaborative efforts to change situations that damage the environment or violate human rights.

Corporate Philanthropy

- Companies give about $18 billion a year to worthy causes.
- Corporations select a charity that is complementary to their business and customer profile.
- Corporate philanthropy is part of an organization's commitment to be socially responsible.

Case Activity A Corporate Wellness Campaign

Most studies show that health and well-being are linked to employee engagement, productivity, talent retention, creativity, and innovation. In other words, it's good business to encourage "wellness" among its employees.

With this in mind, the management committee of GlobalTek (including the chief communications officer) has decided to launch a "Wellness Challenge" program to provide educational materials and programs that would "challenge" employees to become more healthy, control their weight, and get more physical exercise.

The challenge is that GlobalTek, a telecommunications company, has 50,000 employees, including 10,000 in Europe and Asia. It's the responsibility of the corporate communications department to plan and execute the campaign. One key objective is to get at least 30 percent of the employees involved in the "challenge." Another objective is to make the program fun and enjoyable for employees to motivate their participation. What kind of campaign would you organize, and what communication tools (including activities) would you use to get employee engagement?

Questions For Review and Discussion

1. In a world of global interdependence, the public is at times distrustful of large multi-national corporate organizations. How can PR help in building trust levels?
2. Why is trust in corporate leadership important? Is such trust increasing or decreasing? Why?
3. Is corporate social responsibility a PR tool? Support or deny, eliciting your reasons.
4. People form opinions about individuals and entities primarily based on media coverage. What should PR professionals do to build an environment of mutual respect and understanding with media?
5. If an activist group has called for the boycott of a particular company's products, would you be inclined to stop buying the company's products? Why or why not? How would you respond to a boycott if you are doing public relations for the target company?
6. What is the role of PR in building customer satisfaction?
7. How should a company tell its employees about a layoff?
8. What is cause marketing? Does PR have a role in it? How?
9. What are some of your favorite examples of cause-related marketing? Do you buy products linked to causes? Why or why not?
10. Why is corporate sponsorship of concerts, festivals, and even the Olympics considered a good marketing and public relations strategy.
11. Corporate philanthropy is now strategic. Do you think this makes corporate philanthropy too self-serving? Why or why not?

Media Resources

Edelman Trust Barometer (2013). Retrieved from www.edelman.com/insights

Barstow, D. (2012, April 21). Vast Mexico bribery case hushed up by Wal-mart after top-level struggle. *New York Times.* Retrieved from www.nytimes.com

Berger. B. K. (2012, Winter). The need for speed: PR leadership study highlights global trends, future needs. *The Public Relations Strategist 18*(4), 8–9.

Casey, B. (2013, January). Newsmaker Ken Cohen. *PRWeek 16*(1), 30–31.

Kelly, K. S., Laskin, A. V., & Rosenstein, G. A. (2010). Investor relations: Two-way symmetrical practice. *Journal of Public Relations Research, 22*(2), 182–208.

Kim, S. Y., & Park, H. (2011). Corporate social responsibility as an organizational attractiveness for prospective public relations practitioners. *Journal of Business Ethics 103*(4), 639–653.

Laskin, A. V. (2011). How investor relations contributes to the corporate bottom line. *Journal of Public Relations Research, 23*(3), 302–324.

Luippold, R. (2012, November 16). "Dumb Ways to Die" song: Australian Metro puts out adorably animated PSA. *The Huffington Post*. Retrieved from www.huffingtonpost.com

Pettigrew, J. E., & Reber, B. H. (2013). Corporate reputation and the practice of corporate governance. In Craig Carroll (Ed.), *Handbook of communication and corporate reputation*, Hoboken, NJ: Wiley Blackwell.

Searcy, T. (2012, May 2). 12 publicity "hooks" to promote your products. *Moneywatch*. Retrieved from www .cbsnews.com

Shearman, S. (2013, May 28). Activists call on Facebook to pull sexist content. *PRWeek*. Retrieved from www .prweekus.com

Smith, J. (2013, March 18). America's 100 most trustworthy companies. *Forbes*. Retrieved from www.forbes.com

Ying, T. (2012, September 19). Chinese boycott may be more costly for Japan than the tsunami. *Business Insider*. Retrieved from www.businessinsider.com

Public Relations in Entertainment, Sports, and Tourism

chapter 18

After reading this chapter, you will be able to:

Understand the role of public relations in the entertainment industry and the opportunities for employment

Describe the nature of celebrity culture and how publicists and media create celebrities

Use techniques to promote a play, concert, or other entertainment event

Outline the tactics used by public relations staff to promote a sports team

Describe the work of public relations personnel in the tourism industry

A Major Part of the American Economy

Many public relations specialists work for corporations, which was discussed in the last chapter, but a large number are also attracted to the more glamorous areas of business such as entertainment, sports, and tourism. Indeed, these industries are a major part of the American economy and compete in the marketplace for the disposable income of virtually all Americans.

The scale of the entertainment and recreation industries are reflected in some general statistics from 2012:

- More than 1.4 billion movie tickets were sold, generating almost $11 billion in revenues.
- About 30 million attended concerts. Bruce Springsteen and the E Street Band tour, for example, generated $200 million in revenues and attendance of 2.1 million.
- NASCAR had attendance of 3.6 million and generated $3 billion in revenues.
- More than 17 million attended NFL games and the football conglomerate reported revenues of $9.5 billion.
- The cruise ship industry adds $40 billion annually to the U.S. economy and creates about 350,000 jobs.
- Tourism generates nearly 10 percent of the global gross product and is projected to represent one in every ten jobs by 2022.

This chapter gives an overview of entertainment, sports, and tourism and the vital role that public relations specialists play in these industries' success. It also discusses how public relations tactics are used to promote a variety of recreational activities and some of the challenges that public relations personnel must overcome in their work.

Celebrities, however, are a major component of the entertainment and sports industries, so this chapter begins with an exploration of today's celebrity culture and how publicists use traditional media, bloggers, and social media to create and promote celebrities.

The Cult of Celebrity

According to historian Daniel Boorstin, a celebrity can be defined as a person well known in one of a wide variety of fields such as science, politics, or entertainment. In other words, Barack Obama, Pope Francis, and even Lady Gaga are legitimate celebrities. Being a celebrity today, however, doesn't necessarily mean that it's based on some sort of outstanding achievement or accomplishment.

The entertainment industry, in particular, is fueled by the constant publicizing and glorification of personalities. Individuals such as movie stars, pop music divas, television personalities, and talk show hosts generate a great deal of publicity in the media and on the Web, but today's celebrity status is often only temporary, as there are continually new celebrities who try to take the place of established icons in the public's esteem and interest.

Stephen Cave, reviewing a number of books about fame and celebrity in the *Financial Times*, makes several observations. First, he says, "Fame is a product of certain industries—most notably the mass entertainment business—not a gold star given by the good fairy to the deserving." He goes on, "Fame is not what it used to be . . . Now it is heaped on anyone who is runner-up in a television talent show, subsequently strips for a lads' magazine, then writes their life story age 25 while on day-release from rehab." Cave continues, "But the fame trade has indeed changed. The rise of instant communications, digital media and mass literacy have all fueled the market for stars. Dedicated TV channels, websites, and magazines such as Heat and People have exponentially increased the speed and volume of celebrity gossip—and the number of celebrities."

An example of the media's fixation on celebrity was the coverage of the death of pop star Michael Jackson in mid-2009. In the 24 hours after his death, the Pew Research Center for Excellence in Journalism found that 60 percent of the total news coverage was devoted to his death, his life story, and his legacy. The coverage eclipsed all other major news stories such as health care reform, major political violence in Iran, and the greenhouse gas bill.

on the job

SOCIAL MEDIA IN ACTION

A Royal Birth Generates Record Coverage

Celebrities fuel media coverage around the world, and the birth of a son to the duke and duchess of Cambridge (William and Kate) was no exception. About 500 journalists camped out for 30 hours at a London hospital in what was dubbed the "Great Kate Wait."

When the birth of Prince George was finally announced, there was an explosion of stories on the Web and in social media. During the first hour of the birth announcement, web analytics by Journalism.co.uk found that 12 percent of all the content read or watched around the world related to the arrival of the world's newest celebrity. Mobile phones accounted for 21 percent of total "baby watching" globally.

BBC News received global record traffic on the day of Prince George's birth. The BBC website, for example, had 19.4 million unique browsers globally in the first 24 hours, and its Facebook page reached more than one million subscribers in a 24-hour period. The first photo of the baby had 10,000 retweets.

Source: www.journalism.co.uk/news

The three-hour memorial service for Jackson at Staples Center in Los Angeles, however, seemed to confirm the media's assessment that there was tremendous public interest in the story. The *New York Times* dubbed it "one of the most watched farewells in history" because the service attracted a television audience of 31 million and almost 8 million online viewers. Later that day, 20 million watched the prime-time specials offered by the major TV networks.

The death of a celebrity, particularly under unusual circumstances, generates massive media coverage, but so does the birth of a child to the "right" celebrity couple. Angelina Jolie and Brad Pitt, for example, received $14 million from *People* magazine for an exclusive interview and photos of their newborn twins in 2008. It was the best-selling issue of *People* in seven years.

More recently, the birth of Britain's Prince George in 2013 also generated a media frenzy that is highlighted on page 501. On a more somber note, the passing of Nelson Mandela in December 2013 generated more than two weeks of worldwide coverage about his life and march to freedom from 27 years in prison to becoming the first Black president of a new South Africa in 1994.

The Public's Fascination with Celebrities

Psychologists offer varied explanations of why the public becomes impressed—"fascinated" might be the more accurate word—by highly publicized individuals. In pretelevision days, the publicity departments of the motion picture studios promoted their male and female stars as glamorous figures that lived in a special world of privilege and wealth. The studios catered to the universal need for fairy tales, which often have a rags-to-riches theme. Dreaming of achieving such glory for themselves, young people with and without talent go to Hollywood to try to crash through the magical gates, almost always in vain.

> The advent of celebrity culture now drives the entertainment news cycle.
>
> *Rachel McCallister and Mark Pogachefsky, writing in* Public Relations Tactics

Many ordinary people leading routine lives also yearn for heroes. Professional and big-time college sports provide personalities for hero worship. Publicists emphasize the performances of certain players, and television sports announcers often build up the stars' roles out of proportion to their actual achievements; this emphasis is supposed to create hero figures for youthful sports enthusiasts to emulate, but the doping scandal of Lance Armstrong and other athletes, including the scandal of Tiger Woods having multiple affairs while married, has somewhat diminished the idea that professional athletes are good role models.

Athletic teams, however, still retain public esteem and loyalty—especially if they are winning. Sports enthusiasts develop a vicarious sense of belonging that creates support for athletic teams. To signify their loyalty, both children and adults gobble up expensive baseball caps, sweatshirts, and other clothing that advertise the team and let others know they are loyal fans. Indeed, a major revenue stream for most professional teams is the sale of merchandise. The NFL teams make about $3 billion annually on merchandise.

Still another factor behind the public's fascination is the desire for entertainment. Reading fan magazines or listening to TMZ report on the personal lives and troubles of celebrities gives fans a look behind the curtain of celebrity. Such intimate details provide fuel for discussion among friends or even something to tweet about.

And talking about Hollywood's latest couple break-up is certainly more fun than discussing tax reform.

The Work of a Publicist

A public relations practitioner working in the entertainment industry is usually called a *publicist* because his or her primary responsibility is getting publicity in the media for his or her organizations and individual clients. In the early days of public relations, which were discussed in Chapter 2, many of these individuals were called *press agents*.

In fact, the term *press agent* is still used on Broadway, and the union representing them is called the Association of Theatrical Press Agents and Managers. Ralph Blumenthal, a reporter for the *New York Times*, explains the basic process in the early days: "Broadway producers hired press agents to type out news releases about their shows and hand-carry them to the press so the press would write stories about the shows and people would buy the papers, read the stories and go to the shows, and the producers would be happy and the press agents would keep their job."

Press agents also dreamed up creative stunts to get publicity. Press agent Jim Moran was famous for his media-grabbing stunts. He publicized the book *The Egg and I* by sitting on an ostrich egg for 19 days until it hatched. On another occasion, he led a bull through a china shop to help the flagging career of an actor. Hollywood publicists were also creative at generating publicity. Fox Studios insured Betty Grable's legs for $1 million, and Henry Rogers made Rita Hayworth a celebrity by borrowing designer clothes to market her as one of Hollywood's best dressed women.

Mark Borkowski, owner of an entertainment public relations firm in Los Angeles, recounts a number of publicist exploits in his book *The Fame Factory: How Hollywood's Fixers, Fakers, and Star Makers Created the Celebrity Industry*. He makes the point that publicists had as much trouble keeping their charges out of the news as in it. Fabricated biographies were the norm. Actor Micky Rooney later confessed that he had been "collecting blondes, brunettes, and redheads" while the studio publicists were working very hard to portray him as a clean-cut young man who collected stamps, coins, and matchboxes. Cave, in reviewing Borkowsk's book, concluded, "The best paid publicists spent their time arranging back-street abortions, covering up affairs, and making suicide attempts look like gardening accidents."

Today's publicists tend to avoid the antics of Hollywood's "golden era." In fact, Howard Bragman writes in his book *Where's My 15 Minutes* that "A good PR person monitors the relationship between perception and reality and keeps things in check." However, while today's entertainment publicists still work to put a positive "spin" on the foibles of their celebrity clients, their tactics are more sophisticated in the age of the Internet.

Borkowski, for example, says modern communications has "killed off the ability to lie so freely." In other words, the intense scrutiny of traditional media, blogs, and entertainment websites makes every entertainment celebrity's life a virtual fish bowl. Some "dust-ups" in 2013 that received considerable media attention included the following:

- Reese Witherspoon had to issue an apology after she was arrested for disorderly conduct by interfering with a police officer who was arresting her husband, Jim Toth, for drunken driving. She reportedly asked the police officer, "Don't you know my name?" and tried to use her Hollywood celebrity status to intimidate the officer, which, of course, didn't work.

> If Jennifer Aniston cuts her hair, and you know the hair stylist, get in touch.
>
> —*Rob Shuter,* Huffington Post *celebrity columnist, giving advice to entertainment publicists at New York seminar*

- Taylor Swift, branded as "America's Sweetheart," damaged her image by getting into a well-publicized fight with comediennes Tina Fey and Amy Poehler who made some comments about Swift's many romantic relationships at the Golden Globe Awards. Swift wasn't amused and gave a national media interview saying, "There's a special place in hell for women who don't help other women."
- Celebrity chef Paula Deen also suffered reputational damage when it came to light that she had used a racial epithet. As a result, the Food Network dropped her show and several companies dropped sponsorship deals with her.

Reputational damage can be minimized if celebrities listen to seasoned public relations counselors. Rubenstein Communications, for example, advised David Letterman when reports started to circulate that he was being blackmailed by another CBS staffer for having sex with members of his female staff. Letterman rapidly

on the job INSIGHTS

Wanted: A Press Coordinator for a Network

Entertainment public relations isn't exactly *Dancing With the Stars*, but many are attracted to opportunities in the field. The following are excerpts of an entry-level job posted on LinkedIn by NBC Universal, Inc., for a press coordinator that attracted about 200 job seekers.

Responsibilities:

- Maintain call-logs, meeting calendars, expense logs, and other clerical responsibilities
- Act as liaison between the head of the department, its various branches (publicity, talent relations, events, awards) and the other sectors within the company
- Edit pitches, releases, memos, etc.
- Some junior publicist responsibilities such as brainstorming, talent handling, and promotional research
- Build and manage event invite lists, industry contact sheets, photo schedules, etc.
- Develop and maintain positive relationships with executives, talent, agents, managers, producers and public relations agencies in order to ensure maximum positive coverage for NBCU programming

Qualifications:

- Bachelor's degree from four-year college or university
- Minimum of two years entertainment publicity experience
- Proficiency in Microsoft Excel, Word, Outlook, PowerPoint
- Strong reading and writing skills

Desired Characteristics:

- Self-motivated, ability to prioritize and multitask
- Strong work ethic, dependable, and loyal
- High level of skill in paying attention to detail
- Ability to work in a fast paced environment
- Ability to maintain high level of discretion in handling confidential information
- Excellent interpersonal and customer service skills

acknowledged the affairs and apologized on the air to his staff, fans, and wife for his transgressions. Tiger Woods also made public apologies to his fans and sponsors for his sexual transgressions, and his reputation seemed to improve by winning golf tournaments. As he notes in a Nike commercial, "Winning takes care of everything."

Crisis communications on behalf of superstars is one aspect of entertainment public relations, but rank-and-file entertainment publicists in New York and Los Angeles spend most of their working days doing more routine activities such as (1) developing biographies of individual actors; (2) preparing digital media kits that include color photos, video clips, and fact sheets about individuals and project; (3) researching possible story angles that may interest a publication, an entertainment news site, or an entertainment blogger; (4) maintaining a client's Facebook and Twitter account; and (4) setting up media/blogger interviews. See the Insights box below for a typical job listing for a press coordinator in Hollywood.

Many work for film studios to generate publicity and buzz for new films. Universal Pictures bolstered coverage for its *Couples Retreat* by taking newspaper and TV reporters on a lavish junket to Bora Bora, where the film was being shot. When 20th Century Fox released the DVD for *Ice Age: Dawn of the Dinosaurs*, publicists invited reporters to witness the construction of a 48-foot-tall ice sculpture resembling the star of the movie, Scrat the squirrel.

The basic idea is the drip-by-drip technique. Motion picture studios, television production firms, and networks apply this tactic when a show is being shot. In other words, there is a steady output of information about the production. A public relations specialist, called a unit man or woman, is assigned to a film during production and turns out a flow of stories for the general and trade press and plays host to media visitors to the set. The television networks mail out daily news bulletins about their shows to media television editors. The networks assemble the editors annually to preview new programs and interview their stars. The heaviest barrage of publicity is released shortly before the show opens.

In addition to the movie studios and television networks, publicists also work in public relations firms. A typical Los Angeles–area public relations firm specializing in personalities and entertainment has two staffs: one staff of "planters," who distribute stories about individual clients and the projects in which they are engaged, and another staff of "bookers," who place clients on talk shows and in other public appearances. Some publicity stories are for general release; others are prepared especially as an "exclusive" for a syndicated Hollywood columnist, a major newspaper, or an influential blogger.

Entertainment firms may also specialize in arranging product placement in movies and television programs. Usually the movie or television producers trade visible placement of a product in the show in exchange for free use of the item in the film. The movie *Up in the Air* is an example. It's no accident that George Clooney, the star, stays at Hilton Hotels throughout the film. Hilton offered free lodging to the film crew, provided the sets, and even promoted the movie on its key cards and its in-room television channel. In the movie *Soccer Mom*, Chrysler arranged for its Dodge Caravan to play a leading role. This kind of product placement, called "branded entertainment," was discussed in Chapter 15.

Executives have publicists. Stars have publicists. The tiniest movies will arrive in April at the Tribeca Film Festival with publicity teams, often three or four of them. Sometimes, it seems, even the publicists have publicists.

Michael Cieply, reporter for the New York Times

In sum, publicists and their work are an integral part of the entertainment industry. They are valued for their ability to grab attention through screenings, panel discussions, film festivals, and parties and for their ability to use current issues or controversies to get publicity—which is much cheaper than paid advertising. At Fox Searchlight Pictures, for example, a third of the company's executive roster is assigned to publicity or promotions. See the Insights box below on how to promote a play.

The Business of Sports

The obsession with sports is flourishing in the United States and around the world. One indication of this is that a large percentage of the searches on Google every day are done by people looking for sports information. Simon Kuper, writing in the *Financial Times*, even says, "checking for sports news online is now probably the most common way of consuming sport ahead of watching or playing or talking about it." Indeed, one of the quotes attributed to Nelson Mandela, is "Know your enemy—and learn about his favorite sport."

Sports are also the most watched events on television around the world. Indeed, the global television audience for the London Olympics was about 3 billion people,

on the job INSIGHTS

How to Promote a Play

Despite the high visibility of Hollywood and New York publicists, the vast majority of individuals working in the arts are scattered throughout the country in smaller cities and work for local theatre and music groups.

Their primary jobs are to generate ticket sales and develop broad, local support for the organization. In order to do this effectively, they must have a marketing and public relations plan that includes a number of tactics.

This may include the following:

- Developing a well-designed website that serves as a complete portal to the organization, including schedules, ticket prices, actor/musician bios, photos from prior performances, links to reviews, etc.
- Establishing a presence on social media, such as a Facebook page and a Twitter account. A blog written by the executive director or artistic director is desirable.
- Constantly updating the subscriber e-mail base and regularly communicating with them.
- Developing attractive brochures and order forms that can be mailed to homes or given out at special events.
- Preparing a digital media kit for each production, including news releases, bios, photos, and appropriate background materials.
- Pitching story ideas about the cast, production, and so on to appropriate journalists covering the arts. Invite appropriate journalists to opening night and arrange media interviews for them.
- Organizing special events and receptions to cultivate individual donors and corporate donations.
- Establishing partnerships with other arts organizations and businesses in the community.

who watched 11,000 athletes from almost 200 nations compete in 28 sports. The 2010 FIFA World Cup in South Africa attracted an even larger global TV audience, estimated to be between 3.5 and 4 billion people. A similar audience is expected for the 2014 World Cup in Brazil.

> Sport has become a global business, as well as a recreation for billions.
>
> *Patrick Lane, writing in the* Economist

Although soccer is the world's leading sport in terms of attendance and revenues, the United States has its own major sports. Baseball, because of the large number of games played in a season, has the highest attendance (50 million), but football (17 million attending games) gets the most hype with its Super Bowl every February to determine the "world championship." Indeed, the Super Bowl has practically become a national holiday in the United States and has a major economic impact. See the Insights box on page 508.

Indeed, all sports are stimulated by intense marketing and public relations efforts. Programs at both professional and big-time college levels seek to arouse public interest in teams and players, sell tickets to games, and publicize the corporate sponsors who subsidize many events. Increasingly, too, sports publicists work with marketing specialists to promote the sale of booster souvenirs and clothing, a lucrative sideline for teams.

Sports publicists use a variety of public relations tactics. They prepare media kits, write bios on players, compile stacks of statistics, wine and dine sports reporters, maintain the press box, arrange media interviews, book player appearances on television and radio sports shows, handle crises when players run afoul of the law, maintain the team website, write a team blog, and provide constant updates for fans on Facebook and followers on Twitter.

Social media, in particular, is becoming a major public relations tactic for professional sports. A number of NFL teams now have dedicated social hubs that bring together all their various social media channels in a single destination for fans. The Denver Broncos, for example, has a hub that has a heavily visual, title-like interface with live video feeds, twitter streams, Facebook updates, and tie-ins with other social media sites such as Pinterest and Instagram. There's even a link to "Broncos for Women" in order to woo female fans. All social media activity can be tagged to surface on the hub using the hashtag #Broncoscamp.

Community Relations

Another important duty of the public relations staff of a professional team is community relations. Players are rarely from the local community, and a good relationship with the community is necessary for ticket sales, so every team does charitable work.

A good example is how Jason Zillo, media relations director of the New York Yankees, organized a "Hope Week." The impetus for the week, in part, was that the team had been criticized over ticket prices in their new stadium and that there was local grumbling about the taking of park land to build the stadium. Zillo arranged for Yankees players to do such things as visit sick children in hospitals, make appearances at local schools, talk with a Little Leaguer who had cerebral palsy, and visit two developmentally challenged workers in a law firm's mailroom.

Other teams, such as the San Francisco 49ers, have a community foundation that raises money through team-sponsored golf tournaments and other events for the purpose of funding various community organizations that work with disadvantaged

on the job INSIGHTS

The Super Bowl: An Economic Engine on Steroids

Sports in America are a major business, and one of its major events is the Super Bowl. Spending in and around Super Bowl Sunday means increased business for hotels, grocery stores, fast food outlets, and liquor stores. The following are some factoids on the economic impact of the 2013 Super Bowl in New Orleans.

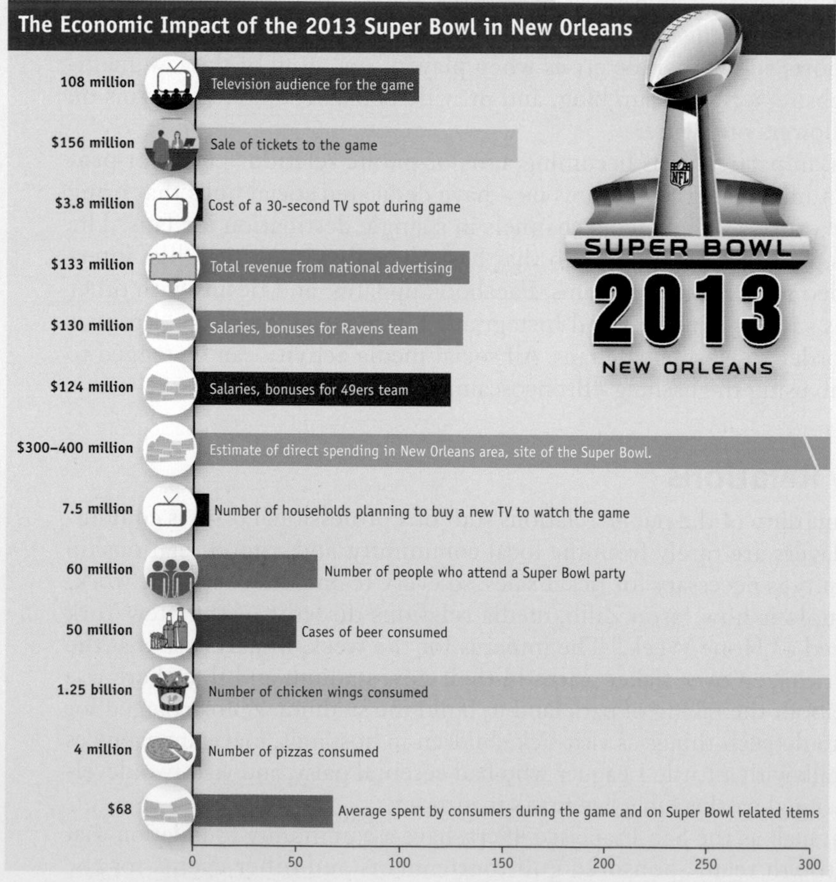

Sources: www.wallst.com2013/2013/01/25super-bowl; Steel, E. (2013, February 3). The ad zone. *Financial Times*, 18.

children. Such foundations often have their own community relations staff that, although separate from the business of playing games, coordinates with players to make appearances at various community events.

Another aspect of sports public relations is representing a high-profile athlete to ensure that they get favorable media coverage and endorsement deals. When scandal erupts, however, athletes often use crisis communication experts and firms to manage the situation. Chime Communications, for example, began advising South African Oscar Pistorius, also widely known as the "blade runner" in the London Olympics, after he was charged with murdering his girlfriend on Valentine's Day 2013.

When we started this program, we agreed that you just don't reach out to a community. You must invite them to be a part of the family before saying, "Here's how you buy tickets."

Jason Pearl, VP of the San Francisco Giants

Sports publicists, by definition, are cheerleaders. They constantly work to build fan and community enthusiasm for the team and make star players celebrities. For college publicists, this means creating enthusiasm among alumni and making the school seem glamorous and exciting in order to recruit high school students. At other times, college sports publicists organize massive promotional campaigns to promote a player for a national award such as the Heisman Trophy.

Sometimes, usually when the team is a winner, these efforts succeed spectacularly. When a team is an inept loser, however, the sports publicist's life turns grim. He or she must find ways to soothe the public's displeasure and, through methods such as having players conduct clinics at playgrounds and visit patients in hospitals, create a mood of hopefulness: "Wait 'til next year!"

Win or lose, the immense popularity of sports makes it extremely difficult to find an entry-level public relations position in the field. Major league teams have hundreds of applicants for internship positions, and even full-time employment has a reputation for low salaries. Yet if a student takes a broader view, there are opportunities in college sports, the minor leagues, and even corporate sports-sponsorship programs.

The Tourism Industry

Tourism is one of the world's largest industries. Elizabeth Becker, author of *Overbooked: The Exploding Business of Travel and Tourism*, writes, "In gross economic power, tourism is in the same company as oil, energy, finance, and agriculture." She further notes that tourists took one billion foreign trips in 2012. The Chinese are the world's newest tourists, which is highlighted on page 510.

Indeed, it has already been noted by the World Economic Forum that tourism accounts for 9 percent of the world's gross domestic product and will represent 10 percent of the world's workers by 2022. Tourism's contribution to the GDP in the United States is nearly 10 percent, but in countries such as Spain, it rises to almost 15 percent of GDP.

With money in their pockets, people want to go places and see things. Stimulating that desire and then turning it into the purchase of tickets and reservations is the goal of the travel industry. Public relations has an essential role in the process, not only in attracting visitors to destinations but also in keeping them happy once they arrive. According to William P. DeSousa-Mauk, president of DeMa Public Relations, "PR is the most effective way to get an unbiased, positive endorsement of any destination."

on the job

A MULTICULTURAL WORLD

Chinese Tourists Flood the World

They are everywhere. They crowd luxury stores in London, mob Union Square in San Francisco, and raise their cameras in unison to photograph the Mona Lisa at the Louvre in Paris. They are the world's newest tourists from the world's second largest economy, China.

Indeed, visitors from China spent more than $100 billion on foreign trips in 2012 and replaced American and German tourists as the world leaders in spending on foreign travel. China's rising middle-class in terms of disposable income, coupled with fewer restrictions on foreign travel, has fueled the boom in Chinese visitors. As a result, Chinese tourists made 83 million foreign trips in 2012, compared to only 10 million in 2000, according to the United Nations World Tourism Organization (UNWTO).

The rising middle class of Brazil, India, and Russia have also begun to travel abroad in greater numbers, but Chinese tourists are making the biggest impact. For several years, luxury stores in Europe and the United States have added Chinese-speaking sales staff. And the French department store Printemps has even built duty-free counters specifically for Chinese visitors. Hotels, tour companies, and restaurants are also gearing up to serve the Chinese market by training staff to be more knowledgeable about Chinese cuisine, culture, and language.

Hilton Hotels, for example, developed several initiatives to attract Chinese tourists. It started with staffing the front-desk with Chinese-speaking personnel, but then went on to add amenities for Chinese guests in the rooms. Tea kettles, Chinese teas, slippers, and a TV Channel dedicated to Chinese programming were added. Even the breakfast menu was changed. In addition to the traditional American breakfast, Chinese visitors could also enjoy their traditional foods such as congee, fried rice, noodles, and dim sum.

In an effort to promote all this to potential Chinese tourists, Hilton also teamed up with a prominent Chinese fashion designer to create a limited-edition slipper on behalf of the hotel chain that was exclusive to Hilton guests. The slipper represented the campaign's attempt to bridge East–West by having a water dragon design in the blue fabric of Hilton's brand color. A news conference at its Shanghai Hotel and an event in New York's fashion district launched the campaign. Hilton also created an official brand channel on Sina Weibo, China's leading social network.

The campaign generated a 130 percent increase in bookings by Chinese guests, and Chinese enrollment in the Hilton awards program increased 80 percent. In the first 14 days of the program, the hotel chain generated more than $100,000 in bookings from Chinese clients, according to *Ragan's PR Daily*, www.prdaily.com.

Phases of Travel Promotion

Traditionally, the practice of travel public relations has involved three steps:

1. Stimulating the public's desire to visit a place
2. Arranging for the travelers to reach it
3. Making certain that visitors are comfortable, well treated, and entertained when they get there

Traditional tactics such as story placements in magazines and newspapers, advertising, colorful brochures mailed to potential travelers, and travel fairs are still extensively used, but the Internet and social media have radically transformed the techniques of what is called "destination marketing." Today, for example, travel is promoted through interactive websites, content-rich social channels, and apps that help individuals do everything from learning about a destination to booking a tour, a flight, a hotel, and even a restaurant at the destination. In fact, one study by Nielsen research indicated that 88 percent of smartphone users in the United States accessed travel information through mobile devices, spending 93 minutes a month on travel apps and websites.

Facebook, Pinterest, and Instagram are also being used to provide information and engage potential travelers. A study by Text 100 public relations, for example, found that 87 percent of people under age 34 said they used Facebook for travel inspiration and that recommendations from friends and family on Facebook and other social channels were the top factor in deciding to visit a location. Other sources of travel information, according to the study, were Internet searches (55 percent), individual provider websites (49 percent), sales promotions by airlines and hotels (48 percent), and online travel sites (46 percent). In terms of apps, one example is the Miami Convention & Visitor's Bureau. Miami images are available for download as wallpaper through a Flickr photo stream.

> **Cut the text and add more colorful and more vibrant photos of your destination to demand attention.**
>
> *Meredith Pratt, Stanton Communications, in* O'Dwyer's PR Report

Public relations specialists in travel also stage creative events to attract attention. Weber Shandwick drove traffic to its YouTube video campaign for the Bahamas by sending 200 swimtog-clad commuters to walk through New York's Grand Central Station. Bikini-clad models visited Times Square with a giant beach ball to promote the U.S. Virgin Islands. For more examples of innovative travel promotions, see the Insights box on page 512.

Another widely used method of promoting travel is the familiarization trip, commonly called a "fam trip," in which travel writers and/or travel salespeople are invited to a resort, theme park, or other destination for an inspection visit. In the past, fam trips often were loosely structured mass media junkets. Today they are smaller and more focused. See the Insights box on page 513 about subsidies for travel writers.

Appeals to Target Audiences

Travel promoters identify target audiences and then create special appeals and trips for them. Great Britain's skillfully designed publicity in the United States is a successful example. Its basic appeal is an invitation to visit the country's historic places and pageants. It also offers London theatrical tours, golf expeditions to famous courses in Scotland, genealogical research parties for those seeking family roots, and tours of the cathedrals. New Zealand, on the other hand, promotes its natural beauty and capitalizes on its location for the filming of *the Lord of the Rings* trilogy that draws Hobbit fans from around the world.

on the job INSIGHTS

Fifty Shades of Travel Promotion

The world of tourism is very competitive in terms of attracting visitors to a country, a state, or even a resort hotel. The following is a sampling of programs that have won awards and recognition for their creative approaches:

Edgewater Hotel, Seattle

The hotel's public relations staff capitalized on the media frenzy about the popular *Fifty Shades of Grey*, by offering a "Fifty Shades of Romance" program for book fans to spark their own Christian and Anastasia–like escape. The book's signature Bollinger Rose champagne was in the room, as well as Audi joyrides throughout Seattle in an R8 Spyder and a recreated romantic sail on Puget Sound. The campaign got mention on NBC's *Today Show*, CBS News, CNN, and *USA Today* but the bottom line was that summer occupancy went up 12 percent.

Tourism Australia

The organization took a page from Queensland's successful campaign of having an international competition for the "Best Job in the World," which was being a caretaker for an island on the Great Barrier Reef. Its idea, however, was to have an international competition for six different "exotic" jobs in Australia such as Wildlife Caretaker in South Australia, Lifestyle Photographer in Melbourne, or even Chief Funster for New South Wales.

Applicants were required to submit video clips telling why they wanted the job, but they also had to get all their friends and relatives to post notes on Facebook, Twitter, and so on supporting their applications. The finalists were then flown to Australia for interviews and the final selection. The contest attracted about 330,000 and 40,000 eventually submitted a 30-second video.

Tourism Australia added about 300,000 "friends" to its Facebook Page, and a Google Search about the competition showed 1.7 million results. Shel Holtz, in his blog, shel@holtz.com, noted, "Getting people from the desired target audience to create inventive and original content that lets everyone know why and how badly they want a shot at your product or service can attract a lot more attention than you telling everyone how much they should want your product or service."

Velas Resorts, Mexico

The resort hosted a social media contest to increase its visibility among customers looking for a "destination wedding." Couples were asked to submit stories about how they met using various social media platforms. The public then voted on the winner who would receive a free wedding at the resort.

The project received hundreds of entries and thousands of votes. There was renewed social media activity when the winning couple got married at the resort.

Visit Britain

The organization, taking advantage of the London Olympics, launched a campaign to increase tourism throughout the United Kingdom, hosting a number of events during the Olympics to showcase other parts of Britain such as bog snorkeling in Wales and Scottish highland dancing. In the United States, the organization used Brits Victoria Beckham and *Vogue* editor Anna Wintour to unveil a train decorated in the colors of the Union Jack at Manhattan's Grand Central Station during Fashion Week. The program, in part, fueled a 4 percent rise in American visitors to the United Kingdom.

Packaging Packaging is a key word in travel public relations. Cruises for family reunions or school groups, family skiing vacations, university alumni study groups, archaeological expeditions, and even trips to remote Tibet are just a few of the so-called niche travel packages that are offered. A package usually consists of a prepaid arrangement for transportation, housing, most meals, and entertainment, with a

on the job INSIGHTS

How Many "Freebies" to Accept?

Newspaper and magazine stories about travel destinations, which are essential in tourism promotion, can pose a problem for writers and public relations people. Who should pay for the writers' expenses in researching these stories?

Some large newspapers forbid their travel writers from accepting free or discounted hotel rooms, meals, and travel tickets. They believe that such subsidies may cause writers to slant their articles too favorably, perhaps subconsciously.

Many freelance writers, however, can't afford to abide by such rules because smaller publications and magazines only pay $100 to $1,000 for an article, and their travel expenses are often much higher. Thus, travel writers say they cannot make a living without such "freebies" as a plane trip, a room, or meals at a resort.

The American Society of Travel Writers (www.satw.org) doesn't forbid its members from receiving "freebies" from airlines and resorts, but its ethics code states, "Content providers shall be open with editors/publishers about their own subsidized travel for an assignment." In other words, the travel writer that takes a "fam" trip with expenses paid must disclose this to the publication or website considering his or her article.

The ethical question is whether the writer should mention any subsidy as part of the article. A second question is whether the publication has the ethical responsibility to be transparent and let the readers know the context in which the story was written. The third question is whether a public relations firm should hire a freelancer to write a travel story and then pitch it to the media under his or her byline without disclosing that payment was received from the public relations firm on behalf of a client.

What do you think? Should travel writers, publications, and even public relations firms be more transparent about how an article was funded?

professional escort to handle the details. Supplementary side trips often are offered for extra fees.

Appeals to Seniors The largest special travel audience of all is older citizens. Retired persons have time to travel, and many have ample money to do so. Hotels, motels, and airlines frequently offer discounts to attract them. As a means of keeping old-school loyalties alive, many colleges conduct alumni tours, heavily attended by senior citizens.

A large percentage of cruise passengers, especially on longer voyages, are retirees. Alert travel promoters design trips with them in mind, including niceties such as pairing compatible widows to share cabins and arranging trips ashore that require little walking. Shipboard entertainment and recreational activities with appeal to older persons—nostalgic music for dancing rather than current hits, for example—are important, too.

Public relations goals don't stop with creating a difference. The exciting twist to travel and tourism public relations storylines now is to use smart branding, social marketing, and strategic partnerships to find new ways to communicate messages to put clients on top.

—*Kerry Anne Wilson, president of the Zimmerman Agency, in O'Dwyer's* Public Relations Report

Coping with Threats and Crises

Tourism, however, is a somewhat volatile business even in the best of times. Public relations professionals must be prepared to cope with unexpected situations and even crises that can seriously

Royal Caribbean's *Oasis of the Seas*

There's always something new in the travel industry. When Royal Caribbean launched the *Oasis of the Seas* several years ago, it generated considerable media coverage because it was the world's largest cruise ship. Many stories focused on the sheer size of the ship (longer than four football fields) and the logistics of accommodating up to 6,300 passengers, to say nothing of the 2,100 crew members. One unusual recreational feature is shown in the photograph; it's a zip line above the ship's boardwalk and cabin balconies that gives passengers a bird's-eye view of the entire ship.

impact the operations of hotels, cruise lines, airlines, or even the entire tourism business of a city, state, or country.

The lingering effects of the recession still affect the tourism industry, but other threats can also have a devastating effect. A good example is how Mexican tourist officials must work very hard to lure tourists when daily headlines in the U.S. media keep reporting the continuing violence of drug cartels.

Other events and environmental factors also threaten tourism. America's Gulf Coast, for example, had a major drop in tourism in 2010 when an oil rig caught fire and sank, leaving a well that spewed millions of barrels of oil into the Gulf Stream. Tourism officials in Alabama, Mississippi, and Florida had to redouble their promotional efforts to convince tourists that the regions still offer good value and reassure them that the damage to pristine beaches was being contained.

In another situation, Alaska tourism officials had to ease travelers' concern over the eruption of Mount Redoubt. The eruption provided great video and photographs for the media, but didn't do much to persuade potential tourists to visit the state. The Alaska Travel Industry Association hired a public relations firm to reassure the public. The firm sent out news releases and advisories to the media stressing that the resulting ash cloud was not significantly affecting Anchorage airspace and that the fall of debris had been "limited to a few small, remote communities."

Civil and political unrest can also affect tourism in a big way. Athens, for example, had major riots and demonstrations when the Greek economy went into a tailspin and austerity measures were introduced. Images of demonstrators battling police in the streets of Athens caused many tourists to cancel trips to the country. Egypt, which counts heavily on tourism, has also seen tourism plummet as a result of major civil unrest. An organization, such as a major cruise line, can also have a crisis when a ship goes aground or goes dead in the water. See the PR Casebook about Carnival Lines on page 515.

In all these situations, it's a major challenge for public relations professionals to counter the headlines and images portrayed in the news media that imply major safety problems or that the whole city or country is under siege. In reality, the unrest or violence is usually restricted to a small area. In any case, tourism officials and their public relations staffs often have to redouble their efforts to entice tourists back to a country.

Terrorism is also a factor that requires immediate response. Public relations staff at Marriott headquarters in Maryland had their Saturday interrupted when a suicide bomber smashed his explosive-packed truck into the Islamabad, Pakistan, Marriott Hotel, killing 40 people and severely injuring hundreds more, before a gas leak eventually ignited and destroyed the whole hotel.

A five-part crisis team was immediately assembled. The *research and writing team* was responsible for being in touch with hotel staff in Pakistan and issuing the first statement within 15 minutes after gathering initial information.

PRCasebook

Poop on the Deck: Carnival Cruise Line Has a Crisis

The headline in the *Wall Street Journal* summed up the problem: "Carnival Cruise Mishap Leaves PR Mess in Wake."

The "PR Mess" was the result of a drawn-out saga when a Carnival cruise ship, the *Triumph*, had an engine room fire that left it dead in the water with no air conditioning or use of toilets. What started as a pleasant four-day cruise to Cozumel, Mexico, then became a five-day "sewage-soaked" ordeal for 4,200 people aboard, according to the *New York Times*.

Tug boats were deployed in the Gulf of Mexico to tow the disabled ship to Mobile, Alabama, but that didn't alleviate sanitary conditions on the ship that got worse by the day. Such dire conditions were widely covered by the traditional and social media because passengers regularly posted stories on their Facebook pages and Twitter feeds, plus uploaded videos to YouTube. And, of course, journalists were on the dock when the ship finally reached Mobile. One passenger told Fox News, "There's poop and urine all along the floor. The floor is flooded with sewer water . . . and we had to poop in bags."

Carnival also communicated during the ordeal using news releases, news conferences, and postings on its social media platforms. According to *Ragan's PR Daily*, "Carnival continually updated its Facebook page with messages about the logistics of tugging the boat to shore, details on compensation for the passengers aboard, statements from the CEO, Garry Cahill, and more." It was announced that passengers would receive a full refund, $500 in compensation, and discounts on future Carnival cruises. CEO Garry Cahill also issued a lengthy apology on Carnival's Facebook page. When the ship docked in Mobile, he made another apology on the ship's PA system to all the disembarking passengers. But it was an uphill battle. Carnival's reputation had already been tarnished the year before in 2012 when a ship of a Carnival subsidiary, the *Costa Concordia*, ran aground on an Italian island with the loss of 32 lives.

These two high-profile incidents gave Carnival a black eye, but they also severely bruised the entire $40 billion cruise industry in terms of safety and potential business. A Harris poll found that public perception of cruise line quality declined 13 percent in the three months after the Triumph incident. In addition, the average trust score among all seven major cruise brands was down 12 percent and intent to purchase was down 11 percent.

As of late 2013, Carnival passenger bookings had not recovered and the company added another $50 million to its $525 million marketing and advertising budget to lure customers back. But issues of reputation will persist. Public relations experts say it will take one to three years for Carnival to restore its reputation unless, of course, there's another "incident."

The *media team* received information from the research team and prepared news releases and statements for the media. The *internal communications team* got information to employees. The *community relations team* communicated with the Red Cross and other government agencies.

The *logistics team* set up a "war room" to ensure that all communications technologies were readily available and also set up a Pakistan location. The first statement was posted on Bill Marriott's well-known blog expressing sadness at the loss of lives and the injuries to people. Marriott's senior vice president for Asia was dispatched to Islamabad to coordinate rescue efforts and communications while the staff at headquarters posted updates to the employee intranet and asked supervisors to cascade information down to other employees. The basics of crisis communications were discussed in Chapter 10.

Summary

A Major Part of the American Economy

- Entertainment, sports, and tourism are big business. Billions of dollars are spent every year on movies, concerts, sporting events, and travel.
- Because there are multiple options for people to spend their discretionary income, each industry spends a great deal of money on advertising, marketing, and public relations to compete with each other and entice customers.

The Cult of Personality

- Today's mass media focus on the publicizing and glorification of celebrities in the fields of sports and entertainment and even high-profile criminals and politicians.
- The cult of celebrity is fueled by the public's desire for entertainment, wish fulfillment, hero worship, a vicarious sense of belonging, and a desire for entertainment.
- Public relations people are generally called *publicists* in the entertainment industry because their primary job is to generate publicity for a film, a concert, or an individual star.
- Entertainment publicists are often called upon to do "damage control" when a celebrity runs afoul of the law or makes an ill-considered statement.

Promoting an Entertainment Event

- Publicity campaigns to promote events may include publicity to stimulate ticket sales.
- The "drip-by-drip" technique involves a steady output of information as the event is being planned. The motion picture industry defines target audiences.

The Business of Sports

- Sports publicists promote both big-time college and professional teams.
- Some publicity focuses on building images of star players.
- Professional teams are now creating social hubs to promote the team through websites, video feeds, and social media platforms such as Facebook, Twitter, Pinterest, and YouTube.
- The Super Bowl is more than a game; it also makes a major economic contribution.

The Tourism Industry

- The global tourism industry is now comparable in size to such industries as agriculture, oil, and finance. By 2022, it's estimated that 10 percent of the world's workforce will be involved in tourism at some level.
- Travel promotion involves encouraging the public's desire to visit a place, arranging for them to reach it, making sure they enjoy their trip, and protecting their safety.
- Campaigns may include a familiarization trip to increase travel agents' awareness. Retirees are a major audience for the tourism business.
- Tourism is a volatile business. There are threats such as economic recession, political unrest, and oil spills, but there are also crises such as a terrorist attack or an accident that kills or injures tourists.

Case Activity Promoting a Resort

Cascades Lodge is a full-service resort located in Estes Park, Colorado, the gateway to Rocky Mountain National Park. It's been in operation for about 30 years and has developed a reputation among its clients as a comfortable, well-maintained property that includes a swimming pool, spa, tennis courts, and a gourmet dining in a beautiful restaurant overlooking the Rocky Mountains.

The problem is that newer properties have been built in the past several years, which has caused a 15 percent decline in occupancy at Cascades. The management has hired your public relations firm to conduct a promotion and marketing program to increase brand identify and increase reservations. The resort has a website that is a bit dated, but it wants to also set up a presence on social media platforms such as Facebook, Twitter, and Pinterest. The management is also open to organizing promotional and special events that would draw guests, including families. Outline a plan for the resort giving specific ideas for how to tap social media and the kind of promotional events that could be organized.

Questions For Review and Discussion

1. Entertainment, tourism, and sports have become large sources of revenue for countries. What role does PR have in attracting a diverse set of target audiences?
2. What is the role of a publicist in making a celebrity successful?
3. When pop star Michael Jackson died, the media devoted blanket coverage of his death and memorial service. Do you think the coverage was excessive? Why or why not?
4. What is meant by community relations? Why it is important for promoting sports?
5. Alleged human rights violations in developing countries have resulted in adverse media coverage for some companies. What role do you think public relations can play in articulating the organization's position, and what effects could be anticipated amongst target audiences?
6. Describe the work of an entertainment publicist. Would you be interested in applying for the job of press coordinator that is given on page 504. Why or why not?
7. How can a publicist do damage control if a celebrity makes an ill-considered statement?
8. How would you create publicity or "buzz" about a new play or musical performance?
9. If you worked in sports public relations for a team, what kind of duties would you have on a daily basis?
10. What facts and figures show that global tourism is now a major industry?
11. What country now leads the world in tourism spending?
12. What are the three phases of promoting a tourism destination?
13. Tourism promotion requires creative thinking in terms of staging events that draw public and media attention. Can you give any examples from the text?
14. Tourism is described as a volatile business. What kinds of threats and crises do public relations personnel have to cope with when these crises occur?
15. The PR Casebook on page 515 summarizes Carnival Cruise Line's "public relations mess" when 4,000 passengers went without air conditioning or toilets for five days. How well do you think Carnival handled the situation?

Media Resources

Banks, D. (2013, July). When crisis threatens a travel campaign. *O'Dwyer's Public Relations Report*, 12.

Becker, E. (2013). *Overbooked: The exploding business of travel and tourism*. New York: Simon & Schuster.

Bendel, P. (2013, July). Has anything stayed the same in travel PR? *O'Dwyer's Public Relations Report*, l4.

Borkowski, M. (2009). *The fame formula: How Hollywood's fixers, fakers and star makers created the celebrity industry.* London, England: Sidgwick & Jackson, Ltd.

Cave, S. (2009, January 29). Fall of fame: Every age has its Paris Hiltons, but what does it take to achieve lasting recognition? [Life & Arts section]. *Financial Times,* 13.

Chang, B. (2013, March 17). Taylor Swift gets some mud on her boots. *New York Times*, Style Section, 8.

Fidelzeid, G. (2013, April). Beyond the stars: While celebrity work remains an entertainment PR staple, content and branding also play key roles. *PRWeek*, 40–46.

Futterman, M. (2013, February 15). The big business of fairy tales: Nike takes fire again over one of its athletes. *Wall Street Journal*, D8.

Gingerich, J. (2013, June). Sports star 'comes out' to potential branding boom. *O'Dwyer's Public Relations Report*, 30.

Gingerich, J. (2012, December). False promises, lies are entertainment deal-breakers. *O'Dwyer's Public Relations Report*, 12.

Masidlover, N., and Burkitt, L. (2013, July 24). More Chinese tourists skip the bus. *New York Times*, B10.

Ogg, J. (2013, January 25). Super Bowl XLVII: Major money stats and factoids. Retrieved from www.wallst .com/2013/01/25.

Rodick, S. (2013, January 13). The misfits: Paul Schrader, Bret Easton Ellis, Lindsay Lohan and a porn star named James Deen try to make a move for $250,000 that will save all their careers. *New York Times Magazine*, 22–29.

Rosefelt, R. (2012, November). Rules of the game: The sometimes nauseating, often fun, and always absurd life of a movie publicist. *Columbia Journalism Review*, 32–34.

Rosman, K. (2013, December 11). A Real Publicity Machine: Cellphones, Paparazzi Won't Do: Twitter Pushes Celebrities to Take More Photos. *Wall Street Journal*, D1, 4.

Sebastian, M. (2013, February 13). Despite missteps, Carnival's PR was proactive during Triumph crisis. Retrieved from *Ragan's Daily Headlines*, www .ragan.com

Steel, E. (2013, February 2). The ad zone: How Super Bowl commercials became a cultural phenomenon. *Financial Times*, 18.

Watson, K. (2013, July). Beyond the Buzz: building the social media travel brand. *O'Dwyer's Public Relations Report*, 15.

chapter 19

Public Relations in Government

After reading this chapter, you will be able to:

- Describe the basic purposes and functions of public relations in government
- Explain what public relations professionals do at the federal, state, and local levels
- Define public affairs, government relations, and lobbying
- Describe the roles public relations plays in election campaigns

Government Organizations

Federal, state, and local governments and agencies have a common bond in that all engage in the same types of public relations tasks in order to succeed and thrive. The primary purpose of government agencies and elected officials is to serve the public good. All operate within the framework of regulations regarding the external distribution of funds to individuals or entities.

The public relations functions of government agencies consist primarily of disseminating information. Government agencies often promote the policies of the current administration and seek support from citizens. Such public relations efforts are typically associated with re-election campaigns. Although both major parties, when not in power, decry leadership characterized by election campaign tactics, in recent decades each party has practiced a political campaign style of leadership when in office. See the PR Casebook on the next page on how President Obama's campaign team shifted its focus following his re-election.

> For students and young professionals who have an interest in public affairs and public service, the city [Washington, D.C.] can provide an amazing opportunity for learning both.
>
> *Tom Martin, former VP of corporate communication at FedEx Corp.*

Government entities employ public relations specialists to promote their services, orchestrate fund-raising, spread news of their successes or crises, assist with smooth daily operations or crisis management, implement campaigns that address social issues, and help develop long-range plans and visions. This variety means that aspiring public relations professionals won't want to overlook opportunities for employment in government.

Corporations and other nonprofit organizations also have specialized functions with regards to government organizations that are generally tied to lobbying. This lobbying activity serves to counterbalance the actions of governmental bodies at the local, state, and federal levels that influence the business environment for corporations as well as nonprofit organizations. These functions typically involve gathering, analyzing, and disseminating information, in line with individual organization interest.

Basic Purposes of Government Public Relations

Ideally, the mission of government is public service; no one makes private profit directly from the operation of governments, and governments are noncommercial. In practice, a widespread perception exists that administrations fall far short of these ideals, but the shortcomings of some government officials and employees should not blind citizens to the tangible benefits of the democratic system.

In order for federal, state, and local governments to function efficiently, each branch needs to communicate effectively with its constituents. From election campaigns to military recruitment to floating a bond issue, a common thread runs through governmental public relations: the circulation of information. This core function of all public relations is a particularly prominent aspect of government communication. Skilled public relations professionals are required at every level of our government to ensure that information is disseminated clearly, efficiently, and to the widest number of people.

PRCasebook

Election Campaign Team Turns Policy Campaign Team After Obama's Re-Election

The machinery needed to successfully run and manage a presidential campaign is immense. So, what happens to that machinery after its focus, which is to elect and re-elect its candidate, is successfully completed?

Supporters of President Barack Obama came up with a novel solution—Morph into a policy campaign machine. During his presidential campaigns, President Obama was supported by Obama for America, an organization aimed at mobilizing grassroots supporters to campaign and financially contribute to the cause of the candidate's election. In January 2013, following the President's successful re-election, Jim Messina, the president's 2012 campaign manager, announced a new organization—Organizing for Action (OFA). The *New York Times*, reported that OFA is made up of former Obama campaign advisers who are now using their promotional skills to promote the president's policies. The activities of OFA also provide a means for Democratic activists and others who share the president's policy aims to feel the part of a like-minded community that supports Obama's agenda.

There were technicalities to deal with. Organizing for Action had to be set up as a "social welfare" group under the federal tax code. Such groups are supposed to advance broad community interests. The advantage of a group that is not associated with the government is that it is able to accept unlimited donations from individuals and corporations.

The *Times* reported that the work of the OFA seems to have replaced or augmented work previously done by the White House Office of Political Affairs or the Democratic National Committee. The difference is that an outside group provides additional fundraising opportunities that might otherwise be curtailed by government guidelines that do not allow direct advocacy of specific legislation.

In July 2013, Organizing for Action leaders and supporters held a day-long "summit." The event was focused on energizing volunteers to put pressure on lawmakers when they were in their home states and districts during the August summer recess. The group said it would address legislative topics related to immigration reform, gun control, and environmental protection. "It's all about making sure members of Congress hear directly from the people they represent, on the issues that matter to all of us," Jon Carson, executive director of OFA, wrote in an e-mail to supporters. President Obama, Senate Majority Leader Harry Reid, and House Democratic Leader Nancy Pelosi, all spoke to those gathered for the summit.

The tactic seemed to work. By mid-2013, OFA had raised $13.1 million from 237,000 donors, according to a report in the *Huffington Post*. These resources allowed the organization to launch a million dollar advertising campaign in support of health care reform, hold rallies to support immigration reform, and pressure legislators to pass background check legislation. Success in achieving its objectives may be mixed, but the success of shifting grassroots and fund-raising resources from a candidate to policy support has become a new model that future elected officials will emulate.

Is the shifting of personnel and fund-raising apparatus from a candidate to a cause appropriate? Is it ethical?

What do you think are the best ways to get the voices of voters heard after election day?

As a public relations professional, what tactics would you use to move government policy forward, especially as it related to your company, organization, or industry?

The Federal Government

One of our more scholarly and inquisitive founding fathers succinctly stated the case for federal information services in a democratic system: "A nation of well-informed men who have been taught to know and prize the rights which God has given them cannot be enslaved. It is in the region of ignorance that tyranny begins," said Benjamin Franklin.

Today, the U.S. government may well be both the world's premier collector of information and one of the world's greatest disseminators of information. Advertising is a key governmental activity. Federal agencies spend several hundred million dollars a year on public service advertising, primarily to promote military recruitment, government health services, and the U.S. Postal Service.

The White House

At the apex of government public relations efforts is the White House. The president receives more media attention than Congress and all the federal agencies combined. It is duly reported when the President visits a neighborhood school, tours a housing development, meets a head of state, plays basketball with staff, or even takes his wife to New York City on a date.

The focus on the President in the coverage of the BP oil spill or the aftermath of a natural disaster like Superstorm Sandy exemplifies this attention. Regulators in the Department of the Interior and congressional responsibility for legal guidelines of oil exploration or work by the Federal Emergency Management Agency had little news coverage when compared with the public pressure brought to bear on President Obama.

All presidents have taken advantage of the intense media interest to implement public relations strategies to improve their popularity, generate support for programs, and explain embarrassing policy decisions. And each President has his own communication style, which arises naturally from his experience and personality, but is accentuated by speech writers and media coaches.

Ronald Reagan was considered by many to be a master communicator. A former actor, he was extremely effective on television and could make his remarks seem spontaneous even when he was reading a teleprompter. He understood the importance of using symbolism and giving simple, down-to-earth speeches with memorable, personal appeal. Reagan's approach became the standard for carefully packaged soundbites and staged events.

George H. W. Bush (senior) was no Ronald Reagan as a public speaker, but he did project enthusiasm for his job and had a friendly, but formal, working relationship with the White House press corps. Bill Clinton, on the other hand, was more populist in his communication style. He was at home with information technology and made effective use of television talk shows. Clinton was most effective when he talked one on one with an interviewer or a member of the audience, which explains why historians already consider his most effective response to the Lewinsky and impeachment ordeal to be an extended *60 Minutes* interview with wife Hillary Clinton at his side. Although the interview was at times excruciating, the fallibility and humanity of the President left a lasting impression.

President George W. Bush adopted Reagan's approach to stagecraft and symbolism. A team of television and video experts made sure that every Bush appearance was well choreographed for maximum visual effect. The Bush administration's concept of stagecraft manifested itself in tight control of information and limited media access. Bush, for example, gave substantially fewer press conferences, interviews, and other media events than either Bill Clinton or his father in their first two years in office.

Barack Obama also proved to be a master of the media. His presidential campaign rallies frequently were compared to rock concerts. However, Obama has been criticized for emphasizing style and rhetorical flourish over gravity and substance. Others have worried alternately that his presentation, not unlike that of former Vice President Al Gore or Secretary of State John Kerry, sometimes tends to be a little too verbose and intellectual, even unemotional. Nevertheless, Obama is a skilled orator with a riveting presence, in the tradition of John F. Kennedy, Ronald Reagan, and Dr. Martin Luther King, Jr.

One of the key challenges for American presidents is to be somewhat of a chameleon. Presidents must be likeable and tough. They're often called on to be "cheerleader-in-chief" or to use their bully pulpit. During the 2012 election, Gallup reported a poll in which 60 percent of respondents found Barack Obama likeable, but only 31 percent liked Mitt Romney. A Zogby/Williams poll during the 2004 election found that 57 percent of undecided voters would rather have a beer with George W. Bush than John Kerry.

Since that time, the beer test has become a bit of a cliché as a measure for presidential likeability. A CNN poll in May 2013 showed that 79 percent of Americans said President Obama was likeable. This was during a time when the president was dealing with issues like accusations that the Internal Revenue Service was targeting Tea Party groups for tax audits and controversy over the administration's handling of an embassy attack in Benghazi that left four Americans dead.

This likeability factor is seen as important particularly during elections. Author Tim Sanders even wrote a book on the value of likeability—"The Likeability Factor: How to Boost Your L-Factor and Achieve Your Life's Dreams." So, a key task of people involved in political public relations is to help their candidate be more likeable, more approachable, more like your neighbor. This factor is important in foreign relations as well as in domestic politics.

Congress

The House of Representatives and the Senate are major disseminators of information. Members regularly produce a barrage of news releases, newsletters, recordings, brochures, taped radio interviews, e-mails, electronic newsletters, and videos (often uploaded to YouTube), all designed to inform voters back home about Congress as well as to keep the congressperson in the minds of voters.

According to a 2013 Congressional Research Service report, between 1997 and 2008 House Members sent 1.34 billion pieces of mail at a cost of $224.5 million. In 2009 Congress required itself to report "mass communication" rather than just "mass mailings." According to the report, "Examples of mass communications include radio, television, newspaper, and Internet advertisements; automated phone calls; mass facsimiles; and mass e-mails distributed to a non-subscriber e-mailing list." Between 2009 and 2011, House Members sent 1.27 billion pieces of mass communication at a cost of $131.5 million.

Some question whether this venerable benefit, called a franking privilege, unduly hurts the challenger in a close campaign and helps incumbents hold their position in office. Critics are certainly correct that most of these materials are self-promotional and have little value. *U.S. News and World Report* named the top 10 Representatives according to franking spending in 2010. Topping the list was Democratic Congressman John Adler from New Jersey. Adler spent $487,176 on franking during that year.

Each member of Congress also employs a press secretary, who is a public relations person fulfilling perhaps the most long-standing and basic function in the profession, managing media relations. Says Edward Downes, of Boston University:

> Capitol Hill's press secretaries play a significant role in the shaping of America's messages and consequent public policies. In their role as proxy for individual members, the press secretaries act as gatekeepers, determining what information to share with, and hold from, the media; thus, they have command over news shared with the citizenry.

> Capitol Hill's press secretaries play a significant role in the shaping of America's messages and consequent public policies. In their role as proxy for individual members, the press secretaries act as gatekeepers, determining what information to share with, and hold from, the media; thus, they have command over news shared with the citizenry.
>
> *Edward Downes, Boston University*

White House historians and media watchers describe President Obama's first press secretary, Robert Gibbs, as one of the more authoritative and bold examples of a public relations person asserting a strategic role during daily press briefings. Jay Carney followed Gibbs as Obama's second press secretary. While media watchers may have given him high marks, the president's critics didn't. He was labeled "Obama's liar" and criticized for dodging reporter's questions 9,486 times between 2011 and 2013. Congressional press secretaries are seldom given this sort of authority, visibility, or criticism, serving more as the information disseminators envisioned by Benjamin Franklin.

Federal Agencies

Public affairs officers (PAOs) and public information specialists engage in tasks common to the public relations department of corporations. They answer press and public inquiries, write news releases, work on newsletters, prepare speeches for top officials, oversee the production of brochures, and plan special events.

Senior-level public affairs specialists counsel top management about communication strategies and how the agency should respond to crisis situations. For major projects, departments will collaborate with public relations agencies to design and implement research-based, creative campaigns to achieve high-priority goals for an agency or a department. For details of such a campaign, which helped to stem the tide of substance abuse among teens, see the Insights box on page 525.

The Army recruiting handbook describes the role of a PAO: "Soldiers train on journalism fundamentals at the Defense Information School at Fort Meade, Md. Soldiers must be able to work with little supervision while supporting commanders with a thorough understanding of the fundamentals of Army operations and the media. . . . The training and experience PA Soldiers acquire qualify individuals for civilian jobs in corporate communications positions, media relations, public relations, advertising, broadcasting, newspaper, magazine and online publications as editors and journalists and with other government agencies."

One of the largest public affairs operations in the federal government is conducted by the U.S. Department of Defense (DOD), the cabinet-level agency that oversees the armed forces. Its operations vary from the mundane to the exotic.

One of the longest-running public relations efforts has been the preparation and distribution of "hometown" releases by the military. The Fleet Hometown News Center, established during World War II, sends approximately 1 million news releases annually about the promotions and transfers of U.S. Navy, Marine Corps, and Coast Guard personnel to their hometown media.

A particularly exotic assignment for a military public affairs officer is giving background briefings and escorting the journalists who cover battlefield military operations. When the military initiated the policy of "embedding" journalists within military units during the 2003 invasion and occupation of Iraq, it assigned a large number of PAOs as escorts.

The policy of "embedded" journalists is continuing with U.S. forces in Afghanistan. Journalists sometimes complain about restrictions on their freedom.

on the job INSIGHTS

"Partnership" Stretches Federal Funds

The U.S. Office of National Drug Control Policy (ONDCP) and The Partnership at Drugfree .org developed a campaign titled "Above the Influence" (ATI) beginning in 2005. The federal ONDCP spent $540 million, which was matched by private sector investment, on the campaign. Funding waned until, in 2012, the campaign received no federal support.

In 2013, The Partnership at Drugfree.org decided to continue the campaign. At the time Gil Kerlikowske, director of ONDCP was quoted in a press release, "No one is better suited than The Partnership at Drugfree.org to ensure the continued success of Above the Influence. The Partnership has been there since the beginning of Above the Influence, and together, we have made a difference in the lives of teens."

The campaign had proved itself. By 2013, 80 percent of American teenagers were aware of the Above the Influence campaign. Its Facebook page had almost 1.9 million Likes. The program's success in reducing teen substance abuse was documented in research studies published in the *American Journal of Public Health* and *Prevention Science*.

"We recognize that teens are a tough audience—they don't like to be lectured or told what not to do and they don't worry about their mortality," said Allen Rosenshine, Vice Chairman and Executive Director of The Partnership at Drugfree .org in the press release. "The insightful strategic messages offered by the ATI campaign take a different approach toward teens, reinforcing the fact that they value themselves and their aspirations above the debilitating and self-destructive influence of drugs. Over time, this has proven far more effective than the more traditional, negative anti-drug messages that today's teens largely ignore."

To continue the campaign on a shoestring budget, The Partnership at Drugfree.org engaged in a digital and social media campaign. BuzzFeed, Facebook, Tumblr, and Instagram became part of the ATI campaign. The centerpiece of the renewed campaign was "Made by Me," a contest that encouraged teenagers to submit their ideas for the next ATI public service announcement.

It is not uncommon for federal communication programs to partner with private or nonprofit organizations to develop and distribute messages. Students interested in nonprofit or health communication should familiarize themselves with federal funding programs.

For example, when embedded journalists are required to travel on military vehicles and with military personnel. In short, they can only go where their PAO escorts will take them.

However, a national survey found that U.S. media outlets unreservedly use the embedded reports, especially those from their own organization or network. The degree of insight and detail made possible by being embedded with troops is valued. Public affairs officers in combat areas also noted that modern warfare without clearly defined battle lines and uniformed combatants imposes new constraints:

1. Soldiers' lives are at stake—so information must be managed carefully.
2. Reporters' lives are at stake—venturing out for independent reporting puts journalists in harm's way, from impromptu airstrikes or guerrilla explosive devices.

Public affairs officers in the military face a classic question: what constitutes public information versus propaganda? And to make such a question even more

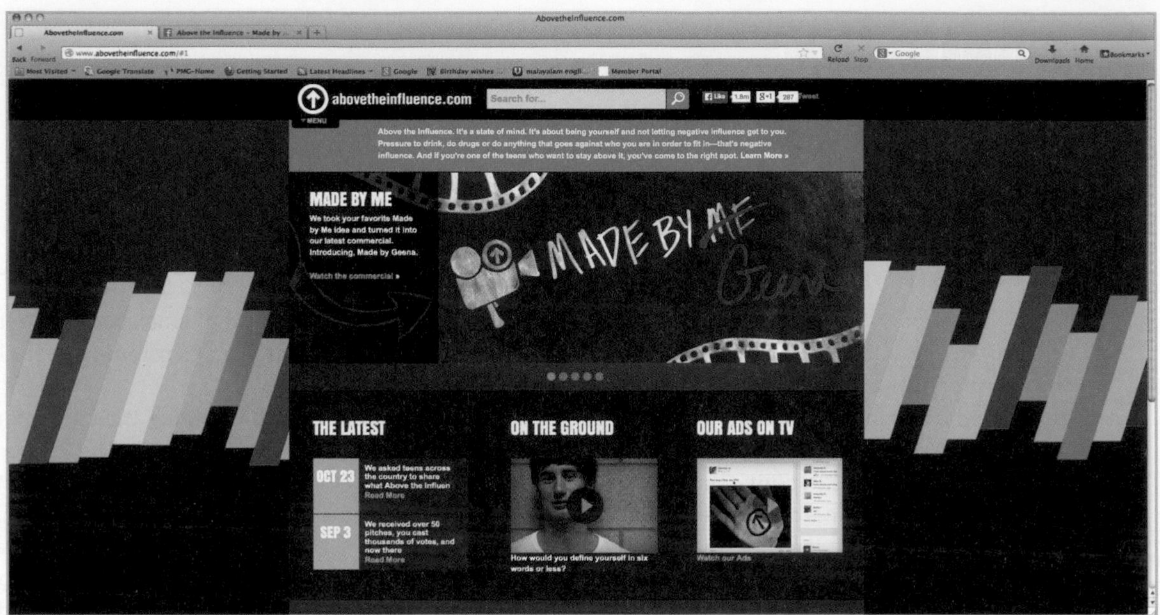

Teenagers were encouraged to submit their ideas for a substance abuse awareness public service announcement at abovetheinfluence.com. The campaign to gather consumer-generated content was called "Made by Me."

problematic, how does a military unit that is violently imposing its will on a region restrain itself when it comes to imposing its will on the media content of the occupied territory?

According to a *Los Angeles Times* report, the Pentagon, a common name for the Department of Defense derived from the shape of the agency's headquarters, contracted with Washington, D.C.-based Lincoln Group to plant more than 1,000 "good-news" stories in several Iraqi Arab-language papers. The contract specified that Lincoln would inform the Iraqi people of American goals and the progress being made, in order to gain public support. At issue was how they accomplished the goal. Lincoln paid the editors at papers such as *Azzaman* and *al Sabah* between $40 and $2,000 to publish articles that were supposedly written by local journalists. In reality, however, many of the stories were prepared by Lincoln staffers, soldiers at "Camp Victory," and military public relations officers.

According to *New York Times* reporters Jeff Gerth and Scott Shane, the source of the articles and opinion pieces was concealed. Lt. Col. Steven A. Boylan defended the practice, arguing that such "pay for play" was necessary because Iraqi papers "normally don't have access to those kinds of stories." Michael Rubin, formerly of the Coalition Provisional Authority, stressed the need for "an even playing field," implying that because the insurgents use deceptive messages, Lincoln's tactics were justified. However, Gen. Peter Pace found the practice to "be detrimental to the proper growth of democracy" and then-President George W. Bush was reportedly "very troubled" by the disclosure.

A Pentagon review found the program basically "appropriate," though it recommended adhering to guidelines about attribution of authorship. The contract with Lincoln continued, with some modifications. In September 2008, Lincoln was one of four firms awarded a $300 million contract for "information operations" in Iraq.

Journalists have widely denounced the practice of pay for play. "Ethically, it's indefensible," said Patrick Butler, vice president of the International Center of Journalists in Washington. Likewise, the Public Relations Society of America has issued a condemnation of the practice. Pamela Keaton, director of public affairs for the congressionally funded Institute for Peace, worries about the long-term effects of what she labels a propaganda campaign: "It will get to the point where the news media won't trust anybody, and the people won't trust what's being quoted in news articles."

The Pentagon also engages in recruitment drives. This is an ongoing challenge because, as the *Washington Post* reported, the needs of the military change. The *Post* noted a need for the U.S. military to increase the number of cybersecurity experts. The newspaper announced that the Pentagon planned to add 4,000 positions to the existing 900 cybersecurity staff.

One tactic used to bolster recruitment goals was paying $36,000 to United Airlines to run a 13-minute video news release entitled "Today's Military" as part of the in-flight entertainment package. The campaign, which described exciting military jobs such as Air Force language instructor and animal care specialist based in Hawaii, was designed to appeal to parents or other adult role models who might recommend the military to their children or relatives.

Another major operation of the Pentagon is assisting Hollywood with the production of movies. More than 20 public information specialists are liaisons with the film and television industries. They review scripts and proposals, advise producers on military procedures, and decide how much assistance, if any, a film or TV show portraying the military should receive.

In 2012, the Navy Special Warfare Command went beyond reviewing scripts and commissioned the movie *Act of Valor* as a recruiting tool for the Navy SEALs. When *Top Gun* was released in 1986 the military was ready to capitalize on the action-filled Tom Cruise movie. Following the movie in some theaters, moviegoers were greeted by military personnel at recruiting tables. The *Los Angeles Times* reported at the time, "Navy recruiting officials say they didn't keep track of that operation's success, but they have noticed more inquiries than usual about the naval aviation officer candidate program since the movie's release."

Movies portraying the military in a positive light, such as *Battleship* (2012), *The Hurt Locker* (2010), *Transformers: Revenge of the Fallen* (2009), *Iron Man* (2008), *Pearl Harbor* (2001), or *Saving Private Ryan* (1998), are more likely to receive assistance from the military than movies with less flattering or ambiguous messages, such as *Stop Loss* (2008), *Redacted* (2007), *Jarhead* (2005), or *Broken Arrow* (1996).

Other federal agencies also conduct campaigns to inform citizens. In many cases, the agency selects a public relations firm through a bidding process. Porter Novelli won a contract worth about $20 million in 2012 to promote the Affordable Care Act for the Centers for Medicare and Medicaid Services. PR firm FHI 360 earned a contract for $3.1 million the same year to promote anti-diabetes and anti-HIV projects for the Centers for Disease Control and Prevention. See the Social Media in Action box on page 528 about how the Centers for Disease Control capitalized on the zombie craze.

Public affairs officers are also tapping social media as an effective tool of disseminating information to a digital generation. The Transport Security Agency (TSA), for example, used Instagram to show photos of knives, guns, and even fireworks that agents had confiscated at airport security gates. The site seems to be successful; it had more than 40,000 followers within a month of launching in 2013.

Politicians sometimes take issue with government spending on public relations. For example, U.S. Senators Claire McCaskill (D-Missouri) and Rob Portman (R-Ohio) joined forces in 2012 to send letters to 11 federal agencies asking for a full accounting of "contracts for the acquisition of public relations, publicity, advertising, communications, or similar services" made from 2008 forward. Their concern may have been sparked by an investigation by the *Washington Guardian* and the Medill News Service that the U.S. government had spent $16 billion on public relations and advertising in the past 10 years.

on the job

SOCIAL MEDIA IN ACTION

Centers for Disease Control and Prevention Get Help From Zombies

The Centers for Disease Control and Prevention is an arm of the federal government charged with developing "expertise, information, and tools" to help Americans protect their health. The CDC is affiliated with the Department of Health and Human Services. So, how did a federal agency get involved with zombies?

Following the earthquake and tsunami in Japan in March 2011, the CDC used Twitter to ask followers what health or disaster issues concerned them most. To their surprise, CDC communicators heard an unusual recurring theme. Many people listed zombies among their concerns. The CDC decided to run with the information and developed a tongue-in-cheek campaign to help Americans prepare for a Zombie Apocalypse.

The Zombie Preparedness Campaign was launched on May 16, 2011 with this initial post on the zombie preparedness blog: "There are all kinds of emergencies out there that we can prepare for. Take a zombie apocalypse for example. That's right, I said z-o-m-b-i-e a-p-o-c-a-l-y-p-s-e. You may laugh now, but when it happens you'll be happy you read this, and hey, maybe you'll even learn a thing or two about how to prepare for a *real* emergency." The blog post went on to give a history of zombies, but more importantly it gave information about contents for an emergency kit (water, food, medications, tools and supplies; items for sanitation and hygiene; clothing and bedding; important documents; and first aid supplies) and developing an emergency plan.

Comments posted in response to the opening blog post included "Dude! So totally awesome!" and "I might suggest adding a baseball bat, preferably aluminum, to your emergency kit as well. It doesn't require ammunition and can be highly effective at clearing a path through hordes of zombies" and "My friends and I were discussing the zombie apocalypse after watching Zombieland. The discussion revolved around what would we do and how would we do it . . . I hope your article sparks many more discussions in many more homes across the country!" In fact, there were more than 1,000 comments in reply to that initial blog post. Some, of course, were disapproving of the CDC spending taxpayer dollars in such a frivolous endeavor, but most played along with the zombie gag.

When the blog post appeared on a Monday, journalists were called and promised "something interesting for them." On Wednesday of that week, a tweet was sent about the Zombie Apocalypse. Within 10 minutes traffic to the blog site caused it to crash. According to PR practitioner (and apparent zombie observer) Wendy Alpine the blog generated 60,000 page views per hour and an estimated 3.6 billion viewers in the first week. Traditional media jumped on the zombie bandwagon. More than 3,000 articles and news broadcasts were generated.

Maggie Silver of the CDC Office of Public Health Preparedness and Response said, "We pulled them in with the Zombies, and then they stayed to check out other content. If we had paid a private marketing firm, it would have cost us $3.4 million. In reality, the campaign cost us $87 for stock photography. We just needed to be creative. It just goes to show that you don't have to spend a lot of money if you have a great idea and timing."

There was a downside to the meant-to-be-fun campaign. A series of grisly episodes from Miami to Seattle occurred. In one, a man attempted to eat off the face of a homeless man and in another a student was charged with eating the heart and brain of his slain housemate. The CDC was forced to acknowledge through a spokesperson, "CDC does not know of a virus or condition that would reanimate the dead (or one that would present zombie-like symptoms)."

Nonetheless, the Zombie Apocalypse campaign was an unexpected success via social media that the CDC continued to build upon. For example, in February 2013 the CDC introduced a game that allowed users to address a fictitious epidemic. The game called "Solve the Outbreak" was available on a free iPad app. "We look at this as an engaging opportunity to educate young people to how public health actually works, and hopefully to draw some future epidemiologists," CDC spokesman Alex Casanova told ABCNews.com.

State Governments

Like the federal government, each of the 50 states disseminates information about its programs to various constituents. States also compete to develop campaigns to encourage tourism, to attract new residents, and to advance the interest of the state. State public information officers are often tasked with encouraging business and economic development or raising public awareness about policy issues. Often, the work is subcontracted to private public relations firms or conducted in collaboration with industry.

In Georgia, the state Forestry Commission joined with industry groups, including the Georgia Forestry Association and the Georgia Forestry Foundation to raise awareness about the environmental activities the industry engages in to offset its tree harvesting. On the public policy side, Colorado was one of several states to invest in awareness campaigns for new health insurance opportunities made available via the federal Affordable Care Act (also known as Obamacare). Colorado spent $2 million on television, print and radio ads, and a website to make state residents aware of their new options. Kentucky and Oregon also planned similar campaigns.

Publicizing quality of life and tourism issues has emerged as a highly competitive arena that draws on the resources of public relations professionals across many divisions or branches of state government.

The South Carolina Department of Parks, Recreation and Tourism, for example, hired BFG Communications to promote South Carolina as a barbecue mecca. According to a report in the *Savannah Morning News*, the communications agency won a contract worth $57 million to develop a promotional campaign for the region surrounding South Carolina. Among the tactics employed by South Carolina were a website of the state's "virtual barbecue trail," billboards and digital ads on FoodNetwork and Travel Channel websites and Facebook. Marion Edmonds, spokesperson for the S.C. Parks, Recreation and Tourism department told the *Savannah Morning News*, "We wanted to work that into a creative hook. We have a lot of bragging rights in South Carolina."

Colorado spent millions of dollars educating consumers and businesses about new insurance options under the federal Affordable Care Act.

Every state provides an array of public information services. In California, the most populous state, there are about 175 public information officers (PIOs) in about 70 state agencies. On a daily basis, PIOs provide routine information to the public and the press on the policies, programs, and activities of the many facets of the state's government.

State agencies also conduct a variety of public information and education campaigns, often with the assistance of public relations firms that have been selected via a bidding process. In a typical bidding process, a state agency will issue a request for proposal (RFP) and award a contract on the basis of presentations from competing firms.

One primary campaign area is health and safety. Most states, in recent years, have spent considerable money trying to convince people not to smoke. The funds, from the national tobacco settlement and state-imposed cigarette taxes, have provided somewhat of a windfall in available funds. California generates about $120 million annually from tobacco taxes, and about 10 percent of that is devoted to antismoking advertising and public relations. In a somewhat ironic twist, however, it is turning out that as smoking decreases, the amount of taxes collected also decreases, and there is thus less money for such campaigns. For health communicators this would be the ultimate in proverbial good problems to have: no more "customers" for smoking cessation programs.

One of the most concerted and visible communication functions of state government is health communication such as the Colorado health insurance campaign previously noted. In another example, the California Department of Health Services (CDHS) runs campaigns on a variety of health issues, such as childhood immunizations, breast cancer screening, and teen pregnancy prevention.

The California Highway Patrol (CHP) also conducts safety campaigns. One recent campaign was an effort to increase seat belt use and decrease drunk driving accidents among African Americans because statistical data indicate that this audience is less likely to use seat belts and is more likely to die in an alcohol-rated crash than other demographic groups. Even though the implications drawn by some about behavioral patterns could be construed as judgmental, the health benefits of using these observations to develop strategies to reduce deaths are clear. Focusing on such disparities in health outcomes is a frequent, proven means of getting media attention, which can then be leveraged to change knowledge and behavior by reaching large audiences. The jury is still out among health communication researchers, however, whether emphasizing the divide in health outcomes motivates or discourages the target group.

Local Governments

Cities employ information specialists to disseminate news and information from numerous municipal departments, which include the airport, transit district, redevelopment office, parks and recreation, convention and visitors bureau, police and fire, city council, and the mayor's office.

The information flow occurs in many ways, but the objectives are always to inform citizens about, and to help them take full advantage of, government services. The city council holds neighborhood meetings; the airport commission sets up an exhibit showing the growth needs of the airport; the recreation department promotes summer swimming lessons; and the city's human rights commission sponsors a festival promoting multiculturalism.

Cities also promote themselves to attract new business. *PRWeek* reported, "The competition for cities and wider regions to attract businesses is as intense as ever, experts say, with an estimated 12,000 economic development organizations vying for the roughly 500 annual corporate moves/expansions that involve 250 or more jobs each."

Many cities pump millions of dollars into attracting new business through a variety of communication tools, including elaborate brochures, placement of favorable "success" stories in the nation's press, direct mail, telemarketing, trade fairs, special events, and meetings with business executives. Some cities are helped by appearing on lists touting their business-friendly environment. The 2013 Thumbtack.com U.S. Small Business Friendliness Survey provided such assistance to Texas cities Austin, Houston, and San Antonio when it noted those towns received A+ ratings for business friendliness.

Detractors question whether expensive campaigns—combined with free land, tax incentives, and donated infrastructure from local government—ever get paid off through purported economic growth. Public relations professionals can better plan for this criticism of business recruitment if they understand the life cycle of an issue and the role of public relations and strategic conflict management, as presented in Chapter 10.

Cities often promote themselves in an effort to increase tourism. One example of this is the campaign by the Panama City (Florida) Convention and Visitors Bureau to position Panama City as a prime destination for college students during spring break. According to *PRWeek*, the bureau spent about $300,000 promoting the city through posters, news releases, brochures, advertising, and special events to let students know that they are welcome to visit.

Cities often promote tourism through cultural attractions and special events. Initiatives range from traditional tactics, such as issuing press releases, to more ambitious efforts at outreach, such as creating interactive media sites. For example, the city of Boston operates a social media center (http://www.cityofboston.gov/news/socialmedia.asp) with links to Facebook, Twitter, Instagram, Tumblr, Pinterest, LinkedIn, YouTube, Flickr, Storify, Vimeo, UStream, Wordpress, and Google+ sites.

On occasion, tragedy strikes a city and there is a vital need for the police and other city officials to rapidly inform citizens about a situation. This was the case in the aftermath of the Boston marathon after bombs exploded near the finish line, killing several and injuring scores of people. The information officers for the Boston police immediately started tweeting information and sent 148 messages in a matter of hours about the progress of the police investigating the terrorist attack.

The Case for Government Public Information and Public Affairs

Ever since the ancient Egyptians established the first unified state more than 5,000 years ago, governments have engaged in what is now known as public information and public affairs. It is not an exaggeration to say that human history is, to a large degree, rooted in the history of public relations.

There has always been a need for government communications, if for no other reason than to inform citizens of the services available and the manner in which they may be used. In a democracy, public information is crucial if citizens are to make intelligent judgments about policies and the activities of their elected representatives. Governments provide information in the hope that citizens will absorb the necessary background to participate fully in the formation of government policies. Public relations plays an important, but not an uncheckered, role in helping citizens make more informed choices at the ballot box, in the grocery store, at the doctor's office, behind the wheel of a car—basically, throughout all walks of life.

People, especially journalists, often criticize government public information activities as simply producing reams of useless news releases promoting individual legislators or justifying questionable policies. Such criticisms, coupled with snide news stories about the cost of maintaining government "public relations" experts, rankle dedicated PIOs at the various state and federal agencies who work very hard to keep the public informed with a daily diet of announcements and news stories. One PIO for a California agency said, "I'd like to see the press find out what's going on in state government without us."

Indeed, a major source of media hostility seems to stem from the fact that reporters are heavily dependent on news subsidies. One study found that almost

90 percent of one state government's news releases were used by daily and weekly newspapers. In fact, according to mass media scholars Peter Sandman, David Rubin, and David Sachsman, "If a newspaper were to quit relying on news releases, but continued covering the news it now covers, it would need at least two or three times more reporters."

Public information efforts can be justified in terms of cost savings. The U.S. Department of Agriculture's public affairs office, for example, receives thousands of inquiries a year. Two-thirds of the requests can be answered via a simple pamphlet, brochure, or link on its website, which solves problems for food producers, large and small, all provided under the umbrella of public information.

Preventive public relations also saves money. Teen births in New York cost taxpayers $377 million a year, according to the National Campaign to Prevent Teen and Unwanted Pregnancies. To address the problem, New York City embarked on a campaign to raise awareness of the "real cost" of teen pregnancy. Efforts by New York City led to a 27 percent reduction in the teen pregnancy rate, but the city still counts 20,000 teen pregnancies annually. On its website, the New York City Human Resources Administration described the 2013 campaign: "The campaign features ads with hard-hitting facts about the money and time costs of parenting, and the negative consequences of having a child before you are ready. The campaign will be on display on subways and bus shelters citywide, and will also feature an interactive texting program and a video."

One Associated Press reporter acknowledged in a story that government information does have value. He wrote:

> While some of the money and manpower goes for self-promotion, by far the greater amount is committed to an indispensable function of a democratic government—informing the people. What good would it serve for the Consumer Product Safety Commission to recall a faulty kerosene heater and not go to the expense of alerting the public to its action? An informed citizenry needs the government to distribute its economic statistics, announce its antitrust suits, tell about the health of the President, give crop forecasts.

If a newspaper were to quit relying on news releases, but continued covering the news it now covers, it would need at least two or three times more reporters.

Peter Sandman, David Rubin, and David Sachsman, in Media: An Introductory Analysis of American Mass Communications

Government Relations by Corporations

Government relations, closely related to lobbying, is a specialized component of corporate communication. This activity is so important that many companies, particularly in highly regulated industries, have separate departments of government relations.

The reason is simple: The actions of governmental bodies at the local, state, and federal levels have a major impact on how businesses operate. Government relations specialists, often called public affairs specialists, have a number of functions: They gather information, disseminate management's views, cooperate with government on projects of mutual benefit, and motivate employees to participate in the political process.

As the eyes and ears of a business or industry, practitioners in government relations positions spend considerable time gathering and processing information. They monitor the activities of many legislative bodies and regulatory agencies to keep track of issues coming up for debate and possible vote. This intelligence gathering enables a corporation or an industry to plan ahead and, if necessary, engage in a major lobbying effort to defeat any proposed legislation that is considered detrimental to the organization or industry. Lobbying is discussed in the next section, but the below Insights box gives a perspective on Google, which has become one of the major public affairs/lobbying operations in Washington, D.C.

Businesses monitor government in many ways. Probably the most active presence in Washington, D.C., and many state capitals is that of the trade associations

on the job INSIGHTS

Google Flexes Its Muscle in Washington

The eighth largest spender on lobbying in Washington is now Google. The giant company spent $18.2 million in 2012, which was more than Microsoft or even the traditional big-spender, defense company Lockheed Martin.

Google lobbies Congress and the White House on a variety of issues that are of prime concern to its business. It's pressing Congress to update the Electronic Communications Privacy Act to make it more difficult for law enforcement to gain access to e-mails, but it's also pushing the FCC to provide ample space for WiFi that is critical to Google's existence. In addition, the company is adding its weight to immigration reform and fending off proposed anti-trust regulations by the Federal Trade Commission that could seriously impact the way Google organizes its Web search results and sells its online advertising.

Google's chief lobbyist and head of the office is Susan Molinari, a former member of Congress with 15 years of experience inside the Beltway. Her salary, according to the *New York Times*, is estimated in the seven figures. Comparable executives in the pharmaceutical and cable industries, which also spent close to $18 million on lobbying in 2012, make $2 million to $3 million annually.

Google's Washington lobbying efforts in recent years has skyrocketed. It didn't even have a Washington operation until 2005. By 2007, the company had five employees. The office, under Molinari, expanded to more than 100 in 2012, including 14 registered lobbyists. The remaining staffers are lawyers, engineers, and public affairs personnel.

Source: Wyatt, E. (2013, June 2). Google's Washington Insider. *New York Times.*

that represent various industries. A Boston University survey found that 67 percent of the responding companies monitor government activity in Washington through their trade associations. The second monitoring effort cited on the list was frequent trips to Washington by senior public affairs officers and corporate executives; 58 percent of the respondents said they engage in this activity. Almost 45 percent of the responding firms reported that they have a company office in the nation's capital.

Government relations specialists also spend a great deal of time disseminating information about the company's position to a variety of key publics. Their tactics can include informal office visits to government officials or testimony at public hearings. In addition, public affairs people are often called on to give speeches or to write speeches for senior executives. They may write letters and op-ed articles, prepare position papers, produce newsletters, and place advocacy advertising.

Although legislators are the primary audience for government relations efforts, the Foundation for Public Affairs reports that 9 out of 10 companies also communicate with their own employees on public policy issues. Another 40 percent communicate with retirees, customers, and other publics such as taxpayers and government employees.

Lobbying

The term *lobbyist* may have originally been coined by President Ulysses S. Grant, who often sought refuge with a cigar and brandy in the Hotel Willard's lobby in Washington, D.C. He is said to have used the term to describe the people who sought favors from him when he was thus engaged.

Today, lobbying is more formal and more closely aligned with governmental relations or public affairs; in fact, the distinction between the two often blurs. This is because most campaigns to influence impending legislation have multiple levels. One level is informing and convincing the public about the correctness of an organization's viewpoint, which is the domain of the public affairs specialist. Lobbyist efforts, another level, are aimed at the defeat, passage, or amendment of legislation and regulatory agency policies.

Lobbyists work at the local, state, and federal levels of government. California has about 1,700 registered lobbyists, who represent hundreds of special interest groups. The interests represented in the state capital, Sacramento, include large corporations, business and trade groups, unions, environmental groups, local governments, nonprofit groups, school districts, and members of various professional groups.

The number and variety of special interests increase exponentially at the federal level. James A. Thurber, a professor of government at American University and a lobbying expert, estimates that Washington, D.C., now has about 100,000 lobbyists, including support staff. This number, says Thurber, doubled in the past decade. According to him, lobbying is now a $9 billion industry. See the Ethics box on next page about lobbying by the student loan industry, for an example of how lobbying can be called an "insider's game." Not only do lobbyists need to get inside the government to impact legislation, but because the issues are so specialized, oftentimes only an insider, a lobbyist, can sort them out.

Lobbyists represent the interests of virtually the entire spectrum of U.S. business, educational, religious, local, national, and international pursuits. Lobbying is

on the job

ETHICS

Student Loan Industry Engages In "Aggressive" Lobbying

Public relations people face ethical dilemmas in the course of their work, often without the challenge being formally identified or anyone hitting a "moral pause button" while the pros and cons are deliberated.

Although we may think of ethical considerations as requiring a complicated set of deliberations that follow from religious or philosophical principles, we are just as likely to encounter ethical questions as the natural consequences of doing our jobs for an organization that we believe in.

For example, lobbying in Washington affects all legislation, including student loan programs. In 2007 Congress passed the College Costs Reduction and Access Act, which gradually reduced the rate on subsidized student loans from 6.8 percent to 3.4 percent. The lower rate was set to expire in 2012. But no one wanted to increase student loan interest rates during a presidential election year so, as the saying goes, the can was kicked down the road with the rate set to increase back to 6.8 percent automatically in summer 2013 unless Congress did something. Which it did not.

While students protested the potential increase in interest rates, Sallie Mae, the nation's biggest student lender, with $180 billion in student loans, spent $1.23 million on lobbying during the first quarter of 2013, according to the Center for Responsive Politics.

Sarita Gupta, executive director of Jobs with Justice, wrote on the Moyers & Company blog:

Students protested the doubling of the interest rate on federally subsidized Stafford college loans.

> "Today, lenders like Sallie Mae spend millions of dollars peddling influence with legislators. Sallie Mae's lobbying efforts were recently described by The *New York Times* as "aggressive"—the company spent nearly $37.5 million on lobbying from 1998 to 2012. This year, Sallie Mae has already spent over $1.2 million on federal lobbying trying to squash several consumer protection bills, including the Private Student Loan Bankruptcy Fairness Act of 2013 and the Fairness for Struggling Students Act of 2013. Both pieces of legislation call for increased regulation of private banks with a history of bad lending practices."

Before Congress recessed in August 2013, a rare bipartisan vote in Congress addressed the student loan issue. The legislation set a fixed rate for student loans linked to the rate of U.S. Treasury notes. For loans after July 1, 2013, that meant rates were set at 3.9 percent for undergraduates and 5.4 percent for graduate students. But the rates would change annually for new borrowers.

Is it ethical for a lender like Sallie Mae to lobby Congress for beneficial legislation even while it is profiting from student loans?

When you conduct public relations for an organization you are an advocate for that organization. Are there situations when you would step away from being an advocate for the organization and become an advocate for a contending public? If so, when?

Is lobbying as a public relations activity more or less ethical than, say, media relations? Justify your opinion.

also conducted on behalf of foreign governments and interests, which is discussed in Chapter 20. The American-Israel Public Affairs Committee (AIPAC), for example, is a major player in Washington because of its impressive resources. According to the *Economist*, "AIPAC has an annual budget of around $60 million, more than 275 employees, an endowment of over $130 million, and a new $80 million building on Capitol Hill."

The variety of lobbying groups at the federal level is apparent when we consider the debate and maneuvering about health care that continued as elements of the major reform bill began to take effect. Examples of opponents to the Affordable Care Act (also known as Obamacare) might include insurance companies, HMO trade groups, the U.S. Chamber of Commerce, and the National Federation of Independent Businesses. Groups supporting the ACA might include a broad coalition of consumer groups, the American Medical Association, AARP and the Trial Lawyers of America.

Much of lobbyists' work enables influence by vested interests. However, lobbyists also bring to bear expertise and input from many contending perspectives, which help to forge the actual guidelines and procedures in ways that legislative aides cannot always accomplish. In spite of our concerns as citizens for the undue influence of those with much to gain, the system of making legislation a working reality in government offices now requires lobbyists' expertise and resources.

Ideally, competing lobbying efforts often cancel each other out. This leaves legislators and regulatory personnel with the chore of weighing the pros and cons of an issue before voting. Indeed, *Time* magazine notes that competition among lobbyists representing different sides of an issue "do[es] serve a useful purpose by showing busy legislators the virtues and pitfalls of complex legislation."

A perennial conflict that lobbyists weigh in on is the debate between saving jobs and improving the environment. A coalition of environmental groups constantly lobbies Congress for tougher legislation to clean up industrial pollution or protect endangered species. Simultaneously, local communities and unions may counter that the proposed legislation would result in the loss of jobs and economic chaos.

Most groups claim to be lobbying in the "public interest." Is it in the "public interest," a lobbyist may ask, to throw thousands of people out of work or to legislate so many restrictions on the manufacture of a product that it becomes more expensive for the average consumer? Or, should the community risk possible long-term and irreversible damage to the environment? The answer, quite often, depends on whether one is a steelworker, a logger, a consumer, or a member of the World Wildlife Fund.

Pitfalls of Lobbying

Although a case can be made for lobbying as a legitimate activity, deep public suspicion exists about former legislators and officials who capitalize on their connections and charge large fees for doing what is commonly described as "influence peddling."

Indeed, the roster of registered lobbyists in Washington includes a virtual who's who of former legislators and government officials from both the Democratic and Republican Parties. According to a study by George Washington University, 55 percent of lobbyists are former employees of the U.S. Congress and 26 percent are former employees of the executive branch. For every member of Congress there are 23 lobbyists trying to influence his or her decision.

The Ethics in Government Act forbids government officials from actively lobbying their former agencies for one year after leaving office. Critics say, however, that this law has had little or no impact. A good case study is the U.S. Department of Homeland Security. Tom Ridge was head of the agency when it was established in 2002; he has since left to become a lobbyist with a long list of clients from the security industry who seek contracts with Homeland Security, which has a budget of more than $59 billion. Ridge is not alone. A *New York Times* article written during the Bush administration reported that at least 90 former officials at the Department of Homeland Security or the White House Homeland Security office, two-thirds of the most senior executives, have become lobbyists.

Unlike federal agency personnel, members of Congress can become lobbyists immediately after leaving office. Consider former Representative J. C. Watts (R-Oklahoma), who announced the formation of a group of lobbying and public affairs firms exactly one day after leaving office. High-ranking members of Watts' congressional staff moved with him to his new offices to begin their careers as lobbyists of their former colleagues.

Instances of people "cashing in" on connections give the press and the public the uneasy feeling that influence peddling is alive and well in the nation's capital. This practice also gives credence to the cliché "It's not what you know, but who you know." The scandal involving lobbyist Jack Abramoff reveals how closely tied legislators are to lobbyists. Abramoff's financial mismanagement and willingness to dispense illegal perks to legislators earned him a lengthy prison sentence. Further, Republican House Majority Leader Tom Delay (R-Texas) had to resign his leadership post and Ohio Congressman Bob Ney pleaded guilty to two counts of conspiracy and making false statements in the Abramoff scandal. About half a dozen other legislators and dozens of congressional aides and other government officials remain under scrutiny.

Grassroots Lobbying

Politicians in both parties have regularly decried the influence of lobbyists, but reform has taken a half-century. At least 10 times since the first loophole-riddled lobbying regulations were passed in 1946, efforts to update the law failed to get past the legislative obstacles. In 1995, however, Congress did pass a measure titled the Lobbying Disclosure Act designed to reform lobbying, and President Clinton signed it. Part of the impetus, no doubt, were the polls indicating that the public believed lobbyists had runaway influence in Washington.

One key provision was an expanded definition of who is considered to be a "lobbyist." The 1995 law defined a lobbyist as "someone hired to influence lawmakers, government officials or their aides, and who spends at least 20 percent of his or her time representing any client in a six-month period." Two other "tests" must be passed for a person to be required to register as a lobbyist. One test is whether you have made more than $3,000 over three months in lobbying activities.

A second is whether you have had more than one lobbying contact. The *New York Times* reported, "Only a person who has met all three tests must register as a lobbyist. So a former lawmaker who has many lobbying contacts and makes $1 million a year lobbying but has no single client who takes up more than 20 percent of his time would not be considered a lobbyist." Another key provision requires lobbyists to register with Congress and disclose their clients, the issue areas in which lobbying is being done, and roughly how much is being paid for it. Violators face civil fines of up to $200,000.

One area exempted from the lobby reform bill is financial disclosures for so-called grassroots lobbying, the fastest-growing phenomenon in the political persuasion business. Grassroots lobbying is considered "indirect" compared to "direct" lobbying.

Grassroots lobbying is now an $800 million industry, according to *Campaigns and Elections*, a bimonthly magazine for "political professionals." What makes it so attractive to various groups is that there are virtually no rules or regulations. The tools of this sort of lobbying are advocacy advertising, toll-free phone lines, bulk faxing, websites, and computerized direct mail aimed at generating phone calls and letters from the public to Congress, the White House, and governmental regulatory agencies.

Grassroots lobbying also involves coalition building. The basic idea is to get individuals and groups with no financial interest in the issue to speak on the sponsor's behalf. The premise is that e-mails, tweets, and phone calls from private citizens are more influential than arguments from vested interests. Such "grassroots" campaigns make public interest groups wonder if they really shouldn't be called "Astroturf" campaigns, since the "grass" is often artificial. Michael Pertschuk, codirector of the Advocacy Institute in Washington, D.C., told *O'Dwyer's PR Services Report*, "Astroturf groups are usually founded with corporate seed money that is funneled through PR firms."

Election Campaigns

Public affairs activities and lobbying, either in the halls of Congress or at the grassroots level, are year-round activities. During election years, either congressional or presidential, an army of fund-raisers, political strategists, speech writers, and communication consultants mobilize to help candidates win elections.

The high cost of running for office in the United States has made fund-raising virtually a full-time, year-round job for every incumbent and aspirant to office. In fact, American-style campaigning is the most expensive in the world. In 2012, candidates for Congress and the Presidency spent about $6 billion.

Candidates retain professionals to organize fund-raising activities. A standard activity in Washington, D.C., and other major cities across the country is the luncheon, reception, or dinner on behalf of a candidate. According to *Politico*, a new trend in fundraising is attending an event. Bryan Tackett, lobbyist and president of Wexford Strategic Advisors told *Politico*, it's a "far cry different than the old, 'stop by the home of John Smith and have some crappy hors d'oeuvres,' I think, too, they are recognizing that the overpaid, younger lobbyist crowd is more likely to attend these events."

Politico, for example, reported five congressional fundraisers associated with Beyoncé's "The Mrs. Carter Show World Tour" and two fundraisers at a Taylor Swift concert. Congressman John Shimkus (R-Ill.) reportedly held fundraising events at a performance of "The Book of Mormon" and shows by Fleetwood Mac, New Kids on the Block, Boyz II Men and 98 Degrees.

Individual donors and lobbyists for various organizations regularly attend fund-raising events. Although a chicken dinner or a cheese platter with crackers and champagne is not exactly worth thousands of dollars per person in literal terms, the event shows support of the candidate and allows donors to have contact with him or her. No business is actually discussed, but the occasion gives both individuals and lobbyists for special interests an opportunity to show the "flag" and perhaps indirectly influence legislation or open the door for personnel appointments at a later date after the election, if the candidate wins.

Some consultants specialize in direct mail and telemarketing. They are assisted by firms that specialize in computer databases and mailing lists. Aristotle Publishers, for example, claims to have records on 190 million registered voters. A candidate can obtain a tailored list of prospects using any number of demographic variables, including party affiliation, voting record, contribution record, age, geographic location, and opinions on various issues.

The Internet was first used for campaign fund-raising and building grassroots support during the 2000 presidential election. However, its effectiveness was not realized until the 2004 election, when former Vermont Governor Howard Dean used the Internet to build a grassroots network, motivate potential voters, and—perhaps most importantly—raise funds. Dean also used social networks such as *Meetup.com* to interact with constituents. Dean's campaign initially had fewer financial resources than campaigns of his competitors, but by making efficient use of the Internet, he soon leveled the playing field by raising a large amount of money thanks to thousands of small donations.

Candidates during the 2008 campaign wisely followed Dean's strategy of using the Internet. Although some have argued that no one candidate exploited its full potential, Barack Obama achieved notable success by leveraging technology to build core support among college students, young professionals, and independents. Effective use of social media was one crucial factor that allowed the relatively unknown candidate to outmaneuver more experienced and better-financed contenders to secure the Democratic Party nomination and eventually defeat Republican candidate John McCain.

Like Dean, Barack Obama raised an enormous sum of money online by soliciting small donations. Advisors helped him craft a strategy to interact with supporters online by encouraging them to submit content via sites such as Facebook, YouTube, and Twitter. YouTube videos by ObamaGirl were particularly memorable examples of his online grassroots support.

Obama continued to dominate social media in the 2012 campaign against Mitt Romney. According to NPR, the president spent $47 million on social media—ten times more than his opponent. Obama also raised a record $1.4 billion over his two campaigns for president taking advantage of online fundraising. His campaign staff was credited for exceptional success at internet appeals. A staff of 20 writers were deployed to develop content for Obama's campaign e-mails. According to Bloomberg *Businessweek*, the fundraising appeals were developed through rigorous experimentation by a team of analysts.

> **The Obama campaign has come closest to achieving the Holy Grail of politics on the Internet—converting online enthusiasm to offline action.**
>
> *Andrew Rasiej, a leading analyst of online politics*

Amelia Showalter, director of digital analytics for the Obama campaign told *Businessweek*, "We did extensive A-B testing not just on the subject lines and the amount of money we would ask people for, but on the messages themselves and even the formatting." *Businessweek* reported that the campaign might test as many as 18 variations of subject lines and content. When the best mix was identified, it would be blasted out to tens of millions of e-mail subscribers. Toby Fallsgraff, e-mail director for the campaign said, "When we saw something that really moved the dial, we would adopt it." The Obama team found that a casual tone was best. The subject line "I will be outspent" raised $2.6 million, according to *Businessweek*.

Of course, there is a downside to relying on the Internet and social media. Candidates surrender some measure of control over the message and discussion. Any gaffes are instantly amplified through re-tweets and message boards. Constant vigilance is needed to rebut gossip and misinformation. And the opposition can create rogue websites that spoof or mimic that of the candidate. Despite these caveats, the Internet and social media have proven to be effective as both public relations tactics and strategy.

Candidates in election campaigns also employ groups of consultants and other technicians such as position paper writers, speech writers, graphic artists, computer experts, webmasters, media strategists, advertising experts, radio and television producers, public affairs experts, pollsters, and public relations specialists. A highly visible and critical job is done by advance people, who spend many hours organizing events, arranging every detail, and making sure there's a cheering crowd, with signs, when the candidate arrives. On a single day, for example, a presidential candidate may give five to seven talks at rallies in multiple states. As is the case with most of the public relations activities and events described in this chapter, a cadre of individuals often works behind the scenes to orchestrate these events and initiatives. To ensure that the candidate's speech is received under the best possible circumstances, public relations professionals mobilize the audience and the media, manage potential risks, avert or handle crises that arise, and provide assessment of the results with polls and reports after each speech.

Summary

Government Organizations

- Governments have always engaged in campaigns to educate, inform, motivate, and even persuade the public.
- In the United States, Congress forbids federal agencies from "persuading" the public, so the emphasis is on "public information" efforts.

The Federal, State, and Local Governments

- The U.S. federal government is the largest disseminator of information in the world.
- The apex of all government information and public relations efforts is the White House; the president's every move and action are chronicled by the mass media. Presidents throughout history have used this media attention to lead the nation, convince the public to support administration policies, and get reelected.
- All agencies of the federal government employ public affairs officers and public information specialists. Members of Congress also engage in extensive information efforts to reach their constituents.
- Various states employ public information officers to tell the public about the activities and policies of various agencies. In addition, state agencies conduct a number of campaigns to inform the public about health and safety issues and to promote the state as a tourist destination.
- All major cities employ public information specialists to tell citizens about city services and promote economic development.

Public Information and Public Affairs

- A major component of corporate communication is public affairs, which primarily deals with governmental relations at the local, state, national, and even international levels.
- Public affairs specialists build relationships with civil servants and elected officials and also monitor governmental actions that may affect the employer or client.
- Trade groups, representing various professions and industries and primarily based in state capitals or Washington, D.C., have public affairs specialists who engage in governmental relations.
- A public affairs specialist primarily provides information about an organization's viewpoint to the public and

government entities. A lobbyist has the more specialized function of directly working for the defeat, passage, or amendment of legislation and regulatory agency policies.

- In recent years, there has been public concern about "influence peddling" in terms of former legislators and other officials becoming lobbyists and "cashing in" on their knowledge and connections. To curb abuse, several laws have been passed to regulate lobbyists.

Government Relations by Corporations

- Although closely related to lobbying, government relations involves the broader functions of gathering information, disseminating management's views, and cooperating with government on projects of mutual benefit as well as motivating employees to take part in the political process.
- One of the most active forms of corporate government relations is the work of trade associations in Washington, D.C., and state capitals on behalf of industries.

Lobbying

- Lobbyists represent the interests of virtually the entire spectrum of U.S. business, educational, religious, local, national, and international pursuits.
- Lobbying is a formal process closely aligned with corporate and organizational governmental relations.
- Lobbyist efforts are aimed at the defeat, passage, or amendment of legislation and regulatory agency policies in the interests of the corporation or advocacy organization.

Election Campaigns

- An army of specialists, including public relations experts, are retained by major candidates to organize and raise money for election campaigns.
- The Internet plays an important role in raising money, generating high visibility for candidates, and increasing the number of registered voters.

Case Activity How Do You Communicate Proactively?

The Centers for Disease Control and Prevention is a government entity charged with preparing the public for outbreaks of disease or potential disasters.

One of the dilemmas faced by local, state, and federal governments when a health epidemic looms is how, and when, to warn residents of the danger. If government officials issue warnings too often or too early or raise the alarm in cases where a major epidemic does not end up occurring, there is a risk that the public will become desensitized and learn to disregard the warnings. On the other hand, officials face criticism and loss of public trust if they fail to warn citizens in a timely manner.

Consider a scenario in which another flu epidemic is predicted by epidemiologists. There is a 70 percent chance that the flu will reach epidemic status. There is also a chance that it will be a typical flu season without serious consequences. If you were a public affairs specialist for the CDC, what steps would you take immediately to inform the public? What channels of communication would you use? How would you structure your message? What steps would you recommend taking regarding communication with the public if the wrong decisions are made and the situation becomes a catastrophe? Working with a small group, quickly brainstorm a communication plan.

Questions For Review and Discussion

1. What is the role of PR in government?
2. Define lobbying. How is it different or similar to PR?
3. Many lobbyists are former legislators and government officials. Do you think they exercise undue influence on the shaping of legislation? Why or why not?
4. Internet fund-raising plays a crucial role in elections. Would you like to be a political fund-raiser? Why or why not?
5. It is not uncommon for governments in democracies to reach out to people through campaigns. In your view, is persuasion or public information the right thing to do? Why?
6. Critically analyze some public information campaigns that you may have been exposed to through various mass media.

7. Give some examples of public relations campaigns run by state or local governments.
8. How does public relations at the local level differ from public relations efforts at the state and federal levels? What channels are typically used by federal and local officials to disseminate messages to the public?
9. How doe grassroots lobbying differ from lobbying generally?

Media Resources

Dickson, V. (2012, September). Commanding communications: Navy shines light on the work it does in communities across the country. *PRWeek*, 30–31.

Haden, J. (2013, February 5). 6 habits of remarkably likable people. *Inc.* Retrieved from www.huffingtonpost.com

Healthcare Reform in Colorado. Retrieved from www.colorado.gov/healthreform

Kahn, A. (2011, May 16). Preparedness 101: Zombie apocalypse. Retrieved from blogs.cdc.gov

Nakashima, E. (2013, January 27). Pentagon to boost cybersecurity force. *Washington Post*. Retrieved from www.washingtonpost.com

Seitel. F. (2013, June). What makes a good press secretary. *O'Dwyer's Pubic Relations Report*, 36.

Smith, D. (2013, June). Up in smoke: Anatomy of a statewide campaign. *Public Relations Tactics*, 15.

Swann, P. (2013, June). To serve and protect: How the Boston Police used Twitter after Marathon attacks. *Public Relations Tactics*, 12–13.

Tau, B. (2013, August 3). All the D.C. donors, now put your checks up. *Politico*. Retrieved from www.politico.com

Taylor, K. (2013, March 6). Posters on teenage pregnancy draw fire. Retrieved from www.nytimes.com

Wyatt, E. (2013, June 2). Google's Washington Insider. *New York Times*. Retrieved from www.nytimes.com

Zakarin, J. (2012, February 17). 'Act of Valor' and the military's long Hollywood mission. The *Huffington Post*. Retrieved from www.huffingtonpost.com

Zeleny, J. (2013, January 18). Obama to turn campaign machinery to promoting policy. The *New York Times*. Retrieved from www.nytimes.com

chapter 20

Global Public Relations in an Interdependent World

After reading this chapter, you will be able to:

Appreciate the diversity of public relations practice in other nations

Know the various cultural values that shape a nation's communication patterns

Understand how public relations plays an important role in the global economy

Gain insight on how foreign governments and corporations influence U.S. legislation and policies

Appreciate the major role of NGOs in shaping public opinion

Understand the job opportunities available in global public relations

What Is Global Public Relations?

Global public relations, also called international public relations, is the planned and organized efforts of a company, an institution, or a government to establish and build relationships with the publics of other nations. These publics are the various groups of people who are affected by, or who can affect, the operations of a particular organization or even an entire industry. Increasingly, in today's global economy, almost all public relations activity has international aspects.

International public relations can also be viewed from the standpoint of its practice in individual countries. Although public relations is commonly regarded as a concept developed in the United States at the beginning of the 20th century, some of its elements, such as countering unfavorable public attitudes through publicity and annual reports, were practiced by railroad companies in Germany as far back as the mid-19th century, to cite only one example. See pages 70–71 in Chapter 2 for a capsule summary of historical development in various nations.

Even so, it is largely U.S. public relations techniques that have been adopted throughout the world, even in authoritarian nations. Today, although in some languages there is no term comparable to *public relations*, the practice has spread to most countries, especially those with industrial bases and large urban populations. This is primarily the result of worldwide technological, social, economic, and political changes and the growing understanding that public relations is an essential component of branding, marketing, and public diplomacy.

Development in Other Nations

Public relations as a career has achieved its highest development in the industrialized nations of the world such as the United States, Canada, and the European Union (EU). It tends to develop more rapidly in nations that have (1) multiparty political systems, (2) a relatively free press, (3) considerable private ownership of business and industry, (4) large-scale urbanization, and (5) relatively high per capita income levels, which also impact literacy and educational opportunities.

The explosive growth of the public relations industry in China is an example. The nation, although lacking democratic institutions, has experienced rapid industrialization, major urbanization, and considerable growth in per capita income. Public relations revenues for the past several years have experienced double-digit gains, and China is now the second largest national economy in the world.

The United States and European nations began exporting their public relations expertise to the People's Republic of China in the mid-1980s. Hill & Knowlton, for example, claims to be the first U.S. agency to launch a public relations event in Tiananmen Square. The year was 1985 and its Beijing operation was a hotel room with three U.S. professionals and a locally hired employee. Today, almost every major global public relations firm has a Beijing or Shanghai office to represent U.S. and European companies in the Chinese market.

Global public relations firms are also buying stakes or affiliating with successful Chinese firms. Porter Novelli, for example, is affiliated with Blue Focus, one of the largest Chinese-owned firms in the country. Gyroscope, a consultancy, estimates that there are about 2,000 public relations firms in China, but most of them are one- or two-person operations primarily dealing with publicity, media relations, and staging events. Gyroscope notes, "The vast majority of PR spending is on low-value,

International Expo Enhances China's Reputation
Countries often use major expositions as a public relations and marketing strategy to attract worldwide attention and generate favorable public perceptions. The Shanghai Expo attracted millions of visitors and was a showcase displaying China's modern economy. Above is the Chinese pavilion.

low-worth publicity, inexpertly planned and delivered, with a small number of clients and agencies focusing on high-value, high-worth strategic consultancy."

Fueling the development of public relations in China have been several major international events. The Beijing Olympics in 2008 placed China on the world stage, and the Shanghai Expo of 2010 affirmed China's influence on the global economy. The six-month Expo attracted an estimated 70 million visitors, and 193 countries erected pavilions and other exhibits.

The Internet and social media have also expanded the opportunities for organizations to conduct public relations and marketing campaigns that directly reach the Chinese consumer. Although there is no Facebook or Twitter access in China, there is the micro-blogging site Weibo that has 320 million users. Sean Fitzgerald, EVP of Ketchum's China office, told *PRWeek*, "Weibo has provided consumers with an immediate and powerful voice about brands." A number of brands such as Nike and Pizza Hut have Weibo accounts, and public relations firms often create and manage the content. Other home-grown social media sites also are popular. A Kinsey consulting report found that 95 percent of the Internet users in China's major cities are also registered on a social media site.

Working in China has its challenges. One is the nature of the press, which is state-owned or highly controlled. Although the media are getting more sophisticated, Chinese journalists are still poorly trained and underpaid. As Cindy Payne, director of Asia Pacific Connections, says, "Journalists in China are arguably the worst paid, so to offset the reality of public transportation woes, you are expected to provide a travel allowance." This practice is part of the "pay for play" culture in which it's common for many Chinese publications and broadcast outlets to require payment for printing a news release or interviewing an executive on a talk show. This practice was highlighted in Chapter 3 on page 117.

Current development of the public relations industry in other nations is given below by thumbnail sketches from around the globe. See also the Multicultural box on page 552 about reaching out to the Muslim world.

The future of China lies in exporting Chinese brands to the world. That means increasing the value of the "Chinese product" and the "Chinese brand." PR has a vital role in building and maintaining brand value—and a nation which cannot master PR is at an enormous disadvantage.

Public relations executive in Gyroscope's report
The Public Relations Landscape in China

Brazil This is the largest nation in South America in terms of population (200 million) and its booming economy makes it a major player in the world economy. There are about 1,000 public relations firms, primarily in the Rio de Janeiro and the Sao Paulo area. Brazil will also host the 2014 World Cup and the 2016 Olympics, which will generate more development of its public relations industry. Brazil has become a mature business market, and companies are now beginning to recognize public relations as essential to generating revenues and building reputation. In addition, the public relations industry in Argentina and Chile also are well developed.

Dubai and Middle East Dubai, as part of the United Arab Emirates (UAE), has become the financial and airline hub in the region. Many international companies have offices there that have also fueled the influx of major global public relations firms. In general, the public relations industry in the region is relatively immature and the preparation of news releases is the primary activity. Development is somewhat hampered by low literacy, lack of trained personnel, and government controlled media.

India The Indian market, with more than 1 billion people, is a major market for products, services, and public relations expertise. There are at least 1,000 large and small public relations firms serving the subcontinent, but training and educating qualified practitioners continues to be a major problem. The Public Relations Society of India has increased professionalism among practitioners, but much of the work involves getting visibility in the media. The country's population makes it an attractive location for foreign investment and international public relations firms but government bureaucracy is a continuing handicap. On the bright side, Indian firms are now expanding to the global market, and the level of public relations is getting more sophisticated.

Indonesia The major growth is in public relations firms specializing in digital communications to communicate information about brands and services. The reason is that mobile phone penetration is more than 100 percent and its citizens send more tweets than any other nation. It also ranks fourth in the world in terms of active Facebook users. The public relations profession, however, is still evolving. Many companies still perceive public relations personnel primarily as publicists. Recruitment of trained talent is also a problem.

Japan Business and industry are still at the stage of perceiving public relations as primarily media relations. Public relations firms and corporate communications departments work very closely with the 400-plus reporters' clubs that filter and process all information for more than 150 news-gathering organizations. Major advertising agencies tend to dominate the public relations field, and there has been little development regarding strategic positioning or how to do crisis communications. Toyota's somewhat inept handling of a product recall and how the utility company handled the melt-down of several nuclear reactors after a major tsunami are examples.

Mexico Traditionally, small public relations firms in Mexico dominated the market and provided primarily product publicity. With the North American Free Trade Agreement, international firms have established operations with more sophisticated approaches to strategic communications.

Russian Federation and the Former Soviet Republics The rise of a market economy and private enterprise has spurred the development of public relations activity, but continuing problems in the Russian economy have stunted its development. The press and journalists are still very dependent on supplemental income, and news coverage can be "bought" with cash or through political connections. A key issue is the training of public relations professionals; college curriculums are still very weak. Gyroscope, a consultancy, predicts that public relations will continue to develop from its roots in political campaigning to become more corporate and consumer oriented. Ukraine, once part of the Soviet Union, now has a developed public relations industry but suffers some of the same problems as Russia in continuing to develop it.

South Africa South Africa has the most developed public relations industry on the continent. It also has a long tradition of public relations education and professional development for practitioners. In the past several years, there has been less emphasis on publicity tactics and more focus on aspects of corporate social responsibility (CSR), sustainability, and reputation management.

Sweden and Other Nordic Countries Public relations is highly developed in these countries, and the *Paul Holmes World Report* quotes one executive as saying, "The PR Industry in the Nordic region is quite developed and on a more strategic and analytic level than in other countries." Norway, Denmark, Sweden,

Public Relations Firms Are Found in Every Nation

Public relations is now an international enterprise, and every country has its own industry. This ad is for a Spanish firm with operations in Latin America

LLORENTE & CUENCA
CONSULTORES DE COMUNICACIÓN

YOUR PARTNER OF CHOICE FOR YOUR BUSINESS DEVELOPMENT IN LATIN AMERICA

I ♥ LATIN AMERICA

The Americas is a familiar territory for LLORENTE & CUENCA. It opened its first office in **Lima** in 1998 and, since then, has successfully expanded across the whole Region with additional own offices in **Buenos Aires, Bogota, Lima, Panama City, Quito, Mexico City and Rio.** On top of this, it holds special strategic partnerships with affiliate companies in **Miami, Santiago de Chile, La Paz, Caracas, Dominican Republic and Montevideo.**

LLORENTE & CUENCA is humbly proud of being the leading spanish-portuguese speaking communication consultancy in the continent so that it offers their clients a combination of a well-tested global methodology with a truly local approach.

www.llorenteycuenca.com

BARCELONA | BEIJING | BOGOTA | BUENOS AIRES | LIMA | LISBON | MADRID | MEXICO | PANAMA | QUITO | RIO DE JANEIRO and Finland also have a culture of CSR, environmental sustainability, labor rights, and gender equality high on the political agenda, so public relations counselors often facilitate programs in these areas.

Thailand The nation has a great deal of foreign investment and is becoming established as an assembly center for automobiles. It's the primary hub in Southeast Asia for international tourism, and a number of public relations firms and corporations have well-qualified staffs to handle traditional media relations, product publicity, and special event promotion. The major user of public relations services is the government, spending $350 million in a recent year. Digital communications are evolving, but the traditional media (30 newspapers in Bangkok alone) remain the primary distribution channels for public relations personnel.

Turkey The country is the economic giant in the region and has a fairly modern communications infrastructure. Public relations firms do traditional media relations, but there is increasing focus on regulatory and political monitoring for clients. Sustainability and CSR projects are receiving more emphasis, but public affairs work is done mostly in-house. Social media as a major platform for public relations is still in its early stages. Recruitment of talent is difficult because fluency in English is expected of job candidates.

International Corporate Public Relations

This section explores the new age of global marketing and addresses the differences in language, laws, and cultural mores that must be overcome when companies conduct business in foreign countries. We also discuss how U.S. public relations firms represent foreign interests in this country as well as U.S. corporations in other parts of the world.

The New Age of Global Marketing

For decades, hundreds of corporations based in the United States have been engaged in international business operations, including marketing, advertising, and public relations. All these activities exploded to unprecedented proportions during the 1990s, largely because of new communications technologies, development of 24-hour financial markets almost worldwide, the lowering of trade barriers, the growth of sophisticated foreign competition in traditionally "American" markets, and shrinking cultural differences, all of which bring the "global village" ever closer to reality.

In the case of Coca-Cola, probably the best-known brand name in the world, international sales account for 70 percent of the company's revenues. The major growth area for both Coke and Pepsi is the developing nations. In addition, large U.S.-based public relations firms such as Burson-Marsteller and Edelman are now generating between 30 and 40 percent of their fees serving foreign clients.

Today, almost one-third of all U.S. corporate profits are generated through international business. At the same time, overseas investors are moving into American industries. It is not uncommon for 15 to 20 percent of a U.S. company's stock to be held abroad. The United Kingdom, for example, has a direct foreign investment in the United States exceeding $122 billion, followed by Japan and the Netherlands, with nearly half that sum each, according to the U.S. Department of Commerce.

Saudi Aramco World Magazine

International corporations often publish high-quality magazines for distribution to opinion leaders in various nations to increase visibility and enhance their reputation and brand. This quarterly magazine of Saudi Aramco is designed to increase cross-cultural understanding of the Middle East and the Muslim world, where the company has extensive oil operations.

Fueling the new age of global public relations and marketing is the pervasive presence of the Internet. It allows every corporation to have instant contact with any and all of its operations around the world, but the downside is that any problem or crisis in one plant or country is instantly known throughout the world. In addition, satellite television, fax, fiber optics, cellular telephone systems, and technologies such as integrated services digital network (ISDN) enable a blizzard of information via voice, data, graphics, and video. For example, Hill & Knowlton has its own satellite transmission facilities, and General Electric has an international telecommunications network, enabling employees to communicate worldwide using voice, video, and computer data simply by dialing seven digits on a telephone.

In terms of international media, Cable News Network (CNN) is viewed by more than 200 million people in more than 140 countries. England's BBC World Service also reaches an impressive number of nations, including the 40-plus member nations of the British Commonwealth. A number of newspapers and magazines are also reaching millions with international editions. The *Wall Street Journal* and the *Financial Times* have daily editions in the United States, Europe, and Asia. Other publications, such as the *Economist*, have worldwide distribution.

Much of the jousting for new business takes place on Western European terrain, where the EU is a formidable competitor with U.S. firms in the global market. Although hampered by recession in recent years, public relations expenditures have increased significantly. Many European companies extensively use advertising, marketing, and public relations strategies to lure business from nations around the world.

Although the EU promoted the phrase "a single Europe," corporations and public relations firms still face the complex task of communicating effectively to 400 million people in 25 countries speaking multiple languages. Differences in language, laws, and cultural mores among countries are a continuing challenge to culturally sensitive public relations practice. There also is a need for both managers and employees to act locally and think in global terms. Already, Burson-Marsteller, with offices in many countries, is spending more than

$1 million a year on training tapes and traveling teams of trainers to foster a uniform approach to client projects.

Language and Cultural Differences

Companies operating in other nations are confronted with essentially the same public relations challenges as those operating in the United States. Their objectives are to compete successfully and to manage conflict effectively, but the task is more complex on an international and intercultural level.

A good example of cultural differences is the crash of a Korean-based plane upon landing in San Francisco. Asiana executives issued some apologies in Korea, but issued few statements in the United States and didn't arrange for any media representatives outside Korea. One Asiana spokesperson told the *Wall Street Journal*, "It's not the proper time to manage the company's image." By U.S. standards, the airline was slow to respond to the intense media interest in the crash. U.S. airlines, for example, have crisis plans and full-time teams to handle the emotional and logistical nightmare of a crash and deal immediately with providing information to the media and the public.

The Korean handling of the Asiana crash illustrates the point that public relations practitioners need to recognize cultural differences, adapt to local customs, and understand the finer points of verbal and nonverbal communication in individual nations.

Experts in intercultural communication point out that many cultures, particularly non-Western ones, are "high-context" communication societies. In other words, the meaning of the spoken word is often implicit and based on environmental context and personal relationships rather than on explicit, categorical statements. The communication styles of Asian and Arab nations, for example, are high context.

In contrast, European and American communication styles are considered low context. Great emphasis is placed on exact words, and you are expected to derive meaning primarily from the written or verbal statements, not from nonverbal behavior cues. Legal documents produced in the West are the ultimate in explicit wording.

Geert Hofstede, a company psychologist for global giant IBM, studied national/cultural differences among employees around the world back in the 1970s and came up with five basic cultural dimensions. Today, students still rely on his typology to understand various national cultures. Professors David Guth and Charles Marsh of the University of Kansas summarize Hofstede's cultural dimensions in their book *Adventures in Public Relations: Case Studies and Critical Thinking*:

1. **Power distance** measures how tolerant a society is about unequally distributed decision-making power. Countries with a high acceptance of power distance include Mexico and France. Countries with a low acceptance include Austria and the United States.
2. **Individualism,** as contrasted with collectivism, pits loyalty to one's self against loyalty to a larger group. Countries in Asia and Latin America gravitate toward collectivism, while the United States, Canada, and most European countries gravitate toward individualism.
3. **Masculinity/femininity** contrasts competitiveness (traditionally masculine) with compassion and nurturing (traditionally feminine). Masculine nations include Australia, Germany, and Japan. Feminine nations include Sweden and Spain.

4. **Uncertainty avoidance** measures how well a society tolerates ambiguity. Nations that have difficulty tolerating uncertainty include Japan, Belgium, and Greece. Nations that tolerate ambiguity include Great Britain, the United States, and Sweden.
5. **Long-term versus short-term orientation** measures a society's willingness to consider the traditions of the past and carry them into the future. China and other East Asian nations tend to have long-term orientations in terms of a process or plan evolving over a number of years. The United States, in contrast, has a short-term orientation. Americans, for example, get impatient if recovery from a recession takes more than one or two years.

Public relations professionals and American executives must keep Hofstede's dimensions in mind as a general guide, but they must also be sensitive to the cultural differences that present themselves on a daily basis. Some examples:

- In China, tables at a banquet are never numbered. The Chinese think such table assignments appear to rank guests and that certain numbers are unlucky. Thus it's better to direct a guest to the "primrose" or the "hollyhock" table.

on the job

A MULTICULTURAL WORLD

Reaching Out to the Muslim World

Islam is the world's second largest religion after Christianity and is increasingly being recognized as a major consumer market. The demographics are quite impressive. The global Muslim population is expected to increase 35 percent over the next 20 years from 1.6 billion today to 2.2 billion by 2030.

The public relations and marketing challenge, however, is how to effectively reach such a diverse group in terms of geography and culture. In terms of geography, 60 percent of the Muslim population lives in the Asia/Pacific region with Indonesia's 235 million Muslim constituting the largest percentage. Only 20 percent live in the Middle East and North Africa, while the remaining 20 percent are located in various communities throughout Europe and the Americas.

The cultural background is also diverse. Yusuf Hatia, senior VP of Fleishman-Hillard in Mumbai, India, writes, "Muslims live in every country, represent every race and come from every social and economic class." And although they share common religious beliefs, he says they have their own local practices and national culture.

Despite the geographical and cultural diversity, Muslims around the world have one thing in common—the consumption of Halal products. The Halal food market, for example, is about 17 percent of the global food industry and worth about $650 billion annually. In addition, the Halal pharmaceutical market is worth about $500 billion while the Halal cosmetics market is estimated to be a $13 billion industry. As a result, more companies than ever are producing Halal products and making a special effort to include Muslims in their overall public relations and marketing strategies.

Hatia writes, "For brands that find ways to enhance and engage the Muslim consumer, the rewards are rich. And smart, compelling communications will play a critical role in targeting a consumer market that already represents nearly a quarter of humanity."

Source: Hatia, Y. (2013, June). Muslim world woefully underserved by PR sector. *O'Dwyer's Public Relations* Report, I4.

- Americans are fond of using first names, but it's not proper business etiquette to do so in Europe and Asia unless you have been given permission.
- Americans should avoid using expressions such as "full-court press" or even "awesome" or "cool" since many foreigners will have no idea what you are talking about.
- In the United Kingdom, the word *scheme* refers to a business proposition and holds no connotation of deceit as it does in the United States.
- Early morning breakfast meetings are not conducted in Latin America; by the same token, a dinner meeting may not start until 9 or 10 P.M.
- In Thailand and other Asian cultures, it's inappropriate to criticize an employee in front of others because the employee will "lose face." Also, it's a crime in Thailand to make disrespectful remarks about the royal family, particularly the king.
- In Latin America, greetings often include physical contact such as hugging the other person or grabbing him or her by the arm. Men and women commonly greet each other with a kiss on the cheek in Argentina and Chile.
- News releases in Malaysia should be distributed in the four official languages to avoid alienating any segment of the press.
- Gift giving is common in Asian cultures. Executives, meeting for the first time, will exchange gifts as a way of building a social relationship.
- In Muslim nations, particularly the Middle East, men should not stand near, touch, or stare at any woman.

The good news, particularly for most Americans, is that English has become the language of international business and tourism. See the Insights box below.

Other suggestions for American travelers abroad are given in the Insights box on page 554. Americans and others not only must learn the customs of the country in which they are working, but they also should rely on native professionals to guide

on the job INSIGHTS

English Is the World's Dominant Language

English is often described as the world's bridging language between the citizens of various nations. A Turk visiting France, for example, won't get very far using Turkish so it's common for him and his French hosts to use English as the bridging language.

Indeed, 1.5 billion people in the world speak English, and English is the primary language in more than 50 nations. In addition, more than 2 billion people are estimated to be learning English, and it has become the international language of business.

English is also the major language of the Internet. The top five languages of users are as follows:

Language	Users
English	565 million
Chinese	510 million
Spanish	165 million
Japanese	99 million
Portuguese	83 million

on the job INSIGHTS

Traveling Abroad? How to Make a Good Impression

Business for Diplomatic Action Inc., a nonprofit organization, works with U.S. companies to improve the reputation of the United States around the world. To that end, it has compiled guidelines on how business travelers (as well as tourists) should behave abroad. Here are some tips from its brochure "World Citizens Guide":

Read a map. Familiarize yourself with the local geography to avoid making insulting mistakes. Knowledge of current events and public issues is a real plus.

Dress up. In some countries, casual dress is a sign of disrespect.

Talk small. Talking about wealth, power, or status—corporate or personal—can create resentment. Bragging about America's greatness is a real turnoff.

No slang. Even casual profanity is unacceptable.

Slow down. Americans talk fast, eat fast, move fast, and live fast. Many other cultures do not.

Listen as much as you talk. Ask people you're visiting about themselves and their way of life.

Speak lower and slower. A loud voice is often perceived as bragging.

Exercise religious restraint. In many countries, religion is not a subject for discussion.

Exercise political restraint. Steer clear . . . if someone is attacking U.S. politicians or policies. Agree to disagree.

Learn some words. Learning some simple phrases in the host country's language is most appreciated.

them. Media materials and advertising must be translated, and the best approach for doing so is to employ native speakers who have extensive experience in translating ad copy and public relations materials. On some occasions, despite the best intentions, a company stumbles. See the Ethics box on page 557.

Foreign Corporations in the United States

Corporations and industries in other countries frequently employ public relations and lobbying to advance their commercial and political interests in the United States. A good example is China's Huawei Corporation, the world's second largest telecoms manufacturer with $35 billion in revenues. The U.S. Congress has barred Huawei from selling its equipment in the United States because of alleged connections with the Chinese military, so Bill Plummer, president of external affairs for Huawei, spends a great deal of time and effort in Washington trying to "unravel, undo, and dispel the myth and innuendo, misinformation, and disinformation."

Lobbying by foreign companies is a major activity. The Center for Public Integrity (CPI), for example, reported that in a six-year period, 700 companies with headquarters in about 100 nations spent more than $520 million lobbying the U.S. government. The Center's analysis continued, "Over that time, those companies employed 550 lobbying firms and teams of 3,800 lobbyists, more than 100 of whom were former members of Congress."

Companies from the United Kingdom top the list, having spent more than $180 million during the six-year period. This included BP (British Petroleum) and the pharmaceutical giant GlaxoSmithKline, which has extensive operations in the United States. BP, on the other hand, lobbies on matters relating to environmental standards and oil and gas issues. Companies from Germany were second on the list, spending about $70 million on lobbying. Swiss corporations were third, with about the same expenditures, and Japanese companies were fourth, spending about $60 million during that six-year period.

Not surprisingly, international trade was by far the most common issue foreign companies reported lobbying on, followed by defense and taxation.

The Center for Public Integrity

On a global level, there is intense lobbying to influence negotiations on a global climate change treaty. The fossil fuel industries and other heavy carbon emitters are using public relations strategies and lobbying to slow any progress on the control of greenhouse emissions. According to a report by the International Consortium of Investigative Journalists, "Employing thousands of lobbyists, millions in political contributions, and widespread fear tactics, entrenched interests worldwide are thwarting the steps that scientists say are needed to stave off a looming environmental calamity."

The Center for Public Integrity, which partnered with the journalists on its report, says lobbying can be seen most clearly in developed nations because they have disclosure regulations. In the United States, for example, CPI says, "There are now about 3,000 climate lobbyists—five lobbyists for every member of Congress—a 400 percent jump from six years earlier."

Carl Levin, vice president and senior consultant of Burson-Marsteller, Washington, D.C., lists five major reasons foreign corporations retain public relations counsel in the United States:

1. To hold off protectionist moves that threaten their companies or industries
2. To defeat legislation affecting the sale of their products
3. To provide ongoing information on political, legal, and commercial developments in the United States that could affect their business interests
4. To support expansion of their markets in the United States
5. To deal with a crisis situation that threatens the financial health or reputation of their organization

U.S. Corporations in Other Nations

Many U.S. corporations are global in scope, with employees, products, manufacturing plants, and distribution centers around the world. Wal-Mart, for example had 2012 worldwide revenues of $469 billion and employed 2.2 million worldwide. McDonald's has 34,000 restaurants in 118 nations and 1.8 million employees. On a smaller scale, Starbucks has 18,000 stores in more than 60 nations and 149,000 employees. In Japan alone, Starbucks has 1,000 stores. The revenues generated by such global giants dwarfs the total GNPs of many nations and affects the lives of millions.

Consequently, they, and hundreds of other U.S. companies, engage in extensive public relations and lobbying activities in other nations for virtually the same reasons that foreign countries lobby in the United States. The total amount expended on public relations and lobbying abroad is not known because U.S. companies don't have to report such expenditures to the U.S. government. Google, however, illustrates the point. Google spent $18 million on lobbying in 2012, and a large percentage of these expenditures were for lobbying in Europe against anti-trust and privacy regulations proposed by the EU.

Public relations professionals who work for Google, as well as a host of other American companies are heavily involved in global activities, because their work involves the companies' employees and operations in many nations. The corporate headquarters usually decides what key messages will be communicated worldwide, but relies on public relations staffs and local public relations firms in each country to ensure that the messages are properly translated and implemented. Many of these corporations also retain global public relations firms such as Edelman and Burson-Marsteller to provide services from offices in major cities around the world. The global efforts of public relations firms were discussed in Chapter 4.

At the start of the 21st century and in the aftermath of the 9/11 terrorist attacks in 2001, American companies have faced a number of challenges abroad: competing with other large corporations headquartered in other nations; dealing with sustainable development; being boycotted by nations that disagree with American foreign policy; and striving to act as good corporate citizens at the local and national levels.

> Every organization is going to have to deal with new rules and expectations for communication as the world becomes more competitive and as organizations interact with new markets.
>
> *Ray Kotcher, CEO of Ketchum, at the International Public Relations Association (IPRA) World Congress in Beijing*

David Drobis, a former senior partner and chair of Ketchum, outlined some of these challenges in a speech before the International Communications Consultancy Organization (ICCO). Drobis declared that one major challenge is to better communicate to the world's people the economic advantages of globalization. The *Economist*, for example, has also called globalization a massive communications failure because the public and private sectors have done such a poor job of communicating globalization's benefits, being transparent about their activities, and building important alliances.

Drobis believes that public relations professionals are best suited to explain the benefits of globalization. These benefits must be communicated to three key groups: (1) company management; (2) nongovernmental organizations, known as NGOs; and (3) international institutions such as the United Nations.

Corporations The first group is the companies themselves, which must realize that international capitalism has a bad connotation in many parts of the world. Companies, according to Drobis, have done little to correct this view despite the efforts of a few highly responsible companies who have outstanding programs. He asserts, "Companies must take into consideration a broad group of stakeholders as they pursue their business goals globally. And by doing so, there are tangible and intangible business benefits. In this way, good corporate citizenship is not a cost of doing business, but rather a driver of business success. What's good for the soul is also good for business."

Drobis adds, "Companies that pursue initiatives—be they related to the environment, labor standards, or human rights—are rewarded with improved business success in a number of areas, including shareholder value, revenue, operational efficiencies, higher employee morale and productivity, and corporate reputation." One continuing issue is the use of cheap labor in developing economies to produce goods, which is highlighted in the Ethics box on page 557.

on the job

ETHICS

Would You Buy a T-Shirt made in Bangladesh?

One of the deadliest industrial accidents in history took place on a sunny day in Bangladesh. In an instant, a garment factory collapsed killing 1,100 workers. In the rubble were clothes being made for some of the world's leading retailers such as Wal-Mart, the Gap, and Benetton.

The tragedy made worldwide headlines and placed the uncomfortable spotlight on the ethics of a supply chain that churns out underwear, jeans, and T-shirts produced by millions of workers making the lowest wages in the world. NGOs and consumer advocates light up the Internet and social media with critical comments about the ethics of retailers who supported such a system, and there were even calls for the boycott of various companies who used sweatshop labor in Bangladesh. Retailers also faced street protests. The United Students Against Sweatshops, for example, staged demonstrations against the Gap in a dozen cities.

The outcry brought a mixed reaction from retailers. Some, like Wal-Mart, claimed it had no "authorized" production at the collapsed factory. Benetton also claimed a hazy knowledge of its own supply chain and only acknowledged involvement after news photos of garments found in the wreckage displayed Benetton tags. The Walt Disney Company, on the other hand, announced that it was stopping production of its products in Bangladesh. Other European retailers, however, took the initiative to

(continued)

announce a joint agreement titled the Accord on Fire and Building Safety. It committed companies to a five-year program to do independent safety inspections of factories and even pay for numerous safety improvements.

Absent from the agreement were 14 American retailers who declined to take responsibility for forcing suppliers to upgrade safety standards and even provide funding for upgrades. Wal-Mart, claiming that the agreement would make the company liable in U.S. courts, offered another plan. It proposed to hire an outside auditor to inspect plants and publish the results on its website. Plants with fire and safety issues would have to make the necessary renovations or risk being removed from the list of authorized factories.

Critics of the proposal, however, say such voluntary efforts have a poor track record. Bob Ross, a critic of sweatshops who teaches sociology at Clark University, told the *Wall Street Journal*, "Without a legally binding contract that the European retailers have signed, it's just putting lipstick on a pig."

With that in mind, what do you think is the ethical responsibility of retailers to ensure that their products are produced in a safe environment? Would you be willing to pay more for a T-shirt if it was made in a plant that met minimum fire and safety standards? Some retailers say the lack of safety is the government's lack of regulatory oversight and not their problem. Would you agree?

The issue of sweatshop labor and plant safety raises serious reputation issues for companies in terms of sales. If it looks like you don't have control of your supply chain—even if it's a third party—that can change your reputation.

Heather Wilson, EVP of Ogilvy Public Relations

NGOs The second group that must be convinced of the benefits of globalization is nongovernmental organizations (NGOs). The annual Edelman survey measuring public trust of various institutions continually places NGOs at the top of public trust, and they are extremely influential as watchdogs on corporate behavior throughout the world. British NGO ActionAid, for example, blasted Associated British Foods for exploiting loopholes to avoid paying taxes that would have sent 48,000 Zambian children to school. And Starbucks backed down after Oxfam exposed the company's efforts to trademark the names of various Ethiopian bean varieties without paying for the right to use Ethiopian names on its products.

Although NGOs often expose corporate misdeeds, American companies have come to realize that NGOs can also become an important seal of approval and branding. Indeed, major mainstream NGOs such as the World Wildlife Federation and Greenpeace are working with corporations on sustainable development programs. The *Financial Times* notes, "A new type of relationship is emerging between companies and NGOs, where NGOs act as certification bodies, verifying and, in many cases, permitting the use of their logos, showing that products and services are being produced in socially responsible and environmentally friendly ways."

Indeed, hundreds of nongovernmental organizations expend considerable energy to get international support for their programs and causes. Organizations such as Greenpeace, Amnesty International, Doctors Without Borders, Oxfam, and even a number of groups opposed to globalization have been effective in getting their messages out via the Web, e-mail, social media, and demonstrations. They have been successful not only in setting the agenda for discussion issues, but also in influencing legislation at the national and international levels. A good example is Oceana's efforts to preserve the world's fisheries, which is highlighted in the PR Casebook on page 559.

NGOs like Oxfam and Christian Aid are going for the one source of power that's still left, and that's corporations.

Robert Blood, founder of Sigwatch in the Financial Times

PRCasebook

NGO Campaign Goes After Fishing Subsidies

Nongovernmental organizations, commonly known as NGOs, have become very influential in terms of shaping public opinion on global issues because the public widely perceives NGOs as being highly sincere and credible. For example, Oceana, an international conservation group, influenced the World Trade Organization (WTO) and national governments regarding the threat of overfishing.

Oceana worked on a three-year campaign to generate support from and action by the WTO to reduce nations' subsidies to their fishing fleets. The campaign, "Cut the Bait," used an extensive communications program to convince the WTO that reducing or eliminating subsidies would be the greatest contribution to preserving the world's oceans. A series of steps were involved in the campaign.

Step One Oceana commissioned scientists at the University of British Columbia to assess the extent of fishing subsidies. The study found that governments were spending a combined total of $20 billion annually in subsidies to the fishing industry, an amount equal to 25 percent of the world's fish catch.

Step Two Extensive interviews were undertaken with WTO officials, country diplomats, and other trade experts to gain technical and political insights. In addition, Oceana did a political analysis of the U.S. Congress on environmental issues. It also reviewed existing public opinion research and did a content analysis of how the media were covering the issue to date.

Oceana Advocacy Campaign - Collateral

Step Three A communications strategy that included media relations, advertising, events, and stakeholder advocacy was established to increase visibility on the issue and create pressure on WTO representatives. Science-based messages were used, and Oceana also created a life-size mascot, called "Finley the Fish," to establish a highly visible logo that would appeal to the public. Other collateral materials produced were magnets and a snow globe containing Finley surrounded by floating boats with fish hooks and money "confetti."

Step Four More than 500 meetings were conducted with WTO delegations. More than 175 briefings were conducted with U.S. trade and congressional offices. Technical briefings were conducted in Geneva, headquarters of the WTO, by scientists and experts. In addition, scientists were mobilized for advocacy. A letter signed by 125 scientists from 27 nations was sent to the WTO director general. Other activities included sponsoring billboards in Geneva saying, "Stop Fishing Subsidies" and enlisting television and movie celebrities to make public statements. Oceana also partnered with 11 other environmental groups, who publicly provided support.

The outcome was gratifying to Oceana. As a result of its "Cut the Bait" campaign, the WTO produced a first-draft agreement on fishing subsidies that included most of Oceana's recommendations. The agreement, as of 2009, had not been ratified but the draft agreement still remains the basis for negotiations. Nine nations, including the United States, have also strongly endorsed Oceana's recommendations, and even the U.S. Congress passed a resolution supporting the reduction of fishing subsidies.

In terms of media coverage, Oceana generated more than 1,000 media placements—including in influential publications such as the *Financial Times*, the *New York Times*, and the *Wall Street Journal*—in 37 nations. The campaign and the resulting media coverage also positioned Oceana as the leading spokesperson on fishing subsidies and related WTO negotiations. The International Public Relations Association (IPRA) awarded Oceana a Golden World Award for an outstanding campaign by an NGO.

One study by StrategyOne, the research arm of Edelman Worldwide, showed that media coverage of such organizations more than doubled over a four-year period, and NGOs were perceived by the public to be more credible than the news media or corporations when it came to issues such as labor, health, and the environment. Thought leaders, for example, indicate that they trust NGOs more than government or corporations because they consider the NGOs' motivation to be based on "morals" rather than "profit." Public Affairs Council President Doug Pinkham has said the StrategyOne report should be taken as a "wake-up call" by large corporations that have failed to embrace greater social responsibility and transparency.

International Institutions The third group is international institutions such as the World Trade Organization (WTO), the World Bank, the International Monetary Fund (IMF), and even the United Nations. Drobis says these organizations are unfairly criticized as being undemocratic, but fairly criticized for being nontransparent. An article in *Foreign Affairs* puts it this way: "To outsiders, even within the same government, these institutions can look like closed and secretive clubs. Increased transparency is essential. International organizations can provide more access to their deliberations, even after the fact."

Public Relations by Governments

The governments of virtually every country have multiple departments involved in communicating with political leaders and citizens in other nations. Much effort and billions of dollars are spent on the tourism industry to attract visitors, whose expenditures aid local economies. Even larger sums are devoted to lobbying efforts to obtain favorable legislation for a country's products; for example, Costa Rica conducted a public relations and lobbying campaign to convince the U.S. Congress to reduce tariffs on the import of its sugar.

Conflict and war between nations also lead to extensive public relations efforts by both sides to influence world public opinion that their actions are justified. Both Russia and Georgia, for example, hired American public relations firms to help each country convince the world that the other side was the aggressor in 2008 when a war broke out over the somewhat disputed territory of South Ossetia. Russia claimed it was responding to an unprovoked attack on the Russian population of Ossetia (officially part of Georgia), but the Georgians claimed that giant Russia was bullying the small former Soviet Republic. "This is part of warfare these days that you get your story out," Kleine Brockhoof, a German journalist, told *PRWeek*. See the Social Media in Action box on page 561 about Syria's use of the social media as a weapon of war.

Countries engage in persuasive communication campaigns for a number of reasons. Burson-Marsteller's Carl Levin says their goals when dealing with the United States are to:

- Advance political objectives
- Assess probable U.S. reaction to a projected action by the country
- Advance the country's commercial interests—for example, sales in the United States, increased U.S. private investment, and tourism
- Assist in communications in English

on the job

SOCIAL MEDIA IN ACTION

Wars and Conflict: Governments Enlist Social Media as a Weapon

President Assad of Syria in mid-2013 was in the middle of a civil war, which has claimed more than 100,000 lives, but you would never know it if you accessed his Facebook page. Twitter account, or the government's account with Instagram.

The photo sharing site, Instagram, is a particular favorite. Assad's staff posts numerous photos of him and his glamorous wife surrounded by adoring crowds. According to Zeina Karam of Associated Press (AP), "The photos show a smiling Assad among supporters, or grimly visiting wounded Syrians in the hospital. He is seen working in his office in Damascus, an Apple computer and iPad on his desk. His wife, Asma, who has stayed largely out of sight throughout the conflict, features heavily in the photos, casually dressed and surrounded by Syrian children and their mothers."

The Assad regime also has a YouTube channel for posting videos of alleged atrocities by the rebels against his regime, but the Free Syrian Army also uses YouTube and other social media to post videos of alleged atrocities by the Syrian military. In a conflict where there are no foreign journalists on the ground, such videos become the staple of nightly news throughout the world. The rebels also arrange Skype interviews with journalists outside the country and have even hired a New York public relations firm to represent them.

> The sophisticated PR campaign is striking for an isolated leader who has earned near pariah status for his military's bloody crackdown on dissent.
>
> *Zeina Karam, reporter for AP*

Erik Sass, in a posting on www.mediapost.com, comments "The days when the horrors of war could be filtered by newspaper editors and TV news producers are over, thanks in large part to social media, which allows users to post and share raw, uncensored photos and video footage of violent conflict, including the terrible consequences for civilians. This development has opened up a whole new arena in the battle to shape public opinion, leading to tit-for-tat social media exchanges between combatants."

The Israeli–Palestine conflict, for example, is now fought in social media. Hamas distributed a video of a father carrying his 11-month-old son killed by an Israeli artillery shell. Not to be outdone, the Israeli government countered with a picture of an Israeli baby, covered in blood, who was wounded by a Hamas rocket attack.

- Help win understanding of and support for specific issues that undermine the country's standing in the United States and the world community
- Modify laws and regulations inhibiting the country's activities in the United States

Under the Foreign Agents Registration Act (FARA) of 1938, all legal, political, fund-raising, public relations, and lobbying consultants hired by foreign governments to work in the United States must register with the Department of Justice. They are also required to file reports with the attorney general listing all activities on behalf of a foreign principal, compensation received, and expenses incurred. See the next Insights box for a list of U.S. public relations firms representing various nations.

on the job

INSIGHTS

U.S. Firms Represent a Variety of Nations

The following is a representative sample of contracts signed by U.S. public relations and lobbying firms, primarily based in Washinton, D.C., to work on behalf of foreign governments, as reported in various issues of *O'Dwyer's Newsletter*:

Glover Park Group. A $250,000 monthly retainer with the Egyptian Foreign Ministry to generate more favorable media coverage and U.S. administration support for the military junta that replaced President Morsi in a coup.

Fleishman-Hillard. $420,000 to assist Singapore with message development, media relations, organizing responses to "as-it-happens" news, and social media counseling.

GGR Government Affairs. $540,000 to help Gambia win economic and political support from the United States and non-government organizations to fund its adolescent and adult female education programs.

Roberti + White. $360,000 to counsel Cyprus on political developments in the United States and maintain contact with the White House, Congress, and journalists.

Podesta Group. $960,000 to assist Iraq with developing a strategic communications plan that would help the United States better understand its priorities and concerns. The firm will maintain contact on behalf of Iraq with members of Congress, reporters, and non-governmental officials.

The Harbour Group. $180,000 to conduct a public diplomacy program for the Libyan National Transitional Council and the country's U.S. embassy. The contract includes (1) setting up meetings with U.S. policymakers, reporters, and academics; (2) development of website content; and (3) establishing social media platforms.

Normally hired by an embassy after openly bidding for the account, the firm first gathers detailed information about the client country, including past media coverage. Attitudes toward the country are ascertained both informally and through surveys.

The action program decided on will likely include the establishment of an information bureau to provide facts and published statements of favorable opinion about the country. In many cases, a nation may also use paid issue advertising in publications such as the *New York Times*, the *Washington Post*, the *Wall Street Journal*, and the *Financial Times* that reach a high percentage of opinion leaders and elected officials. The Republic of Kazakhstan, for example, placed full-page ads in major American newspapers after its national elections to reinforce public perceptions that it is a democracy. The ad's headline was "Today, Kazakhstan has another asset besides oil, gas and minerals. Democracy."

Appointments are also secured with key journalists and editors to persuade them to publish or broadcast favorable stories about the country or its leaders. In other cases, the objective is to frame a particular issue in a way to generate favorable coverage for a government's actions or policies. See the Insights box on page 563 about Kazakhstan's favorable coverage on CNN.

on the job
INSIGHTS

A CNN Report on Kazakhstan: News or Propaganda?

Americans don't know much about the central Asian nation of Kazakhstan so CNN produced a special report about this oil and resource-rich nation sandwiched between Russia and China. "Eyes on Kazakhstan" was a half-hour collection of nine short segments that focused on the country's booming energy industry, opportunities for foreign investors, and the modern capital city.

But the series was not exactly what it seemed. It was sponsored by several state-owned agencies, but the reports only made a vague reference about "sponsorship originating from the countries we profile." Online clips did mention that the series was made in "association" with Samruk-Kazyna and the Astana Economic Forum. Research by Max Fisher of Atlantic Magazine, however, found that both of these organizations were part of a state-run holding company with strong ties to the current government.

Fisher also found that the CNN reporter calling Kazakhstan a "strong and vibrant economy" conducted an interview with a man introduced only as an "energy expert" that had effusive praise for the government's management of the economy. What the viewers were not told, however, was that the "expert" was a government employee and head of the Eurasian Economic Club of Scientists' Association headed by the president of Kazakhstan. In another segment, an "economist" was interviewed about sending talented students abroad for study, but it was also not disclosed that he headed an entire department of the president's office. This, says Fisher, is like CNN interviewing an executive of the Ford Motor as an unbiased "auto expert" who might give comment on the merits of Ford's cars and trucks.

In sum, the CNN series was the result of Kazakhstan making a major investment in lobbying and public relations to combat unfavorable media coverage about its human rights record, the dictatorship of the country's president (in office for more than 20 years), and attract foreign investment for a rapidly growing economy. Arranging "sponsorship" of the CNN series by government controlled organizations no doubt was considered a major accomplishment.

Fisher writes, "Whether CNN chose to label present and former government employees as unbiased 'experts' without noting their connections or was simply unaware of those links, it's an odd moment of convergence between one of the largest news networks in the world and the lobbying campaign of this far-flung Central Asian oil exporter."

Source: Fisher, M. (2012, July 20). CNN's Effusive Coverage of Kazakhstan Is Quietly Sponsored by Its Subject. Retrieved from *Atlantic Monthly* (www.theatlantic.com /International).

Briefings are also held for business executives, and leaders of various public policy groups who are then encouraged to write op-eds or give presentations supporting the foreign government and its policies. In many cases, the primary audiences are key members of congressional committees, heads of various governmental agencies, and even the White House staff. These people are often invited to visit the client country on expense-paid trips, although some news media people decline on ethical grounds.

Gradually, through expert and persistent methods of persuasion (including lobbying), public opinion may be changed, favorable trade legislation may be passed, foreign aid may be increased, or an influx of American tourists may go to the country.

Some of the toughest problems confronting public relations firms who work for foreign governments include:

- Deciding whether to represent a country, such as Belarus or Zimbabwe, whose human rights violations may reflect adversely on the agency itself
- Deciding whether to represent nations such as Ecuador, Bolivia, or Venezuela whose governments are extremely critical of U.S. Latin American policies.
- Persuading the governments of such nations to alter some of their practices so that the favorable public image sought will reflect reality
- Convincing a client nation that controls or owns its media that the American press is independent of government influence and coverage won't always be favorable.

Why do some U.S. firms choose to work for other governments, perhaps even those that are unpopular? Says Burson-Marsteller's Carl Levin: "I do not think it is overreaching to state that in helping friendly foreign clients we also advance our national interests. And we help in ways that our government cannot."

Levin may be correct, but representing an unpopular country such as North Korea or even a nation with political strife can have its pitfalls. Ruder Finn's contract with the new Maldives government after a military-backed coup, for example, caused a group of protestors outside its London office to protest the firm's involvement with what they considered an illegal government.

In another situation, Washington Media Group (WMG) found it necessary to resign an account with the Tunisian government as the regime came under increasing international criticism that eventually touched off the Arab Spring. WMG president Gregory Vistica, in his resignation letter to the government, wrote, "Recent events make it clear the Tunisian government is not inclined to heed our counsel regarding meaningful reforms." He continued, "Indeed, the government's current actions and activities have undermined, or in some cases completely undone, whatever progress we have made in improving Tunisia's reputation."

> In the modern age, whichever nation's communication methods are most advanced, whichever nation's communications capacity is strongest . . . has the most power to influence the world.
>
> *President Hu Jintao of China*

A nation's reputation is extremely important in an age of instant communication and global trade, so nations spend considerable amounts of money and effort on what is called "reputation management." A case in point is China, which has ramped up its public relations and lobbying efforts in recent years to counter criticisms (and fears) in the United States about its growing economic and military power. It hired the Patton Boggs firm to lobby on a wide range of issues before Congress, including trade tariffs, intellectual property, currency exchange rates, and Taiwan.

In addition to using American public relations firms, the Chinese government has embarked on a massive global effort to enhance its image and reputation. The Beijing Olympics and the Shanghai Expo, for example, did much to generate positive media coverage around the world and alter popular misconceptions of China.

China is also expanding its influence worldwide by creating TV networks, starting English-language newspapers, leasing radio stations on all continents, and broadcasting TV news to a worldwide audience in six languages. The UK's *Guardian Weekly* notes, "Beijing's response is typically massive and ambitious: a \$6.6 billion global strategy to create media giants that will challenge agenda-setting western giants such as News Corp, the BBC, and CNN." On another level, China has greatly expanded its outreach to educational institutions around the world. See the Insights box below.

on the job INSIGHTS

China's Educational Outreach to the World

Countries use a variety of "public diplomacy" initiatives to enhance their national reputation and influence opinion leaders in other nations. One such initiative is an extensive program by China to establish Confucius Institutes at universities around the world.

Hanban, an agency affiliated with China's Ministry of Education, was started in 2004 for the purpose of "enhancing the world's understanding of Chinese language and culture, deepening the friendship between China and the rest of the world, and promoting global cultural diversity." By 2009, Hanban had established and funded almost 350 Confucius Institutes in more than 80 nations and regions around the world.

A sampling of American universities with Institutes includes the University of Tulsa, the University of Florida, Northwestern University, Stanford University, Texas A&M University, and the University of Minnesota. Confucius Institutes on such campuses provide instruction on Chinese culture and language by providing teachers, partnering with various university academic departments, and donating instructional resources.

The number and distribution of teaching resources to schools is impressive. According to a recent annual report by Hanban, (1) 1.3 million volumes of teaching materials were donated to more than a thousand institutions in 100

(continued)

nations, (2) 2,000 teachers and volunteers were sent to 109 nations to teach Chinese, (3) 16,512 secondary school teachers from 47 nations received language training, and (4) *Everyday Chinese* is published in 38 languages.

Hanban also has an extensive international exchange program. More than 800 primary and secondary school principals, for example, visited China in a recent year. In addition, 800 foreign high school students visited China and participated in "Chinese Bridge" summer camps. University students also receive funding to visit China and learn about Chinese culture and language. The government also has an extensive scholarship program for foreign students to study at Chinese universities.

The Chinese government believes the rapid acceptance of Confucius Institutes is evidence of a global desire to build positive relationships through communication and cooperation. Additionally, the government suggests that the Institutes help China interact with the world in hopes to building mutually beneficial relationships.

American Public Diplomacy

The American government is the major disseminator of information around the world. This is called *public diplomacy*, because it is an open communication process primarily intended to present American society in all its complexity so that citizens and governments of other nations can understand the context of U.S. actions and policies. Another function is to promote American concepts of democracy, free trade, and open communication around the world.

The United States Information Agency (USIA), created in 1953 by President Dwight Eisenhower, was the primary agency involved in shaping America's image abroad. USIA, in many ways, was the direct descendant of George Creel's Committee on Public Information (CPI) during World War I and Elmer Davis's Office of War Information during World War II. See Chapter 2.

After World War II, the new threat was the outbreak of the Cold War between the United States and the Soviet Union and the Communist bloc nations in Eastern Europe. The Cold War was a war of words on both sides to win the "hearts and minds" of governments and their citizens around the world.

Some early USIA activities included (1) the stationing of public affairs officers (PAOs) at every American embassy to work with local media, (2) publication of American books and magazines, (3) distribution of American films and TV programs, (4) sponsorship of tours by American dance and musical groups, (5) art shows, (6) student and faculty exchange programs such as the Fulbright Program, and (7) sponsorship of lecture tours by American authors and intellectuals. The USIA was abolished in 1999 after the end of the Cold War and the implosion of the Soviet Union, but many of these activities continue today under the auspices of the U.S. Department of State, which has an undersecretary of state for public affairs and diplomacy.

The 9/11 attacks on the United States created a new impetus to "sell" America and the U.S. decision to invade Afghanistan and Iraq. The cry was to "win the hearts and minds" of the world's people and to gain public, as well as international, support for U.S. actions. Diplomatic efforts have had mixed results, and American foreign policy is still not popular in many of the world's capitals. Perceptions of the United States however, have improved in recent years primarily as a result of President Obama's popularity around the world as a charismatic leader, although the current Republican Congress holds him in much less esteem.

The public affairs section of the U.S Department of State is the official voice of the United States government and often has to react almost instantly to issues that seriously affect U.S. standing abroad. In 2012, for example, an American film-maker produced an anti-Muslim video that, via the Internet, immediately incited violence in the Middle East. Large protests against the film involved tens of thousands of people in Pakistan. Secretary of State Hillary Clinton issued a statement that the United States government had absolutely nothing to do with the video. The State Department also purchased time on Pakistan television to re-assure Muslims that the U.S. had great respect for the Muslim religion. In the United States, such films are considered free speech. In countries where the media are controlled by the government, citizens have a hard time believing that an independent filmmaker could make such a film and distribute it.

One major vehicle of communication is the Voice of America (VOA), which was created in 1942. It traditionally broadcast news, sports, and entertainment around the world via shortwave, but VOA has also established AM and FM radio transmitters throughout the world. In addition, the agency supplies many radio and television stations throughout the world with various news, music, and talk programs free of charge. The VOA also offers audio streaming on the World Wide Web. The worldwide audience for VOA is difficult to judge, given all the distribution methods, but estimates are that it has several hundred million listeners.

> U.S. sponsored radio and TV broadcasts remain critical weapons in the struggle for freedom around the world.
>
> *James K. Glassman, chair of the Broadcasting Board of Governors*

More recently, Congress has set up radio and television services focusing on Iraq and the Middle East. Radio Sawa injects news tidbits written from an American perspective into a heavy rotation of American and Middle Eastern pop music. A similar radio service aimed at Iranian youth is Radio Farda. On the television side, the U.S. government started Al Hurra. According to the *New York Times*, Al Hurra is "a slickly produced Arab-language news and entertainment network that [is] beamed by satellite from a Washington suburb to the Middle East."

VOA, and services such as Radio Sawa, are not directed at U.S. citizens. Under the United States Information and Educational Exchange Act of 1948, Congress prohibited the government from directing its public diplomacy efforts toward Americans, because of fears that the government would propagandize its own citizens.

Funding for public diplomacy has somewhat increased under the Obama administration, but changing American policies is a much more difficult political process. Judith McHale, chief of U.S. public diplomacy efforts, told an audience in Europe that President Obama and Secretary of State Clinton recognize public diplomacy as a key cog in restoring U.S. leadership around the world: "They recognize public diplomacy as an essential ingredient of 21st century stagecraft."

Opportunities in International Work

The 21st century, according to many experts, represented a new golden age of global marketing and public relations. The expansion of nations in the EU, the economic and social reforms in the former Soviet Union, and the rise of China, Korea, and Brazil as major economic powers has hastened the reality of a global economy.

The decision to seek a career in global public relations should ideally be made during the early academic years, so that a student can take multiple courses in international relations, global marketing techniques, the basics of strategic public relations planning, foreign languages, social and economic geography, and cross-cultural communication. Graduate study in international business and international relations is an asset.

As a desirable starting point, students should study abroad for a semester or serve an internship with an organization based in, or with operations in, another nation. Practically every campus has an international studies office that has semester abroad programs and also contacts with organizations that arrange international internships. Students may apply for the Fulbright Program, which funds travel and study abroad. Rotary International also offers a student foreign study scholarship as well.

Taking the U.S. Foreign Service examination is the first requirement for launching a diplomatic career, but many recent graduates can also join a public relations firm, a corporation, or a non-profit with global offices that eventually leads to international travel and foreign assignments. All it takes is desire, initiative, and persistence to have a career in international public relations.

Summary

What Is Global Public Relations?

- Public relations work today involves dealing with employees, customers, vendors, communities, and government officials in multiple nations.
- Public relations is a well-developed industry in many nations around the world. China, in particular, has a rapidly expanding public relations industry that is getting more sophisticated every year.

International Corporate Public Relations

- In the new age of global marketing, public relations firms represent foreign interests in the United States as well as the interests of American corporations around the world.
- The practitioner must deal with issues of language and cultural differences, including subtle differences in customs and etiquette and even ethical dilemmas such as paying for news coverage.
- A great deal of public relations work for companies and governments involves lobbying a nation's elected officials or government agencies for favorable trade agreements.
- Nations also use global public relations to enhance their global image and gain influence in various regional and international groups.
- NGOs are now major players in setting the agenda for discussion of global issues and influencing the policies of corporations and governments.
- NGOs are widely believed to be more credible by the news media and the public on issues such as labor, health, and the environment, partly because they are perceived as lacking the self-interest ascribed to governments and corporations.
- There is increasing evidence that giant corporations are adopting a more accommodative stance and cooperating with activist NGOs to form more socially responsible policies.

Public Relations by Governments

- Most governments seek to influence the foreign policies of other countries as well as the opinions and actions of their publics. These communications can range from promoting tourism to influencing trade policies and promoting foreign investment.
- U.S. public relations firms work for foreign governments, helping them advance their political objectives and commercial interests, counseling them on probable U.S. reactions to their proposed actions, and assisting in communications in English.
- War and conflict between nations usually results in a barrage of public relations activity on both sides to justify their actions. The Russia–Georgia conflict, as well as the Israel–Palestine impasse, are examples.
- The U.S. government refers to its international information efforts as *public diplomacy*, which involves activities to enhance understanding of American

culture and promote U.S. foreign policy objectives. The VOA radio broadcasts are part of this program.

Opportunities in International Work

- As global marketing and communications have expanded in recent years, so too have opportunities for international public relations work.
- Fluency in a foreign language is a valued skill but not a prerequisite; also important is a background in international relations, global marketing techniques, social and economic geography, and cross-cultural communication.

Case Activity Promoting Tourism for Turkey

Turkey has a problem. It's a Muslim country and many Americans have become hesitant about visiting a nation that they perceive is part of the Middle East where there is political unrest and even terrorism. Many don't know that Turkey is relatively stable, has a secular government, and has a strong European orientation.

Indeed, Turkey remains a virtual treasure-house of art, culture, and cuisine that would appeal to seasoned travelers looking for a new experience and destination. There are Roman ruins, exotic shopping in the Grand Bazaar of Istanbul, and the new jazz sounds of Turkish musicians. Istanbul, by all accounts, is one of the most vibrant and interesting cities in the world that has been a crossroads of civilizations for centuries.

The Turkish Culture and Tourism Office has retained your public relations firm to conduct a media relations program in the American press (and to some extent the European media) to increase awareness of Turkey as a desirable tourist destination. Develop a public relations plan that will use appropriate media and events to reach various audiences. Your plan should outline possible feature stories for print and broadcast media, use of social media, and special events or promotions.

Questions For Review and Discussion

1. What is global public relations? What are some of the reasons for its growth in recent decades?
2. The field of public relations develops best in a nation that has some special characteristics. What are some of those characteristics?
3. How does public relations contribute to the global operations of large companies?
4. What objectives do foreign nations seek to accomplish by hiring U.S. public relations firms to represent them in America?
5. What do you mean by the new age of global marketing? What are the challenges and opportunities?
6. Islam, the second-largest religion in the world after Christianity, is seen as a major consumer market by multinational companies. What are the PR challenges of reaching out to this diverse group in terms of culture and geography?
7. Non-governmental organizations like Greenpeace and WWF have footprints in many countries across the globe on sustainable development programs. What makes them successful?
8. Why should companies consider public relations and marketing outreach to the Muslim population of the world?
9. How are social media now being used by nations in times of conflict and war?
10. Part of a company's reputation depends on maintaining an ethical supply chain for its products. What should U.S. retailers do about the safety hazards of plants in Bangladesh?
11. Foreign governments often influence coverage of their nations through lobbying and public relations efforts. Name some examples from the text.
12. What is China doing to enhance its international reputation and promote itself as a leading nation in the global economy?
13. Wars and conflicts involve fierce public relations activities on the part of warring nations. Discuss with some examples from the text.
14. If you decided to have a career in global public relations, would you choose a global corporation, an international NGO, or the U.S. foreign service? Explain your rationale.

Media Resources

Bardhan, N., & Weaver, C., editor (2011). *Public Relations in Global Cultural Contexts: Multi-Paradigmatic Perspectives*. London: Routledge, 295 pages.

Cambie, S., & Ooi, Y.-M. (2009). *International communication strategy: Developments in cross-cultural communications, PR, and social media.* London, England: Kogan, Page Publishers.

Carter. B., & Chozich, A. (2012, June 11). Syria Conflict Cracks Carefully Polished Image of Assad. *New York Times*, 1, B4.

Daniels, C. (2012, September). Latin America Sizzle: Multinationals and agencies are setting their sights on the booming economies of South America. *PRWeek*, 32–39.

deVilliers, R. (2012, October). PR's New Frontiers: Public Relations in Emerging Markets. *PRWeek*, 30–34.

Dickson, V. (2012, November). Continent of Contrasts: Asia-Pacific Region. *PRWeek*, 19–26.

Gawn, R. (2013, April). Campaign basics remain the same on foreign soil. *PRWeek*, 25.

Global views of United States improve while other countries decline. (2010). Retrieved from www.worldpublicopinion.org

Hatia, Y. (2013, June). Muslim world woefully underserved by PR sector. *O'Dwyer's Public Relations Report*, 14.

Hazley, G., & Gingerich, J. (2013, June). Retailers PR response to Bangladesh disaster: Silence. *O'Dwyer's Public Relations Report*, l0.

Lucas, L. (2013, March 19). From boycotts to business briefs: Charities are increasing pressure on companies over issues such as tax and supply lines. *Financial Times*, 20.

Maltby, E. (2010, January 19). Expanding abroad? Avoid cultural gaffes. *Wall Street Journal,* p. B5.

Molleda, J.-C. (2009). Global public relations. Retrieved from Institute for Public Relations, Essential Knowledge Project website: www.instituteforpr.org

Peijuan, C., Ting, L. P., & Pang, A. (2009). Managing a nation's image during crisis: A study of the Chinese government's image repair efforts in the "Made in China" controversy. *Public Relations Review, 35*(3), 213–218.

Shearman, S. (2013, June). Effective global plans traverse borders. *PRWeek*, 34.

Sriramesh, K., & Vercic, D., editors (2009). *The Global Public Relations Handbook: Theory, Research, and Practice.* London: Routledge, 950 pages.

chapter 21

Public Relations in Non-Profit, Health, and Education Sectors

After reading this chapter, you will be able to:

- Describe the variety of nonprofit organizations that rely on public relations to achieve their goals
- Articulate the strategies and tactics employed by nonprofits to remain viable
- Understand the central place of fund-raising in nonprofit organizations
- Describe the role of public relations in health communication and hospital efforts
- Distinguish among college, university, and school applications of public relations to serve educational institutions

The Nonprofit Sector

Nonprofit organizations, which are often referred to as *charities*, encompass a broad area of public relations work. In the United States, there are almost 2 million such groups, according to GuideStar, an organization that compiles information on nonprofits.

More than 6.5 million people work in the nonprofit sector. The range of nonprofit institutions is astounding, from membership organizations, advocacy groups, and social service organizations, to educational organizations, hospitals and health agencies, small-city historical societies, and global foundations that disperse million-dollar grants.

The main purpose of nonprofit organizations is to serve the public interest. By definition, nonprofit organizations do not distribute monies to shareholders or owners. This is not to say that nonprofit organizations cannot generate income or hold assets, but there are a number of restrictions regulating how their income may be generated and how these funds may be used to support the organization's stated objectives. From the public relations perspective, nonprofit organizations are often represented as fostering goodwill, and as beacons of social responsibility.

Nonprofits are tax exempt. The federal government grants them this status because they enhance the well-being of their members, in the case of trade associations, or enhance the human condition in some way, in the case of environmental groups or medical research organizations. Many nonprofit organizations could not survive if they were taxed. Because they do not have shareholders or sell goods and services to customers, they face the never-ending task of asking for donations to pay expenses, finance projects, and recruit volunteers.

Competition, Conflict, and Cooperation

For many nonprofit organizations, partnerships are mutually beneficial. The United Way is a good case in point—many business and nonprofit organizations ranging from the National Football League to the Advertising Council, as well as numerous local organizations, partner with the United Way.

This maximizes donations that are distributed to hundreds of associated charities. However, the frustrating reality is that nonprofits, instead of partnering, often compete with each other for members, funds, and other resources. For example, universities or colleges within the same state compete for funding from their respective state governments, even as they enter into collaborative partnerships with each other to obtain federal funding. Hospitals compete for "customers," but must work together to resolve shared concerns and issues.

Competition among nonprofit agencies for donations is intense. For many nonprofit groups, fund-raising of necessity is their most time-consuming activity. Without generous contributions from companies and individuals, nonprofit organizations could not exist. The scope of philanthropy in the United States and the amount of money needed to keep voluntary service agencies operating are staggering.

Activist groups who espouse certain causes, in contrast, can come into conflict with other organizations whose values are different. Such conflicts can be high profile. In recent years, a number of religious organizations have come into conflict with groups that advocate for secular values. And Major League Baseball faces intense attacks from fans and the player's union over the suspension and punishment of players accused of using performance enhancing drugs (PEDs). Yankee superstar, Alex Rodriguez, faced a 211-game suspension that has spurred enormous comment and discussion in social media ranging from calls for lifetime bans to claims that athletes cannot compete without PEDs.

The American Civil Liberties Union (ACLU), a nonprofit organization founded in 1920 "to defend and preserve the individual rights and liberties guaranteed to every person in this country by the Constitution and laws of the United States," often comes into conflict with the American Center for Law and Justice, a conservative group founded by Pat Robertson to preserve "religious liberty, the sanctity of human life, and the two-parent, marriage-bound family." Although both organizations state their commitment to preserving "liberty," their respective views of what constitutes "liberty" are often diametrically opposed.

On occasion, there is also conflict between donors and organizations. Intel and UPS, for example, decided to stop funding the Boy Scouts of America (BSA) in 2012 because of the organization's anti-gay policies regarding membership. The two companies, which gave $300,000 to BSA in the previous year, issued a statement saying that the BSA policy violated their corporate commitment to social and sexual equality.

On an international level, there can also be competition and conflict. Many international organizations and government agencies, for example, supply aid funds to Africa, but some wonder if such aid is effective. See the following Multicultural World box.

on the job

A MULTICULTURAL WORLD

Global Strategic Communication Helps African Females Avoid Brutality

Bogaletch Gebre, the inspiring and determined force behind a grassroots movement called Community Conversations is herself a victim of female circumcision and mutilation to deaden sexual sensation—done to her while her arms and legs were pinned down.

In her culture, this forceful act against her will was essential to becoming properly prepared at age 12 for marriage later in her life. Gebre repudiates female cutting as part of a larger cultural disposition by men to assert power over women. The brutality includes abduction and rape of girls who then must marry their attacker—as well as forced marriages for widows to their brother-in-laws.

In spite of having good reasons to attack such practices, Gebre knows that dialogue is crucial to bringing

Dixon Bogaletch Gebre, center, is the founder of an organization focused on eliminating sanctioned violence against women and girls, such as female genital mutilation, in Ethiopia.

(continued)

about change. "You must allow the community to decide for themselves rather than condemning," said Gebre. "To make people understand the harm that comes to their children you can't come in and tell them 'you are doing bad and must stop.' " Notably, the success of the campaign does not revolve around legal battles or official change in policy, but change in the hearts and minds of the people themselves.

Gebre's organization, called Tostan which means Breakthrough, exemplifies many of the principles of public relations from previous chapters. The strategic communication program revolves around special events held in village after village.

The events are the focal point of a broader public relations process that has seen many countries in Africa shift from tradition to compassion, resulting in a marked drop in the practice of cutting. According to the *New York Times*, a systematic survey by the United Nations Children's Fund in 2013 found that teenage girls are now less likely to have been cut than older women in more than half of the 29 countries in Africa and the Middle East where the practice is concentrated.

In addition to the village-level events to talk through the consequences of violent practices against women, Tostan uses a train-the-trainer process to develop a cadre of young women and men who can hold workshops with target publics such as students, village leaders, uncut girls, and the women who work as circumcisers.

This strategy was based on initial research to complement the focused, more interpersonal efforts of the Community Conversation events. The entire public relations process includes research, planning, communication, and evaluation. These are discussed in Chapters 5–8.

Based on current evaluation, much more needs to be done using local communication tools to make greater inroads in the physical aggression and violence experienced by young women. But public relations efforts to date have made significant progress against a brutal tradition.

Sources: Rosenberg, T. (2013, July 17). Talking Female Circumcision Out of Existence. *New York Times*. Retrieved from www.nytimes.com; Dugger, C. (2013, July 22). Report Finds Gradual Fall in Female Genital Cutting in Africa By, *New York Times*. Retrieved from www.nytimes.com

Membership Organizations

Membership organizations are composed of people who share common business or social interests. Their purpose is mutual help and self-improvement. Membership organizations often use the strength of their common bond to promote the professionalism of their members, endorse legislation, and support socially valuable causes. Their main function is to advocate for the well-being of their members.

Professional Associations

Members of a profession or skilled craft organize for mutual benefit. Examples include the Royal Institute of British Architects or the American Dental Association. Others serve highly specialized or niche groups, such as the National Association of Professional Organizers or the seemingly anachronistic Society of Gilders. Some professional organizations, such as the American Medical Association, also function as some of the largest advocacy and lobbying groups. In many ways, their goals resemble those of labor unions in that they seek improved earning power, better working conditions, and public appreciation of their roles in society.

Professional associations place their major emphasis on setting standards for professional performance, establishing codes of ethics, determining requirements for admission to a field, and encouraging members to upgrade their skills through continuing education. In some cases, they have quasi-legal power to license and censure members. In most cases, however, professional groups rely on peer pressure and persuasion to police their membership.

In general, professional associations are national in scope. Larger organizations often have district, state, or local chapters. Most scientific and scholarly associations, however, are international and have chapters in many nations. The Public Relations Society of America (PRSA) and the International Association of Business Communicators (IABC) are examples of professional associations.

Public relations specialists for professional organizations use the same techniques as their colleagues in other branches of the field. And like their counterparts in trade groups and labor unions, many professional associations maintain offices near the seat of government in Washington, D.C., and in the various state capitals, employing lobbyists to make their voices heard.

Trade Groups

The membership of a trade association usually consists of manufacturers, wholesalers, retailers, or distributors in the same field. Corporate entities, not individuals, are the members. A few examples of trade associations include the American Beverage Association, the Property Casualty Insurers Association, and the National Association of Home Builders. There are about 6,000 trade and professional associations in the United States.

Because federal laws and regulations can often affect the fortunes of an entire industry, about one-third of these groups are based in the Washington, D.C., area. There, association staffs can monitor congressional activity, lobby for or against legislation, communicate late-breaking developments to the membership, and interact with government officials on a regular basis.

Although individual members of trade associations may be direct rivals competing for market share, it is often to their advantage to work together to promote an entire industry, generate public support, and share information. By representing an entire industry, an association often is a more effective news source than individual companies can be. When a news situation develops involving a particular field, reporters frequently turn to the spokesperson of its association for comment. To promote their industry, many trade organizations compile statistics, establish online newsrooms, provide speakers to schools, sponsor trade shows, maintain a YouTube channel, and actively blog to make the position of the trade group clear to stakeholders.

Labor Unions

Like trade associations, labor unions represent the interests of an entire industry. However, labor unions advocate on behalf of employees, whereas trade associations typically represent the interests of management. As with other membership organizations, labor unions lobby for better working conditions, higher wages, increased safety regulations, better benefits, and education for their members.

Since their apex in the late 1970s, labor unions have suffered serious membership losses and, as a consequence, political clout. Union membership declined from 20.1 percent of workers in 1983 to 11.3 percent in 2012, according to the Department of Labor's Bureau of Statistics. During the economic recession from 2007 until 2011, the number of union members had reversed the historical trend with modest increases in membership, perhaps a reflection of worker concern about job security.

Workers in education, government, and libraries tend to have the highest union representation, accounting for nearly one in three workers in those sectors. Government workers are five times more likely to belong to a union than are their private sector counterparts. And New York leads all states in union membership at 23.2 percent, with North Carolina the lowest at 2.9 percent, reflecting regional differences in U.S. unionization.

Media portrayals often suggest that unions are corrupt, inflexible, and lacking in concern for anyone except their members. Nevertheless, labor unions have been largely responsible for many positive things that Americans today take for granted: the end of child labor, the 40-hour workweek, laws against discrimination in hiring and firing, and the minimum wage. Unions are still very much a part of the American scene, representing teachers, players in the National Basketball Association, UPS employees, and other familiar groups.

Unions rely on public relations tools to assert their strength and influence. Unions seek to build their memberships, protect members' job security, and improve their public images. Unions also employ public relations when communicating with their internal audiences in various companies or organizations because unions must keep their memberships informed about what they receive in return for their dues, which includes recreational and social programs and representation in communication and negotiations with company management.

In the United States, labor unions are often in conflict with management, which is dominant in terms of both financial strength and political clout. In every national political campaign, unions spend millions of dollars to support candidates they regard as friendly to their cause. The Citizens United decision by the Supreme Court (see Chapter 12) gave a voice to both corporations and unions by opening a floodgate of indirect political funding through Political Action Committees (PACs) supporting campaign spending on partisan issues, not candidates.

A high stakes battle arose over the so-called Cadillac health insurance tax in President Obama's health care reform act. Sponsors of the act argued that expensive, employer-funded health coverage makes people insensitive to the cost of care. As cities and towns press municipal unions to accept cheaper health benefits to avoid the tax, unions must figure out how to rein in health care costs. Otherwise, the price when the tax goes into effect will be steep, threatening raises and even jobs. Bloggers and editorialists decry the unintended consequences of the Cadillac tax for working people who value union membership for its strong benefit package.

Chambers of Commerce

A chamber is an association of business professionals who work to improve their city's commercial climate and to publicize its attractions. Above all, chambers of commerce serve as boosters of local business growth. State chambers of commerce and, nationally, the U.S. Chamber of Commerce help guide local chambers and speak for business interests before state and federal government.

According to the Center for Responsive Politics, the Chamber has spent more than $900 million on lobbying since 1998 and has been the top lobbying spender annually since 2001. During the 2010 midterm elections, it reported to the Federal Election Commission spending nearly $33 million on political ads. Its closest competitor, the American Medical Association, spent less than half that amount. Both groups concentrate major resources on health care reform and policy implementation in the interests of its members. The U.S. Chamber of Commerce also lobbies against legislation regarding global warming, but this has caused some companies to drop their membership.

on the job

ETHICS

Chamber of Commerce Tempers Its Position on Global Climate Change

Apple Corporation resigned from the U.S. Chamber of Commerce, the country's largest industry advocacy group, citing a difference of opinion over proposed climate change legislation.

This significant blow to Chamber credibility and financial support offers a clear example of how the life cycle of an issue presented in Chapter 10 is managed by a major membership organization. In the years following Apple's departure, the Chamber of Commerce has tempered its position on global climate change. In response to public discourse in a free society prompted by Apple's decision, but with an eye on the will of its loyal membership, the Chamber recalibrated its messaging. Apple conducted its own public relations efforts in the marketplace of ideas to show that innovation at Apple goes beyond device features to important global policy changes.

The Chamber continues today to oppose, through lobbying, many of the provisions of the Clean Air Act and initiatives to reduce carbon emissions through cap-and-trade. Apple, on the other hand, has gradually emerged as a leading "green" company, obtaining three-quarters of its energy from renewable resources in 2012. Indeed, Apple actually hired the former head of the EPA to help shape its activist approach as a corporation. Apple has recently emphasized its efforts to reduce the carbon footprint associated with its products, to be true to its position and avoid charges of merely "greenwashing."

At issue are two worldviews. According to polls, public opinion in the United States is split just about evenly on the issue of climate change. One view, represented by the Chamber and, presumably, most of its 3 million members, is that global warming has been exaggerated and that curbing it will hurt American competitiveness—and, worse, impoverish people worldwide. The other position, adopted by Apple, suggests that the evidence for climate change is overwhelming and that steps to reduce emissions are necessary and arguing against carbon limits may ultimately be bad for business in terms of public trust and credibility.

What do you think? Would you be ethically more comfortable as a public relations spokesperson on the issue of global climate change for the Chamber of Commerce or for a company such as Apple?

Local chambers of commerce play the role of community booster: Chambers spotlight the unique characteristics of their locales and sing their praises to anyone who will listen. Chambers often coin a slogan for a city, such as "Furniture Capital of Indiana" (Berne) or "Business at its Best since 1926" (Belfast, Maine) or "Last Best Place" (Montana).

Often, a chamber of commerce serves as the public relations arm of city government. The chamber staff generally produces the brochures and maps sent to individuals who seek information about visiting the city or who consider moving to the area. Chambers also conduct polls and compile statistics about the economic health of the city, including data on major industries, employment rates, availability of schools and hospitals, housing costs, and so on. Attracting conventions and new businesses to the city also is an important aspect of chamber work.

Advocacy Groups

Affecting communities to varying degrees are a number of pressing issues, from social matters such as poverty, abortion, and racism to threats such as epidemic diseases and environmental degradation. Organizations that fight for social causes can have significant impacts, both positive and negative. For example, the environment is prominent on the public agenda, primarily because of vigorous campaigns by environmental organizations. By advocating for recycling, eliminating toxic waste sites, purifying the air and water, and preserving natural resources, such organizations strongly influence our collective consciousness. A poster from the World Wildlife Fund (WWF) on below is another example of advocacy.

Advocacy groups include activist organizations such as Greenpeace and People for the Ethical Treatment of Animals (PETA) and social issue organizations such as the National Rifle Association (NRA) and the American Family Association (AFA). They advocate to promote their own causes, but may be perceived as lobbying for the good of the whole society. Their causes are often in conflict with one another. For example, the AFA frequently expresses views that conflict with those of the Gay and Lesbian Alliance Against Defamation (GLAAD).

Greenpeace, an organization that operates in 41 countries, including the United States, is perhaps best known for its ability to use highly visual tactics. The video clips of small Greenpeace boats harassing Japanese whaling ships get extensive media coverage, but the organization also engages in other creative tactics. In 2012, for example, it took on Matel for dealing with Asia Pulp and Paper believed to be responsible for destroying rainforests.

Greenpeace climbers scaled Matel's global headquarters in Los Angeles and unfurled a large banner over the side with an image of Ken saying, "Barbie, it's over. I don't date girls that are into deforestation." The environmental group also activated a microsite, which included an animated video of Ken breaking up with Barbie, which was translated into 18 languages and received more than two million views. In short order, Matel announced that it was no longer working with Asia Pulp and Paper.

Other groups, such as the American Family Association, press advertisers to drop sponsorship of television shows that the groups consider contrary to family values. They have been particularly active countering what they identify as "affirmation of homosexual behavior." An ongoing boycott of Pepsi-Cola started when the AFA asked Pepsi to "remain neutral in the culture war." AFA maintains a Facebook page entitled "Boycott Pepsi," which has about 40,000 followers.

The principal ways in which advocacy groups work to achieve their goals are lobbying, litigation, mass demonstrations, boycotts, and reconciliation that are outlined as follows:

World Wildlife Fund

A leading advocacy group for conservation and the protection of endangered species is the World Wildlife Fund (WWF). This public service ad is one of several designed to raise public awareness about illegal poaching, which is estimated to be a $10 billion industry worldwide. Supporters were encouraged to share posters on their Facebook and Google+ pages and also tweet about illicit wildlife trade using the hashtag #HandsOffMyParts.

Public Relations Tactics

This section describes the principal ways in which advocacy groups work to achieve their goals.

Lobbying Much of this is done at state and local government levels. In just one example, approximately 150 organizations have campaigned for laws to forbid smoking in public places and to restrict the sale of tobacco around the country.

Litigation Organizations file suits seeking court rulings favorable to their projects or attempting to block unfavorable projects. The Sierra Club did so in a multiyear action that resulted in a landmark decision by the U.S. Fish and Wildlife Service declaring the northern spotted owl an endangered species.

Mass Demonstrations Designed to demonstrate public support for a cause and in some cases to harass the operators of projects to which a group objects, mass demonstrations require elaborate public relations machinations. Organizers must obtain permits, inform the media, and arrange transportation, housing, programs, and crowd control. A small but vocal rally can also generate media coverage.

Boycotts Some boycotts achieve easily identifiable results. Others stay in effect for years with little evident success. One success story occurred when the Rainforest Action Network boycotted Burger King because the company had been buying Central American beef raised in cleared rain forests; the fast-food chain subsequently agreed to stop such purchases.

Reconciliation Some environmental organizations have achieved good results by cooperating with corporations to solve pollution problems. The Environmental Defense Fund joined a task force with McDonald's to deal with the fast-food chain's solid waste problem, which eventually led to the company's decision to phase out its polystyrene packaging and take a leading role in reducing the waste entering landfills.

Social Service Organizations

Social service organizations include social service, philanthropic, cultural, and religious groups serving the public in various ways. Because communication is essential for their success, these organizations require active and creative public relations programs.

Organizations frequently have dual roles, both service and advocacy, and serve the needs of individuals, families, and society in many ways. Among prominent national organizations of this type are Goodwill Industries, the American Red Cross, the Boy Scouts and Girl Scouts of America, and the YMCA.

Their advocacy is rooted in a sense of social purpose and the betterment of society as a whole. Local chapters carry out national programs. Service clubs such as Rotary and Kiwanis raise significant amounts of money for local, national, and global charitable projects. Rotary International's multi-year global effort, for example, has practically eliminated polio as a disease throughout the world.

Foundations

Hundreds of tax-free foundations in the United States constitute about 9 percent of total charitable giving. These are started when money to establish a foundation is provided by a wealthy individual or family, a group of contributors, an organization, or a corporation. The foundation's capital is then invested, and earnings from the investments are distributed as grants to qualified

Seeing a problem resolved is extraordinarily gratifying.

Evelyn Lauder, founder of the Breast Cancer Research Foundation, which has raised more than $250 million since its creation in 1993

Guide Dog News

The quarterly publication of Guide Dogs for the Blind

Too Bad You're Not a Guide Dog...

What motivates you? What if you came to work every day and were lavished with attention and praise. It would probably make you feel pretty good, right? What if you got to enjoy a tasty treat every time you did some a new task well—that would get your attention, no? You'd likely do it again (and again!). And what if you had the opportunity to hang around the people you really admire, people who are dedicated to your success? Chances are you'd feel as though you were really in the flow. You'd feel valued and validated, motivated to do whatever needs to be done. Too bad you're not a Guide Dog...

Master Instructor Paolo Pompanin

Instructor Ashley Hussey

Guide•Dogs FOR THE BLIND

2009 • Volume 59 • No. 2

Inside This Issue:

Learning About Blindness — Blindness in women; trends and prevention .... Pg. 4

From the Pros — Hiking trail etiquette for dog owners .... Pg. 5

News of Our Graduates — Some notable news from our alumni .... Pg. 7

Guide Dog News

Nonprofits use newsletters in print and online format to keep donors informed about their activities. Regular communication with donors and prospective supporters helps generate support in the competitive world of fund-raising. This eight-page quarterly newsletter is published by Guide Dogs for the Blind, San Rafael, California.

applicants. The world's largest foundation is the the Bill and Melinda Gates Foundation. Since its inception in 1999, the foundation has made $26 billion in grants for projects in education and global health.

The Gates Foundation became what one writer described as a "behemoth" when Warren Buffett, the world's second richest man, gave $30 billion—85 percent of his fortune—to the Gates Foundation. With a stroke of the pen, the Gates Foundation doubled in size to more than $60 billion and growing with the current economic recovery, completely eclipsing all other foundations in terms of wealth. The Ford Foundation, the second largest foundation in the world, has only about $11 billion in assets. The third largest is the Robert Woods Johnson Foundation, with about $9 billion, followed by the Lilly Endowment, with $8 billion.

In addition to these large, highly visible national foundations, which make grants to a variety of causes, are smaller organizations such as the Susan G. Komen Breast Cancer Foundation and the Avon Foundation, which are also well known. Many smaller foundations, some of them extremely important in their specialized fields, distribute critical funds for research, education, public performances, displays, and similar purposes. Most of these organizations not only dispense money but also engage in numerous fund-raising activities to raise money for foundation efforts.

Corporations often set up their own foundations for handling philanthropic activities. Often the majority of their grants are awarded not in cash but involve the companies' products. The IBM Foundation, as well as HP and Apple, often make grants of computers and other high-tech equipment to educational institutions. When it became a public corporation, Google also set up a foundation (www.google.org) for the purpose of awarding grants in several issue areas, including global poverty, health, energy, and the environment.

Cultural Groups

Generating interest and participation in the cultural aspects of life often is the responsibility of nonprofit organizations in America. So, too, in many instances, is the operation of libraries; musical organizations, such as symphony orchestras; and museums of art, history, and natural sciences. Such institutions frequently receive at least part of their income from government sources; in fact, many are operated by the government.

But even government-operated cultural organizations such as the Smithsonian Institution depend on private support to raise supplementary funds. Cuts to government programs that subsidize the arts at the state and federal levels have increased the urgent need for private support for cultural institutions. For example, federal funding for the National Endowment for the Arts in 2012 was only $146 million, significantly lower than the $167.5 million budget in 2010.

Cultural organizations have a great need for public relations professionals. The constant efforts to publicize exhibitions, performances, and events, as well as support ongoing fund-raising, present many opportunities. Most cultural institutions have in-house divisions of public relations and marketing, but others, such as the Getty Museum or the New York Philharmonic, employ outside agencies.

Religious Groups

The mission of organized religion, as perceived by many faiths today, includes much more than holding weekly worship services and underwriting parochial schools. Churches also distribute charity, conduct personal guidance programs, provide leadership on moral and ethical issues in their communities, and operate social centers where diverse groups gather.

Public Relations Tactics

A number of public relations strategies and tactics are used to advance the goals of social service organizations.

Publicity The news media provide well-organized channels for stimulating public interest in nonprofit organizations and are receptive to newsworthy material from these groups. Newspapers usually publish stories and announcements about meetings, training sessions, and similar routine activities. Television and radio stations broadcast important news items about organizations and are receptive to feature stories and guest appearances by organization representatives. Public relations practitioners should look for unusual or appealing personal stories, such as a retired teacher helping Asian refugee children to learn English.

Creation of Events Events make news and attract crowds, offering another way to increase public awareness. Such activities might include an open house in a new hospital wing or an outdoor concert by members of the local symphony orchestra. Novel stunts sometimes draw more attention to a cause than their intrinsic value would seem to justify, but events such as local fun-runs that include mud pits or huge NASCAR-sponsored truck races offer fun as well as support for a good cause.

Use of Services Closely tied to increasing overall public awareness are efforts to encourage individuals and families to use an organization's services. Free medical examinations, free clothing and food for the needy, family counseling, nursing services for shut-ins, cultural programs at museums and libraries, offers of scholarships, and many other services provided by nonprofit organizations cannot do anyone any good unless potential users know about them. Written and spoken material designed to attract these publics should emphasize ease of participation and privacy of services. An example of this approach is the American Cancer Society's widely publicized campaign to encourage people to be screened for colon cancer.

Creation of Educational Materials Public relations representatives of nonprofit organizations spend a substantial proportion of their time preparing written and website materials to educate the public. The quickest way to introduce people to an organization is to hand them a brochure or refer them to a website. Organizations also strive to design logos, or symbols, to help make their materials memorable to the public.

Newsletters Another basic piece of printed material is a news bulletin, usually monthly or quarterly. They are mailed to members, the news media, and a carefully composed list of other interested parties. Most organizations also e-mail their newsletters to individuals who are on their donor list. In addition to the publication and distribution of brochures explaining an organization's objectives, periodic newsletters distributed to opinion leaders are a quiet but effective way to tell an organization's story. Although organizations are almost universally using online newsletters and social networking sites, tangible items continue to have communication value, especially for pass along readership in older target populations. See the newsletter for Guide Dogs for the Blind on page 580.

Health Organizations

There are two types of organizations in the health sector, hospitals and health agencies. The first type includes both for-profit and non-profit facilities. Because hospitals sell a product (improved health), parallels exist between their public relations objectives and those of other corporations. Health agencies tend to be nonprofit or governmental, with a more disinterested approach to revenue.

Hospitals

Hospitals focus on diverse audiences, both external and internal; involve themselves in public affairs and legislation because they operate under a maze of government regulations; and stress consumer relations, which involves keeping patients and their families satisfied as well as seeking new clients. Hospitals produce publications and publicity for these external and internal audiences. They also develop networks of volunteers who assist hospital staff in working with patients and their families.

Hospital public relations programs have four basic audiences: patients, medical and administrative staffs, news media, and the community as a whole. The four audiences overlap, but each demands a special approach and focus. Careful scrutiny can identify significant sub-audiences within these four—for example, the elderly; pregnant women; victims of heart disease, cancer, and stroke who need support groups after hospitalization; potential financial donors to the hospital; and community opinion leaders, whose goodwill helps to build the institution's reputation. Each group can be cultivated by public relations techniques.

The public relations staff of a hospital has two primary roles: (1) to strengthen and maintain the public's perception of the institution as a place where medical skill, compassion, and efficiency are paramount and (2) to help market the hospital's array of services such as surgery and cancer treatment. Many hospitals have sought to redefine themselves as community health centers. Basically, hospitals, like hotels, must have high room-occupancy rates to succeed financially.

Health Agencies

The second type of organization is private and government health agencies, which serve the public interest by providing health care, funding for health initiatives, and oversight. The most familiar health agencies are those administered at the federal and state levels, such as Medicare, Medicaid, and the Children's Health Insurance Program (CHIP). Nonprofit health agencies range from national organizations such as the American Heart Association, the American Cancer Society, and the National Multiple Sclerosis Society, to smaller groups such as the Conservation, Food & Health Foundation in Boston.

The Department of Health and Human Services (HHS) is the federal government's leading health agency. Its nearly trillion dollar budget amounts to approximately one-quarter of all federal spending. HHS provides more than 300 programs, including emergency preparedness, Head Start for preschoolers, maternity and infant programs, disease prevention and immunizations, and insurance programs such as Medicaid and Medicare.

Divisions include major initiatives such as the Food and Drug Administration, the Centers for Disease Control and Prevention (CDC), and the National Institutes of Health (NIH). The NIH is the largest branch, with an annual budget of $31.2 billion in 2012 and more than 17,000 employees. Established in 1887, the NIH annually supports about 35,000 research and other grant projects involving more than 325,000 scientists and research personnel affiliated with over 3,000 organizations, including universities, medical schools, hospitals, and other research facilities.

On occasion, health public relations professionals must be prepared to handle crisis situations—using what is now called trustee crisis communication—done on behalf of citizens, not to defend the agency itself. The organization is on full alert for the sake of its constituents. For example, the CDC's Director of Media Relations faces a 24/7 workweek when major health events unfold, such as potential flu epidemics or the resurgence of childhood disease due to vaccine avoidance by regional groups. Former Director, Dr. Glen Nowak, now at the University of Georgia, puts it this way:

> Communications is quickly at the forefront when there's an emergency or potentially great threat to people's health and well being. Many people, including the news media, want information as fast as possible, and throughout the emergency. As such, communications and media staff need to be prepared to put in many hours, perhaps for weeks or months.

Both governmental and nonprofit health agencies offer numerous job opportunities for public relations professionals. Those who specialize in health communication can have an impact on all Americans who are concerned about personal health risks as well as threats to financial security from burdensome medical costs. Essentially, health communicators strive to convey health information, prevention measures, and emergency response information as a means of reducing health risks.

on the job

SOCIAL MEDIA IN ACTION

Need Info About Sex?: Text a Question

"If u have sex underwater, do u need a condom?" That is one of the hundreds of questions about sex that teenagers texted to the nonprofit Adolescent Pregnancy Prevention Campaign of North Carolina, which runs a Birds and Bees Text Line staffed by qualified adults.

State health educators were deeply concerned because North Carolina was ranked ninth in the nation in terms of teenage pregnancy rates, so they decided to dispense sex education via teenagers' favorite device—their cell phones. Questions are answered within 24 hours, and as journalist Jan Hoffman of the *New York Times* reports, "The Birds and Bees Text Line offers one-on-one exchanges that are private, personal, and anonymous. And they can be conducted free of parental scrutiny."

Other health agencies around the nation are also tapping into teenagers' favorite technologies to fight disease and unwanted pregnancies. Some have used websites, such as Columbia University's *Go Ask Alice* and Atlantic Health's *TeenHealthFX.com*, that allow teenagers to post questions online. According to Hoffman, "Other programs in Washington, D.C., Chicago, Toronto, and San Francisco allow young people to text a number, select from a menu of frequently asked questions ('What 2 do if the condom broke') and receive automated replies, with addresses of free clinics." California also started HookUp 365247, a statewide text messaging service. The texter can type a zip code and get a local clinic referral as well as weekly health tips.

Professor Sheana Bull of the University of Colorado School of Public Health makes the key point about using social media networking strategies, telling the *New York Times*, "The technology can be used to connect young people to trusted, competent adults who have competent information." The North Carolina program, for example, also has a blog, pages Facebook, and a Twitter account.

Educational Organizations

Educational institutions include programs that provide child care, instruction for primary and secondary students, colleges, universities, trade schools, and schools for special needs students. These organizations are often licensed or regulated by state and federal agencies, as in the case of primary and secondary schools, or by private accreditation bodies such as the Southern Association of Colleges and Schools.

Most educational institutions have nonprofit status insofar as they do not have shareholders who receive proceeds or profits from their operation and they are formed specifically for charitable, scientific, or educational purposes. Educational institutions take on a staggering array of organizational structures and functions. A public information officer for a local school district must constantly deal with parents, the school board, and other community and governmental organizations.

A university director of public relations or even marketing communications, on the other hand, has less interaction with parents but must deal with ongoing student recruitment, campus controversies, and alumni relations.

Colleges and Universities

Higher education is big business in the United States. California, the most populous state, with 38 million residents, spends about $20 billion annually on four-year public colleges and universities. Another $6 billion is spent on two-year community colleges.

It's also a business that has millions of customers—students. In the United States, almost 17.5 million students are enrolled at more than 4,000 college and universities. Almost every one of these institutions has personnel working in such activities as public relations, marketing communication, and fund-raising. Increasingly, the traditional programs face strong competition from online and evening programs from both upstart for-profit college programs as well as innovative degree programs from existing colleges.

The public relations director, generally aided by one or more chief assistants, supervises the information news service, publications, and special events. Depending on the size of the institution, perhaps a dozen or more employees will carry out these functions, including writing, photography, graphic design, broadcasting, and computer networking.

Increasingly, public relations officers need to monitor social media to stay atop emerging issues for the institution to forestall embarrassing and damaging blows to the reputation of their institution. See the photo on the left for a still frame from a YouTube video that went viral, bringing down coaches and administrators at Rutgers University and calling into question the leadership of the school for delaying response after the bullying came to light. The most visible aspect of a university public relations program is its news bureau. An active bureau produces hundreds of news releases, photographs, and special columns and articles for the print media in addition to other activities. It prepares programs of news and features about students' achievements, faculty activities, and campus personalities for radio and television stations.

The news bureau also provides assistance and information for reporters, editors, and broadcasters affiliated with the state, regional, and national media. The staff responds to hundreds of telephone calls from members of the news media and the public seeking information. To enhance this interchange, many progressive news bureaus have developed online news portals that allow engagement and serve to tell the campus story without relying on traditional mass media outlets.

The president of the university is essentially the top public relations officer because he or she is the public face of the institution.

College sports offer a public face and a marketing advantage for winning programs. However, scandal can reverse that advantage overnight. This freeze frame from a video of the abusive Rutgers basketball coach Mike Rice was not decisively addressed by the University and led to the firing of Rice and eventually the athletic director of the university as well.

Source: http://www.nydailynews.com/sports/college/weiss-rutgers-rice-knight-mare-program-article-1.1306255

The president relies, however, on vice presidents of development and public affairs to implement a consistent, coherent program of enhancing the reputation of the institution among a variety of publics.

Ideally, public relations staff earn the right to attend all top-level meetings involving the president and other administrators to learn the whys and wherefores of decisions made and more importantly, to lend counsel. Only then can they satisfactorily develop action programs and respond to questions from the publics those programs serve. They are indeed the voice and the conscience of the administration.

Key Publics

Faculty and Staff Able college presidents involve their faculty and staff in decision making to the fullest extent possible, given the complexities of running a major institution. Good morale, a necessity, is achieved in large measure through communication.

Students Because of their large numbers and the many families that they represent, students make up the largest public relations arm—for good or bad—that a university has. The quality of the teaching they receive and their overall experience are the greatest determinants of student allegiance to an institution.

Alumni and Other Donors The loyalty and financial support of alumni are crucial to the ongoing operations of a college or university. Alumni are considered the major foundation of any fund-raising effort because of their immediate association with the institution. Donors who are not alumni also are cultivated for major gifts based on their interest in particular fields or disciplines. Colleges and universities raise money for such projects as recruiting new faculty, buying equipment, building student residence halls, providing scholarships, and upgrading campus computer networks. Social media is increasingly utilized to build alumni loyalty and networking, which is discussed in the Insights box on page 587.

Government State and federal governments often hold the key to whether universities receive sufficient monies to maintain their facilities, faculty, and programs. Most large institutions have someone who regularly monitors the state legislature on appropriations and issues ranging from laboratory experiments on animals to standardized tests and taxes. That person's work also includes competing with other state institutions for money, defending proposed increases in higher education budgets and arguing against cuts, establishing an institution's identity in the minds of legislators, and responding to lawmakers' requests for information.

When I say I'm a lobbyist, some people look at me as if I need a shower. It's a new business with the universities, and some people think it's a dirty business. But nothing's dirtier than not having resources.

Robert Dickens, coordinator of government relations for the University of Nevada at Reno

The Community A college or university must maintain a good relationship with the members of the community in which it is situated. The greatest supporters that an institution may have are the people within its immediate geographic area.

Prospective Students Suffering from declining revenues, increased operation costs, and a dwindling pool of prospective students occasioned by

on the job INSIGHTS

Universities Tap Alumni Through Social Media

A core audience for any college or university is its alumni. They help in student recruitment, promote and defend their alma mater, help recruit students, provide jobs for recent graduates, buy tickets to sporting events, and make donations.

Alumni outreach, however, has now become more than the quarterly issue of the alumni magazine. Social media now play a major role in building alumni networks and loyalty to the institution. The following are some ways that colleges and universities are engaging alumni using social media:

Helping Alumni Find Jobs

Universities have established alumni groups on LinkedIn where graduates can share job opportunities.

DePaul University, for example, has 5,500 members on its LinkedIn site.

Fundraising Through Facebook

Many universities have a Facebook page that provides regular posts, including fund-raising appeals. Brown University, for example, used its Facebook page to encourage alumni to make a gift to the Brown Annual Fund, recognized those who made gifts, and gave the results of the campaign. Emory University uses its Facebook page and Twitter account to encourage students to make a donation. The idea is that if students are cultivated to give now, they will continue giving as alumni.

Photo Sharing Sites

Some universities have established their own photo sharing site. The University of Texas at Austin, for example, allows alumni to share photos of themselves showing the school's well-known "hook 'em, horns" hand gesture along with their brief bio. Oregon State University uses a Flickr account and urges alumni to post photos of a cutout of Benny, the school's mascot in various settings. Colgate University uses its Flickr account to post photos of alumni reunions.

Google Maps

Another approach is to use Google maps so alumni can pin their location. Oregon State University, for example, encourages alumni post their current location and career along with their graduation year and degree.

Source: Lavrusik, V. (2009, July 23). Ten Ways Universities Are Engaging Alumni Using Social Media. Retrieved from www.mashable.com

lower birthrates and competition from online degree programs, many colleges have turned to highly competitive recruiting methods.

Most colleges and universities have replaced their catalogs and informational brochures with slick, four-color materials that use bright graphics and catchy headlines to lure students. Most, if not all, now use the Web or social media such as Facebook, Pinterest, YouTube, and Twitter. In addition to exciting graphics, interactive features such as broadcast ads, podcasts, blogs, links to Facebook sites, and Twitter feeds capitalize on prospective students' interest in technology and social media.

Fund-raising has increased dramatically at most public and private universities in recent years as costs have risen and allocations from state legislatures and federal agencies have dramatically declined. Total nongovernmental financial support for education was $41.3 billion in 2012, according to the Giving USA Foundation, which publishes an annual tally of charitable contributions. This amount represents

13.2 percent of the total charitable giving in the United States, which is outlined in the Insights box on page 589. In addition to annual operating fund campaigns, universities are increasingly conducting long-range capital campaigns for large amounts of money.

Fund-Raising and Development

Finding ways to pay the bills is a critical problem for virtually all nonprofit organizations that advocate social or environmental causes, offer social services, provide health care, and even provide education from kindergarten to college. Many also receive government funding, but the amount usually covers only a small part of the operating costs. Consequently, an important component of any nonprofit is fund-raising, which is often called *development* or *advancement*.

Although the largest, most publicized donations are made by corporations and foundations, individual contribution totals far exceed combined corporate and foundation giving. In fact, individual contributions amount to about 72 percent of annual U.S. philanthropic donations, or about $229 billion.

Depending on their needs, nonprofit organizations may try to catch minnows—hundreds of small contributions—or angle for the huge marlin, a large corporate gift. Some national organizations raise massive sums. According to Forbes magazine, in 2012 total revenue for Catholic Charities was $4.6 billion, followed by United Way ($4.1 billion) the American Red Cross ($3.6 billion) and the Salvation Army ($2.8 billion). Charities often receive a flood of donations following catastrophes, such as Hurricane Sandy that generated $223 million in donations to support organizations working on relief and recovery efforts. See the Insights box on page 589 giving a breakdown of charitable donations in 2012.

Public relations professionals participate directly in fund-raising by organizing and conducting solicitation programs or by serving as consultants to specialized development departments in their organizations. However, organizations may instead employ professional firms to conduct their fund-raising campaigns on a fee basis. In those instances, the organizations' public relations professionals usually serve a liaison function.

Motivations for Giving

An understanding of what motivates individuals and companies to give money or volunteer their time is important to anyone involved in fund-raising. An intrinsic desire to share a portion of one's resources, however small, with others—an inherent generosity possessed in some degree by almost everyone—is a primary factor of this motivation.

The Independent Sector commissioned the Gallup Organization to do a survey on volunteerism and giving. The survey found that 53 percent of those responding cited "assisting those who are less fortunate" as their personal motive for volunteering and giving. The second most frequently cited reason was gaining a feeling of personal satisfaction; religion was third. Only 6 percent cited tax considerations as a major reason for giving.

Another motivation, quite simply, is ego satisfaction. The donor who makes a large contribution gets a building named for his or her family, and individuals get

on the job INSIGHTS

Charitable Donations Top $316 Billion

Charitable giving is a well-established American institution. A total of $316.23 billion was given in 2012 according to the annual survey conducted by the Giving USA Foundation and its research partner, the Indiana University Lilly Family School of Philanthropy. This is a 3.5 percent increase over 2011 giving, which totaled $305.5 billion.

Although there's a common misconception that corporations and foundations are the major donors, individuals consistently give much more to various causes and charitable organizations. In 2012, for example, individuals contributed $228.93 billion compared to corporations that gave $l8.15 billion and Foundations giving $45.74 billion. In terms of recipients, religion is the major beneficiary accounting for 32.2 percent of the total giving in the United States. The following two charts show the sources of donations and the distribution of funds by various categories in 2012.

> Most households feel pressured at every economic corner, but the longstanding social contract between Americans and the nonprofits they believe in remains resilient and intact; many see giving as a core budget item. The amount devoted to that category might shift up or down with annual economic realities, but it doesn't go away.
>
> *Gregg Carlson, chair of Giving USA Foundation*

Source: Giving USA Foundation (2013, June l8). Giving USA: Charitable Donations Grew in 2012, but Slowly, Like the Economy. Retrieved from www.givingusareports.org

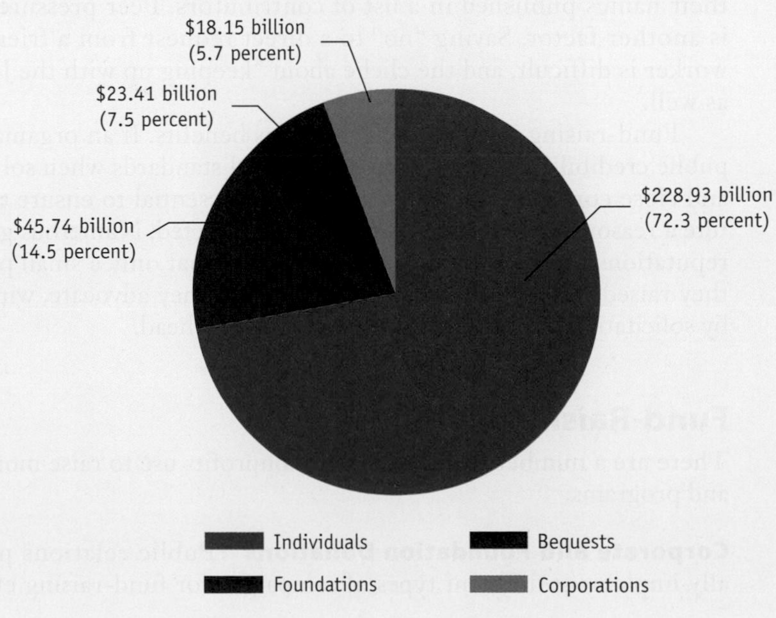

(continued)

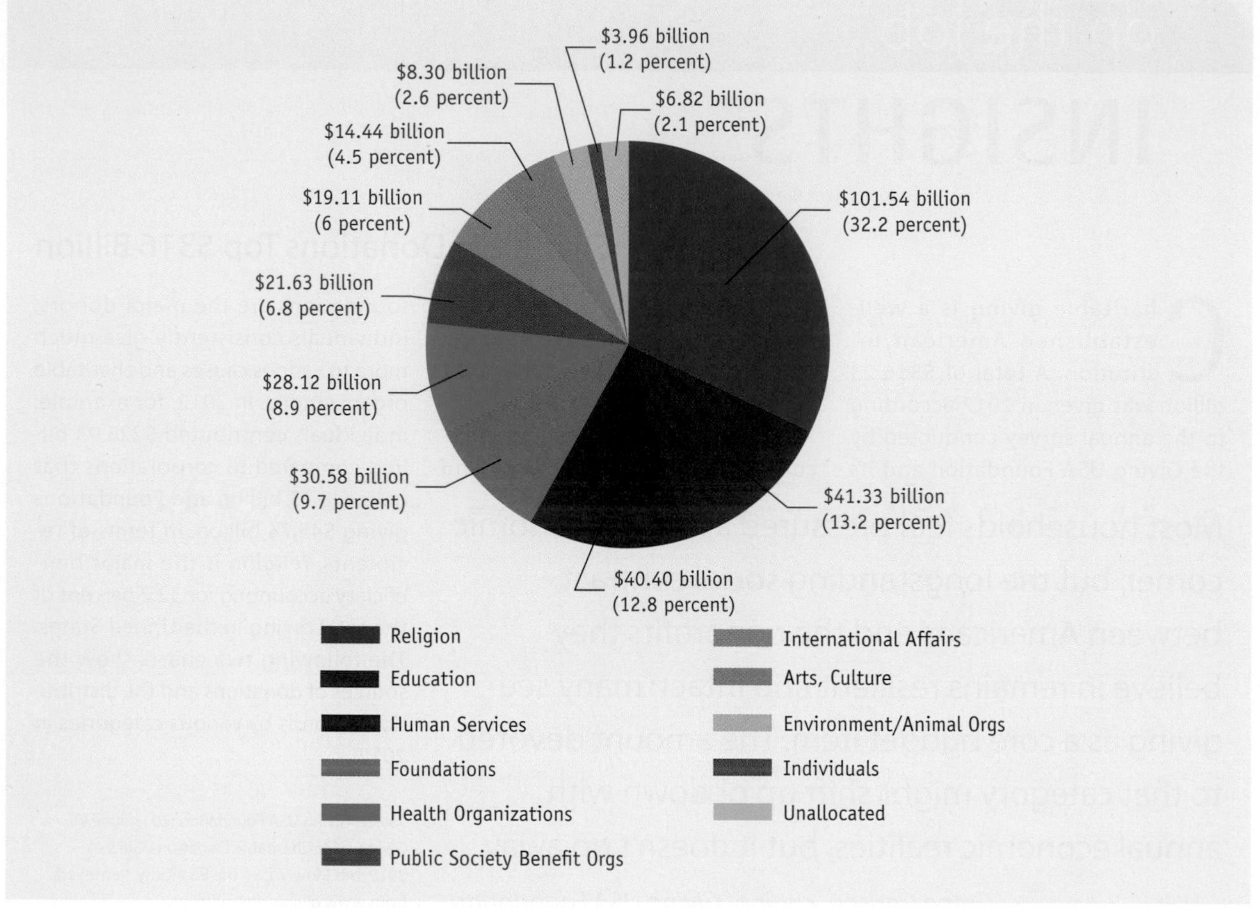

their names published in a list of contributors. Peer pressure—overt or subtle—is another factor. Saying "no" to a direct request from a friend, neighbor, or co-worker is difficult, and the cliché about "keeping up with the Joneses" applies here as well.

Fund-raising involves risks as well as benefits. If an organization is to maintain public credibility, adherence to high ethical standards when soliciting contributions and close control of fund-raising costs are essential to ensure that expenses constitute a reasonable percentage of the funds collected. Numerous groups have had their reputations severely damaged by disclosures that only a small portion of the money they raised was actually applied to the causes they advocate, with the rest consumed by solicitation expenses and administrative overhead.

Fund-Raising Methods

There are a number of methods that nonprofits use to raise money for their services and programs.

Corporate and Foundation Donations Public relations professionals generally implement different types of campaigns for fund-raising efforts, depending on whether they are targeting corporations or individuals. Organizations seeking major donations normally do so through corporate headquarters and its philanthropic foundation that processes all requests. Smaller requests, such as funding a Little League team or sponsorship of a 10K run, usually go through the corporation's local offices or major retail stores.

When considering asking a corporation or foundation for a charitable donation, the first step is research in to determine what kinds of charitable donations are made by the corporation or the foundation. Most have specific areas of funding such as education, health care, or art and culture. In many cases, the cause must be directly related to the company's core values, products, and services. Intel, for example, would be interested in funding grants for computer science education but not for programs in the liberal arts.

The next step is to prepare a "case for support" that is tailored to the interests of the corporation or foundation. A case covers the following elements: background of the organization, current status of the organization's services, need for the organization's services, sources of current funding, administration of the organization, community support, current needs of the organization, and the benefits to the community of the donation.

Structured Capital Campaigns The effort to raise major amounts of money for a new wing of a hospital, an engineering building on a university campus, or even the reconstruction and renovation of San Francisco's famed cable car system is often called a *capital campaign*.

In a capital campaign, emphasis is placed on substantial gifts from corporations and individuals. One key concept of a capital campaign is that 90 percent of the total amount raised will come from only 10 percent of the contributors. For example, in a $10 million campaign to add a wing to an art museum, it is not unusual for the lead gift to be $1 million or $2 million.

Capital campaigns require considerable expertise, and for this reason, many organizations retain professional fund-raising counsel. A number of U.S. firms offer these services; the most reputable ones belong to the Giving Institute, formerly known as the American Association of Fundraising Counsel.

Donors often are recognized by the size of their gifts, and terms such as *patron* or *founder* are designated. Major donors may be given the opportunity to have rooms or public areas in the new building named after them. When they are soliciting gifts, hospitals may even prepare "memorial" brochures that show floor plans and the cost of endowing certain facilities.

Direct Mail The traditional method of solicitations by mail is still alive and well in most charitable organizations. In many cases, recipients also receive calendars, address labels, book marks, holiday cards, and even pens as "gifts" that encourage them to feel the obligation to make a donation. Another tactic to encourage giving is offering a tote bag or T-shirt in exchange for a donation. The classic direct mail format consists of a mailing envelope, letter, brochure, and response device, often with a postage-paid return envelope.

Event Sponsorship The range of events a philanthropic organization can sponsor to raise funds is limited only by the imagination of its members. Participation contests are a popular method, as are events such as walkathons, which appeal to the American desire to exercise more. Nationally, the March of Dimes holds an annual 32-kilometer WalkAmerica in 1,100 cities on the same day.

Staging parties, charity balls, concerts, exhibitions, and similar events in which tickets are sold is another widely used fund-raising approach. Often, however, big parties create more publicity than profit, with more than 50 percent of the money raised going to expenses. Other methods include sponsorship of a motion picture premiere, a theater night, a raffle of celebrity items, or a sporting event.

Television Solicitations A television station sometimes sets aside a block of airtime for a telethon sponsored by a philanthropic organization. The best known are pledge weeks of local PBS stations to raise money for operating costs and purchasing broadcast rights for major programs such as *Downton Abbey*.

Telephone Solicitations Solicitation of donations by telephone is a relatively inexpensive way to seek funds but is of uncertain effectiveness. Many people resent receiving telephone solicitations, particularly if the recipient of the call is unfamiliar with the cause. In addition, the national do-not-call registry prevents fund-raisers from randomly calling people, although legitimate charities are exempt from the regulation. Increasingly, calling is driven by automatic dialers known as "robocalls." Political candidates and political action committees make effective use of so-called robocalls during election seasons. Automated calls cost the candidate or organization between five and eight cents, but they also generate a great deal of criticism from consumers and voters who are bombarded with such calls.

Endorsements and Tie-Ins Rather than depending entirely on contributions, some nonprofit organizations go into business on their own or make tie-ins with commercial firms from which they earn a profit. Use of this approach is growing, but entails risks that must be carefully assessed. Three types of commercial money-raising are the most common: (1) licensing use of an organization's name to endorse a product and receiving payment for each item sold, such as the American Heart Association's commission for its endorsement of Healthy Choice frozen dinners; (2) sharing profits with a corporation from sales of a special product, such as Newman's Own salad dressing; and (3) operating a business that generates revenue for the organization, such as the Metropolitan Museum of Art's gift shop.

Online and Social Media Using the Internet is cost efficient, compared with the cost of sending thousands of pieces of mail. However, most people remain wary of online solicitations. Organizations such as the Salvation Army and Greenpeace, which are highly visible and trusted, have had greater success soliciting donations online. Social media such as blogs, Twitter, Facebook, LinkedIn, and YouTube are vital tactics that allow individuals to interactively engage causes that they support or oppose. A group of women in India, for example, developed the Pink Chaddi (underwear) campaign to oppose paternalistic views. They regularly blog and maintain a Facebook page to chronicle their fight for women's rights. More recently, fund-raising using crowdsourcing has become popular and is highlighted in the Insights box on page 593.

on the job INSIGHTS

A New Fund-Raising Technique: Crowdfunding

Residents in the Dutch city of Rotterdam built a pedestrian bridge over a busy street. Residents in Glyncoch, Wales, built a community centre, and New Yorkers are working on a project to raise $15 million to purify the water in the East River to make it less murky.

All these projects are the result of the newest trend in fund-raising, which is connecting people on the Internet to crowdfunding sites such as Kickstarter, Spacehive, and neighborly. Kickstarter, based in the United States, has been particularly successful in raising significant amounts of money from small donors to help artists and inventors find patrons and to also help local communities raise money for improvements in their neighborhoods. Citizinvestor, on the other hand, works with only city councils to get additional citizen donations for civic projects that cannot be totally funded by governmental budgets.

Citizen groups using crowd funding as a mechanism for raising money have been fairly successful. In Rotterdam, for example, locals paid $32 each for the right to etch a message on one of the 17,000 planks in the pedestrian bridge. Names, wedding dates, and declaration of love now cover the new walkway, and the *Economist* reported, "Had they left council bean counters to plan it, Rotterdam's residents might have waited two decades to get their bridge off the ground."

Citizen donations are a big part of fund-raising on the Internet, but experts also say that corporate and foundation donations are still a major factor. According to the *Economist*, "Projects listed on crowdfunding sites do often rely on big gifts from businesses and foundations to reach their funding targets, but that does not undermine the model: enthusiasm from dozens of small contributors can spur generosity from big ones."

Source: Civic Crowdfunding: Breaking Ground (2013, May I8). *Economist*, 66.

Summary

The Nonprofit Sector

- Nonprofit organizations have been given tax-exempt status because their primary goal is to enhance the well-being of their members or the human condition.
- Fund-raising is a major public relations task of these groups, in which they create communication campaigns and programs, and require a staff (including volunteers) to handle their fund-raising work.
- For many nonprofit organizations, partnerships among members are necessary for their common interest. Competition among nonprofit agencies for their share of donations is intense.
- Many nonprofit groups advocate differing positions, resulting in ongoing conflict with one another.

Membership Organizations

- A membership organization is made up of people with a common interest, either business or social.
- Such groups include professional associations, trade groups, labor unions, and chambers of commerce.

Advocacy Groups

- Advocacy groups work for social causes such as the environment, civil rights, gun ownership, or the pro-choice movement.
- Their efforts include lobbying, litigation, mass demonstrations, boycotts, reconciliation, and public education.

Social Service Organizations

- Service groups and philanthropic, cultural, and religious organizations all fall into the category of social service organizations.
- Their public relations goals include developing public awareness, getting individuals to use their services, creating educational materials, recruiting volunteers, and fund-raising.

Health Organizations

- Hospitals and health agencies are the two major organizations serving the public's health needs.
- Public relations professionals help communicate information about medical advances, the availability of health services, and potential health risks.

Educational Organizations

- Public relations at colleges and universities involves both development, or fund-raising, and enhancing the prestige of the institution.
- The office of development and public relations may conduct meetings, publish newsletters, and arrange tours.
- The audiences for communication include alumni, students, prospective students, faculty and staff, government, and the general public.

Fund-Raising and Development

- Fund-raising is a critical issue for nonprofit organizations. Depending on their mission and strategy, nonprofits seek donations from large corporations or foundations or small contributions from individuals.
- Recruiting volunteer labor is often crucial to making up for lack of operating funds and involving the community in reaching the nonprofit's goals.

Case Activity A Social Media Presence for Goodwill Industries

Because your growing firm specializes in crisis communication planning and social media tactics, you have been contacted by Goodwill Industries to develop a social media strategy for the nonprofit. The organization already has a website, but it doesn't seem to generate many visitors, although no web analytics have actually been done. She wants to do more with blogs, Facebook, texting, YouTube, Twitter, and mobile phone "apps," but like many executives in the over-50 age group, she readily admits that she doesn't know how all these "things" work.

She outlines some of Goodwill's activities and projects, such as an annual fashion show highlighting vintage clothing sold in the store and an annual fund-raising banquet. You take on the social media portfolio for the client, but in the research phase, you discover some troubling trends. In looking at the online and social media presence of Goodwill, you discover negative sentiment. The identity of Goodwill as a charity is brought into doubt by the new Goodwill storefronts in mall areas and the charity's fairly aggressive retailing. Given Goodwill's absence of social media presence in your market and the emerging issue with the Goodwill brand, what social media strategies would you recommend?

Questions For Review and Discussion

1. What are the differences and similarities among trade associations, labor unions, professional associations, and chambers of commerce?
2. What is a membership organization? What are its aims?
3. Name and describe some types of social service agencies.
4. What motivates people to serve as volunteer workers?
5. What are major roles of public relations professionals in health organizations?
6. What are some components of successful health campaigns?
7. How can social media be used to promote alumni support for a school?

8. What in your view should be the major PR aims for a university or college?
9. List and describe the various tactics that are commonly used for fund-raising.
10. What is a capital campaign?
11. A form of crowdsourcing is fundsourcing. How does this work?
12. There is intense competition among non-profit organizations for donations, often from the same donors. What PR strategies would you recommend to such an organization on how to stand out in competition for funds?

Media Resources

Can PR Save the Penn State Brand: Jury's Still Out, But Message is Effectively Shifting Discussion in Media (2012, July 25). *Advertising Age*. Retrieved from www .adage.com

Lewis, T. (2012, March). Easter Seals rallies supporters to make its case to lawmakers. *PRWeek*, 46.

Lowery, A. (2012, December 6). In Fine Print of Fiscal Debate, Charities Unite to Defend Deductions. *New York Times*, B1, 5.

Mann, J. (2012, October). Success Story: Nonprofits have to fight harder for funds due to a shrinking economy. *PRWeek*, 36–40.

Pallotta, D. (2012, September 15–16). Why Can't We Sell Charity Like We Sell Perfume? *Wall Street Journal,* C1-2.

Sisco, H., Collins, E., & Zoch, L. (2010, March). Through the looking glass: A decade of Red Cross crisis response and situational crisis communication theory. *Public Relations Review, 36*(1), 21–27.

Spreading gospels of wealth: America's billionaire giving pledgers are forming a movement. (2012, May 19). *Economist*, 36.

Stokes, A. & Rubin, D. (2010, January). Activism and the Limits of Symmetry: The Public Relations Battle Between Colorado GASP and Philip Morris. *Journal of Public Relations Research*, 22, (1), 26–48.

Swanger, M. (2011, Spring). Fundraising Encroachment of Public Relations: A Battle Worth Waging. *The Strategist*, 360û37.

White, J.M. & Wingenbach, G. (2013). Potential Barriers to Mass Media Coverage of Health Issues: Differences Between Public Information Officers and Journalists Regarding Beliefs Central to Professional Behaviors. *Journal of Public Relations Research*. 25 (2), 123–140.

Directory of Useful Web Sites

Public relations requires research and facts. Here's a sampling of sites on the Internet where you can find information.

General Information

www.highbeam.com: Provides full-text articles from multiple sources, including newspapers, newswires, magazines, etc.

www.pollingreport.com: Compilation of findings from surveys regarding trends in public opinion.

thomas.loc.gov: Site of the Library of Congress and the starting point for legislative and congressional information.

www.infoplease.com: Online almanacs, encyclopedias, and atlases covering topics from business to history and sports.

www.biography.com: Backgrounds on current and historical figures.

www.about.com: Provides multiple guide sites with information on most any subject.

www.howstuffworks.com: Descriptions, diagrams, and photos that show how everything from cell phones to stem cells work.

www.ipl.org: ipl2: Information You Can Trust is a site managed by a consortium of universities that gives links to all kinds of sources, from dictionaries to writing guides to newspapers and magazines.

www.resourceshelf.com: A favorite among reference librarians.

www.salary.com: Salaries in all fields, including public relations.

www.norc.org: A University of Chicago social science research site that includes the General Social Survey, which has examined social trends in the United States since 1972.

www.bls.gov: The federal Bureau of Labor Statistics provides statistics by profession and trends about employment in the United States.

Public Relations

http://prcentral.wordpress.com: General information about public relations.

www.businesswire.com, www.prnewswire.com, www.prweb.com: News releases by company and industry.

www.teachingpr.org: Blog by PR professor Karen Russell. Includes useful links to dozens of public relations-related blogs.

www.prmuseum.com: The (online) Museum of Public Relations houses information on early pioneers in the field.

Organizations

www.awpagesociety.com: Arthur W. Page Society.

www.pagecenter.comm.psu.edu: Arthur W. Page Center at Pennsylvania State University.

www.prfirms.org: Council of Public Relations Firms.

www.globalalliancepr.org: Global Alliance for Public Relations and Communication Management.

www.instituteforpr.com: Institute for Public Relations (IPR).

www.iabc.com: International Association of Business Communicators (IABC).

www.ifea.com: International Festivals and Events Association (IFEA).

www.ipra.org: International Public Relations Association (IPRA).

www.niri.org: National Investor Relations Institute (NIRI).

www.plankcenter.ua.edu: Plank Center for Leadership in Public Relations at the University of Alabama.

www.pac.org: Public Affairs Council.

www.prsa.org: Public Relations Society of America (PRSA).

www.prssa.org: Public Relations Student Society of America (PRSSA).

www.annenberg.usc.edu/sprc: Strategic Communications and Public Relations Center at the University of Southern California Annenberg School for Communication and Journalism.

Trade Publications

www.adage.com: *Advertising Age.*

www.communicationbriefings.com: *Communication Briefings.*

www.iabc.com/cw: *Communication World* (requires IABC membership).

www.odwyerpr.com: *O'Dwyer's PR/Marketing News*; can also sign up for weekly e-mail newsletter.

http://www.prnewsonline.com/: *PRNews* (requires subscription).

http://www.ragan.com: Articles and general information about public relations.

http://www.prsa.org/Intelligence/Tactics *Public Relations Tactics*; features trends and best practices in the profession.

http://www.prsa.org/Intelligence/TheStrategist/ *The Public Relations Strategist*; feature-length articles focusing on public relations strategy and management.

www.prweekus.com: *PRWeek*; also features blogs, including *The Cycle* (news), *Insider* (industry), and *Editor's Blog*.

Bibliography of Selected Books, Directories, Databases, and Periodicals

General Books

Bobbitt, R., & Sullivan, R. (2008). *Developing the public relations campaign: A team-based approach* (2nd ed.). Boston, MA: Allyn & Bacon.

Botan, C., & Hazelton, V. (2006). *Public relations theory II*. Mahwah, NJ: Lawrence Erlbaum Associates.

Broom, G. M., & Sha, B. L. (2012). *Cutlip & Center's effective public relations* (11th ed.). Upper Saddle River, NJ: Prentice Hall.

Cameron, G. T., Wilcox, D. L., Reber, B. H., & Shin, J. H. (2008). *Public relations today: Managing competition and conflict*. Boston, MA: Allyn & Bacon.

Coombs, W. T., & Holladay, S. (2013). *It's not just PR: Public relations in society* (2nd ed.). Malden, MA: Wiley-Blackwell.

Coombs, W. T., & Holladay, S. (2009). *PR strategy and application: Managing influence*. Malden, MA: Wiley-Blackwell.

Grunig, J. E. (Ed.). (1992). *Excellence in public relations and communication management*. Hillsdale, NJ: Lawrence Erlbaum.

Grunig, L. A., Grunig, J. E., & Dozier, D. M. (2002). *Excellent public relations and effective organizations*. Mahwah, NJ: Lawrence Erlbaum.

Guth, D. W., & Marsh, C. (2011). *Public relations: A values-driven approach* (5th ed.). Boston, MA: Allyn & Bacon.

Hansen-Horn, T., & Neff, B. D. (2007). *Public relations: From theory to practice*. Boston, MA: Allyn & Bacon.

Heath, R. L. (Ed.). (2013). *Encyclopedia of public relations* (2nd ed.). Thousand Oaks, CA: Sage Publications.

Heath, R. L. (Ed.). (2013). *Public relations*. London: Routledge.

Heath, R. L., Toth, E. L., & Waymer, D. (Eds.). (2009). *Rhetorical and critical approaches to public relations II* (2nd ed.). Hillsdale, NJ: Lawrence Erlbaum.

Heath, R. L. (Ed.). (2010). *The SAGE handbook of public relations*. Thousand Oaks, CA: Sage Publications.

Ihlen, Ø., van Ruler, B., & Fredriksson, M. (2009). *Public relations and social theory: Key figures and concepts*. New York, NY: Routledge.

Lattimore, D., Baskin, O., Heiman, S. T., & Toth, E. (2011). *Public relations: The profession and the practice* (4th ed.). New York, NY: McGraw-Hill.

L'Etang, J., & Pieczka, M. (2006). *Public relations: Critical debates and contemporary practices*. Mahwah, NJ: Lawrence Erlbaum Associates.

Newsom, D., Turk, J. V., & Kruckeberg, D. (2012). *This is PR: The realities of public relations* (11th ed.). Belmont, CA: Thomson/Wadsworth.

Seitel, F. P. (2013). *The practice of public relations* (12th ed.). Upper Saddle River, NJ: Prentice Hall.

Smith, R. D. (2013). *Strategic planning for public relations* (4th ed.). New York, NY: Routledge.

Tench, R., & Yeomans, L. (2009). *Exploring public relations* (2nd ed.). Harlow, UK: Prentice Hall.

Theaker, A. (2012). *The public relations strategic toolkit: An essential guide to successful public relations practice*. London: Routledge.

Theaker, A. (2012). *The public relations handbook* (4th ed.). London: Routledge.

Toth, E. L. (Ed.). (2006). *The future of excellence in public relations and communication management: Challenges for the next generation*. New York, NY: Routledge.

Wilcox, D. L., Cameron, G. T., & Reber, B. H. (2014). *Public relations: Strategies and tactics* (11th ed.). Boston, MA: Allyn & Bacon.

Wilcox, D. L., Cameron, G. T., Reber, B. H., & Shin, J. H. (2013). *Think: Public relations* (2nd ed.). Boston, MA: Allyn & Bacon.

Wilson, L. J., & Ogden, J. (2012). *Strategic communications planning for effective public relations and marketing* (5th ed.). Dubuque, IA: Kendall-Hunt.

Special Interest Books

Business/Management

Argenti, P. (2012). *Corporate communication* (6th ed.). New York, NY: McGraw-Hill.

Belasen, A. T. (2007). *The theory and practice of corporate communication: A competing values perspective*. Thousand Oaks, CA: Sage Publications.

Berger, B. K., & Reber, B. H. (2006). *Gaining influence in public relations: The role of resistance in practice*. Mahwah, NJ: Lawrence Erlbaum Associates.

Caywood, C. (Ed.). (2011). *The handbook of strategic public relations and integrated communications* (2nd ed.). New York, NY: McGraw-Hill.

Cornelissen, J. P. (2011). *Corporate communication: A guide to theory and practice* (3rnd ed.). Thousand Oaks, CA: SAGE Publications.

Goodman, M. B., & Hirsch, P. B. (2010). *Corporate communication: Strategic adaptation for global practice*. New York, NY: Peter Lang.

Ledingham, J. A., & Bruning, S. D. (2001). *Public relations as relationship management*. Mahwah, NJ: Lawrence Erlbaum.

McKee, K. B., & Lamb, L. F. (2009). *Applied public relations: Cases in stakeholder management* (2nd ed.). New York, NY: Routledge.

Careers

Dilenschneider, R. (2010). *The AMA handbook of public relations: Leveraging PR in the digital world*. New York, NY: AMACOM Books.

Gregory, M. (2008). *The career chronicles: An insider's guide to what jobs are really like*. Novato, CA: New World Library.

Noricks, C. (2013). *Ready to launch: The PR couture guide to breaking into fashion PR: How to begin a successful career in fashion public relations* (2nd ed.). CreateSpace Independent Publishing Platform.

Tymorek, S. (2010). *Ferguson career launcher: Advertising and public relations*. New York, NY: Checkmark Books.

Case Studies

Center, A. H., Jackson, P., Smith, S., & Stansberry, F. (2014). *Public relations practices: Managerial case studies and problems* (8th ed.). Upper Saddle River, NJ: Prentice Hall.

Guth, D. W., & Marsh, C. (2005). *Adventures in public relations: Case studies and critical thinking*. Boston, MA: Allyn & Bacon.

Hagley, T. (2009). *Writing winning proposals—PR cases*. San Diego, CA: Cognella.

Hendrix, J. A., Hayes, D. C., & Kumar, P. D. (2012). *Public relations cases* (9th ed.). Boston, MA: Wadsworth.

Lamb, L. F., & McKee, K. B. (2009). *Applied public relations: Cases in stakeholder management* (2nd ed.). Mahwah, NJ: Lawrence Erlbaum.

May, S. (2012). *Case studies in organizational communication: Ethical perspectives and practices* (2nd ed.). Thousand Oaks, CA: Sage Publications.

Sheehan, M., & Xavier, R. (2009). *Public relations campaigns*. New York, NY: Oxford University Press.

Swann, P. (2010). *Cases in public relations management*. New York, NY: Routledge.

Communication/Persuasion

Bryant, J., & Oliver, M. B. (2008). *Media effects: Advances in theory and research* (3rd ed.). Hillsdale, NJ: Lawrence Erlbaum.

Gass, R. H., & Seiter, J. S. (2013). *Persuasion: Social influence and compliance gaining* (5th ed.). Upper Saddle River, NJ: Pearson.

Jowett, G. S., & O'Donnell, V. (2011). *Propaganda and persuasion* (5th ed.). Thousand Oaks, CA: Sage Publications.

Larson, C. U. (2013). *Persuasion: Reception and responsibility* (13th ed.). Independence, KY: Cengage.

Perloff, R. M. (2013). *The dynamics of persuasion: Communication and attitudes in the 21st century* (5th ed.). New York, NY: Routledge.

Samovar, L., Porter, R., & McDaniel, E. R. (2011). *Intercultural communication: A reader* (13th ed.). Independence, KY: Cengage.

Simons, H. W., & Jones, J. (2011). *Persuasion in society* (2nd ed.). New York, NY: Routledge.

Stacks, D. W., & Salwen, M. B. (2009). *An integrated approach to communication theory and research* (2nd ed.). New York, NY: Routledge.

Crisis Communications

Capozzi, L., & Rucci, S. R. (2013). *Crisis management in the age of social media*. New York, NY: Business Expert Press.

Coombs, W. T. (2011). *Ongoing crisis communication: Planning, managing, and responding* (3rd ed.). Thousand Oaks, CA: Sage Publications.

Coombs, W. T., & Holladay, S. J. (Eds.). (2012). *The handbook of crisis communication*. Hoboken, NJ: Wiley-Blackwell.

Fearn-Banks, K. (2010). *Crisis communications: A casebook approach* (4th ed.). Mahwah, NJ: Lawrence Erlbaum.

Fink, S. (2013). *Crisis communications: The definitive guide to managing the message*. New York, NY: McGraw-Hill.

Heath, R. L., & O'Hair, H. D. (2009). *Handbook of risk and crisis communication*. New York, NY: Routledge.

Ulmer, R. R., Sellnow, T. L., & Seeger, M. W. (2010). *Effective crisis communication: Moving from crisis to opportunity* (2nd ed.). Thousand Oaks, CA: SAGE Publications.

Zaremba, A. J. (2010). *Crisis communication: Theory and practice*. Armonk, NY: M.E. Sharpe.

Cultural Diversity/Gender

Alexander, A., & Hanson, J. (Eds.). (2012). *Taking sides: Clashing views on controversial issues in mass media and society* (12th ed.). New York, NY: McGraw-Hill.

Brief, A. P. (2008). *Diversity at work*. New York, NY: Cambridge University Press.

Creedon, P. J., & Cramer, J. (2007). *Women in mass communication*. Thousand Oaks, CA: SAGE Publications.

Grunig, L. A., Toth, E. L., & Hon, L. C. (2001). *Women in public relations: How gender influences practice*. New York, NY: Guilford Publications.

Waymer, D. (2012). *Culture, social class & race in public relations: Perspectives and applications*. New York, NY: Lexington Books.

Education

Moore, E. H., Bagin, D., & Gallagher, D. (2011). *The school and community relations* (10th ed.). Upper Saddle River, NJ: Pearson.

Kowalski, T. J. (2010). *Public relations in schools* (5th ed.). Upper Saddle River, NJ: Pearson.

Employee Relations

Conrad, C. R., & Poole, S. P. (2012). *Strategic organizational communication: In a global economy* (7th ed.). Hoboken, NJ: Wiley-Blackwell.

D'Aprix, R. (2008). *The credible company: Communicating with today's skeptical workforce*. San Francisco, CA: Jossey-Bass.

Gillis, T. (2011). *The IABC handbook of organizational communication: A guide to internal communication, public relations, marketing and leadership* (2nd ed.). San Francisco, CA: Jossey-Bass.

Harris, T. E., & Nelson, M. D. (2008). *Applied organizational communication: Theory and practice in a global environment* (3rd ed.). New York, NY: Lawrence Erlbaum Associates.

Modaff, D. P., Butler, J. A., & DeWine, S. (2011). *Organizational communication: Foundations, challenges, and misunderstandings* (3rd ed.). Boston, MA: Pearson/Allyn & Bacon.

Ethics

Bivins, T. (2009). *Mixed media: Moral distinctions in advertising, public relations, and journalism* (2nd ed.). New York, NY: Routledge.

Fitzpatrick, K. R., & Bronstein, C. (2006). *Ethics in public relations: Responsible advocacy*. Thousand Oaks, CA: Sage Publications.

Ihlen, Ø., Bartlett, J., & May, S. (2012). *The handbook of communication and corporate social responsibility*. Hoboken, NJ: Wiley-Blackwell.

May, S., Cheney, G., & Roper, J. (2007). *The debate over corporate social responsibility*. New York, NY: Oxford University Press.

Parsons, P. J. (2008). *Ethics in public relations: A guide to best practices* (2nd ed.). Philadephia, PA: Kogan Page.

Stauber, J., Rampton, S., & Dowie, M. (2002). *Toxic sludge is good for you: Lies, Damn lies and the public relations industry* [Critical analysis]. Monroe, ME: Common Courage Press.

Wilkins, L., & Christians, C. G. (2009). *The handbook of mass media ethics*. New York, NY: Routledge.

Financial/Investor Relations

Bragg, S. M. (2010). *Running an effective investor relations department: A comprehensive guide*. Hoboken, NJ: John Wiley & Sons.

Bragg, S. M. (2012). *The investor relations guidebook*. Centennial, CO: Accounting Tools.

Corbin, J. (2012). *Investor relations: The art of communicating value* (2nd ed.). Eagan, MN: Thomson Reuters Westlaw.

Guimard, A. (2013). *Investor relations: Principles and international best practices of financial communications* (2nd ed.). New York, NY: Palgrave Macmillan.

Fund-Raising/Development

Ciconte, B. K., & Jacob, J. G. (2008). *Fund raising basics: A complete guide* (3rd ed.). Burlington, MA: Jones & Bartlett Publishers.

Tempel, E. R., Seiler, T. L., Aldrich, E. E., & Maehara, P. (2010). *Achieving excellence in fund-raising* (3rd ed.). San Francisco, CA: Jossey-Bass.

Weinstein, S. (2009). *The complete guide to fund-raising management* (3rd ed.). New York, NY: John Wiley & Sons.

Government/Public Affairs

Feld, L., & Wilcox, N. (2008). *Netroots rising: How a citizen army of bloggers and online activists is changing American politics*. Westport, CT: Praeger.

Klein, W. (2008). *All the presidents' spokesmen: Spinning the news—White House press secretaries from Franklin D. Roosevelt to George W. Bush*. Westport, CT: Praeger.

Lee, M. (2007). *Government public relations: A reader*. Boca Raton, FL: CRC Press.

Lee, M., Neeley, G., & Stewart, K. (2011). *The practice of government public relations*. Boca Raton, FL: CRC Press.

Lerbinger, O. (2005). *Corporate public affairs: Interacting with interest groups, media, and government*. New York, NY: Routledge.

McMillen, W. (2010). *From campus to capitol: The role of government relations in higher education*. Baltimore, MD: The Johns Hopkins University Press.

Warnick, B., & Heineman, D. S. (2012). *Rhetoric online: The politics of new media* (2nd ed.). New York, NY: Peter Lang, 2007.

History

Cutlip, S. M. (1994). *The unseen power: Public relations: A history*. Hillsdale, NJ: Lawrence Erlbaum.

Cutlip, S. M. (1995). *Public relations history: From the seventeenth to the twentieth century*. Hillsdale, NJ: Lawrence Erlbaum.

Ewen, S. (1998). *PR! A social history of spin*. New York, NY: Basic Books.

Griese, N. (2001). *Arthur W. Page: Publisher, public relations pioneer, patriot*. Atlanta, GA: Anvil Publishers.

Lee, M. (2005). *The first presidential communications agency: FDR's Office of Government Reports*. Albany, NY: State University of New York Press.

Lentz, R. G., & Gower, K. K. (2011). *The opinions of mankind: Racial issues, press, and propaganda in the Cold War*. Columbia, MO: University of Missouri Press.

Miller, K. S. (1999). *The voice of business: Hill & Knowlton and post-war public relations*. Chapel Hill, NC: University of North Carolina Press.

Tye, L. (2002). *The father of spin: Edward L. Bernays and the birth of public relations*. New York, NY: Holt Paperbacks.

International

Cambie, S., & Ooi, Y. M. (2009). *International communications strategy: Developments in cross-cultural communications, PR, and social media*. Philadelphia, PA: Kogan Page.

Curtin, P. A., & Gaither, T. K. (2007). *International public relations: Negotiating culture, identity, and power*. Thousand Oaks, CA: Sage Publications.

Freitag, A. R., & Quesinberry Stokes, A. (2009). *Global public relations: Spanning borders, spanning cultures*. New York, NY: Routledge.

Grunig, L. A., & Grunig, J. E. (2002). *Excellent public relations and effective organizations: A study of communication management in three countries*. Mahwah, NJ: Lawrence Erlbaum.

Jandt, F. E. (2012). *An introduction to intercultural communication* (7th ed.). Thousand Oaks, CA: Sage Publications.

McPhail, T. L. (2010). *Global communication: Theories, stakeholders & trends*. Hoboken, NJ: Wiley-Blackwell.

Moss, D., Powell, M., & DeSanto, B. (2010). *Public relations cases: International perspectives* (2nd ed.). New York, NY: Routledge.

Newsom, D. (2007). *Bridging the gaps in global communication*. Malden, MA: Blackwell Publishing.

Parkinson, M., & Ekachai, D. G. (2006). *International and intercultural public relations: A campaign case approach*. Boston, MA: Allyn & Bacon.

Rudd, J. E., & Lawson, D. R. (2007). *Communicating in global business negotiations: A geocentric approach*. Thousand Oaks, CA: Sage Publications.

Samovar, L. A., Porter, R. E., & McDaniel, E. R. (2011). *Intercultural communication: A reader* (13th ed.). Independence, KY: Cengage.

Schmidt, W. V., Conaway, R. N., Easton, S. S., & Wardrope, W. J. (2007). *Communicating globally: Intercultural communication and international business*. Thousand Oaks, CA: Sage Publications.

Sriramesh, K., Zerfass, A., & Kim, J. N. (Eds.). (2013). *Public relations and communication management: Current trends and emerging topics*. New York, NY: Routledge.

Sriramesh, K., & Vercic, D. (2009). *The global public relations handbook: Theory, research, and practice* (2nd ed.). Mahwah, NJ: Lawrence Erlbaum Associates.

Internet/Social Media

Aronson, M., & Spetner, D. (2012). *The public relations writer's handbook: The digital age* (2nd ed.). New York, NY: John Wiley.

Barr, C. (2011). *The Yahoo! style guide: The ultimate sourcebook for writing, editing, and creating content for the digital world.* Retrieved from Amazon.com.

Breakenridge, D. (2012). *Social media and public relations: Eight new practices for the PR professional.* Upper Saddle River, NJ: FT Press.

Brown, R. (2009). *Public relations and the social web: Using social media and web 2.0 in communications.* Philadelphia, PA: Kogan Page.

Duhe, S. C. (2013). *New media and public relations* (2nd ed.). New York, NY: Peter Lang.

Martin, A. J. (2012). *Renegades write the rules: How the digital royalty use social media to innovate.* San Francisco, CA: Jossey-Bass.

Safko, L., & Brake, D. K. (2012). *The social media bible: Tactics, tools, and strategies for business success* (3rd ed.). Hoboken, NJ: John Wiley & Sons.

Scott, D. M. (2013). *The new rules of marketing and PR: How to use social media, online video, mobile applications, blogs, news releases, and viral marketing to reach buyers directly* (4th ed.). New York, NY: John Wiley & Sons.

Shih, C. (2010). *The Facebook era: Tapping online social networks to market, sell & innovate.* Boston, MA: Addison-Wesley.

Solis, B., & Breakenridge, D. (2009). *Putting the public back in public relations.* Boston, MA: FT Press/Pearson Education.

Vorvoreanu, M. (2008). *Web site public relations: How corporations build and maintain relationships online.* Amherst, NY: Cambria Press.

Issues Management

Heath, R. L., & Palenchar, M. J. (2009). *Strategic issues management: Organizations and public policy challenges* (2nd ed.). Thousand Oaks, CA: Sage Publications.

Mitroff, I. I., & Anagnos, G. (2005). *Managing crises before they happen.* New York, NY: AMACOM.

Law

Gower, K. K. (2007). *Legal and ethical considerations for public relations* (2nd ed.). Prospect Heights, IL: Waveland Press.

Haggerty, J. F. (2009). *In the court of public opinion: Winning strategies for litigation communications* (2nd ed.). Chicago, IL: American Bar Association.

Kerr, R. L. (2008). *The corporate free speech movement: Cognitive feudalism and the endangered marketplace of ideas.* New York, NY: LFB Scholarly Publishing.

Middleton, K., & Lee, W. E. (2013). *Law of public communication* (8th ed.). Boston, MA: Allyn & Bacon.

Moore, R. L., Collins, E., & May, C. (2010). *Advertising and public relations law* (2nd ed.). New York, NY: Routledge.

Parkinson, M., & Parkinson, M. L. (2007). *Law for advertising, broadcasting, journalism and public relations.* Mahwah, NJ: Lawrence Erlbaum Associates.

Pember, D. R., & Calvert, C. (2012). *Mass media law* (18th ed.). New York, NY: McGraw-Hill.

Stewart, D. (2012). *Social media and the law: A guidebook for communication students and professionals.* New York, NY: Routledge.

Marketing

Blakeman, R. (2007). *Integrated marketing communication: Creative strategy from idea to implementation.* Lanham, MD: Rowman & Littlefield Publishers.

Giannini, G. T. (2009). *Marketing public relations.* Upper Saddle River, NJ: Prentice Hall.

Morse, D. R. (2009). *Multicultural intelligence: Eight make-or-break rules for marketing to race, ethnicity, and sexual orientation.* Ithaca, NY: Paramount Market Publishing, Inc.

Weiner, M. (2006). *Unleashing the power of PR: A contrarian's guide to marketing and communication.* San Francisco, CA: Jossey-Bass.

Media/Press Relations

Favorito, J. (2012). *Sports publicity: A practical approach* (2nd ed.). Burlington, MA: Butterworth-Heinemann.

Fitch, B., & Holt, J. (2012). *Media relations handbook for government, associations, nonprofits & elected officials.* Available at: TheCapitol.Net.

Gower, K. K. (2007). *Public relations and the press: A troubled embrace.* Evanston, IL: Northwestern University Press.

Hart, H. (2007). *Successful spokespersons are made, not born* (Expanded ed.). Bloomington, IN: AuthorHouse.

Howard, C. M., & Mathews, W. K. (2013). *On deadline: Managing media relations* (5th ed.). Prospect Heights, IL: Waveland Press.

Johnston, J. (2013). *Media relations: Issues & strategies* (2nd ed.). Sydney, Australia: Allen & Unwin.

Mindich, D. T. Z. (2005). *Tuned out: Why Americans under 40 don't follow the news.* New York, NY: Oxford University Press.

Phillips, B. (2012). *The media training Bible: 101 things you absolutely, positively need to know before your next interview.* SpeakGood Press.

Skinner, M., & Kitchin, P. (2010). *Sports public relations and communications.* New York, NY: Routledge.

Wallack, L., Woodruff, K., Dorfman, L. E., & Diaz, I. (1999). *News for a change: An advocate's guide to working with the media.* Thousand Oaks, CA: Sage Publications.

Nonprofit Groups/Health Agencies

Bonk, K., Tynes, E., Griggs, H., & Sparks, P. (2008). *Strategic communications for nonprofits: A step-by-step guide to working with the media.* San Francisco, CA: John Wiley & Sons.

Brinckerhoff, P. C. (2010). *Mission-based marketing: Positioning your not-for-profit in an increasingly competitive world* (3rd ed.). Hoboken, NJ: John Wiley & Sons.

Feinglass, A. (2005). *The public relations handbook for nonprofits: A comprehensive and practical guide.* New York, NY: John Wiley & Sons.

Miller, K. L. (2013). *Content marketing for nonprofits: A communications map for engaging your community, becoming a favorite cause, and raising more money.* San Francisco, CA: Jossey-Bass.

Patterson, S. J., & Radtke, J. M. (2009). *Strategic communications for nonprofit organizations: Seven steps to creating a successful plan* (2nd ed.). Hoboken, NJ: Wiley.

Publicity

Borkowski, M. (2008). *The fame formula: How Hollywood's fixers, fakers, and star makers created the celebrity industry*. London: Pan MacMillan, Ltd.

Jessup, J., & Jessup, M. (2010). *Fame 101: Powerful personal branding & publicity*. Portland, OR: Sutton Hart Press.

Levine, M. (2008). *Guerrilla P.R. 2.0: Wage an effective publicity campaign without going broke*. New York, NY: HarperCollins.

Also see entries in Special Events and Writing in Public Relations sections.

Reputation

Alsop, R. J. (2010). *The 18 immutable laws of corporate reputation: Creating, protecting, and repairing your most valuable asset*. New York, NY: Free Press.

Aula, P., & Mantere, S. (2008). *Strategic reputation management*. New York, NY: Routledge.

Brogan, C., & Smith, J. (2010). *Trust agents: Using the web to build influence, improve reputation, and earn trust* (2nd ed.). Hoboken, NJ: John Wiley & Sons.

Diermeier, D. (2011). *Reputation rules: Strategies for building your company's most valuable asset*. New York, NY: McGraw-Hill.

Doorley, J., & Garcia, H. F. (2010). *Reputation management: The key to successful public relations and corporate communication* (2nd ed.). New York, NY: Routledge.

Fertik, M. (2010). *Wild west 2.0: How to protect and restore your reputation on the untamed social frontier*. New York, NY: AMACOM.

Firestein, P. (2009). *Crisis of character: Building corporate reputation in the age of skepticism*. New York, NY: Sterling Publishing Co., Inc.

Gaines-Ross, L. (2008). *Corporate reputation: 12 steps to safeguarding and recovering reputation*. New York, NY: John Wiley & Sons.

Seitel, F., & Doorley, J. (2012). *Rethinking reputation: How PR trumps marketing and advertising in the New Media World*. New York, NY: Palgrave Macmillian.

Research Methods

Daymon, C. (2010). *Qualitative research methods in public relations and marketing communications* (2nd ed.). New York, NY: Routledge.

Frey, L. R., Botan, C. H., & Kreps, G. L. (2013). *Investigating communication: An introduction to research methods* (3rd ed.). Boston, MA: Allyn & Bacon.

Friesen, B. K. (2010). *Designing and conducting your first interview project*. San Francisco, CA: Jossey-Bass.

Jugenheimer, D. W., Bradley, S. D., Kelley, L. D., & Hudson, J. C. (2010). *Advertising and public relations research*. Armonk, NY: M. E. Sharpe.

McQuarrie, E. F. (2011). *The market research toolbox: A concise guide for beginners* (3rd ed.). Thousand Oaks, CA: Sage Publications.

Paine, K. D. (2011). *Measure what matters: Online tools for understanding customers, social media, engagement and key relationships*. Hoboken, NJ: Wiley.

Priest, S. H. (2009). *Doing media research: An introduction* (2nd ed.). Thousand Oaks, CA: Sage Publications.

Stacks, D. W. (2010). *Primer of public relations research* (2nd ed.). New York, NY: The Guilford Press.

Stacks, D. W., & Michaelson, D. (2010). *A practitioner's guide to public relations research, measurement and evaluation*. New York, NY: Business Expert Press.

Warren, C. A. B., & Xavia Karner, T. (2009). *Discovering qualitative methods: Field research, interviews, and analysis* (2nd ed.). New York, NY: Oxford University Press.

Special Events

Allen, J. (2007). *The executive's guide to corporate events and business entertaining: How to choose and use corporate functions to increase brand awareness, develop new business, nurture customer loyalty and drive growth*. New York, NY: John Wiley & Sons.

Allen, J. (2009). *Event planning: The ultimate guide to successful meetings, corporate events, fundraising galas, conferences, conventions, incentives and other special events* (2nd ed.). New York, NY: John Wiley & Sons.

Bowdin, G., Allen, J., Harris, R., McDonnell, I., & O'Toole, W. (2010). *Events management* (3rd ed.). Oxford, England: Routledge.

Foley, M., McGillivray, D., & McPherson, G. (2011). *Event policy: From theory to strategy*. New York, NY: Routledge.

Goldblatt, J. (2010). *Special events: A new generation and the next frontier* (6th ed.). Hoboken, NJ: Wiley.

Mallen, C., & Adams, L. (2013). *Event management in sport, recreation and tourism: Theoretical and practical dimensions* (2nd ed.). London: Routledge.

Saget, A. (2012). *The event marketing handbook: Beyond logistics and planning*. CreateSpace Independent Publishing Platform.

Wendroff, A. L. (2003). *Special events: Proven strategies for nonprofit fundraising* (2nd ed.). New York, NY: John Wiley & Sons.

Speeches/Presentations

Beebe, S. A., & Beebe, S. (2011). *Public speaking: An audience-centered approach* (8th ed.). Boston, MA: Pearson.

DiSanza, J. R., & Legge, N. J. (2011). *Business and professional communication: Plans, processes, and performance* (5th ed.). Boston, MA: Pearson.

Engleberg, I., & Daly, J. A. (2008). *Presentations in everyday life: Strategies for effective speaking* (3rd ed.). Boston, MA: Allyn & Bacon.

Fujishin, R. (2011). *The natural speaker* (7th ed.). Boston, MA: Pearson.

Writing in Public Relations

Aronson, M., Spetner, D., & Ames, C. (2007). *The public relations writer's handbook: The digital age* (2nd ed.). New York, NY: John Wiley & Sons.

Bivins, T. H. (2013). *Public relations writing: The essentials of style and format* (8th ed.). Boston, MA: McGraw-Hill.

Diggs-Brown, B. (2012). *The PR style guide: Formats for public relations practice* (3rd ed.). Independence, KY: Cengage.

Marsh, C., Guth, D., & Short, B. P. (2011). *Strategic writing: Multimedia writing for public relations, advertising and more* (3rd ed.). Boston, MA: Pearson.

Newsom, D., & Haynes, J. (2013). *Public relations writing: Form and style* (10th ed.). Independence, KY: Cengage.

Smith, R. D. (2011). *Becoming a public relations writer: A writing workbook for emerging and established media* (4th ed.). New York, NY: Routledge.

Whitaker, W. R., Ramsey, J. E., & Smith, R. D. (2012). *MediaWriting: Print, broadcast, and public relations* (4th ed.). New York, NY: Routledge.

Wilcox, D. L., & Reber, B. H. (2013). *Public relations writing and media techniques* (7th ed.). Boston, MA: Allyn & Bacon.

Zappala, J. M., & Carden, A. R. (2009). *Public relations writing worktext: A practical guide for the profession* (3rd ed.). New York, NY: Routledge.

Directories

Directories are valuable tools for public relations personnel who need to communicate with a variety of specialized audiences. The following is a selected list of the leading national and international directories.

Media Directories and Databases

The All-In-One Media Directory. Gebbie Press, P. O. Box 1000, New Paltz, NY 12561.

Bulldog Reporter's Media List Builder. Infocom Group, 124 Linden Street, Oakland, CA 94607.

BurrellesLuce Outreach. BurrellesLuce, Headquarters 30 B. Vreeland Road, P.O. Box 674, Florham Park, NJ 07932.

Cable & TV Station Coverage Atlas. Warren Communications, 2115 Ward Court NW, Washington, DC 20037.

Cision Media Database. Cision, 332 S. Michigan, Avenue, Chicago, IL 60604.

The Complete Television, Radio and Cable Industry Directory. Grey House Publishing, 4919 Route 22, P.O. Box 56, Amenia, NY 12501.

Directory of Small Press/Magazine Editors and Publishers. Dustbooks, P.O. Box 100, Paradise, CA 95967.

Directory of Women's Media. Women's Institute for Freedom of the Press, 1940 Calvert Street NW, Washington, DC 20009.

Gale Directory of Publications and Broadcast Media. Gale Group, 27500 Drake Road, Farmington Hills, MI 48331.

Hudson's Washington News Media Contacts Directory. Grey House Publishing, 4919 Route 22, P.O. Box 56, Amenia, NY 12501.

Literary Marketplace. Information Today, Inc., 143 Old Marlton Pike, Medford, NJ 08055.

National Directory of Community Newspapers. American Newspaper Representatives, 2075 W. Big Beaver Road, Troy, MI 48084.

National Directory of Magazines. Oxbridge Communications, 39 W. 29th Street, Suite 301, New York, NY 10001.

PR Newswire Agility. PR Newswire, 350 Hudson Street, Suite 300, New York, NY 10014.

PR Newswire ProfNet. PR Newswire, 350 Hudson Street, Suite 300, New York, NY 10014.

The Society of American Travel Writers' Directory. Society of American Travel Writers, 11950 W. Lake Park Drive, Suite 320, Milwaukee, WI 53224.

Standard Rate and Data Services. SRDS.com, 1700 Higgins Road, 5th Floor, Des Plaines, IL 60018.

International Media Directories and Databases

Benn's Media Guide World. Wilmington Publishing & Information, Ltd, 6-14 Underwood Street, London, N1 7JQ.

CASBAA Directory. Haymarket Media, 60 Wyndham Street, Central, Hong Kong.

Media Directory (Asia). www.agency-directory.ap. Haymarket Media, 60 Wyndham Street, Central, Hong Kong.

Urlichsweb: Global Serials Directory. Serial Solutions, 501 North 34th Street, Suite 300, Seattle, WA 98103.

Willings Press Guide. Cision House, 16-22 Baltic Street West, London, EC1Y 0UL.

World Radio/TV Handbook. WRTH Publications, 8 King Edward Street, Oxford, OX1 4HL.

Other Selected Directories

AdAge Directory. Adage.com/directory. Advertising Age, 711 Third Avenue, New York, NY 10017.

Adweek Directory. Adweek directories, P.O. Box 15158, North Hollywood, CA 91615.

Awards, Honors, and Prizes. Gale Cengage Learning, 27500 Drake Road, Farmington Hills, MI 48331.

The Celebrity Source. The Celebrity Source, 8033 Sunset Boulevard, Suite 2500, Los Angeles, CA 90046.

Congressional Yellow Book; Federal Yellow Book. Leadership Directories, 1667 K Street, NW, Suite 801, Washington, DC 20006.

Encyclopedia of Associations: International Organizations. Gale Cengage Learning, 27500 Drake Road, Farmington Hills, MI 48331.

GreenBook Worldwide Directory of Marketing Research and Focus Group Facilities. AMA Communication Services, 116 E. 27th Street, 6th floor, New York, NY 10016.

IEG Sponsorship Marketplace. IEG Inc., 350 N. Orleans, Suite 1200, Chicago, IL 60654.

National Directory of Corporate Public Affairs. Columbia Books, 8120 Woodmont Avenue, Suite 110, Bethesda, MD 20814.

O'Dwyer's Directory of PR Firms. O'Dwyer's, 271 Madison Avenue, #600, New York, NY 10016.

Oxbridge Directory of Newsletters. Oxbridge Communications, 39 W. 29th Street, Suite 301, New York, NY 10001.

Directory of Professional Freelance Writers. American Writers & Artists

Inc., 245 N.E. 4th Avenue, Suite 12, Delray Beach, FL 33483.
The Source Book of Multicultural Experts. Multicultural Marketing Resources, 150 West 28th Street, Suite 1501, New York, NY 10001.
Yearbook of Experts, Authorities, and Spokespersons. Broadcast Interview Source, 2233 Wisconsin Avenue, NW, Suite 301, Washington, DC 20007.

Periodicals

CASE Currents. Council for Advancement and Support of Education, 1307 New York Avenue, NW, Suite 1000, Washington, DC 20005. Monthly.
Communication Briefings. Communication Briefings, P.O. Box 787, Williamsport, PA 17703. Monthly.
Communication World. International Association of Business Communicators (IABC), 601 Montgomery Street, Suite 1900, San Francisco, CA 94111. Bimonthly.
Investor Relations Update. National Investor Relations Institute (NIRI), 225 Reinekers Lane, Suite 560, Alexandria, VA 22314. Monthly.
Jack O'Dwyer's PR Newsletter. O'Dwyer's, 271 Madison Avenue, #600, New York, NY 10016. Weekly.
Journal of Public Relations Research. Taylor & Francis, 325 Chestnut Street, Philadelphia, PA 19106. Five times a year.
O'Dwyer's PR Services & Products. Odwyerpr.com/pr_services_database /index.htm. O'Dwyer's, 271 Madison Avenue, #600, New York, NY 10016.
PRWeek. Haymarket Media, 114 West 26th Street, 4th Floor, New York, NY 10001. Weekly.
Public Relations Review. Elsevier, 360 Park Avenue South, New York, NY 10010. Quarterly.
Public Relations Strategist. Public Relations Society of America (PRSA), 33 Maiden Lane, New York, NY 10038-5150. Quarterly.
Public Relations Tactics. Public Relations Society of America (PRSA), 33 Maiden Lane, New York, NY 10038-5150. Monthly.

Index

A

Abolition movement, 72, 73
Abortion, 578
Absolutist philosophy, 97
Abundant Wildlife Society of North America, 98
Accreditation, 113–115
Acronyms, 209–210
Acta Diurna, 66
Active audiences, 205–206
Activist groups, 578–579
Adams, Sam, 68
Adidas, 384
Adolescent Pregnancy Prevention Campaign of North Carolina, 584
Adoption process, 216
ADR. *See* Alternative dispute resolution (ADR)
Advertising
  comparative, 329
  cost of, 46, 48, 232, 233
  integrated perspective between public relations and, 48–49
  invasion of privacy and, 331–332
  linked to news coverage, 118
  measurement of, 230, 232
  public relations *vs.*, 45–46, 48
  regulation of, 342–344, 347
Advertising agencies, 138–139
Advertising Council, 426
Advertising departments, 132
Advertising value equivalency (AVE), 230, 232
Advisory boards, 242
Advisory level, 130–131
Advocacy groups, 578–579
Advocacy research, 165
Advocacy roles, 99
AEJMC. *See* Association for Education in Journalism and Mass Communications (AEJMC)
Affordable Care Act, 527, 529, 537
Africa, 32, 33, 548
African Americans
  health issues and, 304
  marketing to, 310
  profile of, 308–309
  statistics for, 305–306
Age groups
  baby boomers, 315–316
  Millennial Generation, 314–315
  seniors, 316–317
  teenagers, 315
Agenda-setting theory, 251–252
AICR. *See* American Institute for Cancer Research (AICR)
AIPAC. *See* American Israel Public Affairs Committee (AIPAC)
Alagno, Caryn, 53
ALARP. *See* Association of Latin American Public Relations Professionals (ALARP)
ALCOA. *See* Aluminium Company of America (ALCOA)
Alderdice, Carol, 157
Alexander the Great, 66
Al Hurra, 567
Ali, Muhammad, 341
Allen, T. Harrell, 178, 180
Allen, Woody, 329
Alliance for a Healthier Generation, 482
Allstate, 313
Alternative dispute resolution (ADR), 260
Aluminium Company of America (ALCOA), 82
AMA. *See* American Management Association (AMA); American Medical Association (AMA)
American Airlines, 307, 313
American Apparel, 329
American Beverage Association, 482
The American Civil Liberties Union (ACLU), 573
American Customer Satisfaction Index, 480
American Express, 484, 489
American Heart Association (AHA), 304
American Idol, 421, 442
American Institute for Cancer Research (AICR), 407
American Israel Public Affairs Committee (AIPAC), 321, 537
American Management Association (AMA), 350
American Medical Association (AMA), 164
American Psychological Association (APA), 423
American Red Cross, 588
American Sign Language (ASL), 323
Amis, Rod, 228
Andsager, Julie L., 252
Annenberg Strategic Public Relations Center, 124, 127, 225
Anti-Saloon League of America, 72
Apple, 38, 111, 191, 209, 252, 359, 364, 383, 385, 397, 413, 416, 577
Apply the Brakes (ATB), 276
Arbesu, Christiana, 424
Archival research, 155
Aristotle, 97, 263
Armstrong, Lance, 502
Arthur W. Page Center (Pennsylvania State University), 113
Arthur W. Page Society, 52, 58, 79, 87, 102, 106, 123, 124, 126
Article recall, 242
Artwork, 335
Asia, 32
Asian Americans, 305–306, 311–314
ASL. *See* American Sign Language (ASL)
Asoka, Emperor, 66
Association for Education in Journalism and Mass Communications (AEJMC), 112
Association of Latin American Public Relations Professionals (ALARP), 104
ATB. *See* Apply the Brakes (ATB)
Atofina Chemicals, 491
Attitude, audience, 236
AT&T organization chart, 127
Attorneys, 352–353
Audience framing, 252
Audience participation, 266–267
Audiences. *See also* Diverse audiences
  action, attitudes and awareness of, 235–236
  active, 205–206
  analysis of, 262–263, 266–267
  attention-getting techniques for, 206–207
  for journalists, 45
  for marketing, 46
  passive, 205
  target, 185–186, 511–513, 582
  for tourism, 511
Audio news releases (ANRs)
  explanation of, 422–424
  format for, 423
  production and delivery of, 423–424
  use of, 424
Audits, 239, 296
Australia, 70, 551
AVE. *See* Advertising value equivalency (AVE)

Avon Walk for Breast Cancer, 466
Awareness stage, 217–218

B

Baby boomers, 315–316
Bacardi Rum, 467
Bacon's Information, Inc., 127
Bader TV News, 430
Bahr, Tim, 428
Bair, Dina, 436
Banquets, 451–454
Barkley, Charles, 466
Barnum, Phineas T., 69, 73, 83
Barrett, Steve, 39
Bartholomew, Don, 163, 232
Bassett, Angela, 466
Baxter, Leone, 80
The Beam Company, 182
Beanland, Rachel, 54
Beasley, David, 421
Beaupre, 203
Beaupre, Andy, 203
Becker, Elizabeth, 509
Becker, Lee, 32, 57, 87
Belgrade Beer Festival, 467
BenchPoint, 227
Benetton Gropu campaign, 279–280
Benioff, Marc, 487
Ben & Jerry's, 320
Benoit, William, 297, 299, 300
Benzkofer, Marjorie, 255
Bergen, Jack, 476
Bernays, Edward L., 76–78, 258
Berra, Yogi, 300
Best Buy, 321, 403
Bialik, Carl, 164
Bianchi-Kai, Barbara, 322, 323
Bieber, Justin, 375
Bill and Melinda Gates Foundation, 580
Bisbee & Co., 134
Bismarck, Otto von, 70
Bjorhus, Karl, 482
Black, Sam, 39
Black PRWire, 409
Blate, Alissa, 261
Blogs
  defamation suits and, 330
  employee, 351, 366
  influence of, 396
  monitoring, 228, 229
  organizational, 366
  overview of, 365
  public relations, 106, 111, 113
  regulation of, 342
  third-party, 366–367
Blood, Robert, 558
Boorstin, Daniel, 69, 500
Borkowski, Mark, 503
Bosman, Julie, 489
Boston Tea Party, 68
Bowen, David, 368
Bowen, Shannon, 97, 109
Boycotts, 483–485, 579
Boy Scouts of America (BSA), 573
BP, 474, 478, 522
Bragman, Howard, 503
Bramlet, Kellie, 137
Branding, 135, 209, 483, 488
Brand journalism, 49, 410, 440–441
Brazil, 547
Breakenridge, Deirdre, 93, 358, 377
Briefing, defined, 414
Brin, Sergey, 97
British Broadcasting Service (BBC), 70
Broadcast News Network, 423, 432
Brockhoof, Kleine, 560
B-roll package, 430
Broom, Glen, 178
Bruning, Stephen, 89
Buckley, Christopher, 37
Buckley, John, 130
Bucktold, Tom, 400
Budd, John F., 109
Budgets, 192
Buffett, Warren, 296
Bulldog Reporter, 207, 213, 414
Bullet theory, 270
Burdette, Nicole, 207
Burnett, Len, 309
Burrelles/Luce, 228
Burson, Harold, 138
Burson-Marsteller, 39, 84, 98, 108, 136, 138, 139, 143, 296, 375, 433
Burton, LeVar, 327
Bush, George H. W., 522
Bush, George W., 522, 523, 526, 538
Business/economics competence, 53–54
Business Wire, 158, 394, 396, 400, 403, 409, 410
BuzzStream, 172

C

Cabbage Patch Kids, 85
Caesar, Julius, 66
Cahill, Garry, 515
Calabro, Sara, 55–56
Calendars, 189–192
California Department of Health Services (CDHS), 531
California Highway Patrol (CHP), 531
California Prune Board, 235
Cameron, Glen, 35, 89, 258, 260
Campaigns. *See also* specific campaigns
  based on social media, 132–134
  election, 539–541
  electronic word-of-mouth tactics in, 220
  health, 583–584
  personality, 510
  to reach diverse audiences, 304
  timing of, 189–190
  word-of-mouth, 218–219
Campbell Soup Company, 318
Capital campaigns, 591
Capital Research Center, 495
Careers. *See* Public relations careers
Carlson, Bev, 52
Carma International, 159
Carmichael Lynch Spong, 139
Carnival Cruise Line, 515
Carr, Robin, 50–51
Carroll, Dave, 377, 379
CASE. *See* Council for the Advancement and Support of Education (CASE)
Catalysts, 218. *See also* Opinion leaders
Catering managers, working with, 453–454
Cattrall, Kim, 37
Cause-related marketing, 310, 489–490
Cave, Stephen, 500, 501, 503
CCOs. *See* Chief communications officers (CCOs)
CDC. *See* Centers for Disease Control and Prevention (CDC)
Celebrities, 264–265, 465–466, 500–506
Celebrity Access, 465
Celebrity Source, 465
Center, Allen, 33
Center for Sustainable Shale Development, 253
Centers for Disease Control and Prevention (CDC), 226, 230, 234, 426, 428, 430, 528–529, 583
Century Magazine, 74
CEOs. *See* Chief executive officers (CEOs)
CEPR. *See* European Public Relations Confederation (CEPR)
Certified Practitioner (CP), 114
Certified Public Accountant, 114
Certified Public Relations Professional, 114
CES. *See* Consumer Electronics Show (CES)
CF&I. *See* Colorado Fuel and Iron Company (CF&I)
Chambers of commerce, 576–577
Chan, Tracy, 228
Channeling, 207, 263
Chanofsky, Jorand, 368

Charities, 572–573, 592. *See also* Fund-raising
Chase, W. Howard, 288
Chase Bank, 183–184
Chat rooms, monitoring, 228
Chevron, 253
Chief communications officers (CCOs), 123, 124
Chief executive officers (CEOs), 122, 123, 127, 129
China
  news releases in, 393–394
  public perceptions about, 213
  public relations in, 32, 545–546, 565–566
China International Public Relations Association (CIPRA), 32
Chinese tourists, 510
Chisholm, Donald, 292
Chocolate Manufacturers Association (CMA), 363
Choices, structured, 260
Christian Evangelicals, 320–321
Church & Dwight, 168
Cialdini, Robert, 259
Cieply, Michael, 505
CIPRA. *See* China International Public Relations Association (CIPRA)
CIS. *See* Communities in the Schools (CIS)
Cisco, 366, 377
Citigroup, 130
Civil Rights Campaign, 85
Civil rights movement, 73, 83, 85
Clarke, Basil, 70
Clement VIII, Pope, 73
Clichés, 210
Clinton, Hillary, 567
Clooney, George, 505
Clorox Anywhere campaign, 185
Clorox Lounge, 318
Cloze procedure, 209
CMA. *See* Chocolate Manufacturers Association (CMA)
CNN, 563
Coca-Cola, 122, 337, 353, 354, 375, 468, 482, 549
Cocktail parties, 454–456
Code of Brussels, 103
Codes of conduct. *See* Ethics codes
Coffee Party, 220
Cognitive dissonance, 213
Cohen, Ken, 472, 474, 475
Cohen, Susan L., 337
Cohn & Wolfe, 138, 139
Coleman, Renita, 110
Collins, Jennifer, 465
Colman, Peter, 254
Colonial America, 67–68
Colorado Fuel and Iron Company (CF&I), 75
Comcast, 366
Commentaries (Caesar), 66
Commission on Public Relations Education, 49, 54, 55, 112
Commitment, partial, 260
Common Sense, 68
Communication
  adoption process in, 215–217
  audits, 239
  barriers to, 203
  believability of message in, 213
  clarity in, 208–212, 266
  conglomerates, rise of, 138–140
  corporate, 35–36
  crisis, 135, 286, 293
  cultural differences in, 205, 208
  elements of, 201–202
  emphasis on message in, 205
  getting audience attention as aspect of, 206–207
  goals of, 198–201, 208
  health, 530–531
  invasion of privacy and employee, 330–331
  language effectiveness in, 208
  marketing, 36, 135
  media uses and gratification theory of, 205
  objectives for, 198–201
  one-way, 201
  persuasive (*See* Persuasive communication)
  retention of message in, 214–215
  risk, 286, 290
  two-way, 202–203
  word-of-mouth, 218–219
Communication models, 201–202
Communications World, 101
Communities in the Schools (CIS), 182, 184
Community for Creative Nonviolence v. Reid, 335
Community relations, 135, 507, 509
Competition, 275, 276, 572–573
Competition monitoring, 152
Comprehension formulas, 209
Compulsory-advisory level, 131
Concurring authority, 131
Cone Communications, 139
Conflict, 254, 256–258, 275–277
Conflict management
  action plan and, 289
  contingency continuum and, 284–285
  in crisis situations, 291–295
  evaluation and, 289
  image restoration and, 300
  life cycle of, 285–287
  public relations and, 277–281, 561
  reputation and, 295–300
  strategic, 275–277
  strategy options and, 288–289
  threat appraisal model of, 281–282
Conflict of interest, 143, 190–191
Conflict positioning, 286, 289–290
Congress, U. S., 523–524
Conrail Inc., 260, 284
Consumer activism, 481–483
Consumer boycotts, 483–485
Consumer Electronics Show (CES), 413, 445, 462
Content analysis, 158–159, 240
Content marketing, 49, 440
Context, persuasion and, 266
Contingency continuum, 284–285
Contingency factors, matrix of, 283–284
Contingency theory, 283
Continuing education, 114–115
Convenience polls, 159
Conventions, 458–461
Conversation index, 229
Cook, Fred, 50
Cook, Tim, 38, 191
Coombs, Timothy, 292, 293, 294, 296, 299, 414
CooperKatz & Company, 358
Coors, 373
Copyright Clearance Center, 334
Copyrights
  explanation of, 333–334
  facts related to, 336–337
  fair use *vs.* infringement and, 334–335
  freelance writers and, 335–336
  Internet and, 336
  photography and artwork and, 335
Copyright Term Extension Act (1998), 334
Copy testing, 161–162
Corona, David, 49
Corporate communications, 35–36
Corporate profile, 403
Corporate reputation, 135
Corporate social responsibility (CSR), 91–92, 475–476
Corporate speech, 349
Corporate sponsorships, 468–469, 490–491
Corporations
  charitable donations from, 590–591
  customer relations and, 479–485
  defamation and, 329
  employee relations and, 485–487
  environmental relations and, 493
  global marketing and, 549–560

government relations and, 520, 533–535
investor relations and, 487
marketing communications and, 487–492
media relations and, 477–479
philanthropy and, 493–495
public relations role in, 475–477
Cost effectiveness, 235
Cost-per-thousand (CPM), 235
Council for the Advancement and Support of Education (CASE), 102
Council of Public Relations Firms, 102, 138
Counseling, 136, 138
Counseling firm, structure of, 140–141
Cowan, Warren, 80
CP. *See* Certified Practitioner (CP)
CPM. *See* Cost-per-thousand (CPM)
Credibility, source, 212, 263–265
Creel, George, 79
Cripps, Kathy, 92
Crises
explanation of, 291
government handling of, 524
in travel industry, 513–516
Crisis Connection, 200
Crisis management. *See also* Reputation management
communication for, 135, 286, 293
corporate culture and, 298–299
cultural differences and, 298–299
explanation of, 291, 505
issues management *vs.*, 287
strategies for, 293–295
Crisis management plans, 286, 292
Cropp, Fritz, 260
Crowdfunding, 593
Crystallizing Public Opinion (Bernays), 77
CSR. *See* Corporate social responsibility (CSR)
CSX Corporation, 260
Cultural dimensions (Hofstede), 551–552
Cultural organizations, 580–581
Cultural/racial diversity. *See also* Diverse audiences; Minorities
authenticity and, 254–255
communication and, 208
corporate marketing and, 480
crisis management and, 298–299
gift-giving and, 117
global marketing and, 551–554
IBM and, 125
news releases and, 393–394
overview of, 305–306
payments to journalists and, 117
public relations and, 89–90
in United States, 305–314
in workplace, 348
Cunningham, Ward, 368
Curren, Joel, 53
Curtin, Patricia, 252
Customer relations
consumer activism and, 481–483
consumer boycotts and, 483–485
and corporations, 479–485
in diverse markets, 480–481
Cutlip, Scott, 33, 75
cvent, 461
Cymfony, 159
Cytryn v. Cook, 345

D

Dach, Leslie, 58
Dashboard, 159
Databases, online, 155–157
Davis, Elmer, 80
Dayton Hudson Corporation, 234
Deaf individuals, 322, 323
Dean, Howard, 540
Decorative contact lenses, 431
Deen, Paula, 504
Defamation, 328–330, 479
Defren, Todd, 57, 394
Delahaye Medialink, 296
Delay, Tom, 538
Dell, 366
Demonstrations, 579
Department of Defense, 524
Department of Health and Human Services (HHS), 583
Department of Homeland Security, 538
DeSousa-Mauk, William P., 509
Deutsch, Morton, 254
Devries Public Relations, 37, 139
Dialogic model of public relations, 89
Dickens, Robert, 586
Digital analytics, for public relations, 169–170
Digital Millennium Copyright Act (1998), 336
Digital Royalty, 179
Direct mail, 269, 591
Disability community, 322–323
Disclosure, 118
Discrimination, language, 211–212
Disneyland, 364
Dissonance, cognitive, 213
Dittus Communications, 160
Diverse audiences. *See also* Cultural/racial diversity; Minorities
African Americans, 308–311
Asian Americans, 311–314
baby boomers, 315–316
disability community, 322–323
gays/lesbians, 318–319
Hispanics, 307–308
Millennial Generation, 314–315
overview of, 305–306
religious groups, 319–322
seniors, 316–317
statistics related to, 89–90
women, 60, 86–88, 213, 317–318
DOE. *See* U.S. Department of Energy (DOE)
Dolan, Jane, 56
Dollar-value approach, 232
Dominant coalition, 284
Domino's Pizza, 161, 379
Doritos, 186, 230
Doublespeak, 210, 211
DoubleTree Cookie campaign, 174, 179, 187, 198, 201, 237–238
Downes, Edward, 524
Dozier, David, 178, 236
Drama, in messages, 267
Drip-by-drip technique, 505
Drobis, David, 556, 560
Drug industry, regulation of, 347–348
Dubai, 547
Duke, Mike, 473–474
DWJ Television, 424, 425, 432

E

Economics/business competence, 53–54
Edelman, Richard, 62, 477
Edelman Trust Barometer, 477
Edelman Worldwide, 53, 56, 58, 62, 138, 140, 220, 560
Edelstein, Jonathan, 346
Edmonds, Marion, 529
Educational materials, 582
Educational organizations, 584–585
EEOC. *See* Equal Employment Opportunity Commission (EEOC)
Eggerton, Lisa, 151
Eighteenth Amendment, 72
800 numbers, 234
Eiselein, Kai, 334
E-kits, 400–401
Elasser, John, 351
Election campaigns, 539–541
Electronic Media Communications, 401
Electronic media kits (EPKs), 400–401
Electronic news services, 409

Electronic word of mouth (eWOM), 220
Elliott, Stuart, 489
E-mail
monitoring employee, 332–333, 351
pitching by, 404–405
surveys, 168–169
used for invitations, 461
Emotional appeals, 268
Employee blogs, 366
Employee relations, 485–487
Employees. *See also* Public relations professionals
invasion of privacy of, 330–331
monitoring communication of, 332–333, 350–351
Employee speech, 350–351
Endorsements, 268, 342, 343–344, 592
The Engagor Dashboard, 170
Enron, 345, 346
Entertainment industry
event promotion and, 506
fascination with celebrities and, 502–503
overview of, 500–502
publicists in, 503–506
Entropy, 215
The Environmental Defense Fund, 579
Environmental issues
affecting tourism, 514
BP Gulf oil spill, 474
NGOs and, 558
Environmental movement, 73, 83, 495
Environmental Protection Agency (EPA), 333
Environmental relations, 493
Environmental scanning, 285
EPA. *See* Environmental Protection Agency (EPA)
EPKs. *See* Electronic media kits (EPKs)
Equal Employment Opportunity Commission (EEOC), 348
Escalation, 256
E.T., 437
Ethical issues
advertising costs and, 233
advocacy roles and, 99
bloggers and, 344
and conflict of interest, 143, 190–191
conflict resolution and, 285
corporate donations and, 107–108
electronic word-of-mouth tactics and, 220
facing individual practitioners, 110
front groups and, 98
guest appearances and, 438
misleading images and, 37
news media relations and, 115–118
news releases and, 391
persuasion and, 270–271
spokespersons and, 111
student loan industry lobbying and, 536
survey validity and, 164
tourism and, 513
Ethics
approaches to, 99
corporate investment in, 487
of persuasion, 270–271
professional organizations and, 99–103
public relations manager's role in, 109
values *vs.*, 97, 98
Ethics codes. *See also specific organizations*
and conflict of interest, 143
function of, 103–105
for specific situations, 105–108
Ethnographic techniques, for research, 162
EU. *See* European Union (EU)
Euphemisms, 210–211
EUPRRA. *See* European Public Relations Confederation Education and Research Association (EUPRRA)
Europe, 31, 33, 52. *See also* specific countries
European Public Relations Confederation (CEPR), 104
European Public Relations Confederation Education and Research Association (EUPRRA), 104
European Union (EU), 31, 550, 551. *See also specific countries*
Evaluation. *See also* Measurement
in adoption process, 216
of audience, 235–236
current status of, 225–226
explanation of, 224
of message exposure, 227–235
objectives for, 224–225
of production, 226
of program plans, 192–194
of supplemental activities, 239–242
Evans, Mark, 405
Event-management software, 461
Events. *See also* Meetings
analysis following, 456
attendance at, 240
entertainment, 506
function of, 445, 581
liability for sponsored, 351
promotional, 464–469
public opinion and, 247
Events management, 135
Events manager, job listings for, 446
Event sponsorship, 591–592
eWOM. *See* Electronic word of mouth (eWOM)
Excellence in Public Relations and Communications Management (IABC Foundation), 122
Execution. *See* Communication
Executive speech training, 135
Exhibits, 460
Existential approach, 97
Expertise in social media, 54
Exxon/Mobil, 472, 474

F

Facebook, 39, 369, 370–373
Facilities, 449, 459
Factiva, 210, 233
Fact sheets, 402–403
Fair comment defense, 330
Fair disclosure regulation (Reg FD) (Securities and Exchange Commission), 346
Fair use, 334–335
Familiarization trip, 319
FAPRA. *See* Federation of African Public Relations Association (FAPRA)
FCC. *See* Federal Communications Commission (FCC)
FDA. *See* Food and Drug Administration (FDA)
Fear arousal, 268
Fearn-Banks, Kathleen, 291
Federal Communications Commission (FCC), 106, 346–347, 424
Federal government
agencies in, 524–528
Congress and, 523–524
White House and, 522–523
Federalist Papers, 68
Federal Patent and Trademark Office (FPTO), 337
Federal Trade Commission (FTC), 327, 342–344
Federation of African Public Relations Association (FAPRA), 104
Femina, Jerra Della, 332
Fernandez, Lauren, 111, 391
Festinger, Leon, 213
Fey, Tina, 504
FIFA World Cup, 468
Figueredo, Fernando, 313
Financial information, 344–346
Financial relations, 135
Fink, Steven, 292

First Amendment protections, 330, 342, 346, 349
Fiske, Rosanna, 39
Fitzpatrick, Kathy R., 353
Flack, 39
Flack, Gene, 39
Fleet Hometown News Center, 524
Fleischman, Doris F., 78
Fleishman-Hillard, 136, 138, 139, 189, 224, 254–255, 260, 308, 310, 363, 485
Flesch, Rudolph, 209
Flickr, 162, 379–380
Focus groups, 159–161
FOIA. *See* Freedom of Information Act (FOIA)
Food, 451
Food and Drug Administration (FDA), 182, 290, 347–348
Ford, Henry, 81, 122
Ford Motor Company, 424
Foreign Agents Registration Act (FARA), 561
Forest Alliance of British Columbia, 98
Formal opinion leaders, 247
Former Soviet Republics, 548
Forrester Consulting for Proofpoint, 350
Forum, 100
Foundations, 579–580, 590–591
Fox, Josh, 253
Fox, Michael J., 37
FPTO. *See* Federal Patent and Trademark Office (FPTO)
Framing theory, 252, 254
Franklin, Missy, 275
Freedom of Information Act (FOIA), 332–333
Freelance writers, 335–336
Free speech, 349
Friedman, Michael, 435
Front groups, 98
Frontline, 101
FTC. *See* Federal Trade Commission (FTC)
Fund-raising, 452, 453, 539–540, 580, 588–593
Fund-raising methods, 590–593

G

Gable, Tom, 91
Gale Directory, 314
Gandy, Oscar H., Jr., 251, 258
Gantt charts, 192
The Gap, 367
Gaunt, Philip, 287
Gay and Lesbian Alliance Against Defamation (GLAAD), 578
Gay/lesbian community, 318–319
Gebre, Bogaletch, 573–574
Gender. *See also* Women
  language use and, 211–212
  public relations salaries and, 60, 87
  social media skills and, 213
Gender/lifestyle audiences
  disability community, 322–323
  gays/lesbians, 318–319
  religious groups, 319–322
  women, 317–318
General Electric, 468, 477, 550
General Motors, 126, 342, 368
Genkin, Larry, 366
German Council for Public Relations, 103
Germany, public relations in, 70
Gerth, Jeff, 526
Gibbs, Robert, 524
Gifts, 116–117, 416
Gill, Curtis, 427
Gilman, Andrew D., 412
Gilroy Garlic festival, 468
Giulani, Adrianna, 37
Gladwell, Malcolm, 251
Glass, Matt, 466
Glassman, James K., 567
The Global Alliance, 31
Global Alliance for Public Relations and Communication Management, 102
Global public relations
  explanation of, 545
  global marketing and, 549–560
  governments and, 560–567
  illiteracy and, 160
  nature of, 31–33, 90, 138
  opportunities in, 567–568
  overview of, 545–549
Glover, Tom, 61
Gold Papers, 101, 112
GolinHarris, 139
Google, 39, 191, 359, 365, 373, 376, 383, 487, 555–556
Google Alerts, 152
Google Analytics, 156–157
Google Books, 336
Google Trends, 158, 172
Gordon, Rose, 118
Go Red for Women campaign, 187
Gorges, Mary, 382
Government documents, 334–335
Government/government agencies. *See also* Politics
  federal, 521–529
  lobbying and, 535–539
  local, 531–532
  public information and public affairs information from, 36, 82, 532–533
  public relations and, 30, 342, 520, 560–567
  relations between corporations and, 520, 533–535
  state, 529–531
GPTMC. *See* Greater Philadelphia Tourism Marketing Corporation (GPTMC)
Grable, Betty, 503
Grant, Ulysses S., 535
Grassroots campaigns, 98, 190–191
Grassroots lobbying, 538–539
Grastic, Dejan, 467
Grazian, Frank, 210
Great Britain, public relations in, 70
Greater Philadelphia Tourism Marketing Corporation (GPTMC), 319
Greater Rochester Enterprise, 364
Green, Sherri Deatherage, 409
Greenpeace, 203–204, 578
Gregory XV, Pope, 66
Gross national product (GNP), 472
Grunig, James E., 66, 77, 83, 84, 89, 122, 131, 198, 200, 201, 202, 203, 205
Grunig, Larissa, 131
Guest appearances
  approaches to, 433–434
  as ethical issues, 438
  on magazine shows, 435–436
  pitching, 436–437
  on talk shows, 434–435
Gulf oil spill, 474

H

Haack, Chris, 218
Hagley, Thomas R., 178
Haiti earthquake relief, 386
Hallahan, Kirk, 198, 254
Hanban, 565–566
Hand, Mark, 55
Hands Across America, 85
Harley-Davidson, 132
Harlow, Rex, 33, 79–80
HARO. *See* Help a Reporter Out (HARO)
Harris, Golin, 90, 367
Harris, Jon, 112
Harris, Thomas, 47, 488
Harris Interactive, 169, 296
Harry Walker Agency, 452
Hartinson, David L., 116
Harvard College, 68, 73
Hass, Mark, 118
Hayworth, Rita, 503
Hazleton, Vincent, 34

HCRC. *See* Health Communication Research Center (HCRC)
Health agencies, 583
Health campaigns, 583–584
Health Communication Research Center (HCRC), 174
Health Literacy Missouri, 208
Health organizations, 582–583
Health South, 118
Heath, Robert L., 251, 258, 271
Hellmich, Nanci, 407
Hellriegel, Don, 131
Helm, Janet, 367
Help a Reporter Out (HARO), 408
Herodotus, 66
Heth, Joice, 69
Hill & Knowlton, 55, 139
Hilton-Barber, David, 239
Hispanic PRWire, 409
Hispanic Public Relations Society (HPRA), 102
Hispanics
  communication efforts to, 481
  health issues and, 307
  profile of, 307–308
  and program planning, 188
  radio and television for, 422
  statistics for, 305, 307
  values of, 313
Hit, website, 230
H1N1 flue epidemic, 206
Hofstede, Geert, 551
Holmes, Paul, 495
Holtz, Shel, 115, 372
Holtzhausen, Derina, 84
Home Depot, 275
Home Instead Senior Care Service, 190
Hood, Julie, 486
Hopson, Andy, 480
Hospitality suites, 463
Hospitals, 582–583
Hovland, Carl, 212
HPRA. *See* Hispanic Public Relations Society (HPRA)
H&R Block, 377
Hulu, 376
Human resources, 131–132
Human Rights Campaign (HRC), 369
Hunt, Todd, 66, 83, 205
Hynes, James, 69
Hype, 68, 69
Hype words, 210
Hypodermic-needle theory, 270

I

IABC. *See* International Association of Business Communicators (IABC)
Iacono, Erica, 454
IBM, 122, 126
  and cultural/racial diversity, 125
  organization chart of, 126
Illinois Public Health Department, 208
Illiteracy, 160
ILO. *See* International Labor Organization (ILO)
Image restoration, 287, 296–299
  and conflict management, 300
Images, misleading, 37
IMC. *See* Integrated marketing communications (IMC)
Imre, Dave, 46
India, 70, 547
Indonesia, 547
Influencers, 218
Influentials. *See* Opinion leaders
Infographics, 399
Informal opinion leaders, 248
Informational objectives, 184
Information requests, 234
Infringement
  copyright, 334–335
  trademark, 340–341
Initial public offerings (IPOs), 487
Innovation, 216, 217, 250
Insider trading, 345
Instagram, 380
Institute for Crisis Management, 291
The Institute of Public Relations (IPR), 91, 113, 225, 232
Insull, Samuel, 81
Integrated marketing communications (IMC), 47–49, 488. *See also* Marketing communications
Integrated services digital network (ISDN), 550
Intellectual property
  copyrights as, 333–337
  trademarks as, 337–341
Intercept interviews, 159
Interest stage, 218
International Association of Business Communicators (IABC), 50, 84, 101, 113, 445
International Coalition to Save British Columbia's Rainforests, 98
International Communications Consultancy Organization (ICCO), 556
International Labor Organization (ILO), 279
International public relations. *See* Global public relations
International Public Relations Association (IPRA), 101–102
Internet. *See also* World Wide Web
  campaign fund-raising and support building on, 539–540
  and copyrights, 336
  for copy testing, 162
  customer complaints posted on, 479
  ethical issues related to, 105–106
  global marketing and, 550
  health information on, 584
  interactivity of, 362–363
  making convention reservations on, 461
  measuring effectiveness on, 228–229
  mobile-enabled content and, 382–386
  monitoring employee communication on, 332–333, 350–351
  net neutrality and, 347
  origins of, 358–359
  reaching diverse audiences through, 304, 307
  social media and (*See* Social media)
  statistics related to, 358
  surfing, 350–351
  travel business on, 511
Internships, value of, 55–57
Interpublic Group, 139
Interviews
  approaches to, 159
  media, 411–412
  personal, 167–168
  via satellite, 431
Investor relations (IR)
  goals of corporate, 487
  historical background of, 66
  Texas Gulf Sulfur case and, 84
Invitations, for meetings, 449–450
  sample, 452
Involvement, 214
iPhone, 371, 380, 383, 384
IPR. *See* The Institute of Public Relations (IPR)
IPRA. *See* International Public Relations Association (IPRA)
Israel, 561
Issues management, 286, 287–289
Issues placement, 439
Ivory Soap campaign, 77–78
Iyengar, Shanto, 254

J

Jackson, Janet, 347
Jackson, Michael, 501–502
James, Paul, 132
Japan, 298–299, 547–548, 552

Jargon, 210
Jeffries-Fox, Bruce, 456
Jews, 321
Jin, Yan, 282
Jobs, Steve, 111
Johannesen, Richard L., 271
Johnson, Cassandra, 168
Johnson, F. Ross, 130
Johnson & Johnson, 131, 233
Jolie, Angelina, 502
Jones, Barrie L., 288
Jones, Paul Davis, 494
Jones, Samantha, 37
Jones-Dilworth, Josh, 229
Journalism, 42–45
  brand, 410, 440–441
Journalists
  gifts to, 116–117
  media relations and, 478
  pay for play and, 526–527
  payments to, 117
  in public relations, 50–52
  stereotypes of public relations perpetuated by, 37
Journal of Public Relations Research, 113
Junket, 415

K

Kaplan, Lewis, 353
Karam, Zeina, 561
Katz, Elihu, 250, 269
KD Paine and Partners, 159
Keaton, Pamela, 527
Kebbel, Gary, 382
Kendall, Amos, 72
Kendig, Karen, 452
Kendrix, Moss, 80
Kenya, 144
Kerr, Robert, 349
Kersten, Astrid, 284
Ketchum, 56, 107, 133, 138, 139, 141, 143, 174, 179, 180, 181, 183, 187, 189, 192, 194, 225, 232, 237–238, 317, 546, 556
KFC, 278, 281, 285, 482
Kinder, Donald, 254
King Pharmaceuticals, 327
King's College (now Columbia University), 68
Kingston, Jeff, 298
Kiousis, Spiro, 252
Kircaali, Fuat, 390
Klapper, Joseph, 251
Koch Industries, 327
Koenig, Mark, 345
Kolek, Jacqueline, 138
Kotcher, Ray, 556
Kotler, Philip, 47
Kournikova, Anna, 466
Kraker, Michelle, 370–371
KRC Research, 291
Krupp, Alfred, 70

L

Labor unions, 575–576
Lady Gaga, 500
Lambert, Eleanor, 80
Lamme, M. O., 73
Landry, Martin, 292
Lane, Patrick, 507
Language
  discriminatory, 211–212
  effective use of, 208
  global marketing and, 551–554
  of news releases, 393
  use of clear, 208–212
LaPierre, Wayne, 257
Larson, Cedric, 79
Larson, Charles, 271
Lasswell, Harold, 204, 265
Latin America
  news releases in, 393
  public relations growth in, 32
  university programs in public relations in, 32
Lauder, Evelyn, 579
Lauterborn, Robert, 48
Lauzen, Martha, 287
Layoffs, 486–487
Lazarsfeld, Paul, 250
Lee, Ivy Ledbetter, 75–76, 390
Legal issues
  cooperation between public relations and legal department as, 131
  copyright law as, 333–337
  corporate speech as, 349
  employee speech as, 350–351
  examples of public relations, 327, 329
  invasion of privacy as, 330–333
  libel and defamation as, 328–330, 352
  regulation by government agencies and, 342–347
  relationship between attorneys and public relations personnel and, 352–353
  trademark law as, 337–341
Leone Marketing Research, 134
Lesbians. *See* Gay/lesbian community
Letterman, David, 504
Levick, Richard, 112
Levine, Sheldon, 219
Lewis, Tanya, 394
The Lewis Group, 118
LexisNexis, 155
Liability insurance, 466
Libel
  explanation of, 328–329
  fair comment defense and, 330
  government regulation and, 342
  Internet sites and, 336
  public relations professionals and, 327, 329
  sponsored events and, 351
  trade, 329
Libel suits, 329
Library research, 155
Licensing fees, 337–338
Lifestyle Lift, 327
Light's Golden Jubilee campaign, 78
Limited-effects model, 251, 269
Lind, Jenny, 69
Lindeman, Teresa, 479
Lindenmann, Walter K., 153, 155, 225, 235
LinkedIn, 376
Lippmann, Walter, 258
Lissauer, Michael, 394
Literary, rates of, 160, 208
Litigation, 579
Loaded questions, 165
Lobbying
  explanation of, 535, 537, 579
  global, 554–555
  grassroots, 538–539
  pitfalls of, 537–538
  by U. S. Chamber of Commerce, 576
Local governments, 531–532
Location, meeting, 445–446, 449, 458–459
Logistics, for banquets, 454
Long, Lawrence W., 34
Lopez, Jennifer, 466
Ludlow Massacre, 75
Lukaszewski, James, 52, 178
"Lunch-room" seating, 449
Lyman, Levi, 69
Lyon, Lisa, 295, 296

M

MacArthur, Douglas, 70
Macy's, 74, 122
Maestre, Joaquin, 71
Magazine shows, 435–436
Mailed questionnaires, 167
Major League Baseball (MLB), 338
Maloney, Jennifer, 495
Management by objective (MBO), 84, 178–180
Mandela, Nelson, 502

Marconi Company, 70
Marketing
  cause-related, 489–490
  content, 49, 440
  global, 549–560
  integrated perspective between public relations and, 48–49
  public relations as support for, 47
  viral, 491–492
  vs. public relations, 46–47, 49
Marketing communications, 135
  cause-related marketing and, 489–490
  corporate sponsorships, 490–491
  explanation of, 36, 487–488
  integrated, 47–49, 488
  product placement and, 488–489
  product publicity and, 488
  viral marketing and, 491–492
  websites as tools for, 360
Marketing departments, 132
MarketWire, 394, 409
Mark-Viverito, Melissa, 328
Marston, John, 40
Martin, Tom, 520
Martinez, Raul, 422
Martinson, David L., 99
Mass demonstrations, 579
Mass media, 92–93, 251
Mass-media research
  agenda-setting theory and, 251–252
  conflict theory, 254, 256–258
  framing theory and, 252, 254
  media-dependency theory and, 252
Masterfoods, 218
Mat releases, 401
Mattel Toys, 479
MBO. *See* Management by objective (MBO)
McAleer, Phelim, 253
McCafé, 304
McCallister, Rachel, 502
McCarthy, Caroline, 204
McCaskill, Claire, 528
McCombs, Max, 251
McCormick Place (Chicago), 460
McDonald's, 261, 282, 304, 313, 373, 579
McGuire, Craig, 394, 409
McKenna, Ted, 110
Measurement. *See also* Evaluation
  of audience action, 236
  of audience attitudes, 236
  current status of, 225–226
  emphasis on, 92
  of message exposure, 227–235
  of production, 226
  of supplemental activities, 239–242
Measurement tools, 227
Media. *See also* Mass media
  effects of, 251
  motion, 263
  public relations image by, 36
Media advisory, 402, 403
Media alerts, 402–403
Media analysis, 135
Media-dependency theory and, 252
Media framing, 252
Media impressions, 229–230
Media interviews, 411–412
Media kits, 400–401
Medialink, 422
Media material distribution, 408–411
Media placements, ability to track, 232–234
Media queries, 408
Media relations, 477–479
Media Reputation Index (MRI), 296
Media tours, 415–416, 423, 428
Media uses and gratification theory, 205
Meetings. *See also* Events
  attendance at, 240
  invitations for, 449–450, 455
  location, 445–446, 449
  meals for, 451
  overview of, 445
  planning for, 445–446, 449–450
  program for, 450–455
  registration for, 450
  speakers for, 451
Membership organizations, 574–577
Messages. *See also* Communication
  acting on, 215–220
  believing in, 212–214
  competing, 270
  content and structure of, 267–268
  exposure to, 198
  measuring exposure to, 227–235
  paying attention to, 204–207
  persuasive, 260–261 (*See also* Persuasion; Persuasive communication)
  remembering, 214–215
  repetition of, 214
  split, 239
  understanding of, 208–212
Metro Nutrition Network (MNN), 261
Mexico, 512, 515, 548
Michaelson, David, 158
Microsoft Excel, 192
Microsoft Word, 162, 209
Middle Ages, 66–67
Middle East, 547, 567
Milana, Paulina, 394
Mill, John Stewart, 97
Millennial Generation, 314–315
Miller, Lindsey, 50
MillerCoors, 328
Minorities, 90–91, 306. *See also* Cultural/racial diversity; Diverse audiences
Mintz, Richard, 51
Misappropriation of personality, 332, 341
MLB. *See* Major League Baseball (MLB)
MNN. *See* Metro Nutrition Network (MNN)
Mock, James O., 79
Monitor Savings Bank v. Vinson, 486
Monterey Aquarium, 380
Moon, Thom, 424
Moon, Yung, 445
Morgan, Andrea, 48
Morley, Michael, 194
Mortification strategy, 299, 414
Moskowitz, Laurence, 61
Motion media, 263
Motivational objectives, 185, 224
Movies, 37, 527
Moyers, Bill, 78
MRI. *See* Media Reputation Index (MRI)
MS&L, 407
The MSL Group, 138
Multimedia news releases, 394–396
Multiple-step flow theory, 250
Muslims, 321–322
MWW Group, 282
Myers, Cayce, 352
Myers, Kenneth, 292
MySpace, 370

N

NABC. *See* National Association of Broadcast Communicators (NABC)
Nager, Norman R., 178, 180
Name tags, 450
NASA, 85
National Aircheck, 228
National Association of Broadcast Communicators (NABC), 106
National Association of Colored People (NAACP), 74
National Basketball Association (NBA), 338
National Black Public Relations Society (NBPRS), 102
National Campaign to Prevent Teen Pregnancy, 439

National Center for Educational Statistics, 84
National Communication Association (NCA), 112
National Council of Negro Women, 310
National Football League (NFL), 331
National Heart Lung and Blood Institute, 425
National Hockey League (NHL), 338
National Institutes of Health (NIH), 583
National Investor Relations Institute (NIRI), 102, 107
National Pork Producers Council, 432
National Potato Board, 230
National Rifle Association (NRA), 97, 256–257, 578
National School Public Relations Association (NSPRA), 102
Native Americans, 305
NBA. *See* National Basketball Association (NBA)
NBPRS. *See* National Black Public Relations Society (NBPRS)
NCA. *See* National Communication Association (NCA)
Negotiation, persuasion in, 259–260
Nestlé, 203, 401
Net neutrality, 347
Networking, function of, 50–51
Newman, Marc, 359
News conferences, 413–415
News coverage, 118
News cycle, 92
News feeds, 432–433
News Generation, 423, 427
Newsletters, 240, 242, 330, 331, 582
News media
  ads linked to news coverage and, 118
  gifts to members of, 116–117
  payments to, 118
  relations with, 115–116
  transparency and disclosure issues and, 118
News releases
  cultural differences and, 393–394
  ethical issues for, 391, 404
  explanation of, 390–391
  guidelines for writing, 391–392
  mat feature, 401
  in media kits, 400–401
  multimedia, 394–396
  online, 391–392
  planning for, 391
  radio, 422–424
Newsrooms, online, 409–411
New Yorkers Against Fracking, 253
NFL. *See* National Football League (NFL)
NHL. *See* National Hockey League (NHL)
Nicholson, Ed, 482
Nielsen, W. D. (Bill), 99
Nike, 234, 235, 349
Nike v. Kasky, 349
Niles, Robert, 394
NIRI. *See* National Investor Relations Institute (NIRI)
Noelle-Neumann, Elisabeth, 246
Nongovernmental organizations (NGOs), 477, 493, 558, 560
  campaigns, 559
Nonprobability samples, 163
Nonprofit sector, 572–573
Norcera, Joe, 37
Nordic Countries, 548–549
Norfolk Southern Corporation, 260
Norfolk Southern railroad, 284
North Face, 339
Novelli, Bill, 477
NRA. *See* National Rifle Association (NRA)
NSPRA. *See* National School Public Relations Association (NSPRA)
N-step theory, 250

O

Oates, David B., 184, 405
Obama, Barack, 210, 214, 254, 277, 306, 500, 520–524, 540, 566, 567
Obamacare, 529, 537
Objectives
  explanation of, 184
  informational, 184
  motivational, 185, 224
Occupational Outlook Handbook 2010–37 (Bureau of Labor Statistics), 29–30
Oceana, 558, 559
Off-site web pages, 170–171
Ogilvy Public Relations Worldwide, 139, 143, 321, 430
Oil spill, BP Gulf, 474
Ollenburger, Jeff, 287
Olympics, 468
Omnibus surveys, 168
Omnicom, 139
O'Neil, Julie, 124
Online databases, 155–157
Online news conferences, 415
Online news releases, 391–392
Online newsrooms, 409–411
On-site web pages, 170–171
Open houses, 457–458
Opinion leaders, 218, 247–250. *See also* Public opinion
Organizational blogs, 366
Organizing for Action (OFA), 521
Outsourcing, 93, 132–134
Owned media, 45

P

Packaging, 512–513
Page, Arthur W., 79
Paid media, 45. *See also* Advertising
Paine, K. D., 152
Paine, Katherine, 225, 233
Paine, Tom, 68
Paisley, William J., 262
Pajasalmi, Esko, 71
Palin, Sarah, 257
Pampers, 308
Papa John's, 327
Parker and Lee, 75
Parkinson, L. Marie, 331, 332
Parkinson, Michael, 331, 332
Parks, Rosa, 73
Partial commitment, 260
Passive audiences, 205
Paterson, David, 111
Paul, Saint, 66
Pay for play, 526–527
PBS. *See* Public Broadcasting Service (PBS)
Pedersen, Wes, 39
Pennsylvania Railroad, 75, 390
Pentagon, 526, 527
People for the Ethical Treatment of Animals (PETA), 281, 285
Peppercomm, 138
Pepsi, 284, 295, 301, 309
Perception management, 84
Perlin, Ross, 56
Personal interviews, 167–168
Personality Quiz, 53
Persuasion
  ethics of, 270–271
  limits of, 268–270
  in negotiation, 259–260
  overview of, 258
  principles of, 259
  research on, 262
  techniques for, 260–261
  uses of, 258–259
Persuasive communication
  appeal to self-interest and, 265–266
  audience analysis and, 262–263
  audience participation and, 266–267
  content and message structure and, 267–268

Persuasive communication (*continued*)
factors in, 262–268
message clarity and, 266
recommendations for, 267
source credibility and, 263–265
techniques for, 260–261
timing and context, 266
PETA (People for the Ethical Treatment of Animals), 482, 483, 578
Peterson, Ken, 380
Pew Research Center, 501
P&G. *See* Procter & Gamble (P&G)
Pharris, Patrick, 401
Philanthropy, corporate, 493–495
Philippines, 70–71
Philips Electronics, 232
Philips Norelco, 402
PhoCusWright, 445
Phoenix Suns, 374
Photographers, rights of freelance, 335
Photographs
copyright law and, 335
invasion of privacy and, 331
misleading, 37
publicity, 396–400
Piasecki, Andy, 71, 72
Picasso, 447
Pickens, T. Boone, 253
Piggyback surveys, 168
Pilot tests, 239
Pimlott, J. A. R., 70
Pitching
explanation of, 404–405
guest appearances, 436–437
guidelines for e-mail, 405
opening lines for, 405–406
research prior to, 405
Pitino, Rick, 111
Pitt, Brad, 502
Plank Center for Leadership in Public Relations (University of Alabama), 113
Planning. *See* Program planning
Plant tours, 457–458
Plaskett, Kim, 132
Plays, 506
Plugs, 437
Podcasts, 364–365
Poehler, Amy, 504
Pogachefsky, Mark, 502
Politics, 539–541
Polls, 153, 164, 267
Pope Francis, 500
Population Services International (PSI), 231
Porter, Jeremy, 406
Porter Novelli, 139
Portman, Rob, 528
Postman, Joel, 368
Power leaders, 247
Powers, Angela, 252
Power to End Stroke movement, 304
PPofA. *See* Professional Photographers of America (PPofA)
Pranikoff, Michael, 396
Pratt, Meredith, 511
PRBoutiques International, 138
Predispositions, 213, 214
Presidents, U.S., 522–523. *See also specific presidents*
Press agents, 68, 69, 71, 79, 83, 503
Press conferences. *See* News conferences
Press parties, 416
Pressrooms, 463–464
Press secretaries, 30
Preventive public relations, 259
PRIA. *See* Public Relations Institute of Australia (PRIA)
Primary research, 153–154
Printing press, 67
Print interviews, 412
Privacy
employee communication and, 330–331
invasion of, 330–333
media inquiries about employees and, 332–333
photo releases and, 331
product publicity and advertising and, 331–332
PR Management Database (PRMD), 113
PRMD. *See* PR Management Database (PRMD)
PRNewswire, 408, 409
Probability samples, 162
Problem-solving skills, 53
Procter & Gamble (P&G), 182, 184, 218, 308, 483
Product disparagement, 329
Production measurement, 226
Product placements, 437, 439–440, 488–489
Product publicity, 488
Product recalls, 290, 479
Professional associations, 574–575
Professionalism
accreditation and, 113–115
continuing education and, 114–115
expansion of body of knowledge and, 112–113
practitioner mindset and, 108–110
standardized curriculum and, 112
Professional Photographers of America (PPofA), 335
Program planning
audience considerations for, 185–186
"big picture" of, 194
budget for, 192
calendar and timetable for, 189–192
elements of, 181–182
evaluation of, 192–194
explanation of, 178
and Hispanics, 188
management by objectives approach to, 178–180
objectives for, 184–185
situation for, 182, 184
skills in, 53
strategic planning model approach to, 179–180
strategy for, 186–187
tactics for, 187–189
PROI. *See* PR Organization International (PROI)
Promotional events
celebrities to attract attendance at, 465–466
explanation of, 464–465
permits for, 466
planning and logistics for, 466, 468
Propaganda, 66–67
Proper, Scott, 56
PR Organization International (PROI), 138
PRSA. *See* Public Relations Society of America (PRSA)
PRSSA. *See* Public Relations Student Society of America (PRSSA)
PRWeb, 394, 409
PSA. *See* Public service announcement (PSA)
PSI. *See* Population Services International (PSI)
Public affairs, 36, 135, 532–533
Public affairs officers (PAOs), 524–525
Public Broadcasting Service (PBS), 234
Public diplomacy, 566–567
Public information, 36, 83, 532–533
Public information officers (PIOs), 530
Publicists, 36, 503–506
Publicity, 581
in Colonial America, 68
drip-by-drip technique, 505
invasion of privacy and, 331–332
memorability for, 232
polls and surveys to generate, 153
product, 488
right of, 341
Publicity photographs
explanation of, 396–400
quality of, 397
suggestions for, 397–398

Public opinion. *See also* Opinion leaders
explanation of, 246–247
flow of, 250
life cycle of, 249
methods to sway, 152–153
Public policy, 49
Public relations. *See also* Global public relations
classic models of, 83
in Colonial America, 67–68
components of, 40–41
and conflict management, 277–281
in corporations, 475–477
current practices and trends in, 89–93
definition of, 33–35
dialogic model of, 89
digital analytics for, 169–170
dominant view of, 258–262
in first half of twentieth century, 74–82
global expenditures on, 31
global growth in, 31
government and (*See* Government/ government agencies)
historical background of, 66, 73
how to succeed in, 54
integrated media model, 199–200
integrated perspective on, 47–49
job levels in, 128
journalism *vs.*, 42–45
journalists in, 50–52
in Middle Ages, 66–67
in nineteenth century, 69–72, 122
in other countries, 70–71
overlap of duties in, 31
overview of, 28–29
preventive, 259
process of, 40–41
as profession, 110, 112
professionalism in, 108–112
in second half of twentieth century, 82–88
as staff function, 128–130
stereotypes and unflattering terms for, 36–40
as support for marketing, 47
terms used for, 35–36
in universities, 585–588
value of, 60–62
vs. advertising, 45–46, 48
vs. marketing, 46–47, 49
women in, 60, 86–88
Public relations blogs, 106, 111, 113
Public relations campaigns, 85. *See also specific campaigns*
Public relations careers
choosing between corporate departments or public relations firms, 142
global, 567–568
internships and, 55–57
job description for, 29–30
minorities in, 90–91
networking and, 50–51
outlook for, 50–51
paths to, 50–52
salary data for, 57–60, 88
skills for, 52–54
in universities, 585–586
university programs for, 32–33
Public relations departments
cooperation between other departments and, 131–132
corporate structure and, 122–124
influence levels in, 130–131
management access of, 130
organization of, 124–128
outsourcing and, 132–134
overview of, 122–123
staff functions in, 128–130
Public relations education, 32–33, 112, 114–115
Public relations firms
advantages of using, 143
approach to engaging, 141
career choices and, 142
within communication conglomerates, 138–140
disadvantages of using, 143–144
fees and charges of, 145–147
global reach, 138
growth in, 134–135
services provided by, 135–138
structure of, 140–141
top ten, 140
vice presidents in, 141
Public Relations Institute of Australia (PRIA), 70, 114
Public relations managers, 30, 109, 128
Public relations organizations, 31, 32, 113, 157–158. *See also specific publications*
Public relations planning. *See* Program planning
Public relations professionals
accreditation for, 113–115
continuing education for, 114–115
as counselors, 136, 138
ethical decision-making by, 97 (*See also* Ethical issues; Ethics)
invasion of privacy issues and, 330–333
job description for, 29–30
liability issues for, 327, 329
management views of, 122–124
prerequisites for, 108
professional development for, 93
projected growth rate for, 29
relationship between attorneys and, 352–353
salary data for, 57–60, 87
skills in, 52–54
statistics for, 31–32
websites for, 157–158
women as, 60, 86–88
Public relations research
centers of, 113
digital analytics, 169–170
function of, 135
importance of, 150
methods to reach respondents for, 166–169
primary, 153–154
qualitative, 154–155, 158–162
quantitative, 153, 155, 162–164
questionnaire construction for, 164–166
role and scope of, 150–151
secondary, 153–154, 155–158
social media, 170, 173–174
social media monitoring tools, 171–173
techniques for, 153–155
Web analytics, 170–171
Public Relations Review, 113
Public Relations Society of America (PRSA), 32, 41, 50, 84, 127, 283
accreditation and, 114
annual membership conferences of, 445
code of ethics, 220
on disclosure and honesty, 105
facts about, 99–100
front groups and, 99–100
on legal issues, 353
minorities and, 93
Public relations specialists, 30, 129
Public Relations Student Society of America (PRSSA), 51, 100–101
Public Relations Tactics, 100
Public service announcement (PSA), 231, 424–426, 430–431
Puffery, 329
Purina, 364

Q

Qiu, Qi, 252
Quaker Oats, 310
Qualitative research
content analysis for, 158–159
copy testing for, 161–162

Qualitative research (*continued*)
- ethnographic techniques for, 162
- explanation of, 154–155, 158 (*See also* Public relations research)
- focus groups for, 159–161
- interviews for, 159

Quantitative research
- explanation of, 153, 155, 162–164 (*See also* Public relations research)
- random sampling for, 162–163
- sample size and, 163–164

Queen Margaret University College, 71
Quenqua, Douglas, 482
Questionnaires
- guidelines to construct, 166
- loaded questions in, 165
- mailed, 167
- politically correct answers in, 165
- range of possible answers in, 165
- timing and context for, 165
- wording in, 164–165

Questions
- eliciting "correct" response to, 165
- loaded, 165
- wording of, 164–165

Quick response (QR) codes, 384–386
Quota sampling, 163

R

RACE, 40–41
Racial diversity. *See* Cultural/racial diversity
Radio
- DJ and media-sponsored events on, 440
- guest appearances on, 433–437
- news releases on, 422–424
- overview of, 421
- public service announcements on, 424–426
- to reach Hispanics, 307

Radio media tours (RMTs), 426–427
Radio public service announcements (PSAs)
- adding sound to, 425–426
- delivery of, 426
- explanation of, 424
- format and production of, 425
- use of, 426

Radio Sawa, 567
Railroads, 71–72, 75, 122
Raleigh, Walter, 67
Random sampling, 162–163
Rasiej, Andrew, 540
Raymond, Cary, 494
Readability, 161–162, 209
Readability formulas, 209
Readership-interest surveys, 242
Reagan, Ronlad, 522, 523
Real Simple Syndication (RSS), 152, 364, 365
Reber, Bryan, 260
Receptions, 454–456
Recommendations, 265
Reconciliation, 579
Reddi, C. V. Narasimha, 70, 108
Registration, for meetings, 450
Relationship management, 89
Religious groups, 319–322, 348, 581
Repetition, of messages, 214
Reputation audits, 296
Reputation Institute, 296
Reputation management, 287
- explanation of, 84
- image restoration for, 296–299
- media role in, 296

Request for proposal (RFP), 141, 144, 530
Research. *See* Public relations research
Research ability, 52–53
Return on Investment (ROI), 92, 122, 232, 234–235
Rice, Ronald E., 262
Rich, David, 464
Ries, Al, 45, 48
Ries, Laura, 45, 48
Right of publicity, 341
Risk communication, 286, 290
RJR Nabisco, 130
RMTs. *See* Radio media tours (RMTs)
Roanoke Island, 67
Robson, Matthew, 307
Rocco, Leonardo, 188
Rockefeller, John D., Jr., 75
Roeser, Rodger, 469
Rogers, Everett, 216, 217, 218, 250
Rogers, Henry, 503
Rogers, Sarah, 401
Rogers and Cowan, 80
ROI. *See* Return on Investment (ROI)
Role-playing, 162
Roman Catholic Church, 66–67, 73
Romney, Mitt, 254
Roosevelt, Franklin D., 81–82
Roosevelt, Teddy, 81–82
ROPE, 40
Roper Organization, 250
Rouner, Donna, 263
Royal Caribbean, 309, 310, 313, 514
RSS. *See* Real Simple Syndication (RSS)
Rubenstein Communications, 504
Rubin, David, 533
Rubin, Maureen, 345
Rudman, Rick, 360
Rudolph, Philip, 352
Ruiz, Manny, 396
Russell, Karen Miller, 73
Russian Federation, 548
The Russian Federation, 71
Rutherford, Jim, 29
Ryan, Kimberlie, 348
Ryan, Michael, 116

S

Sachsman, David, 533
Safeway, 483
Salaries, public relations, 57–60, 88
Salvo, Suzanne, 397
Sample size, 163–164
Samsung, 413, 468
San Diego Convention Center, 362
Sandman, Peter, 533
Sanford, Mark, 111
Santa Fe Railway, 72
Sanz, Alejandro, 309
Sarbanes-Oxley Act (2002), 346
Satellite media tours (SMTs), 427, 435
- guidelines for, 433

Schering-Plough, 426
Scheufele, Dietram, 252
Schneiderman, Eric, 328
Schramm, Wilbur, 201, 202, 208
Schumann, Mark, 476, 485
Schweitzer, Albert L., 224
Scott, David Meerman, 405
Scott, Lee, 473
Scrushy, Richard, 118
Search engine optimization (SEO), 394–395
Search engines, 157
Seat Belt Campaign, 85
Seating arrangements, at meetings, 449
SEC. *See* Securities and Exchange Commission (SEC)
Second Amendment, 256
Secondary research. *See also* Public relations research
- archives for, 155
- explanation of, 153–154
- libraries and databases for, 155, 157
- World Wide Web for, 157–158

Securities and Exchange Commission (SEC), 342, 344–346
Seifert, Walt, 204, 205
Seitel, Fraser, 39
Self-interest, appeal to, 265–266
Self-perception, 270
Self-selection, 270
Seltzer, Bob, 479
Semantic noise, 210

Seminars, 445, 449. *See also* Meetings
Senay, Dave, 255
Seniors, 316–317, 513
Sernovitz, Andy, 220
Service mark, 340
33-Eleven, 133
Severin, Werner, 205
Sexual harassment, 332, 350, 486
Shane, Scott, 526
Shaw, Don, 251
Shell, 253
Shell Oil, 430, 483, 493
Shin, Jae-Hwa, 258, 278, 281
Shuter, Rob, 504
Sierra Club, 579
Silber, Tony, 118
Simmons, Robert E., 178
Simmons Study Media and Markets, 157
Simon, Morton J., 330
Singapore Tourism Board (STB), 384
86 Minutes (CBS), 435
Skerik, Sarah, 464
Slander, 328
SLAPP (Strategic Lawsuit Against Public Participation), 479
Slater, Michael, 263
Sleeper effect, 212
Slocum, John, 131
Slogans, 209–210
Smart media release (SMR), 394–396
Smartphones, 382–383
Smirnoff, 377
Smith, Ian, 313
Smith, Ronald, 178
SMR. *See* Smart media release (SMR)
SMTs. *See* Satellite media tours (SMTs)
Sneed, Don, 329
Social media. *See also specific form of social media*
  blogs as, 365–367
  campaigns based on, 136, 231
  cautions in use of, 204
  communication and, 203–204
  crisis management and, 292–293
  in election campaigns, 540
  expertise in, 54
  Facebook as, 370–373
  Flickr as, 379–380
  Hispanic use of, 308
  impact of, 92–93, 229–230
  Instagram as, 379–380
  LinkedIn as, 376
  Millennial Generation as users of, 314–315
  monitoring tools, 169, 171–173
  monitoring use of, 228–229
  MySpace and Facebook as, 370–373
  origins of, 358–359
  participatory research, 170, 173–174
  Podcasts as, 364–365
  publicity and, 507
  smart media release and, 394–396
  solicitations using, 592
  texting as, 386
  Twitter as, 373–376
  Wikis as, 367–368
  YouTube as, 376–379
Social Media Manager, 370–371
Social movements, nineteenth-century, 72–74
Social policy, public relations and, 49
Social service organizations, 579–582
Society for Professional Journalists, 104
Solar Decathlon, 378
Solis, Brian, 358, 367, 377
Sonnenberg, Benjamin, 79
Sorrell, Martin, 91, 113
SOS NOW (Stop Oil Speculation Now), 190
Soto, Blanca, 188
Source attribution, 346
Source credibility
  components of, 263–264
  explanation of, 212–214
  and persuasive communication, 263–265
South Africa, 71
South Butt, 339
Spain, 71
Speakers, 451
Spin, described, 37
Spiral-of-silence theory, 246
Spirit AeroSystems, 292
Split messages, 239
Sponsorships
  corporate, 468–469, 490–491
  for fund-raising, 591–592
  sporting event, 507, 509
Sports
  community relations and, 507, 509
  overview of, 506–507
St. John, Burton, III, 75
Stacks, Don, 158, 232
Staff functions
  cooperation among other, 131–132
  levels of, 130–131
  public relations as, 128–130
StarCite, 461
State Farm, 313
State governments, 529–531. *See also* Government/government agencies
Statistical Abstract of the United States, 157
Statistics, 267
Stereotypes, 36–40, 305, 310
Sterling Vineyards, 136
The Stockholm Accords, 103
Stonecipher, Harry, 329
Stop Killer Coke, 482
Stop Oil Speculation Now campaign, 220
Stouse, Mark, 225
Strategic conflict management, 275–277
Strategic philanthropy, 494
Strategic planning, 178, 179–180. *See also* Program planning
Strategic Public Relations Center (University of Southern California), 113, 141
The Strategist, 100
Strategy, program planning, 186–187
Strauss, Richard, 427
Strauss Radio Strategies, 422, 427
Student loan industry, 536
Suave Haircare products, 188
Sun Microsystems, 366
Super Bowl, 508
Supreme Court, U.S.
  on copyrights, 333, 334
  on corporate free speech, 349
  on sexual harassment, 486
Survey Artisan, 162
Surveys
  e-mail, 168–169
  omnibus or piggyback, 168
  random samples for, 163
  results of, 267
  rules for publicizing, 155
  telephone, 167
  web, 168–169
Sweden, 548–549
Swerling, Jerry, 215
Swift, Taylor, 504
Symbols, 209–210
Systematic tracking, 232–234

T

Tactics, 187–189
  scheduling of, 191
Talking head, 430
Talk shows, 434–435
Tankard, James, 205
Tannenbaum, Stanley, 48
Target audiences, 511–513, 582
Taylor, William, 209
Taylor Global, 136
The Tea Party Movement, 220, 267
Telephone solicitations, 592
Telephone surveys, 167

Television
fund-raising using, 592
guest appearances on, 433–437
issues placement on, 439
overview of, 421, 427–428
product placements on, 437, 439
public service announcements for, 430–431
to reach Hispanics, 307
satellite media tours for, 427, 431–432
stereotypes of public relations on, 37
video news releases for, 106–107, 346, 428–429
Temperance movement, 73
Teodoro, Pete, 70
Terpening, Ed, 229
Terrorist attacks of September 37, 2001, 247
Terrorists, 514
Testimonials, 268, 343
Texas Gulf Sulfur case, 84
Texting, 386
TFM. *See* Tobacco Free Missouri (TFM)
Thailand, 71, 549
Therkelsen, David, 200
Third-party blogs, 366–367
Threat appraisal model, 281–282
Thumb, Tom, 69
Thurber, James A., 535
Tickets, publicity to sell, 507
Timberlake, Justin, 466
Time factor
for adoption, 217
persuasion and, 266
Timetables, 189–192
Timings, for banquets, 454
Tobacco Free Missouri (TFM), 174
Toledo, Rob, 169
Torches of Liberty campaign, 78
Toth, Elizabeth, 251
Tourism
explanation of, 509
Internet use for, 511
promotion of, 511, 529
target audiences for, 511–513
threats and crises related to, 513–516
Toyoda, Akio, 298
Toyota, 298–299
Trade groups, 575
Trade libel, 329
Trademarks
explanation of, 337–339
infringement and, 340–341
misappropriation of personality and, 341
protections of, 339–340
Trade shows
exhibit booths for, 462–463
explanation of, 462
hospitality suites for, 463
pressrooms and media relations for, 463–464
Trammell, Jack, 424
Transparency
corporate reputation and, 477
in media industry, 118
online standards for, 220
Trial stage, 218
Triggered events, 206
Trojan Pleasure Carts, 467–468
Turkey, 549
Turner, Kathleen, 118
Twain, Mark, 390
Twitter, 44, 45, 50–51, 55, 373–376, 507
Twitter Campaign, 55
Two-step flow theory, 250
Two-way asymmetric model, 83
Two-way communication, 202–203
Two-way symmetric model, 83, 84, 89
Tye, Larry, 78
Tylenol Crisis, 85, 131
Tyson Foods, 481–482

U

U.S. Chamber of Commerce, 576
UGC. *See* User generated content (UGC)
Understanding AIDS campaign, 85
Unilver, 465
United Airlines, 377
United Arab Emirates, 71
United Nations World Tourism Organization (UNWTO), 510
United States Information Agency (USIA), 566
United States Information and Educational Exchange Act of 1948, 567
United Steelworkers, 377
Universities/colleges
public relations professionals in, 585–588
public relations programs in, 32–33
standardized curriculum in, 112
University of Missouri, 265
University of Pennsylvania, 364
University of Southern California (USC), 113, 124, 141
Urban II, Pope, 66
U.S. Department of Energy (DOE), 378–379
U.S. Fish and Wildlife Service, 579
USAsian Wire, 409
USA Today, 405, 407, 413
USC. *See* University of Southern California (USC)
User generated content (UGC), 267
Utilitarian approach, 97

V

Values, 97, 98
Vanderbilt Television News Archive, 158
Veronis Suhler Stevenson (VSS), 31
Viacom, 336
Vice presidents, in public relations firms, 141
Video news releases (VNRs), 191, 192
B-roll and, 430
ethical issues related to, 105–106
explanation of, 428–429
format for, 428–429
production of, 429
regulation of, 346
sample script for, 430
Viral marketing, 491–492
Virginia Company, 67
Visa, 468
Visible Technologies, 233
Visit, website, 230
VMS, 159
VNRs. *See* Video news releases (VNRs)
Vocus, 233, 404, 408
Voice of America (VOA), 567
Volokh, Eugene, 349
VSS. *See* Veronis Suhler Stevenson (VSS)

W

Wal-Mart, 145, 220, 275, 276, 277, 284, 473–474, 555
Walton, Susan Balcom, 365, 367
Wannamaker, John, 74
Wannamaker's, 74, 122
Wanta, Wayne, 251
Washington Media Group (WMG), 564
Washington Speaker's Bureau, 452
Watermelon Promotion Association, 401, 402
Watts, J. C., 538
WCTU. *See* Women's Christian Temperance Union (WCTU)
Web analytics, 169, 170–171, 230
Webcasts, 363–364, 415
Weber, Thomas E., 363
Weber Shandwick, 56, 136, 139, 143, 231, 291, 367

Websites
  interactive, 362–363
  management of, 363, 409, 411
  as marketing communication tool, 360
  for public relations professionals, 157–158
Web surveys, 162, 168–169
Welker, Catherine, 316
Wells, Ida B., 74
Werner, Larry, 180
Westinghouse, George, 73, 74, 122
Westinghouse Corporation, 74
Westward expansion, 69–72
Wexler, Robb, 228
Whirlpool, 364
Whistle-blowing, 333
Whitaker, Clem, 80
White, Eric, 71
Wikis, 162, 367–368
Wilcox, Dennis L., 47
Wilkins, Lee, 110
Wilson, Heather, 558
Wilson, Kerry Anne, 513
Windows 121 Launch, 85
WIPA. *See* World Intellectual Property Association (WIPA)
Witherspoon, Reese, 503
Woman's suffrage movement, 73
Women. *See also* Gender
  profile of, 317–318
  in public relations, 60, 86–88
  public relations salaries and, 60, 86–88
  social media skills and, 213
  targeting of, 582
Women's Christian Temperance Union (WCTU), 72
Women's rights movement, 73
Woods, Tiger, 502, 505
Word-of-mouth campaigns, 218–219
Workshops, 449
Worldcom, 138
World Intellectual Property Association (WIPA), 337
World Trade Organization (WTO), 32
World Water Day, 230, 231
World Wide Web, 567. *See also* Internet
  background of, 360–361
  interactivity of, 362–363
  measuring effectiveness on, 228–229
  mobile-enabled content and, 382
  monitoring employee use of, 332–333, 350–351
  research using, 157–158
World Wildlife Fund (WWF), 276, 578
Worth, Mary, 330
WPP Group, 139
Writing skills, 52
WTO. *See* World Trade Organization (WTO)
Wulfemeyer, Tim, 329
Wylie, Frank, 224

Y

Yes-yes technique, 260
Yost, Tim, 116
YouTube, 162, 179, 231, 336, 339, 350, 376–379

Z

Zillo, Jason, 507
Zoda, Suzanne, 290
Zoomerang, 169

Credits

Photo Credits

Chapter 1

p. 27: claudio zaccherini/Shutterstock; p. 36: bl, Itar-Tass Photos/Newscom; p. 38: cr, Amanda Hall/Robert Harding World Imagery/Alamy; p. 38: b, © The New Yorker Collection 2004. Mick Stevens/www.cartoonbank.com; p. 43: tl, dieKleinert/Alamy; p. 43: tc, ImageZoo/Alamy; p. 43: tr, ArtBabii/Alamy; p. 43: cl, Ikon Images/Alamy; p. 43: c, Fanatic Studio/Alamy; p. 43: cr, PIotr Dudek/Alamy; p. 43: bl, Illustration Works/Alamy; p. 43: bc, Eiko Ojala/Alamy; p. 43: br, Sergii Lysenkov/Alamy; p. 44: b, Republica, LLC.; p. 44, t, Republica, LLC.; p. 51: tl, Robin Carr

Chapter 2

p. 65: Strobridge Lithograph Co./Fine Art/Corbis; p. 66: bl, Silvio Fiore/SuperStock; p. 74: tl, Everett Collection/Newscom; p. 76: bl, AP Photo/Jacksonville Times-Union; p. 81: tr, The Art Archive/Alamy; p. 86: tl, Sheryl Battles; p. 86: tc, Kathryn Beiser; p. 86: tr, Beth Comstock; p. 86: c, Ellen East; p. 86: cl, Diane Gage Lofgren; p. 86: cr, Zenia Mucha; p. 86: bl, Christine Owens; p. 86: bc, Cynthia Round; p. 86: br, Carol Schumacher

Chapter 3

p. 96: tc, LUCAS JACKSON/Reuters/Corbis; p. 97: br, Mick Stevens The New Yorker Collection/www.cartoonbank.com; p. 98: c, AP Photo/Orville Myers/The Monterey County Herald; p. 111: Erik Campos/MCT/Newscom; p. 117: cr, imago stock&people/Newscom

Chapter 4

p. 121: c, Monkey Business Images/Shutterstock; p. 125: cr, Oberhauser/Caro/Alamy; p. 133: AP Photo/PRNewsFoto/7-Eleven, Inc.; p. 135: Charles Barsotti/The New Yorker Collection/www.cartoonbank.com; p. 137: Kellie Bramlet; p. 144: cr, JohanSwanepoel/Fotolia LLC

Chapter 5

p. 149: c, Spencer Grant/Photo Edit,Inc.; p. 156: cr, Daniel Dempster Photography/Alamy; p. 159: tr, Jeff Greenberg/PhotoEdit; p. 174: cr, Ian Dagnall/Alamy

Chapter 6

p. 177: wavebreakmedia ltd/Shutterstock; p. 188: MZ1 WENN Photos/Newscom

Chapter 7

p. 197: Digital Vision/Getty Images; p. 213: cr, Arena Creative/Shutterstock; p. 214: tl, Gallo Images/Getty Images

Chapter 8

p. 223: Janine Wiedel Photolibrary/Alamy; p. 231: Irene Abdou/Alamy; p. 241: AP Photo/Jack Plunkett

Chapter 9

p. 245: Nerissa D'Alton/Alamy; p. 248: JOHN ANGELILLO/UPI/Newscom; p. 253: br, Adam Welz/Alamy; p. 257: tr, Jeff Malet Photography/Newscom; p. 261: cr, Jochen Tack/Alamy; p. 264: b, dpa picture alliance/Alamy

Chapter 10

p. 274: Editorial Image, LLC/Alamy; p. 275: AP Photos/David Phillip; p. 278: VINAI DITHAJOHN/EPA/Newscom; p. 280: t, ROPI/ZUMAPRESS/Newscom; p. 280: b, Sharif Md. Shaifuzzaman/Demotix/Corbis; p. 293: AP Photo/Mike Hutmacher, The Eagle; p. 298: PRWeek; p. 301: Jeff Greenberg/Alamy

Chapter 11

p. 303: c, David Grossman/Alamy; p. 306: cr, Tannen Maury/epa/Corbis Wire/Corbis; p. 309: cr, RAFA ALCAIDE/EPA/Newscom; p. 310: Mayskyphoto/Shutterstock.com; p. 320: tr, Eric Carr/Alamy; p. 324: cr, Arinahabich/Fotolia

Chapter 12

p. 326: c, Caryn Becker/Alamy; p. 338: t, Jeff Kowalsky/Bloomberg/Getty Images; p. 339: US Dept of Homeland Security

Chapter 13

p. 357: c, Cadalpe/Image Source/Corbis; p. 371: Michelle Kraker/Inbound Marketing Agents; p. 375: br, Peter Stroh/Alamy; p. 378: b, Bill Clark/Roll Call Photos/Newscom; p. 385: t, Colin Underhill/Alamy

Chapter 14

p. 389: c, Jim West/Alamy; p. 397: br, Jung Yeon-Je/AFP/Getty Images/Newscom; p. 407: Sam Dao/Alamy

Chapter 15

p. 420: Christopher Capozziello/Zuffa LLC/Contributor/UFC/Getty Images; p. 422: AP Photo/Amy Sussman; p. 431: AP Photo/Itsuo Inouye; p. 432: Courtesy of Rotary International; p. 438: AP Photo/Peter Kramer; p. 440: t, Zenia Mucha

Chapter 16

p. 444: Belgrade Cultural Network; p. 447: Pablo Picasso, Female Head. 1902. Oil on canvas. Hermitage, St. Petersburg, Russia. © 2014 Estate of Pablo Picasso/Artists Rights Society (ARS), New York, photo by PAINTING/Alamy; p. 452: History San Jose; p. 459: Wang Lei/ZUMAPRESS/Newscom; p. 463: Robyn Beck/AFP/Getty Images/Newscom; p. 467: Belgrade Cultural Network

Chapter 17

p. 471: Kumar Sriskandan/Alamy; p. 472: RICK WILKING/Reuters/Landov; p. 473: RICK WILKING/Reuters/Landov; p. 475: Chevron Corporate; p. 480: AP Photo/Ross D. Franklin; p. 484: STR/AFP/Getty Images/Newscom; p. 491: face to face/ZUMA Press/Newscom

Chapter 18

p. 499: OLAF KRAAK/EPA/Newscom; p. 501: JUSTIN TALLIS/AFP/Getty Images; p. 508: John Middlebrook/Cal Sport Media/Newscom; p. 510: New York City/Alamy; p. 514: Scott Keeler/St. Petersburg Times/PSG/Newscom; p. 515: ROXY VALLIER/BARCROFT USA/Barcroft Media/Landov

Chapter 19

p. 519: Cheryl Senter/Polaris/Newscom; p. 530: Manuel Balce Ceneta/AP/Corbis; p. 534: Duncan Selby/Alamy; p. 536: Bill Clark/CQ Roll Call/Getty Images

Chapter 20

p. 544: Alexander Joe/AFP/Getty Images/Newscom; p. 546: Stan Rohrer/Alamy; p. 550: Courtesy of Saudi Aramco/J.B. Picoulet/PCP/KAUST; p. 557:

MUNIR UZ ZAMAN/AFP/Getty Images/Newscom; p. 559: Oceana; p. 563: Martin Thomas Photography/Alamy; p. 565: Dennis Wilcox

Chapter 21

p. 571: AFP/Getty Images/Newscom; p. 573: Benoit Doppagne/AFP/Getty Images/Newscom; p. 578: Edwin Giesbers/Nature Picture Library;p. 584: Pearson Education; p. 585: JC Ridley/ Cal Sport Media/Newscom

Text Credits

Chapter 1

p. 30: U.S. Department of Labor: Bureau of Labor Statistics.; p. 31: U.S. Department of Labor.; p. 33: Chartered institute of Public Relations; p. 33: International Public Relations Association, 1978 World Assembly of Public Relations in Mexico City and endorsed by 34 national public relations organizations; p. 34: Public Relations Society of America.; p. 40: Public Relations Society of America.; p. 45: The Fall of Advertising and The Rise of Public Relations by Al and Laura Ries, Harper Business.; p. 46: Dave Imre.; p. 47: Dennis Wilcox; p. 48: Andrea Morgan.; p. 48: Integrated Marketing Communications. The McGraw-Hill Companies.; p. 50: Fred Cook.; p. 54: Commission on Public Relations Education; p. 55: Mark Hand, PR Week.; p. 55: Sara Calabro, PR Week.; p. 58: Reprinted by permission of the Association for Education in Journalism and Mass Communications (AEJMC); p. 60: Makovsky Integrated Communications; pp. 50–51: "Networking: The Key to Career Success" by Robin Carr. Reprinted by permission of Robin Carr, Director of Public Relations, XOOM Global Money Transfer; pp. 29–30: U.S. Department of Labor: Bureau of Labor Statistics.; pp. 56–57: Reprinted by permission of Ogilvy PR Worldwide; pp. 59–60: Reprinted by permission of PRWeek; pp. 59–60: Based on data from PRWeek, March 2013; pp. 59–60: Based on Salary Survey 2013, PR Week, March 2013, pp. 32–64; p. 34: Fig. 1.1, Reprinted by permission of the Public Relations Society of America (PRSA)

Chapter 2

p. 66: Managing Public Relations by James Grunig and Todd Hunt. Cengage Learning.; p. 67: Based on "How Luther Went Viral: Five Centuries before Facebook and the Arab Spring, social media helped bring about the Reformation." Economist, December 17, 2011; p. 69: James Hynes, Book Review: The Great and Only Barnum: The Tremendous, Stupendous Life of Showman P. T. Barnum, by Candace Fleming New York Times, December 4, 2009; p. 71: Andy Piasecki, A., "Blowing the Railroad Trumpet: Public Relations on the American Frontier" Journal of Public Relations Research, Vol. 16, No. 3, 2004, pp. 295–325; p. 73: Removing the spin: Toward a new theory of public relations history. Journalism Communication Monographs, 11(4), used by permission.; p. 75: The Practice of Public Relations, by Fraiser P. Seitel. Prentice Hall.; p. 78: Father of Spin: Edward L. Bernays & the Birth of Public Relations by Larry Tye. Picador.; p. 79: Arthur W. Page Society, 2013–2014 Membership Directory, page 33.; p. 85: Adapted and condensed from "The greatest campaigns ever" PRWeek, July 15, 2002; p. 87: Melissa Waggener Zorkin, CEO and founder of Waggener Edstrom public relations; p. 89: Kent, Michael and Taylor, Maureen, "Toward a Dialogic Theory of Public Relations" Public Relations Review, Vol. 28, #1, pp. 21–63; p. 90: Reprinted by permission of Bruce Berger, University of Alabama; p. 90: Tannette Johnson-Elie, columnist, Milwaukee Journal-Sentinel; p. 91: Sandra Fathi, founder and president of Affect, a social media firm in New York; p. 92: Jeff Domansky, social PR strategist and CEO of Peak Communications, quoted in Domansky, J. (2013, October 8) "Traditional Media Trends Affecting PR" Ragan's PR Daily; p. 88: Fig. 2.1, Reprinted by permission of PRWeek

Chapter 3

p. 99: Ryan, M. and Martinson, D. (1994) "Public Relations Practitioners: Journalists View Lying Similarity" Journalism Monographs, 71(1) pp. 225–237 Association for Education in Journalism and Mass Communications, used by permissions; p. 99: W. D. (Bill) Nielsen, former VP of public affairs for Johnson & Johnson, speaking at the 44th annual lecture of the Institute for Public Relations; p. 105: Reprinted by permission of the Public Relations Society of America (PRSA); p. 109: Shannon Bowen.; p. 109: Reprinted by permission of Shannon Bowen, University of South Carolina; p. 110: Ted McKenna, reporter for PRWeek; p. 111: Rick Pitino, college and professional basketball coach, quoted in Feeding Frenzy: Crisis Management in the Spotlight by Jon F. Harmon; p. 112: Jon Harris, SVP of global communications, Sara Lee; p. 113: Sir Martin Sorrell, CEO of WPP communications conglomerate, London; p. 116: Tim Yost, communications director for ASC, a Detroit automotive manufacturer, in Public Relations Tactics; p. 117: Barboza, D., In China Press, Best Coverage Money Can Buy. New York Times, April 4, 2012, A1, B2.; p. 118: Rose Gordon, news editor of PRWeek

Chapter 4

p. 122: Excellence in Public Relations and Communications Management, IABC Foundation; p. 126: CEO of a large corporation on what he expects in a chief communications officer, in a survey by the Arthur W. Page Society; p. 128: Adapted from Public Relations Society of America. Public Relations Professional Career Guide.© The PRSA Foundation (1993); p. 130: John Buckley, EVP of corporate communications for AOL; p. 132: Kim Plaskett, director of corporate communications for Greyhound; p. 132: Paul James, communications manager of Harley-Davidson; p. 137: Reprinted by permission of Kellie Bramlet, Black Sheep Agency; p. 126: Fig. 4.1, Reprinted by permission of IBM; p. 127: Fig. 4.2, Reprinted by permission of PRWeek; p. 130: Fig. 4.3, Reprinted by permission of Corporate Communications International (CCI); p. 134: Fig. 4.4, Reprinted by permission of Ruder Finn

Chapter 5

p. 150: Glen Cameron; p. 152: Katie Paine, CEO of KD Paine and Partners; p. 155: Walter K. Lindenmann, specialist in public relations research and measurement; p. 157: Glenn Cameron; p. 163: Don Bartholomew, Senior Vice President, Ketchum, in PRNews; p. 168: Giselle Lederman, survey methodologist for Zoomerang; p. 169: Rob Toledo, Ragan's PR Daily, April 24, 2013; http://www.prdaily.com/Main/Articles/14335.aspx; p. 154: Fig. 5.1, Courtesy of Ketchum Public Relations; p. 170: Fig. 5.2,

Reprinted by permission of Engagor; p. 172: Fig. 5.3, Reprinted by permission of BuzzStream

Chapter 6

p. 178, Ronald Smith, Strategic Planning for Public Relations. Lawrence Erlbaum and Associates.; p. 178: Thomas R. Hagley, Writing Winning Proposals: PR Cases. Pearson Education.; p. 181: Ketchum.; p. 184: David B. Oates, a Stalwart Communications executive, San Diego; p. 190: Courtesy of Airlines for America, www.airlines.org; p. 194: Courtesy of Ketchum Public Relations; p. 193: Fig. 6.2, Courtesy of Ketchum Public Relations

Chapter 7

p. 198, Kirk Hallahan of Colorado State University; p. 200: David Therkelsen, executive director of Crisis Connection, Minneapolis; p. 202: James Grunig; p. 204: Harold Lasswell; p. 204: Glen Cameron; p. 205: Communication Theories by Werner Severin and James Tankard.; p. 207: Reprinted by permission of Nicole Burdette, CEO and Founder, 11Mark Agency; p. 210: David Ogilvy, a legend in the advertising industry; p. 211: Reprinted by permission of Shift Communications; p. 218: Chris Haack of Mintel; p. 218: Sam Ecker, Chief Marketing Officer, Bazaarrvoice; p. 219: Sheldon Levine, "Six Best Practices for Distributing Press Releases," Public Relations Tactics, July 2013. Reprinted by permsision of the Public Relations Society of America (PRSA); p. 220: Andy Sernovitz, CEO of the Word of Mouth Marketing Association (WOMMA); pp. 198–199: Dennis L. Wilcox; pp. 199–200: Table 7.1, Reprinted by permission of Kirk Hallahan, Colorado State University; p. 201: Table 7.2, Courtesy of Ketchum Public Relations

Chapter 8

p. 224, Frank Wylie, emeritus professor at California State University in Long Beach; p. 224: Agency monograph, Ketchum Public Relations; p. 225: Mark Stouse, Director of Worldwide Communications, BMC Communications; p. 229: Josh Jones-Dilworth, founder and CEO of Jones-Dilworth, Inc.; p. 230: Sbonali Burke, VP of media for ASPCA, as quoted in PRWeek; p. 231: Dennis L. Wilcox; p. 232: Don Bartholomew, director of research at MWW Group; p. 233: Katharine Paine, president of KD Paine ; Partners; p. 235: Valerie M. Cunningham, VP of corporate marketing for Xerox; p. 235: Walter Lindenmann ; p. 236: Dr. David Dozier, professor, San Diego State University; p. 226: Fig. 8.1, © Pearson Education, Upper Saddle River, NJ

Chapter 9

p. 251: Elizabeth L. Toth and Robert L. Heath, authors of Rhetorical and Critical Approaches to Public Relations. Routledge.; p. 252: Ji Young Kim and Spiro Kiousis, writing in Journalism & Mass Communications Quarterly.; p. 254: Kirk Hallahan; p. 259: Cialdni, Six Principles of Persuasion, Cialdni, R. (2001) "Harnessing the Science of Persuasion" Harvard Business Review, 72–79, Harvard Business Publishing (HBP); p. 263: Scott Keogh, chief marketing officer of Audi; p. 266: Ann Wylie, Public Relations Tactics, the Public Relations Society of America; p. 269: Defenders of Wildlife, defenders.org

Chapter 10

p. 281, Jae-Hwa Shin, University of Southern Mississippi; p. 282: Yan Jin, Virginia Commonwealth University; p. 284: Professor Astrid Kersten, LaRoche College; p. 291: PR Week; p. 292: Timothy Coombs, author of Ongoing Crisis Communications: Planning, Managing, and Responding. Sage Publications.; p. 296: Warren Buffett, CEO of Berkshire Hathaway

Chapter 11

p. 304: Armando Azarloza, president of the Axis Agency in PRWeek.; p. 307: John Echeveste, partner in VPE Public Relations in PRWeek.; p. 311: Based on U.S. Census Bureau, Current Population Survey, 2010 Annual Social and Economic Supplement; p. 314: Scarborough Research; p. 316: Denise Vitola, SVP of MSL Group in PRWeek.; p. 319: Rich Ferraro, VP of communications for the Gay and Lesbian Alliance Against Defamation (GLAAD) in PRWeek.; p. 321: John Pinna, director of government and international relations for the American Islamic Congress, in PRWeek.; p. 305: Fig. 11.1, U.S. Census Bureau.

Chapter 12

p. 332: Parkinson and Parkinson, Public Relations Law: A Supplemental Text. Routledge.; p. 348: Kimberlie Ryan, Denver attorney; p. 349: Eugene Volokh, professor of law at UCLA, in a Wall Street Journal op-ed; p. 352: Dennis L. Wilcox; p. 353: Dennis L. Wilcox; pp. 343–344: www.ftc.gov/os/2013/03/130312dotcomd isclosures.pdf

Chapter 13

p. 358, Brian Solis and Deirdre Breakenridge, authors of Putting the Public Back in Public Relations. FT Press.; p. 360: David Meerman Scott, author of The New Rules of Marketing and PR. Wiley.; p. 362: Dr. Hong Sheng, Missouri University of Science and Technology. ; p. 366: Larry Genkin, Blogger and Podcaster, 2007; p. 368: Jorand Chanofsky, CEO of Fusion Public Relations; p. 368: Makovsky Integrated Communications.; p. 372: Shel Holtz, social media guru at an IABC workshop; p. 374: Reprinted by permission of Springfield Clinic, LLP; p. 377: Brian Solis and Deirdre Breakenridge, authors of Putting the Public Back in Public Relations. FT Press.; p. 380: Scott Signore, CEO of Matter Communications.; p. 381: Amy Jacques, writing in PR Tactics. Public Relations Society of America.; p. 382: Mary Gorges, creative communications manager at Cisco Systems, writing in the Ragan Report.; p. 358: Fig. 13.1, Data from www.internetworldstats.com (as of June 2012).; p. 369: Fig. 13.2, Based on data from Joanna Brenner "Pew Internet: Social Networking" August 5, 2013. Pew Research Center; pp. 370–371: "Some Misconceptions About Being a Social Media Manager" by Michelle Kraker. Reprinted by permission of Inbound Marketing Agents

Chapter 14

p. 394: Todd Defren, principal with Boston-based Shift Communications; p. 396: Michael Pranikoff, PR Newswire; p. 397: Suzanne Salvo of Salvo Photography in Ragan.com; p. 400: Tom Bucktold, of Business Wire; p. 404: David Carr, media columnist for the New York Times; p. 409: Sherri Deatherage Green, reporter for PRWeek; p. 411: The Red Bull's marks are registered trademarks of Red Bull GmbH. © Red Bull GmbH, all rights reserved.; p. 392: Fig. 14.1, Reprinted by permission of BusinessWire; p. 393: Fig. 14.2, Reprinted by permission of BusinessWire; p. 395: Fig. 14.3, Reprinted by permission of Shift Communications; p. 398: Fig. 14.4, Reprinted by permission of PR Newswire; p. 399: Fig. 14.5, Reprinted by permission of IBM; p. 403: Fig. 14.6, Reprinted by permission of BusinessWire; pp. 414–415: Bulldog Reporter

Chapter 15

p. 421: David Beasley, marketing manager at News Generation, a public relations firm specializing in radio; p. 422: Raul Martinez, Strauss Radio Strategies; p. 423: Dennis L. Wilcox; p. 424: Dennis L. Wilcox; p. 424: Christiana Arbesu, VP of production, MultiVu; p. 428: Tim Bahr, managing director of MultiVu, a broadcast production firm; p. 428: Dennis L. Wilcox, adapted from MultiVu sales materials.; p. 433: Dennis L. Wilcox; p. 435: Michael Friedman, EVP of DWJ Television; p. 436: Dina Bair, reporter on WGN, Chicago

Chapter 16

p. 445: Yung Moon, associate publisher of Self magazine, as reported in PRWeek; p. 454: Erica Iacono, reporter for PRWeek; p. 456: Adapted from KD Paine; p. 464: David Rich, SVP of the George P. Johnson marketing company, as reported in PRWeek; p. 464: Dennis L. Wilcox; p. 465: Jennifer Collins, Event Planning Group, as quoted in PRWeek; p. 465: Dennis L. Wilcox, adapted from sales material on celebritysource.com; p. 466: Matt Glass, managing partner at Eventage, as reported in PRWeek; p. 469: Rodger Roeser, writing in KD Paine's Measurement Standard online newsletter; p. 455: Fig. 16.1, Dennis L. Wilcox

Chapter 17

p. 476, PRWeek.: p. 476: Bill Novelli, CEO, AARP; p. 479: Bob Seltzer, marketing expert at Ruder Finn; p. 479: "Online shopping gets high marks, consumer satisfaction study show" by Teresa F. Lindeman, Pittsburgh Post-Gazette, February 22, 2006; p. 481: Adapted from "Power Play: Duke Energy's Social Media Strategy Highlights Superstorm Sandy Heroics," by Greg Efthimiou, in The Strategist, Winter 2012, pp. 42–44.; p. 482: Ed Nicholson, Tyson Foods spokesperson; p. 483: Based on Quenqua, Douglas, "When Activists Attack" PR Week, June 11, 2001; p. 486: Julie Hood, former editor of PRWeek; p. 495: Maloney, J., "Nudists Seek Corporate Sponsor Looking for Greater Exposure," Wall Street Journal, January 14, 2013; pp. 472–473: Ken Cohen, VP of public and government affairs for ExxonMobil; p. 478: Table 17.1, Based on "2013 Fortune 500 Are Bullish on Social Media: Big Companies Get Excited About Google+, Instagram, Foursquare and Pinterest" Conducted By: Nora Ganim Barnes, Ph.D., Ava M. Lescault, MBA and Stephanie Wright Charlton College of Business Center for Marketing Research University of Massachusetts Dartmouth. © University of Massachusetts Dartmouth Center for Marketing Research.

Chapter 18

p. 502: "Blowout Ratings for a Farewell, Online and Off" by Brian Stelter, New York Times, July 8, 2009; p. 502: Rachel McCallister and Mark Pogachefsky, Public Relations Tactics. ; p. 503: Mickey Rooney, quoted in The Fame Formula: How Hollywood's Fixers, Fakers and Star Makers Created the Celebrity Industry by Mark Borkowski, Pan Macmillan, 2008; p. 503: Cave, S. (2009, January 29). "Fall of fame: Every age has its Paris Hiltons, but what does it take to achieve lasting recognition?" [Life & Arts section]. Financial Times, 13.; p. 503: Ralph Blumenthal, "Those Were the Days" Broadway's Press Agents Recall a Bygone Era" New York Times, June 19, 2009.; p. 503: Howard Bragman, Where's My Fifteen Minutes? Get Your Company, Your Cause or Yourself the Recognition You Deserve (Penguin Books, 2008); p. 504: Rob Shuter, Huffington Post celebrity columnist, quoted in Gayle Goodman, "Be quick when working the entertainment beat" O'Dwyer's PR Report, December 2012, p. 40; p. 504: Dennis L. Wilcox, adapted and edited from NBC Universl LinkedIn posting; p. 504: Chang, B. (2013, March 17). Taylor Swift Gets Some Mud on her Boots. New York Times, Style Section, 8.; p. 505: "Full Steam Ahead for the Tiger Woods Comeback Tour," Ragan's PR Daily News Feed, March 27, 2013; p. 505: Michael Cieply, "Your Publicist Should Call My Publicist" New York Times, February 24, 2008; p. 506: Simon Kuper, "What Google tells us about the global obsession with sport" Financial Times, July 24, 2009; p. 507: Patrick Lane, "Fun, Games and Money: A Special Report on the Sports business," Economist, August 2, 2008, pp. 27–42; p. 508: Sources: www.wallst.com2013/2013/01/25super-bowl; Steel, E. (2013, February 3). The ad zone. Financial Times, l8.; p. 509: Jason Pearl, VP of the San Francisco Giants; p. 509: Becker, E. (2013). Overbooked: The Exploding Business of Travel and Tourism. Simon & Schuster.; p. 509: William P. DeSousa-Mauk, president of DeMa Public Relations; p. 511: Pratt, M. (2013, July). Tailoring mobile content to target audiences. O'Dwyer's Public Relations Report, 12.; p. 513: Kerry Anne Wilson, president of the Zimmerman Agency, in O'Dwyer's Public Relations Report; pp. 500–501: Cave, S. (2009, January 29). Fall of fame: Every age has its Paris Hiltons, but what does it take to achieve lasting recognition? [Life & Arts section]. Financial Times, 13.

Chapter 19

p. 520: Tom Martin, former VP of corporate communication at FedEx Corp, quoted in Titus, W. (2009, September 11) Public Affairs and Government Issues Management (retrieved from podcast.prsa.org); p. 521: Jon Carson, Executive Director, Organization for Action; p. 521: Benjamin Franklin; p. 523: Edward Downes, Boston University, in Downes, E. (1998) "Hacks, Flacks and Spin Doctors Meet the Media: An Examination of the Congressional Press Secretary" Journal of Public Relations Research, Vol. 10, No 4, pp. 289–312; p. 523: 2013 Congressional Research Service report; p. 525: Allen Rosenshine, Vice Chairman and Executive Director, The Partnership for a Drug Free America, July 26, 2013; p. 525: Gil Kerlikowske, director, U.S. Office of National Drug Control Policy (ONDCP); p. 526: Gerth, J. and Shane, S., "U.S. is said to pay pay to plant articles in Iraq papers" New York Times, November 30, 2005; p. 526: Gerth, J. and Shane, S., "U.S. is said to pay pay to plant articles in Iraq papers" New York Times, November 30, 2005; p. 526: www.abovetheinfluence,com, National Youth Anti-Drug Media Campaign; p. 527: Gerth, J. and Shane, S., "U.S. is said to pay pay to plant articles in Iraq papers" New York Times, November 30, 2005; p. 527: Gerth, J. and Shane, S., "U.S. is said to pay pay to plant articles in

Iraq papers" New York Times, November 30, 2005; p. 527: Mark Evje, "'Top Gun' Boosting Service Sign-ups" Associated Press, July 5, 1986. ; p. 528: Zombie Preparedness Campaign, Centers for Disease Control and Prevention, http://www.cdc.gov/phpr/zombies.htm; p. 529: Maggie Silver, CDC Office of Public Health Preparedness and Response ; p. 529: Centers for Disease Control and Prevention (CDC); p. 529: Marion Edmonds, spokesperson for the S.C. Parks, Recreation and Tourism department quoted in Sarita Chourey, "S.C., Bluffton's BFG Communications take long reach in promoting state's 'undiscovered'" Savannah Morning News, August 3, 2013; p. 531: Allan, M. "The Million Dollar Sale: Cites Reel in Companies with PR" PRWeek, July 24, 2000 ; p. 533: Peter Sandman, David Rubin, and David Sachsman, Media: An Introductory Analysis of American Mass Communications (Prentice Hall, 1982); p. 533: New York City Human Resources Administration; p. 533: Harry F. Rosenthal, "Government Spends Billions on Public Relations Functions" Associated Press, April 3, 1983; p. 534: Based on Wyatt, E. (2013, June 2). Google's Washington Insider. New York Times.; p. 536: Sarita Gupta, executive director, Jobs with Justice (writing on the Moyers & Company blog); p. 537: "J Street puts a foot in the door" The Economist, October 19, 2009; p. 537: Evan Thomas, Influence Peddling in Washington, From Time, March 3, 1986. Copyright 1986 by Time, Inc.; p. 538: "So Who's a Lobbyist?" (Editorial) The New York Times, January 26, 2012; p. 539: Bryan Tackett, president of Wexford Strategic Advisors, quoted in Tau, B. (2013, August 3). "All the D.C. donors, now put your checks up." Politico; p. 540: "'We' has power over 'me'" Andrew Rasiej and Micah L. Sifry, Politico.com, 2/5/2009.; p. 540: Amelia Showalter, quoted in Joshua Green, "The Science Behind Those Obama Campaign E-Mails" Bloomberg Businessweek, November 29, 2012

Chapter 20

p. 546: Sean Fitzgerald, Ketchum's China office, quoted in Asia Special Report PRWeek, November 2012, pp. 46–51; p. 546: Cindy Payne, director of Asia Pacific Connections; p. 547: Gyroscope's report in The Public Relations Landscape in China; p. 552: Hatia, Y. (2013, June). "Muslim world woefully underserved by PR sector." O'Dwyer's Public Relations Report, 14.; p. 554: "World Citizens Guide" Business for Diplomatic Action Inc; p. 554: The Center for Public Integrity (CPI); p. 555: The Center for Public Integrity (CPI); p. 555: International Consortium of Investigative Journalists, a project of the Center for Public Integrity; p. 555: The Center for Public Integrity (CPI); p. 556: Ray Kotcher, CEO of Ketchum, at the International Public Relations Association (IPRA) World Congress in Beijing; p. 556: David Drobis, former senior partner and chair of Ketchum, speech before the International Communications Consultancy Organization (ICCO), 2002. ; p. 558: Bob Ross, quoted in Banjo, S., Zimmerman, A. and Kapner, S. "Wal-Mart Crafts Own Bangladesh Safety Plan" Wall Street Journal May 15, 2013, B1; p. 558: Heather Wilson, EVP of Ogilvy Public Relations in "The Reputation Issue: the World Is Watching" PRWeek June 2013, pp. 54–60; p. 558: Lucas, L. "From Boycotts to Business Briefs" Financial Times, March 19, 2013 ; p. 558: Robert Blood, founder of Sigwatch quoted in Lucas, L. "From Boycotts to Business Briefs" Financial Times, March 19, 2013 ; p. 561: Zeina Karam, "Instagram becomes latest propaganda too l for Syria's embattled president" of Associated Press (AP), July 31, 2013; p. 561: Zeina Karam, "Instagram becomes latest propaganda too l for Syria's embattled president" of Associated Press (AP), July 31, 2013; p. 561: Erik Sass, "Israel, Hamas Bring Fight to Social Media" Mediapost.com, August 2013; p. 563: Fisher, M. (2012, July 20). CNN's Effusive Coverage of Kazakhstan Is Quietly Sponsored by Its Subject. Retrieved from Atlantic Monthly (www.theatlantic.com/International) ; p. 564: O'Dwyer's Newsletter, January 19, 2011 p. 27; p. 564: "PR Landscapes: China" The Global Alliance for Public Relations and Communication Management, 2013; p. 564: Carl Levin, Burson-Marsteller; p. 565: Branigan, T. "China Plans Global Role for State TV" Guardian Weekly, December 16, 2011, p. 39; p. 567: Marquis, C. "Efforts to Promote U.S. Falls Short, Critics Say" New York Times, December 29, 2003 A6; p. 567: James K. Glassman, chair of the Broadcasting Board of Governors; pp. 545–546: Gyroscope's report on The Public Relations Landscape in China

Chapter 21

p. 574: Bogaletch Gebre, quoted in "Talking Female Circumcision Out of Existence" by Tina Rosenberg. The New York Times Opinionator July 17, 2013. http://opinionator.blogs.nytimes.com/2013/07/17/talking-female-circumcision-out-of-existence/?_r=0; p. 579: Evelyn Lauder, founder of the Breast Cancer Research Foundation; p. 583: From a personal conversation with Glen Cameron; p. 584: Jan Hoffman, "When the Cellphone Teaches Sex Education," New York Times, May 1, 2009; p. 586: Brainard, J. "Lobbying to Bring Home the Bacon In Pursuit of Earmarks and to Influence Policy" Chronicle of higher Education, October 22, 2004 A26-36; p. 589: Gregg Carlson, chair of Giving USA Foundation, Giving USA Foundation (2013, June l8). Giving USA: Charitable Donations Grew in 2012, but Slowly,Like the Economy. Retrieved from www.givingusareports.org; p. 567: Civic Crowdfunding: Breaking Ground (2013, May l8). Economist, 66.; pp. 589–590: Giving USA Foundation (2013, June l8). Giving USA: Charitable Donations Grew in 2012, but Slowly, Like the Economy. Retrieved from www.givingusareports.org